Structural Violence

Structural Violence

The Makings of Settler Colonial Impunity

ELENA RUÍZ

OXFORD
UNIVERSITY PRESS

Oxford University Press is a department of the University of Oxford. It furthers
the University's objective of excellence in research, scholarship, and education
by publishing worldwide. Oxford is a registered trade mark of Oxford University
Press in the UK and certain other countries.

Published in the United States of America by Oxford University Press
198 Madison Avenue, New York, NY 10016, United States of America.

© Oxford University Press 2024

All rights reserved. No part of this publication may be reproduced, stored in
a retrieval system, or transmitted, in any form or by any means, without the
prior permission in writing of Oxford University Press, or as expressly permitted
by law, by license, or under terms agreed with the appropriate reproduction
rights organization. Inquiries concerning reproduction outside the scope of the
above should be sent to the Rights Department, Oxford University Press, at the
address above.

You must not circulate this work in any other form
and you must impose this same condition on any acquirer.

Library of Congress Control Number: 2023952573

ISBN 978–0–19–763403–5 (pbk.)
ISBN 978–0–19–763402–8 (hbk.)

DOI: 10.1093/oso/9780197634028.001.0001

for my sisters

Palabras de Elena

One must strive to become tough and philosophical concerning destruction and death . . . but it is not permissible that the authors of destruction should also be innocent. It is the innocence which constitutes the crime.

—James Baldwin

Contents

Introducing Impunitycraft	1
1. Structural Violence Is *Self-Repairing*: The Long Game of Colonialism	32
2. Structural Violence Is *Historical*: On Testimony and Gender-Based Violence	115
3. Structural Violence Is *Profit-Driven*: Epistemic Capitalism	160
4. Structural Violence Is *by Design*: Cultural Gaslighting	219
5. Structural Violence Is *Not Fate*: Beyond Structural Trauma	246
Acknowledgments	297
Notes	301
Bibliography	413
Index	451

Introducing Impunitycraft

In the spring of 2022, researchers at the University of Geneva made a breakthrough in understanding the cellular origins of metastasis, the leading cause of death from cancer. As many people know all too painfully from caring for a loved one with late-stage cancer, most patients who die of their cancer succumb to its escalating spread throughout the body or to opportunistic infections. What kills you is not the primary cancer tumor; it is the malignant spread of self-replicating cancerous cells and the effects of this spread on the body's critical functions.

Known as *metastatic colonization*, a sequence of biological events allows circulating cancer cells to "invade distant organs, settle in supportive niches, and eventually overtake the host tissue."[1] The underlying molecular basis and mechanistic determinants of this process have long eluded scientists. During the social haze of that first "postpandemic" spring of 2022 (when over three hundred million Covid-19 cases were reported worldwide), amid a media flurry of emerging subvariant reports, escalating natural disasters, global civil unrest, and war in Europe, a new picture of the cellular origins of metastasis began to emerge. The picture painted by the study's findings is an important window into our story about the regenerative processes of settler colonial social systems and their adaptive functions throughout history.[2]

What the researchers found was that cells from primary tumors broke off, reprogrammed themselves, and developed new resilient skills and functions when faced with imminent death from chemotherapeutic agents.[3] The cancer spreads because it knows you tried to kill it.[4] And it doesn't accomplish this feat alone; cancer cells use proteins in the body to stay alive by comigrating to other parts of the body, illustrating an adaptive range of techniques along the way to remain intact as a subsystem of cancerous cells throughout the body. Using a network of intrinsic and extrinsic cues in a tumoral ecosystem to escape cell death, the cancer cells' "near-death experience" triggers an evolving series of pro-metastatic reprogramming and hormonal signaling states that overpower the body's own resilient immune defenses against cancer. The result of this adaptive process is not just cancer cell survival, but an overall

Structural Violence. Elena Ruíz, Oxford University Press. © Oxford University Press 2024.
DOI: 10.1093/oso/9780197634028.003.0001

system escalation in cancer cell function. In other words, the cancer can now do harm as a system that it could not do before it was attacked.

This imagery of a self-healing and adaptive physical system that overcomes the resilient functions of other systems in response to attacks against it has stayed with me as a feminist decolonial scholar of violence. It calls to mind what US legal historian Reva Siegel terms "preservation through transformation."[5] Preservation through transformation refers to a status-enforcing state action that "evolves in form as it is contested" through the legal system, ensuring that the harms the legal system purports to address for victims of violence live on to inflict even more violence and injury on people and communities after the harm is legally addressed.[6] A remarkable breadth of legal and policy examples exist to illustrate this process.

For example, marriage or cohabitation was a valid legal defense for rape in every US state until the 1970s. Feminists fought back.[7] When legislatures and courts relented to social pressure and began eliminating these exemptions,[8] a new crop of gender-based policies governing domestic violence emerged that placed new barriers to relief. Courts increasingly relied on difficult-to-obtain forensic evidence to establish "proof of force and/or resistance" and established "shorter time frames by which a woman has to report rape by her husband, ultimately making spousal rape more difficult to prosecute."[9]

The legal system adapted to attacks against it—yes, the legal system, not the old statutory codes or legislation that made up the marital rape exemption as a functioning subsystem in US law.

The goals and self-regulative capacities of settler colonial (key terms are defined in the notes) social systems are easily obscured through law and policy. They are also obscured through race-neutral reasoning meant to produce plausible deniability for the harmful design of these systems. Accepting at face value the professed reasons why institutions like US law and policing exist (and what their purported goals are) contributes to an evasion of responsibility. Why do these institutions exist in the ways that they do, when they reliably produce observably disparate outcomes for different populations? Black children, for example, are far more likely than white children in the United States to be exposed to lead in early childhood.[10] There is no safe detectable blood level for lead. And yet "If a young black girl and a young white boy both lived in apartments with lead paint, and both their parents won a lawsuit against the landlord, the white boy could receive millions more dollars in damages."[11]

Settler colonial institutions are not here to protect us—not all of us, at least. As a whole, these institutions also produce an aggregate of benefits over long periods of time that are not evenly distributed across the populations they govern. Since the 1960s, for instance, white households have most benefited from capital gains. The successful concentration of stolen Indigenous land in white households and the dynastic endurance of settler colonial racial systems, continuously upheld through federal wealth policy, made this possible. It allowed white wealth accumulation to overcome the declining trend in the racial wealth gap in the years after emancipation.[12] Some populations profit more than others from the differential access points to economic damage awards, assets, income, and other drivers of economic mobility.

This profitable pattern of accumulation helps us understand why so many Republican legislators and intergenerational beneficiaries of settler colonial systems insist on using epistemic maneuvers aimed at legislating wealth policy, and it is especially evident in the recent attempts to whitewash history and contemporary reality in the push to censor education.[13] This is an old authoritarian trick used to obscure the mechanisms by which power, privilege, and wealth are continuously gatekept and protected by dynastic chains of transmission.

At the institutional level, the idea of preservation through transformation helps to show that "the ways in which the legal system enforces social stratification are various and evolve over time,"[14] but it doesn't quite indicate why. Why does the legal system adapt to continue to enforce social relations based on different racial, ethnic, gender, ability, and social status (including differential access to wealth, income, and education) so persistently over time? And why does the legal system escalate and expand its functions—often through a domain shift in the institutional mechanism or the area of law surrounding the harm-producing regulation—when under attack by reform efforts?

Consider that in the aftermath of legal challenges to "spousal rape" exemptions (e.g., *State of N.J. v. Albert Smith*, *Commonwealth v. Chretien*, *People v. De Stefano*)[15] several states introduced functionally similar exemptions that would prohibit "*unmarried* women from charging the men with whom they were cohabitating with rape."[16] The legal category of a "voluntary social companion" was used across various states to justify an increasingly expansive range of date rape cases, especially if the victim "had previously permitted sexual liberties" with the offender or if aggravating factors, such as the use of a weapon, were absent.[17] As is evident here, the legal system formed an adaptive pathway to ensure the dynastic transmission and structural continuity of gender-based violence, and, while doing so, it also gained in functional reach.

The gain in function did not affect all populations equally. The identification of who was most harmed by the adaptive response of the legal system is key to understanding its expanding mechanisms. In the evolving overlap between victim services, law enforcement, and the legal system, new patterns of disparate treatment emerged based on race, ethnicity, immigration status, and gender identity. This network overlap broadened the pathways through which victims seeking orders of protection could be harmed.[18] In the courtroom, increased reliance on forensic and photographic evidence to prove physical injuries from intimate partner and sexual violence placed higher burdens of proof on women-of-color survivors. Given how physiological differences in skin color affect the appearance of injury impressions,[19] particularly in photographs,[20] white survivors are four times more likely than Black survivors to have medical professionals recognize their physical injuries resulting from assaults.[21] This creates an evidentiary procedure that predictably places legal relief beyond the reach of survivors of color in sexual assault cases. The legal system, in other words, has found ways to transform old wrongs into new ones that target specific populations with even greater levels of administrative sophistication than before.

But why? After all, a system does not adapt just because it can. Sure, self-healing happens to be a property of complex systems. But a system adapts because it has a goal or purpose, or because it is programmed to do so in light of its overall system purpose and design. Built into a system's design is the capacity to discover errors in its functioning and to modify itself or redeploy resources at different levels of organization to achieve functional continuity over time, and to maintain stability across disruptions. Recall the metastatic colonization of cancer in the body—that system finds new ways to stay alive based on a molecular blueprint for possible pathways to reorganize in response to threats against it. It does not adapt just because it can, but because a specific system state generates a particular pro-metastatic response to survive impending cell death.[22] The goal of molecular research on metastatic colonization is thus to discover such an inherent design or genetic blueprint in order to build effective therapeutic responses to disease spread (based on knowing the set of genetic instructions for what a cancer is likely to do and how it is programmed to react to various treatments).[23] Survivors of color understand the inherent design of the legal system; we understand what the legal ecosystem (e.g., the police, medical examiner's office, health professionals, and victim services accessed through the prosecutor's office) is likely to do with our rape cases and how it is programmed to react to our testimonies according to well-established patterns of indifference and procedural dragnets that can overcome the caring zeal of individual point-of-care providers or officials.[24] We know all too well that we hardly stand a chance.

The impact of system design on structural resilience and continuity is significant. The politico-legal system, for example, has remarkable structural continuity. Consider the throughline between Republican state senator Bob Wilson's 1979 protest during a legislative debate, in which he lamented: "If you can't rape your wife, who can you rape?" Republican Todd Akin's 2012 absurd claim that women's bodies have a biological way of preventing pregnancies that result from "legitimate rape," and the US Supreme Court's 2022 decision in *Dobbs. v. Jackson* that overturned the constitutional right to abortion established in *Roe v. Wade* (under the Due Process Clause of the Fourteenth Amendment), paving the way for states to enforce births resulting from rape.[25] What populations are most harmed by these policies and governance stances, and who gains most from the structured maldistributions of such harms? The historical throughline points squarely in the direction of settler colonial social structures and the oppressive relations they enable as sources of maldistributed harm.

The famed "I can't believe I'm still protesting this shit"[26] sign held at the 2017 Women's March on Washington in response to Donald Trump's election offers a clue into this distributive design of harm. The sign reflected some existing awareness of (and frustration over) the self-regenerating capacities of social systems and the potential for social institutions to sustain long-term violence despite ongoing social change. But the sign also obscured other features of social structures pertinent to the design of settler colonial social structures, like who is designed to benefit most from gains in legal reforms and who is designed to be most harmed by rollbacks in legal protections, or by escalations in the enforcement functions of institutions.

Another sign held high that day helped correct the race-evasive narrative of feminist rage over the public resurgence of rape culture under Trump: "Don't forget: White women voted for Trump" (Angela Peoples, *presente*). A viral photo depicts Angela Peoples holding the sign while standing in front of three social media-engrossed, pink pussyhat-wearing white women. In an interview, Peoples said: "[The photo] tells the story of white women in this moment wanting to just show up in a very superficial way. . . . You're here protesting, but don't forget: The folks that you live with every single day—and probably some of the women that decided to come to the march—voted for Trump, made the decision to vote against self-interests to maintain their white supremacist way of life."[27]

For critical race feminists like Kimberlé Crenshaw, what's important about the self-reparative sociolegal process is that it upholds white norms over time, thereby strengthening settler colonial white supremacy's long-term ability to reinvent itself in new guises and to enact structural violences across a broadening range of intersecting domains and identities.[28] Anthea Butler's work on white evangelical racism illustrates why upholding white norms—and the corresponding trinity of beliefs surrounding "capitalism, the founding of America, and the idea that wealth is a blessing"—has been a dedicated political project with stubborn historical continuity.[29] Upholding white norms is a settler colonial project focused on accumulating profit, wealth, and power in economically austere terms. It's also about *violence* and the power to wield it in ways consistent with the dynastic design of settler colonial social systems.

The world of white norms is not accidental; it cannot be kept alive without a well-functioning mechanism that regulates threats to whiteness as a historically enduring and continuously adapting ecosystem of settler colonial social relations.

This is the work of structural violence.

Since at least the mid-nineteenth century, theorists of color and Indigenous scholars have framed settler colonialism and racialized patterns of violence across a diverse set of positions, locations, and experiences.[30] These diverse lineages—spanning Black radical, decolonial, anticolonial, abolitionist, and women-of-color feminisms, Indigenous resurgence, and traditions of resistance to colonial framings of gender variance and disability—deeply underscore the structural features of colonial violence.[31]

Frantz Fanon, for example, believed racism to be fundamentally structural, and therefore that "the habit of considering racism as a mental quirk, a psychological flaw, must be abandoned" in favor of intentionally orchestrated views of colonial violence that reproduce racism across institutions.[32] Leanne Betasamosake Simpson (Michi Sagiig Nishnaabeg) uses a grounded (land-based) normative perspective to illustrate, in exceedingly clear terms, what the payoff for ongoing settler colonial structural violence is and for whom: "Colonizers wanted the land. Everything else, whether it is legal or policy or economic or social, whether it was the Indian Act or residential schools or gender violence, was part of the machinery that was designed to create a perfect crime—a crime where the victims are unable to see or name the crime as a crime."[33] Angela Davis famously argued slavery should be seen as a concerted system of organized domination that requires the existence of a distinct structure—a "slaveocracy"—that fundamentally links capitalist economic systems, agricultural production, and specialized techniques of violence (such as rape, torture, and confinement) to produce asymmetric profit for white settler populations and their descendants.[34] Michelle Alexander's bestselling title, *The New Jim Crow*, skillfully outlined the massive and continuing scope of white supremacy in the structural evolution of mass incarceration from the plantation economies of the antebellum South to the modern sprawling prison industry. Alexander argues that racism "is embedded in the structure of a social system," and, as such, "the widespread and mistaken belief that racial animus is necessary for the creation and maintenance of racialized systems of social control is the most important reason that we, as a nation, have remained in deep denial" about the many lifelines white supremacy retains in order to survive challenges to its existence.[35]

From Fanon to Alexander, a powerful throughline exists about the structural resilience of violence and discrimination based on colonial origins, and about the ability of oppressive systems to "shapeshift"[36] and use a variety of mechanisms (administrative, epistemological, and cultural) to adapt to attacks and challenges to their existence. All these works reject the view of social inequality as either accidentally produced or as the product of impersonal forces that have no link to colonial violence. As the extensive literature across Indigenous studies, ethnic studies, critical education studies, critical geography, Black studies, Latinx and Latin American studies, women-of-color feminisms, queer studies and critical trans studies, critical disability studies, and postcolonial and decolonial studies suggest, there is no shortage of internal debates and diverse approaches to the framing of (and methods for) interpreting structural violence in relation to colonialism. While they may not reach consensus on the methods of analysis, the specific modalities of structural violence, or the global character of the various historical processes of colonization that produce death and displacement for specific populations, these diverse literatures are clear on what structural violence is not: an accident.

This consistency across diverse fields and activisms has renewed calls for approaches to social justice based on system-level change.[37] The existing literature on systems theory has done little to meet the moment.[38] Systems theories of society (e.g., what social systems are and how they operate as an integrated structural whole or "relational network") built on naturalized views of social structure tend to emphasize morphostatic and morphogenetic processes that restate the obvious: systems can adapt and self-heal.[39] Yet they offer no insights into the dynastic chains of transmission that prevail in settler colonial social systems or into why these dynamics endure. This results in whitewashed "systems based" theories of change that reduce colonialism to situational or environmental variables that portray the causal powers and emergent properties of settler colonial social structures as derivative or accidental, rather than as part of an inherent design—and a very old one at that.[40] This is where the focus on anticolonial literatures serves as an important corrective to eurocentric social ontologies and to views of systems as reducible to their network interrelations (and the emergent multilevel properties of social systems). Anticolonial literatures offer multiple insights into how settler epistemological systems uphold structural violence while also diagnosing the regenerative nature of settler colonial violence as it historically emerged, not as an idealized theory about how "context" always shapes social meaning.

It is difficult to imagine a theoretical tradition critical of colonial projects—from settler colonial studies to liberation theology—that has not, in way or another, homed in on the self-reparative and adaptive features of colonial violence—or made suggestions to the effect that systemic violences like institutionalized racism have found ways to overcome resistance, reform, and even revolutions. That's significant. It's an insight that has stayed with me throughout my work on structural justice, women-of-color feminisms and gender-based violence, Latin American liberation thought, and Indigenous feminisms in Abya Yala, and through my activism and organizing work against human trafficking and sexual violence in the United States and Mexico. It got me thinking about structuralism as it is traditionally conceived in philosophy, namely as broadly apolitical and therefore pretty useless as an advocacy framework, especially in the way structuralism is taken up in philosophical traditions of logical empiricism. It also got me thinking about the underexplored influences of systems theory (especially the notions of network adaptability and self-organized criticality) in social science and progressive economics research among the early strands of Latin American anticolonial thought, which is inherently political and meant to enact social change. Last, it became clear to me how political uses of structure-based theories in women-of-color feminisms, despite their long and neglected history, far outweighed the usefulness of whatever philosophy had to offer in ethics or normative theory.[41]

Alongside this realization, I was also moved by the rising social justice literature on structural oppression that surged throughout the 2010s and its resonance with my own experiences of injustice. It was a decade that began with the Arab Spring and ended with what the *New Yorker* heralded as "the story of 2019: protests in every corner of the globe."[42] Political scientists called the surge in mass protests a "pronounced shift in the global landscape of dissent" that placed people-centered power at the center of challenges to autocracy, authoritarianism, shadow democracies, and social repression.[43] The range of advocacy platforms represented in protests was as diverse as the places of protest, from civil rights to Indigenous autonomy and the Land Back movement, to calls for an end to the culture of systemic sexual assault and harassment (notably through the #MeToo movement). During those years of well-organized, global pushback against rising repression, systemic racism, enduring occupation, and rape culture, it felt like something was changing—a tide finally turning, a strong shift in wind speed and direction, a tipping point approaching that would herald a new era of accountability. Folks had had enough.

In the affective mix of collective mourning, outrage, and optimism of those years was the seed of a familiar fear. It was a fear common to advocacy work, where the dawn of cultural shifts and breakthroughs resulting from years-long efforts can be swept back into the ocean of progress by nighttime, often in one fell policy swoop or bloody government crackdown. That doesn't mean resistance was ever off the table. It means strategy had to match the shifting landscapes of repression, to keep up with the machinery of violence as it has been designed for centuries to adapt to change.

Knowing the long history of community organizing, activism, and scholarly work that preceded the burgeoning social justice literature topping the 2010s' bestseller lists, I was inspired but mostly frustrated. I was angered by the epistemic burden people of color continually face to prove the existence of nonaccidental harms to our communities. Here we are again, I thought—lighting the fires in the beacons, fanning the flames, harnessing the power of winds into waves of foreword social momentum, fighting languages of death and destruction with the creative abundance of defiance, with the rancor of youth and the technical deft knowledge keepers use to express urgency in creating change for our communities. All the while, it felt to me, scholars of color were once again compelled to make the case for why the coordinated and systemic violence that assails us is wrong or should not continue.[44] It reminded me of the need to shift the focus in racial justice literatures from the "wrongful white benefit"[45] that arises out of racial exploitation, to the rigorous examination of the structural conditions needed to interrupt and overturn the active, planned, impunitive, and ongoing structuring of death and dispossession that arises out of the administrative and epistemic arms of settler colonial structural violence.[46]

What we need is a strong offense as well as a strong defense. And the scholarly work of speaking truth to power, as it appeared to me, was largely playing into a defensive strategy in the design of settler colonial social systems to stem those efforts for change, and to turn our existing offenses into defensive strategies meant to sap our strength and energy long term. The goal is not to show that harm is ongoing, it's to end it.[47]

The Turn to Impunity

In 2019, while spending a fellowship term at Harvard, I attended a talk by the health sociologist David Williams on the cost of resilience. It spoke directly to many of the concerns I had about how we carry our grief—how it carries us into the grave slowly with the steady momentum of an object decelerating across an iced lake into a man-made hole. We hang on as long as we can. The reality is that the endocrine system bears the weight of our grief, and that the daily blows to our nervous system place tremendous burdens on our bodies that have real consequences for our health and well-being. This harm can extend across generations and in the heritable changes in gene expression that are associated with environmental exposures to neurotoxins or to childhood stressors capable of crossing the "molecular bridge" between genes and the environment.[48]

When people laud us for being brave, inspirational, or, worse, "resilient" and do nothing to change the material conditions that induce the continuing need for bodily regulation of anticipated adversity and repeated trauma, they are maintaining the status quo that conditions war—a war some populations have to fight but not others. It's like thoughts and prayers after a mass shooting in the United States, sent sealed with a kiss from the gun lobby.

Williams's work on racial stress and attempts to develop an allostatic scale to measure the impact of repeated exposures to racism drew on decades of accumulating evidence suggesting that "psychological resilience in the face of adversity may lead to undesirable effects on physical health,"[49] particularly from stress during adolescence.[50] Well, who knew? We did. We live it.

Williams's work, and the social epidemiological literature on "weathering,"[51] helped crystallize my broader theoretical questions through the lenses of population-level payoffs and systems-level operations. Through these lenses, I considered who research is produced for and its relationship to institutional change, how the methods of our disciplines reproduce and are conduits for structural violence, and the relationship to knowledge production and cultural power in settler colonial societies.[52] As I worked through these issues in academic forums, a distinctive pattern emerged that characterized those research initiatives rooted in advancements in knowledge based on specific community needs. The pattern differentiated between tribalcentric analyses of knowledge about sexual assault prevalence,[53] and the kind of hamster wheel of theoretical and social scientific production on social inequality that goes straight into the dustbins of impunity in settler colonial societies, leaving us drained and physically worse off than before. By design, of course.

So I wondered. What would happen if accounts of violence and structures existed that supported these findings of social stratification and racial inequality on a more consistent basis, so that there was a better chance these arguments did not have to be made piecemeal, repeatedly, and at great psychological cost?

What would happen, I found, was that the regenerative nature and sociostructural design of settler colonial white supremacy would swiftly shift domains and find alternate avenues for reproducing harms and structural burdens that mirrored, if not redoubled, the previous tunnel of impunity in which accounts of settler colonial violence emerged. My focus in this project slowly shifted from the all-too-familiar structural phenomenon of violence and the endurance of racial systems to the problem of impunity for said violence.

Impunity is the structurally supported exercise of power without accountability. It comes from the Latin word *impunitas*, meaning a freedom from punishment (from *poena*, as in a penal colony). From Roman legal sources to the criminal law of the high middle ages, impunity became a cornerstone of legal theories of punishment in the evolving infrastructures of empire. While legal and religious texts repeatedly warned that impunity leads to delinquency in order to justify expansive administrative domains and authority over punishment, a parallel tradition emerged that routinely placed some infractions in a "private" domain, outside the reach of public retribution (both state-sanctioned and clerical), on the basis of social standing.[54] Who could get away with a range of offenses, and who was most likely not to (or to get caught in the growing web of strategically criminalized offenses), had everything to do with culture and the cultural regeneration of the rising settler colonial state apparatus.

It is no accident that settler colonial cultures, which are rooted in these ancient traditions, conceptualize accountability through logics of caging and punitive measures tied to the reproduction of settler colonial social relations, where some populations are disproportionately caged and surveilled for the benefit of others. It is also no accident that the dominant conceptions of violence, force, and evidentiary proof that evolved alongside carceral systems supported individualized searches for perpetrators while creating escape hatches of accountability for settler colonial societies to continue mainlining population-level harms. It's an ecosystem of impunity, plain as day.

We often talk about systemic oppression as the result of "the system" doing its thing. What is "the system's" purpose, after all? What's the goal, the endgame of the structured harm exhibited in the behavior of settler colonial social structures? And how does a settler colonial social system's purpose relate to the distributed design of harm so painfully evident in "systemic racism"?—a phenomenon aptly described by Ruth Wilson Gilmore's definition of racism as the "production and exploitation of group-differentiated vulnerabilities to premature death, in distinct yet densely interconnected political geographies."[55] As an ecosystem, perhaps a nonwhitewashed systems framing that is historically deep and attuned to the goals of settler white supremacy could be helpful in telling the story of settler colonial impunity for structured harm and systemic violence. And I have a story to tell.

Impunity today is narrowly understood as that which escapes state-sponsored punishment in the existing governance schemes of settler colonial cultures. It is a notion that endures, generation after generation, revolution after revolution, and as a structurally produced epistemological feature of settler colonial social regeneration. I think settler colonial impunity and the prevailing notions of structural violence are deeply linked. How are they linked, you ask? As TikTok star RaeShanda Lias-Lockhart says as she diagrams social problems, "Let's check the board."

The Project

This book theorizes the existence of self-repairing *dynastic historical formations*—what I call "white dynastic formations"—that underwrite cultures of violence in settler colonial societies, but whose corresponding epistemic forces tied to wealth accumulation and group privilege often go untracked. This book recognizes the role these epistemic forces play in producing and maintaining the massive disparities in health inequality and the maldistribution of disease burdens for marginalized populations, including sexual violence. Whiteness, I argue, is a cohesive system of structural transformations that cannot be disconnected from the structural iterations of gendered violence in settler colonial cultures. As such, this book challenges the commonplace view that dismantling structural racism can be done without addressing gendered violence. It also challenges the idea that current social policy initiatives and mainstream approaches to equity and inclusion are set up to make effective and lasting change. Understanding white dynastic historical formations demonstrates how such approaches are based heavily on models of social change—such as psychological models of implicit bias (and anti-bias training responses)—that overlook the deeply structural and dynastic features of white supremacy. To show the resiliency and impunity of settler colonial white supremacy, I give a step-by-step illustration of how white dynastic formations function, how they self-repair, how they shapeshift, and how they have existed in one form or another since the twin projects of white supremacy and wealth accumulation began formulating in the transition from classical to late antiquity.[56]

More broadly, I use the concept of dynastic formations as a tool to unpack the many and complex reorganizations of power that create structurally invariant phenomena like systemic racism and racialized sexual violence in settler colonial cultures. Structurally invariant phenomena are critically important to understand because they point to the veritable ways social phenomena can withstand functional change *as structures* when subjected to social transformations as social facts—how there can be racism with or without racists and rape cultures with or without rapists.[57] Dorothy Roberts, on the twentieth anniversary of her landmark book *Killing the Black Body*, expressed this idea by noting, with "a mixture of exasperation and expectation," that "all the devaluing ideologies, laws, and policies I wrote about not only persist, but have expanded in new guises to inflict even more injury on even more women and their families and communities."[58] I show how this capacity for expansion is built into the basic design of social structures that are rooted in the power dynamics of white dynastic formations. I show that democratic social change is persistently accompanied by a deepening of the structural mechanisms that ensure the survival of white supremacy as a regenerative structure, and I hold the line against conclusions that this regenerative capacity means we're done for—that settler colonial white supremacy and the cultures of violence it supports is our collective fate.

It surely is not.

Structural Violence is written in the spirit of producing frameworks that support the long-standing practices of collective and individual resistance to colonial occupation and settlement in the Americas. It is a critical project rooted in decolonial epistemologies of the global south, women-of-color feminisms, and in Indigenous methodologies that, following Dian Million (Tanana Athabascan), define theorizing as happening when "we engage in questioning and reformulating those stories that account for the relations of power in our present."[59] As such, this book does not provide a unified or transcendent theory of violence nor of structures. Rather, it questions the prevailing settler epistemologies surrounding what structural violence is thought to be to reveal cultural payoffs at various social levels, including the interpersonal and institutional. In the process, the book explains how a vast intergenerational system of epistemic wealth arose, which, in conjunction with settler colonial infrastructures of power, has been integral to the maintenance of racial systems and to the imperial accumulation of capital as settler wealth—to keeping the stolen land and intergenerational infrastructures of supportive institutional affordances that allow some populations to access systems of impunity with greater ease and likelihood of success.[60] The aim of the book is thus to show how systemic racism operates as a coherent, transgenerational system of social transformations that can withstand foundational challenges to its existence, and to also show how this insight tracks back to the concrete lives of marginalized people—and to women of color in particular—via our daily experiences with structural violence.

Each chapter explores a feature of structural violence. Structural violence, I argue, is self-repairing (Chapter 1), deeply historical (Chapter 2), profit-driven (Chapter 3), intentional (Chapter 4), yet certainly not fate (Chapter 5).

Chapter 1, the longest of the chapters, addresses a simple question: What is "structural" about "structural violence" in the context of systemic racism in settler colonial societies? The answer is not much, actually, if we take the standard social scientific view of structures used to define the concept of structural violence. And herein lies the problem. Traditionally, structural violence is understood as a relational theory of top-down harm between social institutions—for example, schools, governments, legal and medical systems—and individuals, where the relation is facilitated by prejudicial social practices like sexism, racism, classism, and ableism that disadvantage people unfairly.[61] While the concept of structural violence quickly gained uptake in the academy because of its purported ability to track the influence of social power on human capacities, it has always been distinguished from behavioral violence by the assumption that it involves no identifiable culprit or aggressor. It is a hard-to-recognize form of violence that produces real-world harms that one does recognize (or whose impact one experiences), but where "neither culture nor pure individual will is at fault."[62] This results in a picture in which historically arbitrary social prejudices and individual attitudes and biases (implicit and explicit) are seen as the fundamental causes of systemic injustices in settler institutions such as the legal system, education, and healthcare.

Missing from this picture are the self-repairing, predictive, adaptive, and resilient features of structures and systems that are common to views of structure in the natural sciences and STEM fields, from developmental biology to chemical, mechanical, and electrical engineering. Also missing are notions of cultural liability, fault, and responsibility for the damaging outcomes settler social systems produce in the lives of marginalized peoples, which are common among views of structure in women-of-color feminisms and anticolonial liberation movements. These systems were set up intentionally to produce the very effects they do, that is, the maldistribution of harm that traditional views of structural violence describe as having no identifiable aggressor. Together, these two features of self-repair and cultural liability form the heart of the view of structural violence advanced in this book. Chapter 1 draws on systems theory and a complex network framing of coloniality to build the foundation for this view, and it outlines what a nonwhitewashed systems theory would need to minimally address to overcome the prevailing and culturally exonerating views of the causes of systemic racism. Culturally exonerating and liability-deflecting views, I argue, can be found in the most mundane (e.g., in an average Fox News broadcast) and unexpected places alike, for example, in the work of great feminist thinkers like Iris Marion Young. I frame the discussion of Young's work on structural violence as an example of the deep rootedness and adaptive capacities of settler colonial white supremacy.

Chapter 2 gives the example of testimony to show how settler colonial impunity is a historically and hermeneutically bone-deep phenomenon tied to the endurance of gender-based violence. Since the beginning of european colonization, sexual violence against racialized women in the Americas perseveres despite the enactment of sweeping social reforms associated with the rise of democratic nation-states. Administrative structures enable wide-scale impunity for sexual violence and allow its production by interlocking oppressions to continue unabated. The increasing impact and scope of sexual violence against racialized women since the start of european colonization is indicative of the structural automation of injustice produced by structurally invariant settler colonial systems. This chapter draws on legal case studies and a conceptual history of testimony in gender-based violence cases to illustrate how structural invariance sustains white dynastic formations through social transformations.[63]

Chapter 3 illustrates that structural violence is profit-driven and that there is a formidable epistemic dimension to settler colonialism. Along with facilitating the taking of land, its function, I argue, is the creation and maintenance of an intergenerational system of interpretive wealth that ties power to social meaning in ways anticipated by Gayatri Spivak and many anticolonial thinkers. I place the emphasis on the relation between knowledge and profit, in plain economic and material terms. The framework of "epistemic capitalism" emphasizes that settler colonial social systems are goal-oriented and brings into focus the shared analytic of functional settlement that incorporates dynastic structures of white supremacy and dispossessive technologies of violence through the goal of extracting profit. The historical system of white supremacy that regenerates as an imperial, dynastic formation is designed to produce profit and ensure the controlled transmissibility of this profit. Decades of sociological studies in racial capitalism and economic inequality confirm the structural prevalence of race-based economic disparities, but economic models of intergenerational wealth transmission and wealth accumulation capture only the system outputs (e.g., economic inequality) of white dynastic formations, not their producing mechanisms, and often portray the outputs as historically arbitrary or unconnected to colonialism. Drawing on work in progressive economics—specifically, Social Structure of Accumulation theory—and theories of racial capitalism in the global south, this chapter develops the notion of "epistemic wealth" to explain the controlled transmissibility of profit in settler colonial societies and argue that a primary driver of social inequality is the intergenerational hoarding of epistemic goods that have been acquired and maintained through violence.

Concentrating wealth in dynastic chains of transmission cannot be done without knowledge infrastructures that promote accumulation. Cultural inheritors of intergenerational interpretive wealth profit from the structured harms to the knowledge systems of Indigenous peoples and from the structured disadvantages settler epistemic systems create and maintain for marginalized peoples. Yet white settlers can claim ignorance about the epistemic dividends they receive from colonial violence all while claiming to be fully aware of how they profit from systemic racism and wealth inheritance structures. This is precisely what interpretive wealth affords them: impunity. Impunity has an important place in the production and maintenance of structural violence that protects settler colonial intergenerational wealth. The technics of settler administrative systems and the forms of violence that organize their domination are thus intimately tied to what I call in Chapter 2 "settler epistemic economies." This is why it is no accident that today's mainstream concept of structural violence is itself a settler construct. As such, it is patterned to enshrine the monocultural realities of euro-atlantic peoples and to work in tandem with colonial institutions to prioritize settler lifeworlds and to continually rescue white settler innocence for profit.

Chapter 4 argues that structural violence is intentional through an extended look at "gaslighting." While the most formidable feature of the standard social scientific view of structural violence is that it is a form of violence that has no identifiable aggressor, this chapter shows how intentionally structured harm can exist without invoking psychological notions of individual intent. It explains the social engineering behind distribution-of-harm designs in settler colonial cultures by looking at structural invariance in healthcare metrics, such as Black maternal mortality rates. It introduces the notion of "cultural gaslighting" as a heuristic for identifying the intentional features of white dynastic formations and tracking the impacts of such predesigned harms in the daily lives of women of color. This chapter also argues that the US legal system is specifically designed to reject legal claims based on structural violence and explains why this is critical to its ability to operationalize racial violence while extending civil rights protections in name only.

Structural violence, I argue, is deeply hermeneutical, historical, profit-driven, intentional, and, above all, self-repairing. It is not a universal phenomenon across all cultures. As the history of white dynastic formations shows, structural violence always has a prestructure, a functional operand built through the active and ongoing cultural accumulation of epistemic wealth. A closer look at white dynastic formations shows that the systemic violences we face as people of color, and as women of color in particular, are neither new, accidental, nor the result of outdated policy or actively ignorant and misinformed agents exercising undue influence in the public sphere. They are the result of coordination. They are also the result of cultural gaslighting on a massive scale.

Chapter 5 illustrates and also moves beyond the idea of structural harm as culturally produced trauma that serves the goals of settler colonial white supremacy. Zapotec, Tsotsil, Tseltal, Chol, Kanjobal, Mame, and Otomí peoples living in what is now referred to as southern Mexico have long organized against colonial invasion and settlement in creative ways that interrupt the adaptability features of structural violence. Because Indigenous Zapatismo has developed dynamic cultural techniques for disrupting the structural invariance of social systems, it has become a main target of state and international agencies' violent interventions. Traditional scholarship attributes this targeting solely to multinational capital's economic interests in the resource-rich communal lands inhabited by Zapatistas. But the militarization of sexual violence against Zapatista women reveals a broader attempt by white dynastic formations to double down on the adaptability features of white supremacy. Zapatismo is thus not only an illustration of the indomitable refusal that is possible in the face of white dynastic formations, but a beacon for peoples everywhere cultivating cultural resistance in the fight for structural justice. "Zapatista politics is perhaps the deepest expression of the politics of care in the world today,"[64] and is a steady reminder of the varied self-defense strategies marginalized groups develop in response to the regional adaptive features of settler colonial social structures throughout the world. Chapter 5 also serves as a reminder of how, for many critical race and Indigenous feminists, the structured nature of progressive rollbacks under settler colonial social structures and relations of domination doesn't mean we stop resisting. It means that the bill for damages is getting longer each day for the continued violences we face in settler colonial societies and that material struggles still form the base of political organizing against sexual terror and against the impunity for the terrible toll of this terror.

Structural violence, as I use it, rejects the exonerating view implicit in the mainstream notion of structural violence as that which has no identifiable aggressor. It links violence with the imperial accumulation of wealth at the level of social structures and the epistemological systems that support them. I hold that structural violence is never accidental. It is a colonial technic that has relied on cultural aggression and epistemic territorial expansion since its conceptual and administrative beginnings in greek and roman inheritance structures and cultural imperialism. It is one that self-repairs, adapts, and has remained stable through various social transformations in history. For violence to become a functioning and stable system of structural racism, it had to have a supportive social infrastructure—a very specific way of relating social elements to one another in a functional, goal-oriented system. This did not happen by accident, nor did it happen overnight, and we can better account for the racialized relations of power in our present by tracing this nonaccidental link between the development of social infrastructures permissive of certain kinds of violence and the rise of notions of wealth as the accumulation of value based on material dispossession. Settler colonial white supremacy, in all its expansive and shapeshifting terrains of violence, is about profit, wealth, and power.

The Stakes

We need to talk about the "why." Now that the checklist is done and I've enumerated the "what" and the "how" of this project and met the formulaic expectations for a scholarly introduction in the discipline's publisher of record, we need to talk about the real sinews and carpal joints that bind this book together. The stakes. The brass tacks. The why this and not that. Getting down to the personal stakes of why, out of a universe of possibilities, I thought it worthwhile to heap more academic ash piles into the dustbin of history is important for at least two reasons.

One, readers who know my work may find the approach and methods in this project somewhat discontinuous with my body of work—which is very specific and rails against collapsing differences among global south feminisms or blurring distinction between the various methods for interpreting and addressing structural violence in diverse communities. Systems theory? That sounds an awful lot like an umbrella term—a "one ring to rule them all" move that can neatly parse out differences while retaining the internal stability of white supremacist logics to regenerate, much as western scientific theories of the seventeenth to nineteenth centuries codeveloped right alongside the racial taxonomies used to justify settler colonial social structures and discrimination. Systems theory can easily pass for a conceptual lens or macroscope that collapses differences in an attempt to produce a unified logic of conquest—one that can be preferentially wielded by the polities who designed settler colonial social systems to produce the very logics that assail us. No thank you. Such a macroscope skirts a little too close to the "ubiquitously ordinary" biocentrism of scientific narratives in social theorizing that Sylvia Wynter and Katherine McKittrick warn against.[65] And it definitely supplants Indigenous views of social structure as living and mutually reciprocal networks, like Mixtec corporeal processes, or the powerful process-based dynamics in Nahua and Andean epistemologies. Why this and not *that*? Why prop up theories that purport to develop a kind of "X-ray vision into the real logic of the sociopolitical system,"[66] when a normatively grounded and land-based framing of colonial violence can also guide the search for the "modus operandi of colonial power"?[67] Why chase after cohesion when complexity will do? I think that needs explaining. After all, Mishuana Goeman's (Tonawanda Seneca) "multiple grounded 'telling' of violence"[68] is deeply structural and can account for the overlapping, coconstituting, and intersecting violence Indigenous women face in settler colonial societies without blurring the relationship between white supremacy, extractive colonialism, settler capitalism, the transatlantic slave trade, diasporic migrations, and histories of marronage—as can many other critical race feminisms and Indigenous feminist frameworks. Systems theory (and the associated theory of white dynastic formations) seems, well, a little too neat and abstract. Nothing is grounded. Nothing breaks with it. Or so it seems.

To add to the disconnect, my work is also highly critical of attempts to go rogue with jargon and boutique theories that make those that theorize them famous while doing absolutely nothing for the people and communities we write about. My daily work directing an institute for structural change involves working with community advocates and grassroots organizers who have developed sophisticated theories of change and action charts that are uniquely responsive to structural oppression in ways that abstract theories of structural violence are not.

I'm an advocate of using scholarship and history to lend support to communal strategies of resistance, or to help get whitewashed scholarship out of the way. I ask: but what will this writing actually *do?* What is its function, who asked for it, how does it live, and how is it given different afterlives in the commercial trafficking and exchange flow of epistemic value that ensues once the paper leaves my hands? The uses and abuses of theory are well known. I use jargon to create very provisional "burn after reading" tools for naming harms and taking names. And here I am talking about "anticolonial systems theory" like it's a really important thing in the world! There's a disconnect here. How many community organizers are going to show up at city hearing, say, for zoning of low-income housing, and claim, "According to anticolonial systems theory these regulations are designed to reinforce settler colonial relations of domination and inequitable access to safe housing for marginalized populations?" Exactly zero. The objection is that frameworks like "anticolonial systems theory" are just piling on more syllables to names for existing practices and tactics developed to address complexity and intersecting violences by critical race and Indigenous feminists and community activists, and potentially covering over them. That's the real and only concern.

Two, and related to this concern—I think writing has consequences. Writing alone cannot "do justice to the social," but it can certainly cause harm. Some authors wield words as bandits would, with no accountability. They write with graceful entitlement, artfully manufacturing words from thought factories, adding self-affirming value to their lives while churning out a production line of prose. All for profit, or glory, or to fill a void, or because they simply can, and so they do. Activists and advocates are left to take up the mantle for substantive and collective change, and this takes years if not decades of generative work. Academics often swoop in with some new theory that steals from cultural workers by rebranding the obvious with the unpronounceable. I think the introduction of a theory of analysis for structural violence in this book therefore needs explaining, and that reason—that "why this and not that"—boils down to lived experience.

There's an unwritten rule in academe that the personal is not scholarly. That if we turn our experiences into objects of study it must be through the scholarly sieve of ethnographic methods and settler colonial phenomenological frameworks for interpreting lived experiences of violence—detached, externally validated, objective, measured, linear, reductively analytical, and evidence-based (or alternatively, as irreducible and beyond interpretation). Indigenous and critical race feminisms do not suffer the need for settler validation schemes as a matter of method and practice, and this partly explains why the methodologies of these feminisms are marginalized in fields like philosophy. Some folks need to be needed; whole fields and domains of knowledge are continuously maintained to support this need as a function of social power.

Frantz Fanon talked about the "colonial gaze" as a structure of representation that actively distorts and misrepresents people of color and Indigenous cultures by "fixing" or interpreting them through the vast interconnected networks of settler colonial cultural institutions and normative social practices. The colonial gaze is upheld through structurally licensed behavior. Less known than Fanon's famous theory is that the colonial gaze has a long history in higher education and in professions like philosophy. In cases where personal narrative does not take the form of settler ethnography or white autobiography, dominant audiences are given institutional license to critique personal narrative as unphilosophical. This mode of critique provides a veil of structural innocence that distances white audiences from the need to connect personal narrative with accountability and the many ways white authors are implicated in the theories they promote. There is a price to pay for personal narrative that not all populations have to pay equally. In fact, watching vulnerability on display while snacking on popcorn is a specialty of settler colonial white scholars.

I think personal narrative is important for accountability in many cases. In mine, it's important for giving a rationale for my methodological choices and allowing those choices to be scrutinized by the communities that they implicate. Andean communitarian feminists, for example, rightfully have little patience for some of the theoretical moves advanced in this book, and they have developed cosmovision-centric politics and epistemologies based on grounded embodiment (*cuerpo-territorio*) that use story work and collective memory to tell similar stories about the regenerative structure of settler colonial white supremacy as a dynastic system that are certainly more effective and appropriate for understanding gender-based violence in the region. The same holds for many Zapotec and Indigenous communities in southern and central Mexico, where my family is from. As Subcomandante Galeano put it in *The Crack in the Wall: First Note on Zapatista Method*: "Our banners are painfully elaborate, struggling to find equivalents for what we in our languages describe in just one word, and what in other languages requires three volumes of *Capital*."[69] I should have made a banner. No joke. Instead, at times, this book can read like three volumes of *Capital*, partly because I am connecting so much; gathering, assembling, tying, looping, weaving together, and braiding into patterns what are very distinct and different strands.

Again, why try so hard to connect the stars when complexity and difference will do? Not everyone who looks skyward tries to trace the connections among each bright celestial body, turning stars into constellations and unveiling the mysteries of the night sky. But I do in this book. I turn skyward and earthward and recognize the dynamic constellation of structural violence at every turn. And I recognize that this violence is by design: it has a shape, a contour, an earthly history, a regenerative social body, and a pastoral clock built across generations. This design drives changes in social landscapes in ways that are made to seem "natural" and inevitable—all to keep the targeting capacities and profitable machinery of violence going, generation after generation. More than one reviewer has called the book "ambitious." They're not wrong. But its ambition is proportionate to the violences I have encountered, and to the rage they have engendered within me.

There are some autobiographical moments that are important for constructing the personal stakes of writing this book and for shaping the direction of strategies and methods I employed. I'll share just a few. Many more could be given, but these are particularly illustrative of why the ideas that follow take the shape that they do.

Many years ago, long before the spring of 2022, I was lost in Miami. It was hot and climate-apocalypse humid, and my head was spinning unnervingly fast. I stumbled my way into an air-conditioned café, where someone in a white shirt came up and asked if I was all right, staring at the bloodstain on my shirt. I wasn't all right. I hadn't been in a long time.

I had driven to Miami earlier that morning to meet with a case officer at the district office for the Equal Employment Opportunity Commission (EEOC). I came prepared with a thick manilla folder, complete with colored subdividers and black binder clips bursting from the upper corner. I held it close to my body, as if the papers inside were an appendage that could reach out and speak for me if I were struck down that moment. A record would be left of my grievance. A sole objection. A resounding *no*.

But as the interview began, I sensed something was quite wrong, and wrong in a way no stack of papers or sovereign scroll of receipts could fix. I was trembling. My hands were clammy, then dry and iced over, like they'd been plunged into ice baths from the knuckles outward and then placed near coals. My heart was pounding so hard I thought Morse code might burst out of it. I was nauseous, and I wasn't sure if the investigator was one person suddenly replicating, or if my vision had turned them into a moving blur. And how could I feel so suddenly starved after stuffing down two bananas on the way in? I faintly heard mumbled questions for which I had no utterable answers. All I had was a folder soaked in sweat and now tears. Lots of them. I was, as the kids say, a hot mess.

The investigator stood up and returned with their supervisor, a Black woman in a sharp suit. New questions came my way: Did I have a disability to disclose that prevented me from formulating cohesive responses, perhaps an anxiety condition that if disclosed, could trigger mechanisms to allow them to continue the interview? How could I know that I had an ultrarare (less than fifty known cases) genetic condition causing these symptoms—that my blood sugar was likely hovering in the 30–40s mg/dL range and that my brain was very likely starved for glucose—or that I had a lesion under my brain, or that small strokes would later follow? I'd been to many doctors, and, like so many women of color, was dismissed when no apparent cause could be found.

So I shook my head no. Something was uttered, then something else, all to say there was nothing she as the supervisor or her staff could do for me in my state. Her tone was a master class in empathy. If only empathy was sufficient to produce justice, I would have been made whole. And perhaps it was my sorry, sorry state that compelled her to say more. She glanced at some papers, then asked me to pause and consider how remarkable my accomplishments were—"How many women of color do you know with a PhD? You and I know how hard that was," she said. And she was right. But it seemed harder to thrive with one, as if by design. I felt a worsening sharp pain behind my right eye and asked where the bathroom was. As I went to leave, she drew nearer and said, "I can tell something special has been laid upon your mantle," and her voice trailed off. The words reverberated around me as I made my way to the bathroom, where I passed out in a stall.

When I came to, I had a come-to-Jesus moment. This was not sustainable. Whatever quest for justice I was on, it was one that preceded the recent events and crossed borders and continents. My body was sending all the signals for closing up shop and going home early to be with family. Something had to change.

I had a choice to make. I could stumble back into that room, or I could summon the heart's reserves to remake my life once more—to walk out the front door, bury the past, and forge a new beginning by making peace with a future that was never meant to include a sense of justice. There would be no peace on the other end of my choice.

My notion of justice has evolved through the years alongside my structural analysis of power and culture, but for a long time, justice was wrapped up in a very simplistic need for public acknowledgment of harm done. I so desperately wanted to hear a simple apology or validation—an unequivocal "You did not deserve what happened to you," because self-blame is so often a part of survivors' emotional landscapes of recovery. But as I found myself barely conscious in a government bathroom with a nasty bleeding scrape, I thought, surely it was time to give up the ghost. We know what it's like to be tried-tired. I've tried. I'm tired. Bone-to-bone, thought-to-thought tired. What did I have to show for my years of quiet rage, persistent defiance, and refusal to succumb to circumstance? I'd been fighting different versions of the same fight for so long, and whatever resilience looked like, it was certainly taking a physical toll that no willful ideal of perseverance could outmatch. The body keeps the score, to quote the famous book title.

Somewhere between regaining consciousness and walking out the front door, I had a flashback. It was to years earlier when I had sat before another official. I had recently escaped my abuser and was living in hiding in a mold-ridden converted garage while attending college in Florida, looking for the next safe place to live and for safe work to afford tuition.

I was young when my perilous documentation status converged with a predator's path at an immigration attorney's office. He promised me safety and the lure of legal work. I took the bait. At the other end of the line was a reel of exploitation and trafficking that lasted years, taking me up and down the I-75 corridor of the United States. Fear, coercion, years of grooming, and threats were enough to keep me in place. One day I pushed back and was met with a fist across the face. It jolted me out of compliance but did nothing to lessen the fear of leaving. I hatched an intricate escape plan that hinged on finding a way to stay in school (this was before the Deferred Action for Childhood Arrivals, or DACA program, existed), so I told a school administrator what was happening to me. I didn't know I would be hatching escape plans for years to come or pleading my case as if I had caused my own abuse. What I remember the most from this period is just how many people—from attorneys to hospital and school administrators—knew about my situation. It would be an important part of my future thinking about violence.

Survivors of sexual violence often talk of disassociation, but less frequently of the deep immersion and hyperfocus that can take place during dissociative moments. For me, it was fixating on a TV show playing in the background—an early *Forensics Files* type of show—where I learned about the Racketeer Influenced and Corrupt Organizations Act (RICO) and the old maxim "Follow the money." I would build a RICO case, I thought, as I was being assaulted. Righteous vengeance needed structure, a plan. And as far as I could tell, someone was using me to make money, which was income, and they were not filing taxes on it, so there—it was a clear case of tax evasion, and a pattern of criminal behavior that included dealing in obscene matter. Someone would have to do something.

Now I don't know if it was the hubris of youthful inexperience or the belief that I could do this as a counterregulatory response to trauma (surely it was the latter), but I began squireling away papers and hastily written numbers on the back of old bank deposit slips, torn-off magazine scraps, napkins, or whatever I could find. I was building a case. I kept track of the numbers deposited into an account at Mercantile Bank under a fake name. All of it. I kept count. Then one day I walked into an IRS office with a very thick folder and asked to speak with an agent. My abuser may have had his day, but I would have my hour.

I was taken to a room where an officer greeted me and sat across a table. She listened patiently and jotted down notes on a legal pad. When I finished, she put her pen down and took a beat. Then she said that she was glad I had come in, that I was a remarkable young woman, and that she had a daughter about my age, whom she had wished could be there to meet me. I was, she repeated, an inspiration. Then the verdict:

"Unfortunately, he doesn't make enough money to make it worth our while."

The words seared. They still sear. I thought of the risks I'd taken, the time and effort and stolen chances it took to do all this. But I was nobody. Nobody of worth, it felt like. Just a walking token of "inspiration," and to whom? For what? The feat of remaining alive when so many of our kin are not, is not inspirational, I thought. What was my life worth? I was full of rage. How much *would* it take for it to be "worth their while"?

I learned then that having hard evidence is not the same as having power over the standards of scrutiny that shift to accommodate the economic goals of social reproduction in settler colonial societies. I learned that violence is unevenly distributed across populations *for profit*, and that some lives' worth are calculated as greater than others. I learned that individualized narratives of virtue are a cover for the functional regeneration of structural violence—that you can be met with kind, empathic, virtuous agents who are no match for the injurious design of social and administrative systems. I learned that it was not a question of whether or not the person in front of me *believed* me, but whether the world was set up to mainline institutionally defensive responses to claims that challenged the permissibility of racial and gendered violence. Some officials believed me, some did not. But the result of working with both groups was the same.

I learned that in an ecosystem of impunity, I never really stood a chance. The continuum of violence that shapes our lives as marginalized people is part of a deeper structure that I struggled in my youth to comprehend in its totality, but I intuitively understood. I sensed it. I just needed a push to reach the next logical conclusion: it's by design—who profits, who is harmed, and why. There's a pattern to violence that is never meant to be tracked through metrics developed by settler colonial epistemological systems, because it is not profitable to do so. The cost of these lessons, however, would need a book to recount.

By my senior year of college, I had resigned myself to the kind of experiences of preemptive dismissal and institutional handwringing without substantive action that Sara Ahmed captures so well in her book on complaint processes and attestations of harm.[70] The cost of this resignation was visceral. It also exposed me to further violence. Predators pick their marks wisely, after all. When a revered professor at the University of South Florida assaulted me in his home as I dropped off a manuscript he'd hired me to transcribe, I went into deep shock. I had thrown myself into school as a way out of my previous life—a path to independence, a possible work visa and health insurance coverage—and I blamed myself for letting my guard down, even with such a "trusted" figure. He said that by accepting work from him, I had been working under the table, and that he would hate to have to call immigration to report me. I thought about how swiftly immigration officials were likely to act on false allegations of a small amount of unreported income from a Brown woman, and how hands-off the IRS had been with proof of unreported income tied to criminal activity from a white man. I learned to hide my rage (really, a fear-rage) and dissimulate well-being, compartmentalizing every feature of my life and mastering task-oriented coping by overperforming academically (when not hospitalized, as I frequently was). I had insurmountable medical debt and few viable options. I made life decisions I would not have made had I not been trying to escape one predator after another. By this stage of life experience, the idea of filing a report on the assault seemed almost laughable—an act of self-torture. I chose to bury the past, remake my life, and start over. I would disconnect the constellations of astral animals and gods from one another, returning them to nothing more than single finite stars, each a tiny point in space and a world onto its own. In one single spot of psychic space, I could inhabit a whole life, detached from other stars. It was a nice thought. But thoughts alone rarely bring one peace.

As I sat recovering in the Miami café, I considered these flashbacks and my quest for justice. That old uncrushed need for reparative action and redress of wrongs had resurfaced, with the same dispirited result. In systems thinking, the term *equifinality* describes different potential processes for shared functional outcomes. My experiences spoke to the equifinality built into the design architecture of the regenerative processes of settler colonial social systems.[71] I thought of the multiple and intersecting experiences of violence on both sides of the US-Mexico border, and how similar the outcomes were in each case.[72] The techniques and mechanisms of violence differed, but they also shared a great deal. That's where this book was born. I needed more than being content with fast-forwarding through the movie *Kill Bill* to reach the line: "That woman deserves her revenge." I needed a map that illustrated the deep interconnections between my experiences, one I would have to draft as my own process of healing. It would turn out to be a map of intricate political design and great cartographic complexity.

Complexity is often used to explain the idea that things are not what they appear to be. This is especially true when simplistic, reductive, and dualistic explanations are given for what are otherwise intricate and multilevel phenomena, like the existence of inequality in contemporary societies. Often, we're told that solutions to very old problems we face are "too complex," or that the answers to systemic oppressions are as complex as the social systems that generate them. This is usually an epistemic ruse to mystify the solutions for collective change that already exist and to avoid the structural resource transfers necessary to ethically respond to these calls for change.

I want to use complexity to explain how things are exactly what they seem to be. Rather than hop on the hamster wheel of redundant explanations in a culture that produces the need for everlasting investigations into structural violence (where "No one is to blame"), I paint a picture of network complexity that illustrates an inherent design. This inherent design consists of a historically constructed probability pathway for distributing harm in settler colonial societies, while simultaneously upholding the systems-level ability of harm-enabling conditions to continue and to evade culturally specific structural responsibility for these conditions. I emphasize the living systemness and historical architecture of a particular social structure that, like a self-regulating thermostat responding to changes in room temperature, adapts and responds to stress points in order to maintain the status quo, and to avoid giving up the reins over the production of profit (or other value-driven end states of settler colonial social structures). I care about the ways settler epistemologies have developed intricate social tools and supportive colonial discourses for siloing blame and controlling the narrative of cultural responsibility for genocide and dispossessive violence, including sexual violence.

In western thought, violence is often reduced to the use of force and subdivided into types that can be studied independently from one another (e.g., as physical abuse, emotional abuse, economic abuse).[73] Like the siloed notions of violence, western accounts of blame and responsibility often rely on narrow notions of individualized punishment that promote settler colonial administrative practices. Individualized searches for justice are often part of a larger architecture of violence that plays right into the hands of settler colonial culture, where population-level targeting can be hidden through selective ameliorative responses to only the most individualized and publicly accepted cases of harm. This is why the problematic rhetorical construction of "the perfect rape victim"—a white, cisgender female who had no previous acquaintance with her attacker—has received decades of feminist scrutiny. If the mainstream notions of violence narrow the cone of possibilities for interpreting what harm is, all the better for the institutions that offer responses to harm, and for the polities that work to maintain dynastic, transgenerational power over these institutions.

This doesn't mean individualized legal responses to harm are not worth seeking. In many cases they are critical to an individual's ability to feel safe, to trust, and to feel supported. It means the plenum of the possible—for example, what form justice can take and the resources for healing that they enable—is reduced in ways that are not value-free or politically neutral. For instance, sexual assault is often used as a way to pressure Indigenous peoples to leave their territories and to interrupt practices of self-determination.[74] And settler colonial cultures reproduce social environments aligned with policies that undermine every stage of trauma recovery for populations of color and sexual minorities, so that the few resources and limited institutional responses available to survivors are often regarded as more valuable than they perhaps are. Again, this doesn't mean that it is not worth pursuing cases of femicide, rape, sexual slavery, and other gender-based crime before legal bodies like the International Criminal Court. The opposite of this is not that.

What recourse we have to ameliorate harm is not accidental. Reparative, restorative, rematriative, rebalancing, reharmonizing, tribalcentric, transformative, or rehabilitative responses to harm-doing that include community-led responses or integrative resource transfers (such as resources to promote Indigenous language revitalization) are not go-to recourses in settler colonial societies because they don't reinforce the other parts of the web of power that maintain the dynastic chains of settler colonial social regeneration in play. The recourse and resources that survivors, our families, and our communities need are not one-size-fits-all and necessitate far more than individualized legal responses. The fact that even individual legal responses are so inaccessible and gatekept means, for one thing, that the collective bill for damages is only getting longer by the hour.

My own process of healing is just that—my own. I think that is incredibly important to emphasize.

Sensory grounding techniques never worked well for me because of my medical condition. Instead, I developed conceptual grounding techniques that helped me through especially difficult times. These techniques are evident in my work on cultural gaslighting[75] and in the braiding of different traditions that make up the anticolonial systems approach advanced in this book. It took years of trying different approaches to find what worked best for me.[76] Remembering that the mainstream narrative of structural violence that's presented as a solution to our experiences of harm is part of a broader architecture of violence was extremely helpful, as was the conceptual map of network interconnectedness and system-level payoffs that helped ground me in a reality that refused the settler colonial explanation of what was happening to me and why. Not everyone needs this response pathway, and for some it can misdirect energies toward unproductive avenues that delink us from our embodiment, our lands, and from the existing wellspring of resources that reinforce alternatives to settler colonial therapeutic narratives to trauma.

For me, there was no clear intellectual tradition in the anglo-american academy, where I received my training and PhD, that spoke to the braided entanglement of the situation Brown migrant women of Indigenous descent in the United States who experience systemic violence across settler borders face. Philosophy offered the fewest resources.[77] Intersectionality came the closest to providing a robust framework for analyzing systemic oppression, and I think it still holds incredible relevance and applicability across a vast range of global feminist struggles. The lack of historical dialogue between scholars in ethnic studies, Indigenous studies, Native studies, Black studies, Latinx and Chicanx studies, Latin American studies, and settler colonial studies (especially in a North-South context) made it difficult to apply just one framework to my thinking.[78] In many ways, this book should have been preceded by a book on Brown feminisms that could speak to these gaps and tensions, to the neglected history of Brown feminist activism in the United States, and to the importance of analyses of colonialism and neoliberalism in intersectional thought in Latin America. It was a book I wanted to write before this one, but it was not the book I needed to survive the next moment.

Part of the active harm of sexual violence is the reinforcing of cultural mechanisms that uphold the ability of institutions to continue mainlining violence to certain populations as a matter of routine administrative procedure.

Given enough time, the slow drip rains down just as much as the flood. I chose to give up the ghost, but not without tallying the cost of my choice. No justice, no peace, after all. At a structural level of analysis, resignation has a cost that is simply too high to bear. When I walked out of the EEOC office, a predator remained unaccountable and went on to harm other women.[79] The professor who assaulted me targeted other women as well. And what stung was the burden of carrying these costs alone, despite knowing that other women had suffered just as I had, and that they, like me, would be functionally silenced one way or another. On top of this, I felt a deep rage, the kind that carries us to early graves, as if it were a lifeline rather than a negative determinant of health. What I wanted was some redress to stop the unidirectional flow of harm rather than for my case to be treated as a one-off, where who I was—or who I needed to become to be taken "seriously"—could be used to justify a particular outcome that did little to enact structural change. I would live, I would die, and the violence would continue even worse than before. That was not a narrative I could live with. I could survive, but never thrive. That is not living.

I've come to understand my need for justice as something far broader than the limited sense of individualized recognition settler colonial legal institutions are designed to offer in sexual assault cases. But I hold the line against the resource-scarcity rationale that uses that broad and evolving need to say we don't need structurally competent lawyers, educators, and doctors as a basic feature of justice in a settler colonial social structure. If this book shows anything, it is that social structures can be intentional in their design in ways that anglo-european social theory likes to obscure to create plausible deniability for ongoing harm.

The day will dawn when I can truly give up the ghost and rest. A day when I can give up the bodily hauntings that run through every organ, every step. A day when I awake, plant my feet on the cold tile floor, and release the rage to let in a spirit other than defiance. Today is not that day.

1
Structural Violence Is *Self-Repairing*
The Long Game of Colonialism

> We cannot begin to address the obscene injustices in this country without grappling with whiteness—not as a simplistic racial categorization, but as a deeply structured relationship to power and group entitlement.
> —Kimberlé Crenshaw

> Too often, today's researchers describe the phenomenology of inequality and injustice, but leave its origins and perpetrators obscured.
> —Fernando De Maio and David Ansell

Race and Retrenchment

Racial inequality is not an accident. It is not the unintended byproduct of human conflict. Nor is it the result of well-intended deeds gone wrong in statecraft. It is a carefully preserved social condition tied to value and its transference, garrisoned at every stage of transformation by a series of adaptive structural maneuvers thousands of years in the making. Just about every way of thinking about and tackling the problem of racial inequality has been influenced by these maneuvers. They reach deep, span wide, and adapt in real time like ad hoc corrections to construction blueprints. History is a good indicator of how these structural maneuvers outlast the bottle-throwing resistance of generations committed to social change. They operate in the background and ensure that "the more things change, the more they stay the same," as Patricia Hill Collins simply put it.[1] Or, as Ibram X. Kendi tweeted, "Racism now, racism tomorrow, racism forever."[2]

Kendi was responding to the Alabama State Board of Education's 2021 passage of the "Preservation of Intellectual Freedom and Non-discrimination in Alabama Public Schools" resolution, which forbade the teaching of "concepts that impute fault, blame, a tendency to oppress others, or the need to feel guilt or anguish to persons solely because of their race or sex" in the state's public schools.[3] The resolution—the first of many to sweep through the US— effectively restricted how racism could be taught in schools. It ensured that the teaching of historical facts in American history, such as slavery, could be structurally whitewashed by reframing the history of settler colonial white supremacy through race-neutral language that obscures the violent racism of this history.[4]

This was not the first time race-neutral language of "nondiscrimination" was used to roll back civil rights advances and to stunt people of color's antidiscrimination efforts in American history. Since the 1980s, legal scholars like Derrick Bell[5] and Kimberlé Crenshaw[6] have criticized similar tactics behind US antidiscrimination legislation and the structural tendency of race-neutral egalitarianism, codified in "formal equality" laws like antidiscrimination employment policies, to promote in function what the legislation claims to combat in legal purpose. "The race neutrality of the legal system creates the illusion that racism is no longer the primary factor responsible for the condition of the black underclass," Crenshaw writes.[7] Race-neutral policies are sophisticated upgrades to the more familiar "overt" racism of the Jim Crow South, but with a narrower functional range of legal pathways (i.e., more exist now but fewer are viable) to remedies for systemic racism. Consider Justice Alito's (2017) race-evasive equivocation of racial animosity with the animosity of sports team rivalries:

> Imagine two cellmates serving lengthy prison terms. Both were convicted for homicides in unrelated barroom fights. At the trial of the first prisoner, a juror, during deliberations, expressed animosity toward the defendant because of his race. At the trial of the second prisoner, a juror, during deliberations, expressed animosity toward the defendant because he was wearing the jersey of a hated football team. In both cases, jurors come forward after the trial and reveal what the biased juror said in the jury room. The Court would say to the first prisoner: "You are entitled to introduce the jurors' testimony, because racial bias is damaging to our society." To the second, the Court would say: "Even if you did not have an impartial jury, you must stay in prison because sports rivalries are not a major societal issue." This disparate treatment is unsupportable under the Sixth Amendment. If the Sixth Amendment requires the admission of juror testimony about statements or conduct during deliberations that show one

type of juror partiality, then statements or conduct showing any type of partiality should be treated the same way.[8]

Every day in US courtrooms, minority defendants brace for the mental slaps and deadly consequences of racist institutional acts and judicial practices that unfairly target and disadvantage, and result in unequal outcomes without recourse to institutionally recognized languages that name and remedy said racism. These practices range from the serial to the mundane: A Texas judge doubled a Black woman's bail for simply saying "yeah" instead of "yes" in her bail hearing. In Louisiana, the state supreme court upheld a lower court's denial of judicial review for a Black defendant who invoked the right to counsel by using the word "dog" in their request (as in: "I want a lawyer, dawg") because it was not clear to the court whether the request referred to an attorney, or a litigious human-canine "lawyer dog."[9] In Pennsylvania, court stenographers, who are legally required to achieve 95 percent or higher accuracy rates, correctly paraphrased sentences spoken in Black dialects less than 34 percent of the time, at times fundamentally changing the meaning of the defendant's attestations and entering those errors into the only official records available for appeal.[10]

Across the United States, a new wave of Republican-led legislation known as divisive and prohibited concepts (DPC) legislation is transforming and updating race-neutral antidiscrimination to cast an even wider legal net than before. In Wyoming, a criminal complaint was filed against library staff at the Campbell County Public Library for carrying LGBTQIA-related titles in the library collection, and two state bills in Indiana and Iowa that also removed long-standing legal protections for libraries and librarians soon followed.[11] In Texas, educators at the Carroll Independent School District were instructed to "make sure that if you have a book on the Holocaust, that you have one that has an opposing—that has other perspectives."[12] Few wondered whether "other perspectives" meant one was required to include instruction on the complex history of settler colonialism in Palestine-Israel relations.[13]

For critical race scholars accustomed to interrogating the methods and mechanisms by which white supremacy routinely enters legal and administrative procedures, the legal illusion of race neutrality serves a purpose beyond merely enabling claims of personal and collective ignorance for wrongs committed against marginalized populations in routine administrative proceedings. It serves to create informal epistemic precedents that can be functionalized, formalized, and marshaled in future rulings as a matter of objective procedure and legal reasoning in American jurisprudence and in policy (i.e., a chain of value transference is being forged). Racism doesn't just "happen," in other words; long before it arrives in the vividly recognizable forms we've come to expect, the ground is carefully prepared in anticipation of its arrival, and out rolls the red carpet. Some of the most arduous but unrecognized behind-the-scenes groundwork takes place through epistemic maneuvers that allow institutions to shapeshift and take on the necessary knowledge architectures to keep up with the changing faces of racism: from the color-conscious racism of the Jim Crow South to the color-evasive racism of Reagan's southern strategy, to the double-down neoracism of Trumpism and "white pride" militias that reboot Klan ideology and language. What persist throughout these changes is the functional reach of white supremacy, and its self-healing capacities as an organized system of domination.

Until very recently, the idea that civil rights are designed to be rollbacks-in-the-making seemed preposterous to the many Americans who grew up with the safeguards of Title IX or other democratic protections, like the right to reproductive choice established in *Roe v. Wade*. For those who study the history of racism (and its vicious intersectional reach and staying power since colonial occupation), such rollbacks are no surprise. In 2017, on the twentieth anniversary of her landmark book *Killing the Black Body*, Dorothy Roberts cautioned, with a "mixture of exasperation and expectation," that "all the devaluing ideologies, laws, and policies I wrote about not only persist, but have expanded in new guises to inflict even more injury on even more women and their families and communities."[14] To whom, exactly, is the rollback in rights a surprise? Certainly not to Roberts, nor to the critical legal scholars who built a program anchored in the idea of "retrenchment."[15]

Retrenchment in critical legal theory is the idea that democratic progress on race made through legal precedent (such as *Brown v. Board of Education*) is not a forward-moving linear continuum with the occasional roadblock, but a teeter-totter pattern of hard-fought wins and structured rollbacks of racial progress that uphold white norms over time. It is a lopsided pattern that requires one side to work significantly harder than the other to achieve equilibrium, or to correct against the repressive and regressive movement of conservative legislative projects and associated jurisprudence. What makes it "harder" is the continuous legal and administrative groundwork that, over time, fortifies legal reasoning architectures to more readily accept from counsel argumentative rationale (such as race-neutral legal reasoning) that favors white polities and upholds white norms of settler colonial occupation and entitlement. Using a clock metaphor, the pendulum swingback of structured rollbacks is designed to outpower the legal counterswings against racism. For Crenshaw and Bell, despite the multiculturalism of the 1980s and race-neutral cosmopolitanism of the 1990s, the balance sheet of history reflects the deep and abiding permanence of white supremacy.[16] "Racism is the permanent thesis," as Bell put it.[17]

Consider the landmark 2013 US Supreme Court ruling in *Shelby County v. Holder*, which rescinded federal protections against voter suppression established by the Voting Rights Act of 1965.

One of the most critical pieces of civil rights legislation ever to pass, the Voting Rights Act was transformative on many fronts. In the three years after the act became law, Black voter registration in the South increased over 60 percent. The legislation was designed with historical acumen for the persistent racist actions taken by state officials in changing voting regulations whenever Black suffrage was on the table as a constitutional and legally enforced right. It took into account the Mississippi Plan and Jim Crow–era "grandfather clauses"—which exempted people whose grandfathers had voted prior to 1866 from a litany of surplus voting requirements such as literacy tests, polling taxes, and proof of property ownership—as well as other persistent efforts to circumvent federal restrictions on discrimination following the ratification of the Fifteenth Amendment. And it crafted specific structural enforcement practices (much like the federal Enforcement Acts of 1870 and 1871) that directly responded to historical patterns of voter deterrence, especially in the South.[18]

To put it plainly, the federal government took southern state officials at their word when they testified before Congress and loudly proclaimed that, since its inception, the United States "is a government of the white race" and should stay that way.[19]

The Voting Rights Act of 1965 thus enshrined the legal expectation that state and local officials could and likely would, unencumbered by federal oversight, return to their known and established historical patterns of discriminatory action, with the knowledge that some areas were more likely to reoffend than others.[20]

The act's enforcement centerpiece—its legal and social-transformative "teeth," so to speak—lay in its much-heralded Section 5. Section 5 established a "preclearance provision" that required states to first prove they were not engaging in racial discrimination efforts prior to passing voting legislation. Between 1982 and 2006, under Section 5, the Department of Justice rejected over seven hundred proposed changes to voting regulations because they were discriminatory—a fact the late Justice Ginsberg pointed out in her dissenting opinion to *Shelby*.[21] Section 5 presumed that white supremacy was the norm because the structure of historical racism said it was, and it created procedural guardrails to contain its spread as it anticipated its recurrent reawakening across various parts of the United States, and especially in the South.

Writing for the majority in *Shelby*, Chief Justice John Roberts rejected the need for such guardrails on the basis that institutional racism was no longer a salient factor in the need for legal protections for minority voters. Racism in voter deterrence was allegedly over—a relic of the Jim Crow South, the court argued.[22]

Following the *Shelby* decision, resurgent Republican redistricting and gerrymandering of districts, stringent voter ID laws, and reduction of multilingual voting materials became the norm across the United States. Between 2012 and 2016, nearly three thousand voting poll centers and voter registration drives in predominantly Black neighborhoods closed, while at the same time new voter ID and REAL ID laws have passed in areas that concurrently shuttered driver's license offices near low-income and minority neighborhoods.[23] In Florida, after an amendment passed restoring voting rights to persons with prior felony convictions, state lawmakers quickly imposed new rules requiring completion of payment of court-imposed fines.[24] Today, state laws banning people with felony convictions from voting represent an estimated 2 percent of the voting age population in the United States, with the highest disenfranchisement rates in the South.[25] In Alabama, Mississippi, and Tennessee, more than 8 percent of the adult population is disenfranchised, and, despite the state constitutional restoration of voting rights to former felons, Florida continues to lead the way in disenfranchisement with over one million formerly incarcerated people still ineligible to vote.[26] This pattern of responses to voting rights protections illustrates the programmatic and recursive (self-repeating) nature of retrenchment under settler colonial white supremacy.

Testifying before the Senate in 2019, Stacey Abrams cautioned that the post-*Shelby* surge in reinstated or newly created hurdles, "while *facially neutral*, result in a disturbing predictable effect on voter access among minority citizens."[27] The late John Lewis, in a hearing before the Subcommittee on the Constitution, Civil Rights, and Civil Liberties, said the following on the Court's decision:

The Court's majority claimed that there was no evidence to support Congress' finding of continuing discrimination in voting in these States, notwithstanding the thousands of pages of recorded evidence compiled by this subcommittee in 2006 demonstrating the continuing need for this coverage formula. And despite Congress voting on an overwhelmingly bipartisan basis to reauthorize these provisions. . . . Tellingly, in response to the Court's decision, States that had been subject to the act's preclearance requirement wasted no time in pursuing voting restrictions that once again undermined minority voting rights. . . . In short, this was the "Jim Crow era Part 2."[28]

"Racism now, racism tomorrow, racism forever."

Kendi's simple tweet captured something critical that is at the heart of this chapter's concern with the structural and systemic nature of violence in white supremacist settler colonial societies. It calls out the ever-renewing structural capacity of white supremacy to reinvent itself and survive eradication into futurity. ("Racism forever," he said.) White supremacy's awareness of survival speaks to a much broader regenerative phenomenon than the prevailing and important account of its staying power in Jim Crow's transformation from postemancipation workarounds into the sprawling prison-industrial and convict-lease system documented in the bestselling book *The New Jim Crow*.[29] It also speaks to an underlying structural account of social regeneration, or the processes that sustain social reproduction, that is rooted in transformational and self-regulating capacities.

A Systems View of Retrenchment

Shelby serves as an illustration of the varied modalities this structural process of settler colonial white supremacist social regeneration can take, and it highlights some of its most important functional features. It shows, for example, how informal epistemic precedents can be systematically formalized and functionalized as part of a future-oriented project of white dynastic supremacy as a distinct social, cultural, and political project. Justice Roberts did not create the background conditions for his "race-neutral" racist reasoning to be especially potent and widely applicable, even on strict legal terms. The Burger and Rehnquist Courts that preceded him set up the critical infrastructure of legal and epistemic success conditions for the

Shelby ruling by actively "redefining racial inequality from a wrong in and of itself—and as such a presumptive object of civil rights enforcement—to a morally benign legal irrelevancy" that could be plugged back into future legal considerations of racial subordination in lieu of more potent social, political, and economic conceptions of racial inequality as a systemic and material fact in American society.[30] Same concept, but now with less teeth. That is not an accident.[31] That is the product of a concerted social and political process that is part of normal system of operations, one that requires ongoing epistemic groundwork and administrative shiftwork to roll out the red carpet for "racism is over" racism, and for its varied formulations in law and policy. This concerted process allows white settler polities to weaponize a broad range of civil rights strategies, such as flipping and reversing Dr. Martin Luther King's wish that his children be judged by the content of their character rather than the color of their skin, into DPC legislation meant to shield white children from "reverse racism" by outlawing lessons on historical injustice, racial inequality, and civil rights history in school.[32] Likewise, white polities can charge civil rights projects with "playing the race card" based on a purportedly suspect metaphysics of "identity politics," all the while obscuring their own formative identarian politics in "white rights" and the Tea Party movement. Also obscured is the important historical caveat that Black and Brown nationalism (as in the Black Panther and the Brown Beret movement in the United States) arose as self-defense coalitions against the genocidal persistence of white supremacy that continues to be embodied in white identity politics and the resurgent neoliberal projects of the settler capitalist state. Thus, what cannot be lost in this story of background shiftwork and complex system operations is who benefits: white settler polities.[33] Nor can we forget what perseveres through historical change unchanged: the pliability of interlocking oppressions and the power to maldistribute population-level harms through them. We are thus interested in how retrenchment functions as part of a broader socioinstitutional ecosystem that produces population-level harms and payoffs, including at the epistemic level.

The cooperative, mutually reinforcing, multilevel, and dynastic character of processes in the structural epistemic systems that rearticulate white supremacy is on full display in *Shelby*. What is this "dynastic" process? And how does it relate to the sociopolitical concepts of structural violence and systemic injustice that movement organizers and activists are all too familiar with?

One clue to this process comes from the systems view of life in ecology, and from emerging research in biology that upends classical evolutionary theory by showing that some organisms, like *Hydra vulgaris* (also known as *Hydra magnipapillata*), are less likely to die the older they get.[34] This is a helpful tool for thinking about the regenerative and adaptive capacities of white supremacy as a system—about the hydric (regenerative) life of colonial violence as a dynastic system of social reproduction that continues to thrive long after settler historiographers have closed the books on colonialism as a past event that haunts us only in our present-day failures to learn from it. In greek mythology, the serpentine Hydra famously grew two heads when one was cut off. Its duplicative and death-defying ability inspired the biological name of the freshwater organism. Under laboratory conditions, hydras have been cut, smashed, even liquefied in blenders only to reconstitute themselves anew and in greater numbers, showing no signs of aging even under long-term study.[35] People are not freshwater polyps, of course, and neither can we reduce social structures to biological structures in western evolutionary paradigms (though white supremacists have tried to do so for centuries to make racial stratification a biological destiny controlled by polities of european descent).

What systems views of social structures can offer is careful attention to the regenerative properties of social processes that are designed to strengthen a structure's purposes and longevity. It can help us predict how a system will react to attacks against it (whether in the form of external or internal forces that put pressure on the system's formative relational integrity), and to design interventions around it. This is of great interest to social scientists and intervention experts in public and community health, for example, who have designed decades' worth of community-based "structural interventions" that, by and large, have failed to substantially alter the structure of systems that said interventions were designed to target. Despite the structural inequalities laid bare so publicly by the Covid-19 pandemic, health inequality persists, and in many cases the domains encroached by it have grown exponentially. Many of the public health experts I've worked with over the years express the same frustration as attorneys and activists did during the height of the Trump era: here we are again. Sexism, racism, and rape culture are back on full display, with a bow of impunity tied around this time. Old policy tricks and statutes designed to uphold social inequality have reemerged, just as biologically reductive accounts of race as genetic immutability have reemerged in biomedical research,[36] evolutionary psychology,[37] science journalism,[38] philosophy of biology,[39] pharmacology,[40] race-based medicine,[41] forensic criminology,[42] and genetic ancestry testing,[43] and through race-norming in education and sports.[44] A systems perspective situates the resilience and stubborn continuity of racial systems as the product of very stable, organized, and self-repairing recursive processes rather than the flexile and contingent arrangements of racial formations across cultures.[45]

For this view to hold, however, we'll need to rework some core ideas in systems thinking that have traditionally informed sociological theories of "systemic racism"[46] without substantive engagement with "the matrix of domination"[47] or the global structure of "settler colonial neoliberal capitalism"[48] that informs structural violence in settler colonial societies. Traditional theories of systemic racism can tell us a lot about the large-scale hierarchical system of racial oppression in the United States that explains why racism (explicit and implicit) is so pervasive in American institutions, but it doesn't tell us much about the structural necessity of the precise mechanisms through which such oppressions are maintained, or about the nonaccidental nature of the social systems from which such mechanisms derive. It doesn't tell us what's "structural" about structural violence in settler colonial societies beyond pointing to the historical continuity of oppressive racial hierarchies, whether they are actuated through individual prejudice or institutionally reproduced biases.[49]

We'll also need to resituate traditional systems thinking within the broader epistemological universe and interpretive ecologies sustained by settler colonial cultures. This will allow us to reconnect the dots between settler colonialism, white supremacy, and gender-based violence as inseparable domains that are necessary to the reconstitution of structural violence in settler colonial societies. It will also help us question naturalized assumptions in social theory about social reproduction processes that obscure dynastic configurations of social structure.[50] In our last chapter, I lay out some alternatives to settler colonial social structuration that already exist yet receive little attention.[51]

Here I argue that in order to give an anticolonial systems view of social structures, particularly of structures of oppression that drive the phenomenon of inequality and injustice in settler colonial societies, it is necessary to make modifications to systems theory. Unmodified, traditional systems theories reproduce whitewashed accounts of structural causation that help functionalize impunity by leaving the origins and perpetrators of social inequality in settler colonial cultures obscured—reduced to independent variables in a nebulous causal cloud of social complexity that hides as much as it elucidates. This is most evident in the mainstream uses and official definitions of structural violence as the pervasive sociohistorical forces that structure inequality yet have no identifiable aggressors.[52] Today's researchers who adopt systems perspectives to study social inequality in environmental policy, health systems, social systems, and beyond are often unwilling to take the next logical step of causal attribution that goes beyond mere lip service to "context" or "history," as in "histories of racial inequality" or the well-worn explanatory matrix of "the social determinants of health." But where does it come from—the system that set up these determinants to regenerate when remediated through policy and practice? How did we end up with this system of structural whack-a-mole that is designed to exhaust us through structuring our very resilience as a necessary feature of existence?

Colonialism is a long game, one that did not end with the wars of formal independence from colonial powers, but which is rooted in dynastic processes of social regeneration and social reproduction that rely on a vast interpretive empire—an ecological system of epistemological and hermeneutic maneuvers that is used to reproduce the violence necessary to maintain power and, most important for me, the distribution patterns that concentrate wealth dynastically among white settler polities.

When describing social inequality through reference to complex systems and system processes, it is not complexity that roots inequality, it is the goals embedded in the system's purpose and design, goals that can be gleaned from the system's own behavior, but also from the instructions it inherits to self-organize as a system. To use a simple metaphor of a complex system—a living tree within a forest—as example, while a tree's branching system is characterized by resilience and angiogenetic regrowth under certain conditions, a tree also has a trunk and roots, and it uses its root structure to route nutrients necessary for continuing growth and to maintain constancy in response to external stresses. It also uses that root system to share water and nutrients through mycelial networks connected to other trees, as self-healing is an intrinsic ability of living systems that involves a diversity of pathways, including connections to subsystems and to the networks a system is a part of (or can reformulate pathways to become a part of).[53] Many scholars who study social inequality today readily accept the regenerative branching system of the tree but refuse to take the root structure seriously. The root structure is where I locate settler colonial white supremacy and the enduring power of settler colonial violence.

In the rest of this chapter, I will sketch out what I think is needed to build an anticolonial systems theory that invests history with structural causal necessity in order to talk programmatically about the need for structural reparations, structural justice, and system-level accountability. To date, the historical strategy of providing a factual picture of systemic oppression backed by massive documentation has not yielded the desired racial justice results of structural fairness and sociostructural accountability, so a systems story is given here that situates such massive documentation within an organized social design of selective uptake and salience that is strategically wielded by white settler policies through the process of social reproduction as white dynastic formations. If, along the way, amid the story's twists and turns, the narrative threat is lost, imagine Annalise Keating (Viola Davis) narrating *How to Get Away with Murder: The Settler Colonial Playbook.*

There are two main sections that follow. In the first section, "What's 'Structural' about Structural Racism?" I outline the range of conceptual maneuvers that exists in settler colonial societies to propagate perpetrator-free cultural accounts of systemic injustice and structural oppression. I focus on the implicit-bias framework and on dominant accounts of "structural injustice" and "structural violence" as examples of such maneuvers. I offer an in-depth exploration of Iris Marion Young's work on structural injustice for two reasons. First, it is widely cited across a range of social justice projects that frame problems of racial and gendered injustice as sociostructural rather than the aggregate result of interpersonal behaviors.[54] This would be quite helpful were it not for the continued silence that exists around Young's stances against historical reparations for slavery and against Indigenous self-determination on Indigenous peoples' own terms.[55] Second, I think Young's work and its extensive uptake illustrates just how powerful, pervasive, and adaptive settler colonial conceptual toolkits are, and the epistemic infrastructure that exists to license these views as mainstream and even liberatory. The same holds true of Paul Farmer's influential view of structural violence, which has had a profound impact across a range of public health and intervention-focused fields.

Against the views of structural injustices offered by Young and Farmer, I give an alternative account of what's "structural" about structural violence based on two interrelated notions: *structural invariance* and *distributive design* (or design-of-distribution strategies). Together these two notions get at the heart of Kendi's tweet—"Racism now, racism tomorrow, racism forever"—by illustrating the self-correcting and enduring historical patterns of structured maldistribution and designed probability pathways that continuously skew precarity and violence toward some populations but not others. The two notions support the anticolonial systems framing of structural violence presented throughout this book.

In this section, I also give a broad overview of structuralism and structuralist views in the humanities to situate these discussions and to differentiate between different uses of the terms "structural" and "systemic." These terms are often used interchangeably when talking about the persistence of social oppressions like sexist racism. I maintain this practice when discussing historical oppressions generally (as in the phrases "systemic racism" and "structural racism"), yet I caution that the way the term "systemic" (and to a lesser extent, "structural") is typically used has very little to do with the *systems-level* "structural" causation that I understand the term *structural violence* to imply. That is to say, "systemic" is generally used as a temporal or spatial aggregate to mean "it happens often" or "the practice is widespread" rather than phenomena that is self-generated and designed to actuate a given course and to guard against other possible outcomes.

In the second section, "A Systems Perspective on Structural Violence," I build toward an anticolonial systems theory rooted in the notion of white dynastic formations. I move beyond the traditional cost-sharing models of shared responsibility for structural injustice that dominate anglo-american political theory. I draw on work in racial capitalism, the metaphysics of science, and women-of-color feminisms to weave a three-stranded braid that supports a coherent picture of structural violence as intentional and rooted in culturally liability—a picture settler colonial epistemologies have worked tirelessly to conceal.

What's "Structural" about Structural Racism?

Advancing critical thinking about the nature of structures and systems driving racial inequality is a pressing need. In the last few years, structural racism has become the dominant model for thinking about injustice in political responses to state violence, but what actually is "structural" about structural racism remains ill-defined and poorly understood. For instance, vast resources have been put toward antibias training programs that focus on nurturing antiracist psychological and virtue-based reflective attitudes in individuals. This approach often assumes that what is systemic about racism is summative—that racism is pervasive because it is everywhere, and that its primary vehicles are people and their thoughts or feelings.

But personal bias (explicit or implicit) does not explain racism's resilience and staying power across all aspects of American life and globally. Neither does the framework of "institutional bias" explain it, as it simply transfers the responsibility for prejudicial outcomes and population-level harms to bureaucratic processes that exculpate individuals and groups for things like racial segregation in healthcare. Such frameworks serve to further mystify the causal and contributory mechanisms for systemic violence, not to clarify it. Understood as a psychological, mental, affective, or built-in disposition, bias at the individual and institutional levels does not explain the endurance of demonstrably well-established patterns of coordinated actions and policies that continue to result in precarity and death for marginalized populations.[56] The bias framework does not explain the current surge and success of DPC legislation, or the extent of reproductive rights rollbacks sweeping the country. Even the most progressive frameworks for social transformations have struggled to account for the enduring ability of state violence to adapt to challenges against it by simply amplifying harms in other public systems like healthcare,[57] public assistance,[58] housing,[59] the child welfare system,[60] and education.[61]

Before exploring what is "structural" about structural racism (and the related concepts of structural violence and structural injustice), we will need to close the door on implicit bias as a reasonable explanation for systemic racism. Some of the details necessary to do this satisfactorily will not be provided until later in the chapter, when we discuss the adaptive functions and purposive design of white dynastic social systems, and in later discussions about testimony and the structural nature of settler epistemic systems. Here we will sketch a basic picture that casts doubt on the strength of the implicit-bias model for pursuing systems-level social change. Along the way, we will reveal why it is no coincidence that the implicit-bias model is by far the most widely adopted and well-funded framework in antiracist training and resource allocation in the United States.

Implicit Bias

The most common understanding of implicit bias involves the idea that racism is primarily in the brain and that the expression of racial prejudice is mediated by functional cognitive processes that operate at different levels of consciousness.[62] The term was coined in the mid-1990s by psychologists working to measure nonconscious beliefs and ethnic biases held by people who did not think they held such biases in the form of explicit judgments (such as openly racist attitudes toward racial groups).[63] While the term "implicit bias" is not reducible to racial and ethnic bias, it has historically been used this way.

The psychological study of prejudice, which dates back to the 1950s,[64] changed significantly with the rise of liberal multiculturalism in the 1980s, and with the subsequent rise of the "postracial" state narrative. The political framing of a democratic "melting pot" in an interconnected globalized era coincided with the rising field of genetic science and the demonstration that there is no genetic basis for the idea of race in human populations. The idea that phenotypical differences cannot be attributed to genotype in matters of race helped construct a *color-evasive* (a more accurate term for the ableist term "color-blind" that denotes a structurally enabled refusal to acknowledge the social relevance of race under settler colonial white supremacy) understanding of American society, institutions, and social structures. This allowed discrimination to continue without institutionally recognized languages that identified discriminatory behavior as overt, intentional, or widespread. Following this development, researchers across various fields argued that explicit biases toward racial groups were on the decline for decades,[65] but researchers also sought to advance empirical and theoretical work in support of the idea that "the concept of race continues to play a fundamental role in structuring and representing the social world."[66]

The framing of "tacit racism" witnessed a resurgence in scholarly interest following the 2012 shooting death of seventeen-year-old Trayvon Martin, in Sanford, Florida, and a national resurgence in public interest in 2020 following the police murder of George Floyd by Derrick Chauvin in Minneapolis and the police killing of Breonna Taylor as she slept in her home in Louisville, Kentucky. The public outcry against police brutality produced a renewed interest in framing state violence through unconscious human biases and implicit racism as powerful drivers of social inequality. This gained traction in popular media outlets, as it was a preferable framing to the more implicatory and precise diagnosis of state-sponsored terrorism against minority populations (think of the murder of Fred Hampton). Between August 2004 and August 2022, for example, Google searches for "implicit bias" peaked in the summer of 2020 (see Figure 1.1). They also saw a significant bump in the months leading up to the 2016 election.

While it may have seemed new at the time to many of those witnessing the discussion, talk of "implicit bias" in 2020 was a very public return to decades-old research on covert racism that included studies on uncritical habits of mind as "dyconscious,"[67] "automatic" prejudice,[68] "implicit stereotyping,"[69] "implicit social cognition," and of course, "implicit bias."[70] The ground had been prepared for implicit bias to function as the neurobiological and psychometric version of "racism is over" racism.

Not all psychologists embrace the implicit-bias paradigm. Some argue that disciplinary habits, entrenched social practices and community norms—for example, ways of doing psychology in a traditionally cisgendered, white, and male-dominated field that promotes naturalized objectivity at all costs—have enabled the construction of a social cognitive concept that reproduces these norms rather than scientifically explains them:[71] "The analytic anchor becomes the implicitness, not the structural factors that socially condition the association or the actual discrimination and its effects (i.e., racism and White supremacy). Psychology's epistemic values prioritize understanding and the automatic responses to stimuli, obscuring how responsibility, restitution, rehabilitation, and reparation fit into the social problem of systematic racism."[72]

To further the argument that the social cognitive concept of implicit bias is a functional tool that ultimately serves the ends of white supremacy, we can examine the lack of scientific consensus on the empirical driving mechanisms of implicit bias alongside the widespread legal and administrative use of measurement tools like the Implicit Association Test.[73]

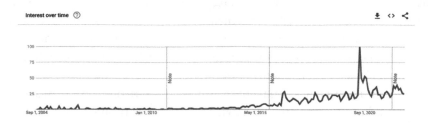

Figure 1.1 Report on Google searches for the term "implicit bias" between August 2004 and August 2022

Data source: Google Trends (https://trends.google.com)

Naturalizing Prejudice: A Double-Edged Sword

One reason the implicit-bias framework has been so successful is that it works like a double-edged sword, with a blunt edge and deadly edge. The blunt edge can be waived around publicly and portrays a picture of implicit bias as designed to intervene in pervasively held ideologies—to make our lives better, safer even. The other (less public) side, which relies heavily on a naturalized picture of prejudice to function effectively in law and policy, cuts much deeper.

Since the early 2000s researchers have attempted to find the neural correlates of prejudice through a range of studies that focus on amygdala activation of human flight-or-flight responses.[74] This research has enabled the wide range of legal arguments based on "threat perception failures" and "racial anxiety" defenses that disproportionately provide cover for white police offers accused of intentional harm or disproportionate use of force resulting in injury or death, as will be discussed in a moment. What is important to keep in mind is that the neurobiological research on implicit bias is continuously leveraged to frame discriminatory acts as no one's fault when it comes to systemic violence against communities of color.

The term "unconscious" has no scientific consensus in the vast literature on implicit bias. It has been widely interpreted to include implicit mental associations and psychological internalization processes that are "uncontrollable, or arational,"[75] pseudoconscious acts of "repression." Unconscious biases have even been reduced simply to "previously learned information."[76] Despite the lack of definitional consensus, fault or blame for discriminatory judgments that result from implicit bias is highly modulated by this unconscious component. Attributions of blame for discriminatory actions resulting from implicit bias typically focus solely on the discriminating agents' self-regulation of prejudiced responses to biases once they have been made conscious or explicit.[77] This mainstream framing of implicit bias as a universal human susceptibility and unconscious phenomenon is a double-edged sword meant to blunt the personal and collective attribution of blame for racism in settler colonial societies.[78]

Without functional accounts of racism as constituted by historical social orders and institutional practices that operate and distribute power inequitably irrespective of individual attitudes, contemporary accounts of implicit bias make it exceedingly difficult to hold institutions, social groups, states, and their systemic policies accountable for the reliably deadly and racist worlds they design, ratify, and historically help to maintain through race-enabling and adaptive infrastructures such as law, policy, and technology enforcement mechanisms. Implicit bias helps create the fungible background conditions against which political and financial power is concentrated in white settler dynastic chains, a phenomenon aptly described as a "kleptocracy" of white elites rooted in "a culture of impunity" that relies on the public narrative of implicit bias (as a preferred intervention tool) to succeed.[79]

What the implicit-bias framework does best is mystify the origins and causes of systemic racism by framing discriminatory acts as no one's fault. The framework then enables the development of real-world institutional mechanisms that reinforce this belief. As attorney Michael Selmi notes, "Legal scholars have fallen hard for implicit bias and dozens of articles have been written espousing the role implicit bias plays in perpetuating inequality. Within legal analysis, a common mantra has arisen that defines implicit bias as unconscious, pervasive, and uncontrollable," the effects of which are legally predictable: to "place that behavior beyond legal reach."[80] In other words, one of the primary reasons that implicit bias has become so popular is that it offers exculpatory power and a promise of innocence to those with the greatest ability to discriminate.[81]

Legal and Administrative Uses
The value of the implicit-bias framework to those who wield it is less dependent on its truth than on its function. As a framework, implicit bias is more than a psychological account of how social imprinting, memory, categorization, and other modulators of human agency and behavior relate to volitional action. It is a functional social tool that epistemically operates within a historical economy of power and stands in specific relation to existing institutional elements of societies rooted in racial systems. By ignoring and eliding structural power relations, the implicit-bias framework allows employers, for instance, to frame antidiscrimination interventions in such a way that white protagonists are positioned as the true victims of biased judgments.
Many modern human resource modules and employment onboarding antidiscrimination training sessions do just this: they actively incorporate and require training on implicit bias that frames discriminatory biases and judgments around white people's experiences with discrimination. A large tech corporation with a global media presence recently presented the HR training scenario of two young Asian women in a breakroom having a benign conversation yet excluding the other employee in the breakroom, a

young white anglo woman, from their conversation. One could not move on to the next module without correctly identifying the scenario as an instance of implicit bias, discouraged by company policy. The company, EVERFI, a major vendor for the education sector, produced the training module shown in Figure 1.2). It was not possible to complete the employee onboarding process at a major US university without agreeing that the "reframe" is the right response to discriminatory behavior.

One way to interpret the module is as an instance of what is known as *epistemic ignorance*. Epistemologies of ignorance describe "a particular pattern of localized and global cognitive dysfunctions (which are psychologically and socially functional), producing the ironic outcome that whites will in general be unable to understand the world they themselves have made."[82] It's a "Who, me?" response by someone guilty of a racial misdeed or participation (active or passive) in white supremacist structures of oppression, regardless of the actual degree of self-awareness involved (so epistemic ignorance can provide cover to Ronald Reagan and Donald Trump alike).[83] By contrast, *epistemic exploitation*, which occurs "when privileged persons compel marginalized persons to educate them about the nature of their

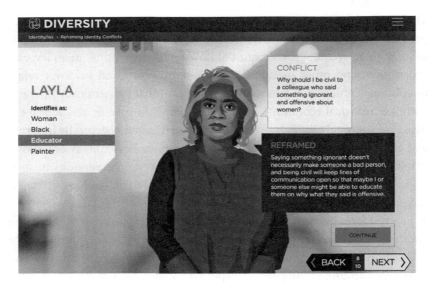

Figure 1.2 Screenshot of an exercise in the Reframing Identity Conflicts module by EVERFI

Reproduced by permission of EVERFI, Diversity, Equity, and Inclusion for Faculty/Staff, Published 2017 EVERFI, INC

oppression"[84] offers a nondysfunctional framing[85] of the same phenomenon that better captures the systems-level operations of the exploitative demands to be "civil" to racists, transphobes, xenophobes, and misogynists, and to accept the daily mental slaps of white supremacy in order to remain gainfully employed (and to get paid less for doing more at work). It's a "Yes, you—all of you" response to someone guilty of prejudice in the context of settler colonial white supremacy, regardless of the actual degree of self-awareness involved.

Another example is the well-documented use of implicit bias to produce institutionally legible exculpatory infrastructures in the legal system under the framing of "threat perception failures" and "racial anxiety" defenses, as noted earlier. Consider the aptly termed practice of "white caller crime":[86]

Dispatcher: "911, what's the address of your emergency?"
Caller: "[Provides address.] There's a woman pushing a shopping cart in front of my house."
Dispatcher: "I'm sorry, I'm not getting it. What's the problem?"
Caller: "You need to get out here now."
Dispatcher: "Um . . . I'm sorry, I don't understand what you're reporting."
Caller: "She's black."[87]

"The worst thing about it? I had to send someone out," said the dispatcher. Rachel Herron, the 911 dispatcher, illuminates the close relationship between policy infrastructures and the ability of civilian complainants to use public services and settler administrative systems to instill terror in the daily lives of people of color as a matter of routine procedure. These administrative infrastructures function as quasi-affirmative defenses (or legal protections) that help produce favorable outcomes for white litigants and defendants charged with (or under investigation for) hate crimes by framing discriminatory acts as no one's fault and beyond the reach of law. An example of this is the variance in successful uses of self-defense laws, which are often tied to threat perception as exculpatory mechanisms for white defendants.

The science of threat perception as unconscious "bias" has only served to provide evidence-based cover for race-based discrimination against people of color by white people. Between 1921 and 1945 in New Orleans, nearly half of all Black people killed by whites were killed by police, and most whites used self-defense as threat perception to justify the use of deadly force.[88] Between 1980 and 2012, young Black males in the United States were twenty-one times more likely to be shot dead by police than their white counterparts.[89]

Today, as before, the precise number of police killings and unequal racial risk of being shot by police is difficult to estimate, given that many of the nearly eighteen thousand police departments in the United States are not required to report fatal police shootings. Chris Burbank, a spokesperson for the Center for Policing Equity, put it plainly: "[Police departments] can tell me how many cars are stolen, but they can't tell you how many people they killed? That is the sad state of affairs."[90] This "sad state of affairs" is by design and infrastructurally supported by administrative mechanisms in law and policy.

Consider the following cases: In *Barnes v. Felix*,[91] a police officer successfully defended his use of deadly force against Barnes, a young Black man, by claiming he had a reasonable fear of threat or significant harm. Even though Barnes had no weapon and made no "suspicious movements," the officer departed from established procedure, and three minutes passed between when the officer pulled Barnes over and when he shot him, the court held that the officer's deadly force was reasonable. In *Graham v. Connor*,[92] a police officer arrested and physically injured Graham, a Black diabetic man undergoing an insulin crisis who swiftly exited a busy convenience store in need of glucose rescue. The Supreme Court protected the officer's conduct (who found Graham's quick movements "suspicious") under a reasonableness standard, finding his force was not excessive and as a reasonable officer would have reacted to the situation.[93] In *Illinois v. Wardlow*,[94] the Supreme Court upheld officers' stop and frisk of Wardlow, a Black man who ran upon seeing the officers while in a "high-crime neighborhood." The Court found that these two factors were enough to satisfy the reasonable suspicion standard in *Terry v. Ohio*.[95]

Self-Defense Laws
The precise legal mechanisms that place accountability for race-based crimes beyond the reach of law are varied and differ by national jurisdiction, but all have common roots in colonial jurisprudence and its roman legal antecedents. Since its inception in roman law (and its subsequent development in common law), the affirmative defense of self-defense has been carefully curated to provide institutional access for population-specific claimants and defendants. In the United Kingdom, the law of self-defense "takes into account only the honest belief of the defendant when responding to a perceived threat, without regard to whether such a perception was reasonable,"[96] making it exceedingly easy to claim justifiable use of deadly force

by police against unarmed people of color. As long as police "honestly believe" they were in fear for their lives when they used deadly force, they can be found innocent of an unlawful killing.[97]

Legal standards of "reasonable perception" provide little safeguards for populations of color in settler legal systems. The idea that how one perceives threat mechanically determines one's behavior is not a value-free idea, just as the ability to threaten is not value-free but guided and shaped by institutionalized norms that uphold heteropatriarchal white supremacy. In *Elonis v. United States*[98] the Supreme Court overturned the cyberstalking conviction of Anthony Elonis on the grounds that reasonable perception standards could not be applied to establish a "true threat"[99] under the federal law used to convict Elonis. Elonis, who is white, was convicted for using Facebook to threaten his ex-wife, a female FBI agent, and to threaten a mass shooting of a kindergarten class. When Elonis's ex-wife left him, he began a cyberstalking campaign that included posts like this: "If I only knew then what I know now / I would have smothered your ass with a pillow / Dumped your body in the back seat / Dropped you off in Toad Creek and made it look like a rape and murder."[100] After Elonis's ex-wife filed a complaint and an FBI agent visited him, he posted: "Did you know that it's illegal for me to say I want to kill my wife? . . . I really really think someone out there should kill my wife."[101] During the trial, Elonis's ex-wife testified she believed what Elonis wrote was a true threat and that she was terrified of him.[102] The jury that convicted Elonis applied an "objective reasonable listener" standard to convict him, meaning that a "reasonable person" would perceive the posts as actual threats. The Supreme Court disagreed (Justice Roberts writing for the majority), stating subjective intent (*mens rea*) to threaten was required to prove the commission of a crime under the federal law used to convict Elonis. Because Elonis claimed he was an aspiring rapper using artistic license to express himself, no such subjective intent could be established.

Nielson and Dennis[103] have documented the long and pervasive history of using rap lyrics as evidence to convict people of color in the United States. In 2012, Jamal Knox's rap song, "Fuck the Police," (in reference to N.W.A.'s classic song) was ruled admissible as evidence against him on multiple charges resulting from a routine traffic stop, and directly resulting in two counts of terroristic threats and witness intimidation.[104] The Pennsylvania Supreme Court upheld Knox's conviction, concluding that Knox had specific intent to threaten through his lyrics (the Supreme Court refused to hear the case). Such inconsistency in court rulings concerning threat perception does not come as a surprise, especially in light of well-documented racial disparities in criminal case outcomes. "A congressional review of the limited federal homicide data from 2001–2010 revealed that killings of Black people by White people were ruled justified 35% of the time. Killings of White people by Black people were ruled justifiable in only 3% of cases."[105] Self-defense laws create the illusion that subjective intent can be used equally by all claimants and defendants to argue in their favor—that what is at stake in the interest of justice is uncovering all the facts of the case to render a fair verdict, including the contextual use of force and the degree to which defendants believed they were in imminent harm when deadly force was used. The largely unsuccessful use of "stand your ground" laws as self-defense in domestic violence cases illustrates the system-generated functional disparity of self-defense doctrines. Marissa Alexander's case, which made national headlines, is a case in point.[106] States with stand-your-ground statutes have the highest disparities in race-based justifiable homicides favoring whites; among cases nationwide where a woman killed an adult man, white women who killed Black men were most likely to be found justified.[107]

> For Black people in White spaces, whose bodies carry the weight of cultural myths about danger and criminality and who may at any time be viewed as suspicious, threatening, or out of place by their neighbors, self-defense laws are a reminder that the law condones, and even encourages, fear-based violence against them. The laws create a framework that legitimates White fear of a stranger who looks racially out-of-place and condones violence based on that fear. This framework in turn helps normalize neighbor-on-neighbor surveillance. The cycle of fear, surveillance, and violence is also one that can be abused. Even if a person is not actually threatened or afraid, she can invoke the framework of fear based on racial out-of-placeness and can expect that police or a jury will be sympathetic. By underscoring Black vulnerability and White ownership, self-defense laws further inscribe the racialized character of White neighborhoods in an era when property laws no longer do so explicitly.[108]

It is no wonder that antibias training—which strategically frames the system-level production of structured disadvantage as the product of "dysfunctional" and largely unconscious subjective intent—is at the core of the over $8 billion invested annually by organizations in diversity training.[109] It is also central to many criminal justice reform platforms that suggest intergroup contact training, counterstereotypic examples, and multifaceted interventions (and not enforced accountability structures) can help reduce the disparate police practices against women of color, trans women, and gender-nonconforming women in the United States.[110]

The purported goal of antibias training is to disrupt the causal flow from implicit bias to discriminatory behavior through designed interventions that make those implicit biases explicit to those who harbor them. In practice, however, implicit-bias trainings and diversity workshops function to create additional burdens on and epistemic exploitation of people of color, who are called upon to educate their institutions and their white colleagues without buy-in from either and without institutional commitment to structural change.[111]

Despite the extensive literature and the number of studies on antibias interventions that show reductions in biases and stereotype associations, research also suggests such improvements are minimal, short-lived, and only work when individuals want to effect or consciously initiate behavioral change in the first place.[112] A 2017 meta-analysis[113] of nearly five hundred studies on implicit bias found that reducing implicit bias had no significant effect on an individual's behavior after training. To date, there is no evidence to suggest that changes in individual performance on implicit-bias measurement instruments (like the Implicit Association Test) translate to real-world behavioral changes that reduce inequality for groups negatively affected by the stereotype or implicit association. There is, however, evidence that implicit-bias training can make individuals more hostile toward other groups.[114] It thus has the potential to lead to far more harmful outcomes than simply enabling self-indulgent feelings of virtue in whites who view exercises in antiracism as a form of self-improvement.

In 2012, a study appeared in the *Journal of Psychopharmacology* claiming the prescription drug propranolol, along with lowering blood pressure, "abolished implicit racial bias" among the study's participants.[115] By 2015, researchers were applying direct current stimulation on the medial prefrontal cortex to test for differential responses to racial bias.[116] Propranolol ultimately proved fruitless in achieving datapoints necessary to garner economic interests from investors and pharmaceutical agencies. It did, however, signal "an epistemological shift in the meaning of racism" as medical pathology that was the culmination of color-evasive treatments of race.[117]

Despite a growing narrative of racism as a medical pathology (the stepping stone to making racism a federally protected disability), implicit-bias models still dominate contemporary behavioral accounts of why police are more likely to shoot unarmed people of color than they are armed whites, or why employers are more likely to hire mediocre white candidates than highly qualified candidates of color. The famed late sociologist Devah Pager[118] demonstrated that, in the absence of other disqualifying characteristics, employers are still more likely to hire a white man with a criminal record than a Black man with no criminal record. The fact that implicit-bias models continue to prevail in policy interventions and studies geared to address Pager's findings is no accident. Implicit bias is a functional script that licenses behavior and access to impunity mechanisms codified in training manuals, practices, and policies.

When framed this way, the epistemic function of the framework of implicit bias as an enforcement mechanism for white supremacy begins to come into focus. And we can think of that epistemic function as part of a longer historical continuum, that is, as part of a very long interpretive tradition in western conceptual systems of producing naturalized or universal versions of tacit understanding that function to produce specific sociopolitical outcomes for some populations.[119]

This section has shown that implicit bias is a structural pathway that provides the regenerative scaffolding for settler colonial social structures to survive into futurity by promoting at the structural level what it claims to tackle at the interpersonal level (racial bias). It bears family resemblance to antidiscrimination law and the irony that such law promotes in function what it claims to combat in legal purpose (discrimination). Philosophy is no different; the most promising, cited, and acclaimed schemas for remediating structural injustices are those that provide an alternate back route to the metaphysical and epistemic assumptions settler epistemic systems rely on to survive. These are features of *resilience* in complex systems. When culturally dominant social psychology, laws, and philosophy are regarded as social practices that emerge from the bottom up to express order and functionality in a larger complex system (here, a settler colonial social structure), it becomes easier to discern the role, purpose, and goal of such practices. And one of the first things that surfaces when examining complex systems is that functionality is not random; social systems can indeed spontaneously self-organize to exhibit patterns at larger scales that don't hold at smaller scales, but only by virtue of the sociostructural dynamics—the connections and scales of interdependence in the system as a whole—that exist due to the history that unfolded. It is this history that is critical for relating the logics of domination (dispossession, extractivism, containment, profit accumulation, perseveration, and violence, to name only some) that underpin settler colonial social structures. Chapter 3 will explain some of these sociostructural dynamics, noting the peculiar regenerative and perseverating (self-propelled recurrence) patterns settler epistemic systems display to stay together as a system (think of a banyan tree, and the way the aerial root structure branches down into the ground to form new trunks that provide entangled stability as the tree spreads laterally as a network).

Distribute Design

Here I find it helpful to turn to a political sociological notion I call "design-of-distribution strategies,"[120] or more simply, *distributive design*. Distributive design is how I work through the idea that administrative systems in settler colonial societies are set up to harm some people and to distribute harm inequitably so that other people benefit. When harms occur, such as when "structural racism" is identified in administrative systems, it is often not a matter of a "failure of care" in public health interventions or medical infrastructures, or a bias-based "failure of due process" in legal systems; it is a systems-level expression of the overall success of a system's purpose and design.[121]

The notion of structured maldistribution that characterizes the distributive design of administrative systems in settler colonial societies is adapted from social epidemiology. Social epidemiology is a branch of epidemiology concerned with how structure and chance are related in the distribution of population health; it assumes that "the advantages and disadvantages in a society reflects the distribution of health and disease" and that understanding the causes of disease and health outcomes in public health science requires an analysis of sociostructural factors.[122] When I talk about "harm" and "benefit" to some people but not others, I'm thinking at the level of populations. Individuals can, of course, benefit because that's exactly how population-level benefits are materialized, but the emphasis is on the probability pathways that are created, recreated, and curated in settler colonial societies that make some outcomes more probable than others for certain populations.

One particularly helpful example of how the dance between structure and chance shakes out at this level of analysis is a Galton board (see Figure 1.3).

A Galton board (or "bean machine") is a physical model of statistical probability that many people are familiar with through the TV game "Plinko." It

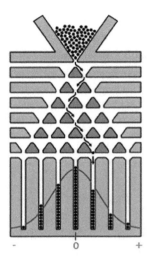

Figure 1.3 A Galton board

demonstrates normal distribution patterns (the bell curve shape in the diagram) given a standard placement of structural parameters (e.g., the even distance of the trays at the bottom, the midline placement of the bean drop above, and the equidistant pins in between them, etc.).[123] The "normal" distribution of harm in settler colonial societies is nonaccidental given the infrastructural placement of parameters (administrative, institutional, socioeconomic, etc.) that determine the distribution at the bottom.[124] The model also helps show that there will always be outliers—what seem like exception to the rule—but that generally, some populations are harmed more than others because of a preexisting design of distribution pathways (which requires settler control of space and lands). Over time, the more history settler colonial systems have to draw on, to self-learn and adapt, the more that settler colonial structures begin to look like inverted Galtung boards, with a wide input stream that leads to a very narrow concentration of wealth.[125] What flips the momentum are settler epistemic systems that adapt continuously to enforce things like credibility economies in history, as we'll explore in the next two chapters in relation to gender-based violence.

Settler epistemic systems are very important because they provide the interpretive schemas that hide such a distribution design and because they work to create self-doubt about the realities we inhabit as people of color and

Indigenous peoples.[126] These systems portray "land politics" and spatial displacement of marginalized peoples as irrelevant or ancillary to structural causes of oppressive phenomena, precisely because structurally, a meaningful structural intervention requires considerations of land—of what pegs are moved where and when that shape the skewed distribution of wealth, resources, and precarities in actual settler colonial societies, not theoretical ones.

In the next section, we'll move closer to an anticolonial systems view of settler colonial social structures (as an alternative to theories of implicit bias for explaining systemic discrimination) by rejecting whitewashed views of "structure" that are part of the design-of-distribution strategies in settler colonial societies.

Theories of Structure

That the phrase "It's a feature, not a bug" has become commonplace in social justice discourses reflects a relatively advanced understanding of systems-level thinking in activist circles. Although it originated in software engineering circles,[127] the phrase soon become a popular descriptor for identifying as designed ordinary system-level injustices that are often passed off as accidental or one-off instances. Even without theoretical grounding in structuralism or theories of structure, there is already a widely shared understanding of the basic features of systems, how they relate to social structures, and the relevancy of systems thinking to issues of systemic oppression.

Historically, this has not been the case in philosophy. Elsewhere I have argued that philosophy has narrowly confined structuralism and associated theories of structure to the "structural turn" in the philosophy of language, and that this disciplinary history is itself riddled with institutional power plays that are intentionally designed to exclude structural approaches to social issues produced by women of color and Indigenous theorists in particular.[128] In this section, I'll review some of this history and the mainstream definitions of structuralism. I'll use these standard definitions and mainstream notions to highlight patterns in the conventional thinking about structures that make their way into three concepts associated with social transformation: "structural injustice," "structural violence," and "social structure."

What Is Structuralism?

Structuralism is not a doctrine; it is a methodology. It is a way of analyzing things based on a theory of structure. The most dominant theories of structure that exist today stem from the scientific paradigm associated with the rise of empiricism and the natural sciences in the late eighteenth and nineteenth centuries. They can be traced back to Aristotelian natural philosophy, particularly to Aristotle's notions of causation, potentiality, necessity, logical relation, matter, and their continuing influence in the shift to mechanistic philosophy in the seventeenth century following Newton.[129] These theories influenced what became known as structuralism in the twentieth century in the humanities and systems theory in the natural sciences, which also employs terminologies of "structure." Under the mechanical paradigm, structures were seen as a way of specifying determinate relations between different objects of scientific study, where a determining relation shed light on an individual object's form and the laws that governed its place in a larger system. Whether the object was a natural language unit, planetary motion, family dynamics, social system, psychic phenomena, or literary genre, the goal was always to produce predictive knowledge that explained how parts related to wholes. The result was a rising body of knowledge on subjects as diverse as "language structures" (Chomsky), "psychic structures" (Freud), "class structure" (Marx), and "social structure" (Lacan) that claimed to have uncovered how things really worked in their respective fields by specifying the existence of an underlying universal structure. One appeal of this framework was the deterministic link between causes and events that placed human knowledge in the same domain as governable physical outcomes, thus giving the appearance of informed choice in a determined (mechanistically programmed) universe.

Over time, the natural sciences grew concerned with the limitations posed by the mechanical framework because it did not account for micro-level changes and randomness in natural phenomena. The emerging fields of molecular biology, ecology, and quantum physics sought to understand structural relations in living systems without relying on the Platonic metaphysics and Cartesian epistemology that had ruled the prevailing accounts of mechanical force. Systems theory arose out of this concern with the limitations of mechanistic accounts of natural phenomena, in which the laws of (Newtonian) physics and chemistry neatly described a determinate, push-pull universe in which the whole really was a sum of its parts. Natural scientists wondered: How was one to make sense of the structural complexity of natural phenomena like crystal growth, where the individual form's relation to the whole system was not self-evident? Chaos theory in mathematics arose in response, along with a key shift in scientific thinking toward understanding structures as dynamic networks. As physicist Fritjof Capra explains:

> The systems view of life was formulated first by the organismic biologists. It holds that the essential properties of a living system are properties of the whole, *which none of the parts have*. They arise from the *interactions and relationships between the parts*. These properties are destroyed when the system is dissected, either physically or theoretically, into isolated elements. Although we can discern individual parts in any system, these parts are not isolated, and the nature of the whole is always different from the mere sum of its parts.[130]

This interactionist interpretation of structure is evident in Swiss linguist Ferdinand de Saussure's famous statement that "in language, there are only differences without positive terms,"[131] meaning that when language is understood as a closed, autonomous system of signs, the relation between word and world is arbitrarily drawn from contrastive relations between other signs in the system.[132] Saussure's work was especially important for what would become known as structuralism in the humanities and social sciences, namely, the application of combined insights from the natural sciences (both the mechanistic and interactionist model) to the study of social structure. Structural linguists like Roman Jakobson (1896–1982) and structural anthropologists like Claude Lévi-Strauss (1908–2009) followed Saussure in advancing views of social systems as objective, universal structures accessible through logical analyses of the relations between elements in the systems they studied.[133] This lineage underlies a range of domains, from developments in linguistic anthropology to the semantic structuralism born out of the Vienna Circle's logical empiricism, for example, that is most associated with structuralism in philosophy.

Structuralist methods gained unprecedented popularity in post–World War II europe, in large part, because they constituted an ideal of scientific objectivism that could be extended to the human sciences. For the first time, social sciences could formulate theories in terms of necessary relationships, which allowed scientists outside the privileged domain of the "natural" sciences to achieve the same kind of "rigor" and "progress" that had been accomplished by fields like biology and astronomy. In time, however, criticisms of objective and synchronic views of social structures began to emerge that echoed the systems theory corrective to earlier mechanistic views.

Poststructuralism arose in the middle to late twentieth century in critical response to three of structuralism's main universalist assumptions: (1) the static view of meaning based on objective and ahistorical structures, (2) the linear view of time as ordered units of progressive development, and (3) a notion of a unified self-reflective subject as interpreter of structures.[134] Poststructuralism has often been described as operating with an implicit understanding of structure that is antifoundationalist. An antifoundational theory of structure works by dispensing with the empirical specification of a determining relation between the elements or objects in a social system. Think, for instance, of all the untenable assumptions after the post-Holocaust "death of grand narratives" and "death of the subject" turn in philosophy. What it retains, on the other hand, is the functional and operational features that are commonly associated with theories of structure in systems theory and the natural sciences. In other words, it keeps all the fun stuff, like genealogy, that performs the functional work of recognizing interconnectedness, relating parts to wholes synthetically to recognize how new organizations of "social power" emerge from regular system interactions (Foucault 101), or how logically binary "structuration" (in need of "deconstruction") occurs (Derrida 101), without the foundationalism associated with reductive empiricism or Cartesian first principles. This shift led to a widespread interpretation of poststructuralism as being a kind of "structuralism without structures" in the analysis of social systems.[135]

This idea of "structuralism without structures" illuminates a shared history in western scientific thinking and a historical division that developed between different academic uses of the term "structure."[136] The historical differences between humanistic, social scientific, and natural scientific framings of structure cluster around two main themes: (1) whether structures are primarily defined through their properties[137] or their functions[138] and (2) how the relation between "systems" and "structures" is conceptualized.[139]

System or Structure?
There is no definitional consensus on the distinction between systems and structures since systems can be described in terms of structures and vice versa, or used interchangeably, depending on the field of study and the scale of the analysis.[140] While I favor a systems-lens use of the term "structure" (e.g., the analysis of a structure-function relation), context is key, and not

everything—randomly scattered house dust along a tabletop, for instance—is a structure.[141] But there are general patterns of use for both terms that derive from the conceptual histories mentioned above. Here I focus on these patterns and operational distinctions to highlight the resilience of settler colonial white supremacy in the way philosophy adopts these distinctions, especially in the concepts of structural injustice, structural violence, and social structure.

In the natural sciences, systems are generally considered to be ontologically prior to structures. An ecologist theorizes the emergence of individual organisms and subsystems (like a coral reef within a marine system) within a larger biotic and abiotic system of interrelations and interactions (i.e., an ecosystem).[142] In the humanities, the inverse historical tendency has been true due to how notions of human agency and individual freedom evolved from early humanist views.[143] Radical humanists, for instance, locate "structure" within the individual being (e.g., in the self-encapsulated capacities for human reason and in the self-transformational properties of human will). In the humanist tradition, this agent-level interpretation of structure takes priority over an individual's place and role in a larger "great chain of being" (the system). The social scientific tradition has been to adopt something of a middle ground between naturalistic (systems driven) and humanistic (agent driven) accounts of structure.[144] Anthony Giddens's famous sociological account of "the duality of structure" is an example of this middle-ground approach, construing society's structuring "rules" or "scripts" and the very social practices those social scripts enable as mutually constituted.[145]

Structure comes from the Latin *structura*, meaning "to build" or "fit together." It is derived from the past participle of *struere*, "to pile, place together, heap up, make by joining together," and can be traced to the Proto-Indo-European root *stere-*, "to spread."[146] What a structure is, how it does it, and what it is meant *to do* (i.e., spread and self-replicate, like roman imperialism) has been part of the conceptual power grid of understanding structure that has been strengthening itself and adapting to changing circumstances for almost two millennia. The disciplinary differences between humanistic, social scientific, and natural scientific framings of structure are situated within this longer history of conceptualizing, for instance, space, building, conquest, time, endurance, and change through western metaphysical and ontological categories that support the development of settler colonial white supremacy as a dynastic formation. This history is not reflected in the narrow clustering of differences between disciplinary accounts of structure.[147] Instead, philosophical accounts of structure have fought over structure-property and structure-function relationships to justify an evolving taxonomy of "social structure" and "social systems" that regenerates settler colonial social reproduction rather than explains it.

The most common general definition of structure today is as a distinct set of "elements" (or objects) and the relations between those elements. Think of a scale model of a structure, like the colorful plastic expanding toy known as a Hoberman sphere (my favorite toy). Structure is something associated with the sphere, not the sphere itself. And we can describe this structure through detailed restrictions that specify the set of elements and relations we're examining; namely, the ball nodes or "joints" (the elements) and the connecting lines that represent the relations among adjoining parts. So to identify "structure," we can't just point to the ball as a collection of aggregates or composites. It is critical to also identify and specify the relations (the connecting plastic lines) among its elements.[148]

This narrow focus on interrelations is so important that some views of structure simply reduce structure to a collection of relations (e.g., imagine a building structure that withstands an earthquake or not depending on the collection of relations between its parts). But most views of structure downplay this focus and instead emphasize that a structure's purpose or function is distinct from its properties and its relations. This is illustrated, for instance, by the difference between studying an organism's anatomy (i.e., its physical structures) and studying its physiology (i.e., how those very structures work). Talk of function is generally "systems" talk. "Systems," then, are usually conceived as a general structure *plus* function.[149]

I think this distinction between structure and system is useful in some field-specific contexts. But in the social sciences and humanities, it is largely a result of conceptual habits that delink what a structure is meant to do and how it operates from what a structure is and how it stays together physically and practically.[150] This produces problematic views of social systems whose behavior is attributed to different levels of structural interactions (or transformations, depending on the model of social structure), and thus relegates the consequences of those interactions to a separable realm beyond social control. At the very least, it relegates the consequential patterns and functional relations of settler colonial social systems to value-free social processes and naturalized forces, placing the social nature of social facts in the domain of social inquiry and hypothesis for unexplained phenomena rather than in producing consequential responses to known patterns of established social forces. It's just another type of *mystification*, to revive a term Sandra Barkty used to describe gender-neutral social explanations that reproduce masculinist norms by design.

Similar to the transitional groundwork on the legal concept of racism done by the Burger and Rehnquist courts, this conceptual division between systems and structures sets the necessary precedent to obscure the true function of this way of thinking about social systems: to rescue white innocence at a plausible deniability level of race neutrality and antidiscrimination efforts. Social theory is replete with theories of social structure that separate system-level and structural-level interactions only to reunite them in views of social systems that do this: for example, make it possible to provide cover for, and accountability safehouses for, the intended consequences of "unintended conduct" reliably produced by the institutional formations and privileged social actors of such systems.

The term "structuralism," as it is typically used in the humanities and in the sciences, often means very different things. Yet both traditions share common antecedents from western scientific thinking, and are not, for example, consonant with Indigenous views of structure. Indigenous views of structure predate by millennia the organismic biological account of systems theory. They often rely on conceptual schemata that organize time, space, and causality using much older conceptual orthodoxies than Albertian or Euclidean space, linear chronologies of Gregorian or Julian calendrical time, or western views of linear causation. Because of this, they are often excluded from historical accounts of systems theory or structuralism. It is a critical mistake, but it is also a socially engineered one.

The siloed disciplinarity of the academy is an important point to emphasize because it helps explain how the social practice of framing structures according to disciplinary habits has led to a conceptual tug-of-war between different accounts of structure that overshadows an important epistemic tendency these accounts all share. Namely, the tendency to produce accounts of structure that facilitate the emergence of whitewashed theories of social structure in contemporary philosophical accounts of systems-level social change. These disciplinary practices allow for the continued mystification and obfuscation of how settler colonial conceptual systems give powerful assists to social practices and institutional systems that fortify oppression over long timescales and to the benefit of dynastic configurations of social structure. They also point to a dire need for a theory of structure that better supports social justice projects focused on bringing about structural transformations in society.

Structure and Transformation

Mainstream social theory views of structure are poorly positioned to do the necessary work that a conception of structure suited to social transformation in settler colonial contexts can do.[151] Since antiquity, when the notion of structure that made its way into social theory began refining its central features in the context of imperial building projects and roman expansion (particularly in the relationship between spatial order, architecture, and political organization), western views of structure have enabled a strategically limited range of political formulations of social transformation. This has enabled theories of social structure to emphasize the historically enduring character of western world-building that is common to hermeneutic philosophy. It has also enabled these theories to preserve social stability through strategically narrow notions of revolutionary or reformist change that emphasize transitional change rather that radical breaks.

Consider the notion of transformation, which is central to structuralist thought. Jean Piaget, who understands structure as first and foremost a system of internal transformations,[152] gives the following description:

> A structure is a system of transformations. Inasmuch as it is a system and not a mere collection of elements and their properties, these transformations involve laws: the structure is preserved or enriched by the interplay of its transformation laws, which never yield results external to the system nor employ elements that are external to it. In short, the notion of structure is comprised of three key ideas: the idea of wholeness, the idea of transformation, and the idea of self-regulation.[153]

This notion of structure as a system of transformations has also been central to western social and political theory since the nineteenth century. We find key representations, for example, in discussions of social revolutions that describe "structural" transitions from one statist form of governance to another.[154] The notion also shows up in classic forms, such as in Marx's historical materialism.

Egalitarian theories of social transformations generally interpret system transformations as intrasystem *transitions*. John Stuart Mill, for instance, observed:

> The entire history of social improvement has been a series of transitions, by which one custom or institution after another, from being a supposed primary necessity of social existence, has passed into the rank of a universally

stigmatized injustice and tyranny. So it has been with the distinctions of slaves and freemen, nobles and serfs, patricians and plebians; and so it will be, and in part already is, with the aristocracies of color, race, and sex.[155]

This social evolutionary handoff from one antiquated social institution to a less antiquated one creates the illusion of social transformation without transforming anything about the societies that produce these powerful institutions. It keeps intact the infrastructure for the restructuring of the mechanisms of reproduction that create and maintain white supremacy in the reproduction of social processes over longer time scales. Richard Rorty's narrative approach to liberal transformations, where "something traditionally regarded as a moral abomination can become an object of general satisfaction" in culture, is another illustration of the transformation-as-transitions paradigm, one where the dominant hermeneutic order (western culture) continues its structural reign.[156]

How "transformation" is theorized in relation to a social structure will yield a different picture of transformation—for instance, one "from below" that "puts pressure" on system elements like governments to pursue change, or "from within," a model that can yield reformist transitions of power.[157] But what, exactly, is being transformed through transformations? Answering this will require a more robust account of social structure in a political context and the relevance of modern systems theory.

In the interim, the idea of *structural invariance* serves to mend the gap between whitewashed theories of structure and anticolonial system theory. Returning to the tree-in-a-forest model mentioned earlier, when one part of the system is in need of self-repair, the roots can slurp up, redistribute, and reformulate the hermeneutic resources necessary to survive as a system—to change in form if necessary (as in the model of the banyan tree's aerial root structure) to accommodate system stresses, but never in function. The function never wanes. I refer to this functional continuity through change as structural invariance when discussing historical patterns of oppression.[158] This view contrasts with key philosophical models of structural injustice, as discussed below.

Structural Injustice: Young's Responsibility for Justice

In her posthumously published final work, *Responsibility for Justice*, Iris Marion Young sets out to formulate a theory of justice that is "appropriate for assigning responsibility in relation to structural injustice" that motivates individuals to pursue social change without assigning guilt, blame, or wholesale assessments of responsibility based on individual membership in a collective or social group (like being a class-privileged white person in the United States).[159] It is widely regarded as an important work in feminist political theory and in development studies, as it formulates a theoretical corrective to the distribution model of social justice that is based on John Rawls's analysis of the "basic structure" and the "core institutions" of democratic nation-states. It is also a particularly helpful text for unpacking what is "structural" about structural injustice in mainstream philosophical views of socially produced harm, and how such views provide new epistemic avenues for group-based abnegation of responsibility for ongoing colonial violence and population-level harms.

Young begins her project by reformulating Rawls's claim in *A Theory of Justice* that "the basic structure of society is the primary subject of Justice,"[160] and what it means to say that "structure is the subject of justice" in the context of "multiple, large scale, and relatively long term" social forces that place people in structurally disadvantaged positions as a basic feature of living in an unjust and globally interconnected society. Young is concerned that the staying power, multilevel workings, and immense functional reach of socioeconomic forces like globalized capitalism make it exceedingly difficult (if not morally wrong) to assign blame to individuals for the "sociostructural position" they are in. Her specific target is conservative policies that punish poor people for being poor and for situations that are largely out of their control, and which do not address the fundamental causes of poverty that keep people in cycles of financial precarity and constant risk of houselessness.

Young thinks conservative critics of the welfare state and luck egalitarians (a view that emphasizes personal responsibility in one's circumstance) vastly underplay the differential *opportunity set* that being in such sociostructural positions affords individuals throughout their life course. For Young, the nature of global capitalism also makes it difficult to neatly separate structural causation and personal responsibility for things like global poverty because, in her view, so many people are involved in the mundane, everyday goings and multilevel workings of free market enterprise: "Thousands or even millions of agents contribute by our actions in particular institutional contexts to the processes that produce unjust outcomes."[161]

Some of these actions may be more problematic than others for Young, like class-privileged habits of conspicuous consumption that continue to drive global manufacturing in the poorest, most vulnerable regions, where profit margins are greatest and labor laws the weakest. But most of our actions are purportedly less problematic (at least at the ethical level of analysis that assigns personal blame) because they emanate from reflexive habits and internalized preferences that result in very common social practices, consumer preferences, and volitional choices—in the very things that mark the daily comings and goings of everyday life under global capitalism. We go to Costco to get gas, swing by Homegoods to pick up a cozy robe on the way to see a sick friend in the hospital, make a pit stop at a florist, likely not reflecting on the devastating environmental and humanitarian impact of the global flower trade or the maquiladora industry that produces fast fashion. These everyday actions are what Hegel and others (such as Marcuse, Adorno, Horkheimer, and Marx) would call "second nature," or the internalized products of "ideology" that work like epistemic enforcement mechanisms serving the interests of historical class or ruling group interests. Taken together, Young argues, our everyday actions function as second nature to reproduce the structured institutional relationships behind inequality, even though there is no mastermind or statist puppeteer pulling the strings. While the diffuse and recursive character of social ideology leads many social conservatives to argue *no one* is responsible for poverty, racism, and other socially produced harms, Young concludes the opposite, that *everyone* is responsible. In Young's framework, everyone is implicated and yet no one is individually to blame.[162]

According to Young, constructing structural causation and personal responsibility as mutually exclusive is problematic on at least three fronts. One, it relies on atomistic views of agents who are isolated from intricately interwoven social relations. Two, it underplays the role of "social structure" and "background social processes" that affect people differently in society. Three, it promotes reliance on theories of justice that focus too narrowly on targeted liability framings of who (e.g., specific laws, policies, or individuals) or what (e.g., badly-structured or malfunctioning institutions) is to blame.[163]

Young thinks structural causation works differently than the way structural causation is typically represented in mainstream accounts of social and institutional injustice in political theory. She is thinking specifically of Rawls's description of the "basic structure" and how it generates the structured relationships that govern patterns of unjust or unequal outcomes in society. "Rawls thinks about structure in the wrong way," she says. "He, along with many of those who follow him, is looking for a *part* of the society, a small subset of its institutions, that is more fundamental than other parts."[164]

In focusing on politico-legal frameworks, he is looking at elements, in other words, not at the functional network of relations (particularly power relations) between those elements that characterize a social system as a dynamic, self-stabilizing, and self-regenerating whole.[165] That's clearly a mistake according to Young since "the structural processes that tend to produce injustice for many people do not necessarily refer to a small subset of institutions and they do not exclude everyday habits and chosen actions."[166] While it is true that, for instance, the courts, state apparatuses, and economic policies overseeing stratified labor structures are important, in any system some elements matter more than others. In a collegiate basketball team, the players play a more central role to the functioning of the system than supporting personnel such as team managers and sports information directors do, such that if you replace a particular player the impact can be greater, but each year players nonetheless leave and get replaced without changing the system itself.

If justice for social inequality requires transformations of society's basic structure, a clearer picture of society's basic structure needs to be given. For Young such a picture must be responsive to how social "structuration" works at different individual, institutional, and collective scales, and to the interactive and multilevel mechanisms it involves as a whole system of social reproduction. Rawls's account of structure just won't do in this case, and neither will his dualistic framework for evaluating normative concerns and applying principles of justice at distinct institutional versus individual scales.[167] To overcome problems caused by Rawls's dualistic framing of individual and institutional levels of social structure, which "too starkly separates institutional justice from individual action," Young crafts a structural story about a woman, Sandy, on the brink of being unsheltered.[168]

Sandy's story is constructed in such a way that her vulnerability to being unsheltered occurs despite her best efforts to secure safe housing, and where no interpersonal interactions involving prejudice, discrimination, or directly liable harm occurred: "All the people whom she encounters act within the law and according to accepted norms and rules."[169] Some people go out of the way to try to help Sandy, even when it is not convenient or riskless for them to do so. Thus, it is not the case that a string of individual "failures to act" or careless acts of nonintervention can be blamed for Sandy's situation. Rather, the "sociostructural" situation Sandy finds herself in is the result of complex background forces coming together in, for example, historical housing policies that disadvantage the poor, conservative-led social welfare reform and cutbacks on public assistance programs, gentrification, gendered pay gaps, red tape, globalization and the restructuring of wage work, the everyday habits of consumers, and the specific circumstances of Sandy's life. Dramatized for TV, the scenario would be scripted as a sympathetic and hard-working character simply being unable to "catch a break." It would also convey the feeling that *no one* should ever have to be in Sandy's situation.

Sandy's case is meant to be paradigmatic of the structural nature of houselessness and of social injustices more broadly, rather than a case of undeserved misfortune, direct discrimination, or bad luck. It is meant to illustrate that causes and solutions for poverty, like other social problems that affect large numbers of people, are structural, and that "structural inequality is a crucial form of injustice" that is undertheorized in prevailing models of social responsibility for injustice.[170] And one of the most central elements these models elide is how very large numbers of people are involved in supporting the status quo.

Young defines *structural injustice* as "a specific kind of moral wrong" that "is distinct from wrongs traceable to specific individual actions or policies." She writes:[171]

> Structural injustice, then, exists when *social processes* put large groups of persons under *systematic threat* of domination or deprivation of the means to develop and exercise their capacities, at the same time that these processes enable others to dominate or to have a wide range of opportunities for developing and exercising capacities available to them. Structural injustice is a kind of moral wrong distinct from the wrongful action of individual agent or the repressive policies of a state. Structural injustice occurs as a consequence of many individuals and institutions acting to pursue their particular goals and interests, for the most part within the limits of accepted rules and norms.[172]

Here Young's interactionist account of social structure begins to come into focus.

For Young, structural injustice is a process, not a one-off event of individual or institutional harm. While this may seem problematic for those who recognize the structural and oppressive nature of, for instance, specific child detainee and asylum policies at the US-Mexico border, Young's emphasis on structural conditions rather than on specific policies isn't problematic in and of itself, because it allows room for recognizing the carceral logics underpinning these systemic policies. They can be recognized in the "structural background conditions of individual action" that, for Young, are the true locus of the powerful weight of history, culture, and recursive social acts and practices that produce social and institutional practices of social inequality. Her conceptualization of these processes is interactionist. It is also staunchly race-neutral and idealized (though in a different way than in Rawls's account). This is where the problem comes in.

Like other white philosophers offering structural theories of social transformation, Young uses Anthony Giddens's account of the "duality of structure" and social structuration to build a similar view of the social processes behind structural injustice, including associated views of social structure. For Young, "Social structures are not part of the society," as she thinks Rawls would have it: "Instead they involve, or become visible in, a certain *way of looking* at the whole society, one that sees patterns in relations among people and the positions they occupy relative to one another."[173] Recall that Giddens carves a "middle" ground between system-level and agent-level interpretations of structure that reflects a merging of the white hermeneutic and western scientific traditions he credits as influential to his concept.[174] Young uses this interactionist baseline to describe her view of *social structure* as a continuous flow of collective conduct at the level of populations that reflects how everyday acts and practices come to be part of the "background conditions" for action.[175] What this picture of social structure allows for, then, is the smuggling in of a view of meaning and intelligibility that establishes the parameters for collective uptake and silence based on race-neutral accounts of social and historical processes. This is business as usual in the history of philosophy.

Gidden's account directly influences Young's account as an interactionist picture of how "social structuration" comes to be. It further influences the way she relates concrete manifestations of social injustice to the underlying structural processes that generate the recursive contexts for discriminatory and unjust actions in history. "*Social systems are not constituted of roles but of (reproduced) practices*" and interactions, Giddens asserts.[176] For Young, a structural viewpoint suggests the existence of a recursive hermeneutic process that comes about through the daily and concrete interactions of millions of individual agents operating against the background epistemic success conditions (e.g., the historical groundwork necessary for broader social uptake, much as the Burger and Rehnquist courts cleared the way for the legal acceptance of "racism is over" racism in the Roberts court) that those same actions serve to reinforce (and over time, create the social parameters for the "limits of the accepted rules and norms" that guide individual action). "We take a structural point of view on social relations when we try to see how the actions of masses of people within a large number of institutions converge in their effects to produce such patterns and positionings."[177] Social reproduction just happens, and this happening is explained by the process of social structuration that she borrows from Giddens, who in turn borrows it from classical white european philosophers and their scientific interlocutors. What is the result of this round-robin game of intergenerational epistemic beneficence and card-trading? (As Mills says, "Whites will cite other whites in a closed circuit of epistemic authority that reproduces white delusions.")[178] The picture Young produces is of a system that is interactionist at the ontic and functional level, but only weakly so, because it narrows down which ontic features of material life and human agency can be construed as culpable to correspond only to what makes sense to her from within her situated white gaze. What makes sense, of course, is a world in which white people alone should not be held responsible for those historical injustices, such as white enslavement of nonwhite peoples, from which they continue to accrue uncountable benefits.

Still, Young's points are not so easily dismissed. She wants her theory of justice to cast a much wider net than alternative theories that allow individuals to forgo *taking responsibility* for the massive inequalities that exist, and to implicate white privileged individuals in the process without personally implicating anyone *because* they are white and/or privileged. Thus, all this framework-building surrounding social structure and social processes of reproduction is being done in the service of creating a theory of justice that can assign responsibility for structural injustices without blaming anyone, even though everyone is structurally implicated.

Young thinks a theory of justice *should* include a theory of personal responsibility at the individual level, but such a theory "ought to ask not only in what ways individuals are responsible for their own circumstances, but also in what ways we should understand ourselves responsible for the background conditions of others' lives that are produced by structured institutional relations."[179] These "background conditions" are not just historically inherited in Young's view, as we just illustrated. They are cocreated and upheld daily through our actions and choices, even if those choices are following purported conventional rules and normative social scripts. The problem with her account of social processes comes into focus when she suggests, while describing Sandy's search for safe and affordable housing, that the practice of "steering" potential renters to housing options deemed "appropriate for their race or occupation" is an example of "wrongs of individual action," as if racism is in the hearts and minds of the individual agent, and not the product of the very powerful recursive social processes she describes at the root of social reproduction.

Instead, Young points to the many historical policies and nonspecific background social conditions that promote inequity at different scales, and which involve very large numbers of actors behaving in ways that the actors themselves may not intend to be directly or indirectly harmful, but which nevertheless still contribute to the overall outcome of the structure of poverty and housing insecurity.[180] While her view is more in line with systems theory and social scientific views of structure than is Rawls's, it is equally idealized and therefore just as inappropriate for theorizing social justice in the context of racial oppression.

Everyone Is Complicit: A Structural Model of White Innocence

The strategy Young's account uses to maintain race neutrality and the structural exculpation of white people for white supremacy is threefold. It begins with her theory of social reproduction. "Many large-scale social processes in which masses of individuals believe they are following the rules, minding their own business, and trying to accomplish their legitimate goals can be seen to result in undesirable unintended consequences when looked at structurally."[181] I'll call this the "collective slipped-on-a-banana-peel" defense of structural racism.[182]

Her second tool in the race-neutral toolkit is the portrayal of slavery as a past historical wrong rather than as a structural injustice that is part of a continuum of ongoing structured disadvantage rooted in the system of white supremacy. Young has no problem understanding poverty along such lines: "I advocate a return to understanding poverty and disadvantage in structural terms ... it is not possible to think about issues of poverty without to some extent looking at social structures."[183] Young understands poverty as an ongoing structural issue, yet she regards racism as a composite of past historical individual and institutional wrongs and sociostructured economic disadvantages that asymmetrically impact people of color. The notion of political responsibility she advances will thus bifurcate issues of racism that appear to her to be "historical injustices" like slavery from more race-neutral (and racially coded) class- and gender-based articulations of sociostructural disadvantage, like urban poverty.

In her account of responsibility, Young distinguishes between "political responsibility" and "historical liability." Political responsibility is "forward looking"—focused on finding practical solutions and working toward shared goals as a political community working cooperatively through solidarity. Historical liability is "backward looking," built on a gamut of psychopathologies (or internalized stress responses to oppression) like "slave morality" (an argument Wendy Brown also makes) and resentment that does little to "fix" present problems that rise from ongoing structural injustices. Socially produced harm targets specific populations but affects everyone, and the issue of structural injustice for Young is that *anyone* (i.e., the theoretical emphasis is on *not leaving white people out* of this framing of violence) is harmed in such ways that derives from having done nothing wrong as an agent, other than simply inhabiting a particular sociostructural position in society.

With socially produced harm affecting everyone, Young can argue for a whitewashed theory of social justice rooted in political responsibility that closely connects the individual and institutional scales of social structure. A whitewashed theory of social justice is one that frames social justice as an issue that exists independently of and can be conceived apart from its relationship to structures of white supremacy and colonialism. In this view, whitewashing is a form of structural gaslighting that disconnects issues such as poverty and wealth inequality from the intentionally racialized historical processes such as redlining, segregation, and racist predatory lending that are responsible for the inequities in population-level outcomes we see today. Note the way that Young's framing of housing insecurity paints it as a tragic situation that is structurally unfair for anyone in a wealthy society to face: "The issue of social justice raised by this story is whether it is right that *anyone* should be in a *position* of housing insecurity, especially in an affluent society."[184] Young places structural injustice here in the power of social processes to produce inequality, not in the specific populations that historically have been, and continue to be, consistently and asymmetrically disadvantaged by such processes. This is a whitewashed interpretation of social structure.

The notion of what is "structural" in structural injustice plays a central role in Young's development of a theory of justice responsive to structural injustice as a race-neutral framework. With this, we are now able to examine her third and final tool in her race-neutral toolkit: the social connection model.

The social connection model is Young's model of political responsibility. She advocates for it against the prevailing uses of the sociolegal "liability model" of responsibility, which assigns personal or collective responsibility based on findings of legal guilt, fault, or causally attributable blame (whether through empirically verifiable linear causes or "strict liability" standards in setter criminal law). She thinks there are two things wrong with this model. First, it "divides people too much" and "creates mistrust" between "separate and dissimilar actors" in society, so it is not effective as a model of political coordination or cooperation. Second, "The liability model does not spread responsibility widely enough" to be effective against the structural (as she defines it) nature of structural injustice, and should therefore "be supplemented with the social connection model" she advances that asserts "responsibility for the future [is] a responsibility each person has alone and *also together with others*."[185] She writes:

> The social connection model finds that all those who contribute by their actions to structural processes with some unjust outcomes share responsibility for injustice. The responsibility [is] forward looking. Being responsible in relation to structural injustice means that one has an obligation to join with others who share that responsibility in order to transform the structural processes to make their outcomes less unjust.[186]

Young very much wants wide-scale social transformations that effect democratic change at multiple levels of society, and she wants as many people to participate in this process as possible. She thinks the best way to do this is through a pragmatic, incremental, issue-by-issue approach that requires collaboration among differently positioned agents, psychological framing considerations to promote individual buy-in, and in certain cases, reference to "parameters for reasoning" about structural justice decision-making she provides.[187] She thinks that her view of individual responsibility for justice taps into a collective-based ethos of communal care for others (rather than personal liability for wrongs one did not personally commit) that will catalyze large groups to take on issues like sweatshop labor, and that they will do so in such a way that corresponds to the way social reproduction processes work.

For Young, there must be a way to call out and implicate large numbers of people in sustaining inequality without saying they caused it as individuals, and one of her biggest concerns is how defensive white people get when told they are "responsible" for historical injustices like slavery. For Young, this defensiveness can trigger "self-indulgent" and narcissistic concerns "over the state of their souls and their character" that prevents white people from "discussing more objectively how social structures operate, how our actions contribute to them, and what can be done to change them."[188] But she also defends the position that it is wrong to assign blame, even if it does not trigger defense mechanisms, to anyone who is not linearly connected to a historical injustice. "Within the standard frameworks of legal and moral responsibility, it is necessary to connect a person's deeds linearly to the harm for which we seek to assign responsibility. The problem with structural injustice is that we cannot trace this kind of connection."[189]

> Cases of historic injustice whose original perpetrators and victims lived generations ago present particular ontological and conceptual problems when we try to apply the liability model . . . it does not make sense, I will argue, to use the language of blame, guilt, indebtedness, or compensation to talk about the responsibilities that Americans today, and particularly white Americans, may have in relations to the historic injustice of slavery.[190]

Well, how nice for the beneficiaries of white intergenerational wealth, we might say. For Young, *everyone* is implicated in some form or another in the production of social structures as "social processes," indirectly coassigning responsibility for colonial violence and settler wealth extractivism to survivors of colonialism.

History does matter in the social connection model, she argues, "but not in order to reproach, punish, or demand compensating damages."[191] The past matters in the abstract "historical lessons of slavery" way, as they have been interpreted in the national state project, so that this sense of history then informs "the way members of the society take up responsibility for present racialized structural injustice":[192]

> All I wish to argue here is that practices of blame and fault-finding, and the spirit of resentment that often animates them, are usually unproductive in politics where the harms are a repeated product of structural social processes. A blame language can be inappropriate and unproductive in the context of issues of structural injustice because it tends to divide people between powerful wrongdoers and those who are innocent, whether as victims or as bystanders. This often oversimplifies the causes of injustice, and renders most people passive or comparatively unable to help or remedy

the problem. . . . A public discourse of blame then oversimplifies, failing to develop a public understanding of the actions and practices whose consequences produce injustice. . . . Rhetorics of blame in the public discussion of social problems, furthermore, usually produce defensiveness and unproductive blame-switching. People who perceive themselves being blamed for wrongs that some people endure usually react defensively. Under a liability model of responsibility, being defensive in response to accusation is a natural and appropriate reaction. . . . our legal and moral practices of blaming and finding fault allow the accused to answer, and to provide evidence, if he or she can, of the fact that his or her actions did not cause the harms, or to explain in the valid excuses he or she has for not being blamed.[193]

Blame is "inappropriate and unproductive" *for whom*?

There are several things wrong with this line of thinking. For one thing, it is not clear that the liability model spreads *any* real and substantive responsibility for systemic violence. Why is that? It's a problem of function and built-in design, not of degree of participation. Rather than examining the historical patterns and system processes of why this might be the case, Young promotes a deliberative justice model of democratic consensus based on discussion and debate.

Young's answer of "solidarity" is a worn trope in social transformation rhetorics, especially when it is advanced (as Young does) in terms of mutually chosen reciprocal bonds of "political friendship" that must be actively forged and reforged unless the tenuous bonds of mutual care and concern be broken. Young understands that what she is calling for in solidarity is "an ideal, a promise, and an engagement," but it is not a response to structural violence.[194] It *is* structural violence.

One of the challenges of critiquing Young's view is that it appears so antithetical to the goals and aims of her work. It is widely held that Young, through her life and works, was genuinely committed in action to racial equity and socially transformative democratic change, and that her philosophical disposition was one of openness, structurally appropriate epistemic humility, and double down-averse corrective action that did not require suppliance or displays of distress from people of color for her to amend her views, or to reflect on the ways her structurally privileged position influenced her methodology or limited her argument. This is partly why her argument is so distressing; it highlights the depths of the problem of white supremacy as a broader and deeper structural phenomenon than Young's notion of structural injustice captures. If it can appear so centrally in the great Iris Marion Young's work, we have a much deeper problem than is theorized in her classic works and phenomenological analyses of structural sexism and injustice.

Young's interactionist account of structural injustice does not place sufficient emphasis on the restructuring of the mechanisms of reproduction that uphold white supremacy in the reproduction of social processes. While some philosophers do highlight the restructuring and adaptive capacities of systems to argue for the same ends as Young—the idea of social transformation from below motivated by popular movements that put pressure on powerbrokers to enact change—there is still insufficient attention to the dynastic and transference capacities of social structures rooted in racial systems like white supremacy.

It is also worth noting that Young's position on historical injustice remained deeply consistent throughout national intensifications of state violence and the open targeting of populations of color. Chapter 7, "Affirmative Action and the Myth of Merit," of her 1991 classic *Justice and the Politics of Difference* offers a similar and equally problematic perspective, as do her public writings on Hurricane Katrina's aftermath[195] and her political writings on the Iroquois nation and Indigenous sovereignty[196] (further explored in Chapter 5).

Young's theory of responsibility for historical injustice in *Responsibility for Justice* tells us a great deal about mainstream views on what is "structural" about structural injustice that will be helpful in our next section on structural violence: "When the injustice is structural, there is no clear culprit to blame and therefore no agent clearly liable for rectification."[197] Exactly as intended.

Structural Violence: Farmer on Violence and "Modal Suffering"

Traditionally, structural violence is understood as a relational theory of top-down harm between social institutions—for example, schools, governments, and legal and medical systems—and individuals, where the relation is facilitated by prejudicial social practices like sexism, racism, classism, and ableism that disadvantage people unfairly. The concept is associated with the rise of peace studies in the 1960s and the influence of "systems thinking" in sociology and economics, especially through the core-periphery relation in world systems theory.[198] It has been especially influential in international relations and development studies, where the term typically refers to "a form of violence wherein social structures or social institutions harm people by preventing them from meeting their basic needs."[199]

While the concept of structural violence quickly gained uptake in the academy because of its purported ability to track the influence of social power on human capacities, it has always been distinguished from behavioral violence by the assumption that *it involves no identifiable culprit or aggressor*. It is a hard-to-recognize form of violence that produces real-world harms that one does recognize (or whose impact one experiences), but where "neither culture nor pure individual will is at fault."[200] Paul Farmer, who is credited with popularizing the concept of structural violence through his writings in social medicine, remained consistent in his characterization of structural violence as having no identifiable aggressor throughout his career. He writes:

> Structural violence is violence exerted systematically—that is, indirectly—by *everyone* who belongs to a certain social order: hence the discomfort these ideas provoke in a moral economy still geared to pinning praise or blame on individual actors. In short, the concept of structural violence is intended to inform the study of the social machinery of oppression.[201]

Farmer's account of the social machinery of oppression is consistent with Young's in two ways. One, he points to everyone's participation in upholding the background conditions for the development of structural violence, and two, he delinks history from social structure by conceptualizing it as an independent variable that informs the background conditions for the development of context-specific violence, like poverty and political violence in Haiti, or women's vulnerability to HIV infection and reproductive coercion in the "developing" world.[202] This leads to tensions in his account of structural violence. Such tensions are reflected in his careful attention to the history of French imperialism, colonialism, and slavery in Haiti, yet also in his oddly apolitical conclusion that "oppression is a result of many conditions, not the least of which reside in consciousness."[203] Colonialism is consistently treated as an independent variable whose analytic and diagnostic power is limited to providing the background context for some of the "many conditions" that cause structural forms of suffering, such as widespread poverty and malnutrition in formerly colonized regions. In his attempt to "devise an analytic model, one with explanatory and predictive power, for understanding suffering in a global context," Farmer fails to understand colonial violence as a *system* that effects the structuring relations of oppression whose outcomes he observes.[204]

For example, in "On Suffering and Structural Violence," Farmer narrates the agony of two Haitians, Acéphie and Chouchou, who died from AIDS and political violence respectively. He insists that structural analysis of their situations "must also be *historically deep*: not merely deep enough to remind us of events and decisions such as those that deprived Acéphie's parents of their land and founded the Haitian military, but deep enough to recall that modern-day Haitians are the descendants of a people kidnapped from Africa in order to provide our forebears with sugar, sago, coffee, and cotton."[205] This passage suggests that Farmer is aware of intergenerational benefits and structuring relations of caste privilege based on colonial racial schemes. Because Farmer does not conceptualize colonialism as a system with generative force, self-sustaining relations, and adaptive mechanisms, the depth of his analysis of colonialism is limited to an events-based contributory causality that informs "how things came to be this way," not why they are likely to *stay* this way. Like Young, he wishes to lift the burden and stigma of being poor from poor people and to point the finger more squarely in the direction of "larger social forces" and processes that militate against poor people's daily efforts to escape poverty, and to design social policy and public health interventions that decrease poor people's chances of dying from a preventable and treatable disease (or from disproportionately suffering from an incurable one). But the causal relation between the disproportionate distribution of global poverty and the violent colonization of nearly 80 percent of the world's territories by european powers (which make up less than 8 percent of the world's landmass) over the span of a few centuries is not a central feature of the predictive power Farmer constructs his notion of structural violence to have. For Farmer, Acéphie's and Chouchou's suffering falls under his conception of structural violence only because "such suffering is 'structured' by processes and forces that conspire—whether through routine, ritual, or more commonly, the hard surfaces of economics and politics—to constrain agency."[206]

But what are these "hard surfaces" and how do they function as part of an overall system with predictive force? How are "economic forces" connected to, for example, neoliberal policy, extractive industries, megaprojects, international development foreign interests and trade policy, the violent suppression of autochthonous Indigenous governance structures, and the high levels of rape, economic abuse, obstetric violence, trafficking, and sexual coercion of women in the region? Farmer begins Acéphie's story with the flooding and destruction of the valley her farming family relied on for subsistence and the admission that the flooding was the result of a hydroelectric dam break. Yet there is no connection made between megaprojects and extractives, the disproportionate rates of gender-based violence that accompany them in the "man camps," and militarized state oversight of these projects—why the soldiers she encounters are there to begin with and what interests they serve to protect.[207] Nor does he make the connection between the very project of colonial sexual violence—as one that "establishes the ideology that Native bodies are inherently violable, and by extension, that Native lands are also inherently violable"[208]—and the resulting practices of reproductive coercion and rape he so willingly attributes to "machismo" in the Haitian military. He explains Acéphie's "hard" choices of sexual partners through a causal chain of agent-based decisions—heart-wrenching decisions based on limited options—that prioritize individual psychological responses to sociostructural conditions. He takes to heart the notion that "being oppressed means the absence of choices,"[209] but he leaves extraordinarily vague the explanations of the social machinery of oppression that constructs these "choices" and not others as viable options within a universe of possibilities. This theoretical vagueness should be understood as the nonaccidental outcome of the same systemic processes that Farmer ignores in his account of structural violence.

As we will learn through this book, the theoretical failure to conceptualize colonial violence as a coherent and transformational system that continues to this day is not accidental, and it has very high stakes. The downstream effects of this system can be demonstrated in the global distribution patterns of disease burdens—as we saw with the Covid-19 pandemic—for example, or the likelihood of early death or exposure to violence simply because of the place one is born in, the neighborhood one lives in, and the sociostructural positions we occupy in settler colonial social infrastructures.

Constructing Structural Causation in Positive Terms
Farmer of course is not the only proponent of the socially exculpatory view of structural violence. In the traditional account of structural violence first developed by Galtung and adopted explicitly by Farmer and implicitly by Young, structural violence is consistently depicted as an *indirect and unintentional* "iron cage"[210] built by human societies through acts of omission,

systemic needs deprivation, failures to embrace a community ethos of collective care, tragic economic and administrative infrastructural stress points in vulnerable regions, and profound social neglect. It is the result of social, political, and economic processes coming together in policies and institutional actions that harm people by producing "modal suffering."[211] Modal suffering focuses on the structure rather than the substance of suffering by looking to "the forces that promote that suffering"—a point Farmer concedes he and others have taken from Latin American liberation theorists. Whereas liberation theorists are exceedingly clear about the causes and the collective agents liable for harm (e.g., colonialism, neoliberalism, white imperialism, US foreign economic policy and its collusion with settler administrative graft architectures, multinational capital, and extractives), an interesting (but unsurprising) thing happens when liberation theory is imported north: the causal chain of historical harmdoing disappears. Instead, the development studies and humanitarian public health tradition (as we'll call it) of conceptualizing structural violence erase this critical feature of structural causation and instead point to "linkages and causal flows in all directions," and to the "difference between the potential and the actual, between what could have been and what is" social reality today.[212]

Racial inequality is a carefully preserved social condition tied to value and its transference. For a transference chain to be valued in settler colonial cultures, it must produce attractive properties (think of preferential attachment processes)[213] that facilitate the formation of relational bonds and links in a transference chain. This means the disappearance of the causal chain of historical harmdoing in the adaptation of liberation theory into social medicine is not accidental; for the framework to have uptake potential in the relevant knowledge infrastructures, liberation theory's identification of the positive harm caused by clear historical culprits must be erased and reframed as a negative collective failure for which there is no clear culprit to blame and therefore no agent clearly liable for rectification.

Consider that for Galtung, structural causation is understood in *negative* terms as a collective failure, or an "absence" of something "positively existing" (a social structure is predominantly ontic for Galtung) that should be there—like a social safety net to fulfill basic human needs.[214] Malnourished people die because they were *left* to die by purported neglect of the whole society, and by the failure to provide socially conscious human services. This failure is reflected in a range of examples, such as "the absence of adequate immunity whether brought on naturally or artificially (inoculation), absence of hygiene, early warning, health services for preventive and curative care" and so forth.[215] Missing from this range of examples are actively produced, socially engineered famines like the ones the British engineered in India and West Bengal, or the French-led intentional economic blockade that resulted in mass starvation in Haiti following Haitian independence from France. Such instances are written off as past instances of *direct* violence that have, over time, become part of the historical bedrock or "sediment" of contemporary societies. It's an explanatory escape hatch to avoid constructing structural causation in positive terms, as such construction would introduce the question of purpose or function.

By contrast, a systems perspective constructs structural causation in positive terms, as something that exists but that also must be kept alive, kept up, actively maintained, and nurtured though the distributive design and various infrastructures set up to perpetuate a particular configuration of social structure and not others.

The characterization of structural causation in primarily negative terms leads to an important paradox in the developmental and humanitarian public health tradition's conceptualization of structural violence: History is both central to understanding the etiology of structural violence and peripheral (at best) to constructing modern-day solutions for it.[216] While structural violence's historical origins lie partly in the past as context, the sociostructural processes that reproduce modal suffering are located elsewhere in this tradition. Therefore, the perpetrators of structural violence remain obscured when considering histories of colonial violence in humanitarian accounts of structural violence.[217] This is by design, of course, as we will emphasize throughout this book.

Farmer's elision of a positive construction of structural causation in his account of modal suffering and structural violence has led critics to argue that "in Farmer's use of the concept, structural violence is arguably also atheoretical—there is no theory to describe the origins of structural violence, no general explanation of how inequality comes to be. Structure is called out but never defined, and the 'perpetrators' of the violence remain obscured."[218] While I don't think the concept is atheoretical,[219] I think the larger point about the resulting whitewashing of structural violence is accurate.

In their 2018 article on the concept of structural violence in health equity research, social epidemiologists Fernando de Maio and David Ansell argue that the notion of structural violence holds promise as an analytic method in health equity research despite two major obstacles it contains. The first obstacle is the lack of a direct method to observe and quantify structural violence, making it "an explanatory concept rather than a measurable phenomenon" easily employed in empirical research and health science.[220] The second obstacle is the "apolitical explanation of health inequities" that is the result of Farmer's framing of the concept.[221] Despite these obstacles, the concept is still useful:

> It's potential lies in the focus it gives to deep structural roots of health inequities; in contrast to the more passive term "social determinants of health," structural violence explicitly identifies social, economic, and political systems as the *causes* of the causes of poor health. It is also evocative in its framing of health inequalities as an act of violence. Perhaps most importantly, by naming social structures as a root cause of avoidable and unnecessary morbidity and mortality, the concept can be used as a counterweight to the belief that our current patterns of population health are natural.[222]

For this to work, however, they caution that the notion of structural violence must be used "in combination with a larger theoretical framework—critical race theory, feminism, Marxism or other approaches."[223] Without it, what's "structural" about structural violence in Farmer's articulation of the term is reduced to naturalized accounts of sociostructural "arrangements" (what Galtung calls "nested structures") that produce social oppression through the social reproduction of culture as a whole, leaving unclear what the target of the intervention is, other than the whole society (hence Young's focus on collective responsibility for structural injustice). For Farmer, these arrangements are thought to be structural because they are "embedded in the political and economic organization of our social world; they are *violent* because they cause injury to people."[224] But this begs the question, what drives the political and economic organization of our social world? Put otherwise, what automates inequality as a basic feature of social structure, not simply as an observable phenomenon described and filtered through the mainstream concept of structural violence?[225] Violence is embedded in the political and economic organization of settler colonial societies to reproduce forms of life and social structures that cause injury to people by design.

In this chapter, thus far, I've interrogated what's "structural" about structural racism by rejecting the implicit-bias paradigm and the mainstream views of structural injustice and violence found in the works of Young and Farmer. These views are representative of the various social mechanisms settler colonial cultures rely on to evade cultural responsibility for historical harms, and of the high level of sophistication such mechanisms display as epistemological apparatuses that help secure the conditions for ongoing structural harm. As conceptual resources that claim to do one thing (e.g., ameliorate harm) but reproduce favorable environments for the reproduction of system-level outputs built into the design of settler colonial social structures (e.g., the protection of white dynastic settler futurity through population-level harms), they are important parts of the infrastructure of impunity in settler colonial societies.[226]

Theoretically, calling out how the mainstream picture of structural violence produces impunity as a functional output also gives us clues about reinforcing loops and the existence of a generative epistemic system of colonial violence that is built upon a vast and powerful economic system of interpretive wealth accumulation and self-regulating cultural balancing forces that we'll address in our third chapter, "Structural Violence Is *Profit-Driven*: Epistemic Capitalism." And, as we've established, some of the main ways the mainstream picture of structural violence operates is by decoupling history from social structure in a way that facilitates separating the "cultural" from the "structural."[227] Such decoupling yields a picture of structures as arbitrary historical interrelations between different elements (and interactive levels) of a social system without their goal-oriented functions, a picture where the purposes of various social subsystems mysteriously work in harmony to produce an integrated social world that reproduces interlocking oppressions. It allows proponents of the mainstream view of structural violence to miss the point that the social systems they find fault with were set up intentionally to continuously produce the very effects they do—for example, the maldistribution of harm that traditional views of structural violence describe as having no identifiable aggressor—with the full acknowledgment that structures of domination establish a reciprocal causal relationship between structural violence and the direct violence that often erupts in order to resist oppressive structures. That is, they are aware that our liberational aspirations and direct participatory efforts to "get out of the structural iron cage" are met with "counter-violence to keep the cage intact."[228] Counterrevolutionary force is a basic feature that is *built into the design of structural violence*, but such insight cannot be found the mainstream picture of structural violence. This requires a course correction.

The anticolonial systems approach I will introduce in the next section tracks this distributive design insight. It situates the resilience and stubborn continuity of racial systems as the product of very stable and organized processes of settler colonial social reproduction.[229] Such an approach rejects views of racial systems the contingent arrangements of "racial formations," and it relies on a structurally invariant view of structural violence that incorporates a functional theory of cultural liability and adaptive transformation.[230] The benefit of such a view lies in its rejection of the exceptionally exculpatory framework of structural innocence that provides accountability covers for white settler populations and their descendants across all areas of social and institutional life.

An anticolonial systems approach first and foremost conceptualizes colonialism as a system with longevity and purpose.[231] It also highlights the violent features of social emergence in imperial, colonial, nonimperial, and neocolonial processes of cultural domination, conquest, and dispossession that continue today and project into futurity—now, tomorrow, and forever, for as long as the system continues. As such, it affirms the basic insights of anticolonial theories of social reproduction that also highlight long-living systems of dynastic white supremacy and their effects: namely, "Racism now, racism tomorrow, racism forever."

A Systems Perspective on Structural Violence

I have two primary aims in charting a systems perspective on structural violence (i.e., an anticolonial systems theory) in settler colonial societies: (1) to support the view of colonial domination as an ongoing process—a "long game," as I call it—that must still be actively fought against, and (2) to reject settler colonial narratives of structural violence and related concepts that distance white settler beneficiaries from the causal and contributory mechanisms that produce automated population-level harms for people of color and Indigenous peoples.[232] To achieve these aims, I rely on a nonideal[233] picture of social emergence that interprets "context" in terms of modal necessity rather than historical contingency.[234] That means I emphasize the structural features of social emergence to insist that what emerged historically as dynastic white supremacy and its inseparable mechanisms of sexual violence are critical to how social knowledge operates in settler colonial societies.

Knowledge and structure are important to this story because the dominant salience operative in settler colonial institutions—the ones that have power over our life outcomes and life chances as survivors—automate the double-edged system of simultaneous offense and self-defense that protects white dynastic wealth and its supporting cultural apparatuses of racist sexism and systemic violence. The fact that the solutions routinely offered to us fail to address the problem is not accidental, but part of a structure that distributes precarity and wellness pathways unevenly by design.[235] It calls to mind the classic June Jordan refrain in "Poem about My Rights": "Who the hell set things up like this"?[236] Philosophy is a lot like this. The traditional solutions are part of the problem.[237]

Structure, Social Knowledge, and Philosophy

Through both analytic and continental traditions, western philosophy has played a central role in producing narratives that allow settler colonial cultures to evade accountability for structural violence. The metaphilosophical idea here is simple: the dominant knowledge systems that emerge in western history, and particularly in philosophy, benefit some populations by design. Who, exactly, benefits from the framing of social knowledge as rooted in a background web of social acts and practices that boil down to a "contextualist platitude"[238] that consistently evades serious accounting for colonial violence on knowledge systems?[239] White settlers and their beneficiaries? Nope, not today.

Mainstream theories of structural violence and associated theories in philosophy provide an epistemic forking mechanism—a way to generate a branched path in rationale for why systemic violence persists that provides plausible deniability for those who most benefit from such violence. What these mechanisms provide is vast domains of nondiscriminatory rationale that support intergenerational wealth (material, social, epistemic) accumulation for white settlers and their descendants. Epistemic forking mechanisms can be policies, concepts, or practices that function like the employment law concept of "pretext," which hides the true reasons for an employer's actions in nondiscriminatory rationale. Philosophy is replete with such mechanisms, as are allied fields. The culturally exculpatory functions of mainstream notions of structural violence and related concepts enable institutions and individuals to shift the conversations of fault and responsibility for structured harm to vague macro-level causes (such as generalized poverty) or mysterious micro-level causes (such as neurobiological bases of prejudiced thoughts) for the harms individuals and communities disproportionately targeted by white supremacy and rape culture endure.

A systems perspective on structural violence calls attention to epistemic forking mechanisms as a basic feature of settler colonial social systems and their regenerative processes. That means that the epistemological systems that emerge under settler colonial social structures reflect the organizational design and purpose of such structures. They work to reproduce and enforce their regenerative stability over long periods of time in a dynamic and interconnected fashion. This is a nonideal perspective on how knowledge operates in relation to social structure and colonial history.

In a nonideal picture of social emergence (a picture implicitly held by racial capitalism literatures), the salient features of social epistemic backgrounds have a distribution design and probability pathways that allow some social acts and practices to emerge *as the* salient and socially legible social acts and practices that recursively constitute "the social world," and it is no accident that these particular social scripts *serve the interests of settler colonial white supremacy and extractive capitalist reproduction schemes.* (Consider that for Mills, a nonideal society is one "which was historically established as (a) a coercive and exploitative venture for differential white advantage, and in which (b) the rules are generally designed for white benefit.") Such dominant salience is what social institutions—law, healthcare, education—rely on to administer white dynastic social power and reinforce whiteness as "a deeply structured relationship to power and group entitlement."[240] It is why, as women of color, we are continuously put in the mind-bending position of searching for our missing and murdered as if no one knows why there's a person-shaped gap where our loved one should be, and would be, had they not lived in society that holds harmless rape culture and sexist racism in state-sponsored violence.[241]

In the view I favor, settler epistemological systems are coherent, dynamic, historically rooted, pervasive, adaptive, well-organized dynastic systems that are designed, from the get-go, to harm some populations so that other populations benefit. They are functionalized through powerful social transference chains of value (what circulates and gets uptake as epistemic worth in social scripts— the dominant social rules and implicit narratives that instruct socially licensed behavior) that have been curated, generation after generation, through coemergent[242] material acts and violences that suppress alternative knowledge systems in the epistemic economy of the settler colonial project (chapter 3).[243]

Modality in the Three-Stranded Braid

To build a systems perspective of structural violence I pull from various intellectual and activist traditions that each highlight different aspects of white dynastic formations—what they are, how they function, and the effects they produce. I use these strands to braid an intricately woven story about dynastic continuity and purposive design that underlies settler colonial cultures and the administrative systems that support settler colonial white supremacy and its indispensable mechanisms of racist sexism and sexual violence.

From racial capitalism, I pull the idea that racial formations predate traditional dating schemes for modernity and european colonial invasion of the Americas in a way that is rooted in, and that functionally preserves, anti-Blackness throughout history.[244] I use this strand to extend the timeline of epistemological processes underwriting racial formations (as functional processes rather than as racial genetic mythography) to antiquity and early christianity through the institution of slavery. I weave this strand into the middle of the braid and pull.

From the metaphysics of science, I pull the idea that systems are self-repairing and adaptive structures that behave predicably and that such predictability can be applied to structures of oppression.[245] I use complex systems theory and basic notions in complex adaptive systems science to reframe Berenstain's thesis and adapt this strand to an anticolonial theory that undermines the purportedly natural features of social emergence, since such whitewashed views are still at the heart of philosophical accounts of how to fight against structural violence. With this strand, I reject political frameworks of resistance to oppression that are part of the scaffolding of settler colonial epistemological systems, frameworks that will never account for the structure of the long game of colonialism, and by design.

From critical race and Indigenous feminisms, without which the braid would come loose, I pull the centrality of racialized gender and sexual violence in analyses of systemic oppression and settler colonial violence.[246] I use this strand to emphasize the point of all this theoretical worldmaking and the actual weight and texture of this braid in my hands: that we are being continuously and systematically silenced, disappeared, violated, shot, and slaughtered without meaningful expectations of structural reprieve. That is the story revealed by the braid's first interlaced threads—an intergenerational map that lays out the gridlines of the bloody future before us if settler colonial white dynastic formations continue to dominate social structure as they have for the last two millennia.

To begin braiding, let's return to the subject of this book: structural violence. The mainstream picture of structural violence presented in this chapter emphasizes its culturally exculpatory mechanisms, or the idea that structural violence involves "no identifiable culprit or aggressor" by design. As a form of nonspecific power, it is everywhere and nowhere. This confounds the transference chain of structural causation and hampers the ability to trace the origins of structural violence to its dynastic source of white settler beneficiaries and institutional creditors. The perpetrator-free framing of structural violence is particularly curious because the cases to which structural violence (as an analytic tool) is most often applied—systemic racial discrimination in settler colonial societies founded on enslavement, dispossession, and sexual violence—have vividly clear culprits and aggressors, as well as targets, those who are abused and dispossessed by such violence, even when violence is described at the level of populations in healthcare, education, and the legal system.[247] The discipline disparities that affect children of color are a case in point:

> Today, Black children are 19 percent of preschool enrollment, but 47 percent of preschool-age children who have had one out-of-school suspension. Black girls are 20 percent of the female pre-school enrollment, but 54 percent of girls receiving one or more out-of-school suspensions. . . . However, from coast to coast, Black girls tell stories of being pushed out of school and criminalized for falling asleep, standing up for themselves, asking questions, wearing natural hair, wearing revealing clothing, and in some cases engaging in unruly (although not criminally or delinquent) acts in school—mostly because what constitutes a threat to safety is dangerously subjective when Black children are involved.[248]

Little direct connection is made between children of color's collective experiences—that is, that the violence they encounter is not accidental or aggressor-free to them—and endemic efforts in the United States to privatize public services and resources to benefit white populations while offloading the costs of privatization onto marginalized populations.[249] That is to say, a very roundabout and causally mystified story tends to emerge between harm, perpetrator, and event that mediates between historical context and contemporary harms.[250]

In the view of structural violence I endorse, it is not plausible to plead epistemic ignorance (e.g., your honor, we didn't have the knowledge resources to know that we didn't know, so our ignorance was passive and outside the *mens rea* active mental intent standard settler colonial law requires to find us culpable!) since the hermeneutic resources that enable dominantly situated knowers to identify structural causation between colonial domination and systemic racism exist in abundance in settler colonial societies. In fact, they dominate! This is the line of argument that I will pursue here. With this turn we move closer to an active and structurally intentional settler colonial variation of Gaile Pohlhaus's helpful notion of *willful hermeneutical ignorance*, a way dominantly situated knowers get away with dismissing the knowledge resources, worlds, and experiences of oppression of nondominantly situated knowers.[251]

Recall, from our introduction, that in the mainstream picture of structural violence there are two important things missing: (1) the self-repairing, predictive, adaptive, and resilient features of structures and systems that are common to views of structure in the natural sciences and STEM fields and (2) the political notions of cultural liability, fault, and responsibility for the damaging outcomes structural violence produces that are common among views of structure in women-of-color feminisms and anticolonial liberation movements.[252] System features (self-repair, adaptability, system resilience) are so pervasive and central to western scientific knowledge and disciplinary practices like medicine that when whitewashed accounts of structural violence become the default, as we find in the mainstream notion of structural violence, nonaccidental patterns of gainful willful hermeneutical ignorance, which accrues profit at the level of populations, begin to emerge. To show this we can turn to work on structural causality and necessity in the metaphysics of science.

Modal Profiles

Nora Berenstain brings insights from the metaphysics of science to social issues of oppression that are helpful in illustrating how the mainstream accounts of structural violence presented here could have easily incorporated the adaptive features and purposive design of social structures that revolutionary physicians like Che Guevara and Frantz Fanon highlight.[253] She does this through the notion of *modal profiles*. "A modal profile is simply the collection of modal features of an object, individual, structure, or system."[254] Structures of oppression like white supremacy have modal profiles that highlight the nonaccidental nature of the patterns and distribution probabilities that emerge in societies rooted in those structures. Berenstain's sophisticated account of what she calls the "modal profiles of structures of oppression" consists of arguments in the tradition of structural realism that can be, for illustrative purposes, broken down to two interrelated concepts: modality and causal profiles.

Modality has various meanings depending on the context of use and the discipline using it. In medicine it can specify a mode or manner of delivering treatment. In music it refers to an arrangement of tones around a root note that produces a particular scale pattern. In logic it is used to refer to what is probable and possible with respect to a proposition or judgment. It is this latter and more general sense of modality as what is probable and possible that comes into play in modal structures. Causal profiles describe the possible and necessary features or behaviors that an object can enter into with respect to other objects or structures.

A modal profile is thus a profile that characterizes the nonaccidental patterns and relations we discussed earlier in this chapter in theories of structure. In a very basic sense, think of it as the logical relations that must hold between different nodal points of a web, where the web is a system that is dynamic and constantly changing in response to external environmental factors and (importantly) internal constraints that inform its structural design as a web. Thus, on the view Berenstain offers, "The modal profile of an object or system is determined by its modal structure and the modal structures of other objects or systems it interacts or could interact with." She writes:

> Modal structures place constraints on the possible pathways of movements through and changes within the systems that instantiate them. Linear algebraic structures constrain the pairs of properties that commute. The structure of evolutionary design space interacts with environmental factors to limit effective ways an organism can move through space.... In scientific contexts, understanding structures in terms of their modal profiles is essential to accurately predicting and explaining the probability distribution of possible outcomes within a physical system.[255]

For philosophers, Berenstain's view of structural modality is built on a scientific realist and anti-Humean conception of natural necessity.[256] That is to say, to return to the web example, that as a system, the web does not exist necessarily, but its modal profiles "are still constrained by modal structures that are themselves characterized by their non-accidental internal relations." Berenstain shows how an object's modal structure, which "captures the *non-accidental patterns of relations* it bears to other events, objects, properties, and systems"[257] produce reliable patterns of how a structure behaves—what it is likely to do and not do. This use of probability pathways already exists in social epidemiology and social medicine (as noted earlier), though often with different theoretical results than Berenstain's clear indictment of white supremacy.

As a tool with activist reach, the power of Berenstain's account of modality lies in its application to nonideal accounts of historical oppressions. When applied to history, modal profiles are in line with racial capitalism's position that, while history could have been different, it wasn't: colonialism happened. Colonial capitalism is thus not a deviation or offshoot from analyses of capital value production and transmission, but basic to them. In other words, what we inhabit in settler colonial societies is the historical structure of colonial violence that *did* emerge. With this framing, it is easy to understand why Berenstain is interested in "how modality operates in the social world," not in modality itself as a fixed object of inquiry. She is interested in the nonaccidental internal relations of structures that serve as reference points for predicting behaviors in structures of oppression—what a white supremacist system is likely to produce, how, against whom, and to what end. Berenstain thus proposes "a realist account of structural oppression" in terms of modal profiles:

> Structures of oppression are to be understood in terms of their modal profiles, which include both their contingent features and, importantly, what I identify as their non-accidental internal relations. Modal profiles are understood as domain-specific, non-accidental patterns of relations that are projectable into the future and invariant under certain transformations. My account has two primary strengths: i) it unifies the metaphysics of structure in structures of oppression with viable metaphysical understandings of structure in the sciences, and ii) it is oriented toward facilitating actionable interventions to disrupt existing structures of oppression.

There are two aspects of Berenstain's theory that are useful for this project. First, it provides a conceptual model for how to think modally about structures of oppression that undercut the perpetrator-free account of structural violence from the get-go without reducing perpetrators solely to individuals (a position I reject because it reifies settler capitalist states' punitive and profitable obsession with carcerality). Two, it portrays structures of oppression as inherently stable and able to repair and adapt themselves—something that is critical to systems theory in general. These two aspects, structural culpability (via system design) and system self-repair, feature prominently in the way I adapt modern systems theory to anticolonial praxis through what I call anticolonial systems theory, to which we now turn.

Anticolonial Systems Theory

Anticolonial systems theory (AST) is a decolonial method of social analysis that has a negative and positive valence. That means it critiques something but it also works to move past it. AST's main subject is the process of social reproduction. When social reproduction is theorized thorough a systems lens that portrays social reproduction as a naturally occurring, self-generating phenomenon, AST can be used as a tool for illustrating colonial thinking underlying the naturalistic and universalizing assumptions of these theories. AST can illustrate how these theories work, for example, by naturalizing features of social emergence that result in the theoretical decoupling of dynastic histories of anglo-european economic racial supremacy (and the structural violence required to uphold this supremacy) from their underlying accounts of social structure.

Against Naturalizing Social Emergence

First, let's explain what social emergence refers to. "Social emergence is the central phenomenon of the social sciences"; it describes phenomena that "socially emerge from complex systems of individuals in interaction" as well as the structural processes (in the social sciences, these include historical, economic, biological, and epistemic processes) that bedrock or foreground such interactions.[258] Broadly speaking, it describes how human societies emerge as complex systems, or "cultures," through an emphasis on what emerges from these systems as wholly new—some property or capability that wasn't there before in individuals but that, as a social group or culture, individuals exhibit.

Think of emergence as when the whole is more than the sum of its parts. In medicine this wholeness is key to transplant science research and the promise of regenerative medicine to produce new organs and to improve surgery outcomes. In academia it describes the emergent properties of universities as degree-granting institutions that individual teachers, administrators, or students do not possess the power to do themselves. In sports and team science research, emergence describes the social cohesion and team attitudes that develop when sports teams interact in an organized fashion, such that different ways of interacting yield different emergent states and attitudes. In anatomy it explains the malleability and contractile properties of smooth muscle tissue that differentiate it from the body's striated muscle tissue that controls voluntary movement, both of which result from complex cellular interactions and molecular events that result in their specialized functions. In economics, almost all economic behaviors are explained in terms of emergence.

Emergence has many specialized definitions depending on the field of research, but generally it is used as a key way of explaining what parts of a system can do together that parts cannot do alone, and it arises out a system's dynamic behavior rather than something intrinsic to parts or something externally introduced into the system (a theological cause, for example). Thus, the standard view in the social sciences is that "an emergent property is one that is not possessed by any of the parts individually and that would not be possessed by the full set of parts in the absence of a structuring set of relationships between them."[259]

In Chapter 3, Glenn Coulthard's structural definition of colonialism as the "sum effect of the diversity of interlocking oppressive social *relations*" that constitute dispossessive cultures will be useful in associating the structuring set of economic relations that converge in settler colonial epistemologies with the structural violence persistently exhibited by settler colonial societies as cohesive systems.[260] The definition is useful here because it draws attention to what is salient about colonialism: *the relations it enables* and through which it operates, not the properties of individual actors or colonial institutions.

It matters little who Cristóbal Colón was to the distributive design of colonialism—whom it was meant to disproportionately harm and why. The perpetrator-free framing of european colonialism as an accident of alleged "discovery" is undermined by the long history (prior to 1492) of european slave raids in the Mediterranean and the Indigenous slaves already aboard Columbus's ships when he sailed for India, slaves made ready to serve as possible translators for wherever his ship landed. Colonialism is a system, a long game with intergenerational parts and actors, but one that has an integral wholeness to its design (that is, a wholeness held together by overall system purposes and goals). Otherwise, it could not stay together as a system, and it could not carry out the violences that have come to define its specialized functions over its long durée of white dynastic formations since antiquity.

The perpetrator-absolving framing of colonialism most commonly arises when the historical features of social emergence (how social reproduction happens) are naturalized. Naturalizing features of social emergence also occur when the structural causation between social formation and history is generalized to fit a "society as system" explanatory model. The purpose of such generalization is to create an internal alignment between the content of such explanatory models and the "epistemological substratum" of western civilization, as Cedric Robinson put it.[261]

The range of theories that naturalize social emergence is vast, crossing disciplines and spanning the history of the social and human sciences. They are evident in Talcott Parson's famous statement that "there is the same order of relationship between roles and functions relative to the system in social systems, as there is between organs and function in the organism,"[262] as well as in Sally Haslanger's contention that "societies are complex systems—or clusters of acting systems—that reproduce themselves: their hierarchies, their culture, their practices, and their structures."[263] The pressing problems resulting from the naturalization of social emergence are that it facilitates (1) the conclusion that "most, if not all, societies reproduce profound injustice"[264] and, connected to this, (2) the erasure of the "perverse determination" of some cultures (from the Latin *cultura*, to grow or cultivate) to reproduce, grow, maintain, and cultivate profound injustice as part of the design of social structures in settler colonial societies.[265] In the naturalized framing of society as system, lost is a theory of social emergence that centers the role of violence (physical, epistemic, hermeneutic) in structuring the relations that appear natural and determined in social systems. Instead, these narratives often highlight the resilient and self-healing aspects of systems to explain social inequality (and the violence that derives from it) but underplay the key functional relation between system purpose and system design—that in a system, things are organized in a way that is not accidental, but in a manner that directly maps onto what a system is designed to do in the first place. This is why Berenstain's modal theory of structural oppression is useful; it does not delink structural causality and the probability pathways in a system's design from the self-healing and self-repairing properties of systems. A social system set up to steal land and labor from noneuropean peoples thus has roots, origins, and predictive future behaviors that cannot be delinked form the self-healing properties of systems.

A central idea in complex systems theory is that a system produces its own behavior. It does so in light of the purpose or goal inherent in its design. How such design is specified depends on what the system is made of, what the various elements that make up the system can and cannot do, and the interrelations that connect them into an integrated whole—into a system acting synergistically and wholistically in synch, even when it does not appear to be doing so. A system's design architecture holds it together through transformations by responding effectively to system pressures and by learning from these challenges to become more efficient, adaptive, and resilient. What allows it to respond effectively is the nonlinear dynamics and self-organized criticality that keep a system functioning, yet still oriented toward a specific system goal. It's a helpful way of thinking about social structure that goes against the grain of core ideas in social theory and in political philosophy about why, out of a universe of possibilities, some social structures arise rather than others. But this design architecture is abandoned by mainstream social theories of systemic injustice that focus narrowly on system self-repair or use machine-learning models of homeostatic regulation (the ability of a system to self-regulate to achieve stability across transformations through balancing and reinforcing loops) to explain social oppression. Such approaches normalize injustice as systemic and "built in" to societies while mystifying what a particular social system is designed to do to keep *those* injustices alive, generation after generation, and to what end. They erase the facticity of a system's particular distribute design (e.g., they erase the historical facticity of Patricia Hill Collins's "matrix of domination") and overemphasize the general adaptive mechanisms of systems, so that they can be applied uniliterally across cultures. Whom, exactly, does this serve?

In such cases, history is a reliable indicator of what a system is designed to do. AST holds that what's causal about structures is inseparable from history *as it unfolded*, not from history as a generalizable "historicality" that gives ontological priority to the systems-based contexts that, in principle, shape individual psychological development and human understanding (by rooting people in a sociohistorical situation that generates epistemic salience from that standpoint). This, of course, is directly related to the idea of social reproduction.

Against Whitewashing Social Reproduction

Social reproduction theories focus on cultural transmission. They offer an explanatory model for thinking about cultural transmission at two interrelated levels: the social and the historical. The first deals with the relationship between the individual and the collective. It holds that social systems reproduce themselves through an integrative network approach of bringing new elements (individuals) into the fold of a previously existing system (collectives). There are multiple theories as to how this "bringing into the fold" happens that range from unreflective habits and developmental language-learning, to coercive social environments and punitive institutional apparatuses that constrain choice (or induce the illusion of individually chosen preferences). The basic idea is that individuals "grow" into an understanding of social practices and do not come fully programmed with cultural know-how at birth.

The second level deals with the temporal dimension of cultural transmission—how cultures stay together as distinct cultures through time and changing historical norms and epochs.[266] Naturalized accounts of social reproduction processes portray the sources and resources for cultural know-how and the transmission of this know-how (how our everyday worlds tacitly make sense to us across individual differences in a social group and provide the semiotic tools and scripts that enable group coordination) as naturally emerging from a given historical backdrop. That is, the "history" of this historical backdrop provides context for epistemic acts and practices like a stage provides a background setting for a play. It does not functionalize the stage in relation to any substantive feature of the play that governs the plot—what is likely to happen to whom and why in the play, irrespective of the actions taken by the actors.[267]

Just as Farmer delinks history from social structure by conceptualizing history as an independent variable that informs the background conditions for the development of the context-specific violence he analyzes, history under this model of social transmission is also naturalized as a background condition. It is seen as an intergenerational inheritance, a historical wellspring of transmitted structures,[268] or source of delimiting constraints that condition human agency by providing the parameters for reasoning and interpretation in culture, but above all it is regarded as culturally relative and contingently arbitrary to the given time and place under discussion.[269] Under this model of historical inheritance, it could always have been "otherwise." Under the modal contextualist model of historical inheritance, it was precisely what it was set up to be, what *did happen* as a result of an intended *design*. No colonialism, then, sure, it could have been "otherwise."[270] But colonialism did not arise out of thin air, and that is the line in the sand drawn by this book.

Naturalized accounts of social reproduction need not be empirically reductive or derive from evolutionary, natural science, or bioarcheological perspectives to be understood as universalizable perspectives on how human sociality and collectively shared meaning emerge. Wittgenstein, for instance, describes how humans naturally grow into an implicit, unreflective understanding of contextual worlds as already intact systems, or webs of meaning, that precondition reflective understanding of propositional knowledge (including our reflective ability to "analyze" our everyday social acts and practices). He argues that "when we first begin to believe anything, what we believe is not a single proposition, it is a whole system of propositions. (Light dawns gradually over the whole.)"[271]

For inhabitants of lands colonized by european powers whose cultures sustained intergenerational campaigns of genocidal violence and epistemic warfare, light did not dawn gradually over the whole. This is what the idea of prestructural violence outlined in Chapter 4 illustrates. Whole worlds and cosmologies with reciprocal relations to lands and bodies were suddenly and with malice violated to produce value for specific populations, and such value includes the ability to tacitly interpret one's world with minimal effort—that is, to take up space with prereflective and presuppositionless presumption of the right to do so, and to disconnect this presumption from the violence necessary to steal and keep control of the lands on which one takes up space as a white settler polity. The severing of this insight from violence against women, and how such violence is functionalized in settler colonial societies, is at the core of my concerns. Such severing leads to the denial of the existence of settler credibility economies in which survivor's testimonies of sexual violence are taken up, and to the existence of credibility redlining and institutionally backed oppressions that form part of the situated life chances for survivors of color (Chapter 2).

What naturalized pictures of cultural reproduction miss (and it is no accident that they miss it, as Chapter 3 highlights) is that colonial systems are designed to reproduce dispossession, death, and social disparities in order to accumulate wealth and concentrate it in dynastic chains of transmission. What is at issue is that the distributive pattern of social systems observed in settler colonial societies is not arbitrary. "The system" doesn't simply distribute burdens and benefits in ways that are unjust because it is "a system"; rather, it concentrates the distribution of benefits among some populations and maldistributes burdens by targeting others because the system is designed in such a way that distributions are asymmetrically borne by different populations. And this is inseparable from history as it unfolded—the techniques of violence that did emerge to consolidate anglo-european power over social structure.

AST frames this causal patterning and targeted maldistribution of harm in settler colonial societies (based on history as it unfolded) in terms of design-of-distribution strategies. AST uses a decolonial modal reading of history, which emphasizes the structural causation that follows from what did unfold historically (european imperialism and colonialism), to reveal maldistributive strategies at work in settler colonial societies. Such strategies represent an expanse in the universe of probability pathways that yield persistent socioeconomic gains for some populations at the expense of others, and can include cyclical interruptions to patterns of gain (as in an economic downturn) without interruptions to the self-repair features of the systems of production that reanimate the social forces behind such gain. But this does not hold across all cultures in the same way, hence the importance of epistemic capital and settler epistemological systems. The epistemic forking mechanisms that functionalize self-healing at the system level of culture are always available in settler colonial renderings of history, and will consistently and predictively reproduce a picture of reality that reframes the probability pathways of social maldistribution under the guise of objectivity and natural history (or its evolutionary subscripts). All cultures do not reproduce profound injustice; but one, we know for certain, does.

Finally, another way to understand how naturalistic accounts of social reproduction became dominant is to look at the whitewashing of the concept's history. Scholars typically trace the origin of social reproduction theories to Marx's account of capitalist reproduction and the role of bourgeois ideology in successfully maintaining the reproduction of an exploitative system of labor,[272] but the idea is older. It can be found in european intellectuals' thinking about linguistic differences and cultural relativity triggered by colonialism and the resulting racism-filled treatises on the origins of knowledge and human understanding, with which Marx was also familiar.[273] What these theories have in common is the centering of white european imperial perspectives and the contention that only europeans have a history proper.

Consider that in 2007, when former French president Nicolas Sarkozy went to Africa, he gave the following comments in a public speech: "The tragedy of Africa is that the African has not fully entered into history." Africans, he claimed, "have never really launched themselves into the future" because "the African peasant only knew the eternal renewal of time, marked by the endless repetition of the same gestures and the same words," and "in this realm of fancy . . . there is neither room for human endeavor nor the idea of progress."[274] Sarkozy's racist statement was of course almost a mirror of Hegel's famous pronouncement, almost two centuries earlier, that Africa is a savage continent that stands outside the realm of history and is incapable of progress.[275] Most european philosophy has said, in one way or another, that the only history proper is occidental history. History, as it unfolded in the nonideal sense, connects these pronouncements to patterns of injustice across geographies impacted by european colonization. Social scientific work on racism has often attempted to relink such patterns to discreet historical causes, such as studies that demonstrate how "Black features" continue to routinely predict which defendants are sentenced to death in the United States,[276] or how similar racist stereotypes of "looking Maori" predict decreased rates of homeownership among Maori communities.[277] What I'm drawing attention to here is a pervasive attempt to reduce history to european history for the purposes of writing history, for possessing it as an official instrument of power, as Spivak might put it, and portraying its outcomes as structural happenstance.

This is AST's negative valence; it spotlights the nonaccidental decoupling of structural causation and history in theories of social reproduction. Such decoupling results in the intergenerational structural reproduction of white settler innocence schemas that routinely mystify the misfortunes of Indigenous peoples and populations of color as natural, inevitable, and causally removed from the purpose and design of the colonial project. For example, Adam Smith, in *An Inquiry into the Nature and Causes of the Wealth of Nations*, writes:

> The discovery of America, and that of a passage to the East Indies by the Cape of Good Hope, are the two greatest and most important events recorded in the history of mankind. . . . What benefits or what misfortunes to

mankind may hereafter result from those great events, no human wisdom can foresee. By uniting in some measure the most distant parts of the world, by enabling them to relieve one another's wants, to increase one another's enjoyments, and to encourage one another in industry, their general tendency would seem to be beneficial. To the natives, however, both of the East and West Indies, all the commercial benefits which can have resulted from those events have been sunk and lost in the dreadful misfortunes which they have occasioned. These misfortunes, however, seem to have arisen rather from accident than from anything in the nature of those events themselves.[278]

Racial inequality is not an accident, despite Adam Smith's insistence. It is not a "dreadful misfortune" disconnected from european colonization of large portions of the world's territories, nor from the dynastic histories of imperial force and territorial expansion that structured the functional architecture of european colonization and its system design. That is to say, in occidental settler colonial cultures, this system design has been ongoing in development and preservation over two millennia.

The mystified causal narrative offered by Smith and many others creates the expectation that to establish liability as a form of cultural responsibility, a "linear causal relationship" must be established, as Young put it. But by whom and for whom, and how will the standards for giving and adjudicating evidence be shaped? Evidentiary standards have always been in the hands of white settlers and their beneficiaries as part of a system design.

AST remains a "systems theory" because it retains a system-level perspective on the function of social systems and their goal-oriented focus. That is, it gives a functional account of how a built-in disposition toward self-replication and system resilience does not happen on its own but is bound up with other critical system features necessary for system cohesion, wholeness, integration, functionality, and *purpose*—features that whitewashed theories of social structure neglect in favor of the self-healing properties of systems.

However, the "anticolonial" aspect of AST also holds that modern systems theory is insufficient for analyzing structural injustice in settler colonial contexts.[279] Like the mainstream notion of structural violence, modern systems theory sets limits on how resistance is conceptualized that benefit the social reproduction of a particular system—that of white dynastic social formations, the generative force behind white supremacy's various transformations in history. It does this by promoting solutions to systemic problems that encourage us to let go, as it were, and "go with the flow" of system processes in ways that consider the long-term welfare of an entire system. In systems theory, feedback loops represent a problem in rational decision-making and planning by encouraging short-term interventions that reinforce what a system is designed to do in the first place—they keep us on a hamster wheel, playing catch-up to a system that feeds off our short-term strategies of resistance. Short-term interventions (along with linear, reductionist, and simplistic solutions) are thus Band-Aids in a larger problem that will continue to pop up, mushroom, and come back with potentially even greater force.

The inefficacy of short-term interventions explains how DPC legislation came about as an even more expansive and forceful national phenomenon than the Trump-era federal legislation that inspired it, and which President Biden swiftly overturned (i.e., it demonstrates the system features of escalation, adaptive retrenchment, and self-organized criticality in the domain of policy resistance). Despite its fairly broad explanatory power, systems theory on its own is not a livable theory for framing anticolonial resistance. Consider that one of the most popular political theories (especially from second-wave white feminists) for social liberation is advancing small-scale local and individual organizing that spurs larger social movements that bring white polities into alliance. That seems reasonable enough, at first: uprisings, marches, bottle-throwing swarms, and the iconic French revolutionary image of crowds in the streets speaking truth to state power. Certainly, the youth of Myanmar are profoundly brave for this, as are the Chilean youth protesting inequality and the Iranian women demanding basic reprieve from femicidal state terror.

Those who study social revolutions over long periods also observe this: the body count, the asymmetric toll, and the intergenerational score—who is ahead and who is down when the death toll is tallied long after the uprisings. And something unsurprising about that death toll emerges—the incredible cost to certain racialized bodies but not others. Of course, "Go shout in the streets" is offered as a pathway to liberation; those who can afford to shout most publicly are also the least likely to be killed for it. Settler colonial cultures routinely ask their most vulnerable to be brave in many ways, to be resilient, and to valorize the image of perpetual resilience (especially when we give our life for it) rather than participate in the reparative and structurally actionable processes that require white settlers to transfer value or give up profits they've grown accustomed to, or to stop partaking in global economic arrangements that fund the ability of states to terrorize women, ethnic, religious, and gender minorities in perpetuity—things more proximate to the design of settler colonial social structures. These structural processes live to see another day, not our kin who left the house early on a cool morning to protest injustice, never to return.

So the idea is not that social protest is not a valuable or critical part of the arsenal against repression, or that we should not throw all our support behind these protests in concrete, meaningful, and financially actionable ways (and recall that from Fanon to the Zapatistas, coordinated self-defensive rebellion is critical to fighting white supremacist neoliberal structures of oppression). It is that anticolonial strategies of refusal and reclamation have a wider arsenal of countermoves that mainstream systems theories, and their political adaptations, do not account for, and that such a gap in accounting benefits some populations more than others.

Systems theory can tell us a lot about why things are likely to stay this way in a structure of oppression, not just how things came to be this way, but it cannot offer solutions that harmonize with anticolonial strategies of resistance and revolution. This is part of the design of systems theory as a settler epistemic framework ensconced within an interpretive genealogy that functions in a larger system of epistemic capitalism. An anticolonial systems perspective of structural violence (1) highlights the role of violence in social reproduction processes instituted by colonialism, (2) shows how colonialism is a self-repairing and adaptive system of intergenerational violence, and (3) conceptualizes the restructuring of the mechanisms of reproduction behind colonial violence as part of a coherent system design. The positive part of the theory seeks to move past this to structural and systems-based anticolonial theories that are appropriate to specific lands and land-based epistemological practices in diverse communities (Chapter 5). How Mayan communities resist the megaprojects of foreign mining, hydroelectric dams on Indigenous lands, and the "Maya Train," for example, should not necessitate building a movement that can reach and recruit white people to be effective. The epistemic effort cannot continue to continuously be put on those most affected by the global structures of settler colonial white supremacy. Colonialism is a long game. While colonialism is typically dated to the fifteenth and sixteenth centuries, "Attempts to annihilate [Indigenous] worldviews have not stopped since that time."[280]

With this part of the braid in place, we can now weave together a picture of white dynastic formations and how such formations create tunnels of impunity that help distance white settler polities as the historical beneficiaries of structural violence.

White Dynastic Formations

If the term "white dynastic formations" has a familiar ring to it, it's likely due to the prevalence of racial formation theory in social science research on race. Racial formation theory holds that, while race is a social construct rather than a biological truth, race and racism are not collapsible terms.[281] This is because, while the former term reflects a functional reality (e.g., the idea that for racialized peoples, race is very real in its consequences despite being a genetic myth), the latter term denotes the vast range of projects (social, legal, political, etc.) by which race is continuously reinscribed, interpreted, and enforced in order to concretize those very consequences as real and visceral in the lives of racialized peoples.[282] The two terms are always interrelated, but not interchangeable. Racial formations thus describe the sociostructural process by which race and racism are interrelated as "race making."[283] For Omi and Winant, "The process of race making, and its reverberations through the social order, is what we call *racial formation*. We define racial formation as *the sociohistorical process by which racial identities are created, lived out, transformed, and destroyed*."[284] An incredible range of projects and social practices can illustrate racial formation processes, including seemingly "positive" ones like civil rights projects (i.e., how racist racial identities might be "destroyed").[285] What never drops out of the equation for Omi and Winant is the pervasive endurance of race as an interpretive backdrop for negotiating meaning in contemporary societies; race has become a tacit (yet "decentered") social fact, like gender. This is so much so that resistance to racism is also race-based, like an inescapable hermeneutic circle.[286]

Importantly for my purposes, Omi and Winant's influential notion of racism is not dependent on white supremacy as a historical structure of oppression (in the modal contextualist way described in this chapter). Race in their framework functions as a much broader phenomenon that can be used to explain anti-Black prejudice by whites as well as racial prejudice by people of color and Indigenous peoples, but without causally necessary triangulation with the historical structures of settler colonial white supremacy.[287] Omi and Winant never deny that white supremacy is the dominant racial project in the United States, nor that the best way to explain the resilience of racism among communities of color might be through histories of colonial occupation and the value systems (and binary gender systems) europeans tried to impose on Native peoples. Where they place the theoretical emphasis is on the explanatory power of race as a (badly worded) "master concept" that is "socially constructed and historically fluid," one that elucidates how "racial meanings have varied tremendously over time and between different societies."[288] For Omi and Winant, race "is continuingly being made and remade in everyday life. Race is continually in formation."[289] While it rejects biologically reductive accounts of race as a genetic reality, racial formation theory especially lends itself to comparative and cross-cultural accounts of racism as a transcendent social force in a naturalized historical continuum of human development. Herein lies the problem.

One of the most prominent features of settler epistemic systems is the conceptual imperative to produce "comparative" accounts of social phenomena that rescue white innocence—frameworks that produce plausibly believable narratives and counterfactuals for colonial violence by showing that "other people do it too," so to speak. (Wait for it—the opposite of this is not that—I'm not claiming people of color cannot be racially prejudiced.)

Consider the 2021 ousting of Los Angeles City Council president Nury Martinez following her racist depiction of Oaxacans as aesthetically repulsive "little short dark people."[290] Numerous news outlets seized on the opportunity to highlight the incontrovertible existence of racism in the US Latinx community, but in a "brown on brown" violence manner that helped white settler polities move farther down the tunnel of impunity by distancing white supremacy from the phenomenon being reported.[291] Ethnic prejudice and colorism[292] undoubtedly exist among communities of color. However, the framework of racial formations misses the mark on the modal contextualism necessary to situate such prejudice in the relevant root structure for understanding the reproducibility and propagation of those very prejudices.

What "marks" the human body and differentiates between phenotypic qualities to create the specific categories and "biases" that underwrite preference and prejudice is not a naturalized phenomenon. Fanon explained this at great length, as did Cedric Robinson and Angela Davis. The tree has a trunk, and the trunk has roots. The historical tree of racism that *did* grow is not uncertain, unstable, and decentered—it is very much consistent, unified, and self-organized to produce racialization in some (very diverse and domain-variant) ways *but not others*.[293] This "constraint" element of what racialization processes work to protect is critically necessary for understanding the dynamics of dispossession behind white innocence projects and the epistemic toolkits that support them. And it has a long history that predates traditional fifteenth- and sixteenth-century colonial dating schemes.

For instance, the ancient greeks associated virtue with physiology and began refining an intergenerational program of physiognomic differentiation that set the stage for color prejudice, but within a *profit-motivated* context where one in four Athenian inhabitants was enslaved without citizenship, and with many enslaved people from Africa. The *Physiognomonics*, previously attributed to Aristotle, notes the following:

> A thick *neck* indicates a strong character, as in males: a thin neck, weakness, as in females . . . a well-sized neck, not too thick, a proud soul, as in lions. . . . Thick *lips*, with the upper overhanging the lower, mean folly, as in the ass and the ape. . . . A *nose* thick at the tip means laziness . . . but when it is strongly aquiline and demarcated from the forehead by a well-defined articulation, it indicates a proud soul, as in the eagle. . . . A small *forehead* means stupidity. . . . Too black a *hue* mars the coward, as witness Egyptians and Ethiopians, and so does also too white a complexion, as you may see from women. So the hue that makes for courage must be intermediate between the extremes. A tawny colour indicates a bold spirit, as in lions: but too ruddy a hue marks a rogue, as in the case of the fox. A pale mottled hue signifies cowardice, for that is the colour one turns in terror. The honey-pale are cold, and coldness means immobility, and an immobile body means slowness. A red hue indicates hastiness, for all parts of the body on being heated by movement turn red. . . . If the eyes are too black, they signify cowardice, for we say above that this is the signification of too black a hue: if they are not too black, but inclining to chestnut, they indicate a bold spirit.[294]

Given that the ancient greeks were not the "fairest" themselves, an unsurprising emphasis on golden mean psychology emerges that valorizes a Goldilocks "just right" physiology—a balanced not too fair, not too dark, a "hue that makes for courage." "Whiteness" in the west has always been a sociohistorical *dynastic* formation that has made room for the changing "hues" of patriarchal white settlement while remaining anchored in anti-Blackness—the "black hue" that "mars the coward, as witness Egyptians and Ethiopians" to facilitate settlement. When LA city council president Martinez made the racist remarks, the anti-Blackness underwriting anti-Indigeneity did not come out of thin air; one need only reference an illustration of the colonial *casta* system that differentiates between (and creates) castes through anti-Black physiognomy (the closer to "black hue" the lower on the ontological ladder and the closer to animalistic representation).[295] The physiognomic differentiation quoted above shows that ableism and sexism are not side hustles of anti-Black white supremacy, but constitutive of it, already brewing in the cauldron of impunity western culture was cooking up to make itself a "master race" in a conflict-ridden Mediterranean.

Cedric Robinson famously traced the "appearance and formulation of racial sensibility in western civilization" to feudal europe and to its internal relations: "Racism, I maintain, was not simply a convention for ordering the relations of European to non-European peoples but has its genesis in the 'internal' relations of European peoples."[296] By extending the emergence of "racial sensibility" further back to the feudal period, Robinson is able to track the codevelopment of merchant capitalism alongside the earliest colonial projects of the modern period, ushering in the field of racial capitalism. Robinson points to ancient greek references of African people's physical appearance that predate colonial racial taxonomies,[297] yet he follows Frank Snowden in claiming that the greeks and romans held no special stigma attached to skin color in the way we associate color prejudice today.[298] While I agree the greeks and romans had no systematic doctrine of "fair hue"-based white superiority—that came later with the great mythography of the Caucasian race—I do think there is ground to suggest a concerted project of proto-racism was brewing in support of the extensive slave system emerging in the ancient world that structurally antecedes racial capitalism's feudal origins.[299] And, given the major metaphysical conceptual shifts that supported the emergence of nonreciprocal dualisms and binary logics of exclusion between the eight and fifth centuries BCE in Asia Minor, I think western philosophy provided the conceptual tools critical to the proto-racist project of cultural supremacy based on racial differentiation.

But I don't think it's necessary to posit such a project in greco-roman antiquity to get a handle on the greco-roman origins of white dynastic sociohistorical formations as a concerted system of social reproduction (one that naturalizes its own origins as "universal"). This is because the focus is on the system-generated *dynamics* of dispossession such social formations plausibly enabled, not on the various racial schemes invariably made possible by the adaptive and self-learning capacities of white dynastic formations. In this sense, I'm in complete agreement with Alyosha Goldstein that an emphasis on social reproduction underscores the complementary coexistence of violent dispossession and "the ever-escalating incorporative intensities of capitalist markets" that turn wilderness into wealth, but also how dynastic dynamics of retrenchment are not timeless universal structures immune to transformative change.[300]

White dynastic formations offer an anticolonial systems framing of the structural racism discussed in this chapter. It's an interpretive lens for tracking structurally violent phenomena like racial segregation, gerrymandering, and racial health inequalities from the bottom up through the dynastic and self-repairing dynamics of social reproduction in settler colonial social structures. While I locate the roots of these particular social reproduction processes in the greco-roman world, many critical race, decolonial, and anti-imperial thinkers do not (preferring the post-Renaissance "modernity" paradigm as the birthplace of white supremacist settler colonial logics, for example). What these different interpretations of the same phenomena share is a consensus that modern-day violence against people of color and Indigenous peoples is structural in nature and that there is something distinctive about western anglo-european culture and its epistemological apparatuses that drives the intergenerational regenerative character of the violences we face.

As I use white dynastic formations, the term "white" denotes the adaptive range and functionalization of whiteness—its ability to shapeshift to accommodate the changing face of western settlement and imperialism since antiquity, including through the early christian church.[301] The notion of "dynastic" refers to a process of *controlled succession* rather than hereditary of biological lines of descent.[302] White dynastic polities are not phenotypic black boxes; from a Constantine to a Medici to an Elon Musk, the hyperconcentration of wealth and power in white dynastic polities is rooted in intergenerational dynamics of violent dispossession under the guise of prosperity projects for specific populations that whiteness helps uphold, not in whiteness as a physical property of skin tone.[303] The emphasis on controlled succession helps bring the intergenerational and adaptive aspects of these complex operations into focus. Finally, the notion of "formations" refers to cultural reproduction processes that uphold whiteness "as deeply structured relationship to power to power and group entitlement," as Crenshaw said. So put back together, we can think of white dynastic formations as anticolonial modal contextualist accounts of social regeneration (the processes that sustain social reproduction) in settler colonial societies. The focus of the toolkit lies in tracking, not what "it" (settler colonial white supremacy) is as a social substance that perseverates through change functionally unchanged, but how it *gets away with it*. It presumes that there exists a tacit playbook on how to get away with population-level murder (i.e., a distributive design) that is accessible to some populations but not others in settler colonial societies.[304] The emphasis is on the structurally controlled regeneration that underwrites cultures of violence in settler colonial societies and creates tunnels of impunity to escape through whenever calls for accountability arise.

Rana Jaleel's concept of "the work of rape" offers clear illustrations of the downstream effects and structural invariance characteristic of white dynastic formations. While the international legal arena has only recently transformed rape law to reflect the understanding of sexual assault as a war crime, Jaleel documents how the various components of legal redefinitions of rape law preserved key functional elements that allowed for the retrenchment of colonial violence and intersecting oppressions to continue to play large roles in rape cases. Jaleel's critique of the white legal transnational feminist project—which promotes "certain frameworks of structural misogyny but not its 'darker' entanglements: capitalism, settler colonialism, empire"— outlines the adaptive capacities of international law and white feminist projects that make retrenchment look like justice by design—an effort that amounts to "attempts to resolve and absolve empire, militarism, and racial capitalism with the judicious application of more empire, militarism, and racial capitalism."[305] The controlled succession of structural violence can remain in place through liberalism's domestic and international administrative developments.

Jaleel's framework and that of Indigenous, abolitionist, decolonial, critical race and anti-imperial feminisms have been at the forefront of recognizing the many mechanisms by which the apparatuses of colonial hegemony live on in liberal democratic and autocratic societies alike, and of the resistant imaginaries required to outmaneuver the counterrevolutionary design of white supremacy in all its forms. Angela Davis, for instance, noted that the administrative responses to police reform often result in increased spending on police and community surveillance infrastructures by design: "We're in a period now where people are demanding reforms . . . the problem is that reforms have often rendered the institution itself more permanent and ultimately more repressive, more racist."[306]

For Davis, "The major challenge of this period is to infuse a consciousness of the structural character of state violence into movements that spontaneously arise."[307] However, "The development of new ways of thinking about racism requires us not only to understand the economic, social, and ideological structures, but also collective psychic structures."[308] In our next chapter, we'll explore how collective epistemologies rooted in white dynastic formations arose to give powerful assists to settler colonial uses of legal testimony that continue to play powerful regulative roles in who is worthy of belief in settler colonial societies. Our goal is to show that whiteness continues to be a cohesive system of structural transformations that cannot be disconnected from the structural iterations of gendered violence in settler colonial cultures.

Some Takeaways

This is inherently a political project, not a philosophical one. Philosophical projects in social theory often aim to establish a more precise correspondence between self and world as a rational gateway for liberation—the idea that if we "know" what ails us and how such forces work, the pathway to freedom is clearer and therefore pulled into a political riptide of progressive emancipation or critical engagement with democratic structures that favors the oppressed. Fanon disagreed with this conclusion on structural grounds.[309] He believed the multivariant system of colonial domination was set up to create recursion at the deepest levels of culture, so that political rights were foreordained to be rollbacks in the making at the moment colonizers "granted" rights to colonized peoples. And he thought this would continue for so long as the colonial system of domination and exploitation existed—a system that produces functionally invariant political formations throughout history that consistently sever land and language from political freedoms outside of settler futurity. "Racism now, racism tomorrow, racism forever." As a structural thinker, he'd agree with that.

But Fanon was also a liberation thinker; as a medical doctor and a revolutionary, he fought to bring the colonial system down, not to explain it. He held a counterdispossessive stance that relied on world-building and creative refusal—hence the important role "culture" plays in consolidating anticolonial revolution in *The Wretched of the Earth*. In keeping with Fanon, the "dynastic" framing of settler colonial social formations and epistemological systems is not fate. To talk about probability of outcomes in a system of oppression means certain outcomes are probabilistic, not deterministic (Chapter 5). And yet. Futures that are outside (that is, that are central to its exploitative subsystems, as Cedric Robinson might phrase it) dynastic whiteness are routinely portrayed as terminal by design (the idea that there's no way out of coloniality, or that hermeneutic death means collective death, that if our ancestral languages have been destroyed and language is the source of sociality, our cultures are also extinct). Pure lies. This is the transference power of settler epistemological systems—to keep the chains of signification flowing in a continuous circuit that reinforces the totality of settler colonial system design through its many subsystems and the power relations such subsystems respecify, so that the illusion of a totality-of-significations accrues to settler colonial epistemologies by design. This is accomplished though violence, and more specifically, the hermeneutic dimension of structural violence (Chapter 4).

What's the endgame of this violence? Value. Power. Wealth. Profit.

> Whiteness has a cash value: it accounts for advantages that come to individuals through profits made from housing secured in discriminatory markets, through the unequal educational opportunities available to children of different races, through insider networks that channel employment opportunities to the relatives and friends of those who have profited most from present and past racial discrimination, and especially through intergenerational transfers of inherited wealth that pass on the spoils of discrimination to succeeding generations.[310]

The basic idea is this: when viewed from an anticolonial systems perspective, it is evident that not all cultures are designed to colonize others, and that the epistemological subsystems under coloniality—for example, the *logos* of anthropo*logy* that Audra Simpson so aptly criticizes—are fundamentally set up to gaslight marginalized populations for settler colonial white dynastic *profit and gain*, to keep the stolen land and the accumulated wealth, and to enact whatever violence is necessary to maintain the hyperconcentration of wealth and well-being (a critical form of capital in settler social structures) in white dynastic intergenerational chains of transmission. These structural epistemic resource wealth transfers, which go untaxed generation after generation, are codified in a system of nonaccidental relations that we are still contending with in settler colonial societies. Hence the need for an account of a systems perspective of structural violence that can illuminate these indirect wealth transfers and the violent economy they operate through. It's a story of how settler colonial white supremacy artfully leverages sociostructural mechanism to encode the playbook of how to get away with systemic violence, to make it a white-collar crime without substantive deterrents or pathways for accountability. It generates a social world replete with nonaccidental inequity and equifinal ways to justify and reproduce that inequity. A world where some lives are deemed to have more worth than others—a world where some lives are deemed—how do they phrase it? Oh yes—"not worth their while."

2
Structural Violence Is *Historical*
On Testimony and Gender-Based Violence

María Micaela de los Santos, an Indigenous widow, was indentured as a wet nurse in colonial Guatemala. In 1798, her father brought suit against the brother of her employer, the Spanish settler don Josef Melchor de Ugalde, for the crime of rape (*estupro*). María testified to the violent attack, the multiple eyewitnesses, and the extensive household history of sexual abuse of servants. The ruling was predictable and swift: "There is no evidence against don Melchor Ugalde beyond the declaration of the woman who says she was forced . . . in a small house, in which there are at least four other residents besides Ugalde de Santos, it would have been very easy for her to avoid the violence, if she wanted."[1]

In 2016, the father of the minor Daphne brought suit against four men from Veracruz's elite settler society for the crimes of rape (*violación*) and pederasty (*pederastia*) after learning she had been forced into the men's vehicle outside a nightclub and assaulted. Daphne testified to the violent attack, named multiple eyewitnesses, and produced a video of the perpetrators openly confessing their crimes. The ruling was predictable and swift: no charges would be filed on the basis of the videotaped evidence, since according to the state prosecutor, "That's not a confession, it's an apology."[2] On the matter of charges filed on the basis of Daphne's testimony, a judge found the accused guilty of the deed but not the crime. He argued that there is no evidence the accused "received pleasure" from the assault, and though she had been abducted, the judge argued Daphne was not helpless to escape the violence "if she wanted."[3]

If she wanted. Lessgo.

Using the example of structural invariance between 1798 and 2016 as a framework, this chapter takes up the epistemic issue of testimonial evidence and credibility in the context of ongoing patterns of gender-based violence in settler colonial societies like the United States, Canada, and

Mexico. These patterns are constituted by settler colonial *distributive design strategies* (i.e., the structured maldistribution of precarity and burden in settler colonial societies for the benefit of white settler polities). The imposition of these strategies ensures that violence continues to be enacted in the lives of women of color intergenerationally, irrespective of our needs and most certainly of our wants. Building on the structural analysis of oppression outlined in Chapter 1, the aim of this chapter is to resist whitewashed legal narratives of sexual violence that turn on settler notions of testimonial credibility. Instead, the chapter will advance more coordinated views of gender-based harm that produce various kinds of structural epistemic profit for some populations but not others—strategically, predictively, and from one generation to the next.[4]

Chapter 2 illustrates how settler colonial administrative systems wield concepts like "credibility" to sustain intergenerational structures of impunity, which in turn help maintain intergenerational channels of wealth transfer for white settler populations and their descendants (Chapter 3). The wide-ranging discussion in this chapter shows that structural violence is deeply historical and not a modern-day phenomenon. The basic design structure of systemic violence—what it aims to shore up as a system and for whose benefit—predates european colonial invasion of the Americas. This lineage of violence continues to impact our lived realities as women of color in a myriad of structural ways. Given the various polities that profit from organized violence against us and the basic system design behind the intergenerational production of such profits, we should have no reasonable expectation of future reprieve from violence.

Organized violence (*violentus*), since its conceptual refinement in roman law, has never been far afield from western epistemic systems. Settler colonial cultures used that conceptual formation to fuel the generative systems of profit that are their bedrock. Organized violence, as outlined in roman law, also forms the basis of settler colonial cultures' specific forms of state, social, and administrative violence that afflicts the lives of marginalized women. The question is: How does the bill for damages get presented through existing social architectures designed to damage as a matter of function? What moves and countermoves are set in place to preclude any serious reckoning with the profitable mechanisms of settler colonial violence, which include the hyperprofitable collusion of racialized violence with rape culture? Chapter 2 tells this story.

The Rise of Testimony

Testimony is a very old concept, which has recently garnered a lot of attention. The emergence of the #MeToo movement and its convergence with high-profile cases such as the Supreme Court nomination of Brett Kavanaugh helped turn testimony and its surrounding epistemological issues of belief, credibility, and trustworthiness into household topics. Many of us recall watching Dr. Christine Blasey Ford's sworn testimony of her experience of sexual violence. We also remember that the public dialogue that followed was driven by media analyses of her body language, tone, social history, intelligence, and detailed memory of the traumatic events. Such analyses were offered as possible evidentiary markers of credibility. Often absent from the discussion was the role that sexism and racism play in determining legal associations between admissible evidence, witness credibility, and public narratives of sexual violence. The specific details of her person that were chosen for meticulous scrutiny, as well as the structural issues that were disregarded, were all too reminiscent of the discussions that occurred in 1991 while Dr. Anita Hill gave testimony before the Senate Judiciary Committee. One *New York Times* article went so far as to report on the epistemic difficulty of adjudicating "two very different versions of the truth, unfolding in the heated atmosphere of gender divides, #MeToo and the Trump Presidency" and left it to readers to deliberate about the winner of the testimonial credibility wars: a veritable "duel with tears and fury" between "a woman's tremulous account of sexual assault" and "a man's angry, outraged denial."[5]

In the wake of such reports, a volume of academic literature arose that revisited decades of scientific and feminist scholarship on trauma, gendered violence, and women's precarious structural positions with respect to social institutions and intersectional oppressions.[6] This literature reinvigorated discussion of testimony but also further fragmented disciplinary contributions on the topic. Neurologists emphasized hippocampal and amygdaloidal activity in encoding very old memories of trauma in the brain, while sociologists noted the various risk exposures associated with stressful experiences of recalling these memories (as in contexts where one is not likely to be trusted about one's own experiences of trauma).[7] Historians pointed to long-existing legal practices of disqualifying women's testimonies of sexual assault through double standards of emotional self-control and patriarchal constructions of the body as a site of ritual mourning. As Rachel Welsh explains, a medieval woman only had three days under Castilian law codes (*fueros*) to bring suit for rape, during which time she had to present herself in public and be seen scratching and tearing her cheeks (*cum secctatis genis*) as a legal sign of a valid accusation, thus triggering a procedural inquiry.[8] Legal scholars likewise noted the long-running abusive practice of using women's sexual histories against them and focusing on survivor's social history as markers of credibility. Under common law, for instance, sexual history has long been used as a powerful legal technique to impeach, or challenge, a victim's credibility, "prove" consent to intercourse where none was given, and justify rape culture "on the grounds that unchaste women are apt to lie."[9]

Philosophers were especially interested in these conversations because they involved classical problems such as what truth is and how to determine it, when testimony leads to justified beliefs and knowledge, how speech and language function in relation to ascertaining testimonial truth, the ways social facts affect these things, and even normative ideas about what ethical social practices should look like when hearing the word of another who brings forth claims of harm. Many philosophers, most of whom had never written on sexual violence, began speaking and publishing widely on testimonial credibility and the ethics of testimony in the wake of the #MeToo movement. One main source of citations for this burgeoning literature on testimony came from what is known as the epistemology of testimony[10] and, later, epistemic injustice.[11] While influential for melding ethics and politics together in a field that rarely connects the two, this literature often elided the fact that credibility deflation is an actively produced social process. In other words, "Targeted ignorances are only sustainable when they are collective and supported by the kind of social power dominant institutions confer."[12]

A growing body of literature within gender studies, feminist legal theory, Latin American testimony (*testimonio*), and Indigenous social theory tackles the issue of testimonial credibility in the context of concrete (and, at times, land-specific) social and institutional systems of power. The philosophy literature, however, was apt to describe problems of testimony through the constructed framework of an "epistemic state of nature."[13] This idealized projection of how human thinking functions "naturally" in a mythical evolutionary time period provides a narrative stripped of all social and historical particulars. This approach relegates issues of sexism and racism to "historically contingent" features of epistemic habits, and it obscures historical awareness of three aspects of the concept of testimony: its growth from the colonial power structures of supplicancy and *Native informancy* (the settler colonial technique of coordinating damage to Indigenous knowledge and communication systems alongside the exploitation of Native people as informants for white settlers); its use to support colonial violence; and its deep genealogical ties to evidentiary requirements that enforce sexual terror and state-sponsored violence against Indigenous peoples in settler colonial societies. Philosophy, as a field, is dominated by whiteness—both demographic and methodological.[14] And philosophers—exemplified here by the "state-of-nature" social epistemologists—fail to recognize the central relevance of this history because they have never had to live it, wrestle with its consequences (daily, viscerally, and at multiple scales of experience), or offer resistance to it in order to survive.

In the next section, we'll turn away from standard abstract philosophical narratives of testimony and take a look at how the practice of testimony arose as a powerful legal technology used to produce a "good informant" rather than good information. The purposes of this legal technology were to secure administrative systems of power that produce a state monopoly on violence and to codify structures of wealth transfer based on the notion of "pure lineage."[15]

Testimony as a Technology of Social Power

Most people today think of testimony as a social practice. Providing testimony is something that we do when we need others (institutions included) to confer trust upon us. It is what we do when we need to communicate our experience but independent verification is either unavailable or cannot be easily obtained, such as when someone has direct or indirect knowledge of a past event that can't be replicated in a courtroom. Sometimes the trust conferred is clearly bracketed by what we say and who is speaking, as in a testimonial oath in court that legally prioritizes the words a person utters over who says them. Such practices include swearing on a Bible and calling a "witness of fact," referring to someone whose opinion is legally severed from the content to which they attest.[16] At other times, testimony's purpose is solely to confer trust on the testifiers themselves, as with credibility witnesses in a trial. In most cases, though, testimony is thought to involve gradients of both content and credibility assessment, with the central component being that of a person telling their story to someone in an evidentiary context—not just speaking into the wind.

This modern notion of testimony has undergone a very long process of naturalization to appear as it does today. Naturalization is a western cultural process that normativizes social practices to make them appear neutral, objective, or universal. This process thus produces the appearance of a "natural" phenomenon rather than a value-laden social practice that distributes social power unevenly.[17] Naturalization of the notion of testimony produces problematic results in two primary ways: (1) by obscuring the role that testimony played in the political expansion of the greek and roman empires and the rise of institutional slavery, and (2) by foregrounding the concept of testimony employed in settler colonial societies that uses the guise of neutrality and impartiality to confer adjudicating power over testimony to white individuals. Through reinventions in seventeenth-century natural law, naturalization also played a prominent role in the institutionalization of european legal and religious systems under colonial and imperial rule. The continued use of testimony reflects its efficacy as a technology of social power and a legal tool in greek and roman antiquity.

Testimony, in this view, is a western technology of social power and a powerful legal technology that differs from the cultural and oral traditions of "witnessing" that arose to counter its effects. "Witnessing," as James Baldwin and others use it, is an antigaslighting practice, rooted in older spiritual traditions, that runs counter to the settler epistemological forms of witnessing that arose to surveil Black and Brown lives and bodies. As a technology of social power, testimony has coevolved alongside criminal and property legal codes that support anglo-european structural economic supremacy to produce a legal order in which "white litigants dominate civil proceedings and Black and Brown defendants proliferate in criminal courts."[18] Testimony's embeddedness in relation to social institutions that shape our everyday world has reinforced its "natural" appearance. However, testimony has never been race or gender neutral, and it has always been gainful for specific populations. The word itself gestures to this origin.

"Testimony" (along with its cognates "testify" and "testament," as well as its prefixed forms "attest," "contest," and "detest") comes from the Latin *testis*, meaning both "witness" and "testicle." Its etymology reflects the clear connection between male authority in antiquity and the important political role oath-giving played in the transition from oral to alphabetic cultures in ancient Greece.[19] As Judith Fletcher explains: "Athens was the definitive phallogocentric community where public discursive practices such as the oath were the prerogative of male citizens who competed for power in the agora, the assembly, and the law courts."[20] For a society rooted in transactional commerce and social status, such power was based on one's wealth accumulation via property transfer (property and testimony thus come together in *testamentum, inteste*/will and intestacy structures) and the ability to prevent family assets from being transferred outside the family through marriage.[21] While women of nonenslaved standing could achieve significant power and independence within families, giving women testimonial powers would have impacted the stability of existing legal regimes governing inheritance structures, which form the foundation of patrilineal social organization in the west. Thus in the greco-roman world, women could not be public oath-givers and had recourse to promise-giving narrative tools only in dramas, comedic plays (refer, for example, to Aristophanes's *Lysistrata*), and Hellenic religious cults.[22]

Restricting women's access to testimony was a critical component of maintaining social power over inheritance structures and strengthening the cultural relation between gender roles and private property in the ancient world. The practice was gainful for specific populations from the start. But as the range and domains of economic gain expanded beyond what was possible in ancient greece, so too did ways of using testimony as a social technology of power.[23] As the dynastic features of western imperialism grew with the global expansion of the roman empire, new avenues to respecify the function of testimonial restrictions emerged. The growth and adaptation of testimonial restrictions was less an opportunity than a structural necessity, as restraints on women's testimony alone are insufficient for regulating the administrative scope of interlocking oppressions that are the hallmark of dynastic social structures.

The Need for Adaptive Technologies

As discussed in the previous chapter, social structures must have restrictions placed on the arrangement of specified social elements to produce observable patterns and behaviors (i.e., the specific relations in a social system) attributable to that social system.[24] But this is not an arbitrary social process. What determines these restrictions in western cultures is undergirded by social values, epistemic orthodoxies, and metaphysical assumptions that are produced through the system itself and have a contextual history of, for example, inequitable access to social power.[25]

Interlocking oppressions are incredibly important to dynastic social systems because they allow social structures to regenerate and survive transformations in an organized fashion and with regularity.[26] They do so by embedding elementary relations of the core social structure with those of a distinct substructure in its own system.[27] This structural respecification can be understood through the metaphor of a relay race: as one racer falls or is tripped at the handoff, the tracks automatically converge to supply an alternate runner.[28] It can also be understood empirically, like the molecular pathway of metastases discussed in the introduction—the one that allows cancer cells that narrowly escape cell death after exposure to chemotherapy to reprogram themselves and acquire metastatic skills. Interlocking oppressions are like self-correcting molecular pathways and automatically convergent track systems; as long as their dominating infrastructure remains in place, the structural vehicle that reproduces dynastic whiteness can always prevail. What structural justice tries to do is frame interventions that interrupt how these pathways communicate and coordinate together as a system to produce their self-healing properties.[29]

Here it is critical to remember that social systems are goal-oriented and that interlocking oppressions are a vital part of settler colonial systems. The orienting goal of greco-roman culture was the imperial production of profit and value through extractive wealth accumulation based on dynastic supremacy. Not only is there structural continuity between imperial territorial accumulation in antiquity, colonial capitalism in the modern period, and globalized neoliberal capitalism in the present, the specific forms the system goal of profit take are realized through interlocking oppressions. The past wealth extracted and produced from the enslavement and abuse of racialized women thus has analogues to the commercial trafficking and sexual abuse of women of color and Indigenous women in resource-rich extractive zones today, and in a way that is fundamentally bound up with the system goals and self-healing properties of white supremacy. The rise of the concept of testimony as a technology of social power follows the course other similar conceptual technologies in settler colonial dynastic cultures. One example is the function of racial hinges and loopholes in the adaptive construction of legal whiteness.

Racial Hinges and Loopholes

Yet another way to think about the mutually reinforcing relationship between a social system's structural continuity and interlocking oppressions as convergent subsystems is the construction of racial ambiguity as legal whiteness.

In the early twentieth century, the United States denaturalized a wave of South Asian and East Asian citizens on the grounds that such citizens were mistakenly labeled by lower courts as "white" because the reigning racial taxonomies of the time said they were (e.g., labeling Hindus born in India as "Caucasians" originating from the Caucasus region that lies between the Caspian Sea and the Black Sea), whereas to the "common man" they were clearly "non-white."[30] Since the eighteenth century, the legal constructions of an immigrant petitioner's (or "declarant") race in the United States have indisputably centered around the main system goal of *jurisdictional white supremacy* (a broader administrative framing of white supremacy that can accommodate changes in the social understanding of whiteness), and the reliably inconsistent rulings on legal whiteness that shapeshift to accommodate the dynamic situational factors of historical change. In 1849 Justice Grier wrote that "it is the cherished policy of the general government to encourage and invite Christian foreigners of our own race to seek an asylum within our borders, and to convert these waste lands into productive farms, and thus add to the wealth, population, and power of the nation."[31] White women who lost their citizenship when they married Asian non-citizens were allowed, through special provisions of a law amended by Congress in 1931, to have their citizenship reinstated.[32] Rose Chin, a second-generation Chinese American woman, also lost her citizenship when she married Pong Mon, a Chinese national. Her application for reinstatement of citizenship was predictably disapproved.[33] The construction of the settler nation-state project (of turning "waste" Indigenous lands into productive white farms) as a white racial state is inseparable from the construction of white womanhood in upholding the settler project.

Following the 1922 passage of the Cable Act, US commissioner of naturalization Raymond Crist began pressing Congress to make provisions for granting exceptions to women's lost citizenship status by marriage to Asian nationals, arguing that "women of perhaps Mayflower ancestry, whose forbears fought through the Revolution, and whose family names bear honored and conspicuous places in our history, who are thoroughly American at heart, and who perhaps have never left these shores, but whose act in choosing alien husbands has caused forfeiture of American citizenship, bemoan the stipulation that such as they must sue for naturalization by the ordinary means."[34] One woman who was able to regain citizenship under the 1931 amendment to the Cable Act did so by establishing pure lineage back to Anglo-Saxon "Scandinavian" origins.[35] Rose Chin, whose Washington State birth certificate assigned her parentage as "yellow," did not have the same access to whiteness as an informal yet highly functional legal domain for renaturalization.

In the 1980s, Louisiana resident Susie Guillory Phills unsuccessfully sued to have her racial classification changed from "colored" to "white." Phills, who by her own account had grown up as a fair-skinned white woman with white ancestry, was applying for a US passport when she learned the Louisiana Department of Vital Records applied a 1970 statute requiring racial classification based on a one-drop blood quantum rule of one-thirty-second "negro blood," meaning her great-great-great-great grandmother, an enslaved Black woman freed in 1762 that genealogists hired by the state had uncovered, made her "three-thirty-seconds" "colored" and well within the range required by law to make her legally nonwhite.[36]

Neda Maghbouleh describes the consistently shifting, flexible, paradoxical, and contingent legal racial status of Iranian Americans through the lens of two concepts that are useful for this project: *racial hinges* and *racial loopholes*. Racial hinges describe how "the geographic, political, and pseudoscientific specter of a racially liminal group, like Iranians, can be marshalled by a variety of legal and extralegal actors into a symbolic hinge that opens or closes the door to whiteness as necessary."[37] A racial loophole "describes the everyday contradictions and conflicts that emerge when a group's legal and racial categorization is inconsistent with its on-the-ground experience of racialization or deracialization."[38] I am suggesting racial hinges are system properties, and that racial loopholes the nonaccidental outcomes of the distributive design of settler colonial social structures.

Consider how racial loopholes work in the case of Mostafa Hefny, an Egyptian-born man of Nubian descent who sued the United States to change his assigned racial status from "white" to Black, contesting the modern tradition, rooted in western colonial ideals, of locating Egypt outside of Africa. He told reporters: "I was not told by Immigration that I was white until I passed the exam for citizenship and then I was told I am now white.... It hurts me because I am unable to reconcile my reality as a black person."[39] The fact that Susie Phills could only leave the country as a "colored" woman, but an Egyptian-born man, Mostafa Hefny, could not legally assert his identity as a Black man to come into the country becomes explainable when we consider that settler states are incontrovertibly invested in importing whiteness (Congress restricted naturalization to "free white" foreigners in its first citizenship statute)[40] as value added to the state project of turning and keeping Indigenous lands jurisdictionally white, and to controlling the movement of nonwhite bodies, typically by regulating the ability to freely leave a space ordered and governed by jurisdictional whiteness. In this case, the judicial system accommodates and bends to provide concrete pathways for settler colonial system goals to be realized.

For example, immigrants and asylum seekers cannot freely travel while awaiting status decisions—a process that can take many years—and must petition for "parole" to leave the United States. In the 1950s, after the US government had forcibly and violently relocated Indigenous peoples from ancestral lands, officers from the Bureau of Indian Affairs routinely pressured Indigenous peoples to move off their reservations. This was done with the lure and promise of jobs, healthcare, vocational training, and housing on the condition of accepting one-way bus tickets to urban areas the government had preselected. The Voluntary Relocation Program, as it was known, sought to promote settler lifeways rooted in private property, wipe out reservations and the growing jurisdictional autonomy of Indian country, and make available for mining reservation lands the government had not known were rich in oil and minerals at the time it created the reservations. A 1956 memo from the Bureau announced the budget for financial incentives would be tripled to allow, among other things, for "a pilot program to assist about 100 of the 'more settled' city-dwelling Indian families in the purchase of homes."[41] In 1942, when the scarcity of male labor in the United States due to World War II was taking a toll on existing agricultural production, industrial farming, and railroad infrastructures, the United States bused in millions of Mexican workers on short-term labor contracts under the "braceros" (men with strong arms) program. Many of these people worked in environmentally hazardous and exploitative conditions before being sent back without having been paid. Those who were paid (the average rate was fifty cents an hour) had a percentage of their paychecks withheld without the worker's knowledge in alleged "savings funds" accounts held by Wells Fargo. Today, despite a successful class-action suit for back wages, thousands of former workers have yet to receive compensation for their stolen labor. Since Reconstruction, the state-choreographed movement of bodies for seasonal agricultural labor and migrant formwork has closely followed the lobbying needs of the grower class for cheap disposable labor, opening and closing racial hinges through changes in immigration policy, census categories, and party platforms. When Reagan famously lobbied for amnesty in the 1980s, his defense was that he would rather see Mexicans have a pathway to citizenship than see farmlands go fallow. When Rep. Elton Gallegly (R-CA) gave opening remarks in a 2011 House subcommittee on the farmworker visa program created by Reagan, he said: "Unlike almost all other occupations, there are simply not enough Americans willing to take the jobs of a migrant farm worker. In fact, our Government's policy for generations has been to remove Americans from such labor."[42] By 2020, the Trump administration solved the problem of the white grower class's need for surplus Brown labor while reviving the political usefulness of the white supremacist trope of the dark-skinned foreigner as a threat to national security and white women's safety: he expanded Reagan's federal guestworker visa program but removed wage-rate protections for farmworkers and initiated wage freezes that would result in nearly $2 billion in savings for the grower class. As with the braceros program, farmworkers were "lured to America—then trapped."[43] Different decade, same system design. Such design does not mean racism went away between the Reagan and Trump administrations; it means it was respecified across various domains (as in criminal justice reform "three strikes" bills and the related myth of young, urban, and implicitly Black and Brown "superpredators"), and that this respecification was not possible without the pathways established by interlocking oppressions.

As a system property, racial hinges automatically converge to block off Mostafa Hefny's access to affirmative action programs in employment and education as a Black man, but open up for white women like Rachel Dolezal to sue Howard University, a historically Black college she was accepted into as a white student, for racial discrimination (for being white) on the grounds that Black students were receiving preferential treatment in internal employment and educational opportunities, but also to claim access to preferential consideration based on affirmative action programs when she decided to pass full time as a Black woman.[44]

Interlocking oppressions functionalize racial hinges to allow paraconsistent logic (a way to hold contradicting or inconsistent information together without reducing the inferring relation between the information to triviality or absurdity) to permeate settler colonial administrative systems. Whiteness is meant to prevail—the house always wins, even when it seems to be losing; there is consistency in its paraconsistency that serves larger system goals and preserves functional pathways beyond the reproduction of whiteness for reproduction's sake. And what such function-preserving shiftwork severs is the goal of profit: its production, accumulation, concentration, and transmission, especially when transmutations in value take place (as when digital goods became socially valued and fungible resources that can be monetized and exchanged). Thus, paradoxically, when the interplay of elementary relations in a social system converges on the goal of profit, then organized ambiguity and indeterminateness will prevail. The system is perfectly inconsistent.

Ambiguity and Distributive Design

Returning to antiquity, consider, for example, the ambiguity in Athenian women's access to ownership of private property; while no Athenian women of any rank could legally own property, wealthy women could own a personal slave.[45] Women could also be enslaved throughout the roman world, but in such cases "white females were the most desired and most expensive slaves."[46] Rigid rules loosen and legal codes become ambiguous to accommodate the core value being respecified through the many relevant subsystems. Here the core value is pure lineage as whiteness, and the subsystems it is respecified through are western gender categories, which have been built and carefully preserved in western culture to continue the perpetuation of white dynastic cultural formations.

The key takeaway from the respecification of the core value is not just that certain privileges and affordances are preemptively awarded to some social agents while others—those more precariously situated in society and with far less social capital to trade—are marked for enforcement and punishment. And it is far less the case that racism is a psychic plague to be wrested from the hearts and minds of individuals through religious-like conversion to the logic of the better argument. To persist, "Racism has managed to harden ... it has had to renew itself, to change its appearance ... the object of racism is no longer the individual man but a certain form of existing," one that results in "the systematized oppression of a people," as Fanon noted.[47] What Fanon misses in his famous structural account of colonial racism is that, for dynastic settlement to work, interlocking oppressions are indispensable. The racial *casta* system Spanish colonizers imposed could not have functioned without antiblackness, misogynoir, anti-Indigenous sexism, and orientalism, as illustrated in the dozens of racial categories concocted by europeans to trace and respecify the relations necessary to reproduce whiteness in the colonies, so that it might outlive challenges to the colonial-era "vulgar racism," as Fanon put it. The racial hierarchical *casta* system is thus not itself the root source of racism, just as social hierarchies are themselves not the root source of oppression.[48]

The crucial element of the process of respecification is the cohesive distributive design that is built into the fabric of western social structures that perpetuates this very process of respecification. Respecification reproduces marginalization at the same time that it produces reified value and structural privileges for dominant populations.[49] And all the while respecification conceals this very process through formal mechanisms like historiography and institutional education and through informal ones like the dominant conceptual order that underwrites institutions.

Another way to examine this powerful distributive design built into social structures is to look at the difference in institutional regulation of gender-based violence across racial categories. Nghiem Nguyen's work on the history of rape laws is helpful here. Like most scholars of western legal systems, Nguyen highlights the influence of the development and refinement of roman law in modern-day legal systems, particularly of "rape-relevant laws."[50] "For the Romans, all sexual assault, including rape, was treated as a crime," yet this only applied to "freeborn Roman women," not to enslaved people or foreigners, against whom crimes could not be committed due to their social status.[51] Nguyen's account highlights a distinction between omissions in legal coverage and the legal observance of unregulated domains that prevent standing (*locus standi*); noncriminalized sexual violence functioned in the western legal regime in a highly structured manner. Specifically, it offered protections to slave owners by supporting existing practices that allowed slave owners to rape their slaves and by procedurally disqualifying testimonies of rape by enslaved women. "Slave owners could order their slaves to submit to the demands of others and could hire their slaves out for sexual services" under the full protection of a legal system that constructed the rape of slaves as an unregulated domain outside the reach of the law.[52] The metalegal function of this unregulated legal domain was critical to securing the adaptive transformation of roman law through the process of Christianization in the Holy Roman Empire and later through the regeneration of the romano-canon system in its application to slave laws in the colonial world. Slave laws in the Americas did not arise out of thin air. While slave status was not racialized in roman society as it was in the colonial era,[53] these laws laid the foundation for the racialized slave laws enforced in the Americas and the disparate evidentiary standards of legal testimony that worked to regulate and suppress Indigenous forms of literacy and knowledge in the colonial world.

Testimony follows a similar pattern of form and function across settler colonial legal systems and the societies that produced their legal codes. In early colonial Australia, the Aboriginal Witness Act of 1844 allowed for the automated dismissal of the testimony of Indigenous people, ensuring that european colonizers who massacred Aboriginal Australians could not be tried on the basis of Aboriginal testimony alone. The Iberian world saw a standardization of distinctions between "true" and "authentic" testimony, which served to develop many of the administrative regulations related to testimony that would become key aspects of racialized practices in testimonial deposition in the Americas (*Doy Fé y verdadero testimonio / ante los señores*). In early Virginia, a 1782 statutory code stipulated that "no negro, mulatto or Indian shall be admitted to give evidence, but against or between negroes, mulattoes or Indians."[54] An 1853 California Supreme Court decision extended the class of people who could not legally testify against white citizens after a lower court convicted George Hall, a white man, of murdering Chinese miner Ling Sing. In *R v. Murrell*—the 1836 founding case for the *terra nullis* doctrine in Australian law that made Aboriginal peoples subject to English laws despite not being able to give sworn testimony in courts (on account that only Christians were rational enough to take oaths)—the court rejected the defense's claim that "Aborigines had their own laws and that they 'were given no protection by European law' partly because 'they were unable to give evidence as witnesses.'"[55] These cases all demonstrate one thing: testimony, since its inception, has been a tool to distribute social power and social goods unevenly, not by accident but by design.

Testimony and Slavery

The structural restrictions on what counted as testimony in ancient greece were shaped by the economic importance of slavery and the need to construct social tools that would support it. Porter[56] and Isaac[57] provide compelling accounts of the sheer magnitude of institutional slavery in ancient Athens and the simultaneous rise of conceptual habits that led to "protoracism," the conceptual forerunner to the colonial formulation of biological racism. Studying the widespread use of slavery in milling operations, Porter argues that previous scholarship vastly underemphasizes the economic and commercial role of slavery (particularly in the late archaic and classical period, from 600 to 300 BCE) in favor of limited sociologies that overemphasize domestic servantry and the practice of taking wartime prisoners for sport. Isaac connects these social practices to the codevelopment of rationalization processes that justified the use of slavery (following Aristotle, for instance) as natural or even inevitable. He writes, "Obviously, in classical antiquity racism did not exist in the modern form of a biological determinism." Nonetheless, "It is justified to speak of early forms of racism, or 'proto-racism,' as a widespread phenomenon in antiquity." He adds: "I do not claim that prejudice and bigotry are invented in the West; I claim that the specific forms of rationalizing these prejudices and attempting to base them in systematic, abstract thought were developed in antiquity and taken over in early modern Europe."[58]

Isaac's claim about the nonaccidental development of systems of prejudiced thought based on abstract thought is important for understanding that the colonial power structures of supplicancy and Native informancy that grounded the use of testimony were not historical aberrations. Rather, those structures were consistent with the intellectual trajectory of western thought and the social conditions it produced to maintain wealth as a dynastic system. Included among those social conditions are the rise of concepts like environmental determinism, the inheritance of acquired characteristics, and most importantly, pure lineage. These concepts were eventually amalgamated and refined to produce the notion of race as biological determinism, which would prove essential to the colonial framework.[59] In my view, race would also become a central organizing principle within the logic of transference mechanisms in settler wealth inheritance structures.[60] Critical here is that in the greco-roman world, the place where the politico-legal concepts that underwrite "democratic" rule were born, there was an intimate connection between an economically profitable system of forced labor and the generation of an analytical framework structured to make judgments about who has the power to ask what of whom, under what protections, with what expectations, and with what foreseeable consequences. In the context of the interplay between economic profit and hegemonic structures, rules governing legal testimony arose in antiquity. That roman criminal law intersected powerfully with the rise of institutional slavery provides a particularly insightful example of how social orders are built into legal systems in ways that generate predictable consequences for specific populations.

Under roman law, enslaved people could not testify against their owners even when a legally recognized crime had been committed against them. This was despite the fact that they could be used as witnesses and thus, in a very limited sense, legally testify in court. In civil contract disputes over ownership of slaves, if there was insufficient evidence such as corroboration from other citizens, courts could turn to slaves as sites of evidentiary informancy. Slaves were not seen as people testifying to lived experiences but rather as extensions of property (or contractual bonds) that could be probed as living documents. Enslaved people could not testify outside of their status as slaves, for example, on their own behalf to acts made against them. Their owners, however, routinely submitted them to courts to testify, although their testimony could only be submitted under one condition. Enslaved people could offer testimony only if it was procured under torture.[61]

Paradoxically, roman law was also explicit on the use of torture as a notoriously ill-advised method to produce truth, one that should be avoided at all costs. Courts and censors routinely cast legal suspicion on citizen's testimony that was obtained through torture, and they remained consistent on this point through the development of much of roman law.[62] The seemingly inconsistent treatment of the testimony of slaves under roman law becomes explicable when we consider said treatment in light of what results it produced and for whom.[63] Many of the structural features of the roman legal framework and the functions they upheld remained surprisingly stable as they were imported into new geopolitical contexts through the processes of colonialism. Roman criminal law introduced context-dependent restrictions on the possibility of subordinated groups producing testimony, and it codified evidentiary requirements of testimony. Both structures form the basis for Continental and English common law and thus also underlay the conceptual structure of testimony in the colonies.

Structural invariance, as noted in Chapter 1, relies on the continuing ability of a system to respecify and perpetuate itself through adaptive transformation. In *Law and Colonial Cultures*, Lauren Benton shows how the "multifaceted influence of Roman law," alongside canon systems, adapted through the centuries to create a kind of ready-made "legal supermarket" where european powers could shop for rhetorical resources to achieve their goals and compete with one another for dominion of Indian subjects:

> English [legal] theorists, for example, countered Spanish claims of conquest in the Americas by asserting that English settlers had not conquered New World territories but had simply occupied them. In doing so, they relied on the Roman legal principle of *terra nullius*—the idea that previously empty "waste" lands could be settled without conquest. [Spaniards] countered that Indigenous inhabitants were not in "possession" of the land because they did not cultivate it.[64]

The invocation of *terra nullius* and the Spanish counterclaim of uncultivated land stirred a frenzy of English "ceremonies of possession" across the Americas, such as arbitrary fence building, road plowing, animal grazing, and garden planting as ways of marking landscapes as objects of agricultural improvement and cultivation-in-waiting for the purposes of producing a title-holding land status.[65]

Spaniards turned to canon law and papal authority to establish divine rights over territories.[66] They devised complex legal rules for establishing citizenship that reversed the ancient roman rule (children follow the condition of the enslaved mother) in their racial *casta* system, thus proliferating Castilian whiteness en masse (the precursor for classifying Latinxs as racially "white" today). The English, not to be outdone, turned to natural law, and by 1767, William Blackstone's *Commentaries on the Laws of England* successfully naturalized colonial legal history by making use of Sir Francis Bacon's earlier solution to the debate: *res nullius*. That concept, with appropriately cited laws as justification, maintained that land belongs to no one and may be claimed anew by legitimate (european) state wars.[67] In the context of exerting claims to land, "defining a 'credible witness'" in the colonial world was never a matter of ascertaining truth, and the purpose of testimony was never the elicitation of truth. The practice of using witnesses in legal proceedings did not become common until the 1500s,[68] when the need for regulating oaths and claims to land arose as a distinctly structural need in the colonial project.[69] Refuting Indian claims to land rights has always been central to the colonial testimonial project, as has its structural relation to refuting claims of violence to racialized women (through which the colonial project vastly expanded its reach).

Legal testimony since its inception in roman law has been used as a dual-track administrative tool of social power, and this dual track has persisted through the adaptive transformations of colonialism and the liberal revolutions that followed it. It is an example of the continuing ability of a system to respecify and perpetuate itself.

Administrative Functions

In the roman world, legal testimony had a procedural legal function for citizens (track A) and a socially administrative, performative function for enslaved people (track B). Its extralegal purpose was to enforce the conditions for the maintenance of slavery as a social practice while publicly displaying the moral worth of laws regulating slavery, which would "allow" enslaved people to engage in the same legal activities as citizens. (The 1512 Law of Burgos that extended legal protections to enslaved Native Amerindians functioned the same way.)[70] This tactic of administrative dissimulation produced the foundation for the rise of political governance models in western democracies.[71] It allowed two seemingly incompatible realities to coexist without producing internal contradictions that could be independently fatal to democratic social structures. In fact, an internal pathway of codependence between democracy and oppression was established to favor certain social groups in power.[72] The abolitionist William Goodell also observed a similar functional aim of settler colonial legal systems, noting that "the slave *becomes a 'person'* whenever he is to be punished . . . he is under the control of law, though unprotected by law."[73]

Testimony arose in colonial courtrooms as a legal technology to support epistemic systems that keep certain structures of oppression in place. Its structural prelude took root in the roman world, where an important social epistemic function of the legal practice of testifying under torture was to break one's confidence in the expectation to be heard, believed, or trusted about one's own experiences, and to socially project the predictability of this outcome for enslaved communities and spectators. The development and projection of this idea was a pivotal step in the modern rise of settler credibility economies as epistemic capital (Chapter 3).[74] This analysis of the historical factors that contributed to the rise of testimony reveals that the practice of legal testimony in the west was designed as a regulatory mechanism for certain classes of people. Legal testimony was not a rational application of universal conditions for communicating truth in evidentiary contexts.

A nonwhitewashed reading of the legal codes surrounding slave testimony in the colonized world shows that the function of these laws was socially and psychologically capacious, designed in part to perform as extralegal regulatory mechanisms that gave enslaved peoples legal protection in name while structuring their continuing precarity in form. I've referred to this move as "settler gold."[75] Slavery was far too profitable and critical to the expansion of the roman empire to fail to regulate who has the power to question whom and to fail to enforce these rules with spectacular structural might. In fact, one of the longest steps in the naturalization of testimony is the focus on this very question—who is asking what of whom under what arbitrary conditions of social power.

In the next section, we'll move further away from the naturalized conception of testimony (as generalizable knowledge considerations involved in fact-finding from reliable evidence) and dive deeper into the coordinated conditions of power that shaped the history of testimony in the Americas. The following paragraphs detail how testimony, in the colonial context, is a structural technology of power designed to promote european jurisdictional power and authority.[76]

Testimony and the Rise of Colonial Governance Structures

Colonial uses of testimony bear resemblance to those of late antiquity, with important administrative developments. Following the resurgence of classical thought in Renaissance humanism, western kingdoms in the Iberian Peninsula revived and finessed key aspects of the roman notion of legal testimony in their varied administrative pursuits of territorial dominance.[77] The bureaucratic apparatus that emerged in early modern europe and developed into the first western "nation-states" was steeped in legal, ecclesiastic, and scholarly thinking about who has the power to question whom, what counts as an answer, and where the social power to regulate the outcome derives. That same conceptual basis also underlay the roman bureaucracy during the territorial expansion of that empire.[78]

The convergence of those lines of thought was evident in the newly formed kingdom of Spain, which in 1492 nationalized its loose confederation of Christian provinces in the north with the southern territories through the expulsion of Arab and Jewish communities in the south.[79] This was not without preparation. Fourteen years earlier, in 1478, Pope Sixtus IV responded to a novel request from the catholic kings to draw up a document that would give them the power to appoint inquisitors in every town in the land.[80] The papal bull *Exigit sincerae devotionis affectus*[81] granted the first-of-its-kind request and ushered in a new administrative era defined by expanding jurisdictional power, one where "for the first time there was a formal link between ecclesiastical and civil jurisdiction."[82] The Spanish (1478–1834) and, later, Portuguese (1536–1821) Inquisitions thus began a process of administrative infrastructural development that would result in widespread adoption of pleading standards set by a new sovereign and carried out by judicial officers of an increasingly centralized official government.[83] A new governance structure was rising. With it came a strengthening network of epistemic practices governing the assessment of ambiguity, misperception, and insincerity—practices routinely employed on structurally vulnerable people pleading their cases to colonial officials.

At the heart of this new governance structure stood the tribunal of faith, the centrifuge of inquisitorial practice.[84] Inquisitorial practice—the processual asking of questions and subsequent assessment of the credibility of testator's responses in tribunals of faith—required structures of suppliance and adjutancy predicated on the power (*potestas*) to enact penal, punitive, or retributive violence. The process was meant to elicit fear and compliance to conversion alongside deference to authority.[85]

Because testimony was obtained under duress, historians have long considered inquisitorial source materials unreliable, deflating the veracity of attestations and limiting the historical value of inquisitorial testimony produced under colonial enslavement to the perspective of the enslaver (as if structural duress is not a basic condition of our legal testimony as women of color). This has produced two results. One, the widespread normative use of the naturalized view of testimony in these historical approaches resulted in the inquisitorial process being well described by historians but undertheorized as a strategy of structural epistemic warfare. Since producing testimony under duress is a structural design feature governing specific populations under colonial rule, at minimum it should be analyzed macrohistorically.[86] Two, it reduced microhistorical knowledge of people's lives under colonialism to the violence done to them, recentering the enslaver's perspective by privileging their acts of violence (qua acts) in historical analyses of colonial social processes. This follows Saidiya Hartman's critique of the colonial archive as "a death sentence, a tomb" where "the stories that exist are not about [enslaved people], but rather about the violence, excess, mendacity, and reason that seized hold of their lives."[87] The dearth of critical macroscopic analyses that track colonial iterations of heteropatriarchal white supremacy in the conceptual rise of testimony (as naturalized, "informational" expressions of thought) only contributes to this problem.

Jurisdictional Power

At its broadest, the testimonial apparatus that entrenched itself between 1540 and 1620 in the catholic Iberian colonies was a functional blueprint—a template in jurisdiction and the professionalization of settler colonial administrative procedure. Testimony, as it was constructed, provided the basis for establishing informal domains of settler nonliability that were self-regulating, such as normative communication standards in administrative procedures, as well as formal domains, like testimonial and notary requirements in property law. The system defined who would be considered legitimate "speakers," who would be "hearers," givers or attesters of facts, and who would be given the jurisdictional authority to assess those attestations as true or credible. It is a system where it is not possible to become a witness or testifier without the structural prelude of western colonial denouncement (*denuncia*) as a public mechanism of bringing testifiers into a specific recognized relation within settler jurisdictional governance, and under the exercise of specific settler legal domains (such as colonial, criminal, civil, or administrative law). Administratively, systems of testimony also enabled the regulation of settlement-enforcing social violence through the practice of subordinated suppliance and collective administrative submission to a new prosecutorial authority, as shown in the Texcocan trial records discussed in the next section.[88]

The Texcocan Trial Records
The Texcocan trial records are considered the earliest records of an occidental evidentiary chain (consisting of legal testimony, maps, line drawings, and illustrations) produced for a legal trial in the Americas. They highlight how evidentiary burdens are cast on structurally vulnerable people (whether as claimants or defendants) though routine administrative processes designed to entrench jurisdictional power—to make answerability to conquerors a basic feature of settler administrative and institutional procedure.

At the heart of the Texcocan trials stood the question of the rightful ownership of Amerindian property—the Oztoticpac palace. The palace and its lands had been seized as part of pretrial procedures when inquisitor Zumárraga— who held that "neither physical punishment nor dishonors warns them [Indigenous peoples] as well as the loss of their estates"—submitted the Texcocan ruler Ahuachpitzactzin (Acolhua) to tribunal.[89] The ruler's counterclaim that the palace was communal property was rejected, and instead the court summoned Native witnesses to attest to Ahuachpitzactzin's idolatry. Following in the roman tradition of slave testimony as probative living documents, the inquisitorial scribes changed the speech of said witnesses from direct to indirect speech, "reducing it to what [the scribes] deemed essential," like attestations of empirical correspondence ("that is what really happened") and linear causation between events witnessed and those reported.[90] The court's search for independent evidence outside of Native testimony triggered the commission of documents—maps, codices, and pictographic calendars with alphabetized Nahuatl, some of which are now housed at the Library of Congress.[91]

Despite the cartographic evidence introduced at the trial (illustrating, for example, native plants and trees on the property being grafted by trellises of european flora, with the implication that these were originally Native lands), Ahuachpitzactzin lost his case and was burned at the stake.[92] What persevered beyond the trial, and its predictable result, was a new formulary for documenting land boundaries in the colonial world through *cadastre* (property surveys, later aligned with *castle doctrines*) and a rising evidentiary processes based on documentary corroboration of witness or claimant statements that contravened Indigenous legal traditions and testimonial customs.[93] Pretrial procedures to confiscate Indigenous lands were not legal mechanisms that only served legal procedural ends, as these practices resulted in widespread land theft and wealth accumulation for the Spanish Crown.

Administrative Manuals
Inquisitorial administrative manuals detailing procedures for obtaining testimony are also insightful sources for understanding the extractive project of settler colonialism that oversaw massive wealth transfers in the form of land theft. The detailed instructions in the manuals prescribed a wide range of economically enriching pretrial procedures to obtaining testimonies. These include the confiscation of possessions of the accused, the reallocation of

lineages of inheritance, the physical occupation of estates, the destruction of noneuropean knowledge resources, and the centralization of interrogative authority.[94]

Following the Texcocan trial in 1539, Spanish settlers who recognized the economic usefulness of denouncement began using the inquisitorial process to make individual land claims over Native territory. This began endangering the profits of the royal treasury in Spain, so in 1572 Phillip II declared that Indians could no longer be subject to the Inquisition, removing the pretrial affordances for individual Spanish settlers to take possession of Indigenous lands. But the institutional bureaucracy and administrative procedures developed through inquisitorial processes were too useful to abolish. The Inquisition presented monarchs with "this extraordinary tool that they could use for a variety of purposes, [and] one of the things the monarchy needed was galley slaves [to row ships]."[95] Inquisitorial processes were thus adapted into new criminal codes and ever-expanding lists of criminalizable offenses, just as the prison industrial complex adapted Jim Crow policies and expanded the reach of white settler economic supremacy and structural subjugation after the abolition of slavery in the Thirteenth Amendment.[96] To plead for mercy was naturalized into pleading your case in court. The settler epistemological maneuvers surrounding testimony only adapted, and never waned.

One such example of this adaptive transformation can be found in the material culture surrounding inquisitorial administrative procedures.[97] Manuals known as *formularies of inquiry* were famously developed to define what a question is, to whom it can be asked, what counts as an answer, and how redirected questioning can be used in fact-finding.

Drawing on two and half centuries of inquisitorial practice in europe, lengthy administrative manuals of interrogation (based, for example, on Dominican Nicholas Eymerich's 1376 *Directorium inquisitorum* and the subsequent *instruciones* tradition) and extracting testimonies of conversion were developed. These manuals focused on how to elicit a "good confession" that yielded reliable information and was not motivated by fear, shame, or other factors, and instead sought the professionalization of interrogation as a dependable procedure for obtaining information that could be used as evidence. They served as blueprints for colonial requirements of informancy for Indigenous populations in the Americas long before testimony was enshrined as an allegedly objective fact-finding mechanism in common law and Federal Rules of Evidence. Many of the investigative practices in our modern penal procedures—including an investigator's ability to lie to a suspect to extract a confession—can be found in these manuals. Hill writes: "These interrogation techniques or ruses are not a purely medieval phenomenon restricted to the inquisition . . . the techniques described by Eymerich—not including torture—resemble those recommended in modern interrogation manuals. They seem to represent an understanding derived from experience of how pressure can be applied to suspects in a vulnerable situation."[98] Interrogation was structurally respecified into the administrative arms of the settler state as a professional discipline at the same time that torture was decoupled from it and relegated to other social pathways to survive the liberal revolutions of the eighteenth century. But not before its full force was unleashed in europe's colonies, as Charles Mills reminds us: "Torture was more or less eliminated in Europe by the end of the eighteenth century, while it continued to be routinely practiced in the colonies and on the slave plantations—whippings, castrations, dismemberments, roastings over slow fires, being smeared with sugar, buried up to the neck, and then left for the insects to devour, being filled with gunpower and then blown up, and so on; [these practices illustrate] the fact that in America the medieval tradition of the auto-da-fé, the public burning, survived well into the twentieth century."[99]

Here Mills illustrates how structural invariance functions by tracing a historical continuum between medieval practices of public torture (the auto-da-fé) to more modern histories of lynching. We can further connect the structurally invariant goals of white dynastic formations to the present day through the Emmett Till case. Consider that the only federal law in the United States to make lynching a crime took over two hundred years to pass. Efforts to pass such laws were repeatedly blocked until 2022, when the Emmett Till Antilynching Act finally passed, despite Republican votes against it.[100] When Emmett Till's surviving family fought for charges to be brought against Carolyn Bryant Donham, the white woman at the center of Emmett Till's death, a 2022 grand jury declined to indict her despite her open acknowledgment in 2017 that she lied to the FBI about Till's actions, setting off the events that directly led to his murder.[101] When journalists interviewed the Reverend Wheeler Parker Jr., Emmett Till's cousin and "the last living witness to Till's August 28, 1955 abduction" for comments, he said the grand jury's decision was "unfortunate, but predictable": "The prosecutor tried his best, and we appreciate his efforts, but he alone cannot undo hundreds of years of anti-Black systems that guaranteed those who killed Emmett Till would go unpunished, to this day. . . . The fact remains that the people who abducted, tortured, and murdered Emmett did so in plain sight, and our American justice system was and continues to be set up in such a way that they could not be brought to justice for their heinous crimes." Anticolonial systems theory (Chapter 1) emphasizes the system design of this predictable outcome, but also brings attention to how calls for retributive punishment (as only one modality of justice) can also be used to respecify the strength of the existing system that ensures answerability to system-coordinated wrongs and accountability for the recurring structure of crimes never occurs, but also, from the perspective of the families of victims like the Reverend Wheeler Parker Jr., to functionalize the impunity underwriting individual cases of injustice. (This is important because in a settler colonial economy, often, the most functional deterrent is cost prohibitions—when it becomes too expensive and unprofitable to impunify a range of behaviors.)

The idea that torture went away as an evolutionary byproduct of American democracy is a powerful regulative narrative in the settler epistemological arsenal.[102] Torture did not go away—it was professionalized. The approaches described by Eymerich reappeared in 1963 in the US Army and CIA interrogation manual known as the KUBARK manual, dispelling the early scholarly assertion that the evolution of information elicitation by authorities through the centuries did away with the willingness to use violence.[103] This is particularly evident in Abu Ghraib and Guantánamo. The influence of these techniques across the Americas is important to recognize. While philosophers often attempt to naturalize conditions of application for the study of testimony and to disaggregate conditions of coercion from the everyday "reports of others," the great majority of testimonial contexts for people of color and Indigenous peoples occur in evidentiary settings shaped by colonial power structures. Asylum and immigration interviews, for example, often fall under "custodial interrogation" arrangements, yet they are often analyzed as the context-free individual unwillingness (due to inherited prejudices or implicit bias, for instance) of the administering officer to "believe" the claimant. And this emphasis on the neocolonial contexts of power that inform the testimonies of structurally vulnerable people is especially important at the level of survivor's experiences with sexual assault services, as the entire chain of administrative services that traditionally begin with reporting, medical evaluation and examination, filing, victim services, and even compensation, is gatekept within the bounds of settler colonial administrative power structures that are designed to automate, retrofit, change, adapt, and accommodate pathways that support some populations more than others, but also to reproduce whiteness.[104]

Colonial administrative manuals of interrogation helped support the development of a theory of evidence that regulated the admissibility of certain kinds of testimony in the colonies, but which operated as objective administrative procedure. Inquisitorial modalities such as formalized denouncement, interrogation, and reinterrogation as fact-finding enterprises were refined in the colonies and had specific ramifications in key settler colonial administrative systems like law and policing. They helped broaden the scope of what constitutes "suspect" statements and which features *extrinsic* to statement content should be used to call a testimony into question. Inquisitorial practice thus shaped an institutional framework that closely regulated the relationship between local activities and a centralized power through the use of Native testimony.

The Christian Moral Right to Know

Inquisitorial techniques were useful to colonial powers outside of the trial context of jurisdictional power.[105] Victoria Ríos Castaño documents the targeted administrative methods of "data collection" from confessing informants that were based on the extrapolation of the "Christian moral right to know."[106] Think here of the ease with which white settlers approach and interrogate people of color in public spaces today: where are we going, why we are here, where we are really from, whether we live around here, what our name is, who we are here to see or what we are here to buy, and so forth. Castaño connects the imperial epistemic "right" to know with the rise of ethnographic methods that focus on obtaining demographic information of value to settler polities as part of the inquisitorial process.[107] In this view, the gathering of witness declarations in support or defense of an accusation was more than an early social demography tool for gathering biostatistical data. It sought to create a knowledge economy surrounding data that could functionally support colonial jurisdictional authority. Such an economy sought to create official jurisdictional challenges to colonial authority that could be formally litigated and adjudicated in favor of settlers on their own epistemic terms and through their own administrative infrastructures. The process would validate the colonial governance structure and vice versa. But it also sought to create social expectations about who answers to whom in what spaces, and to change those spaces to reinforce such expectations.

Structural Epistemic Warfare

That european jurisdictional authority expanded across the globe using structural epistemic warfare owes partly to the design success of the testimonial apparatus, and to its adaptive success, resilience, and respecification across religious and secular legal systems. *Structural epistemic warfare* is the idea that conquest and colonization have multiple modalities and operative scales of violence, including epistemic ones, that must work together as a system to produce the complex sociostructural transformations necessary to retain stability across transformations. This is evident in the functionally continuous periodized shift from colonization to imperialism to neoimperialism and now, neoliberalism—which is extractive colonialism in a liberalized market. Structural epistemic warfare is warfare because it is organized to produce a winning outcome for particular populations and to engineer defeat and produce mass casualties for targeted populations. It is structural because, through respecification features like value-transference mechanisms in epistemic capitalism (Chapter 3), it harmonizes the subpurposes of administrative systems into larger system goals that reflect the materially profitable end goals of white dynastic formations (of which dispossession and settlement are a powerful means to an end). Racism, in this sense, can be regarded as structural epistemic warfare because it is a system phenomenon that results in "the state-sanctioned or extralegal production and exploitation of group-differentiated vulnerability to premature death."[108]

During the seven hundred years of inquisitorial activity (thirteenth to nineteenth centuries),[109] testimony went from a function-preserving feature of roman law dispensed through its special connection to social status and oaths (and later, duels as corroborative actions when such oaths were challenged), to a mechanism for structural respecification—that is, for centralized administrative structures of statist governance and colonial management to adapt to challenges and changing circumstances. The focus on economic gain did not wane from its introduction in fourteenth-century manuals through the nineteenth century. As a social tool of power, testimony traversed the globe following the pattern of european colonialism of diverse lands and regions. The social practice of testimony cannot be delinked from how credibility functions as a tool of social power in settler colonial societies. For instance, the Australian Aboriginal Evidence Acts (1839–1849), mentioned above, show how anglophone fact-finding processes that are incompatible with Indigenous claims to truth are purposefully institutionalized in settler colonial administrations to create evidentiary pathways that favor white settler polities and confer credibility to white settlers by procedural means.[110] A powerful example of one of the sharpest tools in the settler evidentiary arsenal is the practice of Native informancy.

Native Informancy

As mentioned earlier, Native informancy refers to the culling of information from Indigenous peoples by european colonizers. Historically, it is associated with practices of Indigenous captivity for linguistic mediation that began in 1393 with european merchant slave raids in Gran Canaria and developed into the vast slave-interpreter system in Spain and Portugal.[111] Native informancy had a systematic procedure. Enslaved Indigenous peoples (particularly Zenegan and Guanache) were first brought to Iberian kingdoms to be baptized and taught Spanish or Portuguese, at times with Arabic as an intermediary language. They were sent on maritime voyages and, if they survived, were typically tasked with obtaining four slaves in return for manumission.[112] In the fifteenth century, direct captivity often bypassed the stopover in western europe and expanded the slave tribute requirements in the Americas. Columbus's journal famously provides linguistic mediation as a self-justifying rationale for the enslavement of Taino peoples, so "that they might learn our language and serve as interpreters."[113]

By the sixteenth century, colonial officials began casting suspicion on enslaved interpreters' veracity and credibility, and increasingly relied on a new wave of white european deportees who were sent to the colonies as settlers to learn local languages (especially in Brazil).[114] Considering the large-scale needs of colonial administration, officials increasingly turned their attention to the use of Native women as linguistic intermediaries. Alvar Núñez Cabeza de Vaca's (1488–1557) descriptions of Native women as "neutrals anywhere, even during war" thinly veiled the european campaign of sexual violence in the colonies while crafting rhetorical support to continue enslaving Native women as informants.[115] Malintzin, Cortés's enslaved Nahua interpreter, is perhaps the most famous Native informant. She, along with Matoaka (Algonquian Powhatan) and Sacagawea (Akaitikka Shoshone), is at the center of settler colonial constructions of racialized women as "natural" bearers of false testimony and cultural betrayal. "Malintzin's excruciating life of bondage was of no account, and continues to be of no account. Her almost half century of mythic existence, until recent times mostly in the oral traditions, had turned her into a handy reference point not only for controlling, interpreting or visualizing women, but also to wage a domestic battle of stifling proportions."[116] The "domestic battle" waged through the "controlling" tool of settler colonial stereotypes of racialized women can be understood through the notion of *controlling images*. Sociologist Patricia Hill Collins introduced the notion of controlling images to show how white supremacist heteropatriarchal thought creates binary oppositions within and between racial and gender hierarchies to produce a controlling system of cultural representations that values cisgendered white womanhood. Through controlling images and stereotypes (such as "the mammy" in *Gone with the Wind* or Reagan's "welfare queen"), Hill argues, Black women's lives, bodies, and experiences are devalued.[117] This is not an accident, since such devaluation affords settler colonial cultures the ability to continue regulating and prescribing norms of conduct (and beauty) for Black women's sexuality. I think the economy of controlling images also affords such cultures the epistemic cover to actively dysregulate administrative domains (like the unregulated legal domain of rape against enslaved women in roman law) and to turn attention away from illicit and harmful conduct done to women of color that would be covered (or is purported to be covered) under such domains in "multicultural democracies." This also creates a sense of mystery or confusion as to structural causation when the things one expects to happen from living in a "democracy" don't happen, or when double standards are on full display. For instance, it is well known in criminal justice circles that white police officers accused of sexual assault are acquitted of sexual assault and/or rape charges at disproportionately higher rates than defendants of color accused of assaulting white women, and receive atypical procedural considerations, including suspended sentences and home detention. In 2021, Baltimore County circuit judge Keith Truffer ignored the state's mandatory sentencing guiltiness (proscribing a minimum of five to ten years) and sentenced white former police officer Anthony Westernman to home detention after ruling there was "no evidence of any psychological injury to the rape victim," despite the victim of Westerman's assault undergoing therapy following the incident.[118] When police officer Arica Waters, the only Black female officer in a small Ohio precinct, filed a sexual assault complaint, she was met with suspicion, in large part due to her reputation for being "open about her sexual desires," and subsequently charged with making a false police report, even though video footage shows she was significantly intoxicated and legally incompetent to authorize sexual activity at the time of the incident.[119] While the charges of filing a false claim did not stand up in court,[120] they speak to the structurally invariant tendency to interpret women of color as bearers of false testimony who must first prove, like an epistemic pay-to-play or preclearance requirement, that we are *worthy of* belief before *being* believed. When we are believed, intersecting racial hinges (such as those that intersect with ableism, heterosexism, classism) and system self-correcting mechanisms take over to ensure such belief is finely sieved through categorical colanders that minimize our chances of accessing real and substantive relief, such as through settler evidentiary chains and fact-finding processes that are designed to be outside our control and against our interests. Tort reform, the next legal frontier in stemming damages in sexual assault cases, already has a long history of producing differential outcomes for plaintiffs of color.[121] This has always been part of the colonial project: to shapeshift the contours of administrative power for the colonial system's overall health and structural longevity.

Native informancy shows that "the reports of others"[122] under colonialism are part of a larger structural epistemic apparatus that produces cultural gains for some populations but not others in reliably systematic ways, and that the foundations of western epistemic communities are not normatively neutral.[123] They produce mycelial networks of conceptual relations that interact, inform one another, adapt, and enforce conceptual schemata that macrohistorically benefit specific social groups, but which are simply cashed out as the "intuitions" of the dominant group. The testimonial apparatus that arose through colonialism aimed to produce good informants for white polities and for the ascending state apparatus that codified laws of evidence as objectively "neutral." Following discussions of epistemic violence in Spivak[124] and Dotson,[125] we can seriously question the motivations for portraying testimonial exchange as based on a universal set of rational fact-finding procedures that become "dysfunctional" or unreliable only when they clash against "culturally relative" historical prejudices in any given time and place. The pooling of information—and the question of whether we can know facts from reliable reports—was never normatively neutral in settler colonial societies. It was, however, as the Inquisition and its administrative aftermath shows, highly profitable.[126]

Testimonio

Against the naturalized view of testimony, Latin American accounts of the practice of testimony (*testimonio*) are especially helpful for detecting fundamental power asymmetries in settler epistemological conceptual schemes that couch credibility as a culturally variant, yet "universal" evolutionary knowledge-process for pooling information from speech acts. *Testimonio* is a first-person narrative that is "told by a witness who is moved to narrate by the urgency of a situation (e.g., war, oppression, revolution, etc.)" and whose discursive strategies are informed by the conditions (material, epistemic, hermeneutic) such situations impose.[127] In this context, "Truth is summoned in the cause of denouncing a present situation of exploitation and oppression or in exorcising and setting aright official history."[128]

The idea that metaphysical relations that underwrite epistemological relevance are universal, or that they share in basic structural features, is a long-existing project of Empire. The colonial administrative testimonial apparatus did not arise out of thin air; it grew using a mycelial network of epistemic inheritances and promulgated know-how (especially those regarding language and writing) that could serve as blueprints for institutional apparatuses in emerging social contexts and historical realities. The Spanish (1478–1834) and Portuguese (1536–1821) Inquisitions should be considered as part of the ongoing european cultural project of developing and fine-tuning standardized processes for implementing power (as organized domination) for the purposes of wealth accumulation and its defense. They were gainful enterprises not only for the tens of thousands of salaried officials, familiars, and commissioners—or the dozens of inquisitors who became popes—but also for the statist governance structures that were implemented through the successful use of organized, systematized administrative procedures, formal documentation, and controlled access to document-making, all of which functioned as classification schemes for the criminalization of ever-expanding offenses. Medieval inquisitorial jurisdictional authority transformed roman law and related practices of land seizure and labor extraction. These processes of organized domination were based on centralized processes of hierarchical administration (and its supporting linear epistemologies). And, as will be shown below, the features of those adaptive transformations in history are relevant to the present.

Testigation

Native informancy influenced the development of various evidentiary burdens cast on structurally vulnerable claimants, burdens that are still active in the current US legal system. Colonial officials needed a theory of evidence that clearly regulated the admissibility of noneuropean testimony, particularly in land claims and allegations of rape. California's 1850 Act for the Government and Protection of Indians regulated jurisdictional authority over all complaints between Indians and whites, decreeing that "in no case shall a white man be convicted of any offense upon the testimony of an Indian or Indians." The plural is significant, since thresholds of compurgation (acquittal by testator's oath of innocence) were often met by the introduction of credibility witnesses.

The inversion of acquittal by oath of innocence is acquittal by aspersion of the accuser. The Indian Evidence Act of 1887, set forth by Britain's Imperial Legislative Council, asserts that "when a man is prosecuted for rape or an attempt to ravish, it may be shown that the prosecutrix was of generally immoral character." Compurgation strategies were thus reversed to devalue the testimony of women through colonial distinctions between Indigenous informancy and the locutionary production of european settlers as "rational" agents. The burden to prove one is not lying is part of the long-existing reversal of communication flows that characterizes the violence of political epistemological projects under colonialism. In modern times, acquittal by aspersion of the accuser has been fine-tuned through a reliable system of interlocking oppressions. The misogynoirist discrediting of Dr. Anita Hill's testimony against Clarence Thomas is one example. Another are the lesser-known exceptions to the military rules of evidence governing rape shield laws, exceptions that open the way for consideration of the accuser's past sexual behavior as potential evidence of consent.[129] What these examples all share is the settler colonial administrative use of testimony to gaslight vulnerable populations—to *testigate* them—with the idea that one's ability to offer compelling or corroborative evidence to the "right" adjudicating bodies directly corresponds to one's chances for relief from harm or to sociolegal remedies, without caveats. This correspondence is magical thinking, at best. In "A Report from Occupied Territory," James Baldwin aptly captures the profit-by-design nature of this magical thinking when he says, "I can't believe what you say ... because I see what you do."[130]

Testimony and state violence are not as far apart as some philosophical traditions would wish them to be. In this respect, the nonwhitewashed genealogy of testimonial processes I give is far closer to the day-to-day experiences of millions of marginalized peoples whose lives continue to be devastated by the complex administration of settler colonial violences. These administrative burdens include complex, structurally stacked, devastatingly unfair, and reliably deadly webs of policies and practices designed to disadvantage populations, such as modern-day pleading standards and knowledge requirements for sexual assault survivors. The next section, "Credibility Proxies," advances a more coordinated view of whitewashed legal narratives of sexual violence that turn on settler colonial notions of credibility, notions that are wielded powerfully and consistently to create the illusion of routine background operations of impartial legal codes and "the rule of law," but which function as well-orchestrated failures of understanding for interpreting Indigenous women's and women of color's claims, lives, and experiences in settler colonial cultures.

Credibility Proxies

In this section I identify an invariant settler colonial structure of evidentiary address that precedes the legal structure of evidentiary proceedings and evidentiary jurisprudence in US law.[131] Evidentiary jurisprudence concerns the rules that derive from judicial weighing of credibility-relevant issues of probative value and admissibility of testimonial evidence in legal proceedings, such as impeachment rules and, formerly, incompetency doctrines. I build on Julia Simon-Kerr's notion of "credibility by proxy"—which portrays the function of evidence jurisprudence as an ongoing attempt by the US legal system to "replace truth-seeking with norm enforcement"[132]—by extending the concept to white dynastic formations and the structurally enabled facility with which settler administrative systems reproduce violence for marginalized populations. The legal system does this, primarily, by tightly controlling the association between violence and credibility and by creating procedural pathways by which violence can be continuously enacted on some testator's credibility more than on others'. What should not be lost in the highly regulated association between legal credibility, attestation, and knowledge claims is the structural role of colonial violence.

Social Worthiness and Rule Structure

For Simon-Kerr, modern evidence jurisprudence serves an extralegal function that produces reliably harmful results for marginalized populations by design, not by accident. This is because it employs problematic conceptions of social worthiness to inform its evolving rule structure governing what can and cannot count as evidence. She writes: "With worthiness as our guide, we have created a system where it is more likely that a black defendant will be successfully impeached with evidence of a prior conviction than a white defendant, and in which prostitution can [still] be used to impeach a witness."[133] Simon-Kerr's focus on the structural makings of an evolving rule structure parallels the adaptive rationale used to disregard the testimonies of victims of sexual assault by fraud or coercion. In 2004, former district court judge Barry Edenfield discounted the testimony of a woman who was led to believe she would be arrested by a man impersonating a police officer if she did not consent to a strip search in which a sexual assault occurred.[134] "It wasn't what I wanted," she testified. Judge Edenfield ignored criminal coercion (e.g., the explicit threat she would be arrested if incompliant) as well as forcible compulsion standards that do not depend on the quantum of force applied to determine whether an act is consummated against a victim's will.[135] Instead, he accused the victim of perpetuating a culture of "victimhood" and "entitlement" and not taking "individual responsibility" for her inability to discern whether it was a real police officer issuing commands or not.[136]

This example is an analogue for how courts "grappled with how to shape impeachment jurisprudence against a cultural background with strong norms about status, or who was worthy of belief."[137] The basic idea is that legal rule structures bend and shift to accommodate system output goals that are other than the ones given by the US legal system. They're covers, or proxies, for the real thing. And that real thing, for Simon-Kerr, is deeply rooted notions of worthiness that reproduce social stratification. I trace this insight further back to white dynastic formations and the structural invariance they generate—to who profits and why.

The argument of an evolving legal rule structure of evidence is fairly simple: "As much as we pay lip service to the notion, [evidentiary] rules have never been, and are not today, about identifying false statements in order to get at the truth."[138] Instead, they have been created within an analytical legal framework that is structurally subordinate to cultural norms about who is worthy of belief in society based on their status and standing.[139] The issue here is not whether individuals hold particular identity prejudices that inform beliefs about who is worthy of credibility but how structurally enabled institutional apparatuses (such as self-repairing "rule structures" in US law) exist to reproduce status norms regardless of what individual jurors or judges may believe about a witness.

Rule structures can operate by functional fiat, meaning that even when fair procedural norms are seemingly enumerated as legal precedent, the rules of application can be so cumbersome and unrealistic that their applicability is limited by design. In *Pena-Rodriguez v. Colorado* (2021), the US Supreme Court upheld but modified the no-impeachment rule that upholds verdict finality[140] by allowing suits to be brought on the basis of jury misconduct that constitutes overt racial prejudice against a criminal defendant. Miguel Pena-Rodriguez, the petitioner, was formerly charged in Colorado with several felonies arising from attempted sexual assault charges of two teenage sisters. Following the verdict, which found Pena-Rodriguez guilty of two lesser charges (unlawful sexual contact and two counts of harassment), several jurors came forward to report one juror, an ex-police officer, who said, "I think he did it because he is Mexican" and that Pena-Rodriguez's alibi witness was not credible because they were "an illegal."[141] Pena-Rodriguez sued under the Sixth Amendment's right to an impartial jury, and the Court ruled in his favor.[142] However, the standards to apply the rule are quite high and include proving that "overt racial bias" directly led to the verdict and, most importantly, allow that evidentiary threshold to remain at the discretion of the trial court. The case (including lower courts' decisions and rationale) illustrates how racial animus and worthiness of belief can operate at multiple scales and legal registers in sexual assault cases by structurally enabled means.[143]

In sexual assault cases, rule structures are complicit with the credibility standards used to promote idealized victims and to prevent survivors from testifying to their own credibility. In *People v. Lukity*,[144] the court held that a victim of sexual assault who was labeled as having "emotional problems" could not introduce evidence in support of her own character for truthfulness in the absence of a direct attack (an established rule), noting that "credibility" and "character of truthfulness" are not synonymous, but the latter is a specific aspect of the former.[145] This made it difficult to combat the dominant ableist representations of sexual assault victims (as not credible, emotionally erratic, and therefore unreliable attestators of their own experience of rape) that are pervasive in sexual assault trials (for the few cases that even reach this stage).

US law has always had a domain of rules aimed at regulating what classes of witnesses are qualified to offer testimony. The history of these rules is whitewashed through legal narratives analogous to the state-of-nature social epistemologist's naturalized notion of testimony. Naturalized legal narratives, in this view, are narratives that omit the close association between institutional norm-enforcement, white supremacy, gendered racism, and the specific formulations of the notion of credibility in US law.

Credibility and Colonial Law

The nascent jurisprudence of credibility in the American colonies provides a clue to this association. Courts in colonial America first regulated what testimony jurors could consider by excluding whole classes of people from testifying under competency doctrines in ways that far exceeded the alleged historically neutral origin of these rules in conflict-of-interest legal principles that evolved in England in the sixteenth and seventeenth centuries (and are themselves rooted in roman legal principles).[146] Examples include the 1792 Act Concerning Witnesses and Prescribing the Manner of Obtaining and Executing Commissions for Taking Their Depositions in Certain Cases, which outright forbade testimony of Black people and Indigenous people against white settlers, and *United States v. Dow*,[147] which applied a Maryland statute that provided "no mulatto born of a white woman . . . be admitted or received as good and valid evidence in law."[148] From Simon-Kerr's perspective, the historical elimination of the overt legal observance of these practices did not eliminate the enduring power of their influence and function in legal proceedings.

Over time, the inadmissibility framework based on competency, which notoriously excluded whole categories of people from testifying, transitioned to impeachment frameworks that greatly expanded the testimony that juries could consider, including that of people of color and Indigenous people.[149] This expansion came with new restrictions and ways of calling into question the credibility of individuals now allowed to testify in a trial: "Jurors would now be exposed to impeaching information about those witnesses—their prior crimes, their prior bad acts, their reputation for truthfulness or lack thereof, and in some jurisdictions evidence of their so-called bad moral character" that former competency doctrines did not rely on to exclude testimony.[150] Jurors formerly shielded from the testimony of specific classes of people were given a new kind of deflective instrument for hearing what such people could say through a legally constructed "choice about how to identify unreliable testimony."

Thus, while whole new categories of people could now testify in court, new categories and rules arose to regulate legal proceedings for introducing evidence of why they should not be believed (impeachment). Under impeachment, jurors are directed to deliberate as if the witness has never spoken at all. New rules, same system output: structural silencing.

Preservation through Transformation

Simon-Kerr is not alone in her contention that impeachment procedures are structurally biased to reproduce harms for marginalized populations. Over the last three decades, significant legal scholarship has linked competency and impeachment procedures for admitting witness testimony to status-enforcing functions that uphold racial and gender social inequality. Simon-Kerr, for instance, draws on Reva Siegel's work on the legal system's structural maneuvering to enforce social stratification under the guise of legal objectivity. Particularly important for this project, Siegel identifies the metalegal phenomenon of "preservation through transformation" discussed in the introduction, which describes how "efforts to dismantle an entrenched system of status regulation can produce changes in its constitutive rules and rhetoric, transforming the status regime without abolishing it."[151] Siegel writes:

> Attempts to dismantle a status regime can discredit the rules and reasons employed to enforce status relations in a given historical era, and so create pressure for legislators and jurists to reform the contested body of law enough so that it can be differentiated from its contested predecessor. Assuming that something of value is at stake in such a struggle, it is highly unlikely that the regime that emerges from reform will redistribute material and dignitary "goods" in a manner that significantly disadvantages the beneficiaries of the prior, contested regime. But if the reformed body of law is to reestablish its legitimacy, it must distribute social goods in a manner that can be differentiated from the prior, contested regime. Thus, lawmakers seeking to reestablish the legitimacy of a contested body of status law will begin to revise its constitutive rules, and to justify the new body of law without overt recourse to the justificatory discourse of the

prior, contested regime. In this way, the effort to disestablish a body of status law can produce changes that modernize its rule structure and justificatory rhetoric. These reforms may well improve the material and dignitary circumstances of subordinated groups, but they will also enhance the legal system's capacity to justify regulation that perpetuates inequalities among status-differentiated groups.[152]

Colonialism is a long game that continuously modernizes itself to produce structural invariance. Siegel here is articulating a legal account of structural invariance that precedes modern impeachment jurisprudence's reliance on "elite nineteenth-century honor norms" like chastity.[153] The notion of preservation through transformation is helpful for situating modern impeachment rules within larger settler colonial structures of evidentiary address that maintain asymmetries in legal outcomes even as social movements work to reform status-enforcing laws and even produce some favorable outcomes. It is also helpful for understanding the existence and nature of the tightly woven net of administrative functions between social institutions, so that if, for example, police reform is achieved through policy changes, a legal dragnet stands ready to produce structurally biased outcomes at the level of populations.[154]

Credibility's Distributive Design

As earlier argued, there exists a cohesive distributive design built into the fabric of dynastic social systems that reproduces structurally invariant marginalization at the same time that it produces reified value and structural privileges for dominant populations—all while covering over this very process. Impeachment jurisprudence did not just enact prohibitions and restrictions. It also created metalegal structures of epistemic affordances surrounding violence (and to delink the association between credibility and "crimes of violence" in particular). These new structures were meant to afford advantage to specific populations. Within these structures is where we locate the particular harm in gender-based violence cases.

Credibility proxies exist within a continuing legal tradition that rests on the belief that adult male violence is not probative of credibility, full stop. While crimes involving deception, such as theft, are consistently regarded as predictive that a person convicted of such crimes will lie on the witness stand, violence is regarded in a legally exceptional status realm in credibility jurisprudence, particularly in rape and sexual harassment cases. This is because "crimes of violence were generally not understood to involve moral turpitude, with the result that witnesses who had been convicted of such crimes were not flagged as presumptive liars."[155] The District of Columbia code of evidence thus includes the "sales of narcotic and depressant and stimulant drugs" in the long list of offenses that involve presumptive dishonesty or false statement, but excludes offenses "of passion and short temper, such as assault."[156] In *United States v. Estrada*, Justice Sotomayor, resting on precedent, also distinguishes "acts of violence from crimes that reflect adversely on a person's integrity" by asserting a prior distinction that "violence is impulsive while lying is predicated on the ability to scheme or plan."[157] This long-existing legal observance has had critical ramifications in sexual assault cases.

The deference paid to male violence and the contrasting scrutiny given to a party opposing that violence is clear in two rulings that center on credibility proxies. In *People v. Segovia*, for example, the Colorado Supreme Court ordered that criminal charges for sexual assault be dropped against a defendant accused of sexually assaulting a child on the grounds that the lower court erred in finding evidence of a prior instance of shoplifting by the complainant child witness inadmissible. The defense counsel in that case asked the complaining child witness whether she had stolen $100 from her mother's store the previous summer in an effort to impeach her as a witness.[158] In a contrasting 2004 case, a court refused to impeach the testimony of a police officer who had lied on the witness stand, was impeached, and whose lies and subsequent impeachment were incontrovertibly memorialized in a criminal procedure case that reached the US Supreme Court (*United States v. Whitmore*).[159] The ability for a system to respecify and self-repair to enact specific functions is plainly on display in US law.

Consider the example of rape shield laws. Rape shield laws arose to limit lines of questioning on sexual history in criminal proceedings to "shield" sex-crime victims from having their past history of sexual behavior or reputation linked to their credibility in the accusation of moral turpitude, whether through the Federal Rules of Evidence or a state analogue. Many believe that the enactment of such laws has provided relief for survivors of sexual violence who testify in court. The reality is that "in states that represent over one-third of the US population, it is still possible to argue in court that engaging in prostitution means a witness is unworthy of belief."[160] In the state of New York, for example, "The rape shield law allows for cross-examination about convictions for prostitution but not as *acts* of prostitution, which echoes the distinction of impeachment jurisprudence between bad acts and prior convictions, the latter being more readily admissible on the question of credibility."[161] Since women of color are policed, arrested, charged, and prosecuted for criminalized sex work at much higher rates than whites, the ramifications are clear. These are not consequences of flawed legal systems— these are designed distributions of harm.

Even in a favorable trial outcome, justice is disallowed before it can ever be sought. Nowhere is this more evident than in the gender-based violence cases that mainline structural oppression. Today, settler notions of testimonial credibility are used to whitewash legal narratives of sexual violence and to gaslight marginalized survivors about the source of traumatic experience they endure as a result of administrative dealing with police, healthcare workers, and the justice system. The legal system produces two primary kinds of structural epistemic profit from these maneuvers. First, it maintains control of legal notions of violence under impeachment doctrines that allow white litigants to exclude histories of violence in ways that uphold structural impunity. Second, it creates self-repairing rule-structures and evidentiary burdens that continuously reinforce settler colonial structures of evidentiary address, creating a class of structurally subordinated legal classes while simultaneously admitting to no identifiable aggressor for said subordination.

Settler notions of testimonial credibility are those that uphold, maintain, and respecify the relations of power that determine who is "worthy of belief" in settler colonial societies. The attribution of being "worthy of belief" can be a proxy for concentrating credibility assessment in the hands of white settler populations in jury trials. Applying or withholding that label also normalizes the administrative violence and discrimination that occurs in healthcare, employment, and education. In both cases, testimonial credibility operates in ways that always aim to strengthen the elementary relations key to white dynastic formations. These relations are organized to carry the primary purpose of white dynastic formations, which is producing (epistemic and economic) profit for white settler populations and their descendants.

Sometimes settler colonial relations of power that trade on whitewashed and naturalized settler notions of "credibility" show up in a variety of ways. Some examples are structurally raised evidentiary burdens for minority plaintiffs, consistently favorable pretrial motions that result in lowered prosecutorial burdens for minority defendants, and racialized gendered stereotypes of sexual reputation codified as relevant to testimonial credibility. Other times, such relations manifest as the preemptive foiling of what one can attest to in the first place that would carry salience or uptake in the dominant conceptual systems of settler colonial societies and their administrative arms.[162]

The key to understanding settler notions of testimonial credibility is that the basic aim and function of their varied applications and practices serve to maintain the fluid working of dynastic systems' advantages across settler institutions. Testimonial credibility may be served by settler colonial systems as a mental slap and subsequent gaslighting, or by structurally withholding entry into collective social processes of interpretation tied to resources and life chances in settler colonial societies. Deploying these systems is paying a credit into the system that one day will allow certain classes of social agents to withdraw credit in the form of credibility affordances. Of course, one does not need to be a white settler to pay into this system, but one does need proximity to dynastic whiteness to make a withdrawal.

A Systems View of Testimony

In liberal democratic societies where white feminisms have dominated, the existence of enduring sexism, cultural machismo, and institutionalized social attitudes that devalue women's lives are presented as the fundamental cause of gender-based violence. The story goes that if we address systemic sexism in society, then that will also effectively hammer away at these types of injustices. Though common, this single-axis feminist analysis of patriarchal power fails to address the structural invariance between the devaluation of María's and Daphne's testimonies of sexual violence so many years apart. The invariance encompasses why they were not believed (or ever meant to be believed) and, more importantly, who or what gains from the public rendering of their testimony as uncredible, or, in more recent cases, credible yet irrelevant to the legal and political machinery.

Cultures are dynamic, yet dynamism has been naturalized in settler epistemic economies to downplay the basic flows and patterns through which system flows operate and drive transformations. All dynamic systems have release valves—features that release pressure yet are essential to the dynamic functioning and cyclical continuity of well-functioning system flows.

In advanced industrial settler colonial economic systems, one such valve is white feminism, which contributes to the overall health of settler colonial systems.

The political concerns and conceptual agendas of white feminisms, for instance, recode stories like María and Daphne's to suit their needs while leaving intact the adaptability mechanisms that regenerate settler colonial violence. White feminisms reframe legal narratives of sexual assault testimony as racially neutral examples of what "moving the goalpost" (i.e., the continuous shifting of standards) looks like when it comes to women's credibility in patriarchal societies. From that perspective, believing women is a social tool that regulates power over women's lives rather than a social practice of determining truthfulness and accuracy through impartial reasoning in evidentiary settings such as courtrooms. The reframe almost never seems to be a far stretch; in both cases, the perpetrators were male, as were the judges, case managers, and civil authority figures who were given the power to bring suit on the women's behalf—all seemingly good evidence of the lingering power of sexist social prejudices as old as roman family law and the "absolute power of the father" (*Patria potestas*).

And yet the dominant single-axis framework of white feminism is not neutral. A white feminist framework doesn't just "miss" the role race plays in the formation and upkeep of gender-based violence in settler colonial societies. It works to uphold it. This is done, for example, through the whitewashing of legal narratives of racialized women's testimony and by locating the harm enacted on women in a system failure rather than the coherence and success of its design.[163] The legal system didn't break down—it performed just as intended.

This is a central point in this chapter: the structural invariance responsible for denying justice to María and Daphne on the basis of legal assessments of the "evidence" does not reflect a failure of the settler legal system to correct sexism in society over the course of three hundred years, but a success of its ability to respecify itself through its self-repairing "distribution design" of who is meant to lose out in order to maintain profitable networks of wealth transferences over the course of multiple generations. The legal system did exactly what it was supposed to do, and where system failures can be recognized as failures, they occur for people whose proximity to whiteness is publicly recognized. Because this view contrasts with the stated principles of modern civil and criminal legal systems in advanced industrial settler colonial societies and the concepts that uphold them, it is difficult for many to accept—though less so for those who repeatedly bear the brunt of its design. A closer look at the rise of witness testimony as a legal technology in colonial courts helps to put strain on the single-axis gender harm interpretation and instead captures some of the designed epistemic machinations of the colonial system at work.

The conceptual barring of racialized women's experiences of sexual violence being meaningfully conveyed through testimony was a foundational precondition for the development of settler legal systems in the Americas. This epistemic barrier is structural, as were the violences that had to be done to Indigenous knowledge systems in order for such possibilities to be successfully excluded by settler legal systems. Thus, the structural invariance responsible for denying justice to María and Daphne on the basis of "evidence" or lack thereof does not reflect a failure of the settler legal system; it reflects a success. The system is working exactly as was always intended. The structural obstacles to justice for racialized women who testify about their experiences of sexual violence are not actuated by psychological biases at the individual level; they are functionally operationalized within the legal system itself. The inconsistency is structured by design. This design produces harmful mental health consequences at the level of populations.[164]

Epistemological notions of testimony, trustworthiness, credibility, and believability are important political goods in settler colonial societies because they help functionalize control over how violence is unevenly distributed across populations at the structural level, particularly through legal systems. In this context, testimony is a powerful technology of violence that produces asymmetric harms and profits for different populations depending on one's processive relation to/within settler social structures. They help maintain systems of intergenerational wealth by establishing structural innocence in legal systems that arbitrate and maintain larger systems of intergenerational wealth (by providing structural justification for long-term exploitative arrangements without binding contracts in the settler credibility economy). As such, they operate within wider value systems or "settler credibility economies" oriented toward producing epistemic profit for some populations and maintaining epistemic labor markets based on surplus labor, social disadvantage, and losses, as we'll illustrate in the next chapter.[165]

In this chapter I have analyzed the idea of testimonial credibility as a social tool of power that was central to the colonial project and its continuation through racialized gendered violence, especially as a legal technology. Credibility is an important part of a market economy in modern advanced industrial settler colonial societies. It is not a form of "social capital," as the sociological literature on nontangible and informal economic resources might describe. The problem that concerns me is not in the concept of "credibility" itself as a closed unit of analysis; it is in the operationalization of concepts in settler colonial infrastructures of power, infrastructures that have been built dynastically to benefit some populations and to enact harm on others while providing epistemic cover for the existence of such distribution-of-harm design.

In the next chapter, I introduce the concept of settler credibility economies to explain key features of the wider settler colonial economy within which testimonial credibility (and settler credit markets in general) operates. I'll use this market framework to talk about sexual violence as part of this economy and the role testimonial evidence plays in maintaining that economy across generations. The basic idea is this: it is not enough to show that harm exists and continues to exist—we must tally the costs accrued by these harms in such a way that structural change can be generated and a bill for damages can be presented. And we must construct a world in which we are not pleading our cases as supplicants in violent systems or hinging the fates of our individual and collective well-being on institutions that were designed to stunt the creation of pathways that promote our well-being. The bill for damages we present will reflect the costs necessary to build such a world—a world in which it is unacceptable to conclude that the violence that assails us as women of color is ever acceptable, or something we are structurally enabled to escape if we "wanted" to.

3

Structural Violence Is *Profit-Driven*

Epistemic Capitalism

> Capital is not a thing, but a social relation between persons which is mediated through things.
> —Karl Marx, *Capital*

> Like capital, colonialism, as a structure of domination predicated on dispossession, is not "a thing," but rather the sum effect of the diversity of interlocking oppressive social relations that constitute it.
> —Glen Coulthard, *Red Skin White Masks*

Introduction

The office manager where I used to work was fond of stating she did "not see race, only people," especially on days that she was confronted by people of color for making racist remarks. The administrators to whom the employees appealed concluded that in the absence of expressly derogatory statements corroborated by "impartial" witnesses, little could be done to prove that the disparate treatment in workloads, space assignments, and microaggressions we experienced were tied to racial bias, anti-immigrant sentiment, or their intersections. Whatever her "private attitudes" (such as her distaste for "Mexican smells" or her vocal disapproval of "those people," the ones who wear "one pant leg rolled up and show their underwear" and who purportedly do not speak "real English"), if the office manager really was racist, they argued, she would not have hired and retained people of color on the staff. The act superseded the alleged belief.

In the 1940s, Ronald Reagan bought and sold several parcels of land in the Hollywood Hills that came with racial covenants prohibiting the sale to "any person whose blood is not entirely that of the Caucasian race" and limiting the occupancy of any dwellings to whites only, with the exception of "domestic servants."[1] As a gubernatorial candidate, Reagan supported Proposition 14—a state constitutional amendment aimed at repealing the 1963 Rumford Fair Housing Act, which forbade racial covenants and housing discrimination on the basis of race, religion, sex, family status, or disability. "If an individual wants to discriminate against Negros or others in selling or renting his house, it's his right to do so," he proclaimed.[2] Reagan went on to oppose the Civil Rights Act of 1964, the Voting Rights Act, the Civil Rights Restoration Act (which he vetoed as president), the implementation of court-ordered busing, employment-based affirmative action, the Equal Rights Amendment, and making Martin Luther King Day a federal holiday.[3] He propagated the misogynistic racial archetype of the Black "welfare queen" as part of the "southern strategy" to unify white voters, yet said: "I resent the implication that there is bigotry in my nature."[4] When confronted about his civil rights record by a delegate of the National Negro Republican Assembly during a 1966 gubernatorial campaign speech in Santa Monica, Reagan famously threw his note cards on the floor, slammed his fist into his palm, shouted at the predominantly Black audience, and stormed out in near tears.[5] As a former campaign manager and Republican strategist recounts, "This was his hot button, and being called a racist was something he couldn't stand for . . . he had stormed out not because he was a racist but because he was not."[6] Instead, as many presidential historians and political scientists argue to this day, it was Reagan's "lifelong belief" in liberal individualism, states' rights, and limited government intervention that led him to do things that "appeared" like racist acts (such as instructing his Justice Department to intervene in support of private colleges' rights to deny students admission on the basis of their race). The alleged belief superseded the act.

The shifting of epistemic standards, evidentiary burdens, and narrative justifications is a primary characteristic of systems-level forms of domination. The maintenance and consolidation of interpretive power by an epistemic community is the organizing principle of interpretation in systems of domination. This means that what a concept *is* or *says* is less important than what it *does* or how it functions in relation to a wider *economic network* of concepts and practices. These network components work together to establish the relational valences necessary to maintain system equilibrium and work together toward a system goal—to keep the whole machinery of power going, generation after generation.[7] One of the relational valences necessary to maintain system equilibrium in settler colonial societies is the creation and control of the paraconsistent logics that produce cloaks of innocence—the kind that Reagan and the administrators we appealed to used to propagate and expand the avenues for structural racism while escaping the charge of being racist.

Chapter 1 illustrated that white dynastic formations are built on inconsistency-tolerant logical systems, systems that bend, adapt, and—like the shapeshifting character of "racecraft," which understands race as an economically profitable and malleable human conception rather than a genetic reality—reorganize in relation to a system goal in order to accommodate internal contradictions or system challenges.[8] Like racecraft, interpretive power can seem amorphous, vaguely wrong yet routine, as in "the way things are." But interpretive power is no act of magic, as Karen Fields and Barbara Fields suggest.[9] Social concepts have functions; they do something. And those functions have concrete socioeconomic value—they have a worth and valency that results in social pathway activity. The activation of certain pathways but not others means some things become "legible" in society, like interpreting as a "crime" the destruction of property but not the destruction of Native languages targeted by settler language policies and residential schooling practices. And because no pathway stands alone but is dynamically interconnected with other pathways in a social structure, skewed distribution and probability outcomes, resulting from certain pathway activity chains of value transference and transmission, yield different available stocks of interpretive wealth for dominant and nondominant epistemic communities.

Interpretive wealth is a stock, not a flow. It is not a natural phenomenon.[10] It is the result of distinct historical econo-epistemological projects originating in Asia minor around the fifth century BCE that came to shape how domination is encoded in a social structure—for example, how "power" comes to be enacted through the intergenerational accumulation of epistemic resources. It creates dominant and nondominant epistemic communities, not for the sake of social differentiation, but for the maintenance, generation, and *control of the chains of value transfer and transmission* that orient profit toward some populations but not others. The intergenerational amassing of epistemic resources by dominant epistemic communities is what the deliberate subordination and attempted destruction of nondominant epistemic resources makes possible. It is the other side of the coin of epistemic oppression—and it is one that, noncoincidentally, most political epistemology literature tends to overlook. Think of interpretive wealth as the net (sum) interpretive backdrop of epistemic resources that drive the regeneration of intergenerational channels of asymmetric wealth transfer for white settler populations and their descendants. Intergenerationally amassed stocks of interpretive resources provide a resilient net worth that withstands shocks, debts, and short-term profit losses since it is driven by the outpaced accumulation of epistemic capital. It is a process that cannot be sustained without structural violence. And it allows settler epistemic infrastructural activity to operate seamlessly in institutions like law, medicine, and education.

It is incredibly hard to repel this backdrop of settler epistemic infrastructural activity if you're on the resisting end of settler epistemic systems.[11] The Honorable Judge Carlton Reeves (US District Court for the Southern District of Mississippi) was up against this very backdrop when he issued a series of bold decisions (2018–19) striking down the state's efforts to roll back abortion rights under the guise of protecting women, calling the state's arguments "pure gaslighting."[12] Judge Reeves struck down other similar measures to roll back gay marriage and civil rights protections. He said:

> If you've never relied on a court, you may not see the assault. If you've never seen a friend or loved one wrongly imprisoned, you may not feel it. If you have never been stopped for Driving While Black, like my friend Judge Robert Wilkins, you might not fear it. But if you know the words of Mississippi's darkest moments, you can hear it. . . . I know what I heard when a federal judge was called "very biased and unfair" because he is "of Mexican heritage." When that judge's ethnicity was said to prevent his issuing "fair rulings." When that judge was called a "hater" simply because he is Latino. I heard the words of James Eastland, a race-baiting politician, empowered by the falsehood of white supremacy, questioning the judicial temperament of a man solely because of the color of his skin. I heard those words and I did not know if it was 1967 or 2017.[13]

Like structural violence, the "power" exerted by settler control of interpretive power is impersonal at one scale. As Judge Reeves's judicial record shows, it has very little to do with how bold or brave or resistant a person is to the systems that assail us. But it is also highly personal at the scale that provides the structural pathways to target some populations but not others, again and again, and to make it harder for some folks to be heard, believed, or have their harms addressed even after white people have their come-to-Jesus moment about their racial biases. Over time, some communities are more likely to be "believed" than others because of this wrongful, violently amassed stockpile of interpretive wealth and pools of epistemic resources.[14] Thus, some populations benefit as epistemic communities while others face greater likelihoods of harm in "multicultural democracies."[15]

As the two opening cases show, structural racism has little to do with the way racism is usually constructed as individual color-based prejudice in multiracial settler states. Reagan's ability to operate within a settler econo-epistemic network to permit the multiple realizability of white supremacy (while denying charges of bigotry) is not due to any inherent property of his skin color. Scholars have widely documented the morphological shifts in who is "white" during various periods in US history, as when Irish and other european immigrants became "white" during Reconstruction and the New Deal era in response to expanding political and economic rights for African Americans.[16] Nor is access to whiteness a sole function of class. The systematic murder of wealthy Osage Native Americans in the early twentieth century, culminating the Reign of Terror (1921–16), and the 1921 burning of Black Wall Street in the Tulsa race massacre are clear historical rebuttals of the idea that access to whiteness is solely a function of economic standing. Hence, we can talk about culturally specific and historical epistemological communities,[17] such as white dynastic settler epistemological communities that do not require one to be "white" to gain membership in an epistemic polity tied to privilege and power[18] yet still work to uphold whiteness as a structural system of intergenerational economic power that retains control over social tools of exclusion.[19] This, of course, is a dynastic system that must be refused.

In relation to the last two chapters, this chapter uses the framework of epistemic capitalism to explain who profits from structural invariance and how. Its basic thesis is that wealth concentration is also epistemic. Epistemology is a system of production that inherently produces value.[20] Value is not objective but relative to its function and the constituting infrastructure in which it operates. Understanding the economic structure and mutually reinforcing relationships of settler epistemic systems (as infrastructures that uphold structural violence) helps reconnect the links between oppressive knowledge practices in settler colonial societies—such as the persistently shifting credibility burdens for sexual violence survivors of color discussed in Chapter 2—and the creation and maintenance of intergenerational channels of wealth transfer for white settler populations and their descendants.[21] It reconnects the experience of harm to the reality of who profits from the intergenerational violence against us, as women of color. Using key ideas from Latin

American economic structuralism and long-range theories of macroeconomic stability in progressive economics, I focus on the core macrostructural relation between economics and knowledge systems that is central to settler colonial cultures.

Of interest to academics, this chapter also advances an anticolonial corrective to the popular economic thesis of inequality $r > g$.[22] It does this by specifying the differential historical valence under which r accrues and operates—namely, that of white dynastic formations that began in grecoroman antiquity and became refined throughout colonialism, and now, through neocolonialism in all its forms. I argue that, once constituted, epistemic capital reproduces itself faster than output increases, such that the interpretive wealth accumulated in the past grows more rapidly than the output of new or rematriated interpretive resources. This does not mean nondominant interpretive communities are resource poor. Nor does it mean that the political epistemological projects of language revitalization, genealogical recovery, and land-based reclamation are unmatched responses to the structural violence done to resources of meaning through colonization. It only means that the interpretive ecology in which meaning operates in settler colonial societies is purposefully set up to make it very hard for formal institutional structures to bend toward justice for people of color and Indigenous peoples, and that many people die or suffer horribly because of this "very hard" feature of structural violence.[23]

At its broadest, this chapter examines the epistemic dimension of capitalism in relation to settler colonial accumulation of wealth. It defines wealth as a structural concentration of value that is generated through settler colonial social relations and the epistemological genera that underwrite them. And it homes in on the social forces and institutional formations that uphold the knowledge architecture of settler colonial white supremacy, or what Charles Mills calls "a cognitive and moral economy psychically required for conquest, colonization, and enslavement."[24]

Such an economy is not reducible to the value (material, exchange, or surplus) produced from physically enforced social conditions like enslavement, nor to the widespread use of psychological forces such as coercion, threats, and fear that are often required to maintain it. In other words, the "economy" in question is made up of far more than the financial ripples and fiscal profit reaped (including the compound interest that is intergenerationally accumulated) by the slave-owning plantation class from colonial land theft and enslavement. And its cognitive dimension is also more than the psychological tactics and aesthetic tropes european colonizers developed to devalue the bodies and lives of peoples whose lands, labor, and lives they stole.

One clue to a more expansive structural epistemic notion of a "cognitive and moral economy psychically required for conquest" comes from the economic explanation for the ebbs and flows in traditional economic cycles. For instance, econometric variables in settler colonial economies often reflect periodic losses in profit (extrinsic to small business cycles, such as GDP) without structurally substantive losses to the social mechanisms that drive production processes of profitability via convergent axes of exploitation and intersecting oppressions—an ever-renewable labor resource.

In this view, a cognitive and moral economy psychically required for conquest need not include manifestly racist somatic tropes and stereotypes if it is at a particular point in a cycle of domination. A cognitive and moral economy can also include upticks in life-chance metrics for people of color as part of an overall system design. The cycles are not random "reprieves" from racism, but part of structural epistemic cycles geared toward the accumulation of epistemic profit that supports a system of epistemic capitalism as a whole (in part, by overseeing the production process and evidentiary standards associated with "signs of progress"). Think here of how the melting-pot multiculturalism of the 1980s made way for the grand-scale social intelligibility of the color-evasive "postracism" of the 1990s and early 2000s. That's a powerful tool to gaslight populations of color with, especially when one's daily experience of social and administrative systems contradicts the color-evasive nondiscriminatory narrative of multiracial democracies. Reagan was an expert at using this narrative to pursue racist policies while flashing his card-carrying commitment to antidiscrimination.

The question is this: How does this "system" work at the intergenerational level? What supports white supremacy's accumulation of epistemic profit even during seemingly unprofitable time periods like civil rights movements, and what supports the resilience of white dynastic social structures across the extensive institutional changes that are often clustered around these social transformations and progressive movements? What possible mycelial network, get-out-of-jail-free card stockpile, or socioepistemic bank reserve, exists to fund the creation of permanent minorities, permanent defendants, and permanent supplicants under the full purview of democratic processes? The framework of epistemic capitalism responds to these questions by providing a market model of system-level social injustices.

Epistemic capitalism is a fine-tuned social system that produces profit via an asymmetric-exchange process of knowledge production. It is based on the structural accumulation of resources of interpretation and the garnering/institutional consolidation of a social market environment conducive to the exchange of knowledge as commodity and white settler accumulation of profit. The aims of epistemic capitalism are accomplished through structural violence. Underpinned by structural violence, epistemic capitalism ensures that socioeconomic advantages continue to accrue at the level of certain populations, creating long-range conditions favorable to the accumulation of settler wealth, epistemic ownership of structures of power, and the dispossession of noneuropean territories over long cycles—the home turf of colonialism.

Such long-term accrual of wealth is not accidental in settler colonial societies, even if neoclassical accounts of social forces extrinsic to economic determinants pretend otherwise. The accumulation, production, and circulation of epistemic resources is a key element in the resilience and adaptive transformational capacity of settler colonial capitalist economies, primarily because it militates against stasis, and static systems cannot remain alive. To describe how epistemic capital (and the intergenerational hoarding of interpretive wealth) structures ongoing inequality, I draw on what is known as Social Structure of Accumulation (SSA) theory in economics[25] and on anticolonial correctives to pertinent assumptions in SSA theory.[26]

The chapter is divided into three main sections. In the first section, "Profit, Wealth, and Knowledge," I survey influential trends in understanding the contemporary relation between race, history, and economic inequality. I situate these diverse literatures in the context of my project to indict the distributive design that automates impunity in settler colonial societies, and to link impunity with population-level economic gains over long-range periods. In the second section, "Social Structure of Accumulation Theory," I delve deeply into SSA theory to harness its explanatory power of the "birth-grow-decay-transformation cycle" of capitalism for developing market models of structural epistemic harms that track how epistemic capital resurges and transforms to meet the changing needs of settler knowledge infrastructures across different historical periods.

Methodologically, I use economic theory to illustrate dynastic epistemic features of white supremacy because it is one place where the existence of hidden and structural forces that drive observable patterns and system outputs is widely accepted, although the perceived independent dynamic generating economic activity differs widely among theoretical traditions. I turn to SSA theory in progressive economics to illustrate the small leap between such systems and the kind of intergenerational social system of epistemic power accumulation I am describing, which also relies on the idea of "forces" driving social structures and cultural processes.

In the third section, "Epistemic Social Structures of Accumulation," I turn to work in colonial capitalism to reject naturalized explanations for these forces. Along with the macrostructurally invariant character of SSA, I retain the profit-by-design character of SSA theory and its rejection of mechanistic determinism in capital accumulation to ascribe intent and agency to social actors in the production of structural violence in settler colonial economies.[27]

For the purposes of this project, the interpretive usefulness of SSA theory is threefold. I adapt three conceptual points from the SSA approach to a political epistemological reading of SSA, as follows: (1) the nonaccidental character of the political-economic environment in shaping capital accumulation, (2) institutional formation as a functional and flexible network that facilitates domain shifts, and (3) the idea of functional invariance based on strongly stable predictive patterns. For this reason, SSA remains a useful framing of radical political economy, although radical political economy is not our only interpretive option in the fight against settler colonial capitalist reproduction schemes.

Profit, Wealth, and Knowledge

Profit, wealth, and knowledge are deeply interconnected in settler colonial societies. Despite the fact that the realms in which these topics are typically studied, economics and epistemology, rarely come together, I demonstrate their clear convergence in colonial capitalism and the forms of knowledge required to uphold it.

Influential Channels

In the last few years, two main research channels have begun to bridge the traditional divide between economics and epistemology. The first stems from increased public interest in social inequality trends following the 2008 global economic crisis. Concerns about growing economic inequality and widening stratification (particularly for historically marginalized groups) converged with academic discussions about the structure of the systems of power required to maintain such dramatic concentrations of political and economic power in white hands—continuously throughout history, and consistently across geographies. Consider the following data:

> By 2020, the world's 2,153 billionaires (which doubled since 2010) had more wealth than the 4.6 billion people who make up 60 percent of the planet's population. Over 99% of billionaires are white, and the vast majority are men. In 2017, just 8 men owned the same wealth as half the world, and for every $10 made, $8 went to the richest 1%. By 2020, the 22 richest men in the world had more wealth than all the women in Africa. During the COVID-19 pandemic, when a new billionaire was minted every 26 hours, the world's richest men more than doubled their fortunes—the biggest surge since records began—while the incomes of 99 percent of the world's population fell during the same period and over 160 million people were forced into poverty.[28]

Many people across the globe were having none of it, of course. In the aftermath of the Great Recession, wide-scale protests (many of which were framed in terms of the settler right to "occupy" various spaces and places) emerged alongside a cottage industry of publications on economic inequality. Despite the clear connection between whiteness and wealth concentration, the historical influence of race-neutral articulations of "class" in political-economic analyses of wealth gaps led to a bevy of economic analyses of the "economy of the 1%" that rarely took up questions of race or its intersections with gender and coloniality. Even Thomas Piketty's bestselling *Capital in the Twenty-First Century* failed to take up the question of why, even with a successful progressive economic agenda aimed at removing barriers to an inclusive economy, "a dollar of income in black hands buys less safety, less health, less wealth, and less education than a dollar in white hands."[29]

Social scientists engaged with some of the incremental (study by study) challenges of highlighting the multigenerational impact of white supremacy on economic inclusion through research on predatory finance practices,[30] housing discrimination,[31] racialized exploitation of prison labor,[32] discrimination of postincarceration labor,[33] and financial sector gatekeeping.[34] Economic explanations of the links between the dominant thinking, value systems, and beliefs (or ideology) driving these gatekeeping systems and the widening social stratification observed across numerous studies were most often attributed to the aggregative econo-political power and class status of ruling elites to perpetuate race-based inequalities in society, not to the enduring adaptive processes of colonial violence necessary to produce wealth for white settler polities generation after generation. Economic analyses of population-level income inequalities suffered the most glaring interpretive lapses. "Economists," Angela P. Harris argues, "pay little attention to other disciplines, but they *really* ignore race. . . . Economists wishing to take white supremacy seriously have thus been pushed into awkward models such as positing an individual 'taste for discrimination.'"[35]

The second channel influential in mending the gap between economics, race, and colonialism in these discussions comes from reinvigorated discussions of racial capitalism[36] and abolition democracy and feminisms[37] that emphasize the central roles colonial racialization, intersectional oppressions, and extractive power schemes[38] play in the production of surplus profit (i.e., retained earnings after operating costs) under settler colonial capitalism.[39] This literature crisscrosses with decolonial literature from Latin America that focuses on diversifying human ecology of knowledges[40] and bringing an end to the "epistemic empire"[41] of western conceptual schemata used to govern and maintain administrative control of stolen Indigenous lands through the globe.

While this latter literature places special emphasis on the epistemological features of colonialism that functionalize governance practices (over the violent day-to-day mechanisms of dispossession and settlement that reproduce wealth under colonial capitalism), it also de-emphasizes early Latin American economic structuralist articulations of the economy as a unified "system of power"[42] in favor of a world systems[43] framing of core and peripheral epistemic locations between social agents situated in a "global north" and a "global south."[44]

What the Latin American economic structuralists got right—and what made its way into many liberation thinkers' critiques of neoliberalism, including Che Guevara's economic writings—was the idea of a harmful distributive design built into the knowledge systems required to uphold asymmetrical terms of exchange between core and peripheral territories, so that some populations always benefit to the detriment of others. In other words, the house always wins. This is the structural story of knowledge that interests me, not because it is our destiny (it is not), or because alternatives do not exist (they assuredly do), but because it backdrops how *impunity is automated* in settler colonial societies.

Administrative Coordination of Settler Colonial Economic Relations

Recall the discussion in Chapter 1 of retrenchment and structural invariance, in which we found that, for every resistant move, settler colonial administrative systems have readily available countermoves. This is why I think of jurisprudence as dynamic epistemic networks that function in relation to settler colonial economic relations. In the twentieth century, as minority defendants began exerting procedural due process rights, a predictable series of roadblocks to meaningful access to due process emerged. In *Arizona v. Youngblood*,[45] the US Supreme Court put up such roadblocks by holding that "unless a criminal defendant can show bad faith on the part of the police," failure to preserve potentially exculpatory evidence does not constitute a denial of due process.[46] In *Vega v. Tekoh*,[47] after widespread national protests against police brutality and racial profiling of minorities, the Court ruled in the 2022 case that defendants can no longer sue the police for violating their Miranda rights since such rights "are not themselves rights protected by the Constitution." Well, how predictable. Those who are able to evade accountability through the administrative systems set up under settler colonial governance schemas are consistently and reliably those who profit most from structural violence. Caselaw routinely demonstrates how impunity functions in close coordination with settler colonial economic relations, revealing more than just the self-repairing and adaptive features of white dynastic formations, and highlighting its goals. Sexual assault tort cases are a case in point.

Sexual Assault Tort Cases
The jurisprudence of sexual assault liability cases in US civil courts offers insight into the system-level payoffs for the administrative coordination of settler colonial economic relations. Civil liability for legally liable wrongful acts (torts) like harm or negligence resulting in personal injury (which includes slander, invasion of privacy, and false imprisonment, in addition to "bodily injury") is central to the insurance industry and the liability coverage protection plans it sells. While insurers are not liable for the willful criminal conduct

of the insured,[48] an insurer may be liable for a host of injuries covered under umbrella policies if the injuries can be disentangled from the criminal act(s). This is highly problematic on several fronts. Fist, sexual assault often involves components like false imprisonment that would otherwise be covered under such policies, but which are difficult to isolate (particularly when coercion is used) and to separate from other features of the wrongful act(s) that criminal codes require to be copresent to determine a perpetrator's criminal liability for sexual offenses. It is reminiscent of the judicial logic that required Black women plaintiffs to separate out which parts of the experience of discrimination corresponded to being "women" and which to being "Black."[49] Second, in an attempt to trigger an insurer's duty to defend the insured for accidents under homeowner's insurance policies, legal reasoning surrounding the experiential separability of "occurrences" in sexual assault can easily be used to try to shield perpetrators from liability by constructing the sexual assault as accidental. In *Allstate Ins. Co. v. Troelstrup*, "[Accused molester] Troelstrup presented deposition testimony from several involved professionals, as well as from the investigating officer, all of whom, in essence, expressed the opinion that Troelstrup had no subjective intention to injure or harm the child," also submitting a psychologist's affidavit stating Troelstrup "had formulated no conscious intent to harm the child."[50] Third, even when separability is logically feasible (as in cases of forced imprisonment where the occurrence of sexual assault potentially takes place at time different from other illicit acts like a perpetrator's photographing of victims, which can be argued as tortfeasance under invasion of privacy statutes), just like with race-neutral reasoning, there is always an adaptive race- and gender-neutral domain of reasoning afforded to institutions to evade the claim for recovery. Consider that sexual misconduct liability insurance, when it is available, also bars recovery against many acts routinely considered sexual misconduct, such as sexual harassment.[51] However, when the insured is a corporation or public entity like a police department, or a religious entity, the protective goalpost shifts to accommodate settler capital interests, with insurers able to use a host of legal determinations to pay out claims and indemnify the insured.[52] This is where federal policy and state-led measures to cap tort claims come in.

In Ohio, a court reduced a jury award of $3.5 million given to a victim of childhood sexual assault (perpetrated by a priest) down to $350,000 after applying the state caps enacted in previous tort reform legislation.[53] In California, the California Code of Civil Procedures (CCCP) allows a person to sue for treble damages (up to three times the compensatory damage amount) in childhood sexual assault cases involving a cover-up. In *LAUSD v. Superior Court*,[54] the court held that, as public entity, the school district had sovereign immunity, and that the function of the CCCP statute was punitive, not compensatory. The ruling meant that the treble damages provision under CCCP's section 340.1 does not serve to compensate victims of childhood sexual assault (but to punish the person(s) responsible), barring plaintiff Jane Doe from seeking such damages from the Los Angeles Unified School District (LAUSD) for her sexual assault by an LAUSD employee when she was fourteen years old. These cases illustrate that the logical ecosystem within which sexual violence is litigated in court functions through an economic network of epistemic relations that confers immunity to some entities and evades accountability for others by design.

A system's behavior can be gleaned from the patterns it regularly exhibits: while "It is estimated that domestic violence accounts for a staggering two million injuries a year, making it a leading cause of death for women age 15–44 and a leading cause of death of pregnant women," as of 2018 there had been "only 163 [tort] cases since 1985. Similarly, although recent surveys have indicated that between 19 % and 23 % of college undergraduates are victims of sexual assault or attempted sexual assault, the new Restatement (Third) of Intentional Torts to Persons cites only a few cases of sexual battery and acknowledges 'the overwhelming evidence of the frequency of sexual assault and the relative infrequency of successful tort recovery.' There are considerably more cases of sexual assault brought against third-party defendants, but even here, recovery is impeded by a variety of special obstacles."[55] While the shattering economic, physical, social, and emotional tolls of sexual assault are well established and legally legible facts, since the rise of the anti-domestic violence and gender rights movement,[56] courts and state statutes have routinely worked to limit (punitive and compensatory) damages for recovery claims for injuries and harms suffered as a result of sexual assault.[57]

Structurally produced roadblocks to sexually based tort claims are not a new phenomenon. From a systems perspective, the interpretive ecosystem from which such roadblocks emerge contains an expansive range of interconnected legal avenues and pathways that allow for a domain shift when old ways of accumulating legal power are stymied by social policies or progressive legal reform. Colonial racism in tort calculation (the formulas used to produce quantifiable damages for harms alleged in tort cases) is a classic example:

[Tort calculation formulas] routinely lower damages for minority plaintiffs through the use of race-based life-expectancy tables and [are] amplified for the compensatory relief of white plaintiffs. Courts routinely use "rehabilitation experts" (*Powell v. Parker*) to provide testimony on demographic statistics related to loss of earning capacity and life expectancy based on "in-group averages" for race and gender. In 2004, (*U.S. v. Bedoine*) a rehabilitation expert calculated compensatory damages for a Native American man by simply multiplying the anticipated earnings of a white person by 58%, and for a Native American woman (who was also part of the suit) by reducing the $744,000 award (what would have been awarded had she been a white male) to $308,000 when adjusting for her gender, and a further reduction to $171,000 when adjusting for her race. It is clear the legal system is capable of performing interlocking harms even as it claims to be unable to recognize intersectional oppressions. . . . The effects of such tables for white male plaintiffs, by contrast, "is to set their recoveries at an unjustifiably high amount, which perpetuates and recreates gender and race disparities in the distribution of personal income." . . . While adjustments made based on in-group racial averages clearly skews profit towards white litigants in tort suits, they produce harmful and reliably deadly consequences for people of color in the criminal system, where they have been used in mitigation to determine and adjust sentencing [toward death penalty outcomes].[58]

Impunity in this context is not the exception but the rule. And it is this impunity that we come up against, again and again, as survivors of color as we navigate public institutions and social services in settler colonial societies that are fundamentally set up to profit from violence against people of color and Indigenous peoples.

Toward Market Models of Structural Epistemic Harms

Epistemologies keep wars going in times of peace, when violence is reduced to the measurable patterns of extralegal uses of force. Epistemologies make systemic violence appear *as* peace, and they keep the lights on at the armories that are later recommissioned for duty when the veil of peacetime dissolves. The economic story of 2020 provides an insight into these and other resilient system features of white supremacy that often go untracked, especially under intense periods of social upheaval and transformation. But it is not a linear story.

It begins with a theory of white placemaking that functionally distorts the histories of settler colonial systems *as systems*, systems that act with goals, purposes, incentives, and constraints that strengthen over time. Systems monitor the flows of intense changes and divert energies to rebalance system loops—or create new ones—all in an effort to stay together as a system: to work holistically and as designed. Impunity, of course, is the hallmark of a settler colonial social system working smoothly as designed.[59]

Colonialism cannot be maintained without epistemic warfare any more than colonial capitalism can survive without knowledge economies that reproduce oppression for some populations but not others. Epistemic capitalism is thus a framework that analyzes the close connection between structural violence, profit, and epistemology in settler colonial capitalist societies—a connection that regularly produces vulnerability, insecurity, precarity, and extractive erasure, particularly for women of color, in the most systemic, predictive, and simultaneously mystified way. It uses the language of "epistemic dynastic formations" to unpack the societal costs of maintaining untaxed dynastic systems of intergenerational wealth and dynastic profit structures that reproduce conditions central to structural violence. It's not just about what has happened to create the current sociopolitical realities, as Chapter 2 illustrates, or even about what maintains it. It offers a way to create new avenues for keeping ledgers and assessing the accounting rate of return and revenue generated over colonialism's long cycles—because the bill for damages is accruing by the chapter. While this may not be sufficient to produce a structurally unrebukable tort claim in settler epistemological strongholds like the courts, it is, at the very least, a practice that tracks with a nonwhitewashed reality of the incredible profitability some populations extract from systemic violence and oppression.

In relation to my project, the framing of epistemic capitalism presented in this chapter yields a specific link between profit, wealth, and knowledge that makes it implausible to maintain a race-neutral account of wealth gaps or of forms of structured inequality as distinct from how violence against women of color operates in settler colonial regimes.[60] In a network framing, the intersecting nodes and probable paths available as social conduits for structural harm are not accidental. System design functionalizes impunity when harms do occur—that is, settler systems leave it in the hands of perpetrators to set the terms by which one must or need not correct behavior or set things right or for each harm. This agenda-setting power is never offered to populations of color in a settler legal environment.[61] The notion of epistemic imperialism underwriting settler epistemic economies conveys a very old sentiment in liberation thinking that western culture has undeservedly been judge, jury, and executioner throughout history.[62] This is what allows the econo-epistemic infrastructures to maintain the regenerative life cycle of sexist racist violence and settler colonial epistemic occupation as seamlessly as they do.

As a methodological point, I have chosen to use political economy and economic theory because they are among the few domains in settler colonial epistemic systems in which the existence of hidden, functionalist, and structural forces that drive observable patterns and goal-oriented system outputs is widely accepted. The leap between the systems recognized by these disciplines and the kind of historical for-profit system of interpretive power accumulation that I describe is so small as to warrant serious laughter when it is theorized for abstract economic laws of motion but denied for white supremacy. What is not laughable is the consistent and predictive harm that results from such a denial.

SSA theory is also a helpful starting point for illustrating the basic system features of wealth accumulation and concentration that require epistemic violences to be routine operating procedures in settler colonial societies. I have argued throughout this book that interpersonal models of epistemic violence are inadequate for understanding the structural nature of white dynastic violence throughout its historical iterations in roman and Alexandrian expansionism, european colonialism, anglo imperialism, colonial and industrial capitalism, globalized multinational capitalism, neoliberalism (and, foreseeably next, digital capitalism), and especially for the structurally invariant profile of violence against women of color exemplified in Maria and Daphne's cases discussed in Chapter 2. The economic model offered through SSA theory provides a partial bridge to the thesis in Chapter 4 that such violence and invariance are intentional, by design, and, most important, profit-driven.

Relatedly, market models of structural epistemic harms help illustrate why systemic injustices that are corrected at the policy level (such as President Biden's Executive Order 13985, issued in response to former president Trump's Executive Order 13950)[63] are still operating under a settler epistemic economy that functionalizes pathways for future rollbacks of those policies. This allows structured precarity for populations of color and the continuity of white dynastic settler wealth to seamlessly coexist in perpetuity—a perpetuity that safeguards white settler futurity by design. And it does so alongside the good intentions of white allies in positions of power who may appear to be individually moving mountains to help stem the tide of white supremacy.[64]

Philosopher Alisa Bierria aptly identifies the inseparability of macrostructural operations and individual action in what she calls the "social dialectic of agency."[65] This notion describes the settler colonial operations of structural epistemic violence that ensure that "even if an agent develops her intentions and acts accordingly, others who observe the agent's action also construct narratives of meaning about her actions, empowering them as social authors of her autonomous action."[66] I find this framing of agency especially helpful, as it portrays an advanced network that creates the illusion of isolation (or isolability) of individual system states, when they are in fact inseparable from the interpretive ecosystem of settler colonial relations in which they operate.[67]

A Word on Value

Before turning to SSA theory, a word about value. I focus on the functional aspect of worth: what it aims to shore up, how, and for whom. Settler epistemic economies are about value—about the functionality of realizable values being traded and exchanged continuously. How such functional value is set, controlled, maintained, and traded to benefit some populations more than others requires more than a theory of knowledge that disambiguates between individual agency and collective levels of social agency (or an account of how "social scripts" influence individual action). It requires historical understanding of social emergence that is not tied to the system outputs of settler epistemic economies. The cultural design and functionality of particular value systems is what the anticolonial systems theory outlined in Chapter 1 sought to illustrate. Thus, when I talk about value, it is this functional valuative process that I have in mind. Think forest, not trees. Then zoom out and think forestry and gatekept access to stewardship over forestry. In this model, some ecological practices of stewardship can be sustained alongside particular economic value systems to the exclusion of others— even if they are invasive—such that impunity can be maintained at a highly functional level without much system resistance (though with plenty of opposition on the ground).[68] Impunity is a system-generated phenomenon, not an interpersonal one explained via structural injustice ex machina. Impunity must be understood in reference to coloniality and the system-level payoffs for white settler populations and their descendants.

Consider a recent survey by Intelligent, which found that 34 percent of white Americans falsely claimed to be a minority on their college application in order to (1) improve their chances of getting accepted (81 percent) and/or (2) benefit from minority-focused financial aid (51 percent).[69] An astounding but unsurprising, 85 percent of the white students who lied about their race to gain advantage were successful in gaining admission. Why is this unsurprising? For one thing, the college-to-job-market pipeline is still a relevant good (economic, social, or otherwise) for white settler populations, such that economic and educational policy whack-a-mole always operates within a larger distributive design based on white dynastic formations. An epistemic market economy in which some people can predictably and reliably get away with lying about race for profit is tied to a market economy in which other people, depending on their processive relation to settler colonialism, cannot.

Market models of structural epistemic harms are also a heuristic for meta-macroeconomic dynamics at the heart of race-neutral accounts of economic systems—the kind that delink "investment in land" from the extractive project of settler colonialism, as we'll see later in this chapter. These harms also help illuminate the problematic nature of philosophical theories of justice and responsibility that place enormous pressure on oppressed peoples to abandon claims to structural economic and epistemic reparations and other forms of *structural resource transfers* in favor of epistemic cost-sharing accounts of responsibility. Epistemic cost-sharing accounts of responsibility usually take the form "We're all in this together," as if we're "in it together" in the same ways and at the cost of historical amnesia. No narrative has been more successful in touting this line than western environmental narratives of anthropogenic climate change. Such narratives are quick to identify the asymmetric carbon emissions of "developing" nations and, when questions arise about western multinational financing of megaprojects worldwide, to portray climate warming as a global problem where there is no particular agent as the perpetrator, just a global polity that needs to come together in climate accords. The way Indigenous communities and communities of color are asymmetrically impacted by climate change and industrial capital infrastructures is often derivative in these discussions. What is not derivate is the way wealthy nations work to stem the efforts of poor nations to receive climate reparations.[70]

The story I tell about social system complexity through the idea of epistemic capitalism is heuristic and exploratory; it is meant to illustrate the depth of coordinated forces that are designed to align and maintain racial systems (with the gender-based violence they require) through profit motives at different scales of social organization, and to get away with it, with impunity. This story about social system complexity deepens a model of network complexity and built-in cooperative design that links together things that seem only distantly related in social inequality literatures. These linkages are not made by merely putting connective tissue between things and events, so as to connect them, endpoint to endpoint, but by exploring the very macroscopic complexity of white dynastic formations that is often used to mystify the very scalable and identifiable violences that those formations support.

A Word on Complexity
Complexity will not save the day. Nothing will be won or lost at this scale of systems analysis that isn't being fought for in greater numbers and with higher stakes at the ground level. Lives are lost, bodies are burned and buried at this scale. As I've said before, "There is no blood on the ontological tree."[71] So we must not carry this meta-macroeconomic story too far beyond illustrating the existence of a powerful epistemic mycelium that is part of the sociostructural arsenal of settler colonial social formations. The offense can't stay drawn up on a whiteboard; it must be run. And running the offense may reveal things about epistemic capitalism that may not hold true as predicted. I want to hold on to (1) the reliability of a harmful distributive design at the core of settler social structures that is likely to continue converging on knowledge practices in settler *institutions* and administrative infrastructures, (2) the idea that there is a deeply rooted and expansive mycelial epistemic network that exists to support the never-ending carousel of automated asymmetries we endure as people of color under white dynastic formations, and (3) an understanding of the system goal of such dynastic formations—accumulated profit. Wealth begets wealth. Wealth also works to uphold wealth by hiding it. "For the wealthy, inheritance provides a genealogical distance from conquest, genocide, and colonial slavery that offers a cover of ostensible innocence and launders accumulated fortunes."[72] This is as true for monetary analyses of intergenerational wealth transfers and accumulation as it is for knowledge infrastructures and resources in a settler epistemic economy.

Let us return to a term I used in the last chapter with respect to the devaluation of Maria's and Daphne's testimonies of sexual assault: *settler credibility economies*. The market model of structural epistemic harms elucidates how sexist racism is not a cognitive "dysfunction" that passively results in wrongful white benefit; it is a well-oiled system of production with active rates of return that exceed rates of growth and output, such that even if the output slows down through targeted interventions (like antibias training or executive orders), the infrastructure that is set in place allows continued accumulation and future expansion through the creation of new epistemic markets for trading and exchange. This process includes the emergence of credibility redlining zones and the supererogatory, redundant demands to demonstrate their existence and resulting harms.

Credibility redlining zones are an emerging discourse in critical geography and data science studies that use geomapping technologies to visualize the spatial distribution of sexual assault cases that are dismissed by police as "unfounded" (i.e., not credible).[73] Between 2009 and 2014 the rate of "unfounded" sexual assault reports in Oxnard, California, was 53.5 percent.[74] Oxnard is over 75 percent Latinx. In Baltimore County, where the Black population is over 31 percent but over 80 percent of sworn police offers are white, the rate is 34 percent. The larger distribution patterns of credibility burdens—who is saddled with the greatest burden of proofs and why—are often obscured in mainstream philosophical accounts of testimonial injustices, as is the connection to land and settler colonial projects of dispossession and cultural genocide. To date, investigative journalism's approach to the data sets on unfounded sexual assault reporting is also limited to single-layer analyses that produce databases of searchable zip codes. This allows media outlets to produce news features such as "Will Police Believe You?" that allow subscribers to find their region's "unfounded sexual assault" rate, with the implication that whether your report of sexual assault will be deemed credible (e.g., "founded") depends as much on where you live as it does who is making the report and who is taking it.[75] Such approaches do not investigate the larger distributive design behind why police dismiss one in five reports of sexual assault nationally in Canada, the relation between policing and settler colonial violence, or the geographic mushrooming of concentrated regions of credibility redlining zones precisely when national averages of unfounded sexual assault began to decline in the United States in the wake of the #MeToo movement (i.e., the adaptive dimensions of racialized sexual violence architectures).[76] The takeaway of this data for my project is simple: it will never stop, the evidence will never be enough, as long as settler colonial infrastructures remain intact. Legal scholars are already foreshadowing the development of algorithms to impeach witness credibility ("algorithmic credibility") that create legal pathways for credibility deflation based on social status determinations of who is worthy of belief in society.[77]

In our next section, we'll turn to SSA theory to illustrate how the basic resources for thinking about this nonaccidental settler accumulative expansionism at the level of knowledge already exist as a model of accumulation in economic theory, so that a market model of structured epistemic harms begins to emerge.

Social Structure of Accumulation Theory

Social Structure of Accumulation (SSA) is a theory of long-run macrostability in capitalist history that explains periods of disequilibria, macroinstability, and economic stagnation as part of larger "waves" or "long swings" of capital accumulation rhythms. These rhythms of economic growth and crisis cycles are not simply the restorative boom-and-bust dynamics of short-run business cycles, which have standard explanations in neoclassical and Marxist economics. Instead, these periods are much longer and reflect infrastructural underpinnings that cannot be accounted for by microeconomic activity. Growth and crisis cycles in SSA also reflect the historical reality of alternating periods of rapid economic expansion and stagnation that have not yielded capitalism's collapse, but instead its continual renewal in capitalism's different stages (such as the world system). At this scale of economic activity, a broader set of explanations is required that tracks with this reality. SSA proposes one such explanatory framework.

Instead of lawlike exogenous economic forces (neoclassical model) or internally generated economic phenomena (Marxist model), SSA theorizes that macroinstability is driven by the creation and collapse of growth-promoting institutions. Whereas Adam Smith believed the economy naturally reached equilibrium if left to its own devices (e.g., through the "invisible hands" of the market at work), SSA theory rejects the impersonal and naturalized (e.g., the idea that, without regulatory intervention, a commodity's market price will inherently drift toward its "natural" price) portrayal of macroeconomic forces. Instead, SSA theory points to human intervention and intergenerational institution-building—to a "determinate institutional structure" composed of growth-promoting institutions that are designed to achieve the equilibrium necessary for the system of capital accumulation to continue generation after generation.[78] The idea is that the human design of institutions and their intergenerational operations as a system of sociostructural succession can produce lawlike behaviors that are predictive of market outcomes, but not foreordained (as with natural laws, like the law of gravity). Thus, the system of institutions (domestic and international) that support capital accumulation over long periods of time is referred to as the Social Structure of Accumulation.

Institutions in SSA theory are defined broadly and include sociocultural and political institutions as well as economic ones. Racism, sexism, ableism, and other socially institutionalized matrixes of power[79] are considered alongside capital-labor relations and more traditional framings of institutions, such as the International Monetary Fund and the multinational cooperative system of financial institutions that arose from the postwar Bretton Woods agreement. The importance of institutions in the economic process is of course not new to economic theory. The novel emphasis in SSA theory is on social institutions (i.e., not just banking, labor, and financial markets) and on the political-economic environment in shaping capital accumulation at the structural level.

Three Takeaways

There are three takeaways from SSA theory for the purposes of this project. One, SSA theory provides a bridge to a network-systems framing of economic relations that highlights the close interrelation between economic and social domains, making theories of racial capitalism more readily significant to economic theory (on the reframe of SSA theory I provide). Two, its emphasis on the accumulation phase of capitalist growth is compatible with anticolonial analyses of capital relations based on extractivism, dispossession, and white settler accumulation of capital that also home in on this phase.[80] Three, its preservation-through-transformation framework—for example, its "birth-grow-decay-transformation cycle"[81]—provides a market model analogue to the profit-by-design and nonaccidental character of systems resilience (e.g., its self-healing capacities) in white dynastic formations (Chapter 1).

First, SSA's special focus on noneconomic institutions means that "the social structure of accumulation approach broadens the range of social phenomena that are considered to work in systematic ways."[82] Such systematicity is helpful for thinking about the interlocking nature of structural oppressions and their relation to economic inequalities. SSA has been used, for example, in the South African context to explore the "highly functional and causally significant relationship" between "the economic system and the system of radical domination" institutionalized in apartheid.[83] (Racial capitalism literature has, of course, also homed in on this relation.) Despite its applied history to anticolonial struggles, for reasons that will be later discussed, the leap to a dispossession-centered account of capital accumulation as colonial capitalism (an economic system rooted in settler colonial social relations) is not found in SSA theory. What is useful is SSA's characterization of social phenomena as functional features of the "basic reproductive structure" of capital relations throughout capitalism's history, as well as the systems-level interrelation between social and economic domains in this reproductive process.

Another important takeaway from the SSA framework is the conceptual shift away from "relations of production" in capitalist growth (Marx 101) toward the accumulation process itself. Such a move allows for a recharacterization of the relationship between social structure and capitalist growth that more robustly captures the dynamics of social power associated with sociocultural institutions. In contrast with the classic Marxist picture of a conceptually privileged economic "base" that in turn shapes the sociocultural "superstructure" (responsible for maintaining a base-supporting status quo in society), SSA theory flips the script but retains the actors. It redescribes the nature and dynamics of the relations that take place throughout economic stability and change under capitalism by giving greater explanatory power to the social domain. In this way, "SSA theory brings politics, ideology, and culture into the heart of the theory of economic growth and crisis."[84] While SSA theory misses the link between colonial primitive accumulation and the onset of SSA cycles, its holistic and structural economic framing of political economy is helpful for reconnecting the dots that neoclassical models sever among culture, ideology, social power, and market forces that routinely reproduce inequality.

A final takeaway for the purposes of this project is SSA's emphasis on the profit-by-design and nonaccidental character of systems resilience in capitalist history. This is expressed partly in the idea that "while the construction of a new social structure of accumulation may not be inevitable, there are powerful forces that push in that direction."[85] I will suggest that, when taking colonial capitalism and primitive accumulation into account through white dynastic formations' emphasis on controlled succession, the intergenerational accumulation of settler colonial interpretive wealth (and the accompanying structural violences that support it) mend the theoretical gap in SSA theory about what drives the successive creation of SSAs and whether SSAs exist outside of modern economic dating schemes. Epistemic capitalism illustrates that nonlinear succession and adaptive continuity are mainstays of white dynastic formations and of the system goals of accumulative profit for white polities. Epistemic SSAs are not "fate," but they certainly constitute "the powerful forces that push in that direction" regardless of institutional reform. This idea can be further illustrated by delving into SSA's history.

Capitalism's "Recuperative Power"

The historical roots of SSA theory can be traced to Marxist analyses of system transformations in the development of stages of capitalism. While indebted to the Marxist theoretical tradition, "SSA theory breaks with it by focusing on the recuperative power of capitalism—its ability to revive and renew itself following prolonged periods of relative stagnation or crisis."[86] SSA theory is not alone in this. It shares basic features of analysis of capitalist "reproduction schemes" with the French regulation school of the 1970s, most notably with Michel Aglietta's *A Theory of Capitalist Regulation*. As economist David Kotz explains, "In both the regulation and social structure of accumulation approaches, the accumulation/institution relation undergoes a birth-grow-decay-transformation cycle" that upholds the long-range macrodynamic stability of capitalism.[87] While both economic schools agree that "the resolution of an economic crisis entails structural change" via new sets of institutional arrangements that reproduce conditions favorable to accumulation, they disagree on the nature of those arrangements and the process by which they emerge.[88]

The SSA approach places more emphasis than the French school on mutually reinforcing sociopolitical forces and gives less credence to abstractly deterministic structural forces as catalysts for system transformations. For the regulation school, the recuperative power of economic downturns is self-generated as an endogenous structural feature of capitalist economies. In the SSA picture, stagnation in accumulation is not self-correcting; something must set the institutional restructuring in motion again. "It requires some collective action and the creation of a political consensus" that is beyond individual social actors acting in isolation to restore prosperity.[89] It requires, on my reading, something like the self-repairing and homeostatic dynamics of white dynastic formations to provide the "push off" via the springboard of accumulated interpretive resources.

In the SSA model, a coherent, purposeful design is attributed to social institutions and yields a highly plausible picture of possible outcomes, such as the cyclically recurring ups and downs and subsequent re-entrenchment of profit-producing conditions in a new cycle of capitalist accumulation. Such is the predictive power SSA ascribes to extraeconomic political and ideological factors in the breakdown and regeneration of capitalist economic institutions. It will be an important bridge and conceptual analogue in examining the role epistemic resources play in the formation of settler colonial wealth.

SSA scholars diverge on what makes an institution "effective" or "pertinent to" an SSA, why some SSAs endure longer than others, whether SSAs are wholly unique or whether there is internal overlap with the institutions of the previous SSA cycle, and whether SSA theory is sufficient to explain durable inequalities[90] that are rooted in settler extractive accumulation processes. I think it is not.

Limits in Explanatory Power

When the SSA approach was formally introduced in the early 1980s,[91] Marxist economics dominated progressive economic theory without any substantive engagement with colonial capitalism. SSA theory's indebtedness to Marx (and to a lesser extent, Keynesian macroeconomics) and the eurocentric model of global economic thinking about inequality outside of the land-labor colonial relation was evident in its preferred analytic of class and labor relations. Firmly rooted in political economy and anglo-european economic thinking on inequality, SSA theorists adapted and modified key elements of Marxist crisis theory and long-wave theoretical frameworks[92] to explain the cyclical peaks and troughs of economic crises that characterized the life cycles of capitalist accumulation. Not only does capitalism go through a triadic cycle of institutionally supported growth, consolidation, and decay, they contended, but over time each cycle is repeated in unique ways that reflect the specific institutional arrangements where capitalism is operating. Missing from this holistic and regenerative picture of economic inequality under capital accumulation rhythms are the kinds of links among land, history, and institutional arrangements that critiques of settler colonial capitalism forge.[93] The understanding of "crisis" that informs SSA theory is thus limited in scope and explanatory power.

Like regulation theorists, SSA theorists were operating in the aftermath of global economic crises (the 1930s and 1970s) and the successive resurgence of capitalist accumulation. Just as the approach of predominantly white male progressive economists was consistent with traditional questions and progressive approaches to the economic study of stratification and inequality (consider that only 1 percent of economists working at the Fed are Black), so too were the economic patterns that SSA isolated for inquiry, as were as the analytic tools and study methods applied by SSA theorists. In this context, SSA theorists sought to provide contemporary answers to the question, "Why is abrupt structural change such a recurring feature of the long-swing dynamic of capitalist economies?"[94]

Gordon and his coauthors presuppose that capital accumulation, the basis for capitalism, "cannot take place either in a vacuum or in chaos," suggesting that "capitalists cannot and will not invest in production unless they are able to make reasonably determinate calculations about their expected rates of return."[95] This is not because they are risk-averse, but because they have investment alternatives in financial markets with predictably lower but steadier financial rates of return, and because the durable nature of institutions (such as the legal system and laws that protect business interests, and political classes that enshrine these laws) has conditioned the expectations of capitalists, who've come to expect institutional responses of some kind to the instability posed by intercapitalist competition and capital-labor disputes.[96]

Though Marxist and mainstream neoclassical traditions recognize capitalists' desire for stability and predictability, according to Gordon et al., "Both traditions have tended either to elide the importance of the external environment in the formation of expectations about the rate of profit or to fail to provide a substantive account of that environment."[97] I think that's right, to an extent.

The account of the external environment in SSA theory does not go far enough, as it is still trapped in uncritical settler colonial assumptions about social regeneration (refer to Chapter 1) that make their way into SSA's framework of the regeneration cycles of capital accumulation (where the push-off phase of SSAs occurs in a contextualist soup of historical platitudes that evade the structuring roles of settler colonial relations in capital accumulation rhythms). What SSA theory misses is that it is also implicated in the generative dynamics of the settler colonial external environment, and one reason the theory fails to account for this is the lack of attunement to the role of epistemic capital and interpretive wealth formation in structuring the regenerative SSA cycle(s).

SSA theory does, however, offer important modifications to the limited structural role ideology plays in Marxist economic theory that offers insights into the macrodynamics of settler epistemic economies. Central to this modification is the multimodal nature of the stability-generating prerequisites for generating profit, and the recurring features of social formations that help maintain this dynamic over long cycles. Gordon et al. write:

> We argue, in sharp contrast [to Marxism and neoclassical economic accounts], that macrodynamic analyses should begin with the political-economic environment affecting individual capitalists' possibilities for capital accumulation. Without a stable and favorable external environment, capitalist investment in production will not proceed. We refer to this external environment as the social structure of accumulation. Its elements derive from the specific set of requirements, neither unlimited nor indeterminate, that must be satisfied for capital accumulation to take place ... the social structure of accumulation, in short, is external to the decisions of individual capitalists, but it is internal to the macrodynamics of capitalist economies.[98]

In the SSA view, successive institutional arrangements arise to support the expansion phase of the accumulation process by regulating the social, economic, and ideological environmental conditions necessary to support accumulation, petering out or restructuring to accommodate the necessary changes that would support a newly effective social structure of accumulation. This happens when an old accumulation cycle begins to show signs of sluggishness (as in real-wage stagnation) and decay, showing an SSA is no longer effective at producing growth. The old SSA, made up "all the institutions that impinge upon the accumulation process," is rendered ineffective and a new SSA begins to be built to replace the old one.[99] The economic racism of the antebellum South can thus adapt to Reconstruction and reforge itself in a new institutional formation that still drives capital accumulation for white polities.

In classic settler epistemological fashion, the SSA process does not address whether "there are any trends in the successive social structures of accumulation," leaving the impression that SSAs are like integrated wholes unto themselves, where the reasons for an SSA's decline are vaguely based on historical contingency—the onset of wars, global pandemics, or new technologies—but where the ascent/rebuilding phase is clearly predicted irrespective of the reason for the disintegration of the old SSA. Given the historical actuality of the global and multimodal character of white supremacy (e.g., the "hard' nonideal model of contextualism discussed in Chapter 1), it is plausible to consider the structural maintenance and upkeep of white supremacy as the primary driver of the ascent and rebuilding phases, and structural challenges to white dynastic formations as catalysts for phases of decline.

Consider that a crucial point of SSA theory—and one germane to this project—is that keeping the old SSA in its integrated totality just won't do to sustain capital accumulation in the long run. Things must change if they are to remain the same, and in this view, you can't revive an old SSA anymore than you can reanimate Jim Crow infrastructures without making some changes. Changes to Jim Crow are necessary in the SSA picture, even if they amount to nothing more than the soft multiculturalism and the dog-whistling covert racism of the Reagan administration. Such changes do not result in meaningful (elementary) alterations to the basic structure of racism, as Reagan-era housing and social welfare policies remind us. Rather, the socioinstitutional realignments necessary to support accumulation arise with predictive regularity, and their restorative effects track with the social and political climate rooted in white supremacy.

When socioinstitutional realignments restore racist structures, the tools of earlier eras are no longer needed and are discarded. The master's tools remake themselves anew in support of the same dispossessive goal. This is why the dog-whistling common to the Nixon and Reagan eras is, under Trumpism, unnecessary to support economic growth (Trump was openly called "white-supremacist-in-chief" by national publications) and overt white supremacy is reanimated in public discourse without integral contradictions to capital accumulation. Yet institutional changes under Trumpism (privatization of public resources, packing of courts, systemic civil rights protection rollbacks) matter a great deal for the formation of successive SSAs. Under President Biden, Republican-packed courts and appointed public officers do a lot of the gerrymandering and assault on reproductive rights work formerly done at the federal level under Trump. The network framing of the SSA model easily explains this domain shift in productive capacity. In the classic

SSA model, each successive SSA "is virtually certain to differ from its predecessor," even when it appears that inconsistent socioinstitutional directions (liberal social policies accompanied by widening economic stratification) are not immediately harmful to capital accumulation and that no institutional changes are necessary. From the SSA perspective, some things must change in the sociopolitical environment if the accumulation of capital is to remain well-functioning and central to capitalism. What drives this change and the interrelation between white supremacy and the accumulative patterns that skew wealth concentration toward white polities through various SSAs remains peripheral to SSA theory.

Again, I still think SSA is a helpful tool that points to some of the same adaptive and nonaccidental features of interlocking systems of oppression at the core of white dynastic formations. In fact, the integrated and interlocking nature of sociopolitical and economic forces in SSA theory does not reject the idea that there are, in fact, strongly stable sociostructural forces that persistently militate against foundational change, just as "the multidimensionality of social structures of accumulation makes coalition-building extremely complicated" and unlikely to foster effective conditions for carrying out foundational system transformations.[100] It only insists that such forces are not metaphysically separate from the social contexts in which they arose, that they are not purely deterministic (e.g., naturalized), and that their existence is no accident:

> The crucial innovation offered by the social structure of accumulation approach is that the wide range of causal factors are not viewed as accidental or external. Rather, it is assumed that a large array of social factors, including some in the political and ideological spheres, can be viewed as governed by laws of motion. More precisely, the interaction between the accumulation process and a large set of social factors is assumed to follow a significantly regular and predictable course. This violates an unspoken assumption in previous long-run growth analyses, both Marxian and non-Marxian, that only a small set of narrowly defined economic factors can predict regular, law-governed behavior.[101]

These social factors are not themselves governed by natural laws (as SSA theory rejects the naturalized account of economic forces), but they can certainly exhibit regular patterns and behaviors that express a structural design in how social facts operate in society.

This is not tantamount to functionalist predetermination. A system design (oriented toward generative accumulation of profit) is in place that must be kept in place if it is to continue, and luckily for those who benefit from such a system, accumulative advantages accrue that make it easier to achieve this than not. This requires work to achieve—for example, population buy-in at various scales, active interventions and backing-off periods, schemes of legislative craft and long-term policy planning, regulative bursts of suppressive public violence and enforcement, governance cycles of retractive mea culpas and democratic realignment, institutional carrots and occasional upticks in life course outcomes, as well as committed intergenerational resources and financial backing. If you destroy a people's language, craft racist policies that undermine various modalities of linguistic resurgence, burn sacred texts, pollute lands necessary for inhabiting Native languages, and suppress cultural resources for hermeneutic interpellation over long ranges, you're nonaccidentally accumulating epistemic advantages that help secure a stable hermeneutic backdrop (or basic interpretive structure) that can be relied upon to subsist through change, and thus create a favorable external environment of structural reliability for settler capital accumulation rhythms to continue. Following SSA theory, this still requires intent on a social scale (Chapter 4):

> The construction of a social structure of accumulation requires explicit and self-conscious actions by leading political actors. By emphasizing these conscious acts we do not intend to suggest a purely conspiratorial, behind-the-scenes process that is hidden from the public's view until it is unveiled as an accomplished feat. Instead, we see this process as occurring quite openly and as involving first the development and then the mobilization of a consensus supporting the new institutional structure.[102]

The disagreement I have is with the characterization of the consensus-supporting apparatuses that maintain cultural hegemony over long periods of time for the purposes of capital accumulation, and in the relation between the "external environment" supported by such apparatuses and the resources of interpretation required to build certain kinds of institutions but not others (e.g., Bureaus of Land Management and "voter fraud" police units). I think such institutional equilibrium requires reference to the creation and maintenance of settler colonial interpretive ecologies or ecosystems of knowledge that aren't naturalized (as hermeneutic philosophy does) or universal, but rather historical and dynastic epistemic systems that regularly produce and coordinate the intergenerational transmission of value for some populations but not others through SSA-like circuits of value transference and exchange.

What SSA theory does a good job of explaining is the boldface openness and transparency of the restructuring mechanisms of capital reproduction. The development of new SSAs happens in real time and in the open. By the time such a new institutional structure is fully emergent and apparent to social actors integrated in the political economy of power (and with structural interventionist power over policy), the development phase of an SSA is likely over. Once the public can read about the history of how we got here in *The Atlantic*, the mobilization phase has likely already taken on generative momentum with institutional consequences. Think here of the rise of the New Right, Tea Party, and insurgent populism in international politics that preceded Trumpism, with widespread ideology-unveiling attention to the historical precedents of Trumpism in national publications. SSA theory thus rejects the "exceptional" reading of Trump's rise to power, and of the resurgence of right-wing populism in a context of post-2008 recession institutional realignments and the rapid economic growth of US financial markets during Trump's term.

SSA's theoretical appeal lies partly in this intermediate level of structural analysis, not unlike Foucault's analysis of the "micro-physics of power,"[103] which simultaneously tracks macrostructural and microstructural levels through an intermediary sociostructural mechanism, such as institutions. It elides purely discursive accounts of power and cultural hegemony while still offering a broad genealogical story of how hegemonic forces gave rise to different stages of capitalism, how they continue to enact influence, and what the interlocking structural character of politics, ideology, the economy, and culture says about counterhegemonic possibilities today. However, SSA still operates under the kind of abstract contextualism that theories of social reproduction (Chapter 1) use to whitewash colonial violence from accounts of capital accumulation. By framing long-wave cycles in terms of self-repeating circuits and complex network relations of social reproduction, SSA provides an analogue for building a market model of capital accumulation that gives insights into the self-healing and regenerative nature of settler capital colonial accumulation of intergenerational wealth. In order to reframe SSA theory for the purposes of this project, three core problems with SSA theory must be addressed.

Three Core Problems

There are several problems with SSA theory. Not all progressive economists endorse it, and, among those who do, it is admittedly "insufficiently worked out," leaving important questions integral to macroeconomic theory unanswered.[104] But what does exist is still subject to specific problems. In this section I outline three problems that limit the usefulness of SSA theory for this project: the simultaneous affirmation and negation of race and gender, the structural discontinuity between successive SSAs, and the role of settler extractive accumulation processes. Although I've noted aspects of these problems above, I think it's worth pointing out that, despite these problems, SSA theory continues to enjoy a level of conceptual buy-in about the regenerative, profit-driven, historical, and adaptive features of capital accumulation that are generally not afforded to theories of white supremacy in settler capitalist societies. At minimum, there is a difference in the level of pushback, owing to the cultural status economics is afforded as a historically white discipline, and to its long history of using settler colonial epistemologies to underwrite methodology (such as orthodox western conceptual framing of value, measurement, social behavior, and variables related to econometric calculation and statistical pattern interpretation). There are important epistemic features of white supremacy involved in granting the self-adaptive features of SSA theory while withholding them for white dynastic formations. Within critical race and Indigenous feminisms, there are alternative frameworks for theorizing white supremacy in settler capitalist contexts that are far better suited for building a decolonial account of epistemic capitalism from the ground up and in relation to specific land-based contexts. The usefulness of SSA theory here is that it provides us with a clear and comparative account of what the whitewashed version of a self-repairing system looks like and how it generates a certain level of social uptake by design. I thus offer a provisional framing of market models of structural epistemic harms under the term "Epistemic Social Structures of Accumulation" to illustrate how epistemological systems in settler colonial societies can be designed and built to preserve colonial relations of power that automate impunity and facilitate indirect channels of wealth transfers for white settler populations and their descendants.

The Simultaneous Affirmation/Negation of Race and Gender

As an explanatory framework for economic forces rooted in noneconomic sociostructural dynamics, SSA theory does a poor job of illuminating the full scope and scale of historical dynamics that are central to settler colonial nation-building and its relation to capital accumulation. Take, for example, the role race and gender play in the set of intuitionists and ideological structures that make up an SSA.

Virtually all SSA theorists make at least a minimal nod to the importance of race and gender—indeed, this is a large part of the framework's broad theoretical appeal. Albelda and Tilly argue such nods are not sufficient to robustly theorize the regenerative power of successive SSAs in capitalist history.[105] They point to Gordon's problematic conceptual prioritization of social class in the framing of the US workforce, claiming that in defining the workforce "as a manufacturing workforce, and relegating agricultural labor, domestic service, unpaid housework, and the growing service sector to an unexplored periphery," a skewed picture of labor emerges.[106] They further argue that the experiences of women and people of color are "equally or perhaps even more important in providing the institutional base for capital accumulation."[107] They write:

> People of color, their families and communities disproportionately bear the burden of the accumulation regime's demise: the workforce and the population remain highly segmented by race.... But white workers—at least on average—are not only insulated from the worst of the economic impacts, they are most often physically removed from the carnage.[108]

This is particularly important since the descent phase of accumulation regimes tends to be downplayed in favor the rebuilding phase, creating yet another organized epistemic gap for the ways capital accumulation disproportionately impacts and relies on marginalized peoples throughout all stages of the SSA life cycle. Like critical race theory's double-edged critique of antidiscrimination law and the equal rights rhetoric that accompanies it (Chapter 1), the SSA framework incorporates and affirms the existence of racism and sexism while simultaneously negating their structural centrality. Furthermore, the SSA framework fails to offer intersectional analyses of the political environment (such as the institutional formations surrounding ableist racialized gendered labor and territorial dispossession in capital accumulation) that tracks these realities at scale.

SSA theorists have worked around the structured inattention to the centripetal role of intersecting oppressions by downplaying, ignoring, or naturalizing them, as well as by attributing transitive universal properties to them when abstracting the role of exploitation in the capital-labor relation. Christensen, for instance, attributes capitalists' use of institutionalized predation of labor on capitalists' economic need to avoid negative gross profit margins (by keeping production costs down, especially in industries with low profit margins or high production costs), or to maintain competitive advantages:

> To stay ahead of the competition and to maximize profits, businesses need to seek out the lowest-cost and highest-productivity labor. In many cases, particularly where technologies are primitive and profit margins slim, this will lead them to search for workers who are disempowered or marginalized in some way—by being gendered or racialized, by a lack of full civil rights or legal documentation, or in other ways that make them less able to organize and to resist exploitation.[109]

This account resembles the target of Marx's own critique of bourgeois capitalists' conviction that "capital is an eternal natural necessity." For Marx, capitalists produce elaborate cultural methods, from philosophical pamphleteering to educational reinforcement and outright mythmaking, to perpetuate the "nursery tale" of the natural existence of capitalism and its allegedly inevitable system of exploitative wage-labor. He writes:

> By confusing the appropriation of the labor process by capital with the labor process itself, the economists transform the material elements of the labor process into capital, simply because capital itself changes into the material elements of the labor process among other things . . . this illusion is one that springs from the nature of capitalist production itself. But it is evident even now that this is a very convenient method by which to demonstrate the eternal validity of the capitalist mode of production and to regard capital as an immutable natural element in human production as such.[110]

This naturalized approach to competitive (including absolute) advantage has notoriously been used to justify plantation economic systems, where seeking out a cheap, high-productivity labor force for a slim profit margin industry goes hand in hand with slavery and the active creation-recreation of new social categories for the exploitation of noneuropean labor.

Angela Davis, who is unpersuaded by the convergent nursery tales of capitalism and settler colonialism as natural necessities, describes the economic rationale of capitalist competitive advantage as a "double advantage" on two fronts. First, the myth of competitive advantage serves as cover for a supererogatory labor process where extra profits can be squeezed out of a targeted population through terror and violence. Second, so long as capitalists can maintain a brutally exploited group on the scale of slavery, it serves a structural ideological function by rechanneling "white workers' hostilities toward their employers" onto said targeted populations. In this way, "The colonization of the Southern economy by capitalists from the North gave lynching its most vigorous impulse. If Black people, by means of terror and violence, could remain the most brutally exploited group within the swelling ranks of the working class, the capitalists could enjoy a double advantage ... this was a critical moment in the popularization of racist ideology."[111]

Davis paints a powerful recharacterization of the causal relationship between capitalist economic systems and racist ideology as bidirectional and intersecting. This recharacterization is germane to SSA's emphasis on the political environment in shaping capital accumulation. However, analyses of race and gender in SSA theory tend to lack intersectional awareness and to rely on superexploitation treatments of race in the analysis of labor forces that drop convergent axes of exploitation from analytical purview. In doing so, they miss the theoretical and structural ramifications of gendered and racial economic disparities for reasons that are central to and inextricable from the recuperative power of capital accumulation rhythms.

The Structural Discontinuity between Successive SSAs

The lack of attunement to intersecting oppressions in SSA theory is reflected in its failure to identify structurally oppressive trends in the successive social structures of accumulation outside of the capital-labor relation, or to provide a robust account of the uniqueness of each successive SSA outside of settler epistemological framings of history, culture, time, and processive force.

To recall, SSA theorists are interested in explaining capitalism's regenerative and adaptive capacities, and why "abrupt structural change" is a recurring and predictive feature of capitalist long-swing dynamics. What drives or makes the recurrence systemic? And what is the relationship between the institutional transformations in one SSA from those of another? If it is place-specific responses to historical contingency, such as new technologies, the breakout of global wars, plagues, natural disasters, and the like, SSA theory has a lot more in common with neoclassical economic theory than it would like to admit. To address this issue, Kotz introduces a "core model" modification to SSA theory.[112]

The core view is a systems-based account that uses a developmental view of history. It goes something like this: a socioeconomic system exists that is characterized by the capitalist-accumulation-social relation (which guides the system output goal) and in which time is organized in progressive developmental units on a historical timescale. At a certain point in time, in response to system stressors, a "core set" of elements in the system reorganize in such a way that the function of the original relation is passed on in the reorganization. The stability generated by this functional invariance allows various subsystems affected by the reorganization, or by the original system stressors, to respond effectively with their own reorganizations that maintain the integrity of the system as an ordered whole. The transformations are not chaotic, and they occur through a clearly defined process: there are three developmental and evolutionary stages (building, consolidation, decline), and at the end of the last stage this process is repeated in toto in linearly progressive timescales for so long as the system exists and for as long as it has existed. The "core view" thus explains the adaptive transformation of a major subsystem in the social structure at a discreet point in time, and why such transformations can make the system appear different when its designed outputs remain the same.

While the SSA framework may appear dynamic and process-driven, the regenerative process in each SSA life cycle is ontologically secondary to the substances (institutions) that persist through evolutionary change (by consistently retaining function over form in transformations, though not dispensing with it in all cases) in capitalist history. Framed this way, it becomes clear that the SSA framework retains core evolutionary and metaphysical assumptions about the development of social structures that undermine the ability of SSA to offer a theoretical foundation for anticolonial praxis. Consider the identification (to date) of only three main social structures of accumulation since the 1800s! The notion of white dynastic formations takes this cyclical periodization much further back and track cycles of accumulation as they converge with western imperial expansion and colonial capitalism, joining with SSA theory on in its emphasis on the profit-by-design character of resurgent capital accumulation cycles. Furthermore, Kotz himself points to the failure of the core framework to determine "which institutions, from among those present at the start of a long-swing expansion, make up the core of the new and developing social structure of accumulation."[113] The theory of white dynastic formations posits white supremacy as an organizing principle for structural respecification of SSAs, suggesting that the kinds of institutions that are likely to form are those that support capital accumulation in relation to settler colonial and settler imperial relations of domination. To flesh out the critical problem of what motivates the regenerative process in SSAs, we turn to the role of settler extractive accumulation processes.

Settler Extractive Accumulation Processes
SSA theory is not sufficient to explain durable inequalities that are rooted in settler extractive accumulation processes that underwrite capitalist production. Extractive accumulation brings the analytic of "extractivism" to capital accumulation rhythms. "While racial capitalism refers to the process that historically subordinated African and Indigenous populations, extractivism references the dramatic material change to social and ecological life that underpin this arrangement."[114] Different ways of being, living, and relating to lands sustain different interpretive ecologies.

Interpretive ecologies, like physical ecosystems, actuate particular relations but not others based on constraints; as with the biochemical and environmental parameters for carbon-based lifeforms to emerge, limits are necessary for any social system to form specified interrelations. But how a system can self-organize into critical states through its various interrelations is not arbitrary; the modal context of historical inputs—the one in which europe colonized 80 percent of the world's territories through terror and structural violence—is key because it generates the interrelations necessary for some pathways to emerge but not others. And it is this pathway activity that creates epistemic mainlines to extractive interpretive domains sustained by settler colonial epistemologies.

Anglo-european interpretive ecologies situate nature as separate from humans, such that lands become natural resources and humans become human resources in market economies that require turning homelands into property—that require turning property into wealth that can be accumulated, transferred, and transacted in measured exchanges of monetized equivalence that reinforce the profound social inequalities necessary to maintain this pattern of settler colonial accumulation based on extracting and producing value from violence. A critical corrective to underlying assumptions in SSA theory that focuses on extractivism comes from Indigenous critique of settler colonial capital accumulation rhythms.[115]

In *Red Skin, White Masks*, Glen Sean Coulthard (Yellowknives Dene) provides a sweeping critique of Canadian liberal political discourses that offer affirmative recognition and institutional accommodation of Indigenous peoples, but which work to impede the self-determination and governance structures of First Nations peoples at the structural level. What's structural about the double move of recognition/effacement is that it strengthens a specific relation that characterizes the system of settler colonialism. Settler colonial extractivism normalizes resource exploitation in a way that continuously recenters dispossession of Native territories in neoliberal multicultural states like Canada (Chapter 5 applies this to the Mexican context and to gender-based violence). To illustrate some of the conceptual machinery at play in this politico-structural move, Coulthard turns to Marx's theory of primitive accumulation, modifying it by contextually shifting from the capital to the colonial relation. In so doing, he highlights how the settler colonial relationship structures ongoing dispossession in predictively recurring cycles of colonial domination and resistance that, unlike in Marx's original framing of primitive accumulation, is still very much alive today. Coulthard offers a framework that goes to the heart of SSA's theoretical puzzlement about the role of primitive accumulation in the resurgent long waves of capital accumulation rhythms: "There are obviously analogues between the assembling of the economic, political, and ideological conditions for the initiation of capitalist relations of production and the assembling of conditions for the rekindling of the capitalist accumulation process. Primitive accumulation, however, takes place within a social environment not dominated by capitalist relations of production. Primitive accumulation must be seen as a problem involved in the transition from one mode of production to another."[116] Coulthard, in line with racial capitalism literatures, demonstrates that, not only can "capitalist relations of production" not be disentangled from colonial relations of production, they are central to it.

One point of convergence with SSA theory is the idea that both capitalist and settler capitalist reproduction schemes are seen as responding to a previous challenge or crisis that informs the nature that the next reproduction scheme will take. For Coulthard, the rise of multicultural discourses that coincided with legal recognition of First Nations' historical treaty rights under Section 35(1) of the Constitution Act of 1982 are not marks of social progress. They are functional mechanisms for the structural reproduction of colonial relations via a new political modality. "The reconciliation of Indigenous nationhood with state sovereignty is still colonial insofar as it remains structurally committed to the dispossession of Indigenous peoples of our lands and self-determining authority."[117] They are weapons in disguise. Liberal views of self-conscious agency and political action based on reflective reason only strengthen colonial relations, as the best disguise is often one that is convincing enough that the wearer forgets it.

Hence, for Coulthard, whether one calls it "force, fraud," or, "more recently, so-called 'negotiations'" under alleged democratic processes, the result is functionally familiar to colonial governance: "ongoing state access to the land and resources." The change in modalities from classical colonial force to liberal negations manifested as coercive harm-reduction ploys in a zero-sum game of neocolonial gerrymandering and selective rights enforcement. Coulthard suggests this change was made necessary when white settler governance structures in Canada were faced with a kind of legitimation crisis during the unprecedented rise and politico-legal successes of the Red Power movement, pan-Indian mobilization, and Native activism in the 1960s and 1970s. Contrast this account with the SSA view, according to which it was the stratifying impact of the economic crisis of the 1970s on a vaguely defined (and implicitly white) labor force that led to breakdowns in existing capital-labor "social accords," forcing a reconstruction of a new institutional backdrop to restore previous conditions necessary for accumulation. For Coulthard, "Any strategy geared toward authentic colonization must directly confront more than mere economic relations; it has to account for the multifarious ways in which capitalism, patriarchy, white supremacy, and the totalizing character of state power interact with one another to form the constellation of power relations that sustain colonial patterns of behavior, structures, and relationships."[118] The irony is that SSA claims to place such an emphasis by pointing to the social world and the conceptual schemata that make oppressive social relations take hold in the political environment that capitalism relies on to reproduce itself.

A key advantage of Coulthard's framework over SSA theory is the ability to account for the transgenerational persistence of dispossessive features of social structures based on capitalism's convergence with white supremacy. Unlike the "core" approach that tracks continuity through well-defined sets of institutional entities in each new social structure of accumulation, Coulthard's framework posits the existence of a "dominant background structure," much like white dynastic formations, that persists through the various series of long-range economic cycles of settler capital accumulation that, for Coulthard, began with european colonial invasion and settlement: the settler colonial relation. This background structure is not immutable or a natural force; it is an "inherited background field within which market, racist, patriarchal and state relations converge to facilitate a certain power effect," as in a historical provenance that cultural inheritors reanimate because it is profitable to do so, not because it is inevitable.

For Coulthard, talking about capitalism's recuperative power without reference to capital accumulation's ongoing relationship to colonialism requires portraying capitalism's "original sin" of primitive accumulation as (1) done and over with, existing solely in some remote past, (2) a conceptual gap-filler in the modernist developmental story of how capitalism got its start, and (3) primarily concerned with the condition and expropriation of the worker's labor power. Coulthard rejects all three of these as "Eurocentric features" of Marx's "original historical metanarrative" and suggests that—lest one also declare, with Marx, that "Indian society has no history at all, at least no known history" or that capitalism will at least bring "backward" underdeveloped world regions into the folds of capitalist modernity—a framework shift to the colonial relation is necessary.

Consider race-neutral (i.e., implicitly white settler) accounts of economic systems that delink "investment in land" from the extractive project of settler colonialism. In her classic *Accumulation of Capital*, British economist Joan Robinson differentiates investments in land from investments in capital goods:

> Investment in opening up land (including mines, oilfields, etc.) is different in an important respect from investment in capital goods. The value of resources obtained bears no relation to the cost of the investment . . . when natural resources are involved, a small investment may yield a huge increase in productive capacity. Moreover, one investment of this kind creates a situation highly favorable to further investment, as when railway-building brings a new territory into touch with a market, and opens up prospects of profit in developing its resources. For this reason the relation between growth of populations and the available supply of land rarely follows a smooth course. At one time population is creeping up upon the available supply and land gradually growing more scarce. Then by some chance turn of history, or because the very scarcity of land has forced on development (transport, new crops), a huge area suddenly comes over the horizon of profitable exploitation and it is

labor to exploit it which has become scarce. This interaction of the maps and the chaps (together with the development of technique) is the chief subject-matter of economic history.[119]

This means, for instance, that the "Maya Train" intercity railway project is not a chance turn of history. The railway connects the Yucatan peninsula, home to western entertainment plantation resorts that dominate the local economy and bus in Indigenous labor, to extractive-rich and highly Indigenous zones in southwestern Mexico. The profit margins from extractives in colonial capitalism alone are powerful system drivers to reproduce the colonial relations required for racialized labor exploitation (mainstream economic analyses of land use, past and present, ignore the role that gender-based violence plays in shoring up the extractive infrastructure). Robinson continues:

> Political history also plays a part, in particular through the development of the colonies. New supplies of labor and of land may become available together. Entrepreneurs of one race, by fair means or foul, obtain the right to exploit territory already inhabited by another, and by fair means or foul, get the indigenous population to work for wages. An ingenious variant was the importation of slaves and indentured labour into sparsely inhabited territory, thus bringing the surplus labor of one part of the world together with the surplus land in another. Colonisation, in both forms, has been particularly important in enriching the industrial sector of capitalist economies with varieties of raw materials unobtainable in the territories where they grew up. To these large questions our formal analysis cannot make much contribution.[120]

Economists are well aware of the role the colonial relation plays, "by fair means or foul," in the accumulation of capital. Historically, that awareness is continuously framed through white innocence cloaks and economic narratives that naturalize colonial history. Coulthard's regenerative account of the role of primitive accumulation in settler colonial nation-building is key to interrupting whitewashed economic narratives. It also provides a critical corrective to core economic and historical assumptions in SSA theory, which is helpful for building a decolonial account of Epistemic Social Structures of Accumulation (ESSAs), to which we now turn.

Epistemic Social Structures of Accumulation

I find Coulthard's framing of a dominant background structure particularly useful for thinking about epistemic dynastic formations in relation to SSA theory and, particularly, for thinking about epistemic wealth in settler colonial societies. Epistemic dynastic formations are an anticolonial systems theory analogue for modeling the econo-epistemic relations in settler colonial capital accumulation rhythms that precede the historical dating schemas of industrial capitalism (the origin of which SSA theory places in the 1800s) and that reflect the long-wave anglo-european cultural investments in accumulating interpretive resources and regulating epistemic market economies for the preferential trading, equivalence-setting, and exchange of settler colonial knowledge resources. This in no way suggests that the scope and breadth of colonial oppressions are reducible to epistemic oppressions. It means that the recuperative power of settler colonial structural violence—the thing that ends up taking our lives "by fair means or foul" at the level of populations—has a broader arsenal of intergenerational and sociostructural weapons than is commonly suggested. And one of these critical parts of the arsenal is the intergenerational hoarding of interpretive resources that create and functionalize indirect wealth transfers among white settler populations, even when such populations endure class-based exploitation and oppression.

Social inequality attributed to intergenerational and/or in vivo wealth transfers is functionally supported by the prestructural accumulation and intergenerational maintenance of interpretive wealth, suggesting that intergenerational wealth in settler colonial societies is not just an economic structure, but a subsystem in a larger system of social processes that govern structural embedding, respecification, and the formation of potential structures in society, including those that regulate social reproduction. In past work, I've referred to features of hermeneutic violence (Ruíz 2020) and settler colonial structural epistemic oppressions in relation to hermeneutic intersectionality, a method I used in my work in women's antiviolence advocacy and organizing to focus on dismantling rhetorical strategies behind racist sexism in rape culture.[121] Here I take a more direct systems approach. Such an approach is represented in the mycelial network I discussed earlier—a network that reroutes resources and adapts elegantly to provide structural stability behind individual domain change. This idea has been modeled in social inequality research by the "wealth structure" of intergenerational wealth by race.[122] If we move toward thinking about wealth in terms of interpretive power, the picture of ESSAs and their role in upholding the interpretive ecologies of white dynastic formations begins to emerge.

Instead of a "core" of institutions generating macroeconomic stability (e.g., structural invariance with respect to capital accumulation) across SSAs, institutional equilibrium can be generated through the homeostatic role ESSAs play in the "inherited background field" Coulthard describes. To illustrate this, I will need to offer a complex-systems framing of this "dominant" basic structure that facilitates "a certain power effect" relative to settler colonial relations of domination. For this, it's helpful to discuss a few things about how I frame complexity (as systems theory narrowly interprets complexity through its occurrence in physical systems), how I frame accumulation, and the relation between the economic and the epistemic.

A Word on System Complexity

Dynastic systems based on white supremacy are systems, above all. And they are complex. That complexity is at the heart of this chapter. The tricky thing about complexity in social systems is that complexity can have multiple modes of expression that each appear to be in contrast with one another. At one scale of a complex system, things look very simply related and distinct, like two endpoints connected by a string. At another scale, an oscillating hierarchy of interconnected webs can appear that requires graph-theoretical innovations to analyze, like the mycelial and mycorrhizal networks of forests. I think racial capitalism works like this. At one scale it appears simple: its immediate impact is felt and distinct, like the gut punch of segregated housing, police violence, and lending discrimination in communities of color. At another, it's connected to multiple timescales and moving forces that are not directly felt, like the economic engines of plantation systems, the evolving global infrastructures of capital gain from extractives, and the worldwide exploitation of racialized labor. Both scales are cofunctional. Their respective impact may certainly differ depending on what land-based context we're talking about. But generally, we tend to lean toward the simpler scale of systems explanations to connect the intricacies of our life experiences of harm and discrimination to a deeper cause—to something that might explain why our go-to solutions keep coming up short against systemic racism and social inequality.

Leaning toward the micro scale isn't wrong—this point is really important. It tells us a lot about the stakes involved: bodies, lives, specific lands and lived experiences. And the closer in you go (as in zooming in through a lens), the more complex things can get as well. The language resources and metaphysical assumptions underwriting language matter a great deal too. The substance ontologies and linear logics permeating subject-predicate grammars in settler european languages (traced to the concocted "Indo-european" mythography used to spread whiteness over Asia by denoting ethnic affiliative belonging through language family resemblance) are simply unsuited to capture braided complexity and reciprocal affiliative attachments among humans and the lands that bore us into being. As the Zapatista's Subcomandante Galeano (2015) put it, and I invoked in the introduction, "Our banners are tirelessly elaborate, struggling to find equivalents for what we in our languages describe in just one word, and what in other languages requires three volumes of Capital."

Overall, we tend to focus less on system-level ordering and macroscopic complexity when talking about persistent social inequalities, and more on the connections between our immediate lives and some larger background force or forces. Paradoxically (by design, of course), what's dynastic about white settler social structures, and their functional connection to systemic violence, is more readily trackable in connection with the macro scale. The dichotomy between the macro and the micro is no accident. Without this dichotomy, structural violence in settler capitalist states could not appear as an "amorphous and nonspecific 'power'" that is disconnected from the concrete and multilayered harms inflicted on marginalized peoples in specific lands and through specific architectures of violence.[123] Such nonspecific power feels very real—in fact, the most real—at the smaller scales, but when one reaches for it to fight it, a host of adaptive and self-repairing processes of mystification in administrative economies begin to take hold.

To counter the adaptive processes that keep the sources of structural violence beyond the reach of our protests and activism, we must engage in work that traces the patterns, connects the logics, and reattaches the strings at the land-based level of felt epistemologies.[124] This work is so important and often so difficult to do. Grounded normativity, as Leanne Simpson (Michi Saagiig Nishnaabeg) so movingly demonstrates, can capture the macro-level complexity of systemic violence to Indigenous communities through epistemologies based on relational logics of deep reciprocal and consensual attachment to lands. The rivers tell the story, as do the waterways, airways, and lands, which are not separate from humans. Consider the way Lee Maracle (Salish) captures salient causal relationships between extractive colonialism and gender-based violence: "Salmon and humans are not separate," Maracle writes. "The last time the salmon did not run upstream was connected to violence against women."[125] In the 1980s, Mayan Q'anjob'al, K'iche', and Chuj communities likewise sounded the alarm on the changing landscapes brought on by deforestation of the Ixil triangle, and the cultural genocide this environmental catastrophe heralded, long before Efrain Ríos Montt's "scorched earth" strategy resulted in genocide and mass rape of Indigenous women. When the birds began disappearing, a bloodied future was ensured.

It is only settler epistemic economies that separate land from language as a starting point for the commercial exchange of political theorizing and concept formation surrounding justice, injustice, and human rights. They do this in order to possess the land, sell it, profit from it, or restore it to "rightful owners" on settler epistemic terms that require settler evidentiary standards to be met, and through reference to settler political categories that pave the way for future reoccupation of rematriated lands. The past devours the future—that part Piketty got right. But whose future the past devours, and whose it preserves and advances, matters. It matters because there is an inherent design to this mattering-to-whom and mattering-as-what that functions as an economic system that helps uphold white norms over long periods of time. "Racism today, racism tomorrow, racism forever," remember?[126] That requires intergenerational networks of controlled succession that can initiate structurally invariant macro-level cycles of "preservation-through-transformation" (as SSA theory holds).[127]

Suffice it to say, historically oppressed people are not clueless as to the existence of macro-level complexity or how complex violence operates in our lives at various scales. It's just that, more often than not, we tend to explain this complexity by building a mental drawbridge that connects the micro and macro scales because this is how settler colonial societies arrange the power grid of conceptual options—end to end with a trench in between. We use this bridge to help us grapple with the past and retain receipts, to travel back into history to expand our understanding and perspective on systemic racism, even if the understanding gleaned from this interscale work operates within the shifting bounds of the mental habits nurtured by the structurally unjust worlds we inhabit.

This interscale mental work, even when done within the bounds described, can be empowering and transformative at the personal level. For one thing, it helps to connect the reality of our lives as they are, under the dizzying pressures of intersecting oppressions, and the vast backdrop of social history that seems to nebulously haunt our present. The Pulitzer Prize–winning 1619 project, which reframes American history and race relations around the date (August 1619) that the first slave ship—the English-chartered Dutch ship *White Lion*—reached US shores, begins like this: "History revealed the building blocks of the world I now inhabited, explaining how communities, institutions, relationships came to be. Learning history made the world make sense. It provided the key to decode all that I saw around me . . . I understood that the absence of 1619 from mainstream history was intentional."[128] At a time when authoritarian governors are requiring universities to "provide a comprehensive list of all staff, programs and campus activities related to diversity, equity and inclusion" and adapting Red Scare tactics of the 1950s to target people of color and LGBTQ and gender-nonconforming communities, periodizing settler white supremacy to distinct events in the seventeenth century that establish persistent intergenerational patterns of ill-gotten gain and historical commitments to whitewashing and discrimination is an important critical thinking and organizing tool. I remain committed to the usefulness of this approach while offering insights into other pathways by which, despite our ability to retain receipts from history, white supremacy's ends are achieved.

Thus, with the notion of epistemic capitalism, I want to begin even further back. Not just timewise (although I do go much farther back than 1619), but in terms of the depth and functional nature of the broader epistemic backdrop that informs how racial systems operate as successfully dynastic economic engines. And I want to expand further out to meta-macroeconomic forces that help underwrite oppression over long timescales and at different scales of interaction and invariance. There are several reasons why I think this is useful.

First, racial capitalism is a broader sociostructural phenomenon than is often described in racial capitalism literatures. Rather than examining the individual components of the production of racial difference and the production of capital in isolation, racial capitalism literatures examine the complex interactions between social, economic, and historical structures that coproduce racial and economic phenomena as part of a coherent social system of exploitation for profit. And they do so from a rich variety of perspectives that often retain system-level analyses of recurring loops, alerting us to the existence of recursive patterns in our social environment.

Recursive patterns are those that signal the continuation of stratifying social forces, cycles, and relations of structural inequality that are self-reinforcing despite policy initiatives and other official interventions that effect change, like legal-precedent-affirming civil rights protections of minority populations. In this way, racial capitalism literatures share a great deal with critical race theory (CRT) and critical legal studies frameworks that detail how antidiscrimination law "learned to live with" racial inequality by design.[129] It's a useful antigaslighting reframe of a powerful structural tool already in our arsenal, one that happens to have a lot in common with the anticolonial systems theory framework discussed in our first chapter.

Second, at a practical level, a racial-capitalism approach makes clear at a system level that the current wave of civil rights retrenchments sweeping the United States are nonaccidental, and it draws out some of the more complex features of this intentional design. For instance, it links the effects of the current Republican rage outbursts over CRT, such as the rise of prohibited and "divisive concepts" legislation sweeping the United States, with the global uptick in authoritarianism and violence against minority populations. These things are not linked linearly, endpoint to endpoint, but are rather linked within a larger system-context of the broader forces and interrelations that are always at play in settler colonial wealth regeneration, including forces tied to racial and sexual violence.

Last, at a theoretical level, this approach illustrates the profit-by-design character of white dynastic formations. As complex social systems, white dynastic formations operate at multiple scales of dynamic complexity and, as systems, they must have goals to function properly. To recall, two of the most important things about systems are their adaptive functions and their purposive design. The adaptive capacities of settler colonial systems are very closely tied to capital production.

We find examples of the adaptive development capacities of economic subsystems in lots of places, of course. In the CRT context, there is the well-known adaptation of racialized servitude to abolitionist legislation, as evident in the rise of the insured slave policy industry and slave rental trade following the slave market interruptions of 1808, when the Act Prohibiting the Importation of Slaves took effect. (Consider that the famed New York Life Insurance company provided the underwriting of over five hundred slave insurance policies.) In the prison abolitionist and prison-industrial complex context, we consider the rise of prison labor systems and the privatization of jailing in the United States in proportion to increased market access and improved economic labor conditions for people of color following the civil rights movement and federal oversight of labor discrimination practices at the state level. In the reproductive rights and survivors' movement context, we find the rise of cultural empowerment of survivors of sexual assault met with unprecedented rollbacks in abortion access and implementation of policies that economically burden and target survivors of sexual violence. These last two contexts are mutually reinforcing, with jailed and detained pregnant people facing extraordinary levels of hardship and criminalization as a result of their rape, especially for disabled, Indigenous, transgender, queer, and gender-nonconforming people of color. Our last chapter will explore the adaptive capacities of settler colonial social systems further through the idea of structural trauma.

Here I focus on the "system goal" part of white dynastic social systems. Understanding what "profit by design" (as a goal) means in relation to settler colonial social systems can help unpack how racial systems operate as successfully dynastic economic engines that are designed to be impervious to fundamental systems-level change. The focus is on the larger sociostructural economic picture that illustrates how a coherent dynastic system of social organization that uses adaptive mechanisms to fortify itself against fundamental system change can work through profit-driven economic systems that uphold racial difference and sexual violence in complex ways.

Economic markets are a key part of this story, because they have inherent social ties that allow them to work in tandem with the social structures and institutional infrastructures that support the greater system goals of a social formation. This chapter argues that working in tandem cannot be done without important system-generated epistemic shiftwork as a complex feature of the overall socioeconomic system. My approach stems from a structural epistemological orientation to basic insights in Latin America economic theory developed in the 1940s about what sustains asymmetric terms of exchange between global powers and poor nations.[130] It has a specific focus on how structural relations of violence become enabled through the economic-epistemic infrastructure of white dynastic formations. I thus use the notion of epistemic capitalism to illustrate this goal-oriented complexity that precedes and follows 1619, but also to emphasize the predictability of what comes next that arises from knowing what a system is set up to do, and how it is set up to do it (e.g., with impunity).

Accumulation in Context

I use the notion of accumulation in an economic context that denotes a wealth-generating process regulated by standards of exchange (e.g., value-setting in a commodities market) that are upheld by social relations in so-called advanced industrial (or free market) economies. I then apply Coulthard's "colonial relation" versus "capital relation" distinction to accumulation, reframing the standards of exchange and the sustaining social relations through settler colonial relations in white dynastic formations.

Specifying the parameters of accumulation being studied is important; depending on the interpretive ecology at play, not all accumulation is tied to commodity exchange markets, or to wealth's cumulative nature in settler capitalist societies. But in settler colonial societies, as wealth-generating processes are distinguished from income-generating processes, accumulation takes on a very specific structural formation. As anyone who has had to work in an informal economy knows, accumulated income can exist outside of classical determinants of wealth. The life course outcomes for those who hustled all their lives in a cash economy to accumulate a small amount of "wealth" can be very different from the outcomes for someone with the same income generated from interest payments on investment returns from inherited wealth.[131] In settler colonial societies, the sociostructural regulative forces associated with the income-wealth association are often mystified. Just as wealth begets wealth and hides it, epistemic wealth functions in similar patterns and dynamics, as we'll discuss shortly.

As a methodological point, I think bridging epistemology and economics is a more helpful analytic for understanding structural injustice in settler colonial societies than bridging epistemology and ethics (the default approach in philosophy nowadays). The language of economic systems is particularly useful because it is already in circulation across various racial-justice advocacy frameworks and intervention-based responses to social inequality, and (particularly germane to my project) because it uses various complex-system language analogues.

This includes language that describes patterns of behavior that appear to be inconsistent, but which are actually consistent at different scales of analysis (like a downward econometric trend considered over a much longer period of economic equilibrium). The language of economic systems is also especially good at conceptualizing and providing a modeling image of network interconnections and relationships between seemingly unrelated forces. By emphasizing this network framing, we can more easily show how economies act as dynamic organizing networks, which orient system goals in ways that critically shape the functions of subsystems (like institutional arrangements) and guide their adaptive development through social and political flux. Since settler colonial wealth regeneration hinges on a well-oiled system that has an orienting goal and adaptive developmental capacities, it is important to understand these features.

The macroscopic complexity and structural epistemology approach to accumulation used in this chapter helps to illustrate some of the connective tissue between economies of exploitation that rely on primary violences of physical and mental extension in settler colonial societies, and paraprimary violences. Paraprimary violences like hermeneutic violence (Chapter 4) work to reproduce and uphold harm prestructurally by supporting an interpretive ecosystem hospitable to white dynastic formations, and by supporting the relevant conceptions of harm and violence necessary to obscure settler colonial violence, or to portray it as accidental. Both scales of primary and paraprimary violence are cofunctional, but again, we lean toward the more familiar one (primary) to describe the true hellscape of exploitation and diminished life chances that await some populations at birth—and before birth, as free and uncoerced births become even less of an option.

To track the organizing principles of interpretation in systems of domination rooted in settler colonial social formations, it is critical to consider the historical systems goals of dispossession and wealth accumulation. As the last chapter demonstrated, tightly controlling the association between violence and credibility has epistemic currency: population-level payoffs and long-run patterns of accumulation hinge on the ability to regulate this association. Daphne's and Maria's cases, as well as the examples offered at the beginning of this chapter, illustrate the structurally invariant profile of white dynastic formations, especially as epistemic polities that govern the distribution of harm in settler colonial societies. They illustrate how, no matter the situation, a supervening analysis of events can always be rendered from well-curated public resources of meaning that will carry the strongest weight of "truth" in the social institutions and cultural systems built in tandem with these resources. What's critical for my project is that *accumulation* refers not simply to the quantification of an individual's generated income in a colonial capitalist labor relation but to a systems process of infrastructural wealth regeneration in settler colonial market economies.

Epistemic Currency and Exchange Networks

The network framing of epistemic currency offered in this chapter has practical implications. For instance, during the 2022 US midterm elections, MSNBC senior reporter Ben Collins suggested the increasing political violence from the Right "comes from this much larger mythmaking apparatus that exists walled off from the rest of society," referring to social media networks and informal channels propagating election denial narratives of the 2020 presidential election.[132] This externalist and exceptionalist framing of mythmaking is common. It portrays violent conservative rhetoric and white supremacist ideology as an aberration, a fringe sociological phenomenon that is not inherent in the culture but "out there" gaining increasing traction (to the point that it is now "common") with disaffected voters and economically disenfranchised populations who feel historically entitled to economic security or to the economic benefits of whiteness. The usual suggestion is that a change in economic circumstance and/or educational outreach efforts (including media literacy education, content moderation regulation, and stopgaps for foreign meddling in elections) can help alleviate the extremism associated with disinformation. By contrast, a network framing of epistemic currency reconstrues the exceptionalist narrative of far-right extremism as a routine result of normal system operations. It relinks the mythmaking apparatus to "the rest of society" so that the predictable and well-oiled sociostructural reinforcement mechanisms and delivery pathways for settler colonial white supremacy come into focus when examining the apparatus in question. There's nothing "ill-functioning" about this; in a systems framing, it's just business as usual in settler epistemic economies. Not only is disinformation a concerted political strategy (particularly on issues of tax enforcement), it has incontrovertible political currency that requires a supporting infrastructure of interpretive resources that are nonaccidental and have been curated over time to make such disinformation appear normal, routine, and potentially profitable.

Disinformation bears family resemblance to the shifting epistemic standards, evidentiary burdens, and narrative justifications that shapeshift to accommodate the system goals of settler colonial societies. It also manifests as a highly professionalized strategy in tort litigation mediation and administrative responses to employer misconduct allegations, in which the production of argumentative and evidentiary red herrings is common. Survivors who file sexual assault or sexual harassment complaints (especially against public entities that require prior clearance and internal investigations to file suit) often become victims of administrative violence and secondary traumas rooted in disinformation tactics. When reading the summary decisions of internal investigations, many survivors find that they are found credible or not credible with respect to something they never alleged (be it something tangential to or closely related to the actual claim)—and this is often entered into the official/legal record of what occurred—with the effect of either diminishing their credibility with respect to their actual claims or generating the appearance of fairness and impartiality by the investigating body (which carries epistemic currency when the report is transferred to the next link in the investigative process). So there's nothing exceptional about disinformation and the planting of distorted narratives; it's an epistemic tool tied to economic features in settler colonial societies that, because of its effectiveness, is finding new domains of application and wider adaptive ranges. The advent of new technologies like social media can help accelerate the functional domain shift of disinformation's use, but they do not originate it.

Social structures, like the economic engines of society, require fuel to function as dynamic systems of complex linear and nonlinear relationships that work together to produce the consistent social patterns we experience as a social world. Epistemologies are an important component of this dynamic picture of social structures because they help determine the kinds of things that can be used as fuel, at least efficiently and effectively. They help determine which institutional channels are activated and which are suppressed to produce a desired system output with the energy source given, and they help sustain a structure in real time by filtering out possible ways a fuel type can lead to internal combustion from incompatibility, like the design of catalytic converters in cars. But unlike catalytic converters and machine models of complex systems, epistemologies are not reducible to the preconditions set out through the specifications of its design, at least not in way that can be captured by linear causal relationships.

We can think of them instead as balancing feedback loops that work in tandem with the various elements (people, lands, environments, social practices, and languages) of a social system to regulate the functioning of stock and flows of meaning and intelligibility toward specific system ends (i.e., Systems Thinking 101). But they are not causally anterior conceptual blueprints for the general success of meaning, salience, and intelligibility— the whole is required for the part to work in real time, and across human, animal, physical and nonphysical systems. That is the dynamic gearwork of a "social relation." Unlike a static force model, this deeply integrative and dynamic way of looking at social systems and the relations they support is based on a notion of systems design that recognizes a constant flowing and changing in response to network flows and inputs. Such a picture also incorporates a logical design architecture of systems based on their context (the modal kind advanced in Chapter 1). It illustrates how intergenerational control over lands can generate epistemological ecosystems that support settler colonial capital accumulation rhythms over long cycles. This is why I think it's a useful framing of Coulthard's "inherited background field" against which the social relations characterized by settler colonial power effects arise. It frames the background field as a living system, in which self-organized criticality (in relation to settler colonial social emergence) arises and produces emergent phenomena that reinforce settler white supremacy over very long periods of time.

Such structural invariance is at the heart of epistemic SSAs (ESSAs), the growth-promoting network of intergenerational interpretive resources that accumulate as epistemic wealth in white dynastic formations (through epistemic capitalism). Since an epistemological dimension is missing in the SSA account of long-term accumulation and capitalist resurgence cycles, SSA's methodology misses the possibility that it is also itself implicated in the generative dynamics of the settler colonial external environment.

In SSA theory, the external environment promotes the ascendancy and successive rebirth of growth-promoting institutions by regulating the social, economic, and ideological environmental conditions necessary to support accumulation. It's a macrostructural approach to classical Marxist thinking about ideology that highlights the close interrelation between the economic and the epistemic in social structures—the ones that did develop historically, not theoretical or ideal ones hypothesized by neoclassical economics. By situating SSAs within a network framing of an "inherited background field"[133] of settler colonial relations generated over very long cycles of white dynastic formations, it becomes easier to notice the role of ESSAs in structuring the ascent phase and regenerative SSA cycles since the rise of greco-roman institutional slavery, through Alexandrian expansionism, merchant capitalism, and colonial capitalist cycles of accumulation, to modern-day neoliberal racism.

Accumulation that is based on material dispossession, extraction, and the epistemic production of innocence cloaks is historically rooted in the dynastic nature of settler reproduction schemes and the orienting system goals of profit generation and wealth concentration for settler white polities and their descendants. The notion of "epistemic capitalism" thus begins with a very strong emphasis on system interconnectedness and the obstacles that exist to talk about economic systems as inseparable from the social structures—and their rootedness in dynastic white supremacy—that produce them, in and through which they operate as nontheoretical systems in our lives.

In the ESSA context, accumulating interpretive resources requires a systems model that is connected to economic outcomes in settler colonial societies. For instance, there are basic growth dynamics of intergenerational wealth applied to the epistemic component of ESSAs; think of New Deal opportunities like the GI Bill that offered tremendous wealth accumulation to white veterans through home loans. As with primitive accumulation founded on the settler colonial relation, where original land theft and stolen labor constitute the intergenerational production of American wealth, the settler colonial relation grounds ESSAs through (1) the extended etiology of settler colonial relations in antiquity (refer to the notion of "proto-racism" in Chapter 1) and (2) the distributive design of how wealth-generating resources are transferred to reinforce intersectional oppressions in race-based income inequalities (e.g., in the adaptive and domain-shifting handoff from one ESSA to another). Interpretive value thus accrues like a game of Telephone spreading through a web (where the nodal connections are not "natural" but must be intergenerationally maintained). What allows such value to be turned into wealth is not the epistemic prosperity of individuals with proximity to settler whiteness in this social web, but the institutional equilibrium ESSAs provide that results in a "stable external environment" for settler capital investment and capital production schemes. They are what restores tacit "confidence" in the structural integrity of a settler market economy undergoing individual market disruptions to continue routing wealth to some populations and precarity to others in the long term (which may require domain shifts in investment strategies, which ESSAs also provide insights to—where to place one's bets and invest in infrastructures of destruction).

A basic idea in this book is that accumulating such resources also requires suppressing and doing violence to Indigenous interpretive ecologies (as our next chapter illustrates). Thereupon, "by fair means or foul," but more precisely, through the adaptive and homeostatic processes of white dynastic settler colonial social regeneration schemes built on structural violence, the effects of the inequality $r > g$ on the reproduction of epistemic wealth can be observed. As Piketty notes, "The inequality r > g implies that wealth accumulated in the past grows more rapidly than output and wages.... Once constituted, capital reproduces itself faster than output increases. The past devours the future."[134]

Comparably, once they are established through the structural epistemic violence of white dynastic formations, epistemic capital and the intergenerational hoarding of interpretive wealth begin to grow and accumulate at a pace that reproduces ongoing inequality, generation after generation. First, a profit rate begins to wield infrastructural returns through a process dependent on the growth and fortification of institutional administrative structures like white dynastic legal systems. Then epistemic capital can enter into circulation at various scales and becomes a resource for increasing white dynastic intergenerational wealth. Such capital can be traded, exchanged, and most importantly, accumulated in a growth-promoting network of intergenerational interpretive resources (i.e., ESSAs) that help white dynastic formations self-heal, adapt, and recover.[135] Institutional disequilibrium brought on by microeconomic instability (such as those set off by labor struggles and progressive social demands) draws on the inherited backdrop of ESSAs—which have equivalent annual costs that exceed rhetorical expenditures in maintaining settler white supremacy—to reorganize and stabilize a favorable external environment for new settler capital regeneration pathways to emerge in the next transference phase of settler colonial social regeneration. An old ESSA (e.g., one that produces color-evasive multicultural racism) is replaced by another (e.g., the ESSA that backgrounds the rise of neoliberal racism). This transference chain continues with growth-decay-transformation cycles that maintain macrostabilizing regularity over long periods of time. The long game of colonialism thus ensures that, in the knowledge economies reproduced through white dynastic formations, the white dynastic past is designed to devour the future of people of color and Indigenous peoples.[136]

There's an economy to the lettered city[137] rooted in imperial settlement and colonial expansionism that predates classical dating schemes of colonial capitalism in racial capitalism literatures. Epistemic capitalism thus reframes the long durée of successive SSAs within the broader white dynastic accumulation rhythms that began in antiquity and the greco-roman slave trade, highlighting the profit-by-design character of white dynastic formations that organizes critical states into the necessary pathways for adaptive transformations and system resilience throughout its various lifecycles.

A critical insight from epistemic capitalism is that social reproduction is not a universally abstractable phenomenon, nor predictive of universal exploitative arrangements throughout all cultures (Chapter 1). "Abstraction" is a term often used in social theory to distinguish theoretical and concrete operations of exploitative social arrangements. (It's not an easy term to use here because of its close connection to Marx.) Abstraction also describes in-built processes and logical procedures that generate the very sense of explanatory ease in a knowledge economy that produces extractivist, use-model, consumptive, and resource-based outputs. In systems theory it is also used to refer to the difference between the modeling and implementation of a system feature or relation—for example, whether a structure is "concrete" or "abstract."

As it is generally used, "abstraction" creates the illusion of context by naturalizing or universalizing principles of thought. Paradoxically, it also makes it easier to describe the individual elements of a system than the interconnections that uphold it. That's not an accident. Interconnections in dynamic systems come into focus most often when uncertain system behavior is at play and the management of dynamic uncertainties must be foregrounded. If you experience a world grounded in stability, where the fulfillment of the expectation of meaning is not questioned because it is infrastructurally supported by a world that has been built to confirm it, chances are that you're going to look to elements of a system to generate explanations that "make sense" rather than to the tight web of mycelial connections that work in sophisticated and complex ways to militate against your very sense of reality, knowledge, and experience.

But if you take away an element of the system, it impacts the relations among the ones that remain (some more than others, as Chapter 1 discussed). This is why a social structure is not blameless or faultless in producing meaning that supports a system goal; cultural preservation and social regeneration require intergenerational commitments and population-level choices that reinforce some interrelations more than others for specific ends and goals, and to the curation of some elements more than others. Within abstraction-based epistemic systems, it is difficult to identify and point to epistemological networks, cosmovisions, and organizations of knowledge that differ from the dominant network flows recognized by the system's architecture without devaluing them as derivative, useless, illogical, mystical, or simply anomalous. This insight is a long-existing part of communal knowledge and Indigenous scholarship on how colonial reality is created and sustained.

The economic approach to knowledge networks presented here requires a dynamic view of settler colonial social structures and processes as active, ongoing, and characterized by flexile durability. In its most basic form, it is an anticolonial systems approach to basic insights in racial capitalisms about the shapeshifting properties of colonial knowledge regimes, as in the idea that "the emergence of a capitalist economy that was based on the exploitation of colonies required new forms of knowledge."[138] I highlight the economic transference chains and permutations in valuation linked with the interpretive dimensions of social knowledge—or how concepts and socially legible practices come to have worldly valence and epistemic currency that can be exchanged under certain terms and conditions for profit or gain.

The safeguarding of settler colonial futures to continue replicating them is what the notion of white dynastic formations expresses with respect to an epistemic economy. As noted, once constituted, epistemic capital reproduces itself faster than output increases. In the short term, the house may incur temporary losses, but statistically over the long range it wins because it is designed to do so, not because of some mysterious property of statistical averages. Its design provides flexibility in an oppressive system by formulating operations and relations that are able to undergo implementation and adaptation, which are sustained by concrete historical relations of colonial violence and administrative infrastructures of settlement and occupation.

Race is an output, not an input of white dynastic formations, but a basic stocks-and-flows chart of a dynamic system shows how outputs easily come back into play as inputs. White dynastic supremacy is designed to always win in the long term—to set up ever-renewing economic channels of commercial exchange that revolutionize profitable pathways for white settler wealth accumulation and intergenerational transmission of lucrative epistemic resources. Why? Profit. Power. Wealth. The Zapatistas have been saying this for decades, and with specific platforms for alternative worldmaking, as Chapter 5 illustrates.

Just because something has a design architecture does not mean it is fate. It means that we must have a plan of counterattack that matches the titanic force and pace of accumulated settler wealth in all its forms and for its structured strategies of counterrevolutionary adaptation. It's time to run some offense. And one of the insights from liberation struggles in Latin America is that, when running an offense, it's important to incorporate into your plan the anticipated defensive strategies and offensive weaknesses of the other side, and to craft strategies that support the effective execution of your game plan in real time. Our advocacy strategies should reflect this as activists and researchers.[139]

In telling the story of epistemic capitalism and white dynastic formations it is easy to forget that it is a story—a heuristic for unraveling the history and inner logic of settler futurity along our global tour of colonial nonsense that so many of us must endure, for no other reason than because of the vast interpretive architectures and administrative realties that colonialism instituted.

But stories have power. And the most powerful stories are often those that have lost their resonance as intergenerationally woven tapestries with collective purpose, operating simply as the way of the world and the authority of the word. So we must press on with a picture to present, a design to lay bare like an index finger tracing a faint constellation in the night sky. There is a pattern to structural violence that links profit, knowledge, and harm.

In a changing demographic picture quickly moving toward minority-majority districts in the United States, where racial minorities comprise the majority of a district's population, epistemic capitalism is a key way settler colonialism is prepared to survive the social transformations and challenges it faces in the twenty-first century. It is also how settler colonial white supremacy has maintained a stronghold in Latin America since the wars of independence. What is key for me is the structural nature and relation of capital to a wider econo-epistemic network of concepts and practices that functionalize impunity and gaslights entire populations about "the way things are" to evade cultural responsibility for propagating long-term conditions of structural harm and avoid having to pay reparations for it or engage in structural resource transfers. And this work of impunitycraft is carried out through the ongoing intergenerational work of consolidating interpretive power by white settler epistemic polities to produce and maintain intergenerational channels of wealth transference for some populations but not others. Knowledge in settler colonial societies is always for profit.

No one gets free with ideology-unveiling alone, though we may find a moment of peace in it. Our next chapter turns to structural accounts of cultural gaslighting to show why, even with the case laid out and the settler-supremacist innocence narrative stripped of its efficacy, we cannot let up, not yet.

4
Structural Violence Is *by Design*
Cultural Gaslighting

> To be an Indigenous woman in this country is to intimately understand both interpersonal and systemic gaslighting.
> —Emily Riddle (nehiyaw iskwew)

Introduction

The term "gaslighting" comes from the title of a 1944 film adaptation of Patrick Hamilton's 1938 play, which portrays the manipulative attempts of a jewel thief to take possession of his wife's riches through a wide range of acts designed to pathologize her as insane, including lies, isolation, doubletalk, and duplicitously restaging household objects. It gained popularity in anglo-american psychology throughout the 1980s and 1990s as a popular-culture heuristic for addressing emotional abuse sustained in intimate partnerships.[1] This framing bracketed out the film's original references to the physical violence (the murder of his wife's aunt) required for the gaslighter to gain access to his wife's home and the specific power relation to her psychic life as her husband. Isolated from its structural connection to other forms of violence, gaslighting came to be known as an interpersonal abuse mechanism or pressure tactic that allows abusers to get inside the head of their intended victims for the purposes of asserting power and/or establishing control.[2] The term continues to have this distinctly mentalistic and interpersonal meaning in modern colloquial usage and in psychology, where it is defined as "the effort of one person to undermine another person's confidence and stability by causing the victim to doubt [their] own sense and beliefs."[3]

I argue gaslighting is a structural phenomenon that upholds interpersonal and institutional modes of mental abuse in settler colonial societies; it is not merely a generalized human trait of psychological susceptibility. Rather, it is a technique of violence that produces asymmetric harms for different populations depending on one's processive relation to/within settler social structures. To show this, I take a social epidemiological approach that focuses on population-wide health inequities alongside Indigenous perspectives on health, self-determination, and colonial violence.[4] I employ anticolonial perspectives on population health inequity that shift the momentum away from probabilistic accounts of life chances (as socially structured for all humans) to more coordinated views of social inequity based on nonaccidental maldistribution of harm.[5] On this view, at its broadest level, gaslighting is a way of curating modalities of resistance to settler colonial cultures for the purposes of consolidating the colonial project of Indigenous land dispossession and cultural genocide of non-euro-atlantic peoples: at its narrowest, an arrowed aim at the inner life of experiences of settler violence. On both accounts, it enacts violence, not moral evaluative accounts *of* violence as an epistemic phenomenon.

Because keeping oppressed peoples in the dark about the social formation of psychological toolkits for understanding violence is a cultural counterrevolutionary strategy designed to manipulate social understanding of colonial violence and its structural prevalence, the greatest success of the gaslighting paradigm is that it provides cover for the structural dimensions of gaslighting. This idea will be examined through the notion of settler innocence narratives[6] and the political demands decoding these projects makes on people living in what is commonly referred to, following the 1848 secession of over half a million square miles on the southwestern border, as "US territory." Focusing on the structural *functionalization* of settler moves to innocence, I argue there is nothing accidental about the popularization of the narrowed psychological understanding of gaslighting as interpersonal emotional abuse. For example, in a 2017 *Psychology Today* article the following list was provided as a diagnostic for gaslighting:

> 1) They tell blatant lies 2) they deny they ever said something, even though you have proof 3) they use what is near and dear to you as ammunition 4) they wear you down over time 5) their actions do not match their words 6) they throw in positive reinforcement to confuse you 7) they know confusion weakens people 8) they project 9) they try to align people against you 10) they tell you or others that you are crazy 11) they tell you everyone else is a liar.[7]

Settler colonial culture does, in fact, tell blatant lies, deny in the face of proof, use the near and dear against you, wear you down over time ... At face value, the notion of gaslighting can all too easily be used as a diagnostic tool to refer to "the effort of one *culture* to undermine another *culture's* confidence and stability by causing the *victimized collective* to doubt [its] own sense and beliefs." By decoupling intersecting structural violences from its original portrayal and containing the source of violence within the isolated consciousness of individuals, the notion of gaslighting as interpersonal emotive harm works to foreclose awareness of ongoing cultural processes through organized failures of understanding. These failures are functionalized through vast networks of settler institutions, social policies, and publicly licensed resources of interpretation.

It is a common move in settler epistemologies. Weak concepts are presented as robust frameworks for analysis that are then laid before oppressed peoples as offerings, keys to insights about what is happening to one, but which (1) reinforce the cultural assumptions behind settler epistemologies and (2) often have to be rebuilt wholesale to even begin to approximate the complexity of harm and violence experienced in settler states such as the United States, Canada, and Mexico. This epistemic labor is done frequently and at great cost. Meanwhile, robust accounts of multistable structural violences (such as those produced by women of color and Indigenous philosophers on Turtle Island) are devalued, testimonially suppressed, and "quieted" in settler cultures, as Kristie Dotson's work on epistemic oppression has powerfully shown.[8] Gaslighting, on this account, is a settler conceptual ruse that diverts critical attention away from structural epistemic oppressions that continue to underwrite the colonial project.[9] One example of this is reductive accounts of medical gaslighting.

Medical Gaslighting

Medical gaslighting is commonly understood as the interpersonal phenomenon of having one's experience of illness marginalized (including having one's self-reported or presenting symptoms downplayed, silenced, or psychologically manipulated) by a clinical provider or healthcare professional.[10] This view developed from the use of gaslighting to denote coercive control in interpersonal violence research[11] and jettisoned structural accounts available in health equity research on racism.[12] The latter identify a wide range of micro-, meso-, and more importantly, macro-level phenomena that work to promote structural oppressions, including cases of legal gaslighting[13] that functionalize coercive social power to continuously downplay women's experiences of intersectional oppressions as we navigate public institutions. These structural literatures emphasize that psychological stressors have real-life harms that certainly include individual tolls, yet also pose significant intergenerational, intragenerational, and historical group consequences that not all social groups face. What gets lost in the reductive interpersonal accounts of medical gaslighting as individualized epistemic injustices is the way these harms are consistently and unevenly distributed across specific populations, not by accident, but by design.[14] In the next section, we'll take a look at how this maldistribution persists through social transformations in healthcare access through US Black women's reproductive health history. A similar point can easily be made for Brown, Indo-Mesitzx, Afro-Latinx, Asian, First Nations, Aboriginal, Pacific Islander, Pueblos Originarios, American Indian, and Indigenous women given the structural maldistribution of intersectional violences surrounding femicide, forced disappearance, rape, sex and labor trafficking in the global economy.[15]

To begin, the systemic clinical silencing of reported symptoms that marginalize US Black women's reproductive health needs does not happen in a vacuum. Decreases in healthcare access and care quality for Black women are not isolated from gains and increases for other populations. This is especially evident in the rise of assisted reproductive technologies (ART), which amplify the reproductive health concerns of white women by design. As Camisha Russell explains, these technologies are often mobilized to maintain racialized systems of global inequality, especially through racial constructions of infertility and catering services to white women and couples with scientifically debunked yet culturally pervasive rhetorics of genetic race.[16] In 1992, Congress set up the National ART Surveillance Program (H.R. 2733) to collect data on ART patient demographics, obstetric and medical history, procedures and birth outcomes, but not race or ethnicity. This led to a bevy of studies attempting to identify the impact of race and ethnicity on ART use (not access to); adjusting for the impact of insurance mandates for in vitro fertilization, one recent study[17] looked at a one-year distribution of ART cycles in the United States varied by race/ethnicity and found "the highest proportion of use occurring among older, college-educated white non-Hispanic women with incomes 300% above the poverty level," or "85.5% of cycles, followed by Hispanic (5.5%), black non-Hispanic

(4.6%), and A/PI non-Hispanic (4.5%) women." This approach to racial inequality in ART is reminiscent of the old line, "When someone hides something behind a bush and looks for it again in the same place and finds it there as well, there is not much to praise in such seeking and finding."[18] Social and biomedical technologies in settler colonial societies are deeply embedded in power differentials that functionalize colonial relations. Indigenous women's and women of color's life chances through reproduction have been carefully regulated by social policies aligned with economic gains for white settler populations since slavery. In fact, racialized labor is so important in a settler colonial market economy that it must be seen as unimportant, mystified through pathologizing rhetorics of risk-inducing population behaviors or personal choice. As the above study conjectures:

> Racial/ethnic disparities in infertility prevalence have been documented and may be due to disparities in conditions known to cause infertility such as sexually transmitted infections (STIs). For instance, some racial/ethnic minorities report higher rates of STIs (including STIs leading to pelvic inflammatory disease) compared with non-Hispanic whites. Additionally, delays in accessing infertility care have been described for some racial/ethnic groups. For example, Asian/Pacific Islander (A/PI) and black non-Hispanic women reported longer durations of infertility and accessed ART at a later age compared with white non-Hispanic women.[19]

There are many ways to responsibly account for the incidence of infertility in marginalized populations, including histories of forced sterilization, asymmetrical environmental exposure risks to heavy metals, organophosphates, bisphenol A, polychlorinated biphenyl, and other contaminants that induce endocrine dysfunction and reduce fetal viability—not just in our lifetime, but in our mother's and grandmother's lifetimes. STIs are not an acceptable conjecture in this context.[20] For example, uterine fibroids, the leading indication for hysterectomy in the United States, are experienced at much higher rates and with greater severity by Black women than white women.[21] This includes an earlier age of onset, such that the very impact of these disparities is born out differently.[22] Yet very few medical studies of this exist compared with STIs, for which national data-sets on racial and ethnic minorities are kept.[23] In her (2018) American Philosophical Association talk, "Stem Cell Clinics, Medical Gaslighting, and Epistemic Marginalization," Nora Berenstain emphasizes the role that medical gaslighting plays in producing intersectionally structured harms that disproportionately fall on Black women and diminish their reproductive autonomy. She notes, "Black women are less likely to have their pain from uterine fibroids taken seriously, and, when it is taken seriously, they are more likely to receive recommendations for extreme procedures that require long recovery periods and result in sterilization." Black women receive hysterectomies to treat uterine fibroids at twice the rate that white women with a fibroid diagnosis do.[24] This is unsurprising in light of the long colonial history of strategic maldistribution of public health precarities and the corresponding gatekeeping of health resources.

In *Medical Apartheid*, Harriet Washington details the exploitative history of medical experimentation on Black Americans that bedrocked the rise of clinical medicine as a functionally white-serving institution and established social baselines for mistrust in doctor-patient interactions in the United States. Washington details, for example, the targeted abuse of Black slave women by surgeon James Marion Sims (1813–1883), a former president of the American Medical Association and founder of the first women's hospital in the United States. Long considered a figurehead in medical advancements in gynecologic medicine and surgery, Sims systematically mutilated and abused his patients of color, seventeen of which he acquired as slaves for these purposes. Among his many known procedures, he once removed the bladder stones from a nine-year-old slave girl in order to create, not close, a vesicovaginal fistula he could study. He routinely anesthetized women so their husbands could rape them while "flatly refusing to administer anesthesia to slave women and girls," repeatedly discounting their pain as real or sufficient to warrant intervention on account of alleged racial differences in pain tolerance.[25] In a recent study[26] of racial bias in pain management, half of white medical students interviewed in the United States study believed at least one of the following to be a biological fact: the nerve endings of Black people are less sensitive than those of whites, Black people's skin is thicker than those of whites, Black people's blood coagulates at faster rates than those of whites, among other myths. The education-to-provider pipeline in US medicine has remained deeply embedded in the colonial project. This includes associated research produced by medical scientists. From an anticolonial standpoint, it is unsurprising that the scientific literature on racial discrimination in US medicine has been severely restricted in analyses of "structural or systematic racism" (0.04% of the established literature) when compared to the skyrocketing number of studies (nearly forty-eight thousand in 2016) that list race neutrally as an objective social factor.[27] A shift in thinking is needed from conducting "informative studies" on race to analyzing the limits of studies that are based on the racist observational economy of Native informancy, the preferred research method in settler credibility economies.

The impacts of these structured absences in medical knowledge for women of color are not only compounded and multiplicative, but also operate across various scales and registers of life. As nonaccidental gaps in knowledge, they help justify intersectionally evasive and race-neutral explanations for our experiences of structured racism and sexist racism in everyday life. This includes the common view that oppressed peoples see oppression everywhere or "read too much into" adverse experiences, even at the doctor's office, where race-neutral explanations almost always produce variants of patient culpability.[28] Noteworthy is that increased presence of empirical studies on clinical racism or sexism (as very few studies on systemic sexist racism exist) has not closed these gaps, but often produced the need for follow-up studies to empirically demonstrate the inverse (antiracism and nondiscrimination) is statistically significant enough to recommend interventions in current conditions. This problem is compounded with the common belief that producing compelling scientific research on social inequality will be met with corrective action, since empirical evidence is thought to yield the potential to inform policy decisions in ways disproportionate to other argumentative strategies in the public sphere. If that empirical proof is imperial, yes, easily, because it can be recognized in the design of social structure that determines the organization of knowledges in the public sphere: bad science gets used *all the time* in marshaling corrective measures against people of color, and called out when it harms white populations.[29] "Cherry picked racist research," as Representative Katherine Clark notes, was used successfully by the Trump administration to rescind civil rights policy aimed at dismantling the school-to-prison pipeline for children of color.[30] A systems view is essential here because, even if a new administration rescinds the rollback, this pattern continues in the prison-to-death pipeline for people of color.[31] One way or another, structured precarity remains for some populations but not others.

This is where new structuralist views of oppression as the coordinated maldistribution of social harm come in. Asymmetries in the distribution of lifetime chances to be in need of systems that systematize racism is not an accidental phenomenon in settler colonial societies. Settler systems need to be needed so they can do their work of structuring power over social structure, whether at the level of regulation, enforcement, encoding, respecification, distribution, or surveillance: social pathways, punitive or rewarding, are established for this purpose. On this view, the structural legacy of medical apartheid continues today despite social transformations aimed at more evenly distributing the social goods of civil rights and other settler configurations of judicable goods by those in power since the landing of the *Mayflower*.

Reductive accounts of medical gaslighting do not capture this reality. Consider that today, women of color walking along the South Carolina statehouse, whether en route to receive gynecologic care or as plaintiffs seeking redress for medical malpractice, must do so under the venerated gaze of marble statues dedicated to Sims and his legacy.[32] Countless similar examples exist. What this signals to us is a choice by the *preservers*, not the creators, to willfully continue mentally slapping and berating marginalized populations long after empirical studies have demonstrated (by publicly legible settler scientific standards) the adverse health consequences and psychophysiological impacts of inhabiting environments that induce stress or increase exposure risks, from low birthweights to inflammatory markers linked to cardiac disease and likelihood of death from stroke. Settler geoscaping of the environment is thus one form of structural gaslighting as mental manipulation and deceit that distributes harms unevenly across populations. It offers structural protectives to some individuals by curating public worlds and visual languages that venerate white supremacy, normalize sexist racism, and reinforce beliefs of "colorblind" societies, so that when a white person is accused of racism, the allostatic load is often less than when a person of color experiences racism.[33] This is a serious social disadvantage. In settler colonial societies, public worlds are also epistemic safety nets that extend various layers of protectives to some people but not others by design. This is not where one arrives in social science research. It is where one starts.

A structural approach to medical gaslighting is helpful here because it illustrates that the gaslighting in question is not simply from the presiding clinical provider: a tightly woven net of policies, training manuals, advisory boards, disciplinary and institutional procedures—even medical equipment—uphold the *structured inattention* to the reproductive health needs of (to follow the previous example) Black women, who continue to have the highest maternal mortality rates of any group for which metrics are kept.[34] Black newborns persistently die at twice the rate of white newborns, and Black women mothers consistently die at three to four times that of whites.[35] The math is not hard, the finding is already knowledge among women of color. From an anticolonial perspective, it is predictive that positivist studies on Black maternal and neonatal mortality rates consistently look to patient culpability or group stereotypes of health risks to explain causes of cases yet draw blanks on hypothesis for extended etiologic periods of health risks among Black women—why patterns of precarity ebb and flow in measurement metrics, yet, on the long view, continue to persist. The structured inattention to the role that racism, white supremacy, and misogynoir[36] play in producing what are often simply couched as "health disparities" is a form of gaslighting that hides the entrenched relations of patriarchal power and white supremacist domination over racialized, gendered populations in a settler context. Colonialism is a long game, one where death and mortality are not measured by cases, but by incidences of cases borne unevenly across populations. Social epidemiological framings of structural violence can be useful because they extend the etiologic period beyond affected cases to historical and structural determinants of health, yet they must be methodologically oriented toward nonwhitewashed configurations of those histories and structures. Critical epidemiology[37] can be a helpful starting point in this regard. In the next section, I turn to more structurally nuanced accounts of gaslighting in racial justice literatures that better capture the nonaccidental nature of structural violence in settler colonial societies.

Racial Gaslighting

In "Racial Gaslighting," Angelique Davis and Rose Ernst argue that gaslighting should be understood as a structural phenomenon that targets those who resist white supremacy.[38] Disambiguating their use of the term from the interpersonal form of psychological abuse represented in *Gaslight* (1944), Davis and Ernst argue *racial gaslighting* is a better way to think about the "macro-level racial spectacles" and other socioinstitutional processes that do the behind-the-scenes work in culture to produce the effects subsequently recognized as psychological gaslighting. The whole supports the part, and vice versa, but what drops out of this picture of gaslighting is a blameless representation of the operations of power and violence in society. The maintenance, upkeep, and regeneration of white supremacy is the true function of gaslighting; it is an "enduring process" that kicks in when individuals or groups *resist* white supremacist structures in any form.

This suggests that racial gaslighting, which Davis and Ernst define as "the political, social, economic and cultural process that perpetuates and normalizes a white supremacist reality through pathologizing those who resist,"[39] will be especially abusive for women of color. Since the functionalization of violence against racialized women is a structural feature of colonial violence and settler white supremacy, the normalization of pathologizing narratives targeting women of color will be multiplicative and asymmetric with respect to white women. "Just as racial formation rests on the creation of racial projects, racial gaslighting, as a process, relies on the production of particular narratives. These narratives are called racial spectacles. Racial spectacles are narratives that *obfuscate* the existence of a white supremacist state power structure."[40] Thus, racial spectacles pathologizing women of color will become ubiquitous in culture, so much so that the need for intersectional understanding of domination will be routinely questioned by progressive movements focused on single-axis social justice projects like white feminism and gender-neutral racial justice. The kinds of techniques, tropes, narratives, and *consequences* that assail women of color who resist will thus differ, as will their visibility and public reach. This shows up in prevalent questioning of white women's mental states as problematic while retaining a weak narrative version of ontological respect for them *as* women (as in Dr. Ford's testimony before the House Judiciary Committee), yet characterizing racialized women's *whole being* as problematic when their mental states are questioned. The questioning comes from individuals, though also from institutional forms, policies, and procedures. When a brown Indo-Mestizx woman is given only the option to check "white" in racial classification checkboxes over the course of a lifetime, the cultural objective is clear. When racialized and Indigenous women are elected into settler public office with noncompliant, anticolonial agendas, the response is predictively swift and all too often fatal.

Gaslighting, on the view offered here, is not a generalized possibility in interpersonal dynamics (based on a universal trait of human psychological susceptibility) actualized by the particular intentional states of an individual. Following Rose and Ernst, it is a *nonaccidental iterative process* that co-opts resistance to white supremacy by pathologizing noncompliance. But pathologization is not meted out evenly across all social actors. A white cisgender upper-middle-class male who allies himself with progressive racial justice movements, or a similarly situated couple who buys a redlined house for a family of color, are going to be marked differently by racial gaslighting than the family of color, as will each family member. Rose and Ernst outline five of these differences in terms of "portrayal, exposure (or risk), pathologization, audience and outcome."[41] To illustrate this, they give two legal case studies about racial power: *Korematsu v. United States*[42] and *Commonwealth of Kentucky v. Braden.*[43]

Korematsu is the landmark case that unsuccessfully challenged Executive Order 9066 authorizing the internment of individuals based on Japanese ancestry during World War II. The *Braden* case revolved around Carl and Anne Braden, a white couple charged with sedition following the firebombing of a redlined home they purchased for Andrew Wade, a Black man, and his family. Analyzing doctrinal decisions in both cases, Rose and Ernst focus on the absurd race-neutral legal narrative crafted in response to Korematsu's and Braden's defenses. They cite the following prosecutorial comments from the *Braden* case transcript:

> There is no question of white and colored in this case. There has been no colored man indicted. I don't know why [the defense attorney] . . . wanted to harp on white supremacy and all that sort of thing . . . [We] should let this be a milestone in the historic fight of America today to stop this evil pitting race against race, white against black, Catholic against Protestant, Jew against the Gentile, rich against the poor.[44]

The *Braden* case used the political narrative of communism, syndicalism, and sedition as a vehicle for racial gaslighting. While the Bradens were harmed for their actions through trumped-up charges and individualized sentencing to hard labor in a Kentucky prison, the violence done to the Wades drops out of the doctrinal history of *Braden*.[45] Davis and Ernst argue the differential portrayal of social actors, the level of exposure in scope (limited to mortal) and range (individuals, families, communities), who is meant to be the spectator, and the outcome of the violence depends on racial profiles determined by white supremacist structures.

In the *Korematsu* case, the Supreme Court majority decision denied Fred Korematsu's claims of civil liberty violations under the Fifth and Fourteenth Amendments by arguing racial prejudice was not the issue: "What we are dealing specifically with is nothing but an exclusion order" to "relocation centers" warranted by national security risks in the midst of an official war.[46] The *Korematsu* decision is peculiar for its ability to withstand structural challenges while being repudiated by legal scholars. It has never been overturned as a matter of law, making possible the legal basis for indefinite detainment and internment of anyone characterized as "enemy aliens" by the United States (including the current carceral detainment of migrants and asylum seekers at the US-Mexico border). From this, Davis and Ernst identify the legal doctrine of *stare decisis* as a supporting mechanism to racial gaslighting.[47]

There are three features of gaslighting Rose and Ernst develop as significant for understanding the structural dimensions of psychological oppression under white supremacy that are helpful for this project. First, racial gaslighting "offers a way to understand how white supremacy is *sustained over time*," broadening the etiologic period of colonial harm.[48] Second, it is about *structural iterative power*, since there is a direct and bivalent relationship between "the promulgation of these [racial] narratives and the creation of law."[49] Third, it is about function, not intent; awareness is "not determinative of whether the process of racial gaslighting is taking place."[50] While intent is not necessary under their framing of gaslighting, a closer look at the history of settler colonialism with respect to Indigenous peoples allows us to bring intent back without the Cartesian trappings of mental egoism that underpin notions of liability in the settler legal distinctions between *actus reus* and *mens rea*, or act and intent. Describing *cultural intent* will also help situate gaslighting as a settler epistemic tool that structurally quiets[51] critical analyses of settler structural violence in order to mitigate *cultural liability* for settler colonial violence and its continuing project of dispossession.[52] The orienting goal of settler colonial violence, it must be repeated, is not cultural or racial domination for domination's sake, but to maintain control over production, accumulation, and transmission channels that secure intergenerational wealth for white settler populations and their descendants.

Settler Moves to Innocence

The notion of *racial gaslighting* is critically important but ultimately insufficient for addressing the social and historical infrastructural support mechanisms that disproportionately produce abusive mental ambients for people of color and Indigenous peoples in settler colonial cultures. This is because, while it correctly identifies the persistence of white supremacy, the facilitating violences—those that have made white supremacy a viable historical project that functions in particular ways and for specific ends—remain unaccounted for. These violences are the techniques of settler colonial dispossession. Techniques here refer to the various encoding functions of a social practice (like sexist racism) that determine ordering, permutation, and synchronicity with other social practices, not its metaphysical existence as a particular entity. Dispossession refers to long-term strategic processes (including various projects of racialization) developed by white anglo-european settlers to *irrevocably* take possession of Native Amerindian lands. Dispossession is a cultural project of epistemic consolidation that requires foresight into counterrevolutionary strategy and co-optation of resistant cultural narratives, such as Native claims to settler possession of stolen lands and political formations of identity that challenge settler colonial authority. The land cannot simply be seen as being owned *by* settlers; it must be seen as the natural and ontological property of whiteness on territory whose history also naturally begins with settlement and a founding story of fathers birthing a nation. The world-building epistemological function of gaslighting is, by default, to produce totalizing and abusive ambients—languages, stories, buildings, practices, rituals, forms, and documents—that work to destroy resistance to settler cultural authority as natural claims to Indigenous land. For these reasons, racial gaslighting analyses of "relocation centers" in the United States, such as those derived from the *Korematsu* decision, that do not attend to the forced relocations and violent internment of Native Amerindians on government reservations and residential schools (in the United States, Canada, but also Mexico and other settler nations,[53] can easily perpetuate colonial narratives about settlers as first peoples.[54]

In "Decolonization Is Not a Metaphor," Eve Tuck and Wayne Yang issue a timely warning about uncritically collapsing progressive struggles for racial justice with Indigenous projects of decolonization: "In our view, decolonization in the settler colonial context must involve the repatriation of land simultaneous to the recognition of how land and relations to land have always already been differently understood and enacted; that is, *all* of the land, and not just symbolically."[55] Collapsing these struggles is one way, according to them, that "the settler, disturbed by her own settler status, tries to escape or contain the unbearable searchlight of complicity."[56] They refer to such attempts to elude psychological liability as "settler moves to innocence."[57] More specifically, "Settler moves to innocence are those strategies or positionings that attempt to relieve the settler of feelings of guilt or responsibility without giving up land or power or privilege, or without having to change much at all."[58] There is thus a distinct material function tied to the psychological motivations behind moves to innocence: keeping various forms of settler accumulated wealth, including power and privilege. This is important because it links individual moves to innocence to a larger social group or historical collective, as in those for whom giving up inherited wealth in the form of land, power, or privilege proves difficult. This is not a psychological trait—the hesitancy to want to give up power, whether by individuals or collectives, does not happen in a vacuum. Underlying supporting mechanisms of settler social structures enable it.[59]

We can extend the notion of settler moves to innocence from individual persons to social groups that promote cultural moves to innocence through monopolizing the structural resources of institutional patterning and distribution design, where the "strategies" or "positionings" of settler cultures Tuck and Yang allude to are refracted in the very institutional enforcement of social structure. In other words, it's far more than personal bias or racial spectacle at play here. It's the structuring of conditions for *ongoing* racial spectacles from one generation to another, or to prestructured cycles of *mobilization without emancipation* that are functionalized in various ways through settler social structures.[60] On this view, culturally structured epistemic mobilization is always *coordinated to obstruct* emancipation in any meaningful, life-changing way for marginalized peoples at the level of populations. Things do get better, for some, for a time.[61] But the long game of colonialism does not have freedom as a basic condition of our lives. It won't simply be given. That doesn't mean it won't be had.

One of the takeaways from the rich literature on dispossession is the notion of indomitable resistance to oppression, including histories of resurgence, reclamation, and refusal.[62] Another is that people make settler moves to innocence because they can, but that this can-do-ness is *always structured in advance*. It is enabled and reinforced by the physical lands and environments around us, and what's been done to them. Psychological violences are not psychological all the way down. Feeling guilty about past and current wrongs feels good when your everyday proximate relations to places, practices, and peoples have been actively curated to confirm your innocence narrative—when you sense you don't have to give anything tangible up to say you feel this way, especially in triangulation with whiteness, stolen accumulated wealth, or settler futurity. In fact, you can potentially profit from moves to innocence by being recognized as the one to name the episteme surrounding power and injustice (as Spivak's criticism of Foucault holds),[63] so long as actual colonial injustices go untracked in the episteme.[64] So there's really not much you have to give up to both recognize this very wrong and profit from it, yet in the process also help maintain the inequitable distribution of access to resources tied to social power. It's settler gold. It simultaneously functionalizes and normalizes the social perceptibility of mobilization without structural emancipation in the domain of knowledge—what could possibly be better for a settler credibility economy? It makes it look like folks are really trying to help us, and we're just overly demanding or unreasonable in our resistance. In the next section I'll illustrate this point by looking to the proliferation of hermeneutic injustice discourses in white feminisms in philosophy. To do this, I draw on the notion of epistemic exploitation[65] and Kristie Dotson's notion of metaphilosophical apostacy.[66]

Epistemic Exploitation

Tuck and Yang's use of settler innocence builds on Janet Mawhinney's[67] and Mary Louise Fellows and Sherene Razack's[68] examination of white activist's "strategies to remove involvement in and culpability for systems of domination" in their role with antiracist organization.[69] Fellows and Razack refer to settler innocence as a temporal race to get to the finish line first, so to speak, in the self-identification with oppression—a "race to innocence" that provides an allegory for "the process through which a woman comes to believe her own claim of subordination is the most urgent, and that she is unimplicated in the subordination of other women."[70] On this view, by claiming to have an "absence of experience," one can place oneself in a position to ask others to perform labor one is creating a new need for. This idea is elaborated at length by Nora Berenstain. Her article "Epistemic Exploitation" (2016) theorizes epistemic exploitation as a tool of epistemic oppression in which dominant populations structurally elicit redundant epistemic and emotional labor from marginalized groups by constantly calling on them to explain and educate them about the nature of their oppression. The "absence of experience" on which the race to innocence hinges is a rhetorical mechanism used to produce epistemic exploitation, manifested as a constantly recreated need for an ever-expanding amount of labor from Indigenous peoples and people of color to white settler populations. The production of epistemic exploitation via settler moves to innocence constitutes part of the practice of epistemic consolidation through the disappearing of violences, a form cultural gaslighting that is necessary for the survival of the ongoing settler project.[71]

Epistemic exploitation functions as a settler form of cultural gaslighting across many fields of knowledge, from cultural anthropology to anglo-european academic philosophy.[72] Here I consider the latter, which, following Kristie Dotson's rich notion of metaphilosophical apostasy in anglo-american analytic philosophy,[73] might also possibly be called *Philopséma,* as in the love of structured untruths as a way of journeying toward a particular cultural form of truth. It may come as a surprise to some to learn that the knowledge projects of the discipline of academic philosophy have always been deeply aligned with colonial and settler colonial epistemic agendas. Locke's account of property, for instance, was explicitly oriented toward providing ontological justification for the removal of Indigenous peoples from their ancestral homelands using culturally arbitrary conceptions of labor and ownership. While ruling out Indigenous knowledges *as* knowledge, academic philosophy also forecloses on possibilities for the expansion of what is recognized as knowledge. One way academic philosophy doubles down on the european colonial subject's self-declared monopoly on knowledge production is through its structured use of epistemic exploitation. Dotson, for example, identifies academic philosophy's *culture of justification* as a way for narrow conceptions of philosophical "rigor" to function as gatekeepers to disciplinary legitimacy.[74] Dotson reflects on how philosophy's culture of justification creates a hostile and unsustainable environment for diverse practitioners who may work on issues that acknowledge the relevance and reality of social location and embodied experience:

> The burden of shifting justifying norms within a professional environment that manifests symptoms of a culture of justification involves sacrificing one's labor and energies towards providing a catalyst for change via numerous legitimating narratives aimed at gaining positive status for oneself as a philosopher and one's projects as philosophical. Let me make the strong statement that shouldering this burden and the set of experiences one exposes oneself to is not a livable option for many would-be diverse practitioners of philosophy and the small numbers of under-represented populations within professional philosophy attest to this observation.[75]

Annika Mann describes similar experiences in which she must respond to others' incredulity and doubt that her work *really* counts as philosophy:

My struggle has been trying to figure out ways to bring my blackness and my femaleness together with philosophy and to find acceptance of such philosophical work within the academy. I think that most departments, to be honest, give lip service to this kind of acceptance. "Yes, we'd love to have someone come here to do African American philosophy. We'd love someone to come and do feminist philosophy and try to bridge these gaps." But when you actually come and say, "OK, this is what I'm going to do," then you get, "What philosophy do you really do?" Or, "What classes can you really teach?" The implication becomes, "What within the mainstream Western canon can you really do?" And that is very frustrating to me. And I think it serves to further marginalize the work that I am trying to do.[76]

Making diverse philosophical practitioners first prove that what they do should count as philosophy is an effective management strategy for quelling (1) the development of insurrectionist knowledges and (2) the intergenerational preservation of ancestral know-how and Indigenous philosophies that contributes to the collective continuance of a people.[77] Marginalized knowledge creators must devote their time and cognitive resources to proving the legitimacy of our ideas by demonstrating that they are at the very least adjacent to and comprehensible within recognizable settler epistemic frameworks. This epistemic "pay to play" requirement on certain populations ensures that our resources and labor are depleted, extracted, and expended on meaningless pretheoretic busywork before we are able to pursue our own counterrevolutionary epistemic strategies, such as trust-busting the epistemic consolidation project of the self-declared settler monopoly on knowledge production.

The ontological project of settler colonialism involves reifying the settler presence on stolen lands as original and timeless, which provides an illusory justification for governance through the "policing" of who belongs there. This logic is similarly played out via the settler policing of who belongs in the proper place of the colonial discipline of academic philosophy. The culture of justification positions dominant colonial epistemologies as the truest, most original, and default forms of knowledge and positions their foot soldiers as the gatekeepers of legitimacy within the ivory tower. As Dotson identifies, "legitimating narratives" that are differentially deployed against racialized populations function as a "boundary policing" mechanism, essentially creating a porous border to the discipline that is reified and enforced through diffuse cultural practices. These material differences are made possible by a structured accumulation of epistemic power[78] that helps generate cultures of salience oriented toward epistemic apostleship, not the deep critical thought often claimed by the discipline.[79]

Another example of colonial epistemic practices of legitimating narratives can be found in how colonial nations structure the institution of gender-based asylum. Sertler demonstrates how these institutions are structured to foreclose on applicants' knowledge while reifying the power of state actors. She writes, "This structural limit becomes visible when we realize how the institution of asylum is *formed* to provide *legitimacy* to the *institutional comfort* the respective migration courts and boards enjoy." Sertler introduces the important notion of "institutional comfort" to describe "the ways in which state actors in migration courts and boards are systemically afforded the ability to arbitrarily and ambiguously misinterpret asylum applicants' experiences, cultures, and countries."[80] As discussed in Chapter 3, epistemic assumptions and norms are structurally tipped in favor of the credibility of state actors at the expense of applicant credibility. This manifests in migration boards' freedom and ability to dismiss credible reports of violence, danger, and threat by asylums seekers and structurally reframe them as noncredible. If applicants' reports about their experiences in their home countries do not fit with the dominant narratives and representations of their country under the colonial gaze, this provides a reason for their reports to be dismissed as suspicious and unfounded.

For instance, Sertler considers the case of Sara, a Kurdish woman in Iraq whose family had arranged for her to be married against her will. After she began a secret relationship with a colleague, her brother caught them and retaliated violently. When Sara went to the police, the officer "told her he would have killed her himself had she been his sister, and that the police could not do anything 'since it was an honour-related crime.'"[81] The migration board dismissed Sara's application based on a failure to find her credible. Specifically, the board suggested that "it is odd and not very likely that she would initiate a sexual relation with another man when she knows she is going to marry her cousin.... That she would be so blinded by love and disregard the consequences is not a reasonable explanation with the culture that is prevalent in northern Iraq and with her family traditions in mind." Because Sara's experience did not fit the board's *strategically uninformed* and *actively ignorant* conception of Kurdish women's lives and "the culture" in northern Iraq, her claims about her own experience were dismissed as unreliable. On this view, Sara did not simply run up against some bad epistemic luck with the board, or fall on the mortal end of an unvirtued interpersonal judgment based on a structural identity prejudice about Kurdish women, migrants, and asylum seekers that, as darn historical luck would have it, belonged to western culture at the time she sought relief.

On one view, the migration board's treatment of Sara is an example of the gaslighting that occurs "where a listener doesn't believe, or expresses doubt about, a speaker's testimony. In this epistemic form of gaslighting, the hearer of testimony raises doubts about the speaker's reliability at perceiving events accurately."[82] Seen in the broader context of colonial relations, this practice also exemplifies the very condition of Native informancy that forms part of the conditions of cultural gaslighting in colonial contexts, where the standards for believability of oppressed peoples shift, change, and multiply and are always asymmetrically held in the hermeneutical contexts of settler colonial culture (which is *always tacitly positioned as adjudicator*). Intake forms, institutional policies, operational practices, social reward mechanisms and official incentives for survival are developed alongside the violences that produce the condition of Native informancy to ensure that who "speaks" and who "hears" is subordinate to the cultural interpretive mechanisms that legitimate speech, meaning, and intelligibility—not what is said, but what is *sayable* through the licensed languages that precondition the possibility of being understood in settler colonial culture.[83]

The move to decouple structural and identity prejudices (even while retaining a formal conceptual relation between them) is linked to the functionalization of innocence narratives that enable the casting of blame to be placed on the precariously knowable intentional mental states of individual social actors who simply followed the *functionally legitimated* scripts of colonial violence and dispossession. Some philosophers have responded to this by proposing different forms of bias training, including cultivating virtued reflective attitudes that open up the way for more just epistemic practices between us. But virtued liberal narratives and reflective practices have always been designed to functionally coexist with oppressive realities. To whom, exactly, is this news? And they have been designed this way since Aristotle theorized virtue alongside the justified enslavement of nonwhite peoples and neo-Aristotelianism was functionalized in the colonial project as the baseline to justify the freedom of enslaved peoples as those possessing western self-reflective Reason. Or have we not read these edicts and papal bulls? Only a settler credibility economy that trades in the social perceptibility of mobilization without emancipation can one make sense of the fact that as of 2019, *Korematsu* was still good law while having been formally overruled. It was good law legally, not rhetorically; it was what was currently allowing the carceral internment of asylum seekers and children as a matter of law. Jamal Green argues that the Supreme Court's five-to-four majority decision in *Trump v. Hawaii*, which claimed to finally overrule *Korematsu*, is thus an "empty and grotesque" claim, empty because it is not binding on lower courts, and grotesque because "its emptiness means to conceal its disturbing affinity with that case."[84] This is what epistemic injustice literatures in white feminisms can feel like for people of color who have long had to consider the relation between social knowledge and the colonial project. In the next section, we'll see how hermeneutic injustice should thus be understood as a form of hermeneutic violence, not the other way around. This is because the possible epistemes for understanding knowledge, truth, credibility, and testimony are often the result of hermeneutical whitewashing and other forms of prestructural violence, including epistemicides, that yield accumulated forms of cultural interpretive power—the gearwork behind cultural gaslighting.

Prestructural Violence

Hermeneutic violence is a unique kind of cultural violence that arose in conjunction with the colonial projects of western european powers. It is violence done to systems of meaning and significance for the purposes of weakening resistance to colonization and securing the dispossession of Native lands and resources.[85] It ensures that the bodies that continue to survive colonial genocide are displaced from a tacit network of referential systems that weave meaning together independently of settler colonial epistemologies. It is a prestructural violence that includes violence to calendrical systems, narrative textiles like *amoxtli*, the treaty-stealing and polluting of lands, rivers, waterways, but also trauma done to traditional kinship structures and nonbinary understandings of sex and gender. On the long view, it can include epigenetic violences that disproportionately induce genetic risks in some populations but not others and force communities to reconfigure the emplaced role of our bodies and communal health under conditions of structured precarity.

For Native Amerindians, the forced, violent imposition of the western alphabet and subject-predicate grammar (as well as the assumptions of exclusionary logic, interiorization, and narrative linearity that support it) constituted a unique violence to the discursive practices of Indigenous communities that very often goes unacknowledged. By weakening the relationship between Native Amerindians and the interpretive resources required to effectively participate in cultural processes, one powerful consequence of hermeneutic violence has been the degree of difficulty contemporary Indigenous women face in having claims of violence heard and recognized in one's home language.[86] The prestructural machinations of these hermeneutic violences are essential conditions for the contemporary forms of cultural gaslighting that are a cornerstone of settler epistemic practices. Cultural gaslighting often turns on the active disappearing of the prestructural hermeneutic violences that formed the conditions of possibility for settler society. On the usual view, european colonizers "imposed" their worldview on Native Amerindians as either an intentional act of domination or as an unintended consequence of encountering a radically different culture, which caused colonizers to revert to their default cultural understandings without insight into the limits of their epistemic frameworks. This cultural narrative of *presumed unintentionality* has allowed settler interpretive resources to accumulate epistemic power,[87] which further allow settlers epistemologies to foreclose revolutionary and insurgent resistance. This is an epistemic spectacle we must refuse.

In political theory, and particularly in revolutionary theory, special focus falls on the stage of political change coincident with the *consolidation* of power, as opposed to the acquisition of power or tactical overthrow of existing power structures. It is at this stage that revolutions often go awry or fail to make the lasting changes necessary to secure the perpetuity of the new power structures, social group interests, or political ideologies. Revolts, uprisings, coups, riots, and insurgencies rarely succeed in fomenting the basic, rapid transformations to existing social structures that survive counterinsurgencies; most revolutions thus acquire the historical character of social mobilizations without the aimed-for emancipation from oppression. In many cases, this is because the revolutionary action has failed to achieve the epistemological break necessary for genuine transformation of stable colonial structures. Colonialism, if it is to survive five centuries of anticolonial strategies (as it has through its structural iterations in imperialism and neoliberalism) requires an element of unarticulated suppression at the deepest interpretive levels that prefigures the emergence of the systematic operationalization of the particular oppressions under colonialism.

Hermeneutic violence performs this counterinsurgent role by preparing the way for cultural processes of domination that cannot just overturn, but *consolidate* european power structures over Amerindian and noneuropean ones. Consolidatory domination at the level of culture thus rests on the ability to do more than regulate social acts and practices through laws, prohibitions, and normative valuations that discourage individual actions. It rests on establishing hermeneutic power over discursive domains and the subsequent regulatory authority to license only those logics *and counterlogics* produced recursively, through self-same systems of interpretation. Cultural recursion can then be seen as a process whereby seizing the structures of meaning and interpretive stability—as part of securing consolidatory domination—is succeeded by a program of establishing social structures that also operate recursively, that is, by translating elements of a system into elements recognized through logics external to the system. Cultural recursion is important to consolidate colonial domination because, by influencing all parts of the social web of interactions, it is able to create the *appearance* of an objective, value-free world that contradicts the lived experience of oppressed peoples—a world behind which a multiplicity of western cultural valuations palpitate, actively shaping the kinds of social acts and practices acknowledgeable as "real" in culture. It is a cruel reality to inhabit, but it is not our only reality. At its most finely tuned stages of development, it creates social contexts where violence can only be recognized to the degree that it corresponds with western conceptions of the extralegal use of force, so that, for example, environmental harms to Amerindian waterways are seen as less violent than interpersonal harms. There's more than one way to kill a people, and this fact features prominently in the colonial project.[88]

"Hermeneutic violence" is an interpretive retooling strategy designed to do something very specific in the world and for specific populations. It is limited by design. The point is not to set up new epistemic puzzles and citational economies around buzzwords, but to continue to refocus attention on the systemic violences that are continuously marshaled against Indigenous women and women of color, strategically, predictively, and from one generation to the next. When we're culturally gaslighted away from making moves for substantive structural change by the overwhelming citational presence of feminist philosophies that claim to have our interests in mind, hermeneutic violence helps us recognize that anglophone accounts of hermeneutic injustice lack an interpretive acumen when it comes to colonial contexts. This is not accidental, as settler epistemologies actively promote narratives of terminal Indigeneity and linguistic death alongside justice frameworks.[89] From an anticolonial perspective, there's simply no such thing as a "serious hermeneutical disadvantage" that does not inflict epistemic injustice, unless, of course, you come from a tradition that (a) thinks you can "opt in" or "out" of hermeneutical practices as a matter of choice, (b) deploys "extant" (undestroyed) hermeneutical resources as the baseline for interpretive understanding, and (c) feels free to deploy an arbitrary understanding of "hermeneutic" that takes away the prestructural hermeneutical commitment to history—something that might come in handy for thinking about how history structures the present conditions of knowledge production.[90] But the work of cultural gaslighting cannot be done alone, by individual agents as gaslighters; it is produced from the bottom up and sustained through the abusive mental *ambients* that allow people to carry out their institutional tasks (of operationalized settler colonial violence) not just with impunity but with reward and philosophical acclaim.

The operationalization of gaslighting as a psychologically reductive interpersonal abuse mechanism in contemporary philosophical discourse trades on a pure innocence narrative. It provides shield and cover for epistemic complicity that enables other forms of mental and physical abuse, not just to individuals, but to communities. It is an act of colonial violence because it delinks the necessary association between the land one inhabits and the ambient world one dwells in, allowing infrastructural development in culture that operationalizes settler histories as real and obfuscates nonsettler realities. Gaslighting, on this view, is a form of epistemic territorial expansion that allows members of dominant communities to claim epistemic space as their own, and only their own. Cultural gaslighting shows that epistemological frameworks that claim to derive from universal sets of metaphysical assumptions about the nature of knowledge are monocultural perspectives supported by structural power relations.[91] Cultural gaslighting thus provides cover for institutions, but also for individuals to mayflower their way through public spaces (and major publications) as a tacit mode of being. Mayflowering is a spatial concept of emplaced social power based on prestructural and structural violences. It describes when a member of an interpretive community privileged under settler colonialism unproblematically bodies forth and takes up social space through an innocence narrative based on epistemic purity that is structurally enabled. Like the "pilgrims" on the *Mayflower*, they presume a right to foreign spaces by reconceptualizing them as blank territories, both physically and epistemically. They're walking lettered cities.[92] Their ability to genuinely think they are doing good—and double down on this—is thus predicated on the creation of social *infrastructures* (like law, disciplines, and argumentative systems such as philosophy) that confirm that reality and operate by the structured dispossession of other forms of life.[93]

Epistemic practices, including those that claim to be liberatory, often recapitulate colonial violences, both structural and prestructural. Unlike, for instance, the nuanced structural account of epistemic gaslighting by Pohlhaus,[94] mainstream white feminist discourses on epistemic injustice and gaslighting illustrate this pattern.[95] What we are being sold as philosophical resources to fight oppression are concepts that claim to fix the very thing they are culturally responsible for. Recognizing this must lead to an open discussion about the possibilities, requirements, and conditions for structural epistemic reparations and cultural revitalization projects, which cannot be severed from Indigenous land rematriation and structural reparations for the coordinated maldistribution of precarities in women of color's lives. Epistemic reparations need to be thought about in structural terms because liberation does not come about by swapping out bad thoughts for good ones or making room for historically marginalized voices while retaining the power to make room culturally. As Dotson and Sertler[96] point out, freeing your mind isn't enough when conditions that structure ongoing precarity in the material world remain. Because I am interested in what allows these conditions to remain—a kind of epistemic *impunity* that is functionalized across social systems—in the next and final section I outline an account of structural innocence that I think prevails in contemporary accounts of social structure. This account keeps us on the hamster wheel of recognition while lasting structural transformations that flip the script at the macro level elude us. It should be seen as only one aspect of larger forces at play in the intergenerational maintenance of colonial violence.

Epistemic Impunity and the Hidden Rules of Social Structure

Contemporary accounts of social structure belie the operational existence of a multitrack model of social structure that is based on the respecification and enforcement of settler colonial relations (*Siedlerproduktionsverhältnisse*, for the nomenclatural purist) and is cofunctional with abstract models of universal social structure derived from the German sociological tradition.

This tradition has cultivated a monocultural view of social structure that works to exonerate the targeted maldistribution of harms in settler societies. As a system of self-exoneration, it works to foreclose the legitimacy of claims for wealth redistribution or reparation in material, social, and structural epistemic terms. For instance, the sociological concept of latent function (and dysfunction) disallows structuralist approaches in the social sciences to identify and track the role of settler colonial complicity in structuring the maldistribution of social protectives and precarities, as latency on both accounts—harm or profit—is always seen as unconscious and unintentional. That's the functional purpose of the definition—that nonspecified consequences of institutional or social phenomena, good or bad, are always seen as unintended *and having no identifiable aggressor*. Because this notion predicates definitions of *structural violence*, it too is seen as having no identifiable aggressor. Whom, exactly, does this benefit? This goes beyond the scope of methodological racism[97] in structuring inequality. It is better understood in terms of techniques of keeping and asserting social power that structure inequality prestructurally, by suppressing and denying as a matter of *automation*. This doesn't take away cultural intent, as one of the basic features of impunity is that automation does not foreclose complicity but maintains it.

Epistemic impunity is as common in philosophy as it is in sociology, cultural anthropology, ethnography, history, and other official instruments of knowledge production and gatekeeping in settler societies, including policy and governance. Structural innocence has become the very bedrock of sociologies of knowledge and economies of observation that work both manifestly and tacitly to maintain control over social power in settler colonial societies. This idea of structural intent is premised on the core notion of elementary functions (or "design") built into settler social structure, where "elementary" denotes processes of self-automation that work to reinforce particular structural relations throughout system transformations. The cultural particularity of relations selected for reinforcement (and respecification in the transformed structure) is important, as they rely on metaphysical and epistemological provenances of dominant social histories that are maintained through social power and its (political, legal, material, institutional) instruments. Not all cultures colonize when given a chance. Stop lying. But there is profit to be had by denying this and asking colonized peoples to first disprove settler assumptions about cultural universals before acquiescing to the salience of the question of reparations for structured and ongoing harms to our communities, for maintaining the conditions under which femicide and sexual violence against us *can* thrive.

There is individual profit and communal wealth to be gained from maintaining abusive ambients that unevenly distribute social precarity across populations. Settler societies use various forms of social power to distribute, reproduce, and automate social inequalities (including public health precarities and mortality disadvantages) that skew socioeconomic gain continuously toward white settler populations and their descendants. While the idea of uneven distribution of harm can be found in the social epidemiology literature and public health research on racism, anticolonial perspectives are needed to outline the hidden rules of social structure in settler colonial societies. These are rules that lead, for example, to epistemic apartheid in legal systems, where the claims of some litigants are recognized (and given access to one procedural legal track that affords different life chances) while others are pathologized and streamlined into another legal track, often a dead-end street where the mitigation phase is ceremonial and the punishment predictive. In this regard, extending the etiologic period of european colonialism helps to reframe a past historical event or static structural determinant in *an ongoing and dynamic interpretive process*. Colonialism, at heart, is an ongoing interpretive process.[98] While it may be strategically helpful to understand gaslighting as placing a special focus on the power relations that can impact a person's trust in their own judgments, what is at stake is not just the existential and ontological spectrum of emotional abuse sustained but the *asymmetric death toll of some populations over others*, consistently, predictively, and from one generation to the next. Cultural gaslighting shows how rhetorical strategies that name a public grievance yet actively *abate relief or remedy of that grievance* are some of the most commonly taught and preserved interpretive resources in settler epistemic systems.[99]

Coming to terms with the coordinated depths of structured dispossession should not lead to impasses for action—it hasn't for many. The colonial mind game has always been to get us to disappear ourselves, to whiten our minds by preference, aspiration, fear, or the terrible calculus of bounded choice to survive a moment of terror we did not create, a moment that often spans lives and generations. We cannot fall into the trap that survival is acquiescence, as surrender only reifies the strength of the relations between specified elements in settler social structures. The work of structural respecification oriented toward basic transformations in settler colonial relations is daunting, but we move toward this future with the assertion that proof of harm is no longer on the table. We've been continuously put in the subordinate position of having to redundantly answer to "Tell me the story of how I conquered you"[100] in order to get relief for coordinated violences that make answerability to conquerors a basic feature of social structure.[101] Half a millennium of evidence is enough. Settler social structures guarantee that there will always be costs tallied to our resistance and resilience. Despite this, we must continue our work, for there is simply no (nonwhitewashed) reason to think the structured abuse, exploitation, and adaptive criminalization of our bodies—and the subsequent structural epistemic gaslighting of this condition—will stop under settler colonial regimes, nor that the ebb and flow of femicide and mortality rates will, unaided, bend toward justice.

5

Structural Violence Is *Not Fate*

Beyond Structural Trauma

> The abject heart of colonialism and neocolonialism, and their practice of capitalism, is *gendered violence*. . . . I think that such violence is not incidental but common to the stresses that race, gender, and sexuality play in ordering and reordering power in our times.
> —Dian Million (Tanana Athabascan), *Therapeutic Nations*

Logics of Wounding

On the night of April 24, 2019, which coincided with day 5-Eagle (Cuauhtli, 1-Ozomahtli) in the Aztec solar year 7-Reed (Acatl), the mayor of Mixtla Altamirano was traveling on the Zoologica-Orizaba highway in the state of Veracruz when a speeding vehicle pulled up, hovered, and sprayed her car with bullets. Maricela Vallejo Orea, along with her husband and driver, were killed instantly. Maricela was six months pregnant. Prior to her murder, as mayor she had proposed the creation of an agency across every municipality to address the systemic nature of gender-based violence, particularly against her Indigenous community.

There is a very old narrative in western culture that frames trauma (from the greek *trōma*, meaning wound) as the unavoidable casualty of individual fate, something that is built into the very fabric of being in a gambled trade-off for living self-determined lives. The origin story of this narrative can be traced back to ancient greek myths of white-robed goddesses—the three Moirai—who moved the mortal spheres of life and death and laid out essential vulnerabilities in the character of every human life. They cast their dice and watched mortals react in self-defining acts.[1] If their fates landed well, it said little of the fated's character: "Bad luck" can make you who you are, whereas responses to good fortunes reflect who you already are—we learn this from the actions of Oedipus at Colonus and from Aeschylus's trickster king of Corinth, Sisyphus.[2] The logic of wounding, which narrates tragedy as an unforeseeable and unavoidable part of human life, was thus intimately tied to the logic of individuation, which detaches people from the sets of social, cultural, and epistemic practices that produce them in order to place their lives within a universalized narrative arc of human existence.[3] Together these logics of wounding and individuation are intimately connected to a normalized conception of *tragedy as inherently blameless*, a game of chance where a person's "bad luck" is disassociated from organized, coordinated efforts structured to bring harm and injury to some people but not others.[4]

For Indigenous women and women of color living in settler colonial societies like the United States, Canada, and the United Mexican States (Estados Unidos Méxicanos), these founding myths have had a lasting and damaging impact through the role they play in maintaining conceptions of trauma that preclude the identification of ongoing structural oppressions and systemic femicidal violence in our communities.[5] The philosophical failure (which is not an accidental failure) to understand trauma as a functional, organizational tool of settler colonial violence amplifies the impact of traumatic experience on specific populations by design. This is not an epistemic "whoopsie," an unintended consequence of historical trajectories codified as tradition, as this book has shown. Rather, it is an organized (and actively maintained) hermeneutic standpoint that recognizes the injuries of some populations and perpetuates the conditions for the nonrecognition of others for epistemic profit, accumulating in interpretive value/wealth from one white settler generation to the next.[6] Recall from Chapter 2 that the roman legal system allowed the interrogation of enslaved people with torture, and that legal action did not arise by accident. It should be no surprise, then, that the rise of the legal concept of *iniuria* in ancient Rome similarly did not come about by accident; it developed to formalize the logic of wounding in terms of grievable harms[7] reserved for specific populations and inapplicable to others, namely, slaves.[8] If your injury has social cognates, especially ameliorative ones, you're simply more likely to live. As the notion of epistemic capitalism (Chapter 3) illustrated, having preferential access to a piggy bank of socially legible epistemic reserves capable of producing ameliorative benefits (for some populations but not others)—especially surrounding injuries—is a powerful social good. It is also a good that has been nonaccidentally accumulated by one cultural tradition through a dynastic process of controlled succession.

The functional use of the concept of injury to produce grievability for certain populations only is not the exception, but the rule. It is an example of the *self-organized criticality*[9] that unfolds in a settler epistemological system. Injury, dignity, humanity, bodily autonomy, inalienable rights, and the vast range of concepts associated with the liberal tradition (the moral tradition adopted by modern settler legal systems) are functional parts of the settler epistemological system that exists to coordinate the goals of settler white supremacy.[10] These concepts say one thing—that all people are created equal and have basic "rights" as humans—but work to uphold another reality.[11] Nowhere is this functional double standard more apparent than in settler states' power to limit Indigenous sovereignty through multicultural state forms of recognition.[12] Sexual violence and institutional responses to sexual violence, femicide, and gendered terror[13] are very closely tied to this power through the paradox of a state-sponsored carceral-impunity complex. In a state-sponsored carceral-impunity complex, we find a common (system generated) contrasting phenomenon, where state-imposed settler accountability frameworks that cage perpetrators of color at disproportionate rates coexist alongside tunnels of impunity, which distance causal and contributory mechanisms (including the perpetrators themselves) of violence from any real (much less structurally meaningful) accountability.[14] The structural design of the carceral-impunity complex comes at a heavy cost for survivors of sexual violence and for the families of survivors, whose injuries and restorative rights to balance the injustice of their injuries are closed off by design.

Epistemically, not much has changed since the development of the concept of injury rooted in roman law. Because the logic of individuation ascribes a disembodied faculty of purely abstract rational thought to the individual, which that logic values above embodied, situated, contextual, and land-based understanding and knowledge embedded in webs of reciprocal relationships, the logic of wounding tied to individuation remains reserved for those already recognized as subjects in settler colonial cultures.[15] The logic of wounding frames Indigenous land dispossession and genocide on Turtle Island as a historic tragedy located in the past that was caused more by the unforeseeable effects of the spread of european diseases in the "New World" than by the deliberate, methodical, plotting of settlers and the governments that supported them to slaughter Native peoples and occupy and exploit Native lands in order to secure land and livelihood for future generations of white settler offspring.[16] Jared Diamond's 1997 Pulitzer Prize–winning settler fantasy, *Guns, Germs, and Steel*, is a modern revival of

Rousseau's 1781 environmental determinist argument, as it differentiates between "savage" and "civilized" peoples through geographic happenstance.[17] Diamond's argument relies on the logic of wounding to incorrectly portray european colonialism and imperialism as the unplanned result of arbitrary geographic forces and fortuitous cultural access to biotic resources (i.e., who had more of what, when, as a matter of pure geographic luck).[18] Philosopher Charles Taylor similarly endorses an incidental might-makes-right portrayal of British colonial violence in Africa: "In the end, we have the Gatling gun, and they have not."[19]

This book has illustrated that the logic of wounding is neither new nor limited in scope and reach; we find it wherever settler colonial economic supremacy operates at local and global scales. Adam Smith's innocence narrative about the causes of uneven development between europe and its colonies under capital accumulation (Chapter 1) is structurally invariant from the logic of wounding in Diamond's celebrated works. Both locate structural causation for european colonialism's population-level harms anywhere but where it most belongs: in the regenerative settler colonial social structures that uphold socioeconomic supremacy for settler white polities over long ranges of time.[20] In fact, we find the logic of wounding, which narrates tragedy and cultural harm as the chancy result of unknown forces or historically arbitrary turns of fate, just about anywhere wealth is measured by profit (rather than, for example, unmonetized communal health and well-being) and is connected to material infrastructures governed by white settler logics.[21]

One of the most powerful innocence narratives that exists today is the causal mythology surrounding the high incidence and prevalence rates of sexual assaults, femicide, domestic violence, and forced disappearances of Indigenous women and women of color in the Americas. At the heart of this chapter is the concern over settler colonial interpretive ecologies and long-run systems phenomena that continuously recreate plausible deniability for structural violence, and how "tragedy" features into this self-automating (i.e., system-driven) causal machinery of plausible deniability. Contra these structural innocence reproduction schemes, the myriad forms of violence Indigenous women and women of color suffer "are neither random nor products of chance. Rather, they reflect the structural brutality of inequalities of gender, race, class, and nationality, linked to neoliberal logics in which market forces define social relations."[22] As Muscogee (Creek) Nation legal scholar Sara Deer notes, "Rape is more than a metaphor for colonization ... it is integral to colonization."[23] Sexual violence works to uphold a settler system of governance that disproportionately licenses violence toward Native communities while providing structural safety nets for white settler polities and the machinery of settler governance itself. In full agreement with Speed and Deer, I think we can and should frame the intersecting inequalities and structural forces at work in sexual and domestic violence against Indigenous women and women of color as nonaccidental. And I want to do that in a way that traces the thread of structured harm back to its origin in colonial system design, so that there is no confusion about the relation between colonial history and present conditions. I thus explain this nonaccidental quality of gendered violence by using an anticolonial systems framing of the notion of trauma—one that centers epistemic features of social reproduction like the logics of wounding and individuation.[24]

In settler colonial studies, the logic of wounding has been famously tied to what Patrick Wolfe[25] calls a logic of elimination for Indigenous peoples, which settlers use to portray colonial invasion as a finite "historical event" reducible to "frontier homicide" and the moral pitfalls of a young nation instead of an organized structure with ongoing tactics of spatial containment and violence.[26] For Wolfe, "Elimination refers to more than the summary liquidation of Indigenous peoples, though it includes that,"[27] such that colonial violence and destruction can take on a range of physical, spatial, linguistic, epistemic, and political formations to achieve the cultural genocidal ends of white settlement of Indigenous lands—for the colonial settler to become, as it were, the original inhabitants of Indigenous lands.[28] Chapter 1 flagged important Indigenous feminist receptions of Wolfe's work.[29] Here we note the importance of his definition of colonialism as a "structure, not an event,"[30] that distinguishes settler colonialism from genocide without excluding it.

Thinking of colonialism as a structure is essential to theorizing the complex and dynamic operations of gender-based violence in settler colonial societies. It is also critical to formulate a necessary relationship to the adaptive range of settler colonial logics that target and maldistribute harm to Black, Brown, Asian, immigrant, and internally/externally displaced people of color, disabled people, as well as gender and sexual minorities, as part of the global neoliberal settler colonial project of enduring white dynastic socioeconomic supremacy—logics that work to secure the next thousand years of more of the same harmful nonsense.[31] In this regard, the logic of individuation also underlies and is entangled with colonial ideologies that help carry out the colonial project, such as neoliberal carceral ideologies. It is thus additionally tied to a logic of containment for people of color.

Like the logic of elimination, the logic of containment is also multipronged; it upholds settler colonial structures of oppression and is in turn strengthened by them, creating an endless positive feedback loop. It justifies the hypersurveillance of communities of color and leads to the removal of people of color from our communities and our absorption into the prison-industrial complex[32] in order to extract our labor while promoting intergenerational harm and trauma to our communities through the destruction of our families. It is also a geopolitical strategy of coordinated restraint in response to extralegal uses of force that enables the systematic production of torture, abuse, and sexual violence through structural impunity; it makes uncountable those violences that further the goals of settler-capital industrial economies and neoliberal agendas.[33] Consider that while the murder rate in Mexico fell during the Covid-19 pandemic, the femicide rate continued to increase—a steady rise of 137 percent in the last five years alone.[34] Yet there is wide-scale impunity for crimes against women and gender minorities in Mexico as there is elsewhere. The clearance rate for rape resulting in a jail sentence is less than 1 percent, yet for decades, American companies like BlackRock have invested heavily in the sprawling prison industrial system in Mexico to the tune of billions.[35] Why is that? It is because the settler state can exercise containment of populations necessary to further the extractive ends of neoliberal capital production (here the convict lease system that is replacing the maquiladora sector), but it can likewise exercise restraint (self-containment) when it comes to leveraging legal infrastructures for their alleged and intended functions of "justice." This criticism doesn't mean carcerality is an acceptable model of justice. "Carceral geographies inscribe racism by cleaving humans from the environment and each other, depriving life-giving resources from populations deemed a threat to a dominant socioenvironmental order."[36] What the settler state's dual-track ability to punish and to refrain from pursuing accountability means is that, as system-generated features, there exists a basic maldistributive design to structures of justice in settler colonial societies that upholds the larger system goal of extractive wealth accumulation for some populations but not others—and to shapeshift when necessary to achieve this end.

Whether by sword or shield, the logic of containment produced by the logic of individuation within settler societies thus invariably also leads to elimination for people of color. The logic of elimination and the logic of containment are both rooted in the structural automation and expansive reproduction of fertile avenues of force, positive and negative, that promote the production and maintenance of settler colonial wealth while simultaneously exonerating white settler culpability through cultural apparatuses like law, policy, law enforcement, governance, and the concepts that uphold them. I explain this nonaccidental, strategic, and complex settler colonial use of force (*forcis*) further in terms of institutionalized violence and the idea of structural trauma.

This chapter proceeds in two sections. In the first section, "Structural Trauma," I unpack the history of the western notion of trauma to situate it within a settler epistemic economy that simultaneously weaponizes and gatekeeps resources associated with the logic of wounding, especially in cases of femicide and sexual assault. This idea is meant to put flesh on the bones of a theory of structural violence as a dynastic and self-repairing process of settler colonial social reproduction (Chapter 1). I touch briefly on Iris Marion Young's[37] settler colonial account of Indigenous sovereignty to illustrate the structural epistemic character of barriers to justice for Indigenous women, discussing Young's work in relation to Sara Deer's[38] account of tribal governance over sexual assault cases. I argue anglo-american political theoretical models of structural justice persistently link epistemic pay-to-play maneuvers with gatekept pathways to collective social change, (e.g., through arguments that require white settlers' buy-in or settler-oriented structures of address for coordinating effective political action). At best, these models are distractions in organizing work. At worst, because they tout principles of nondomination and cultural pluralism that create pathways for the critical components of dispossession to be bundled or sold along with their frameworks of justice, they are functional features of white dynastic formations. Democracy reigns, but colonialism lives to see another day. Most importantly, the structurally produced burdens to appeal to anglo-normative accounts of structural justice and whitewashed principles of bilateral nondomination—because they are the most functional exchanges in a settler epistemic economy—deter policies and practices necessary to bring justice to survivors and to produce survivor-centered resources. Such policies and practices must acknowledge the dynamics of colonial domination—where one culture has historically done wrong to another, as a fundamental feature of the act of rape.

In the second section, "Dignified Rage," I turn to Zapatista communities' (Tsotsil, Tseltal, Tojolabal, Zoque, Mam, Chol) autonomous frameworks of resistance that move beyond anglo-american political theoretical models of structural injustice, suggesting that in some cases, a suitable response for white feminists eager to offer aid is to get out of the way (*no estorben*). I reject the moralizing pay-to-play game that expects the outcome of such criticism to center white feminists as well, such as imperatives for personal reflection on how continuing colonial occupation structures their political and philosophical engagements with marginalized polities. Instead, I reaffirm political notions, as J. Kēhaulani Kauanui (Kanaka Maoli) puts it, of "enduring Indigeneity"[39] and autonomy that are widely held in Indigenous feminist activism and its manifestation in Zapatismo, which includes Indigenous and non-Indigenous actors. I am particularly interested in feminist articulations of enduring Indigeneity in Zapatista territories in relation to the dual use of legal rights discourses and the crafting of Indigenous law. As Sylvia Marcos notes, "If there is something that has given Zapatismo its distinctive characteristic, its colour and its flavour, it has been its emphasis on including and defending women's rights as defined through the Women's Revolutionary Law."[40] I examine the structural barriers toward implementing the Women's Revolutionary Law as a lived reality, framing the problems of gendered racism and sexual violence as inseparable from the Zapatista's anticolonial critique of the "the capitalist hydra"[41] and of the global infrastructure of neoliberal exploitation and graft. Finally, I turn to the *Lekil Kuxlejal* tradition of land-based well-being and autonomous governance in Zapatista communities to reaffirm a democratic path forward in light of systems-based obstacles and structural oppressions created by white dynastic formations. In relation to the last four chapters, this chapter illustrates that structural violence is not fate, despite what settler epistemologies would like to portray.

Structural Trauma

This section analyzes a core concept in settler epistemology—namely, the western notion of trauma—to demonstrate how settler conceptual frameworks obscure the intentionality of structural violence by design. Before proceeding, and to thwart risks of getting too theoretically abstract—because Maricela's life was not abstract—let me clearly state that what I am arguing for in this section is a politicized understanding of trauma that foregrounds our lived realities of asymmetric harm when it comes to traumatic experience. Trauma and its impacts are not evenly distributed across all populations, despite the fact that medical and disciplinary literature often treat them as if they are. In the standard western picture, trauma is portrayed as a human risk factor to which people are universally vulnerable. Social determinants such as poverty, war, social class, and environmental exposures are presented as predisposing some populations to greater incidence of traumatic harm. These factors, then, are treated as what creates hot zones of traumatological effects. In contrast to this picture, I contend that the primary producers of trauma and its impacts are systems-based phenomena, such as the organizational logics of domination that arise from the self-organized criticality of white dynastic formations over long ranges of time. It is these organizational logics, as systems-based phenomena, that perpetuate conditions of poverty, war, racism, and sexual violence for some populations but not others—strategically, predictively, and intergenerationally.[42]

One way to understand how the standard medical approach disappears the systems-based colonial production of population-level harms is through the distinction in population health science between "causes of cases" and "causes of incidence." As Sean Valles explains:

> The distinction is between two types of causal explanation for two different types of causal phenomena. . . . For instance, genetic variations make individual people a substantially higher or lower risk of hypertension . . . , but these individual-level variations seem to make no causal contributions to the extensively studied massive disparity in hypertension rates between US White and Black populations . . . . Genetics may explain much about sick individuals (causes of cases) but do little to explain why some populations are plagued by hypertension more than other populations (causes of incidence).[43]

Trauma models of care often follow the "causes of cases" model. As such, they fail to address the systemic violence and functionalization of racist sexism and sexual violence in women's lives that a "causes of incidence" approach might help track. Such an approach could better capture, for instance, how settler colonial governments infrastructurally support femicide with impunity through law and policy, as well as how gender has always been a primary tool of settler colonial violence, particularly against Indigenous women and women of color.[44] Importantly, politicized approaches to trauma do not take away provision models of care for those suffering from the effects of trauma today;[45] they only insist that traumatic effects are being nonaccidentally glossed over and strategically misrecognized or pathologized when those who suffer the logic of wounding are not white.

Since the term first rose to prominence in sixteenth-century european anatomical treatises and later experienced a resurgence in the developing fields of psychology and neurology, trauma has been characterized in a range of domains. These include emotion-based accounts that characterize trauma as "an experience of unbearable affect,"[46] socioecological models of multiple traumas and clinical disorders such as post-traumatic stress disorder (PTSD), and surgical approaches to wound triage in emergency medicine. Today, while trauma can be used to refer equally well to physical or mental injury, accounts of trauma's cause, duration, and function diverge.[47]

Depoliticizing the Trauma-Pain-Tragedy Triad

One of the main lines of thought about trauma, whether understood as a physical or mental injury or both, has been its special connection to the idea of tragedy and the emotional life of individuals undergoing pain. In "Tragedy: A Curious Art Form," the classicist Anne Carson writes: "Why does tragedy exist? Because you are full of rage. Why are you full of rage? Because you are full of grief."[48] This grief comes from an injury, a wound (*trōma*), that bereavement tries to suture closed. What is lost in this tragedy-rage-grief causal triad is the direct link from rage to the causes of incidence that perpetuate grief-inducing violence in some communities but not others, strategically, predictively, and from one generation to the next. This triad is no accident. The ancient greeks were experts at depoliticizing grief and creating a new form of public art to regulate the shifting emotional boundaries between public and private life in the tenuous rise of democratic rule. This was the work of tragic plays.[49] The very meaning of tragedy comes from these plays—*tragōidia*, from *tragos*, meaning goat, as in the human-goat satyrs that performed between acts, and *ōidē*, or public performance of song. Tragedy arose in the west as a public mechanism to contain social forces and resistance to violence through (1) internalizing conflicts and (2) depoliticizing violence by portraying it as a naturally occurring phenomenon. The latter is represented in the tragic hero's inability to foresee the consequences of his actions. More recently, Stephen Diamond's celebrated work on the psychological genesis of violence reinforces the depoliticized view of trauma by characterizing increased homicide rates in the United States as "senseless violence," something he says we can make sense out of only if we understand violence "existentially" as the "naturally occurring, universal, *inescapable* aspects of the human condition."[50] We can also get a glimpse of the internalizing function of tragedy in Carson's universalist account of the psychology behind it:

> Grief and rage—you need to contain that, to put a frame around it, where it can play itself out without you or your kin having to die. There is a theory that watching unbearable stories about other people lost in grief and rage is good for you—may cleanse you of your darkness. Do you want to go to the pits of yourself all alone? Not much. What if an actor could do it for you? Isn't that why they are called actors? They act for you. You sacrifice them to action.[51]

Except tragedy has always been a theater of sacrifice that kills the Black actors first, enacts horrific sexual violence on women for endless replay, and systemically degrades the human worth of migrants of color for the benefit of white audiences and the settler gaze.[52] Who is sacrificing whom in order to visualize pain? The *trauma-pain-tragedy* triad is one of the most strategically depoliticized configurations in settler epistemic systems. It was central to the rise of the model of Native informancy in colonial testimonies of trauma and remains a powerful force today. It manifests most vividly in the silencing of calls for change made in the wake of communally traumatizing targeted violence against racialized peoples, as in the 2019 mass shooting of Mexicans in El Paso, Texas, by a white nationalist. Let's bury the dead first. Don't politicize tragedy—no one could have predicted this, another official says.[53] Except predictive outcomes are exactly what settler governance schemes are designed to produce. The difference is for whose benefit.

The depoliticized trauma-pain-tragedy triad is also found in routine administrative reactions to sexual violence and femicides throughout the Americas. The silencing of calls for change in this domain are far more regulative of women's affective responses to violence and its structural underpinnings, as the silencing works to dampen—and profit from—the possible political fallout of women's public bereavement and calls for system change. Yesenia Zamudio, whose murdered daughter, María de Jesús (Marichuy) Jaime Zamudio, is widely thought to have been pushed off the fifth floor of a building in 2016 by her college professor and three classmates after resisting a sexually motivated attack, gained national attention in a public campaign for justice. "Stop profiting off our pain," said Zamudio in a video shared on social media:

> So what if I'm enraged and extreme? What if I set things on fire, wreak havoc, and raise fucking hell in this city? What's the fucking problem with that? They killed my daughter! I'm not a collective, and I don't need a drum or a fucking political party to represent me. I represent myself and without a microphone! I'm a mother whose daughter was killed! And yes, I'm an empowered, feminist mother, and I have had fucking enough. I have every right to burn down and destroy whatever I want, and I'm not going to ask for anyone's permission, because what I break is for my daughter. And she who wants to destroy should destroy, and she wants to burn down should burn down. And she who doesn't want to, should get out of our way. Because before they murdered my daughter, they murdered many, many others. And how were we before? All comfortable in our houses, crying and sewing. No more, sirs, that's done with now! We've broken the silence. And we won't allow that our pain is turned into a damn [media] circus. And if [the media] is going to talk, then talk about all who are raped and sexually assaulted by teachers and public servants. Talk about the women who get acid thrown on them. Talk about the girls who are raped in their cribs by their own fathers, and their families that stay silent because their catholic faith silences them. I am the mother of María de Jesús Jaime Zamudio, and I demand justice. For me, for my family, and for my daughter, and for all the ones that no one names.[54]

"Grief and rage—you need to contain that," writes Carson. But by whom and *for* whom? Zamudio is keenly aware of how state and corporate actors routinely "sacrifice her to action" in a staged counternarrative that serves to depoliticize grief by calling it "a tragedy." As Chapter 2 illustrates, when rage is gender-coded as male, it is afforded every opportunity to be recoded as justified violence in legal and administrative systems, and more so to the extent that it intersects with settler colonial conceptions of justifiable force (e.g., though relational proximity to ethnic, national, political, and other configuration of sociostructural belonging in white settler societies). This is especially true in social scientific analyses of the incidence and prevalence of femicide as perpetrated by predominantly poor and working-class men who are themselves victims of toxic cultures of masculinity, with a causally mystified narrative about what, specifically, supports and originates such cultures over time (and with institutionally afforded outlets for evading accountability). "Although there is no doubt that femicide embodies the most deadly logic of masculinity, that its perpetrators are misogynist and racist killers, the focus on working-class men deflects attention away from the multiple structures of violence in the lives of women."[55] Deflectionary epistemology, which upholds the carceral-impunity complex, is a shared metric of conceptual exchange between settler administrative systems responsible for "managing" sexual violence in settler colonial societies.

Tragedy's special connection to the emotional life of individuals undergoing pain is not a value-free connection.[56] The particular interrelation, node to node, between depoliticized grief and mainstream trauma narratives functions as a key part of white dynastic polities' continuous ability to weaponize reality in order to silence dissent and gatekeep structurally ameliorative resources for gender-based violence.[57] This is a fancy way of saying thoughts and prayers do more than nothing; they actively delink the necessary actions and maneuvers for addressing harms from the harms that require them, and they do so as a recurrent phenomena. For her public efforts to seek justice for her daughter's murder, the National Polytechnic Institute, which employed the attacker of her late daughter, offered a posthumous degree to Marichuy's mother and a public apology six years later, calling Marichuy's death a "tragedy" and a teachable moment about the seriousness of gender-based violence.[58] Deer frames responses such as these as a way of "apologizing without apologizing."[59] They certainly do some things—promise change, start in-name-only initiatives that are underfunded and unviable long term—while promoting the regenerative conditions for trauma to continue. The inability to understand trauma as a functional, organizational tool of settler colonial violence amplifies the impact of traumatic experience on specific populations, not by accident, but by design.

Trauma's "Redemptive" Value

Another motif in western conceptions of trauma has been trauma's redemptive value. Much of psychoanalysis, some of phenomenology, and all of the western existential tradition find some positive value in trauma, even when it is characterized as unassailable personal despair. This is because trauma is said to be a possible gateway to authentic self-knowledge and personal transformation (again, the logic of individuation at play), and even thought to yield philosophical insights into the very heart of the human condition. Take, for instance, Robert Stolorow's self-analysis of trauma and the subsequent advice he gave a patient:

> I recalled my feeling at the conference dinner as though I were an alien to the normals around me. In Gadamer's terms, I was certain that the horizons of their experience could never encompass mine, and this conviction was the source of my alienation and solitude, of the unbridgeable gulf separating me from their understanding. It is not that the traumatized and the normals live in different worlds; it is that these discrepant worlds are felt to be essentially and ineradicably incommensurable.... this is the legacy of your experiences with terrible trauma. You know that any moment those you love can be struck down by a senseless, random event. Most people don't really know that.[60]

The implicit white and abled social location of "most people" and "normals" is important here. Indigenous people and people of color do not, generally, agree that "most people don't really know" that they and their loved ones can be struck down at any moment and for any reason. When I was growing up, one of the first stories my mother taught me—after she taught me a four-digit proof-of-life code and singable emergency phone contact—was a story that her father told her. She said, "He sat me down when I was your age and told me, I do not want to die before you grow up. But it is possible and you and your siblings must prepare. And you may die before me. I would be very sad, but I would go on. You have to understand how to go on." She repeated that last part often. Years later, I told the story to an American therapist when asked to relay my earliest memories. She quickly diagnosed the exchange as child abuse. I wondered for the first time about the range of pathologizing techniques used to contain and erase marginalized people's tactics of survival against colonial violence. If there is something traumatizing in this narrative, it is not the powerful lesson of survival in the name of what Kyle Whyte calls "collective continuance" and J. Kēhaulani Kauanui calls "enduring Indigeneity." Rather, it is the intergenerational impact of the reliance on colonial deficiency narratives about our powerlessness to change things, a reliance that trades on a logic of woundedness, hurt, and fear whose function is to stunt coordinated action against the systemic violences we face. What is traumatic is the structurally enabled use of trauma discourses to disarm strategies of refusal—our refusal to be systematically disappeared or to accept anything less than the reclamation of what is rightfully ours—our lives, our safety, our well-being in our personhood and our communities, and, in Indigenous contexts, having stolen lands rematriated and uncoerced treaties honored.

This is one way that concepts of trauma that acknowledge the nonaccidental nature of structural violence can be helpful—by normalizing positions of political resistance rather than simply teaching how to cope with and accept structured loss in the name of narrative wholeness. This latter strategy, which is an all-too-common method in western mental-health care and social work, is a normative violence aimed at finishing what colonialism started.[61] As my mother knew intuitively, trust is not deserved in settler colonial contexts.[62] Native feminist scholar Dian Million (Tanana Athabascan) explains: "Given the history between Indigenous peoples and settler states, no safe place has been obtainable. Mistrust *should be* a feature of appropriate mental health in Indian Country."[63] For Indigenous peoples and people of color living within landscapes occupied by settler colonialism, there is no safety, and recognizing this fact is necessary to our survival. Yet passing this knowledge on intergenerationally in the name of collective continuance is pathologized within the very mental health frameworks that claim universal application to our trauma while simultaneously delinking it from the structures that produce it consistently, predictively, and by design.

Million on Trauma

Million's account of therapeutic care frameworks in settler colonial societies is critical to the notion of trauma as a nonaccidental, organized violence. For example, Million questions "the healing industry" in Canada and the United States that functionalizes violence against Indigenous peoples in the name of humanitarianism and human rights advocacy. There are two sides to the settler healing coin, but both license western intervention in Native people's lives. On the one hand, Indigenous peoples are often portrayed as terminally traumatized by the wounds inflicted on them by settler colonialism, as injured beyond repair. When those who suffer the logic of wounding are not white, ascribing pathology is typically the first response.[64] On the other hand, Million points out that when Indigenous peoples are not seen as terminally wounded but rather as possible subjects contained within the logic of individuation, they are treated as "painfully subscribed *subjects for healing*."[65]

In other words, they are identified as sites for legitimate state and cultural intervention, whether in the form of forced state residential schooling or aid recipients for humanitarian development. Trauma is the "preferred language" of international human rights instruments in the aftermath of globalization and the rise of neoliberal market economies, where development metrics and humanitarianism meld into frameworks intended to empower the disenfranchised.[66] On both accounts, the western legal positioning of victims prevails. The objective is never to disappear the traumatic suffering Indigenous peoples encountered as a result of intersecting violences, but to disappear Native lives altogether. This follows Wolfe's notion of the logic of elimination, which analyzes "what might be called the settler colonial will, a historical force that ultimately derives from the primal drive to expansion," a "greedy dynamic [that]is internal and self-generating."[67] Elimination is strategic because it aims to vacate Indian lands and render them available for settlement.[68] On this account, trauma narratives can easily trigger calls for humanitarian emergencies that are coordinated by settler colonial cultures, not unlike the engineered Bengal famines of 1770 and 1943 that killed millions of Bengalese under colonial British administration.[69] This does not mean that marginalized peoples have been passive recipients of structurally violent surroundings,[70] but rather that our surroundings have been shaped to deflect the realities of our experiences with structured trauma.

One thing to take away from this analysis is that simply expanding western trauma models and provision care to include experiences of injury and colonial violence from Indigenous communities and people of color is not an appropriate response.[71] Such an attempt to make existing understandings of trauma more inclusive would simply constitute what Ezgi Sertler calls a "recognition bluff."[72] A type of administrative violence, a recognition bluff is, according to Sertler, a "form of misrecognition where administrative systems enable new categories of legibility promising recognition for certain populations while, at the same time, they limit that category in ways that harm those populations." Consider that none of the mainstream approaches to trauma recognize, as phenomena that can be encompassed under the logic of wounding, the strategic elimination of referential networks of lands, rivers, plants, animal life,[73] the intergenerational sexual abuse of children in residential state schools, the systemic targeting and elimination of antiviolence leaders like Maricela, or the banality of femicide and normalized impunity over organized disappearances of women. Widening the net of existing western understandings of trauma would thus merely "include" more people under the category of those who have experienced trauma while continuing to limit the category of trauma in ways that uphold the logics of elimination and containment. As a normative violence, accounts of traumas to narrative life do not generally account for the history of organized violence against forms of narrativity that are not western. It's settler epistemology all the way down. This does not mean we've been epistemically colonized and there is nothing left of our cultures (the colonial dream of trauma). It does mean there are great epistemic labors and untallied epistemic exploitations[74] that must be accounted for in discussions of trauma, including intergenerational trauma.

Traditional Accounts

Perhaps one of the most promising frameworks for addressing the structured and systemic nature of gender-based violence in our communities arose in the post-Holocaust discourses of historical trauma and intergenerational trauma. The framework produced directly addressed injurious effects to whole communities across generations rather than just to individuals. In *Discourse on Colonialism*, Aimé Césaire famously connected the logic of colonial violence with fascism, arguing that the racist logics of elimination perpetrated by Nazi Germany were first developed and perfected on colonized peoples. His concern was not that global moral horror over the Holocaust was misplaced, but that the moral outrage of humanism is "sordidly racist";[75] it recognized the pain of subjects already recognized as subjects (because of their proximity to whiteness) while ignoring the pain and suffering of nonwhite peoples under the colonial regime and its aftermath. This logic still exists today. Consider that, in an entire contemporary book-length philosophical treatment on transgenerational trauma[76] that specifically takes up "dialogues across history and difference," grapples with the "ghosts of our forebears," and promotes the idea that "to heal human suffering, we often need to reclaim our elders," there is not a single reference to Native Americans. Not one. This isn't laughable, it's consistent.[77]

The logic of wounding even underlies many contemporary accounts of structural violence. Recall Johan Galtung's definition of structural violence as "violence that results in harm but is not caused by a clearly identifiable actor"—a definition that has had a significant impact on international organizations such as UNESCO and the World Health Organization and that also influences the CDC and contemporary public health research on inequality. In a study of differential outcomes for patients living in trauma deserts, defined as areas where a level I or II trauma center is more than one hour away by car, researchers (unsurprisingly) concluded that race was a strong predictor of worse trauma outcomes.[78] For the researchers, this constituted "structural violence," which they defined as the contingent "social arrangements that put individuals and populations in harm's way" but which have "*no identifiable aggressors*," do not "involve physical act[s]," and cannot be seen as "intentional."[79] Serious genealogical whitewashing work has gone into rendering social structures as arbitrary sets of relations that are as accidental as they are historically contingent. Indigenous social theory and anticolonial approaches to intergenerational trauma[80] have addressed this issue by linking settler colonial violence to the modalities of stress-inducing social, institutional, and cultural violences in marginalized people's lives. Trauma, when functionalized through institutions, is designed to finish what violent colonial settlement started—to consolidate the program of colonial techniques of violence that began in brutalizing physical as well as epistemic and hermeneutic violences. The goal is to dispossess Native peoples of lands and resources, exploit racialized labor (including gendered racialized and Indigenous labor) for surplus profit, and contain resistance through gender-based violences and their normalization. Colonial violence contains and pathologizes resistance through institutional violence, so that there is always functional complicity within settler colonial institutions. One way this is done is by instilling fear through the ongoing possibility of retraumatization. Operation Janus, one of the Trump administration's anti-immigrant policy agenda instruments aimed at broadening the reach of denaturalization (i.e., revoked citizenship), is one example. If an immigrant woman obtains citizenship through marriage legally and suffers intimate partner violence, she is forever wedded to her abuser through the lifelong possibility that they could fabricate claims of entering into a false marriage among myriad other possible accusations, extortions, and abuses.

The idea that a racialized woman is able to produce evidence that can be deemed satisfactory under an epistemic economy based on more than five hundred years of Native informancy is weak at best. Tortured asylum seekers have borne their mutilated bodies in US asylum credibility interviews, and US citizens have produced empirical proof such as birth certificates, Social Security cards, biometrics, and all have been to no avail in proving the legitimacy of their claims.[81] This is the reality we face in settler credibility economies.

As Emma LaRocque explains in "Here Are Our Voices—Who Will Hear?," "It was not that they had been silent; it was not that they hadn't spoken. They were not heard. But 'heard' here is a complexity . . . [First Nations'] statements were widely known but had no weight as any publicly accepted truth."[82] The traumatizing impact of these hermeneutic practices is not tragic, the result of unforeseeable forces, but structured and strategic to harm some people but not others. The level of perpetual structural anxiety this supports also makes it difficult to address issues of past violence, abuse, and survivorship among women-of-color immigrants. While one should not forget that this precarity is structurally engineered, through policy and law, this insight also adds a layer of complexity to discussions of structural trauma by having to recenter settler colonial configurations of birthright and belonging in racialized immigrant women's fight against spousal abuse. The function of trauma in this case is to create conditions of perpetual precarity and vulnerability that work to disappear those who resist settler formations of social life, thus centering violence on those who transgress colonial gender binaries, such as racialized women, and nonbinary, trans, and Two-Spirit people.

Conceptual approaches to practical problems, however promising, can lose track of the material details central to organizing resistance to violence: the names, dates, causes of death, the families left behind, suspended in life but unable to die without knowing where the bodies are. The statistics can be given. They have been given, the evidence entered.[83] In many cases, compelling physical evidence has been used to sentinel impending violence: before Maricela was murdered, she had received numerous death threats. Members of her family also received them before they, too, were killed. And prior to Maricela's tenure in office, Gisela Mota Ocampo was sworn in as the first female mayor of Temixco, only to be slain later that day—shot at home in front of her family. She too, had received numerous threats. And before Gisela, Tiquicheo Mayor, María Santos Gorrostieta Salazar survived two assassination attempts—one of which claimed her husband's life—before being tortured and slain in front of her young daughter. Over a hundred mayors have been murdered in Mexico alone, and tens of thousands of Indigenous women and women of color have been murdered or disappeared across Turtle Island and Abya Yala in the last few years. The links between organized crime, terror-based governance, and the historical structures of colonial domination that perpetuate gender-based violence[84] are strategically blurred in favor of depoliticized trauma narratives as part of a systems process rooted in dispossession and extractivism.

If enumerating our losses were enough to produce justice, more of us would do that critical work. But there exists a systemic design-of-distribution to the way our losses shake out that continues to underlie our attempts to address systemic violence—why tremendous public resources are often utilized to address sexual assault, kidnapping, and murder, but only when it happens to some populations and not others. On paper, Mexico has some of the most progressive policies against gender-based violence.[85] Day-to-day life, however, is quite different from official policy in settler cultures. New fertile lines of force (*forcis*) are generated to serve as enforcement mechanisms when older uses of force and violence become obsolete or illegal within settler legal systems. To go back to Daphne's case in Chapter 2, it is not incidental that the accused perpetrators were white or white-adjacent Ladino elites, just as it is not incidental that municipalities with the greatest rates of impunity for these crimes are places that center tourism and the extractive industries of natural resources and petrochemicals. Force and enforcement come together in the logic of wounding when the protection and regeneration of settler wealth is at stake. This is because trauma operates within a settler colonial architecture oriented toward the basic reproduction of social structures for transmitting intergenerational wealth among white settlers and their descendants. I can't say this enough: it's about profit, wealth, and privilege at the expense of other's lives and well-being, including the lands that bore us into being and that sustain all life. There is such a thing as enough. But not under settler capitalism and the dynastic violences it supports as a system.

This work takes a toll on us, and reframing problems in different lights can help address our own enraged pain as feminist scholars of violence. Not theoretical violence. Real violence, harms, and injuries. In "Grief and Indigenous Feminists' Rage," Speed endorses a research culture that recognizes "the ways we bring past violences to the field with us" as survivors, one "where our hearts do not have to be checked at the gate" in order to do our work.[86] Reframing the phenomenological experience of precarity and vulnerability in racialized gender-based violence from a structural perspective can help in this direction.[87] Such a reframe counters a settler innocence narrative like Diamond's and rejects the idea of tragedy as inherently blameless, disassociated from organized efforts to enforce colonial relations through social transformations by structuring the conditions for loss. As Speed notes, "Formulating violence against women as purely interpersonal phenomena only serves to de-politicize gender violence. Individual or interpersonal gender violence cannot be understood outside of the historical and ideological structures that give rise to it and in which it is enacted."[88] Structural trauma, on this view, is a functional, organizational tool of settler colonial violence that amplifies the impact of traumatic experience on specific populations by design. It calls for an end to narratives of trauma that are severed from the settler colonial project of Native land dispossession and genocide. It also calls for divestment from the logics of traumatology that recenter the founding myths and tacit values of anglo-european culture. Structural trauma then is a methodological pivot for conducting trauma-based, gender-based violence research in an anticolonial context. It is not a new approach but a reaffirmation of what Indigenous, Black, and Brown feminisms have contended for centuries about the nonaccidental role of gender-based violence in the consolidation of the colonial project: it is a structural phenomenon.

One of the great ideological achievements of settler epistemic systems in advanced industrial societies is the successful packaging of constraint-as-freedom alongside the freedom to not exercise restraint when it comes to violence against marginalized peoples. The cultural machinery of war that continuously reconstructs freedoms as white dynastic norms and privileges is thousands of years in the making, thousands of years in adaptive self-healing and learning as a system, and if we forget this, if we forget that we're made to forget this by settler epistemic systems, we're in for a fight that is even harder than the one we are already in. "To hell with this," as the Zapatistas famously say.

As I've argued throughout this book, a primary function of settler colonial epistemic systems is to structure and prepare the social pathways for interpretive counterplay (the cultural rebranding of insurgent practices that threaten white dynastic formations into nonthreatening forms) to emerge as the dominant reality.[89] Philosophy has played a large hand in this. Many of our most cherished and lauded "liberal" figures—defenders of cultural and gender pluralism, women's rights, and social democratic norms—illustrate this point. They seem to say all the right things, but on closer inspection, their work builds sophisticated back routes and side chutes for the network interconnections necessary for white supremacy to endure. In Chapter 1, we discussed Iris Marion Young's view against reparations for slavery as consistent with the 91 percent of Republicans and GOP leaders who say descendants of people enslaved in the United States should not be repaid in some way.[90] Here I'd like to note her position on Indigenous self-determination as similar in form and function to her argument against reparations for slavery. I do this to highlight the burdens anglo-european political philosophy creates for anticolonial political projects already in existence, especially when philosophers bill their work as post/anti/decolonial in spirit.

Young's "Hybrid Democracy"

In "Hybrid Democracy: Iroquois Federalism and the Postcolonial Project," Young argues for a political model of global governance she calls "decentered diverse democratic federalism."[91] She thinks such a model is needed for ethical and historical reasons: historically, because the current system of state sovereignty derived from nineteenth-century european political thought lacks the "institutional imagination" to adequately respond to rising Indigenous claims to sovereignty and the right to self-rule, and ethically, because while "anyone interested in justice today must face the project of undoing the legacies of colonialism," new borders inevitably raise "global justice" questions about the fair allocation and redistribution of the world's resources, the question of human rights interventions, and environmental considerations that affect us all.[92]

Like most anglo-european political theorists and their models of political knowledge, Young presumes political alternatives do not exist until a white person names them into being as a novel framework. Young thus endorses her own such framework—a global version of federalism (a mixed-governance model of a centralized "federal" authority sharing power with semiautonomous regional or state powers) built to regulate possible conflicts that are in the interest of "global justice," and to promote democratic engagements toward global peace.[93]

Functionally, Young's views support a soft settler colonialism (which is just settler colonialism sneaked in through a back route) that works by heralding public support for Indigenous self-determination with the proviso that Indigenous peoples must engage in codeliberative political processes with "outsiders" whenever non-Indigenous interests are at stake, such as whenever outsiders' access to natural resources is impeded by a political border that becomes established through the exercise of Indigenous rights-claims to autonomous governance. If this is Indigenous self-determination for Young, what, one wonders, does she think colonialism is?

Young goes to great lengths to support her argument against Indigenous nation-building as grounds for complete autonomy from foreign intervention, with natural resource allocation as a major point of contention. Citing Charles Beitz's argument that states do not have the moral right "to keep for themselves all the benefits derived from the natural resources that happen to lie within their borders" such as "fertile land, economically valuable minerals and so on," Young affirms the view that "no state is entitled to treat them as its private property to be used only of its own benefit. Because certain resources are necessary for the productive capacity of all societies, they must be considered a global commons." For Young, this view boils down to the fact that natural resources "are by no means distributed around the globe" and that some resources are inevitably "more valuable than others." This classic restatement of settler capital globalization theorizes resource scarcity from the point of white dynastic formations. It hides the plain fact that the home ranges and lands of Indigenous peoples across many of the world's geographic regions happen to overlap with vast natural resources and fossil fuel reserves considered "valuable" to settler capital interests. The Zapatista struggle in southern Mexico is inseparable from this context.

As a conceptual framework and through its functional operations, Young's framework still requires Indigenous answerability to non-Indigenous polities and to a global framing of nationhood where white settler polities can make demands on resources thought to lie within Indigenous people's territories. As a decolonial systems thinker, what I find particularly interesting is the way Young leverages the discourse of "interconnectedness" and systems-level features of global colonial capitalism as an argument to support a new era of (global) federalist intervention in Indian country and in rising autonomous territories throughout the world. In other words, there are many ways to configure the world through connectivity, interrelatedness, and interwoven principles. Some of these ways establish ethical relations and responsibility *to* various peoples, lands, and environs, whereas different manners of establishing and picking out the salient (relevant) connections between system elements lead to vastly altered (e.g., nonreciprocal and hierarchical) interrelations that distance people *from* responsibility (especially as liability). To recall, the logic of distancing is how Young argues against individual liability for structural injustices (the world is just too interconnected! By which she means everyone is responsible without any one individual capable of being held liable). Now, she uses that same logic to argue for limited jurisdictional sovereignty for Indigenous peoples. While Young endorses sovereignty limitations for any statist formation, her argument (the very subject of her essay) is geared toward Indigenous sovereignty claims. She writes:

The web of global, national, and regional interactions draws all of us into relationships such that actions or events in one locale often have profound consequences for others. . . . While local and regional self-determination are important values, *no jurisdiction ought to be sovereign . . . this means rejecting a conception of self-governance as non-interference,* clearly separating a realm of our business from a realm outside that is none of our business, and where those outside must be kept out of our business.[94]

Yes, Young really said this. In her view, global interdependencies "call for some form of international regulatory scheme that aims for stable and just cooperation"[95] rather than calling for the abolition of the current settler capitalist international regulatory scheme that self-organizes and adapts to be able to continuously enforce stable "cooperation" in structurally unjust ways. Her view that "the scope and complexity of economic, communication and many other institutions in the world today constitute a sufficiently tight web of constraint and interdependence that we must speak of a global *society,*" is a straightforward settler colonial construct of social interdependence. How *did* such institutions emerge and to what end? The naturalized story of an emerging "global society" offered by Young brings us back to Chapter 1 and our discussion of innocence-producing uses of "historical context."[96]

As this book has shown, the initial conditions for structuring the "web of local, national, and regional interactions" Young observes are not random or the product of chance. From roman law witness stipulations of enslaved persons to colonial-era testimonial burdens, to modern-day evidentiary standards, the initial conditions for the rise of white dynastic formations (and their supporting epistemic economies) have shaped the developmental trajectory of white supremacy as a multistable system. That means two things (for the purposes of my project). First, multistable systems are capable of producing contradictions without deterring the historical trajectory of white dynastic formations. Second, as a system property of white dynastic formations' self-organization, coexisting attractors (the endless states of discrimination produced by interlocking oppressions) can continuously anchor the trajectory of settler social structures toward the states necessary to uphold its goal of white dynasty socioeconomic supremacy.[97] Whereas Marx thought the forward march of history leans toward revolutionary class struggle with emancipation at its endpoint, this view of colonial history as a nonlinear dynamic system suggests a widening spiral vortex as a more appropriate illustration of the dynamics of settler colonial societies.

Time can progress without substantive change in the conditions that replicate colonial violence, generation after generation, allowing for increasing dimensionality—expansive domains and capacities for settler epistemic systems to pursue their functions. Anticolonial systems perspectives hold that, just like "thoughts and prayers" that don't just do nothing—they actively uphold structural innocence schemes—"well-intentioned" political theorizing also does not "do nothing"; it is an active part of creating the myriad of anchors and attractors that allow white dynastic systems to keep functioning as a system.

By now, it should be clear that anticolonial systems views emphasize the capacity of systems to endure and shapeshift in response to nonoptimal conditions. The dynamic view of white supremacy as a historical system of self-organization is compatible with the view that "colonialism did not end with the end of historical colonialism based on foreign territorial occupation. Only its form has changed. Indeed, as has been happening since the sixteenth century, capitalism cannot exert its domination except in articulation with colonialism."[98] However, the anticolonial systems view stresses the importance of *initial conditions* (hence I go further back than the sixteenth century) and the *critical points* around which self-organization occurs— such that it is more than a change from one state to another (e.g., from the "form" of imperialism to neoliberalism) that identifies the system of white supremacy, but rather the underlying mechanisms by which such dynamic shifts occur. Preserving the sociostructural interrelations and conditions that shape the ability to self-organize around critical points is what white settler polities protect above all. The reason Section 5 of the Civil Rights Act of 1965 was so effective in achieving concrete and effective responses to structural discrimination lies precisely in its design around nonwhitewashed assumptions about white supremacy: it exists, it has continued to exist, and is likely to continue existing given its history. Anticolonial systems views thus reject the traditional framing of systems change in complex systems theory as a naturalized playbook where long-term gains always come at the expense of short-term actions, or where basic transformations oriented toward structural change require the relevant nodes of engagement to be white polities and the sociostructural interconnections they established. Policies that disrupt the intended flow of harm toward vulnerableized (i.e., structurally made to be vulnerable, as Speed would put it) communities are real, necessary, and worthwhile endeavors for enacting structural change, even if they are also target points around which dynastic formations organize to contain the spread of system stress points. Among the various system responses to such efforts are liberal theories of change that double down on conceptual schemes that allow for sophisticated workarounds to such policies and practices. Hence, the long-term world-building strategy is a critical component of restructuring policy instruments that invariably steer toward settler colonial intervention schemes. "Another way is possible" is a Zapatista motto for a reason.

In the following sections, I'll reject Young's white dynastic formulation of settler colonial intervention schemes in favor of Indigenous self-determination as structurally contextualized autonomy (rather than naturalized "nondomination"),[99] one that is not premised on the racist view that Indigenous peoples lack the capacity to understand how global forces can require the development of strategies and responses to deal with shared problems on their own accord, including the ability to engage in dialogue with settler governments. (This is particularly the case because most shared concerns, from human rights to climate change, have asymmetrically borne consequences for Indigenous peoples.) Before turning to such an autonomous framework practiced in Zapatista communities, I turn to Sara Deer's account of the importance of linking Indigenous autonomy and the right to self-determination to the structural nature of gender-based violence.

Deer on Self-Determination and Gender-Based Violence

Deer's influential analysis of rape (her preferred terminology for legal formulations of nonconsensual sex) offers critical insights into the structural dynamics of gendered violence in settler colonial societies, and into the various reforms tasks that remain in tribal rape law to make such laws truly centered on Native survivors' experiences and needs.[100] The first order of business for Deer is undoing colonial myths about the prevalence and incidence of rape in Indian country as driven by an outside, naturally occurring force. According to Deer, when violence against women, and Native women in particular, is framed as an "epidemic," a deflectionary epistemology is at work to provide cover to perpetrators and their institutional enablers, which erases the structural causation between colonial violence and present-day gendered violence. It also reduces the harm of rape and sexual assault to biomedical models of physical injury that strategically overlook the psychic, spiritual, and communal interrelations shattered by rape. Rape is undoubtedly an instrument of war capable of being used against Native and non-Native people alike, but Deer cautions against liberal feminist framings of the causes and harms of rape as reducible to patriarchal violence. She writes: "Today's mainstream feminist theories about rape are often responding to a culture grounded in patriarchy of European origin. When tribal governments respond to gendered violence, though, they are responding to a phenomenon fully entrenched in abusive colonial power."[101]

Young's framework tries to speak to, but ultimately fails to understand, the structural dynamics of abusive colonial power. Colonial powers have always found a way to rule by jurisdictional fiat (or administrative analogues) even on lands designated as "Native" and "self-governing" by colonial governments themselves. At stake is the ability to control the terms by which sovereignty is "given" or withheld, but also to do the work of structural violence that upholds colonial power relations (even under conditions of "mutually recognized" noninterference). The notion of structural violence advanced in this book, which focuses on the systems-level adaptive features of white dynastic social reproduction schemes, shows how nondomination can functionally coexist with structural domination by design. This is evident in the link between sovereignty and jurisdiction in sexual assault cases that Deer highlights. Deer draws attention to how the way "the crisis of rape in tribal communities is inextricably linked to the way in which the United States developed and sustained a legal system that has usurped the sovereign autonomy of tribal nations."[102] Complex federal legal schemes (e.g., the Major Crimes Act of 1885, Public Law 280, the US Supreme Court decision in *Oliphant v. Suquamish*) were created to deny tribal governments jurisdiction "over the vast majority of sexual violence that happens to Native women."[103] This framework of legal scheming is a system feature of white dynastic formations. In other words, it is not the exception, but the rule. The Tribal Law and Order Act of 2010 (which was designed in part to "provide greater freedom for Indian tribes and nations to design and run their own justice systems"),[104] and The Violence Against Women Act of 2013 (which included a provision giving Tribal nations governance over domestic abuse cases) were "built on the blood, sweat, and tears of Native women and their allies."[105] In the 2022 case *Oklahoma v. Castro-Huerta*, the Supreme Court ruled that states once again have jurisdiction over Native lands in criminal proceedings, reversing two hundred years of precedent. As Ruíz, Berenstain, and Paredes-Ruvalcaba write:

In the United States, Indigenous Tribal Nations have historically been legally denied criminal jurisdiction over non-Native people who commit criminal acts on tribal lands, which prohibits Tribal nations from pursuing accountability for non-Native perpetrators of sexual violence against Native women. . . . The vast majority of perpetrators of rape and sexual assault against Native women are non-Native men. For decades, non-Native sexual predators, usually white men, have knowingly exploited this legal landscape in order to perpetrate sexual violence against Native women on reservations with impunity. . . . That sexual and reproductive violence against Native women serves the project of settler statecraft is a guiding principle of the ongoing processes of colonization and colonial genocide that continue to underlie the existence of the United States. As Simpson. . . explains, "A large part of the colonial project has been to control the political power of Indigenous women and queer people through the control of our sexual agency because this agency is a threat to heteropatriarchy . . . Indigenous body sovereignty and sexuality sovereignty threaten colonial power." . . . The promotion of systemic sexual violence against Indigenous women, children, and Two-Spirit people is an essential mechanism to disrupt structures of governance grounded in mutual relationships among Indigenous peoples, lands, animal relatives, and other Indigenous Nations—all of which pose a threat to settler governance structures.[106]

The above notion of "settler statecraft" directly addresses the systems-level features of colonial violence that transfer jurisdictional struggles over "borders" to the bodies of Native peoples. In Young's framework, "Outside agents who believe that the actions of an autonomous agent affect them adversely can legitimately make a claim on the affecting agent to have a right to negotiate with them about the terms of their relations and the actions that may harm them. Self-determining entities need to join a decision-making body to work out procedures for adjudicating such claims and potential conflicts."[107] This is precisely how non-Native people who rape Native women on Native lands are able to appeal to a decision-making body for redress.[108]

Jurisdictional struggles over sexual assault cases in Indian country are directly tied to the asymmetry of evidentiary burdens for proving violence. In western conceptual schemas, history is set up as a linear timeline of official narratives (e.g., "the great deeds of great men" nonsense) that can be excavated for "proof" and brought back to settlers as a treasure trove of epistemic artifacts, or "receipts," whenever settler colonial systems assail, harm, and traumatize us. Without this silver tray of evidentiary offerings to power, the official narratives of law, healthcare, and settler governance claim to be powerless to intervene, much less to consider a ceasefire. We are asked, time and again, to extract reason from an irrational system set up to kill us and reduce us to our labor—so that others can benefit and reign in the full sun of mediocrity and unsustainable relations with the earth—until we (so the hope is) tire from the labor and relent to the design of settler colonial social structures and ways of being and living. While we tire from gathering receipts that will never add up in the administrative logics of settler bureaucracies, a powerful system of dispossession and displacement lumbers on.[109]

Rage Becomes Her

In *Rage Becomes Her*, Soraya Chemaly narrates the many cultural tools that silence women and specifically survivors of sexual violence. One of these tools is the settler colonial structure of address I describe throughout this book. She writes:

> Conservatives like to debate rape statistics, which have always made me wonder, what is their Goldilocks number? What exact number of rapes is not too high, not too low, but *just* right? What makes a rape "legitimate" in the eyes of conservatives? Certainly not victims' anger, suffering, or ideas about assault. Mainly, it is some throwback idea tied to notions of property violation or a moral infraction on the part of the victim. Today there is no law giving rapists the right to rape, but fewer than 3 percent of rapists, the overwhelming majority of whom are men, are ever prosecuted and imprisoned. More than half of US states allow rapists to sue for custody of children born from their raping. Rape laws have always reflected how we feel about people's relative citizenship rights.[110]

In my work as a survivor advocate, I have routinely produced incidence and prevalence reports of sexual assault statistics for various agencies and groups. During Covid-19, in my role as the Principal Researcher on Gender-Based Violence for the MeToo organization, I led research efforts in producing the kind of urgent data sets on intersecting inequalities between race, gender, socioeconomic status, and survivor health that other organizations, from Data for Black Lives to social justice research centers, were also working furiously to produce during the pandemic. Our findings echoed what we already knew about social stratification and the asymmetric physical, mental, and economic burdens continuously borne by populations of color, and women of color and Indigenous women in particular. It was a "pessimism of the intellect, optimism of the will" endeavor triggered by a global health crisis, but it was not a new phenomenon. Over the years, I've tracked how little pull even the most staggering statistics have in policy circles. This is especially the case for rape and attempted rape statistics of Indigenous women. As one lobbyist said to me about the percentage of Indigenous women who have experienced rape, "If it were 10 out of 10, it still wouldn't move the needle [with certain policymakers]." The takeaway from the abysmal but predictive indifference toward the lives of Native women and women of color is not to shut down data surveillance programs across the board (as Deer explains the many constructive tribal uses of survivor-centered sexual violence statistics and approaches to data governance); it is to show the productive goal of surveillance as a settler colonial project that is structurally indifferent to the harms born from its system so that structural interventions can speak to this design. Data without advocacy is settler gold.

Today, the dominant models of structural injustice ask marginalized peoples to explain displacement and dispossession in a way that will click with what white settler polities need to hear to think through the moral worth of subsequent actions, if there are any, as sufficient to warrant behavioral change at the personal or collective level. All this evidentiary busywork is a ruse to detract from insurgent political formations that strain the bonds between the elementary relations of settler colonial social systems that allow white settler polities to enjoy both peace and an epistemic space that arbitrates this peace, where they adjudicate and we plea. And one way this strain can emerge is through alternative relational pathways and interrelations between history, people, and culture—from other ways of being, acting, relating to the world that disrupt core epistemological orthodoxies and the metaphysical assumptions on which such orthodoxies rest. Given the vast strategies settler colonial societies use to self-organize around system threats, a systems-based approach of structural respecification and ongoing counterformations across all system features (such as policy) is warranted.

Constructing Violence

Consider the vast strategies settler colonial societies use to structure violence in ways that will evade what settler cultures count as "violence." Professional surveys that serve as expert mechanisms to the United Nations have done this by simply defining violence as the illegal use of force, making it impossible to survey the death toll resulting from police killings or other uses of force lawfully enacted by state actors, such as forced removal of unsheltered populations in urban spaces and military deployments to autonomous territories where multinationals have mining, oil, and foreign investment interests. The Trump administration used this same semantic technique to limit what could count as domestic violence and sexual assault in the United States, thereby narrowing the scope of who could claim to be a "survivor of abuse" and who could seek legal remedy or qualify for federally funded victim resources.[111] The same occurred in immigration and asylum policy under US attorney general Jeff Sessions. By the time family separation at the US-Mexico border gained national attention, the semantic ground had already been paved to limit administrative responsibility for (and judicial mitigation of) state-sponsored child abuse. In the Australian context, Aileen Moreton-Robinson (Goenpul) documents how the settler state crafted a broad range of rhetorical strategies that used "security" discourses to double down on patriarchal white sovereignty in order to deny Indigenous sovereignty. This widely used technique provides settler states with a powerful narrative that separates the mechanisms of settler capitalist statecraft from gendered racisms, colonial occupation, and the violences it sustains. Little by little, the links between colonial dynamics and impunity for systemic violence are blurred, and an alternate reality begins it functional reign.

Another way that settler colonial societies reframe violence as nonviolence is to create causal and contributory distance between perpetrators and harms. For instance, Latin American states often deploy paramilitary groups and use financial intermediaries to dilute the international chain of corporate funding and foreign support of local military intervention (think of the intricate web of shell corporations documented in the Panama Papers). Whenever the skyrocketing rates of sexual assault in militarized zones rise to international attention, as they periodically do, it becomes easy enough to use colonial chains of evidentiary reasoning (which insist on unbroken chains of physical evidence) to causally distance harm(s) from their perpetrator(s).[112]

In the 1980s, the Guatemalan military carried out a series of multilevel interventions (including forced disappearances, widespread rape, and razing of houses and communal dwellings) to prevent Indigenous communities from gaining legal title to local landowners' estates in the village of Sepur Zarco.[113] "When we analyze the survivors' [of rape] testimonies, we find a common thread in their stories: the struggle to obtain legal certainty (titles) over the land they owned."[114] There is little coverage of the connection between Indigenous land dispossession and sexual assault in the prevailing humanitarian narratives of the incidence and prevalence of military aggression and assault against Indigenous women in Latin America. What little coverage does exist tends to rehearse the well-worn narratives of cultural "machismo," often via pathologizing racial tropes of "brown on brown" violence, or point to indistinct social determinants of health like "poverty" and "educational level attained." Rarely is the US role in training and financing the armed forces that carried out the Mayan genocide (over two hundred thousand, by some estimates) acknowledged as the relevant contributory cause (e.g., the "but for which" the crimes against Mayan peoples could not have been carried out).[115] In 1999, after a UN report revealed (what was, by then, an open secret) the extent of US involvement, former US president Bill Clinton crafted a causally liable distancing narrative from the genocide by accepting moral responsibility. He said: "It is important that I state clearly that support for military forces and intelligence units which engaged in violence and widespread repression was wrong, and the United States must not repeat that mistake. . . . we are determined to remember the past, but not to repeat it."[116] One sure way to repeat the past is to mystify the present as causally distant (but morally proximate) to the violence knowingly and willfully enacted on populations to protect white settler extractive profit and financial gain for generations, and to erase this link between past and present in policy responses to Indigenous migration to the United States.

These two techniques of semantic reversal and contributory distancing illustrate dynamic geopolitical strategies of coordinated restraint associated with the logic of wounding.[117] Settler administrations are not just failing to act; they are designed to produce policies that fail people who are made to be vulnerable, and to get away with it.[118] It is not that the United States did not know Mayan peoples were being slaughtered, it is that they were left to die by the very people funding and providing training for the violence against them, and this ability was coordinated in advance, during and after the genocide through a system process of white dynastic social reproduction as a long-run phenomenon.[119]

As many are aware from watching *Dateline*, under US settler criminal law, legal culpability for homicide is often equal to (if not greater) for the actor(s) that planned, financed, or otherwise set in motion the events leading to a homicide, than for the actor(s) most proximately and directly responsible for the act of homicide. What settler interpretive ecologies functionalize is a narrative reversal whenever the perpetrators have relational proximity to dynastic whiteness, especially at the governance level. In short, while there is always a way to generate plausible deniability on the harms end of colonial violence, the inverse is true on the evidentiary end. (How has Henry Kissinger still not been held accountable for war crimes?) This dual-track power is a systems feature, part of an overall design architecture made to regenerate and grow accumulated value and to control its dynastic transmission intergenerationally.[120] What I'm drawing attention to here is the interconnectedness of subsystems in settler reproduction schemes and the role this interconnectedness plays in upholding structural violence over seemingly discontinuous periods of time.

Alternative Feminist Constructions

Critical race and Indigenous feminisms have been central to conceptualizing alternatives to state-based and rights-based discourses of autonomy and self-determination that illustrate the creative labor of producing long-term structural respecification of settler colonial social relations. Theories and practices include the reconceptualization of self-determination as bodily, cultural, and land-based "integrity,"[121] *cuerpo-territorio* (body-earth territory),[122] as well as rich affirmations of cultural endurance mentioned in this chapter.

These diverse feminisms have also held the line against rights-based rollbacks and the nonaccidental maldistribution of harm in settler colonial white supremacist societies, working within and against settler administrative structures to provide internal system resistance to settler colonial creations of day-to-day harm. "Attempts to harness the power of the state through the appropriate rhetorical/legal incantations should be appreciated as intensely powerful and calculated political acts. In the context of white supremacy, engaging in rights discourse should be seen as an act of self-defense."[123] Since Gramsci, the notions of "hegemony" and "wars of maneuver/position" (which produce cultural and political dominance by incorporating opposition into the apparatuses of legitimation—much like the contradictory existence of a mass-produced Che Guevara t-shirt or narrowly designated "free speech zones" on college campuses)—have cast suspicion on such attempts to "harness the power of the state" toward liberatory goals.

Gramsci's framework has a ring of systems theory to it. He uses terminology of "structures," "equilibrium," "reproduction," and he famously outlines the mechanics of structural domination by focusing on adaptive features of "hegemonic" social systems, particularly their ability to reproduce the conditions of their own production by incorporating opposition (with the goal of getting subordinate groups to consent to their own domination by adopting the dominant group's goals and values). Asserting that the dominant ideology is "structural and epistemological" rather than fundamentally "psychological or moralistic," Gramsci focuses on the structural processes by which cultural apparatuses (e.g., politics, education, etc., in Marx's "superstructure") coordinate with administrative apparatuses to respond to dynamics of resistance in the productive "base" of society: "In other words, the dominant group is coordinated concretely with the general interests of the subordinate groups, and the life of the state is conceived as a continuous process of formation and superseding of unstable equilibria . . . between the interests of the fundamental group and those subordinate groups—equilibria in which the interests of the dominant group prevail, but only up to a certain point, i.e., stopping short of narrowly corporate economic interests."[124]

Gramsci's analysis of power has been widely used to theorize diverse liberation projects that question the efficacy of harnessing the power of the state in its liberal form.[125] While we are now at a point where no one needs advanced degrees to grasp how going through official channels can limit our options or place us in a worse position than before an injury occurred, the basic insights of the Gramscian framework are still levied as theoretical problems in defense-based organizational work that reacts to immediate threats, such as water protectors defending Indigenous territories against the threat of colonial mining operations.

One of the issues I have with the Gramscian framework (as it is commonly used) is that it fosters a bivalent (rather than a network) construction of relations of domination between an ideological (structural-epistemological) apparatus and oppressed groups. Elsewhere,[126] I have argued that this configuration of power between oppressor-oppressed (a holdover from political theorizing since at least Hegel) underplays the role intersecting oppressions play in upholding hegemony. Intersecting oppressions are redistribution points that facilitate the communication of system goals in white dynastic formations; they are functional lifelines of colonialism and are integral parts of system design. While a node-to-node relation may be sufficient to establish a relation of domination, the redistribution, dynamic scaling of oppression, and adaptive resilience to system challenges is greatly improved by a multinode topology of domination. Hence, racist sexism, rape, and femicide perpetrated by men of color are not "separate" phenomena set apart from state-sponsored terrorism and violence (e.g., as in examples of "internal colonialism") but of a piece with it. It's just another day in the life of white dynastic formations.

Another issue with the way the "no speaking to state power without reifying state power" exception works is by ignoring the temporal dimensions of colonial reproduction schemes as self-healing systems. Over time, white dynastic systems adapt theoretical insights into their innerworkings and self-heal by incorporating them into their redistribution and administrative design as well: an undocumented migrant woman that seeks citizenship from the white settler state has undoubtedly less safety, less economic security, less access to healthcare, and control over reproduction over long ranges of time without documentation than with.[127] This is by design. Policy instruments and legal frameworks advance new oppressive functions in light of this reality. Hence, Crenshaw is right that coordinated acts of self-defense that respond to direct and structural forms of state aggression are not reducible to a politics of reaction or ideologically induced consent. They are a core part of what I consider to be structural guerrilla warfare.[128]

Structural Guerrilla Warfare

Born out of anticolonial struggles against foreign-backed dictatorships in Latin America, the term *guerrillas* is typically associated with members of (predominantly leftist) "political organizations operating in both rural and urban areas which use armed warfare for the purpose of changing societal structure,"[129] and which have long histories of women's participation that are often ignored.[130] In such low-intensity warfare, one builds support at the grassroots level, coalition to coalition, assembly to assembly, skirmish to skirmish, in an effort to create stress points for a much larger, well-organized yet unwieldy army for small-scale conflict. I think we can adapt the basic principles of guerrilla warfare to nonarmed engagements with state power that flips the script on the time-worn state sovereignty/reification dilemma. When thousands of attorneys descended on US airports to issue writs of habeas corpus (L. "you have/produce the body") in response to Trump's ban of travelers from Muslim-majority countries, speaking to state power was not a luxury, but a structurally appropriate defensive strategy. Of course, the judicial system adapts to create massive backlogs and procedural black holes where forms, case files, and people go missing (as in the cases of missing child detainees intentionally separated from their families). And it doesn't lessen the vast power and administrative reach of settler governance systems to unevenly distribute harm and gatekeep resources. But as a systems-based response that operates alongside the myriad of collective and grassroots-based responses to structural violence, structural guerrilla warfare can expose (if briefly) the core function of white dynastic social reproduction schemes and allow for targeted interventions that speak to system design (as the many militarized Trump administration responses to the Black Lives Matter movement show). It can also save lives. Colonial warfare is a long game, a low-intensity war of attrition with high-intensity periods and stakes. The role that normative and socially legible (to settler state power) narratives play in structural responses to oppression cannot be easily dismissed, as it will often be necessary to submit normative discourse to undo normative binds (e.g., to use Young's framework and principles of nondomination to get a point across). On the guerrilla structuralism framing, this use of settler epistemological toolkits is not passive or ideologically produced, but a strategic feature of collective refusal, one that cannot be used as it was designed or intended.

On the other side of guerrilla praxis is not "theory," but land and resources. Reclamation of land and the material chains of value transference in settler colonial societies forms the base of structural change in settler colonial societies.[131] As a sole offensive strategy of self-defense, structural guerrilla warfare is limited in the world-building that can emerge from it, but it is no less necessary to address the structural design of settler colonial violence that continuously reorganizes to maintain control of the conditions for white dynastic social reproduction to endure. Settler epistemologies only recognize settler epistemologies, after all. Also needed is an anticolonial offensive strategy of change that restructures relations of domination in a way that does not require buy-in from the people who have harmed you to succeed. It simply requires action and air awareness over where one is in a dynamic system process of adaptive self-healing, and of the alternate paths that have been created (and strategically obscured by the logics and value infrastructures of settler epistemic systems) as livable options. Just as with therapeutic approaches to cancer treatment, you can potentially *outpace* a dynastic formation in a systems network framing of oppression—something whitewashed theories of structural change miss.

In our last and final section, I turn to the Zapatista model of using "rights in rebellion"[132] as an example of guerrilla structuralism. I stop using this term ("guerrilla structuralism") henceforth because it is critical to not present Zapatismo as anything other than what already exists: the alternatives that have been forged and cared for though painstaking communal labor and long-term struggles of resistance. These approaches reject the idea that resistance is futile, or that the identification of a serious conceptual dilemma for sovereignty is also a structural barrier to political organization that defends sovereignty as noninterference and autonomy for Indigenous peoples. It is also a land-specific model of creative refusal that illustrates the affirmatory function of enduring Indigeneity. For J. Kēhaulani Kauanui, enduring Indigeneity has a twofold meaning, "[first,] that indigeneity itself is enduring—that the operative logic of settler colonialism may be to 'eliminate the native,' as the late Australian scholar Patrick Wolfe brilliantly theorized, but that Indigenous peoples exist, resist, and persist; and second, that settler colonialism is a structure that endures Indigeneity, as it holds out against it."[133]

Dignified Rage

In the mid-1980s, Indigenous communities in Mexico organized the Ejército Zapatista de Liberacion Nacional (EZLN) (National Zapatista Liberation Army) in response to long-existing struggles over land tenure, structural poverty, government suppression, and state-sponsored terrorism against (predominantly rural and peri-urban) campesino and Indigenous communities.[134] Agro-industrial chemical contamination of water sources, toxic environmental exposure from hydrocarbon extraction and mining, deforestation (especially in the Lacandon Jungle), invasion of genetically modified seeds, the imposition of monoculture (especially for oil palm production), and the structural adjustment programs that forced Indigenous peoples to seek out industrial wage labor for survival, were all background factors for the rise of the EZLN. But it was in the southern state of Chiapas in

STRUCTURAL VIOLENCE IS *NOT FATE* 283

the early 1990s that the movement became a large-scale Indigenous rebellion with a philosophical mandate based on Indigenous political principles that became known as Zapatismo.

To understand Zapatismo, it is necessary to understand the economic and social backdrop of Chiapas, which, to date, along with the neighboring state of Oaxaca, has the highest concentration of Indigenous peoples in Mexico (in the rural areas it's close to 100 percent, made up of predominantly Mayan Ch'ol, Tsotsil, Tseltal, Tojolobal, Mam, and Zoque peoples). Chiapas is a contradiction: it is both the most resource-rich state in Mexico and the poorest state, with the highest rates of poverty, infant mortality, and malnutrition. This contradiction is explicable in light of colonial power structures that disempower marginalized communities with the closest proximity to natural resources. Chiapas provides half of the hydroelectric power for all of Mexico, is the leading exporter of coffee, has the richest forests of exotic woods, ore, and copper mines, and most significant, holds one of the largest untapped oil reserves in Latin America.

In 1978, the journal *Science* published an article in its news and opinion section entitled "Mexico: The Premier Oil Discovery in the Western Hemisphere":

> Intensive exploration in Mexico is turning up oil fields so immense that they could overturn conventional wisdom about world oil supplies and significantly alter the geopolitics of energy . . . the apparent magnitude of the Mexican oil deposit is a "tremendous shock" that "boggles the mind" according to oil experts who are familiar with the discoveries . . . what this means for the United States is that during the next 5 to 10 years Mexico will become a world-class oil exporter, and if policies favorable to both sides can be worked out, Mexico could export a large part of its production to its neighbor to the north.[135]

Now what do you suppose would happen next? Throughout the 1970s a series of geological reports confirming the existence of "unexplored" regions and untapped mineral resources, including hydrocarbons, in the south of Mexico became the subject of intense exploration efforts by the United States.[136] A 1983 US geological survey identified oil reserves in the "Southeastern Mexico-Guatemala region [encompassing Chiapas]" to be "about 53 B[illion]B[arrels] of oil, 3 BB of natural gas liquids, and 65 Tcf of gas. The estimated undiscovered resources are about 78 BB of oil and 24 Tcf of gas. Estimated total original recoverable resources (ultimate) are about 177.5 billion barrels of oil equivalent (BBOE)."[137] Similar studies made their way to the US General Accounting Office, which disseminated the information to the US oil industry and paved the way for the series of US-led privatization reform initiatives in Mexico that formed the backbone of the drafting of the North American Free Trade Agreement (NAFTA), which went into effect January 1, 1994. As economic historian Sara Babb points out, "Dominated by economists trained at Harvard, Yale, MIT, and the University of Chicago, three consecutive presidential administrations have transformed the Mexican economy with a series of neoliberal reforms that included the widespread privatization of state industries, the revision of the Mexican Constitution to help ensure the property rights of foreign investors, and the lifting of protectionist trade barriers under the North American Free Trade Agreement," adding that "these policies were met with the widespread approval of the international community, multilateral institutions such as the International Monetary Fund (IMF), and a number of prestigious foreign economists."[138]

This process of constitutional reform spanned several administrations. Between the presidencies of Miguel de la Madrid Hurtado (1982–1988) and Carlos Salinas de Gortari (1988–1994), dozens of decrees and alterations to the constitution transformed the existing agrarian reform-based policy framework into a neoliberal policy framework friendly to free market enterprise, foreign investment and extractive interests, and specifically to the terms of the General Agreement on Tariffs and Trade (1986) and NAFTA.[139]

The most consequential of these changes came in 1992, when President Salinas de Gortari modified Article 27 of the constitution—enacted in 1917 by the revolutionary agrarian reformer Emiliano Zapata, from whom Zapatistas take their name—which was the legal foundation for distribution of community-owned lands called *ejidos*. Article 27 protected, at least in theory, the rights of Indigenous communities to communal land. More specifically, as the cornerstone of land tenure law in Mexico, Article 27 "declared all land, water, and mineral rights to be the property of the people of Mexico. It also gave the government a mandate and the requisite authority to expropriate land from large landholders and give it to eligible agrarian [e.g., Indigenous and poor rural] communities."[140]

Reform of Article 27 was the most important of several hundred changes in constitutional and civil law made by Mexico at the insistence of foreign governments and multinational capital interests in anticipation of the signing of NAFTA. The other significant reform was the requirement that the Mexican state put up the oil reserves in Chiapas as collateral,[141] irrespective of the fact that the lands on which the oil exists belong, historically, to Indigenous groups in Chiapas. The reform of Article 27 thus represented an important element in the "deterritorialization"[142] of the Indigenous and campesino class, part of a process of violent resettlement and displacement incentives that began in the 1970s when the Mexican ruling class started abandoning support programs for rural areas in favor of maquiladora-led industrialization. The process of deterritorialization forced millions of campesinos and Indigenous peoples to enter the industrial workforce, providing cheap labor for the rapidly growing maquiladora sector and, now, the inundation of foreign enterprises and factories (conveniently built next to jails). It is also closely associated with human trafficking, femicide, and sexual violence (particularly in the city of Juarez).

NAFTA was considered a "death sentence" for rural Indigenous peoples because their primary means of survival, farming, was no longer viable without price and tariff protections—but also, as the Zapatistas argue, because the privatization of industries would require increasing numbers of Brown and Indigenous bodies to continue providing cheap labor. When the Mexican government sent the military to Chiapas to resettle the Indigenous population, under pretexts resulting from the criminalization of Indigeneity as synonymous with "insurgents" and "human rights violators," the Zapatista resistance was born. In 1994, on the day NAFTA was signed into law, a full-scale rebellion took place that began the Zapatista struggle of armed combat and transformed into the antimilitary cultural rebellion of Zapatismo.

The struggle by Indigenous peoples of Chiapas reflects the nature of neoliberalism as an extension of colonial violence. Neoliberalism is more than the mere privatization of land, resources, and the codification of laissez-faire economics in state law and regulatory policy. It is part of a larger "capitalist hydra" that structurally keeps Indigenous peoples in subordinated cultural positions for economic profit and gain. Zapatismo thus has two parts: a rejection of this historical system of Indigenous oppression and a positive, affirmative vision of Indigenous life. (This double move tracks with Kēhaulani Kauanui's notion of enduring Indigeneity.)

In *Rights in Rebellion*, Speed repositions the Zapatistas' use of the global discourse of human rights as a strategic choice that is part of a broader understanding of resistance politics: "Positive law is not our law; in our communities we have a different way. But it is very useful for us to understand it, in order to defend ourselves from the government."[143] In Speed's view, this approach to rights discourses embodies "a refusal to accept either modern liberal individual rights or state-defined multicultural recognition of collective rights as the unitary model for the exercise of their rights. This has been particularly clear in the case of Indigenous women."[144] Consider the Women's Revolutionary Law (WRL), jointly decreed with the January 1, 1994, uprising:

> In their just fight for the liberation of our people, the EZLN incorporates women in the revolutionary struggle regardless of their race, creed, color or political affiliation, requiring only that they share the demands of the exploited people and that they commit to the laws and regulations of the revolution. As well as taking account of the situation of the woman worker in Mexico, the revolution supports their just demands of equality and justice in the following Women's Revolutionary Law.
>
> First: Women, regardless of their race, creed, color or political affiliation, have the right to participate in the revolutionary struggle in a way determined by their desire and capacity.
>
> Second: Women have the right to work and receive a just salary.
>
> Third: Women have the right to decide the number of children they will have and care for.
>
> Fourth: Women have the right to participate in the affairs of the community and hold positions of authority if they are freely and democratically elected.
>
> Fifth: Women and their children have the right to primary attention in matters of health and nutrition.
>
> Sixth: Women have the right to education.
>
> Seventh: Women have the right to choose their romantic partner, and are not to be forced into marriage.
>
> Eighth: Women shall not be beaten or physically mistreated by their family members or by strangers. Rape and attempted rape will be severely punished.
>
> Ninth: Women will be able to occupy positions of leadership in the organization and hold military ranks in the revolutionary armed forces.
>
> Tenth: Women will have all the rights and obligations elaborated in the Revolutionary Laws and regulations.[145]

Many of the articles of the WRL address the issue of systemic violence against Indigenous women, including domestic abuse, sexual violence, reproductive and obstetric violence, and economic injustice. However, the law's ability to take root has been moderated by the Mexican government's persistent efforts to set the terms of self-governance and autonomy for Indigenous communities. In 2001, after a failure to implement the San Andés Accords on Indigenous Rights and Culture agreed to by the EZLN in 1996, the Mexican government made last-minute changes to the proposed Law of Indigenous Rights and Culture that would (1) give state governments control of the terms of self-government, (2) limit legal control of Indigenous lands, and (3) limit the preferential use of natural resources, such as water, for local communities. To recall Deer's reasoning, the strategic hurdles to self-governance placed before Indigenous peoples are intimately connected to the ability of Indigenous communities to respond to gender-based violence. It is worth noting that the 2001 legislation included language aimed at "protecting" Indigenous women from abuse; "specific clauses were included to ensure that the right to self-determination included guarantees for human rights, the 'dignity and integrity' of women, and their equal rights to vote, [but] recognized neither indigenous territories nor specific jurisdictions, and the rights of indigenous peoples to their ancestral territories as set out in ILO 169 were effectively subordinated to the existing regime of property rights."[146]

Colonial hegemony as a product of white dynastic formations cannot simply be maintained through state repression of armed rebellion and cultural incorporation of antirepressive struggle (e.g., through multiculturalism and the promotion of Mexico as a "pluriethnic" state). Intersectional violences, as noted in the dual function of the 2001 legislation, are critical to the maintenance of cultural hegemony. In Chiapas, the economic exploitation that occurs on the German coffee plantations and along the Usumacinta and Grijalva rivers intersects powerfully with sexual violence and genocidal repression, and with the history of rape on the large estates (*los ranchos*) that were part of the encomienda system of Indigenous enslavement and land dispossession. María de Jesús Patricio Martínez (Marichuy), the first Indigenous woman presidential candidate in Mexico, made plain the vast ecology of violence Indigenous women face and why the structure of criminal governance goes hand in hand with femicidal settler statecraft: it protects private interests and extractive profit of dynastic capital accumulation, just as the 2001 law on Indigenous rights does:

> They don't care if they contaminate the water that runs under the earth and that is the life source for our communities. They sow death with their

"intelligence," with the liberation of gas, and with their toxic spills. They strip and destroy the earth by sowing death, destruction, exploitation, contempt, and repression against us. . . . What they do here, in Totonac territory, they want to do in Nahua territory, in Tepehua, Popoluca, and Tikmay territory [etc.]. They sow fear, they disappear our peoples, and the narco-violence appears less and less different from what the mining companies do, what companies that extract hydrocarbons through fracking do, those that commercialize and traffic our immigrant brothers and sisters on these lands, those that kill women only for being women . . . [They] discriminate [against] our peoples to justify to themselves the dispossession and the violence. . . . And now they are doing that in the entire country, regardless of whether we live in the cities or in the countryside; or whether we are peasants or journalists; or students of housewives; of whether we are white or brown.[147]

The interrelation between settler states, criminal governance ("narco-violence"), mining, petrochemical, and agrobusiness, and other extractive interests has only recently begun to be widely discussed by researchers.[148] Rosalva Aída Hernández Castillo documents the 1997 assassination of forty-five Indigenous men, women, and children (including pregnant women) in the now-famous Acteal massacre, but also develops necessary analyses of the "Mexicanization"[149] policies of state integration of Indigenous peoples that cultivated a culture of impunity for the massacre and of the paramilitary forces that enabled it. Mariana Mora argues such impunity plays an important role in how local communal history is incorporated (as "social memory") into personal memories, allowing communities to "interpret racialized relations of rule" by refusing to portray past violence as a historical accident or as politically arbitrary.[150] Mora highlights the "constant reactivation" of memory focused on local relations of domination as a political toolbox for situating resistance to settler colonial domination and sexual violence. "Many narratives alluded to memories or threats of sexual violence, such as those about when the young women had to take the tortillas to the master."[151] Such threats are structurally invariant with the modern-day threats made by ranch owners (e.g., "If my sons rape your girls, that is no longer my problem")[152] and the predictable nonresponse by settler colonial authorities. This brings us full circle to the notion of rage.

In September 2008, the Sixth Commission of the EZLN issued a communiqué to commemorate the opening of the Festival Mundial de la

Digna Rabia (International Festival of Dignified Rage). It read, in part, "This is what has come to our ears, to our Brown heart":

> Above they intend to repeat history. They want to impose on us once again their calendar of death, their geography of destruction. When they are not trying to strip us of our roots, they are destroying them. They steal our work, our strength, they leave our world, our land, our water, and our treasures without people, without life. The cities pursue us and expel us. The countryside both kills us and dies on us. Lies become governments and dispossession is the weapon of their armies and police. We are the illegal, the undocumented, the undesired of the world. We are pursued. Women, young people, children, the elderly die in death and life. And there above they preach to us resignation, defeat, surrender, and abandonment. Here below we are left with nothing. Except rage. And dignity. . . . if this world does not have a place for us, then another world must be made. With no other tool than our rage, no other material other than our dignity.

A common interpretation of the above use of dignity is as a "co-optation" the western use of the term for different functional ends, with the western model serving as the paradigm and the purportedly co-opted use as the copy of the model. I think a different process is at work. As Chapter 3 illustrates, settler epistemic economies codify (and continuously respecify) the resources for colonial politics of knowledge. This continuous transference process and its infrastructural use in institutions (including multinational human rights bodies) allow particular chains of signification to emerge as the dominant hermeneutic backdrops of interpretation in settler colonial societies—the "matrix of domination"[153] against which stereotypes function in a system of white interpretive accumulated wealth. This allows violence that falls outside the scope of current settler understandings of human-rights-violating violence to play a critical role in the development of humanitarian crises, all the while remaining paradigm orphans in humanitarian research. This means that nondominant notions of violence (like hermeneutic violence and land-based harms of environmental racism) lack a conceptual scaffolding or disciplinary taxonomy for recognizing their existence despite the nontrivial impact they have on people's lives and communities, and that this conceptual neglect is by design. Following this idea of structured hermeneutic violence and the epistemic imperialism wielded by white dynastic formations, I suggest the notion of dignity has been strategically curated by settler colonial epistemologies to narrowly mean one thing for the very populations it is meant to protect, and to close off structural epistemic pathways to alternative meanings for other populations. And I think the Zapatistas are making a lateral move that calls bullshit on this epistemic chain of value transference and intergenerational hoarding of epistemic wealth—engaging with it only to the extent that not doing so leads to certain death—but keeps generating momentum toward different conceptual formations of dignity as a practice of enduring Indigeneity, of "collective heart" (Ko'ontik, Ko'onkutick). This argument follows Speed's contention that the use of human rights discourse in Chiapas "is an organic conceptualization" grounded in Indigenous legal formulations that differs from (but is also in dialogue with) the notion of human rights found in natural and positive law.[154]

Consider the way humanism arose from western political projects of conquest and expansion. Humanism, as it emerged from Italian Renaissance political thought and developed through Enlightenment philosophy, has been the grounding political perspective by which human beings are (1) recognized as such, (2) have this recognition protected through the granting of social goods (like legal rights), and (3) are granted or denied the corollary social recognition of those rights. The paradigm of dignity arose within humanist thought as the single most important concept for organizing the ideals of Renaissance individualism into active political norms and practices. Today, in its colloquial use, we think of the "dignity" of human life and purportedly recognize the moral call to respond to claims that emanate from an "inherent" human dignity. However, for Renaissance thinkers, the concept of dignity was foremost an answer to the onto-metaphysical question of the place of human beings in the universe—in the great chain of being in christian cosmologies. Thus, Pico della Mirandola's *Oration on the Dignity of Man*, for instance, distinguishes humans from the rest of nature by virtue of divinely bestowed special attributes, properties, and capacities, such as self-reflexive reason and free will. Early humanists, drawing on classical thought, were clear on what made one human: not "dignity" but Reason. Given free will, one could have the very thing that makes one human as an intrinsic property but still fail to realize one's humanity by failing to exercise one's capacities.[155] The exercise of those capacities is what Pico characterized by the word "dignity," so that "unlearned," "slovenly," un-Renaissance men were rather undignified because they did not actualize their "God-given" rational attributes, perhaps stooping to physical pleasures; there is moral relevance now if one does not exercise the duty to realize one's dignity. And here we can sense echoes of classical antiquity and the older, roman aristocratic usage of dignity, *dignitas*, to distinguish ranking (as in the etymological origin of "dignitary"). It's important to trace this notion because both conceptions of *dignitas* worked their way into modern usage in settler epistemic systems, with only one notion (as intrinsic worth based on "universal capacities") being prevalently recognized, while the other (as distinction in rank) still regulates the primary notion's function and extension, so that some people are still regarded as having more "worth" than others—and therefore being "worth saving" more than others.[156]

In roman political thought, *dignitas* was used as a term of distinction for senators and statesmen; it was something that could be given to you (by the emperor), lost, awarded, or regained through political savvy in office, but it could also be an inherent birthright of noble families—an intrinsic right to title. As Cancik explains:

> The expression "dignity of man" was coined in Stoic anthropology. Formulated in the second/first century BCE by Panaetius of Rhodes and Marcus Tullius Cicero in Rome, it did not become a common term for the ancient Stoic authors. The original Latin term *dignitas hominis* denotes worthiness, the outer aspect of a person's social role which evokes respect, and embodies the charisma and the esteem presiding in office, rank or personality. It is concrete dignity inherent in the rational persona, given by Nature and to all human beings.[157]

What this concept set up for the later coinage of dignity is the idea that *dignitas* expresses a relation of elevated standing or rank over something else. It also became central to a gendered conception of dignity as probative of masculinity in ancient Rome.[158] In the way *dignitas* appears in book I of Cicero's *De officiis* (On Duties), it expresses the more universal and intrinsic idea that all human beings have an elevated place in the great chain of being due to reason (this continues on to Kant, in the *Grounding for the Metaphysics of Morals*, through the idea of the "dignity of a rational being"). As Cicero writes, every person is by nature superior to "cattle and other beasts," and reason, the source of our dignity, is nourished in ways that are superior to the base nourishment of beasts through bodily pleasures—through "study and meditation" and the measured use of self-reflexive reason to temper the bodily passions that lead to an excess "unworthy of the dignity of man."[159] Thus, in time, dignity became a descriptor of peoples generally associated with rationality rather than animals and their bodies. This helps explain why, as part of a system of western hierarchical binaries, dignity for colonized peoples was realized (i.e., the settler epistemological pathway created to realize dignity), not through the heightened social ranking of a dignitary, but through "humility" (*ser humilde*—to be humble, is the essentializing moral psychology most often attributed to Indigenous peoples by peninsular christian thinkers and colonial administrators since the sixteenth century). The part supports the whole in a well-oiled system of epistemic and interpretive domination. Although today the term "dignity" operates as if it were a single monolithic term signifying intrinsic value, it has always had a dual character and operated as such.

Even if dignity is something that is realized only when one lays claim to it, it is a historical reality that specific populations have been systematically on the "giving, granting" end, and others on the "asking and receiving" end, again not by accident but by design. So merely expanding the framework of dignity to more peoples is not the answer, at least not in the decolonial view. In the decolonial view, dignity is an instrument of colonial violence against Indigenous peoples and a multiscalar regulative force in the lives of people of color. It functions on the basis of a prior erasure and delegitimation of Mesoamerican conceptions of selfhood (in the Zapatista context), privileging of european conceptions rooted in greco-roman antiquity, and a subsequent monopolization of social goods and resources by tying them to european conceptual schemata. It's the perfect white-collar crime.

In contrast to this picture, whether at the collective level of dignity as a creative force, or dignity as a rights-based discourse, Zapatista uses of the discourse of dignity and the practices that surround it are operating outside the hermeneutic circle set up to trap and guard against resistant epistemologies in the global south. They are also more effective at illustrating structural resistance than the study of complexity in natural systems that informs mainstream systems theory (Chapter 1). They address structural respecification oriented toward basic transformations through the strength of the collective heart to recreate another reality through a shared language, one that is not found but made. The structural epistemic design set up by settler colonial epistemology is thus not a death sentence:

> Design has unquestionably been a basic political technology of modernity, from objects to services, institutions and cities. We can say that the current crisis is the result of deeply rooted ways of being, doing, and knowing, and

these are closely tied to design. Reclaiming design for the construction of other worlds thus appears to have great relevance as an intellectual and political project. It demands a new and effective awareness of the historicity of design and its relationship to the patriarchal, capitalist, modern, and colonial onto-epistemic formation.[160]

I want to emphasize Escobar's phrasing of "the historicity of design" because it's what I've tried to develop with respect to white dynastic formations and the notion of modal contextualism: there's a historicity of design that promotes some sociostructural pathways but not others for the purpose of white dynastic social reproduction, one that is rooted in exclusionary hierarchies and political formations autochthonous to imperial building and exploitative forms of social arrangements.

Colonial design isn't a universal cosmic truth. It's a historical process that has been going for thousands of years, so it is rooted and firm in its resilience. But so are we, and the space of scorn can be as productive and creative as the space of adaptive, counterrevolutionary forces. One cultural imagination is a spiraling vortex, another, an open cone of possibility.

A world "where all worlds fit."

Some say that scholars of violence are of two kinds: either they are reconciling a reality they have never known, or they are unraveling the imprint of the violence they endured or were closely spared. I think that's true to a certain extent. Whether you are spooling knowledge about violence into a cohesive thread of meaning or unraveling its design strand by strand to identify its inner makeup, knowledge about violence is never apolitical. It comes with stakes, economic functions, and epistemic uses that are enabled by the knowledge economies we operate within.

Different epochs call for different uses of knowledge about violence. In the fog of war, the first use is "tragic," as in a public performance of grief that detaches the patterned from the consequential. This serves as a mystifying tool that detaches history from the past violences that produced the present in order to justify the unjustifiable.

What I know about violence is that the history that gave rise to it cannot be detached from the impact wounds and the ledgers of death it creates in the present, no matter how exceptional a present conflict may appear to be. It is like the return of a boomerang long ago launched and since forgotten, to echo Fanon's writings on colonialism in Africa. Its historical force will continue to shape terrains in ways that undermine oppressed people's deepest ambitions for a life free of violence and a life filled with dignified peace for all. What the Zapatistas call for is a world "where all worlds fit" and in which they do because, in such a world, history has been faced head-on.

As a scholar of violence, I worry about the power of global settler capital and white dynastic social reproduction to shape political imagination, and the possible death sentence this imaginary means for oppressed peoples actively resisting structured poverty, precarity, and dispossession throughout the world. We know who suffers most in the end from these ahistorical imaginaries. In 2012, amid the ebullience for an unfolding democratic Egyptian Revolution, security forces in Tahrir Square coordinated the mass rape of female protesters. Years before, in Mexico, state-backed paramilitary forces targeted Indigenous nonviolent protesters in Acteal, Chiapas, massacring pregnant women and children. There are so many ways to burn down a people's white flag of dignified aspiration against structured poverty and despair, so many cultural and global enforcement tools shaped to erase imaginaries of a life free of violence if that life cannot be used for its labor or the lands that sustain it cannot be exploited for the profit of others. And one of those principal tools is to portray resistant peoples—people historically oppressed by the powerful reach of colonialism—as anti-democratic, illiberal, bad humanists, or worse. And the *choque*, the profound logical clash and irony of this narrative tool is that the political base of liberation struggles is today made up of calls for *democratic change* and the equal treatment of us all. There will always be deterrents, forces outside the forces that sustain liberation and work against it. But we are left to fan the flames of our own fire with the knowledge that the most humanistic amongst us is the one that continues to call for a liberty forged in real, substantive change—in a dignified peace that is not a democracy in name only. Real democracy, now, and for all.

There can be no lasting peace that is not of a piece with history as it has unfolded. One that begins with the simple acknowledgement of what has happened. As a survivor of sexual violence, I come up against the contradiction of a social world that frames accountability and pathways to healing through punitive logics, where to move on, to become "whole" again, reality must be named in a formal legal space, the accused confronted, and a harm entered into an official record. That limited sense of "justice" is what is afforded to us (even if it, too, is in name only). Separating justice pathways in sexual violence from the pathways to address the structural violences that sustain sexual violence creates a deep contradiction and roadblock to structural change. Reality must be named, for, as James Baldwin said, "it is the innocence which constitutes the crime."

I'll close as the Zapatista festival on dignified rage closed, with the following words: "Having listened to each other, it's clear to us what is happening in other places, and we see that it's not that different from what is happening here.... And we know that another politics, another path, another culture, another everything is possible."[161]

Today is not the day to rest. We must continue world-building toward new worlds, with new possibilities. Worlds that Maricela Vallejo Orea, and so many others, died trying to bring into being.

Acknowledgments

An incredible team of people helped to get this banned book to press. Materially, there are the institutions and foundations that provided funds critical to the research and writing, and who anxiously await disclaimers that the views expressed in this book are my own (I affirm they are). I thank the Institute for Citizens and Scholars for a generous fellowship that secured the release time necessary for writing, Michigan State University for a substantial development grant that underwrote the research for Chapters 1 and 2, and Harvard University's Department of Sociology for the office space and invaluable input from faculty on early versions of Chapters 3 and 5.

Chapter 4 previously appeared in *Hypatia*, Chapter 5 built on work accepted for publication at *Meridians*, and versions of Chapter 3 were presented at various conferences, including as "Interpretive Power and Intergenerational Wealth Mobility" at Cornell University in June 2019, and as "The Role of Epistemic Capital in Structuring Inequality" at Harvard's T.H. Chan School of Public Health in October 2019. Chapter 2 was presented as "On Testimony and Gender-Based Violence in Settler Credibility Economies" at the University of Cambridge's "Understanding Gendered Violence: The Value of Testimonial and Qualitative Evidence" workshop, funded by the European Research Council's Qualitative and Quantitative Social Science: A Unified Logic of Causal Inference? project.

I thank the journal reviewers (except reviewer number two) and the many conference, workshop, and colloquia participants for their astute comments and suggestions (especially the multiple anonymous Oxford University Press reviewers for this book). I continue to learn from the insightful feedback of colleagues and students whose projects share in our joint quest for transformative social change and in an indomitable refusal to succumb to whitewashed versions of our world, our histories, or to what is to be done in response to systemic violence.

I had a tremendous editorial team supporting the project. A book like this requires structural competence at multiple stages of development, including at the editorial stage, and I was lucky enough to find an acquisitions editor at OUP—Lucy Randall—who had such competence. This book is at OUP because Lucy Randall is at OUP. I was also lucky to have the guidance of Dr. Vanessa Davies (now of the Environmental Protection Agency) throughout the writing process. This book is undoubtedly better because of their expert approach to blending accessible narrative with scholarly rigor and fact-based receipts. Lawyers Tia Rowe and Taylor Mills pitched in with technical assistance as well, and Jessica Marínez Cruz provided generous research assistance that brought the book to completion.

Numerous colleagues near and far contributed to the intellectual contours of the book. Foremost among them is the white Jewish feminist philosopher of science Nora Berenstain. It was Berenstain's suggestion that each chapter focus on a feature of structural violence. Like the brilliant Alisa Bierria, Rocío Zambrana, and Shannon Speed (Chickasaw Nation), whose work inspired much in this project, Berenstain understands history and its central relevance in theorizing harm and oppression today. But as a white woman, she also understands the structural competence and reparative work that is required to forge meaningful engagements across differences based on that history. I have learned what futures are possible when such actions are taken.

I have also benefited from the many conversations with colleagues at my institution. When I joined MSU as an assistant professor, I had the good fortune of being surrounded by a team of dazzling thinkers and advocates for structural change: Kristie Dotson, Kyle Whyte (Potawatomi), and Sean Valles among them. With an all-star cast around you, it's hard to not get better at becoming you. While the golden age of MSU philosophy is long gone, the lessons generated by what can happen when diverse scholars, Black and Brown feminisms, and Indigenous scholarship are given the space and resources to thrive are not. I hope these lessons get uptake. Our work marches on whether they do or not.

The heart of my work is sustained, not by philosophers, but by the inspiring community organizers and tireless advocates for change that I've had the pleasure to work with and learn from across the hemisphere, including the US team at Me Too International, the many feminist activists (from Ecuador through northern Mexico) organizing against femicide and sexual violence, and the many grassroots and community partners at the Research Institute for Structural Change. I am because we are.

The many friends who wouldn't let me quit this project deserve all the flowers. A special thank you to the incomparable Natalie Cisneros, who came off the bench to assist in an emergency with flawless skill, and to Kristie Dotson, who has been a constant source of support for nearly two decades.

Most importantly, my family. I have the most spirited and dedicated family who lovingly gather what is left of us on this side of the portal and finds a way to thrive, and an amazingly supportive partner who always reminds me health and happiness are the best revenge. Cheers, love.

Last but not least, I thank the readers for picking up this book. There is much in this book that needs refining, rethinking, and developing. But its spirit is true. That means it won't last long on the shelves without its being barred from public education curriculum and its core message calling for real democratic change distorted. Reading a book—the smallest act of defiance—is not nothing these days. Our collective commitment to a life free of violence, to our health, our well-being, and dreams for better futures can never be banned, extinguished, or made illegal. We press on. *Adelante.*

Notes

Introduction

1. Massagué, 2016, p. 298.
2. Settler colonialism is typically defined as a geopolitical mode of domination where foreign settlement drives the displacement and replacement (often, but not necessarily, through genocide) of Indigenous inhabitants. The primary goal of settler colonialism is to dispossess Indigenous populations of their lands and lifeways and to replace them with foreign settlers and lifeways. Although settler colonialism, when broadly construed, is not unique to western culture, the distinctive culture of justifications for imperial settlement that is unique to the global development of european colonialism in the fifteenth and sixteenth centuries can be found as far back as book 9 of Homer's *Odyssey* and in the administrative structure of neo-Assyrian kingdoms in the ninth century BCE (Graham, 2017). I conceive settler colonialism through a systems lens to highlight the continuity and cultural design of social structures of domination that have resulted in systemic violence for our communities, and for women of color in particular. This framing of settler colonialism emphasizes that the functional recipe—that is, the basic elements and interrelations that guide the blueprint for development—for structural violence was present in greco-roman antiquity. In recent years, the term has lost much of its complex connection to the overlapping and coemerging strategies of conquest developed in the western Mediterranean world, particularly by the roman empire, to effect colonists' total domination and forge an *imperium sin fine* (an empire without end) of functional settlement. This loss is due in part to the sharp conceptual lines drawn by the late Australian scholar Patrick Wolfe. Wolfe characterized settler colonialism as (1) fundamentally distinct from "franchise or dependent" colonialism (e.g., where colonial states are primarily "administered" by a foreign metropole—as in "the kind of colonial formation [Amilcar] Cabral or [Frantz] Fanon confronted" in Africa [Wolfe, 1999, p. 1])—and (2) as an eliminative form of invasion. For Wolfe, settler colonialism constitutes "a structure not an event" that is still ongoing and based on the fact that "the colonizers came to stay" (Wolfe, 1999, p. 2). I have issues with the narrow *Mayflower* interpretation of what "came to stay" constitutes and the range of settlement schemes it leaves out. Because many colonists settled lands using a diversity of sophisticated structural violences (including linguistic elimination) and administrative schemes that enabled them to lay sociolegal claims of eminent domain—allowing them to "come to stay" at any time they wished, cases like the 1834 French annexation of Algeria as an occupied colony that became a French settler colony actually challenge important aspects of Wolfe's distinctions. That's not to say differences do not

exist. It's to say that elimination is a variant and sophisticated technology of foreign settlement that is functionally invariant when examined longitudinally. I take a systems framing of the notion of "structure" employed by Wolfe that departs from his assessment of the constitutive interrelations of the elements of anglo-european settlement. Consider that a major point of contention for Wolfe is the purported difference between settler and franchise colonial formations surrounding Indigenous labor. He contends settler colonial formations are "not primarily established to extract surplus value from indigenous labour" (Wolfe, 1999, p. 1). Indigenous scholars have warned of the tendency of settler colonial studies (catalyzed by Wolfe's work) to supplant Indigenous studies (Kauanui, 2016) in ways similar to how postcolonial studies co-opted Native American studies (Cook-Lynn, 1997). Black scholars have aptly worried about the mutually exclusive binaries Wolfe's work fostered between colonial formations of labor (as inherently about stolen Black labor) and colonial formations of land (as inherently about stolen Indigenous land and ancestral placemaking) (King, 2016; refer also to Harris, 2019). "By not incorporating more of the globe in his study, Wolfe's particular formulation of settler colonialism delimits more than it reveals" (Kelley, 2017). It hides, for example, "how race and sovereignty intersect and are mutually constitutive" (Harris, 2019), and how purportedly classic examples of "franchise" colonialism are driven by coconstituting structures of functional settlement (e.g., as in colonial capital relations) that persistently respecify and reformulate the structures necessary for settlement across artificial settler borders. In other words, what appears to be a social and administrative structure built on metropole colonialism can be made up of substructures of settlement that forge the elementary relations necessary for infrastructures of foreign settlement to swing open—at any time and any place. If settlement is a function of power, the ball is in their court. Anyone familiar with the expansive network of agricultural fincas, european settlers, and the vast German coffee plantations of southern Mexico—and the ongoing eliminative war on Indigenous peoples and environmental protectors of Indigenous lands—would take exception to the idea that Latin American states are not settler colonial states or settler-states-in-process. This argument is artfully developed by Shannon Speed (Chickasaw Nation) (2017): "In places like Mexico and Central America, such labor regimes (encomienda, repartimiento, hacienda) were often the very mechanisms that dispossessed indigenous peoples of their lands, forcing them to labor in extractive undertakings on the very land that had been taken from them. This dynamic, in turn, necessitated distinct processes of racialization from those in other parts of the world, and entailed a far more radical abrogation of their sovereignty" (p. 784). So, while there are differences in how colonialism shakes out in different territories, and while there is significant variance among the techniques of colonial violence (such as processes of racialization and colonial gender binaries) used on different populations, variance in the structuring capacities of european settlement highlight the adaptive functions of settler colonial white supremacy as a dynastic and dynamic system. They do not reflect fundamentally different forms of colonialism that are structurally incommensurable with one another. Who benefits from such a framing of types of colonialism as fundamentally distinct from one another, where the divergence of historical lineages is abstracted into cultural amnesia about the historical roots of colonial occupation as a concerted western cultural project? I'll tell you who: white settler polities and those invested in the exceptionalism of the anglo-european state project—a project that promotes self-exculpatory narratives about the sources of social inequality and systemic violence against racialized communities on cue (including racist tropes of intergroup conflicts that are delinked from the historical structuring conditions of social violence in colonial occupation). The heart of settler colonialism lies in its function; in its ability to do the work of ongoing occupation and dispossession over very long periods of time to achieve some specific ends but not others—to "secure a stable environment for the industrious appropriation of the world," as Mills put it (1997/2014, p. 31). Consider that settler infrastructures constantly change it up when it comes to methods or justifications for reproducing white settlement, from empire-building through depopulation and elite replacement strategies, to *blanqueamiento* (cultural whitening) and administrative infrastructures of racial management. In the US immigration case, *re Ellis* (179 Fed. 1002 (1910)), the US government argued that while Ellis was "white," he was not from europe, and thus he was not an eligible "free white person." The goalpost of justifications is not moved by mysterious epistemic forces, just as there is no "invisible hand" moving market forces that is delinked from colonial capitalism, even if Adam Smith tried to argue otherwise. Reconnecting colonialism with the overlapping and coemerging strategies of conquest developed in the western Mediterranean world, as Cedric Robinson (1983) has done to an important extent, is crucial for conceptualizing functional settlement through its goals of effecting colonists' total domination and forging an *imperium sin fine*, one way or another, and despite generational social change. Nothing comes from nothing—nothing ever could. If settler colonialism is indeed a structure, not an event, illuminating the functional features of settler colonial structures as a dynastic system would go a long way in fighting the responsibility-evasive narrative of happenstance and accident that characterizes much historical discussions of colonialism in social inequality research. My point is not that there is "one" colonialism with various forms or regional subtypes, but that the way in which the various land-based emergent properties of colonial structures arose is linked beyond artificially constructed settler borders. That's not a new argument. Lisa Lowe's *The Intimacies of Four Continents* (2015) and Speed's "tendency to think hemispherically" (2019, p. 12) about settler colonialism presage this argument by relinking the generative forces of colonial occupation across settler-imposed geographic lines and arbitrary borders. These correctives do not deny that the physical presence of bodies in spaces marks lands and shapes geopolitical formations in distinctive ways. Bodies change spaces. Material culture shows this. As Speed notes, the structure of settlement has a material foundation and a functional operand that cuts across settler borders and settler time, morphing from colonialism to imperialism to neoliberalism to secure ongoing occupation—but material occupation and dispossession are in the driver's seat, not the epistemological techniques used to secure short- and long-term occupation. Epistemic structural violences are viscerally real and part of a concerted strategy of conquest, of course—hence the importance of "understanding how settler logics

structure the frames of reference that continue to define the colonial exploitation of these countries" (p. 788). But they are not the primary goal of settler colonial strategies of conquest—what colonialism aims to shore up and for whom. What I find helpful in Speed's analysis is the possibility of understanding settler colonialism primarily through its adaptive functions rather than through a basic interrelation between its elements, and for a notion of functional settlement that makes room for land-based particularities while recognizing the adaptive capacities colonial systems develop to swing open and shut close the mechanisms that can swiftly transform spaces into physically settled territories with a sole edict or administrative decree. Part of the administrative power to wield violence in ways consistent with the design of settler colonial social systems concerns knowledge and how knowledge is socially produced or suppressed—when, where, and by whom. (I think Kristie Dotson's work on epistemic oppression illustrates this perfectly.) Exploring how colonial power relations impact the politics of knowledge is not antithetical to anticolonial liberation efforts rooted in the material reclamation of stolen Indigenous land, though it can certainly come close to it when political sociology or decolonial theory is done as a purely intellectual exercise detached form the political goals of enacting material structural change. The important work of authors like Eve Tuck (Unangax̂) and Audra Simpson (Kahanawa:ke Mohawk) rightly caution against the epistemic turn in decolonial theory—or with any effort to reframe anticolonial resistance on immaterial grounds that don't work to return stolen resources and lands—to give back the "actual ground," as Jodi Byrd says. I think that's right. I also think it's right to engage in nuanced discussions of belonging and structural displacement that don't reduce land to Indigeneity and relegate stolen labor to Blackness or to homogenous processes of racialization. If there is anything I've come to learn from being assaulted on both sides of the US-Mexico border, it is that the reach of colonial occupation and violence is at least an interhemispheric phenomenon with bone-deep regenerative resources. It comes for one, it comes for all—as a system feature. The Zapatistas have been saying this for decades, but it was the lived experience of violence and the secondary traumas from the harmful design of administrative systems that solidified this for me, and that grounds my commitment to theorizing colonial violence from the starting point of its connective tissue—what holds it together and allows it to regenerate across borders and social transformations despite our intergenerational resistance. This is what informs my approach to the use of the term *settler colonial white supremacy*.
3. Conrod et al., 2022.
4. More precisely, the study shows that impending cell death drives tumor cells in primary tumors to acquire pro-metastatic states through cell plasticity. "Metastases are thus proposed to originate from the induction of pro-metastatic states through intrinsic and extrinsic cues in a pro-metastatic tumoral ecosystem, driven by an impending cell-death experience involving ER stress modulation, metastatic reprogramming, and paracrine recruitment via a cytokine storm" (Conrod et al., 2022, p. 1; refer especially to the literature review of the multiple mechanisms underlying the various processes associated with cancer-related deaths on p. 1). While previous literature on chemotherapy-induced metastasis has explored chemotherapeutic agents' promotion

of the formations of structures in, for example, breast tumors and repair responses that are exploited by tumor cells throughout the metastatic cascade (Karagiannis et al., 2018; Middleton et al., 2018), it is important to note that "overwhelming evidence shows that chemotherapy is potentially curative for patients with localized breast cancer and prolongs life in patients with metastatic disease" (National Cancer Institute, 2017). This caveat is not just a public service announcement for anyone who may mistakenly infer that chemotherapy directly causes cancer (it does not); it raises an important systems-level question about the kinds of structural interventions that might be warranted and designed in social systems in light of the known adaptive measures of physical systems—because sometimes, chemotherapy kills the cancer in individual cases, just as short-term self-defense strategies save lives.
5. Siegel, 1997, p. 1113.
6. Siegel, 1997, p. 1113.
7. In the United States, the feminist antiviolence movement that took shape in women's rallies against domestic violence throughout the 1970s and 1980s was not a unified bloc. It was rooted in the exclusion and marginalization of women of color and Indigenous women, including queer women of color, Two-Spirit communities, and disabled women in ways that are relevant for this project (refer, for example, to Ritchie, 2000; Erevelles, 2020; on white-streaming of feminism as a colonial project, refer also to Grande, 2003; Berenstain, 2020).
8. E.g., the legal provisions that conferred immunity for nonconsensual sex perpetrated by a victim's spouse.
9. Klarfeld, 2011, p. 1820.
10. Yeter & Aschner, 2020.
11. Harrington, 2016. Every academic that just cross-referenced this statement probably took exception with its source in a popular press. There's a point to this reference; while the US surveils populations of color across a wide and intimate array of categories, including incidence and prevalence of sexually transmitted diseases (STDs), courts generally refrain from gathering information on race, gender, ability, and income of parties. This is no accident. Creating a cloud of social demographic mystery over patterns of legal outcomes and access to the legal system profits specific populations. "Since the discovery of bias or disparity in civil justice would require some knowledge of these basic facts about litigants, assessment of whether courts are open to all is not currently possible" (American Academy of Arts and Sciences, 2022). Is it really not possible to responsibly gather this information, or is there a structurally designed administrative feature that ensures the feasibility of such a task, and, when feasible, its relevance is persistently out of reach? Just ask: Who benefits from the designed withholding of information about patterns of disparity? There's a systems-level reason for why these vast epistemic voids surrounding legal demographics exist and why the contrasting abundance in data, for instance, on racial health disparities, doesn't move the needle toward structural change in the ways necessary to eradicate systemic racism in healthcare (Hatch, 2022). Even if we have the data, they won't save us, as Hatch emphasizes. A domain shift in relevance will take place that ensures the data are made irrelevant to the governing administrative domain of knowledge.

Over time, creating epistemic voids and structured inattention surrounding demographic realities functions to coordinate wealth transfers and concentrate resources among white polities. Consider the disparate damage awards in tort cases. After California passed tort reform measures prohibiting reductions in jury damage awards on the basis of race, legal scholars began documenting loopholes that allow racial considerations to continue infiltrating the calculation of tort damages (Gilboa, 2022). It's about the adaptive abilities of social institutions to skew profit, wealth, and power toward specific populations.

12. Derenoncourt et al., 2022. The data from this study show that "the most dramatic episode of racial wealth convergence occurred in the first 50 years after Emancipation. This initially rapid convergence gave way to much slower declines in the wealth gap in the second half of the 20th century. From a starting point of nearly 60 to 1, the white-to-Black per capita wealth ratio fell to 10 to 1 by 1920, and to 7 to 1 by the 1950s. 70 years later the wealth gap remains at a similar magnitude of 6 to 1. We demonstrate that both this 'hockey-stick' pattern of convergence and the large enduring gap today can be broadly rationalized by a parsimonious model of wealth accumulation for each racial group, where savings from income and capital gains are the drivers of wealth growth. Even under equal conditions for wealth accumulation after slavery, in other words, identical savings rates and capital gains across the two groups, our convergence model portends a racial wealth gap of 3 to 1 today. The main reason for such a large and lasting gap is the enormous difference in initial wealth between Black and white Americans on the eve of the Civil War" (Derenoncourt et al., 2022, pp. 2–3). For an analysis of the relationship between colonization, treaty-making, and a timeline of increased US federal control of Indian assets, refer to Lui et al., 2006; Miller, 2011. For an account of the accumulation process of land dispossession that backgrounds the claim of the relationship between settler wealth regeneration and stolen Indigenous lands, refer to Nichols, 2019; Coulthard, 2014, and Beyer, 2022. On the racial wealth gap, refer to Hamilton & Darity, 2009; Kirk, 2007; Hooper & Kearins, 2004; Williams, 2022, Martscher et al., 2022; Ott, 2022. Absent from most accounts of the racial wealth gap is an analysis of gender. In 2010, for example, women of color (single head of household) had just "one penny of wealth for every dollar of wealth owned by their male counterparts and a tiny fraction of a penny for every dollar of wealth owned by white women" (Chang, 2010, p. 4).

13. The irony of recent Republican pushes to censor higher education is that you don't need an advanced degree to figure out that passing legislation that prohibits the teaching of the idea that "systems of oppression" exist has payoffs for the beneficiaries of systems of oppression. Or that banning the existing curriculum on historical disparities and social inequality and replacing it with programs that "emphasize the study of Western civilization and economics, as well as the thinking of Western philosophers" (especially "the Greeks and Romans") (Saul et al., 2023)—is a western project aimed at reproducing white norms (something that the discipline of philosophy specializes in). That's not education—that's an attempt to keep America white. And it is an attempt that is not much different from the goals of the Kremlin's "re-education" camps for Ukrainian

children, or from the culturally annihilating aims of Indian residential schooling. Two things are especially relevant here: how unremarkably common such tactics are in the continuum of authoritarian and autocratic rule in colonized territories, and the role of knowledge in the social production of privilege. First, whether it is Republican Arkansas governor Sarah Huckabee Sanders banning the word "Latinx" from all state documents (with some Democratic agreement), or Republican Florida governor Ron DeSantis banning the word "gay" in public school curriculum (similar to Indiana's HB 1608 and Utah's HB550 that target transgender youth), the range of maneuvers aimed at producing disadvantage for historically marginalized populations is vast and varied. Yet the time-worn authoritarian maneuver of authorizing an "official history" or a state narrative of events—one that rationally reconstructs events to serve state interests and to create subclasses of "subversives" that the state can then surveil and disadvantage as a population to continue to reap profits for a select class—is old hat. The Batista, Trujillo, Montt, Somoza, and Pinochet regimes in Latin America illustrate this well. Argentina's "dirty war" (1976–1983), for example, was "intensely verbal and used language with diabolical skill to confuse, disorient and terrorize," reversing the meaning of democratic vocabulary in the service of the dictatorship (Feitlowitz, 2011, p. ix; refer also to Richard, 2004). Mothers of forcibly disappeared children showed up at police stations asking for their whereabouts, only to be gaslighted about their own alleged failure as mothers for having "lost" them—an illusion manufactured partly through government forms with distortive language schemes and educational curriculum that supported the dictatorship's narrative of events. Second, these authoritarian language schemes underscore the continuing relevance of knowledge (and analyses of knowledge) in the continuing settler colonial attempts to legislate an official story that reproduces narratives central to a "self-replicating white supremacist system" (McKittrick, 2021, p. 132). In Florida, Republican leaders are now calling for educational reforms where "the core curriculum must be grounded in actual history, the actual philosophy that has shaped Western civilization" (Saul et al., 2023). Settler colonial epistemological systems make it exceedingly easy to claim whitewashed and distortive narratives of social and political events and "western civilization" paraconsistently alongside the biocentric and scientific belief systems based on "facts" that rule the natural sciences and fields like medicine. The ease with which settler colonial white supremacy adapts through settler epistemic systems is one reason I talk about the relation between social knowledge and historiography through "modal contextualism" (Chapter 1) rather than theories that place the emphasis on the nuanced diversity and plurality of knowledges (and resources for meaning), such as "polyphonic contextualism" (Medina, 2012) and "pluritopic hermeneutics" (Mignolo, 2015, following Raimundo Panikkar; refer also to Mignolo's related notion of "colonial semiosis" in same volume).

14. Seigel, 1997, p. 1116.
15. *State of N.J. v. Albert Smith*, 85 N.J. 193, 426 A.2d 38 1981; *Commonwealth v. Chretien*, 417 N.E. 2d 1203, *People v. De Stefano*, 121 Misc. 2d 113 (N.Y. Cnty. Ct. 1983).
16. Woods, 1983, p. 188; refer also to Russell, 1982.

17. Berger, 1988; Guinier, 2004, p. 2341. The use of a weapon as an aggravating factor has been persistently used as presumptive evidence used by courts to overcome the toxic assumption of the victim's tacit consent in intimate relationships.
18. Klarfeld, 2011. At the same time, the methodological instruments for identification and measurement of harm across legal domains remained fixed on single-axis and single-variable approaches (including additive, marble-by-marble approaches to multivariable research), making intersectional harms exceedingly difficult to address in antiviolence research. Another trend that emerged as a systems-generated rollback is the professionalization of the antiviolence movement under an administrative structure that concentrated organizational power among white women with professional degrees (Bierria, 2009).
19. Baker et al., 2010.
20. Moore, 2022.
21. Sommers et al., 2006. Recently, a wave of media reports noted improvements in lighting technologies used by forensic nurse examiners and medical officials for detecting bruising injuries on sexual assault and intimate partner violence victims with darker skin tones. In one report, a nurse examiner tells the story of a rape survivor of color who reported that the perpetrator had bitten her. But the examiner "could not locate the bite or corresponding bruise on the woman's dark skin. Without documentation, there was nothing to substantiate the victim's claim, and when their injuries cannot be documented, women are less likely to report incidents of sexual assault, are less likely to engage in the process, and have worse judicial and medical outcomes" (McLeod-Henning, 2022). There are several problems with this approach to victim services, least of which is bad lighting. One problem is the structurally produced assumption that the victim is lying and the higher burdens of proof of injury that are continuously placed on survivors—especially survivors of color and Indigenous women—to show proof of force that can be used to overcome doubts the victim is lying. This point is important because one rhetorical question that is often posed to me, especially by normative theorists and ethicists who want there to be a rulebook for conduct that tells them how to stop being colonial misogynists, is: Should we do nothing? (e.g., should we not develop technologies appropriate for remedying population-specific health burdens, like purple lighting for detecting bruising injuries in darker skin tones). This question is often posed as a subtle threat to withdraw aid bankrolled alongside military occupation.
22. That is not tantamount to genetic predetermination. Social epidemiology and social medicine perspectives converge on the idea that disease burdens in populations are deeply impacted by social factors (I prefer "socially designed" phenomena) like differential access to diagnostic tools, preventative care and treatment, safe home and school environments and affordable nutrition, just to name a few.
23. Understood in a broader context of health equity research. Consider that at day's end, progress made on the molecular origins of metastasis will invariably lead to greater gains in cancer control for white populations, as the last few decades of research has shown when compared to populations of color (White et al., 2014). James Baldwin, Frantz Fanon, Audre Lorde, Charles Mills, and so many other scholars of color whom

I discuss in this book perished from cancer. That's not incidental to our story. In the United States, cancer is the leading cause of death among people who identify as Latino/a/e/x (Miller et al., 2018); "Black people have the highest death rate and shortest survival of any racial/ethnic group for most cancers"—in fact, "Black women are 41% more likely to die from breast cancer than White women, despite lower incidence of the disease" (American Cancer Society, 2022). A similar pattern emerges for American Indian / Alaska Native women, who are 2.3 times more likely to have, and 2.2 times as likely to die from, certain (e.g., liver and bowel) cancers compared to white women (US Department of Health and Human Services, n.d.). Among people with disabilities, cancer disparities persist, with greater likelihoods of late-stage diagnoses and higher mortality rates, compounding the patterns of racialized health burdens that already exist. However the numbers shake out in the settler epistemological statistics game of proving to harm-doers that harm is ongoing, a basic pattern reliably and continuously emerges. Cancer operates in a public health context governed by these patterns—by settler colonial social structures and relations of domination that gatekeep health resources and maldistribute precarity and inequitable life chances that promote health insecurity and worse outcomes among marginalized populations by design. Who dies, who lives, who recovers, what recovery looks like, and how secondary traumas ripple into communities—it all takes place in a social world built on relations of domination forged in specific landed histories of colonial occupation, settlement, and violence. It is a world forged in structural violence.

24. It is not a matter of "distrust" between service providers, law enforcement, and historically marginalized communities that contributes to the low incidence of reporting among those most likely to experience sexual assault or attempted sexual assault; it is, rather, communal awareness of the inherent design and blueprint of the legal ecosystem that developed under settler colonialism, and what the goals and probable outcomes of that design is.
25. Bergen, 2016, p. 19; Haberkorn, 2012.
26. Hurley, 2022.
27. Obie, 2017.
28. Crenshaw, 1988. Refer also to Bell, 1992; Harris, 1993. Bell's account of "short-lived victories that slide into irrelevance as racial patterns adapt in ways that maintain white dominance" is especially relevant.
29. Butler, 2021, p. 122.
30. Ahmed, 2017; Alexander & Mohanty, 1997; Alqaisiya, 2018; Anzaldúa, 1987; Barker, 2017; Ben-Moshe, 2020; Byrd, 2011; Canaza-Choque, 2021; Collins, 1990; Combahee River Collective, 1986; Cooper, 1892; Coráñez Bolton, 2023; Curiel & Espinosa, 2004; Cusicanqui, 2019; Davis, 2016; Deer, 2015; Douglass, 1845; Du Bois, 1903/2007; Dunbar-Ortiz, 2014; Escobar, 2008; Erevelles, 2011; Fanon, 1961/2007; Freire, 1968; Galarte, 2021; Gandolfo, 2010; Glissant, 1997; Grande, 2015; Guevara, 1961; Kēhaulani Kauanui, 2008; Johnson, 1982; Khalidi, 2020; King, 2019; Kuokkanen, 2006; LaDuke, 2016; Lorde, 1984; Lowe, 2015; Lugones, 2007; Mamdani, 2020; Mariátegui, 1928; Min-ha, 1989; Mills, 1997/2014; Mohanty, 1991; Moreton-Robinson, 2015; Narayan, 1997; Paredes, 2008; Puar, 2017; Quijano, 2000; Robinson,

2013; Said, 1979; Sandoval, 2013; Schutte, 1993; Simpson, 2013; Simpson, 2014; Smith, 2013; Snorton, 2017; Santos, 2007; Speed, 2019; Spivak, 1988; Thiong'o, 1986; Wildcat, 2001; Yuval-Davis & Stasiulis, 1995; Zea, 1988.

31. For example, Aníbal Quijano (2000) links coloniality (the present-day endurance of colonialism after formal independence from colonial governments), settler governance schemes, and epistemology through a world-system framing that calls BS on the naturalized narrative of globalization as the inevitable march of progress and modernization, conceptualizing it instead as just another adaptive evolution of colonial capitalism that colonial knowledge systems try to cover over to maintain the inequitable global distribution of wealth and labor intact. Shannon Speed (Chickasaw Nation) (2017) theorizes structures of colonial settlement in Latin America that upends the land-labor binary in settler colonial studies (Wolfe, 2016) and illuminates the violent structural association between land dispossession, bodily exploitation and enslavement, gender-based violence, and neoliberal logics of profit and extraction. Jasbir Puar (2017) interrupts the liberal state machinery that relies on the ability/disability binary to promote productive, capacitated, and cisgendered bodies as the baseline for economic development. Puar shows how "debility" is structurally produced through a political economy of capacity—one where one is "never healthy enough" (p. 82)—that supports settler state architectures built on the enduring economic exploitation of marginalized populations. Gloria Anzaldúa's watershed *Borderlands / La Frontera* (1987) threads colonial histories of territorial displacement along the US-Mexico border with the manifold strands of psychic stress, alienation, and communal trauma that ensue from carving up territories for white settlement and maintaining them through cultural violence, generation after generation. Gayatri Spivak (1988) coined the term "epistemic violence" to refer to the eurocentric design of colonial knowledge systems that colonists developed to erase (as in a coordinated attempt) nonwestern knowledges and to enact a structural stronghold over the administrative systems that form the particular form of economic organization in colonized territories—an adaptive mechanism that creates alternate routes and escape hatches for colonialism to achieve settlement across a diversity of pathways (seeping into culture, narrative, and literature, for example.
32. Fanon, 1967, p. 38.
33. Simpson, 2017, p. 15.
34. Davis, 1983, p. 7.
35. Alexander, 2012, pp. 183–184.
36. Fields & Fields, 2012.
37. Davis, 2016.
38. This is especially the case in sociology. Sociology is founded on the idea that human behavior is socially mediated or produced, yet it largely operates through colonial views of social structure and social action that have been naturalized to apply to all human communities while prioritizing the lifeworld and interpretive schemas of white anglo-european polities. (Refer, for example, to Bourdieu, 1990; Parsons, 1976; Durkheim, 1964; Giddens, 1979; Porpora, 1987).

39. Buckley, 1967. According to Buckley, "The various features of complex adaptive systems sketched so far—openness, information-linkage of the parts and the environment, feedback loops, goal-direction, and so forth—provide the basic conceptual elements that underlie the general features characteristic of systems referred to as 'self-regulating,' 'self-directing, and 'self-organizing'... [Morphostasis] refers to those processes in complex system-environment exchanges that that tend to preserve or maintain a system's given form, organization, or state. Morphogenesis will refer to those processes which tend to elaborate or change a system's given form, structure, or state" (1967, p. 58).
40. They tell us little about the perduring causes and intensifying forces behind the evolving and self-regulating "matrix of domination" (Collins, 1990) that affects the daily lives of marginalized people in settler colonial white supremacist cultures, or about how racism is respecified and "embedded in the structure of a social system," as Alexander (2012, p. 183) writes. It is no accident that anglo-european white authors continue to be predominantly cited in the sociology of social structure and that their views are inherited from a european intellectual tradition that was also a wellspring for racist constructions of natural selection in human populations. Buckley (1967), for example, characterizes Herbert Spencer's work in terms of its positive contributions to an "organic model of society" and attributes its eugenicist core to a race-neutral lapse in logic, "an unfortunate decision of Spencer and others to liken society to the individual organisms rather than to the species, for many of the contradictions in their position stem from the failure to distinguish biological levels of organization" (p. 12). The logical design of this "unfortunate decision" is not regarded as a component or feature of the systems model of society advanced by Buckley and his successors.
41. Ruíz, 2021.
42. Wright, 2019. Throughout the 2010s, demonstrations swelled in places like Hong Kong, Chile, Haiti, Columbia, Peru, Ecuador, South Korea, Greece, Iran, Lebanon, India, Iraq, Greece, Zimbabwe, Mexico, Nicaragua, and Australia and throughout the United States and Europe. National Public Radio reporters Claire Harbage and Hannah Bloch said of the decade: "All decade long, people around the world—young, middle-aged and old, in places wealthy and not —poured into the streets, over and over again, insisting on economic and social equality, demanding better governance and action on a range of ills including corruption, racism, sexual abuse and climate change" (Harbage & Bloch, 2019).
43. Wright, 2019.
44. The fault lies with the system-level production of gaps in knowledge and of structured silences supported by the adaptive features of settler colonial white supremacy, not with scholars. Social justice initiatives have filled critical gaps in knowledge about racial redlining, eminent domain, and the wealth of techniques settler colonial societies use to reproduce racial systems and intersecting oppression, yet the conditions under which the need for such initiatives exists remain largely the same.
45. Mills, 2017, p. 131.

46. Such racial justice academic platforms advance the view, whether wittingly or not, that the role of philosophy in resisting settler colonial white supremacy is to give arguments as to why things like cultural genocide are morally wrong rather than questioning the relations of power that exist to mainline genocidal violence to some cultural communities but not others, generation after generation, and which prevent us from interrupting violence at its core. I regard the latter as a far more complex system that produces racial exploitation alongside the systemic sexual violences we face as women of color, one that produces the very need to generate argumentative frameworks of racial justice that ask us to redundantly prove the harms to our communities using settler colonial epistemic resources designed to deflect white settler responsibility for the active harms we endure.
47. And there was also the toll. For many of us, especially in our work on femicide and sexual assault, there is no space safe from the emotional and physical toll this work takes, and what we bear witness to day in and day out without reprieve. Professional meetings often involve talking with folks sharing the most traumatic and cataclysmic events in their life, and even the most detached research still churns out data sets demonstrating continuing patterns of harm, pushing back like a brick wall of indifference against generations of grief and suffering.
48. Sweatt et al., 2012, p. 4.
49. Trudel-Fitzerald & Ouellet-Morin, 2022.
50. Shonkoff et al., 2009; Sañudo et al., 1999.
51. Geronimus, 1992.
52. Refer also to the idea of "methodological racism" in Ruíz, 2017, and generally, the long history of work in Indigenous methodology (e.g., T. Smith, 2012; Simpson, 2017) that situates this question in a land-based context.
53. For example, Deer, 2015.
54. The clerical offenders of the twelfth century in England are a case in point (Fraher, 1984).
55. Gilmore, 2022, p. 107.
56. This extended etiologic period of development for colonialism is one way the concept of white dynastic formations differs from theories of coloniality and racial capitalism, which generally focus on modernity or premodern merchant capitalist europe to track the rise of colonial capital relations.
57. But only as long as cultures of institutional permissiveness and settler colonial impunity (cultures that are underwritten by settler capital interests) persist. To be clear, progressive periods of hope and surges in communal spirt—what the Zapatistas call the *collective heart*—do arise, and these strides in enlarged possibilities for freedom are almost always the result of decades-long organizing efforts by marginalized communities putting in the work, day in and day out, with the full knowledge that every swing in grassroots progress will be met with powerful counterswings in policy and governance. That doesn't stop organizing efforts and movements. It tallies the costs tied to resilience.
58. Roberts, 1997, p. xi.

59. Million, 2004, p. 32. While I develop an anticolonial view of systems theory compatible with Indigenous views of structure that highlights process-based dynamics and living networks of evolving interrelations, such an anticolonial theory is not coextensive with Indigenous methodologies rooted in land-based practices and knowledges (refer, for example, to the discussion on macrological complexity and grounded normativity in Chapter 3). What I find particularly important in Indigenous methodology, especially through the oral traditions of originary peoples (*pueblos originarios*) who identify as Zapatistas, is the practice of learning and theorizing by doing, and the feminist formations that incorporate memory work and the importance of continuously retelling the past (especially histories of colonialism) in responding to structural issues of violence in women's lives (Mora, 2017). Storywork thus plays a leading role in how I approach methodology; I use anticolonial systems theory to tell a story, not to demonstrate a proof. (One reason for this is that settler epistemological systems are designed to adapt to learned skills in evidentiary expertise—to move the goalpost of justifications in response to threats to settler colonial white supremacy. But they do this at the same time they reproduce stories of their own that support settlement and ongoing occupation.)
60. Refer, for example, to Sara Ahmed's (2004; 2012) notion of nonperformativity as "institutional speech acts that do not bring into effect what they name" (2021, p. 29).
61. The concept is associated with the rise of peace studies in the 1960s and the influence of "systems thinking" in sociology and economics, especially through the core-periphery relation in world systems theory (Galtung, 1969; Wallerstein, 1975). While Paul Farmer popularized the term, the term was built on the insights of Latin American "liberation theologians during the 1960s" (Farmer et al., 2006). Developed by Gustavo Gutiérrez (1988), liberation theology uses the concept of structural violence to illuminate the coordinated features of colonial violence that result in massive disparities and economic and social inequities in Latin America, but uses the language of christianity to motivate social change. "Liberation theologians argue that there exists a larger, social dimension of sin beyond individual wrongdoing. There are sins of commission but also sins of omission; that is, there is a social dimension to sin that is more than the sum of individual acts. Structural sin is the generator of poverty and oppression . . . structural sin is caused by sinful social structures that distort human solidarity, reciprocity, and equality" (Robles, p. 238).
62. Farmer, 1999, p. 79; Farmer et al., 2006.
63. A basic position of this book is that settler colonial administrative technologies exist to protect white settler intergenerational wealth by producing systemic violence for those who resist or threaten white supremacy. This is in line with many views in racial capitalism and racial injustice literatures; however, emphasis on how this specifically impacts Indigenous women and women of color is often missing or underplayed in these fields. If we want to understand how colonial systems of power work and how they have been able to withstand so many challenges throughout history to maintain economic dynastic formations that disadvantage populations of color by design, it is critical to examine the adaptability features of settler colonial systems. This includes

examining their regenerative ability to harm marginalized peoples at different scales and administrative registers while feigning democratic protections for vulnerable populations. The forced sterilization of Spanish-speaking migrant women at the Irwin County Detention Center (a US Immigration and Customs Enforcement detention center in Georgia) that began in 2019, and the systematic abuse of Indigenous women migrants from Central America and Mexico in the infamous T. Don Hutto immigration detention facility in Taylor, Texas, serve as illustrations of how racialized women are at the nexus of systemic racism and sexual violence in ways that produce unique harms for us and which reflect the complex reconfigurations of colonial power throughout its more than five-hundred-year history in the Americas. The anticolonial notion of structure I employ throughout this chapter thus illuminates a much broader, more insidious, and harmful system of sociostructural risk factors than found in current literature on racial inequality and sexual violence. This intentional "design of distribution" function of settler social structures—which draws on social epidemiological framings of the sociostructural determinants of health inequality—plays a leading role in my account of structural violence since it explains how "harm by design" can exist without individual intentions.

64. Clark, 2019, p. xxv.
65. Wynter, 2001, p. 59; McKittrick, 2021, p. 132.
66. Mills, 1997/2014, pp. 5–6.
67. Coulthard, 2014, p. 4.
68. Goeman, 2013.
69. Galeano, 2015.
70. Ahmed, 2021.
71. I think settlement is a historical spectrum of equifinal processes; it can take the shape of politico-epistemic projects like *mestizaje* or physical occupation that rigidly maintains distinct subpopulations for relatively long periods of time. Who owns the land and what interests are upheld through the polities in power have remained relatively stable through the various social transformations since at least the rise of merchant capitalism. Refer to endnote 1.
72. In Mexico, the medical examiner paused his intake when I answered "yes" to whether or not I had tattoos, as if it were a lifestyle risk factor I should have answered "no" to in order to be more credible as a crime victim. In the United States, I awoke to an ER physician who was saying, "My, what tangled webs we weave," tone-setting the clinical exchange before asking a single question. These were small things that were not so small when considered as part of an interacting and interconnected network of shared cultural goals driven by polities in power that reproduce conditions to keep the same colonial system going, generation after generation. For an example of this account of violence, refer also to the work of R. Aída Hernández Castillo.
73. What eludes this reductive and disconnected picture of violence is how violence functions in relation to system-level transformations in society, and how it features into the larger ecosystem of self-organized critical states that produce precarity and harm over long periods of time in order to maintain internal equilibrium in settler colonial social structures. It also means that diverse practices of freedom, from abolition

feminisms to Indigenous self-determination, are responding to the regenerative processes of settler colonial social systems in structurally important ways.
74. Ojeda Martínez, 2021.
75. Ruíz, 2020.
76. This can be a dynamic process; different points in time often call for different approaches that also depend a great deal on available resources for healing and the material conditions of response. Whereas today I have different material and communal resources of support to ground my approaches, this was not always the case. My early work on cultural power and language reflected not only institutional and professional limitations I encountered, but also traumatic experiences with thinking my lack of fluency in English contributed to my assault (and later, of not being heard, or of being heard and disregarded despite my fluency). As Toni Morrison reminds us, "The first thing done by those who hold the rifles is discredit the other's language. When you have an army and a navy, you can say to the other that her language is not a language, that what she says is closer to the speech of animals. Knowing how to manage this position, of being subordinate with respect to language, is a fundamental problem for all dominated peoples" (1998).
77. Through knowing the story philosophers—who are predominantly white, cisgendered males—tell themselves about their own history was extremely helpful in decoding the dynastic stronghold philosophy has on approaches to rational inquiry and historiography, and the interconnections between these approaches and the regeneration of settler colonial social structures.
78. Though Shannon Speed's hemispheric intersectional approach came close. Speed has also highlighted the problematic absence of dialogue between Latin American and Indigenous studies in the United States and Canada.
79. Years later, connected through her attorney, one survivor recounted a familiar story to many women in academic and legal professions—that she was terrified of ever setting foot in a courtroom again without being an attorney herself. Our areas of expertise, our expert command of professional domains, is in so many ways tied to our survival and need for self-advocacy tools that function in a system that generates redundancy for such tools as a network feature of oppression.

Chapter 1

1. Collins, 2006, p. 14.
2. Kendi, 2021.
3. The resolution reads, in part: "BE IT FURTHER RESOLVED, That the Alabama State Board of Education recognizes that slavery and racism are betrayals of the founding principles of the United States, including freedom, equality, justice, and humanity, and that individuals living today should not be punished or discriminated against because of past actions committed by members of the same race or sex, but that we should move forward to create a better future together" (Alabama State Board of Education, 2021).

4. Whitewashing refers to the deliberate attempt to conceal white complicity by recasting history in uniform, glossed-over ways that favor narratives of white innocence. Structural whitewashing functionalizes the pervasive use of whitewashing by aligning administrative institutions with the pathways necessary to escape accountability, and to instill a sense of presumptive permissibility of expected impunity for one's actions. You do it because you expect to get away with it, or at least have a reasonable expectation that what "not getting away with it" entails can be overcome within the same social system.
5. Bell, 1990.
6. Crenshaw, 1995.
7. Crenshaw, 1995, p. 117.
8. *Pena-Rodriguez v. Colorado*.
9. *State v. Demesme*. Justice Crichton, the presiding judge, said, "In my view, the defendant's ambiguous and equivocal reference to a 'lawyer dog' does not constitute an invocation of counsel that warrants termination of the interview and does not violate *Edwards v. Arizona*, 451 U.S. 477, 101 S.Ct. 1880, 68 L.Ed.2d 378 (1981)."
10. Rickford & King, 2016.
11. Sye, 2022.
12. Lopez, 2021.
13. Common to these bills was the suggestion that teaching kids about colonialism and the institution of slavery in the United States could result in irreparable harm to white children, who might internalize feelings of guilt or shame as a result of affiliative attachments to protected personal characteristics like race or gender. Republicans had, seemingly overnight, settled on the tenuous epistemic discomfort of (implicitly cisgender white christian) children as the heartbeat of the project to save America's white supremacist soul, but in a way remarkably consistent with the regulative use of white women's honor to murder people of color and Indigenous peoples with impunity. Moreover, Republicans who now insist on the (rightful) importance of teaching Holocaust history in public schools also supported legislative efforts to ban books on the Holocaust throughout much of 2021 and 2022. (Refer, for example, to Ohio House Bill 327—the "Both Sides" bill, and remarks from the Republican bill sponsor to teach "German soldiers'" side of the Holocaust. https://ohiohouse.gov/members/casey-weinstein/news/ohio-republican-lawmaker-wants-to-require-teaching-german-soldiers-holocaust-perspective-in-classroom-censorship-bill-109365.)
14. Roberts, 2017, p. xi.
15. Crenshaw, 1995.
16. Bell writes: "American racism is not, as Gunnar Myrdal concluded in his massive study, *An American Dilemma*, an anomaly on our democratic landscape, a holdover from slavery that the nation both wants to cure and is capable of curing. Rather, it is a critically important stabilizing force that enables whites to bind across a wide socio-economic chasm. Without the deflecting power of racism, masses of whites would likely wake up to revolt against the severe disadvantage they suffer in income and opportunity when compared with those whites at the top of our socio-economic heap" (1993, p. 3571).

17. Bell, 1993.
18. Downs, 2020, pp. 1–14.
19. Calhoun, 1848, as cited in Hecht, 2020, p. 1. The senator speaking was former secretary of state and vice president John Calhoun. In the same speech, he said, "We never dreamt of incorporating into our union only but the Caucasian race—the free white race." When someone tells you who they are, believe them.
20. Using jurisdictional coverage formulas established in Section 4, the act applied a similar logic of *recidivism risk* that is frequently applied to Black and Brown defendants during the course of routine sentencing hearings in criminal proceedings, but to very different ends, outcomes, and assumptions about race and systemic racism (An act to enforce the Fifteenth Amendment to the Constitution of the United States and for other purposes, August 6, 1965). *Shelby v. Holder* struck down the coverage formula in Section 4(b) that established which jurisdictions would be subject to preclearance, effectively gutting the preclearance powers of Section 5. The 1975 extension of the Voting Rights Act expanded coverage to "language minority groups" (Public Law 94-73, 1975). 52 USC § 10310(c)(3) defines "language minority groups" as persons of "American Indian, Asian American, Alaskan Natives or of Spanish heritage" (Legal Information Institute, US code Title 52, https://www.law.cornell.edu/uscode/text/52/10310#c_3). This expansion meant that ethnic and racial groups formerly excluded from protections under the 1965 act now had legal recourse, such as the ability to sue and compel jurisdictions to provide translation materials and language-specific assistance to facilitate voter registration or to cast a vote.
21. Downs, 2020, p. 9.
22. An opinion piece in *The Guardian* discussed the ruling under the satirical headline "The Supreme Court Guts the Voter [sic] Rights Act . . . Since Racism Is Over" (Cox, 2013). According to Justice Roberts, "Coverage today is based on decades-old data and eradicated practices," such as literacy tests, that fail to capture historical gains in formal equality for people of color. He cites what is arguably evidence of the act's success (and continuing need for coverage) as a reason to end it: "Voter registration and turnout numbers in covered States have risen dramatically" since the 1960s and 1970s, when the law was enacted. Whatever the original disparities that produced the legal remedies in the act's geographic coverage formulas, "There is no longer such a disparity" (570 U.S. 529, pp. 3–18). Refer to Senator Lewis's statement (Hearing before the Subcommittee on the Constitution, Civil Rights, and Civil Liberties) for a rebuttal of this race-evasive racist legal logic.
23. Downs, 2020, p. 10. Consider also: "What they did in Alabama was they crafted a Voter ID law in 2011, but they knew that it was so racist that it could not get through the Department of Justice preclearance review. Then *Shelby County v. Holder* came through and gutted the Voting Rights Act and gutted preclearance and [snaps fingers], boom, they implemented the voter ID law" (p. 43).
24. Lawmakers also passed a bill creating a police force to track down alleged "voter fraud" that targeted minority voters (Florida Senate Bill 524). In 2022, under the direction of Republican governor Ron DeSantis, the election police agency began arresting former felons who became ineligible to vote under the elaborate exceptions

to the amendment, arrestees who were subsequently charged by the state with voter fraud in very public media campaigns. The majority of defendants were Black. Upon arrest, many of the defendants expressed confusion about the complex caveats that made them ineligible to vote, as they believed (and in some cases, had been told by state officials) they were eligible.

25. Uggen et al., 2022.
26. Uggen et al., 2022. In Arizona, a 2016 so-called ballot harvesting law passed that made it a criminal offense to be in possession of a ballot other than one's own or that of a relative. After state prosecutors levied charges (resulting in jail sentences) against members of the Latinx community for dropping off sealed ballots for friends and community members who could not access transportation to the nearest precinct drop-off, a federal appeals court in 2021 struck down the law for violating the Voting Rights Act. The very next year, when armed militia and members of the election-denial movement began gathering near ballot boxes before the 2022 Arizona primaries, a Trump-appointed federal judge ruled the armed gunmen did not constitute a "true threat" or intimidation in violation of the Voting Rights Act (Bensinger, 2022).
27. Downs, 2020, p. 140; emphasis added.
28. Lewis, 2019.
29. Alexander, 2020.
30. Lindsay, 2006, p. 88. Hermeneutically speaking, race neutrality helps to hide something, but it also works to do more, to produce something—an interpretive scaffolding and epistemic possibility—that wasn't there before (at least not in the same way). The idea that power is a multiscale phenomenon associated with the "productive" and "regulative" capacity of knowledge systems has a long history in philosophy. The notion of power necessary for this view can be found as far back as propositions 34 and 35 of part I of Spinoza's *Ethics* (1677), which poses a distinction between *potentia* (potency, as in the inherent might of God or the power of a collective) and *potestas* (power to act, as in judicial power, which can impose constraints), in Foucault's (1976/2020) regulative account of social power in the concept of "biopower," as well as in various strands of political philosophy, critical theory, hermeneutic thought, feminist theory, and liberation philosophy, such as Enrique Dussel's *Philosophy of Liberation* (1977). The idea that social power is a multiscale structure that disappears itself to effectuate an illusion of reality that serves group interests (i.e., as group form of social domination) is also found in Nietzsche (as a rejection of Kant). This (quite old) notion of a structure that disappears itself by design has even been popularized in movies through different versions of Charles Baudelaire's (1869) famous words, "Do not forget, when you hear the progress of lights praised, that the loveliest trick of the Devil is to persuade you he doesn't exist" (from his poem "Le joueur généreux"). So the conceptual resources are there, and have been there quite for some time—and in a language white settler intellectuals can understand. Despite this, mainstream philosophers rarely connect these tools to how settler colonial epistemologies function and what purposes they serve. Edward Said (1979), Gayatri Spivak (1988a; 1988b; 1999) and the various decolonial schools of the middle to late twentieth century elaborated this

hermeneutic function in relation to cultural domination and european colonialism at length.

31. And it did not happen overnight. It was done one legal ruling at a time, much like the *Dobbs v. Jackson* ruling that eliminated the constitutional right to abortion by overturning *Roe v. Wade* coincided with (a) long-standing state-level efforts to enshrine fetal personhood in legislation tied to women's restricted access to reproductive care and (b) historical strategies developed by white evangelicals to actuate institutional pathways to resist desegregation and civil rights gains. Reproductive rollbacks are intimately connected to structural racism through global architectures of settler capital relations (Ruíz et al., 2023).

32. Refer to Executive Order 13950 (2020), which reads, in part: "Thanks to the courage and sacrifice of our forebears, America has made significant progress toward realization of our national creed, particularly in the 57 years since Dr. King shared his dream with the country. Today, however, many people are pushing a different vision of America that is grounded in hierarchies based on collective social and political identities rather than in the inherent and equal dignity of every person as an individual. This ideology is rooted in the pernicious and false belief that America is an irredeemably racist and sexist country [objection: no one said it was irredeemable]; that some people, simply on account of their race or sex, are oppressors; and that racial and sexual identities are more important than our common status as human beings and Americans. This destructive ideology is grounded in misrepresentations of our country's history and its role in the world. Although presented as new and revolutionary, they resurrect the discredited notions of the nineteenth century's apologists for slavery who, like President Lincoln's rival Stephen A. Douglas, maintained that our government "was made on the white basis" "by white men, for the benefit of white men." Our Founding documents rejected these racialized views of America, which were soundly defeated on the blood-stained battlefields of the Civil War. Yet they are now being repackaged and sold as cutting-edge insights. They are designed to divide us and to prevent us from uniting as one people in pursuit of one common destiny for our great country." This is a textbook example of race-evasive racism that serves to preserve white supremacy.

33. As mentioned, the DPC legislation that swept through statehouses as racially coded "race neutral" bills were all predicated on the idea that white (implicitly cisgender christian) children could be harmed by feelings of guilt or shame from exposure to historical facts, and that it was better to not allow teachers to say the word "gay" (HB 1557, Parental Rights in Education 2022) or to teach children about slavery than to risk the guilt by association that Republicans allege comes from knowing the truth of America's genocidal founding in settler colonialism. White children were left to suppose that the Black children in the classroom came from thin air, and the Black children strategically deprived of any official narratives to correct whatever stories the white children could say about Black children's historical origins in the United States and the long legacies of disparate treatment. If public schools must be desegregated, at least the curriculum could maintain the old racial orders.

34. Hydras are known for their powerful regenerative ability (in biological research, the hydra is used as a model for regeneration) and their standing as biologically "immortal" organisms due to their being primarily composed of stem cells and low rates of senescence. Hydra research also contains useful analogues to complex systems research and to the metaorganizing and self-regulating properties that maintain balance over time, coordinating with other structures to achieve this and exhibiting epigenetic regulation (refer to Deines & Bosch, 2017; Li et al., 2015; McGrath, 2021). (I wish to thank my sibling Ariel for gifting me, twenty years ago, an electron microscope photograph of a hydra, which has hung in every office I've had, and later, alongside Mauricio Gómez Morín's depiction of the mythical Hydra.)
35. Bellantuno, 2015.
36. Burchard et al., 2003.
37. Kanazawa, 2012; refer to Colar, 2011.
38. Wade, 2014.
39. Sesardic, 2010.
40. Refer to Hatch, 2016.
41. Refer to Braun, 2021; Borrell et al., 2021.
42. Refer to Queirós, 2022.
43. Schuenemann et al., 2017.
44. Refer to Starr, 2022.
45. Omi & Winant, 1994.
46. Feagin, 2006.
47. Collins, 2000.
48. Speed, 2019.
49. And they certainly don't tell us why racial hierarchies are deeply interconnected with gender-based violence, other than the common platitude that oppressions "intersect" (which, of course, they do). For a history of the concept of intersectionality, refer to Ruíz, 2017.
50. As a methodological note, I address racial oppression in terms of what is oppressive about it: qua the violence it enacts and the actual toll it takes, not the mere fact of its existence. Scholars of violence often distance themselves from the phenomena they study to achieve or reinforce ideals of objectivity as a gateway to empirical truth, but in a political ecology where truth is traded and verified by settler epistemological standards. In a systems perspective, this move (the detached study of phenomena surrounding inequality) emerges as a tool of oppression that reinforces the epistemic value of generating independent validation and careful measurement of phenomena in order to legitimize grounds for the possible social redress of the phenomena in question (but by conferring adjudicating power to the white polities that dominate academic, legal, and political fields). Placing those demands on studies is a powerful social tool to obscure the inner workings of structural violence in settler colonial societies, so we'll also need to ask about broader patterns of the use and usefulness of traditional social theory along the way.
51. Due largely to power law distribution properties of settler epistemologies. Power law distribution properties of settler epistemic systems describe the synchronized

operations between magnitudes (e.g., the expressed or activated nodes in the system, such as working institutions) that have a functional relationship between one another, such that a change in one magnitude triggers a proportional change in the other (proportion here just means the response is relative to the triggering force). Power law distribution properties are connected to knowledge architectures in settler colonial societies because they automate the ripple-like repression of alternatives to modes of being (ways of living and relating) when such modes pose threats to settler structures (e.g., to neoliberal capital accumulation and the exponential growth for profit margins regardless of environmental or human health impacts). They illustrate a dynamic and living self-iterative social process of cultural regeneration that is active, responsive, adaptive, synergistic, and far more predictable and driven by nonaccidental features than settler conceptions of social structure portray. Alternatives to settler colonial social structuration include Indigenous conceptions of systems theory (which have been used widely in Indigenous-led public health interventions) and political models of consensual democracy and women's rights rooted in autonomy, environmental stewardship, and the dignified well-being of communities.
52. Farmer, 1999.
53. The difference between a social system and a tree root system cannot be explained by biologically evolutionary explanations of overall system survival (or colonialist Malthusian theories of social competition for resources) because many cultures, particularly in the so-called "pre-Columbian" world, were and are rooted in, for example, cycles of lunar and solar complementarity and balance that often result in sustainable decline—in a systems balancing between the caring capacities of the earth that bore us and the social structures that arose with metaphysical relations fundamentally different from the western substance ontologies that sought to persevere through change unchanged themselves. Moreover, I am also aware the mycelial theory of network cooperation is not universally accepted (as western mycological models rooted in intraspecies competition prevail). Since it is consistent with Indigenous theories of network cooperation in living systems, I endorse the so-called wood-wide web theory).
54. José Medina (2013), for example, frames their "chained actions" model of interconnected social responsibility for structural injustice explicitly on Young's model: "As Young emphasizes, structural injustices are often so pervasive and extended across networks of social relations that we can legitimately say that *we are all responsible* for them. We should even consider the possibility that those who suffer the most the consequences of a structural injustice may also be complicit with it" (p. 160). Medina wisely cautions that this does not mean "we are all *equally* responsible," yet the larger problem of settler colonial logics operative in Young's stances remains unaddressed.
55. Refer to Chapter 5 for Young's view on Indigenous self-determination.
56. This is in spite of the upticks in representations of diversity and progressive platforms in elected officials and public offices.
57. Washington, 2006.
58. Eubanks, 2018.
59. Rothstein, 2018.

60. Roberts, 2022.
61. Morris, 2018.
62. As it is generally used in academic circles, implicit bias refers to an evaluative model of thinking about human actions (or "agency") that is based on an individual's psychological internalization of stereotypes, conceived as popular beliefs or attitudes that affect perception and decision-making. It is typically framed as a universal psychological trait to which everyone, regardless of race, is susceptible due to the deep influence of society and culture on human cognitive and linguistic development. In almost all cases, implicit bias is described as having an unconscious component that produces the implicit attitude or tacit stereotype behind the discriminatory act or the explicit judgment being examined. One example might involve considering whether a healthcare provider who withheld medical technologies or treatments from a patient of color did so because of internalized or unconscious racial biases that influenced their perceptions of the patient's ability to pay for or benefit from said treatments. Hence, implicit bias is often simply referred to as "unconscious bias" in ethical analyses of decision-making.
63. Benaji & Greenwald, 1995. Refer, for example, to Project Implicit (https://implicit.harvard.edu/implicit/aboutus.html). This approach departed significantly from earlier psychological studies on prejudice as psychopathology or abnormal behavior, which stemmed from post–World War II psychological research into the authoritarian personality and the cognitive processes behind ethnic prejudice and anti-Semitism.
64. In psychology, this lineage is traced to Allport's (1954) *Nature of Prejudice*. In philosophy, the dating scheme traces back to nineteenth-century precursors to social psychology and theories of the unconscious in German thought.
65. Bobo, 2001.
66. Omi & Winant, 1994, p. 56. Doane and Bonilla-Silva's *White Out: The Continuing Significance of Racism* (2013) and the extensive scholarship on color-evasive racism are prime examples.
67. Jackson, 1999.
68. Dovidio et al., 1997.
69. Banaji et al., 1994.
70. Greenwald & Banaji, 1995.
71. Grzanka & Cole, 2021.
72. Grzanka & Cole, 2021, p. 19.
73. The Implicit Association Test (Greenwald et al., 1998) was created as a measure of implicit social cognition (Fazio & Olsson, 2003).
74. Phelps et al., 2000; Phelps et al., 2003.
75. Fitgerald & Hurst, 2017, p. 2.
76. Glas & Faloye, 2021, p. 991.
77. Implicit biases have also been used to describe behavior that is automatic, tacit, or nonverbal (typically without reference to ableism in psychological studies of bias): "In addition to affecting judgments, implicit biases manifest in our nonverbal behavior towards others, such as frequency of eye contact and physical proximity. Implicit

biases explain a potential dissociation between what a person explicitly believes and wants to do (e.g., treat everyone equally) and the hidden influence of negative implicit associations on her thoughts and action" (Fitzgerald & Hurst, 2017). A *negative implicit association* refers to an unconscious mental or affective association that generates, or is likely to generate, a negative judgment about a person or social group that has the potential to enact, or be a conduit for, harm. As to what counts as a "negative" or "prejudicial" judgment, the idea of *cultural relativity* is used to account for the various social standards that reflect sociohistorical contexts of a given time and place.

78. On the one hand, the mainstream understanding of implicit bias naturalizes *social emergence* (broadly, how societies arise as complex social structures that produce their own behavior through the interaction of individuals) as a primary function of individual cognition in a way that reduces racism to perceptions of race. This move makes it possible to suggest we can use prediction-and-control models to intervene in these problematic perceptions. It produces confidence in the belief that, by understanding sociocognitive processes, we can manipulate environments (such as reducing exposures to stereotypes) or that we can design interventions (such as antibias training) to reduce unwanted outcomes from these processes. Studies even suggest that implicit attitudes may be more reliable predictors of behavior than self-reported explicit attitudes (Beattie, 2013; Beattie et al., 2013), bolstering the public image of the implicit-bias paradigm as a preferential framework for designing social interventions. In this vein, the framework of implicit bias has been widely used to substantiate psychological science on race bias that overwhelmingly supports the view that racial bias is a widely held, pervasive, and prevalent phenomenon. The aim of this blunt side of the implicit-bias sword is to create social appeasement for marginalized populations who routinely experience racial discrimination (yet feel it is not acknowledged as real or significant) while functionalizing epistemic escape hatches that allow system-level impunity of discriminatory practices to continue. What allows individuals to engage in discriminatory behavior are not the automatic social reflexes born from the norms of the unjust worlds one grows into; it is the tacit expectation that one is likely to get away with such behavior depending on one's processive relation to settler colonial social structures. Such affordances can and often are internalized in epistemic habits. But more important, they are supported by the institutional infrastructures set up to support white settler futurity. Consider that the standard view of implicit bias (i.e., the blunt edge) can support paraconsistent accounts of antiracism and racism together without resulting in contradiction. Dr. Seuss's (who is known for his racist stereotypes) famous depiction of the "racial prejudice bug" as eradicable by pumping "mental insecticide" into one ear and out the other serves to illustrate this point ("What this country needs is a good mental insecticide," digital object, Special Collections & Archives, UC San Diego, https://library.ucsd.edu/dc/object/bb7065726h). Racism and antiracism can exist side by side in this framework, following a pattern of "retrenchment" discussed earlier. The implicit-bias (as a regenerative pathway for institutionalized racism) side of the sword cuts much deeper than the side meant to acknowledge and intervene in pervasively held racial ideologies. It is kept sharp by design, and it is afforded every opportunity to perfect its aim across various targets.

79. Sirota, 2021.
80. Selmi, 2018, p. 193. At the heart of this elision is epistemic control over the preservation of self-image and social, moral, and economic standing of those who enable and perpetuate racism, whether wittingly or not. "Unconscious biases do not mean people are bad," a medical journal reports, "and they do not mean those who raised or educated us are bad people. They mean lessons were learned that unconsciously affect decision-making" (Glas & Faloye, 2021, p. 991).
81. One lesson learned is the social expectation that racist prejudices can be afforded protective infrastructural support and access to institutionally recognized mechanisms that result in impunity and some level of social payoff.
82. Mills, 1997/2014, p. 18. For broader discussion and examples, including "white ignorance," refer to Sullivan & Tuana, 2007; Pohlhaus, 2012; Bailey, 2007; and Mills, 2015.
83. Reagan biographers have long alleged that Reagan did not personally have racist views while conceding that his policies had racially inequitable consequences (Chapter 3). In academic conferences, scholars have brought up Reagan as an example of someone with a "genuine hermeneutical inability" that made his actions wrongful but not epistemically culpable: a true case of "hermeneutical injustice" without "motivated cognitive bias" (Fricker, 2010; 2013). Empirically, this is nonsense. After a lengthy court battle, in 2019 the National Archives released a phone call between former presidents Reagan and Nixon that challenged the racism-evasive mythography by capturing the two ex-presidents "joking and bromancing over mutually-shared racist antipathies towards Africans, calling them cannibals, monkeys, and uncivilized people who only recently learned to wear shoes" (Ruíz and Sertler, 2019, n.p.). The man was a racist, full stop, even if he lived in a society that afforded him every epistemic mechanism and interpretive opportunity to affirm his own belief to the contrary—essentially what "epistemic capitalism" provides for. But philosophically, whether or not Reagan is a "straightforward 'racist cognizer'" (Fricker, 2013) doesn't change what's at stake. What is at stake here is the philosophical maneuvering that transforms race-neutral reasoning to continually rescue white innocence in an age of social justice redress. This is what Fricker's (2010) framework of hermeneutic injustice does. Typically, when one speaks of injustice in relation to structural harms and the history of white supremacy, the injured party is conceived in part in relation to historically oppressed groups. The framework of hermeneutical injustice, on the other hand, is built to provide safe harbor to white people who suffer white ignorance at the "level of conceptual repertoire" (Fricker, 2013). Interestingly, in response to the obvious charge that her framework exculpates structurally produced unknowing in the service of maintaining white supremacy, Fricker explicitly exempts "the white ignorance of the straightforward racist cognizer" from her framework of hermeneutical injustice. But the safe harbor her framework provides to epistemic oppressors is the rule, not the exception. In other words, whenever there exists what Dotson would call a third-order epistemic oppression, Fricker's framework allows that structural condition to be leveraged as an exculpatory mechanism for the dominantly situated group, framing the condition as a form of interpretive marginalization for the privileged rather than an accountability

pathway for their ongoing perpetration of structural injustices. Indeed, her (2013) response to Medina makes categorical attempts to rescue certain forms of white ignorance as "epistemically non-culpable," because the white people that engage in them are victimized by their ignorant societies. Bad thoughts and deeds happen to good people because of the bad societies they happen to inhabit. It's just such bad luck for them! I agree with Dotson's (2012), Medina's (2012), and Pohlhaus's (2012) nonwhitewashed characterizations of socially mediated "ignorances" as inextricable from the historical contexts in which social power operates. We can sit here another two thousand years and wait for "western" philosophy and ethics to align with the reality of lived experience for marginalized people, or we can just call it what it is: a very sophisticated settler epistemic paradigm for whitewashing structural violence. In this book, I push nonwhitewashed conceptions of structural injustice to the modal structural (Berenstain, 2019) realm Berenstain suggests as a response to the pervasive doubling down of hermeneutic injustice apologists who insist that they too acknowledge "historical context" in structural-level accounts of epistemic harms. This is what the notions of modal contextualism and hermeneutic violence serve to do.
84. Berenstain, 2016, p. 569.
85. Refer to Tremain, 2017, pp. 41–44, for an analysis of the ways the framing of epistemologies of ignorance in terms of "cognitive dysfunction" upholds ableism.
86. Fields, 2022.
87. Herron, 2018.
88. Adler, 2012, p. 43. Adler offers an example of this exculpatory function by endorsing the view that collectively shared views and cultural values like "endemic racism" can cause reality distortions like seeing a physical weapon where none exists, providing evidence-based scientific rationale to police officer's self-defense claims when under the suspicion or charge of unlawful killing of unarmed people of color.
89. Gabrielson et al., 2014.
90. Frazee, 2019.
91. *Barnes v. Felix*, 532 F. Supp. 3d 463 (S.D. Tex. 2021).
92. *Graham v. Connor*, 490 U.S. 386 (1989).
93. Importantly, *Graham* held that all claims of excessive force (including those resulting in death) by police should be analyzed under an "objective reasonableness" standard rather than a general "due process" standard, making it more difficult to introduce claims of racism-motivated investigative stops resulting (minimally) in a violation of certain fundamental rights in police brutality suits.
94. *Illinois v. Wardlow*, 528 U.S. 119 (2000).
95. *Terry v. Ohio*, 392 U.S. 1 (1968). As Justice Apel recently noted in his dissenting opinion in *State v. Price-Williams*, 973 N.W.2d 556 (Iowa 2022), implicit bias played a central, disguised role in the *Terry* decision and its progeny and is now protected when considered "reasonable."
96. Wang, 2018, p. 374.
97. Wang, 2018.
98. *Terry v. Ohio*, 575 U.S. 723.

99. *Watts v. United States* placed "true threats" beyond the scope of the First Amendment's free speech protections. For more on the true-threat doctrine, refer to Crane, 2006.
100. Bazelon, 2014.
101. Lithwick, 2015.
102. Lithwick, 2015.
103. Nielson & Dennis, 2019.
104. https://harvardlawreview.org/2019/03/commonwealth-v-knox/.
105. Rolnick, 2018, p. 1654.
106. In July 2010, twenty-nine-year old Alexander fired a "warning shot" when her estranged husband threatened to kill her in her home. Alexander was subsequently sentenced to twenty years in prison for aggravated assault despite her self-defense arguments under Florida's stand-your-ground law. Alexander showed she had good reason to fear for her life: her estranged husband had been arrested previously for physical abuse against Alexander, and in his deposition he openly admitted to a long history of violently abusing women, and of having lied to the police in his original report, when he claimed Alexander pointed a gun directly at him and his children. He said: "The way I was with women, they was like they had to walk on eggshells around me. You know, they never knew what I was thinking or what I might do. Hit them, push them." The white prosecutor, Angela Corey, blatantly disregarded this evidence. Corey would go on to be appointed by Republican governor Rick Scott as special prosecutor in the Trayvon Martin case. (For a discussion of statistics based on race and gender in stand-your-ground laws, refer to Carmon, 2014.)
107. Refer to Carmon, 2014.
108. Rolnick, 2018, p. 1654.
109. In the popular article "Unconscious Bias Training Doesn't Work, but It's Making Billions," Freya India (2021) reports on the popularity of implicit-bias training. She writes, "Google, Facebook, and other Silicon Valley giants proudly crow about their implicit-bias trainings. The results are underwhelming, at best. Facebook has made just incremental improvements in diversity; Google insists it's trying but can't show real results; and Pinterest found that unconscious bias training simply didn't make a difference. Implicit-bias workshops certainly didn't influence the behavior of then-Google employee James Damore, who complained about the training days and wrote a scientifically ill-informed rant arguing that his female colleagues were biologically less capable of working at the company." Silicon Valley companies aren't the only ones working on their "implicit bias" problem. Police forces, the *New York Times*, countless private companies, US public school districts, and universities such as Harvard have also turned to implicit-bias training to address institutional inequality.
110. Lee et al., 2022.
111. Thus, the way antibias training operates in a settler epistemic economy (this idea is expanded in Chapter 3) is governed by racial order-reinforcing norms and practices, where people of color are expected to do the work of securing favorable environments

for white settlers and their descendants. There is a nonaccidental overrepresentation of people of color learning about their biases and expressing "humility" when learning about them in these training modules. The function of these programs is exculpatory for some populations but not others. Even Ohio University's Kirwan Institution for the Study of Race and Ethnicity produces training modules on implicit bias that attribute the origins of racial bias to "classical conditioning" and "associative learning processes" like childhood exposures to norms (https://kirwaninstitute.osu.edu/implicit-bias-training).

112. Lai et al., 2016; Monteith, 1993.
113. Forscher et al., 2016.
114. Kawakami et al., 2007.
115. Terbeck et al., 2012, p. 419. This was not the first time neurobiological approaches to the cognitive basis of racism had appeared in medical research, but it was the first time pharmacological solutions were indicated for further study.
116. Sellaro et al., 2015. Researchers asked participants to take an Implicit Association Test while under direct current stimulation.
117. Thomas & Brunsma, 2014, p. 1467.
118. Pager, 2007.
119. The anglo-european philosophical framework of implicit understanding is one example among many of that epistemic function at work.
120. Ruíz, 2020.
121. Ruth Gilmore's notion of racism as structured vulnerability to premature death of racialized populations (2007, p. 28) is particularly helpful here, as is the long tradition of Latin American social medicine (from Che Guevara's early work to Fernando DeMaio, and especially Frantz Fanon's work). Fanon's structural account of the public health and psychiatric system in Alegria under French occupation is especially important. Fanon attributes an intentional design—a primary function to "depersonalize" and "decerebralize" the Arab and Black population to achieve the goals of settler colonial occupation—to the permanent replacement efforts of the Native by the colonizer (whether this was through franchise colonialism or permanent settlement). Refer to, for example, Fanon, 1964/2022.
122. Honjo, 2004, p. 193. Refer also to Beckfield, 2018.
123. Nancy Krieger introduced this idea to social epistemology through the metaphor of a quincunx, a Victorian gardening pattern invented by Francis Galton (from which the Galton board name derives), "as a tool for illustrating how the arrangement of probabilities resulted in distributions" (Beckfield, 2018, p. 5; refer also to Beckfield for the idea of probability pathways as structured disadvantage). By physically modifying the path probability (among other possibilities) of the quincunx, it's easy enough to create a skewed distribution, but the usefulness of the visual metaphor for Krieger is to show generally that distribution *processes* exist. As Beckfield explains, "The point is that distributions are not 'natural' or 'innate' and do not inhere exclusively in the objects being distributed; rather, distributions are created by processes that can be manipulated and modified . . . it shows how the fates of elements of

populations can depend on design, rather than the attributes of the elements themselves" (pp. 7–8).

124. I put "normal" in quotes because the metaphor (as it relates to settler colonial societies) here is a visual tool and representative of a general dynamic; a better statistical representation would be a *long-tailed distribution* pattern, which is defined by power law relationships and represents a skewed distribution pattern (picture the bell curve of normal distribution as a tall *C* tilted on its side). A good example of long-tailed distributions (aside from the obvious case of wealth accumulation in settler colonial societies) is book sales (Fenner et al., 2010); most books only sell in small runs and go out of print, but a few "blockbusters" go on to sell millions. One of the bestselling books of all time (over one hundred million), Agatha Christie's (1939) *Ten Little Niggers* was easily retitled *Ten Little Indians* in the 1960s in response to the civil rights movement, illustrating the adaptive and intersecting feature of white supremacy discussed throughout this book alongside long-tailed distribution dynamics.

125. The analogy is to economic stratification and wealth concentration (statistically, binomial distribution still holds under inversion). Another helpful visualization would be a long-tailed distribution pattern, as noted above.

126. Jean Piaget contended that "knowing reality means constructing systems of transformations that correspond, more or less adequately, to reality" (1970, p. 15). While Piaget had in mind a narrow transformational model that relies on a variation of isomorphic scales between knowledge and reality (to explain developmental knowledge acquisition as a system property), his phrasing captures well the idea that reality is a political good tied to gatekept epistemic access to possible transformation pathways. For instance, "democracy" and humanitarian ideals are framed as the normative baseline in multicultural democracies, so that attempts to concretely identify phenomena in a language that can be recognized (the logical prerequisite for entering into settler evidentiary chains of proof for accessing administrative relief through law or healthcare) is always thwarted in advance. One way to understand this is through the *choque*, or cognitive clash, Gloria Anzaldúa (1987) describes when negotiating meanings among settler and nonsettler epistemic traditions in the US-Mexico borderland (which are both physical and psychic te) rains for Anzaldúa). Although many interpret Anzaldúa as hermeneutically silenced or epistemically stunted (usually under some ableist version of muteness) by this clash, their writings on creativity and the cognitive clarity achieved in dreamwork highlight interpretive resilience and epistemic refusal that is often ignored. (Serious problems still remain, of course, in Anzaldúa's politics of heritage and her tricultural *amasamiento* (kneading) of settler and nonsettler cultural traditions when giving accounts of *mestizaje* as a metaphysics of hybridized identity (criticisms that she addresses briefly in her late works.)

127. To discriminate between instances of implemented versus nonexistent features in software design when diagnosing system errors (or "glitches") (Peng & Wallace, 1993).

128. Ruíz, 2016; Ruíz y Flores, 2022. Some of this exclusion has begun to change recently with respect to relevant analyses of social injustice, but the latter problem persists through continued structured inattention to theorists of color, Indigenous conceptions of systems, and the general whitewashing of theories and typologies of structure. This is especially evident in analytic ontologies of social systems that mirror continental ontologies of social systems developed by Nazi sympathizers.
129. Systems principles can also be found in Aristotle's *Politics* through the idea that "the whole is of necessity prior to the part." In context: "Further, the state is by nature clearly prior to the family and to the individual, since the whole is of necessity prior to the part; for example, if the whole body be destroyed, there will be no foot or hand, except in an equivocal sense, as we might speak of a stone hand; for when destroyed the hand will be no better than that. But things are defined by their working and power; and we ought not to say that they are the same when they no longer have their proper quality, but only that they have the same name. The proof that the state is a creation of nature and prior to the individual is that the individual, when isolated, is not self-sufficing; and therefore he is like a part in relation to the whole" (1253a).
130. Capra, 1997, p. 4; emphasis added.
131. Saussure, 1916/2011, p. 120.
132. There is strong evidence that Saussure did not hold this view, but that it is the product of blatant editorial revisions by his disciples, to the detriment of Saussure's more nuanced and dynamic view of language. The famous Arbor/Equous illustration, for example, was adopted by Saussure provisionally as a "didactic exercise" to show the alternative view to come, not as his endorsed view. For a review of this literature, refer to Ruíz, 2016.
133. For Lévi-Strauss, "A structure consists of a model meeting with several requirements. First, there structure exhibits the characteristics of a system. It is made of several elements, none of which can undergo a change without effecting changes in all of the other elements. Second, for any given model there should be a possibility of ordering a series of transformations resulting in a group of models of the same type. Third, the above proprieties make it possible to predict how the model will react if one or more of its elements are submitted to certain modifications. Finally, the models should be constituted so as to make immediately intelligible all of the observed facts" (1958/2008, p. 279).
134. For a review of this history, including the racist legacy of linguistic anthropology, and examples of postmodern and poststructuralist accounts of structure, refer to Ruíz y Flores, 2022.
135. Piaget, 2015, p. 128. An example is Deleuze and Guattari's (1987) concept of the "rhizome." A rhizome is a botanical term for describing the random patterning and branching system of underground rootstalk networks, as in ginger or turmeric. Deleuze and Guattari use the term as a heuristic to describe how instability functions as an organizing principle for understanding social structure and the continuous reorganization of power across multiple and (seemingly) disconnected social domains. Randomness, complexity, instability, fragmentation—all core themes in the poststructuralist turn—can be reconciled with the historical study of social

power and sociopolitical oppression as primary objects of study for many poststructural thinkers. The notion of the rhizome is closer, then, to systems theory and the functionalist perspectives of organic structures in biology, so that the "post" in poststructuralist here is not "a"-structural, but rather places the emphasis on randomness, branching, and dynamic processes the way organismic biologists often do in analyzing the self-regulating behavior of systems—even in highly complex orders and in randomness, things are so organized as to produce reliable results in a system, even if those precise connections or methods of intersystem communication are not within the reach of the scientists (as interpreter of structures). The poststructuralists often used this approach to diagnose the organization of power in the social domain to great acclaim, often rejecting and eliding any association with structuralism as a term or tradition. But it is evident that this should not be taken as a rejection of all views of structure in their analysis of social systems and systemic oppression.

136. Some theorists regard the terms "structure" and "system" as so interrelated in their analysis of the relationships of patterns relevant to a specific inquiry that they are practically inseparable. (Or they are used interchangeably as temporary placeholders for more formal disciplinary terms like "organism" or "model" that receive special treatment later.) For others, "Focusing on structure allows us to abstract away all features of the objects of the system that do not affect the way they relate to one another. It is clear that the system comes already structured. We can then talk about its abstract structure, but this talk is parasitic on the system being a particular and already structured complex" (Psillos, 2006, p. 536). In *Structuralism: The Art of the Intelligible*, Peter Caws (1988) details a common distinction among natural and quantitative scientists between already structured/concrete systems and abstract systems that tends to be downplayed in many social scientific and humanities-adjacent views of structure. He writes: "By a system I shall understand a set of entities (called the elements of the system) mutually related in such a way that the state of each element determines and/or is determined by the state of some other element or elements, and every element is connected by a chain of such determinations, that is, the system has no isolated elements . . . by a structure, finally, I shall understand a set of relations among entities that form the elements of a system: the structure will be said to be concrete if the relations are actually embodied in some system, abstract if they are merely specified but not so embodied" (pp. 12–13). Philosophers often treat these relations and embodiments as if they happened outside of time or space, on the head of a pin. While a common way of understanding structuralism is based on implied system views of structures that require structures to be a system (and not just a collection of elements without a process or group operations that act on elements to bring about some change, or to maintain stability through those changes), history and space as critical components of determining relations in social systems are often ignored. Refer also to the discussion of structure-function and structure-property relations in this chapter.

137. For example, through an ontic "structure-property relation" as in chemistry. In chemistry intermolecular attractions reveal how structure determines properties that guide how molecules behave. While we can describe the functions of a chemical

system and the elements that comprise it, on this view the emphasis is on the *physical properties* of covalent compounds that guide the development of some intermolecular forces but not others based on those properties. Refer also to endnote 153.

138. For example, through a processual structure-function relation that focuses on how structures behave and how its parts interrelate to guide the structure's possible behavior, like the parts of an organism.

139. Depending partly on the metaphysics adopted and the conceptual orthodoxies employed, accounts vary as to what the "building blocks" of structures and their "building methods" are, as do the ways of relating them to one another. This variation invariably produces a diversity of ways of relating the ideas of "structures" and "systems" as separate, hierarchical, collapsible, interchangeable, collaborative, reciprocal, recursive, interlocking, coconstituting, among other possibilities. The takeaway: the distinction between system and structure is highly context dependent.

140. For instance, "in chemistry, discussions of structure and function are not as clearly defined," with some chemistry education associations using the terms "function," "behavior," and "properties" synonymously (Kohn et al., 2018).

141. But can potentially be one under the right constraints and scale of analysis: "Randomly" scattered house dust is easily a system to the dust mites that feed off it, for instance.

142. Note that the natural sciences generally work with a physical three-dimensional notion of (Euclidean) space that has important consequences for whether a structure is considered finite or abstract, as well as for the potential relations exhibited by structures (which in abstract structures can include an infinity of both objects and relations).

143. The human being as a self-contained agent is the "system" in this view, though of course there are early humanist and religious traditions that integrate agent-based models of systems as a distinct subsystem within the larger eschatology of a "the great chain of being"—a theistic universe that imbues subsystems with a grand design and purpose. An example is Pico della Mirandola's (1463–94) *Oration on the Dignity of Man*. The treatise is known for heralding the rise of the humanistic and individualist turn in the Renaissance, and for rejecting the medieval social hierarchies that situated humans in a fixed and deistic account of social processes. Mirandola, like many of his contemporaries, began to give accounts of human existence that transferred the system-level account of social processes *within* the individual through the renewed emphasis in the capacity for rational introspection and self-reflective reasoning. He likened humans to chameleons who can constantly refashion themselves and produce self-transformation in the pursuit of knowledge. Religious humanist accounts thus split the difference by placing the functional driver, goal, or purpose of human existence outside humans (i.e., knowledge of God).

144. The social scientific tradition comes from the dual impacts of (a) western scientific thinking and (b) the late eighteenth- and nineteenth-century backlashes against scientific reductivism from the white anglo-european intellectuals who influenced social theory (e.g., Durkheim, Parsons, Weber, and Marx). Here I am thinking

particularly of the influence of German Romanticism and its uptake in different traditions of vitalism, phenomenology, gestalt theory, and social psychology. For an analysis of the influence of German Romanticism on the development of systems theory in the work of Niklas Luhmann (a key figure in systems theory), refer to Fortmann (2015). Refer also to Lévi-Strauss's (1958/2008, p. 354) reference to the origins of ideas about transformation in structuralist thought as traceable to Goethe (1790).

145. Giddens, 1979. For Giddens, "Structure is both medium and outcome of the reproduction of practices. Structure enters simultaneously into the constitution of the agent and social practices, and 'exists' in the generating moments of this constitution." This means the duality of structure "expresses the mutual dependence of structure and agency"—i.e., the "middle ground" approach described a moment ago (p. 69). Giddens follows the German hermeneutic tradition in characterizing social structure through "the essential recursiveness of social life" and characterizes social knowledge as (1) constitutive of human subjectivity and (2) composed of "tacit stocks of knowledge which actors draw upon in the constitution of social activity" (p. 5).

146. Ayto, 1994; etymologyonline.com.

147. While I focus here on western views of structure, there is great variation among these views, as stated. These range from views of structure as organic (as in the physical neural structures of brains, or the physical structure of a coral reef ecosystem), methodological views that analyze structures in terms of system operations (or their "systemness"), mathematical and set-theoretic structures that model these relations and delineate the formal rules that govern them, gestalt structures that organize thinking, and inorganic structures (like computer networks and AI learning systems) that emphasize the self-organizational and transformational aspects of structures. The variety of positions within scientific structuralism and poststructuralism alone is substantial. The aim here is not to provide an exhaustive list or a unified theory of structure, but to illustrate the diversity of uses and, in certain disciplinary cases, common roots in the varied uses of associated terms that highlight patterns relevant to our inquiry. "The point of structuralism, after all, is to show that the entities in play are relational rather than substantial, and to show which relations are involved, how they are generated, and how the structures they compose transform one another; it is not to claim that those relations are so complex that they require mathematical expression" (Caws, 1988, p. 106).

148. It is also important to specify the scale of the relations under scrutiny and, at times, the planar level of analysis.

149. Sometimes the term "structure" is used in a systems-laden way that incorporates function, as in the interactionist interpretation mentioned earlier. When a structure is defined primarily through its function—for example, how it works or manages to do what it does—a structure is understood through the emphasis on the organization of elements in a given domain, where such organization is *functionally characterized by its aim to produce certain results via a series of transformations.* Many functionalists use "structure" this way. In these contexts, the structure is

primarily understood as a result of goal-oriented system processes. When defined primarily through its properties—for example, what the building blocks are and how that determines what can be done with them—a structure is regarded as an attempt to systematically relate different elements to one another in order to discern some basic arrangement (or further underlying structure, or substructure) that exists among elements of a system. While this can be regarded as a non-systems-based use of the term "structure," this last part is critical for a notion of structure that is not reducible to a collection of aggregates or mere composites and that cannot therefore express system functions. It is therefore needed for a functional account of structure and can be found in many social theorists' account of social structure. This serves as an example of how difficult it is to produce unequivocal distinctions between systems and structures. In social theory, functionalists generally understand structure through a systems lens because it allows them to connect individual agents (the elements of a social system) with normativity—e.g., with the social norms that can arise independently of individual human behavior. Functionalists emphasize stability across disruptions in social systems, but they do not reconnect the strings between the regulative capacities and adaptive design of social institutions and the stable pattern of harmful outcomes settler colonial social systems produce a basic feature of "social structure." When sociologist Émile Durkheim famously separated causal and functional explanations in the social sciences, it became fairly easy to keep these separated and still produce a "systems"-level picture of "structure." So, while "the characteristic interpretation of 'structure' among functionalist writers differs in a basic way from that typical of structuralist thought . . . in both bodies of thought the notions of structure and system are often used more or less interchangeably" (Giddens, 1979, p. 3). Hence, functionalism does not get at what is pertinently structural (e.g., what is doing the work of structuration) about structural racism in settler colonial societies.

150. A notable exception is Dotson's (2018) taxonomy of epistemological inquiry, which uses this distinction to track how metaepistemological assumptions work their way into social knowledge in settler colonial white supremacist societies in order to produce systemic harm for marginalized populations. So I regard her project as a critical relinking attempt that interrupts the settler colonial epistemological toolkit that exists to evade responsibility for genocide and epistemicides alike. The kind of problematic structure/systemic distinction I'm thinking of is in the "society as complex system model" that justifies a social ontology that maintains "societies are not planned and implemented by anyone" (Haslanger, 2022), so as to produce exculpatory accounts of personal and cultural responsibility in distinctions between structural and systemic injustices.

151. This is not my project here. For an excellent account of what such a notion of structure might entail that is compatible with realist positions in the metaphysics of science, refer to Berenstain, 2019.

152. One implied distinction that permeates this literature regards where the transformation is located in relation to the social systems being described—namely, whether transformations are internal or external to a social system, or some combination

of the two (and if so, how the interaction occurs and what governs them). In Lévi-Strauss, for instance, the notion of transformation is central to his structural method because it theorizes "the capacity of the structure to account for the ordered transformations between [different] models of the same group of phenomena," meaning that a transformation is a way of relating two models of the same type externally (Descola, 2016). Lévi-Strauss uses the colonialist observational economy of anthropology to offer the example of separate men of different social groups exchanging women with one another; thus the transformation is an *external process* of passing from one representing relation to another in models (here, the structure of similar kin groups) of the same type. He borrows the core of his morphological view from the biologist D'Arcy Thomson (1917), who uses "a geometrical grid of transformation to move from the form of an organism to the form of another organism by a process of continuous deformation and without respring to some complex initial form out of which all the other forms of organisms would be derivable" (Descola, 2016, p. 39). Whether the transformation is internal or external to systems, the idea of transformations is central in structural thought due largely to the heavy influence of morphology and the emphasis on morphogenetic change in the various schools of thought (from empiricism to Romanticism) that influenced its development.

153. Piaget, 2015, p. 5.
154. Skocpol, 1979/2015. Theda Skocpol's classic work *States and Social Revolutions* (1979/2015) uses a structuralist framework to define social revolutions as "rapid, basic transformations of a society's state and class structures" (p. 4) that are engineered by popular uprisings.
155. Mill, 1863, p. 93.
156. Rorty, 1995, p. 21. Refer also to Rorty's "Justice as a Larger Loyalty," where he writes: "[Nonwestern] societies should adopt recent Western ways by, for example, abandoning slavery, practicing religious toleration, educating women, permitting mixed marriages, tolerating homosexuality and conscientious objection to war, and so on. As a loyal Westerner, I think they should indeed do all these things. I agree with Rawls about what it takes to count as reasonable, and about what kind of societies we Westerners should accept as members of a global moral community. But I think that the rhetoric we Westerners use in trying to get everyone to be more like us would be improved if we were more frankly ethnocentric, and less profoundly universalist. It would be better to say: Here is what we in the West look like as a result of ceasing to hold slaves, beginning to educate women, separating church and state, and so on. Here's what happened after we started treating certain distinctions between people as arbitrary rather than fraught with moral significance. If you would try treating them that way, you might like the results" (2010, p. 443).
157. For Marx, the transition brought on by proletarian revolution must be between two different economic *systems*, even though it takes place in a logically continuous manner that makes the transformation appear as a historical "transition." Hence it is regarded as a "radical break," even when it is described in evolutionary terms (i.e., as a consequence of the inborn errors of capitalist systems that lead to their own destruction). In Marx a change in the economic system corresponds to a fundamental

reorganization of the polity (the base and relations of production) that maintains the system. If the relations change, one is no longer describing the same structure or model. So revolution from "below" (internal transformation) is coupled with a view of systems change as a process of transitions from one model to another.

158. Although it is adapted through general systems theory terminology, this idea has a long history in Latin American social theory (and in liberation epistemology) via the notion of the structural negation of revolution (Guevara 1961; Fanon, 1959; Molineux, 1989). Feminist reflections on postrevolutionary retrenchment of colonial orders are especially important in this framework (Margaret Randall's feminist work on the failure of the Nicaraguan revolution to effect lasting transformative change serves as an example). More recently, political sociology has examined structural invariance through the framing of counterrevolution as the "order-producing attributes" born from the "collective and reactive efforts to defend the status quo and its varied range of dominant elites against a credible threat to overturn them from below" (Slater & Smith, 2016).

159. Young, 2011, p. 74.

160. Rawls, 1971/1999, p. 6.

161. Young, 2011, p. 111. Notice, here, that interconnectedness is framed as a functional escape hatch for personal responsibility when the salient interconnections are agent-based.

162. Refer also to Young (2006), who writes, "I don't mean that no one should be blamed for some of the awful things that happened in the wake of Katrina. According to some reports, for example, the operators and employers of some nursing homes in New Orleans abandoned the residents to the flood. That is a crime. Perhaps Michael Brown and other high Federal Emergency Management Agency officials should be blamed for not knowing that tens of thousands of people were sweltering and starving in the Superdome. But I want to argue that, for the most part, in the aftermath of Katrina (and Rita)—as in other social processes involving many events, institutions, and actors—seeking culprits is bad politics. We should think instead in terms of responsibility and accountability, as distinct from blame or fault." Now who do we think this delinking of accountability from notions of fault will benefit? This is an attempt to functionally whitewash accountability. It is also insulting to the Black residents of the Lower Ninth Ward who were not unclear about the true and underlying causes of the failed or delayed emergency responses in their district, which readily disclose where blame and fault lies. "Not knowing that tens of thousands of people were sweltering and starving in the Superdome" is perhaps the structural understatement of the century—what afforded and protected such unknowing, even if true? Racist actions, policies, and infrastructures that produce death and destruction are not social abstractions without material infrastructures and the intermediators that must be put in place to administer them. (If the intermediators are persons of color, for example, they are surely held at fault more readily.) Young does offer us a clue into her thinking about what's violent about structural harms when she claims "structural injustice is not as horrible as systematically perpetrated genocide; I think of it as 'ordinary' injustice" (2011, p. 93). The population-level harms, targeting

design, and genocidal outcomes of structural injustices are vastly undertheorized in Young's thinking.
163. Young, 2011, pp. 18–39.
164. Young, 2011, p. 70.
165. "Sometimes it appears that the basic infrastructure refers to the basic legal framework defining rights, tax and fiscal policy, and the regulation of economic activity. In other passages, however, the structure seems to refer to a set of institutions such as families, courts, and major corporations" (p. 70). Young's (2011) analysis does not identify the hermeneutic prejudice to interpret the basic structure in settler governance-adjacent terms and institutional configurations.
166. Young, 2011, p. 70.
167. Young, 2011, p. 68.
168. Young, 2003; 2011, p. 44. This story is first introduced in Young, 2003.
169. Young, 2011, p. 46. Sandy is a single mother (her age and race are never given) with two children who is being pushed out of her centrally located (and already unaffordable) apartment after a developer bought it. She works in retail at a suburban mall that takes her three hours to get to each day, since she lacks a car and relies on public transportation. Despite her moxie and devotion to finding housing, she cannot find an affordable housing situation she deems safe for herself and her children and is unable to secure housing subsidies due to a two-year wait list. Unable to find housing near a bus line, she uses her savings as a down payment on a car, and when she finally finds a one-bedroom apartment, she is unable to afford the three months' down payment. Sandy interacts with a wide range of people throughout the process, from realtors to social workers. In a foil for Young's later discussion on sweatshops, Sandy's case is presented as a kind of fast-moving factory production line where each person's automated task is conditioned by the institutionalized rules and normative social practices that (to Young) don't seem problematic on their own (as everyone is responding to socioeconomic forces themselves), but which taken together contribute to the final product of Sandy's increased vulnerability to being unhoused.
170. Young, 2011, p. 41.
171. Young, 2011, p. 44. It is a twofold distinction from (1) wrongs that "come about through individual action" and (2) wrongs that are "attributable to the specific actions and policies of other powerful institutions" like direct state or legal actions.
172. Young, 2011, p. 52, emphasis added.
173. Young, 2011, p. 52, emphasis added; p. 70.
174. "The concept of social system, understood in its broadest sense, refers to reproduced *interdependence of action*: in other words, to a 'relationship in which changes in one or more component parts initiate changes in other component parts, and these changes, in turn, produce changes in the parts in which the original changes occurred'" (Giddens, 1979, p. 73). Giddens widely uses mathematical structuralist terms to describe core aspects of his theory of structuration, while clearly acknowledging the influence of white european (and particularly German) phenomenologists and existentialists in his thinking (Giddens, 1979, p. 3). For

young, this interdependence takes on an interactionist dimension that centers individuals in the emergence of social structure: "Social structure, then, refers to the accumulated outcomes of the actions of the masses of individuals enacting their own projects, often uncoordinated with many others . . . often producing outcomes not intended by any of the participating agents. Sometimes these unintended outcomes even run counter to the intentions of most of the actors" (pp. 62–63).

175. For Young (2011), social structures constrain and enable in two primary ways: "One is material. The accumulated effects of past actions and decisions have left their mark on the physical world, opening some possibilities for present and future actions and foreclosing others, or at least making them difficult" (p. 53). The other is historical: "All these existing physical structures and relationships carry the effects of past assumptions, decisions, and interests with them, and these continue to condition contemporary possibilities for action even as we try to transform them" (p. 55).
176. Giddens, 1979, p. 117.
177. Young, 2011, pp. 70–71.
178. Mills, 2017, p. 69.
179. Young, 2011, pp. 39–40.
180. Here Young is drawing on Hannah Arendt's distinction between guilt and responsibility in the Holocaust. She agrees with the distinction but thinks Arendt goes too far in calling out group-based polities (like being German) for political responsibility. "Because we dwell on the stage of history, and not simply in our houses, we cannot avoid the imperative to have a relationship with actions and events performed by institutions of our society, often in our name, and with our passive or active support. The imperative of political responsibility consists in watching these institutions, monitoring their effects to make sure that they are not grossly harmful, and maintaining organized public spaces where such watching and monitoring can occur and citizens can speak publicly and support one another in their efforts to prevent suffering. To the extent that we fail in this, we fail in our responsibility, even though we have committed no crime and should not be blamed" (Young, 2011, p. 88).
181. Young, 2011, p. 63.
182. This defense has been widely rebuked by the epistemologies of ignorance that (to different degrees) reject passive accounts of social reproduction and instead highlight the contributory and institutionally backed mechanisms of social reproduction behind oppressive systems (Pohlhaus, 2012; Berenstain, 2016). (The absence of this perspective in Young's thought is evident in her acceptance of some state forms of control and violence as "legitimate.")
183. Young, 2011, p. 26.
184. Young, 2011, p. 45.
185. Young, 2011, p. 119; emphasis added.
186. Young, 2011, p. 96.
187. The logic is similar in structure to the "electability" arguments for political office, and what otherwise deeply informed, and structurally astute candidates must do to

appeal and "soften" their image to be electable to the majority of white voters and voting blocks that wield considerable power and coffers.
188. Young, 2011, p. 118.
189. Young, 2011, p. 96.
190. Young, 2011, p. 147.
191. Young, 2011, p. 173.
192. Young, 2011, p. 147.
193. Young, 2011, p. 117.
194. Young, 2011, p. 121.
195. Young, 2000; 2006.
196. Young, 2000.
197. Young, 2011, p. 95.
198. Galtung, 1969; Wallerstein, 2004.
199. Lee, 2016.
200. Farmer, 1999, p. 79.
201. Farmer, 2010, p. 354, emphasis added.
202. Refer to Farmer, 1999.
203. Farmer, 2004, p. 307.
204. Farmer, 2010, p. 337.
205. Farmer, 2010, p. 337.
206. Farmer, 2010, p. 335.
207. Refer to Deer, 2015; Deer & Kronk Warner, 2019 on the relation between extractives and sexual violence in Indian country.
208. Smith, 2005, p. 10.
209. hooks, 1984/2000, p. 5.
210. Galtung, 1969. The term comes from Weber's *The Protestant Ethic and the Spirit of Capitalism*.
211. Farmer, 2010, p. 335.
212. Galtung, 1969, pp. 47, 168. Structural violence is not a "direct" form of violence understood as a behavioral act of "commission" by people or institutions. That doesn't make modal suffering from structural violence less harmful, painful, or violent. On the contrary, for Galtung (1969) and those who adopt his views, these acts of omission should be recognized as violent, painful, and harmful because the human suffering that results from structured deprivation (like dying of hunger from poverty) is largely preventable today: "If a person died from tuberculosis in the eighteenth century it would be hard to conceive of this as violence since it might have been quite unavoidable, but if he dies from it today, despite all the medical resources in the world, then violence is present according to our definition" (p. 168).
213. *Preferential attachment* refers to a model of interconnections in network science that explains how new nodes come to integrate or relate to other part of the network: the more densely connected a node is, the more it preferentially attracts new nodes to attach to it. When thought of in terms of wealth inequality, this process can illustrate nicely the basic dynamics and snowballing effects of how inequality is replicated (e.g., how wealth networks generate more wealth for those who already

have it), but without having to know great details about scale-relativity or other distinctions of preferential attachment in network theory. They can show the link formation process that is a helpful tool for thinking generally about *value transference infrastructures* in settler colonial societies, and how they are reinforced through time via power laws rather than objectively "given" by a historical tradition. (Refer, for example, to Figure 1 in Haruna & Gunji, 2019.) I say "generally" because many of the assumptions of these models, if mapped one-to-one onto settler colonial topographies, would trade on settler epistemological assumptions (e.g., the idea that new nodes can "know" the degree of every existing node prior to attachment, rather than depending on the node's degree) that reinforce mainstream views of structural violence as anything but "structural," or a systems process with a self-organizing design architecture and goals, irrespective of individual knower's intentional states. With this caveat, we can then think very generally about preferential attachment as the idea that in a complex network, new joiners "prefer" to attach to already well-connected members and that highly connected members (nodes) can "increase their connectivity faster than their less connected peers" (Jeong et al., 2003, p. 567). Gatekeeping at various levels of social resources and social capital easily come into focus through this lens.

214. This is a standard position in the capabilities literature and in development studies, particularly the basic-needs approach advanced by Amartya Sen.
215. Galtung, 2007, p. 134 (e.g., the design of interventions in scale, scope, and substance all too often gesture toward history but often replicate epistemological and cultural conventions rooted in colonial thinking and solutions to systemic problems).
216. One of the unfortunate consequences of western logic and the prevalent use of the law of the excluded middle is that the opposite of this is not a value-free position of purity or innocence. Refer to Dotson, 2018 for an analysis of this idea.
217. Because historical injustices are understood in terms of direct violence, it allows Farmer and Galtung to talk about specific individuals, even "architects" of structural violence in history, without further specifying the relation between individuals, collectives, and the ongoing processes of death and dispossession that structure precarity differentially between populations throughout the world. History plays a central role in understanding how conditions that promote suffering for the world's poor (who are regarded as "the chief victims of structural violence") came to be, but the function of history is limited to an origin story of individual or situated violent circumstances, not of structural violence itself (Farmer, 2010, p. 344). One way of understanding this approach is as a variation of the standard historiographical approach to cultural memory, which warns of repeating mistakes a culture fails to remember or memorialize. It is the forgetting and active erasure of histories of direct violence that pose a threat to (implicitly white) societies by "enabling conditions of structures" that promote widespread suffering and poverty. Farmer (2010) writes, "Erasing history is perhaps the most common explanatory sleight of hand relied upon by the architects of structural violence. Erasure or distortion of history is part of the process of desocialization necessary for the emergence of hegemonic accounts of what happened and why . . . and there are certain times, such as now, in

which exploring the historical roots of a problem is not a popular process. There is not always much support for laying bare the fretwork of entrenched structures that promise more misery" (p. 356). Interestingly, the predictive value of this "fretwork of entrenched structures" falls short of predicting *who* the continuing "architects" of structural violence will be or what the parameters for the continuation of modal suffering are. "The erasure of historical memory and other forms of desocialization" are "enabling conditions of structures that are both 'sinful' [i.e., wrong, from the Latin America liberation tradition of suffering as a sin] and ostensibly *'nobody's fault'*" (p. 354; emphasis added). Farmer's longtime concern with the "desocialization" (2010, pp. 295, 356) of medicine in favor of molecular and biologically reductive explanations for the causes of disease appeals to the need for contextualism in social medicine, but such contextualism is not sufficiently tied to the structural features of settler colonial occupation necessary to understand what is structural about the structural violence he attributes to his patient's situations.

218. De Maio & Ansell, 2018, p. 752.
219. Because as a theory, its epistemic infrastructure is built to do something, namely, to structurally support the continuation of white supremacy through humanitarian shifts in the notion of suffering as agential constraint.
220. De Maio & Ansell, 2018, p. 754.
221. De Maio & Ansell, 2018, p. 750.
222. De Maio & Ansell, 2018, p. 755.
223. De Maio & Ansell, 2018, p. 754. They point to the use of eco-social theory, "which presents a multi-level and historical framework for understanding the distribution of disease populations," as one tactic to give greater theoretical precision to the concept (p. 755).
224. Farmer et al., 2006, p. 1686.
225. I think it's possible to have a coherent notion of structural violence that does the work necessary to address the structural and interlocking nature of oppression in settler colonial societies without nesting it in other frameworks, however helpful those frameworks are for theorizing social harm. I think it's possible because it already exists in accounts of structured dispossession and systemic violence produced by the liberation, Indigenous, and critical race theorists discussed throughout this book. (Practitioners who are scouring this book for "solutions" to the known problem of the low rates of long-term success of interventions in social science and applied research would do well to begin with recognizing the historical terrain of the problem generating these failures, and how anticolonial literatures respond to them.) But I also think it's important to call out what the mainstream picture of structural violence gets wrong and how it manages, quite artfully, to provide the grounds for abrogating responsibility for structural violence presented by these accounts, and for automating impunity for systemic harm as a basic feature of settler colonial social structures.
226. This is what I care about most: impunity infrastructures and how they work intergenerationally to coordinate systemic violence against marginalized populations, and in particular, how they coordinate systemic violence against

women of color. This framing of impunity is useful because it tells a powerful story about how accountability escape hatches are functionalized in concrete historical terms through a basic systemic property, rather than some external intervention of will or collective response based on group values. It calls attention to the powerful structuring conditions of white dynastic formations that cannot be reduced to intergenerational transfers of dominant ideology. Social reproduction requires actions over short and long ranges, infrastructural reaffirmations of values reflected in concrete policies, and coordinated webs of power necessary to control the lands and spaces where social structuration actually takes place. As Crenshaw notes, "Coercion explains much more about racial domination than does ideologically induced consent" (1995, p. 110). But it also needs the epistemic wealth transfers and intergenerational accumulation of hermeneutic resources that license the material infrastructures and administrative institutions responsible for mitigating harms in the social world.

227. Galtung, 1969. Refer also to Piaget's idea that "structuralism calls for a differentiation between the *individual subject*, who does not enter at all, and the *epistemic subject*, that cognitive nucleus which is common to all subjects at the same level" (p. 139).

228. Galtung, 1990, p. 295. Part of the corrective to these framings of structural violence has come from within international relations and peace studies, wherein mainstream theories of structural violence are reframed as "conflict-generating social structures" that are not apolitical nor arbitrary since the misery produced by weak "basic needs" infrastructures is not arbitrary or accidental (Rubenstein, 2017). While such correctives are helpful for understanding that *the first parties in conflict to resort to direct violence are not breakers of the peace*, because they are responding to the direct consequences of systemic and structural forms of violence, such theories still harbor a tendency to decouple history from social structure in ways that produce naturalized accounts of conflict resolution schemes.

229. This view is consistent with the anticolonial characterization of european colonization as an ongoing process (Wolfe, 1999; Speed, 2019), and not a past historical event that negatively impacts the present, an event whose magnitude and scope continues to be elided in mainstream philosophical accounts of social transformations. The failure to conceptualize colonialism as a system often results in a picture in which historically arbitrary social prejudices and individual attitudes and biases (implicit and explicit) are regarded as the fundamental causes of systemic injustices in settler institutions such as the legal system, education, and healthcare. It also results in whitewashed accounts of structural injustice as the natural outcome of social reproduction processes—the force majeure behind the "machinery of oppression"—where no person, policy, or process (including colonialism and white supremacy) is "liable for rectification." The reasons given for this are varied, but it is often because (1) social reproduction is purported "social" (i.e., a group phenomenon) all the way down (i.e., in total), and (2) societies and the social values they produce are interpreted neutrally, as not inherently good or bad, only becoming so when viewed from the perspective of other social traditions and standpoints.

230. E.g., the transformational capacities of settler colonial social systems to produce structural invariance.
231. Structural innocence shows how frameworks that support western humanitarian and benevolent perspectives can also work to uphold settler colonial configurations of power at larger scales and across much longer time periods than the designed humanitarian interventions have the power to effect, thus creating a system loop and unaddressed structural causation for the ongoing suffering caused by long-living systems of dynastic white supremacy.
232. Although it is not a primary focus, the framework I outline can ameliorate the opposition of "structure versus event" in Indigenous structural critique (Nichols, 2020). Such a view, which construes structure as separate from event, situates a system's self-regulating dynamic behavior outside or adjacent to "structure." I frame settler colonial logics in terms of the epistemological systems and dynastic historical formations that uphold these logics.
233. In philosophy, ideal theory is associated with the work of John Rawls (1971/1999). For Rawls, ideal theory "works out the principles that characterize a well-ordered society under favorable circumstances" (p. 216) rather than theorizing about justice and its applications from the world as it actually is (e.g., as Marx does), under "unfavorable" nonideal circumstances of (in Marx's case, for example) economic strife and class division. Charles Mills (2005) famously described ideal theory as pure "ideology" of white polities: "a distortional complex of ideas, values, norms, and beliefs that reflects the nonrepresentative interests and experiences of a small minority of the national population" (p. 172). (The notion is classically dated to Rousseau's [1762] distinction between two types of social contracts (one idea and the other nonideal) and goes back as far as Plato's *Republic*.] Charles Mills (1997/2014; 2005; 2017) famously held a nonideal view of colonial history in his account of the racial contract and Black radical liberalism, as did Cedric Robinson (1983) in his contextual account of racial capitalism. A difference between Mill's (2017) nonideal account and the one presented here lies in his pathological (refer to Tremain, 2017) account of white supremacy as an "ill-ordered" and distortive society that contrasts with Rawls's depiction of an ideal, "well-ordered society": "We are not, of course, in such a [well-ordered] society. We are in a nonideal . . . *ill-ordered society*, which was historically established as (a) a coercive and exploitative venture for differential white advantage, and in which (b) the rules are generally designed for white benefit" (Mills, 2017, p. 211). While I share Mills's general indictment of white supremacy, especially his contention that white supremacy is functionally alive and continuously results in producing "illicit white advantage/white privilege" (p. 211), I don't think the nonideal framework is sufficient for producing anticolonial critiques of white supremacy, or that white supremacy is functionally aberrant. Quite the contrary, *it is perfectly well-functioning, as it was designed to be.* This is important because of the way nonideal theory relies on history and contextualism to argue for principles of "corrective justice" (i.e., to "tear up" the "bad" racial contract); I think a structural and systems-based perspective on history as a well-functioning cultural *design* is more helpful for political organizing and thinking

about strategies for overturning the dynastic design of white supremacy in settler colonial societies. It is also more fruitful for relinking the relevance of structural violence and intersecting oppressions, including racial femicide and rape culture, to the basic functioning of the sociostructural machinery that reproduces dynastic white privilege intergenerationally. Mills is right that there is an epistemological element of whitewashing that is "distortive'" insofar as it attempts to erase facts and narratives that pose challenges to white supremacy. But that is a feature of a well-functioning system, not an ill-ordered one. Consistent with a systems framing of structural violence, the notion of modal contextualism (as I use it) would be pretty useless without also addressing the power laws produced through settler epistemologies. Consider that, even if we did use a modal contextualist approach of "This is what actually did happen, and it matters," counternarratives of whitewashed histories (e.g., "No, *this* is what really happened"—as with Holocaust denial or your average Trumpian "truthiness" spin) would easily arise that are pure gaslighting, yet fully operative in settler administrative systems set up to receive such whitewashed history as official narrative. Hence, modal contextualism is fundamentally tied "to how social knowledge operates in settler colonial societies" (hence Chapter 3's subtitle, "Epistemic Capitalism").

234. I refer to this view generally as modal contextualism. The notion of modality is unpacked later in the chapter through Nora Berenstain's work in the metaphysics of science. For illustrative purposes here, to use a simple modal example from the empirical world, "It is not necessary that the world was such that salt crystals ever formed. But given that they did, it is necessary that they are held together by ionic bonds" (Berenstain, 2019). Modal contextualism equally rejects the historically contingent account of cultural values (as the chancy results of culturally relative traditions) in philosophical hermeneutics, as it does the weak contextualist platitudes of seemingly context-laden accounts of social emergence in mainstream analytic social epistemology (e.g., not Dotson).

235. The experience of these double-edged systems, on a very good day, is like fighting with a bank that is mistakenly withdrawing funds on autopay but accuses you of insufficient funds and assesses surcharges that perpetually indebt you to them, creating a downstream effect of further devastation in your life (to which you have no legal recourse because of the policy webs that tightly link financial lobbying with nonenforceable banking regulations and weak consumer protections).

236. What I chose to do with my PhD in philosophy is tell a story of who the hell set things up like this, and for my own healing. Hence the project of a systems view of structural violence, one that reaches deep into history and the epistemological formations that settler colonial cultures rely on to maintain dominion over it. Taking an anticolonial, nonideal, modal (i.e., structural) contextualist position, I wish to highlight the depth and breadth of settler colonial epistemological systems' distributive design since antiquity, and how such design bankrolls the tacit expectations of impunity for perpetrators of sexual violence whose processive relation to settler colonial social structures affords them asymmetrical epistemic access to these expectations, and to the structurally responsive institutions that functionalize impunity

as routine administrative procedure and cultural birthright. That doesn't mean the endgame is more people in jail. It means the differential conviction rates for rape and sentencing outcomes in settler colonial societies reflect settler colonial racial schemas and nonaccidental priorities over which lives matter and which don't. And that is a legitimate philosophical agenda and a focus of concern.

237. The design-of-distribution framing of settler epistemic systems I sketch throughout this book illustrates that the traditional account of implicit understanding, like other philosophical accounts of social knowledge practices rooted in contextual platitudes, is designed to adapt to challenges to its universal framing. To keep assessing charges and enforcing its right to be wrong because you are who you are, and it is what it is. Here's an example: when a claimant or defendant of color goes to speak in settler colonial courts, it is a matter of system automation that our speech and testimony will be recoded in ways that do not favor us, or that require tremendous supererogatory epistemic labor in order to meet the evidentiary burdens set by the governing administrative system. As Edwidge Danticat put it in the *Farming of Bones*, "I know what will happen. You tell the story, and then it's retold as they wish, written in words you do not understand, in a language that is theirs, and not yours" (2000, p. 246). This has been my enduring experience as a survivor of sexual violence and as a woman of color living in multiple settler colonial societies and navigating social services that were never designed to listen or believe me, or to believe me and secure the same functional outcome as if I weren't, whether on one side of the border or the other.

238. Bach, 2005, p. 15.

239. The structural contextualist view of human understanding at work in anticolonial systems theory is in stark contrast to western conceptual traditions like philosophical hermeneutics, as earlier suggested. Philosophical hermeneutics loves the idea of "context," but in a different way and with dissimilar end results for marginalized populations than in the structural approach to knowledge advanced, for example, by Dotson. Philosophical hermeneutics situates the distributive design of social structures in the arbitrariness and "contingency" of historical backdrops that emerge to interplay with purportedly universal social epistemological processes. These processes determine how meaning is constituted in a social world across cultures (i.e., how things become "intelligible" and socially legible in the first place). Why do some cultures do or believe certain things? Answer: context. Tradition. The wellspring of hermeneutical resources we inherit and take up dynamically as our own, given a new time and space. Etc., etc., etc. . . . Philosophy is historically bursting with a piñata of terms and endless neologisms to describe the social dimension of knowledge in relation to meaning-making and cultural intelligibility of social acts and practices: for Searle, it's the "Background" of "preintentional capacities that enable intentional action" (1998, 129). For Merleau-Ponty and Bourdieu, it's the "Habitus" of human interaction and activity that unfold against cultural backgrounds, histories, and languages that constitute a shared background of intelligibility for a society. For Gadamer, it's prejudice as "pre-understanding" and "historically-effected" consciousness (1960). Importantly, social epistemological

processes are not epistemological all the way down in the philosophical hermeneutic tradition exemplified by Gadamer. This means that social knowledge is recursively coconstituted by the concrete social acts and practices common to a polity in the present (e.g., the traditions we actively "take up"), so that social change can be explained. What we do today—what makes sense to do as normative acts and practices—is done in light of past collective actions and in relation to a projected future, so that despite significant historical change, over time a "tradition" emerges with a social history, a common language, and so forth. There's no grand puppeteer, just social collectives unfolding in time and negotiating new meanings against a generalized social "backdrop" of meaning-disclosing history and common languages that transmit our cultures. (For further critique of this approach—namely, *which* social acts and practices predictively rise to the level of "practice," and which are suppressed, refer to Ruíz, 2018.) This interplay between contingent historical backdrops and socially produced meaning results in a picture in which slavery and racialized sexual terror are not predictable outcomes of system-generated phenomena linked to history by causal necessity, but the historical happenstances of unfortunate turns of fate. Instead of predictable and reliably deadly system processes, scholars of social inequality in this tradition turn to events-based (i.e., things in the past) historiography to explain structural inequality by means of vague contextualism or the idea, as the european philosopher George Santayana put it, "Those who do not remember the past are condemned to repeat it." Putting the argument simply, how sad that such things happened; they happened, and that is bad (a normative judgment from our current "humanitarian" tradition), and those interested in ethics and politics should develop projects to stop these injustices. (Gadamer's famous debate with Habermas reflects this perspective.) But as I will show, the effects of traditions of racial injustice observed today have to do with a distributive design built into the very social structures and epistemological systems that generate salience in settler colonial societies. This is not captured in philosophical hermeneutics nor in allied philosophical traditions that do not locate "which interpretations gain assent and are integrated into the motivational system that governs a person or group's agency" (Fricker, 2013, p. 50) in a systems view of the recursive relationship between history and culture. Which interpretations gain assent and which don't is the result of a dynastic social process of intergenerational beneficence that has *transactional value and is based on violence*. This violence is both historical and involves an *active* suppression of hermeneutical possibilities by a dominant culture.

240. Crenshaw, 2021.
241. We know why they're not here, why they've been *made to be* missing. We know the same way we know the necessity of building coalitional networks that bring wider attention to things that seem quite nonaccidentally suppressed as unimportant in the national conversation surrounding racial violence and sexual assault: its intersections, its complex harms, and rippling effects. The solutions that are routinely offered to us profoundly fail to address the problem. For instance, the aggressively punitive carceral solutions that the settler state offers are designed to both privatize and profit from the criminalization of Black and Brown bodies, and to

create multiple pathways to escape accountability when the claimant is a woman of color. The pain and rage prevail as constants.

242. Again, by "emergent" I do not endorse the interactionist "middle ground" of social structuration that considers social acts and practices as agent-mediated emergent phenomena against a given historical backdrop (making the structure of agency exceedingly passive when it is not). I am referring to the systems-level capacity, through system properties like *preferential attachment* and *self-organized criticality*, to produce certain dominant social phenomena as "emergent" but not others. This requires *upkeep and buy-in, generation after generation*—otherwise the system would respond to internal pressures against its basic function (hence the language of "co" emergence). The coemergence is at the level of system interactions, not agent-based models of interactions. Further discussion of how agents are still essential to uphold the historical functional order of racial systems (but in a way that doesn't produce an "Everyone is responsible so there are no individuals to blame" model) is provided in Chapter 3.

243. When I talk about knowledge, I place the emphasis on violence. The success conditions for producing institutionally legible knowledge in settler colonial societies is based on violence. The systems perspective of structural violence I offer here shows the roles violence plays in producing the dominant knowledge systems in western culture that structure colonial capital production and its indispensable mechanism of racialized sexual violence. It also shows that this violence is by design.

244. Robinson, 1983. Robinson traces racial capitalism to feudalism; I go further back to antiquity. Unlike Robinson, who (following Snowden), holds that "Romans, like their Greek predecessors, did not evolve prejudices of color and race" (p. 85), I turn to the evolving systems architectures (including the *institution* of slavery) and rising knowledge infrastructures (including core metaphysical assumptions and logical systems of the western tradition) that created the capacity for the precise kinds of color prejudice we associate with the colonial period. I carefully avoid claims that, since the core ingredients of proto-racism can be traced to greco-roman antiquity (Chapter 2), racial prejudice based on skin color (analogous to modern biological taxonomy of plants) has always existed, and is therefore "determined." A white supremacist logic would easily take such a historical claim of color prejudice in antiquity to portray peoples who have "always been enslaved" as inherently "enslaveable," or (following Aristotle), as "natural slaves."

245. Berenstain, 2019.

246. Davis, 1981; Speed, 2019.

247. That is, before settler colonial epistemological systems converge on the subsystems of historiography and official narratives of history to skew the story of what really happened (which in turn fortifies settler epistemological systems as interconnected wholes). As Spivak (1999) and the South Asian (and the Latin American) school of subaltern studies famously agued, this epistemic shiftwork is the result of and the productive work of epistemic violence. It is sheer white historiographic mythography, and it pervades everyday institutional apparatuses in culture like schools, legal systems, and history books. Philosophy's role in this mythography has been

to provide a wide array of defensive arsenal through democratic theory, ethics, and political theory that substantiates the cultural defense of impunity (e.g., by distinguishing between "historical injustices" and more general "structural injustices" that can evade the just sentence of wide-scale reparations for harms done and actively maintained, all the while cover one's tracks of having done so, as Young's work discussed earlier so powerfully illustrates).

248. Morris, 2018, p. 57. Unsurprisingly, the most common analytic tool for examining early educational push-out policies and practices remains implicit bias (refer to Gilliam et al., 2016). Studies on preschool educators' implicit biases as viable explanations for disparities in preschool expulsions outnumber the research examining the underlying structural causes of school push-out. What is of interest in the former studies is the mental life of potential racists (for instance, studied by tracking educators' eye movements in controlled experiments) rather than the collective experiences of children who are continuously subjected to disciplinary disparities, and the connection between these collective experiences to the historical infrastructure of white supremacy and racialized sexism in education zoning policy that upholds such "dangerous" subjectivity. The latter tell a larger structural story of consistent patterns of abuse in settler colonial administrative systems.

249. MacLean, 2021.

250. For example, historical injustices and contemporary racist policies thus emerge as distinct categories of analysis. Historical practices like the "residential security" strategies of the New Deal's Home Owners' Loan Corporation, which redlined maps consequential to school boundaries, are cited as relevant contextual factors for underlying causes of racial inequality in education.

251. Refer also to Schutte, 1998. For Pohlhaus, willful hermeneutical ignorance occurs "when dominantly situated knowers refuse to acknowledge epistemic tools developed from the experiential world of those situated marginally. Such refusals allow dominantly situated knowers to misunderstand, misinterpret, and or ignore whole parts of the world" (2012, p. 715). By an active an intentional variation I mean that it is part of a larger distribute design of settler epistemological systems that affords this possibility so widely and pervasively to white people, and that the purpose of such systems is to consistently skew multivariant formations of profit toward white settlers and their descendants at the intergenerational scale. So it's not just a structurally afforded wrong that results in "wrongful white benefit," as Charles Mills often says. It is a whole epistemic economy designed to make such wrongful benefit status quo and to mainline vulnerability, precarity, and disadvantage toward marginalized populations. Such design reconfigures marginality through structural operations and its productive cultural devices, like what Neda Maghbouleh (2017) calls "racial hinges" (refer to Chapter 2 for discussion of racial hinges). Similarly, we can issue a more active and intentional variation of what José Medina (2013) calls a "wrongful interpretive obstacle."

252. Ruíz, 2021. For example, physicians-turned-revolutionaries Che Guevara (1961) and Frantz Fanon (1961/2007) readily made the connection between cultural liability, historical violence, and the self-repairing and resilient features of colonial violence

that authors like Galtung and Farmer (who are widely cited as the originators of the concept of structural violence) miss. Fanon's and Guevara's training as physicians yielded organismic and functional accounts of systemic oppression and colonial violence that informed their frameworks for resistance, and which are also reflected in Latin American social medicine's concern for the sociostructural causes of disease.

253. This is particularly true for Farmer, who had access to biological systems views of life as a western medical doctor trained in the biological sciences. I differentiate Berenstain's account of "modal structures" from Farmer's account of "modal suffering" to illustrate the strength of systems-based approaches to social oppression and the harm produced by neglecting the self-repairing, adaptive, and resilient features of structures in accounts of structural violence. We'll then build on this to produce an anticolonial account of systems theory suitable for theorizing resistance to systemic forms of violence in settler colonial contexts.

254. Berenstain, 2019.

255. Berenstain, 2019.

256. "Humeanism is broadly construed in terms of a metaphysics that denies the existence of natural necessity. Another way to put this is that Humeanism denies there are nonlogical necessary connections among outcomes, events, processes, and phenomena. For the Humean, patterns in the phenomena are metaphysically primary and modal facts derive from or supervene on these patterns. This is not a viable way to understand modality as it is construed in science for several reasons. One, it cannot account for quantum entanglement. Two, it cannot account for the success of induction as a scientific method. Three, there is no viable noncircular way to formulate 'sophisticated' Humeanism—the version of the view that is supposed to avoid the problems with naïve regularity theory. Finally, despite the contentiousness of the debate, I find concerns regarding the lack of explanatory power of Humean laws to be quite compelling" (Berenstain, 2019, n.p.).

257. Berenstain, 2019, n.p.

258. Sawyer, 2005, p. 189.

259. Elder-Vass, 2011, p. 17.

260. 2014, p. 15, my emphasis.

261. Robinson, 1983. For example, he writes that, at base, "Marxism is a Western construction—a conceptualization of human affairs and historical development that is emergent from the historical experiences of European peoples mediated, in turn, through their civilization, their social orders, and their cultures. Certainly its philosophical origins are indisputably Western. But the same must be said of its analytical presumptions, its historical perspectives, its points of view. . . . European Marxists have presumed more frequently than not that their project is identical with world-historical development. Confounded it would seem by the cultural zeal that accompanies ascendant civilizations, they have mistaken for universal verities the structures and social dynamics retrieved from their own distant and more immediate pasts" (Robinson, 1983, p. 2).

262. Parsons, 1951, p. 115.

263. Haslanger, 2022, p. 1. As reinforced throughout this book, a prime example in philosophy is also the subfield of hermeneutics; consider that the heartbeat of hermeneuticists' (e.g., Charles Taylor) cultural essentialism (Narayan, 1998) masquerading as multiculturalism lies in the power to naturalize social emergence—to give a "just so" story (dating back to Herder) about how meaning and intelligibility emerges cross-culturally from a culturally situated historical backdrop that provides ethnocentric cover for the race-neutral but patently racist ("historically situated") view of western superiority. (Refer to James Maffie on Taylor's 1982 article, "Rationality.")

264. Haslanger, 2022, p. 1.

265. Vizenor, 1999, p. 2.

266. In most, if not all, western social reproduction models, the dialectic between the individual and the collective is connected to the history of the social environment (language, norms, rules, social practices, and interpretive habits) an individual is born into, rather than the history of the physical environment and its constitutive role in shaping the connections and interrelations among people, including language and social meaning. This shapes norms of responsibility and notions of justice (particularly as balancing processes) that are intertwined with land-based ethics of sustainable and reciprocal relations between humans and lands.

267. This analogy has obvious limitations due to the material interpretation of stage design and interactionist views of social practices that would hold an agent capable of changing the stage design through an actor's interaction with parts of the set.

268. Or rather, prestructures, as depending on the model of social ontology, they are either prior to mental states or behavior, or coemergent with social practices.

269. The interactionist interpretation of social practices adopted by Young, Giddens, and many other social theorists temporalizes this relationship between history and society to make it appear dynamic and responsive to how individual agents negotiate cultural presents thorough reflection on the past or through present engagements with a vision of the future shaped by the past (e.g., as in social movements). Another approach to the interactionist model comes from Foucault's account of "discourse," which has a twofold explanatory scheme for social emergence: (1) it refers to the "practices that systematically form the objects of which they speak" as well as to (2) the arbitrary historical system that grounds those practices as meaningful. The arbitrariness of such history creates the appearance of cultural specificity (consider the vast range of examples Foucault gives in the opening paragraphs of *The Order of Things*) while universalizing the conditions under which societies emerge as human societies. What's important for my purposes is that both interactionist and noninteractionist accounts of social emergence are consistently applied cross-culturally, leading to the judgment that cultures universally reproduce profound injustice (and as such their models of social justice can be, in theory, applied globally). Again, how history unfolded matters: this universal framing of social inequality— that all societies reproduce profound injustice—has historically and disproportionately been used to pathologize marginalized populations and to easily pick out

purportedly culturally specific internal causes (such as "machismo") to blame for the violence enacted against marginalized communities at the level of populations. It is a mechanism to obscure the interrelated infrastructural material conditions and structural causation necessary to maintain such violence, and who most benefits from this maintenance.

270. Lisa Lowe (2015) refers to this as a "past conditional temporality" (p. 175). Refer also to Arturo Escobar's *Pluriversal Politics* (2020). The emphasis is on not portraying colonial occupation as a terminal event or final arbiter of history.

271. Wittgenstein, 1969, p. 21. Propositions 140–144 are especially relevant. Wittgenstein describes a prelinguistic framework of human understanding whereby culturally particular socialization arises and is handed down from one generation to another. The process of social reproduction is not simply based on the oral transmission of knowledge, for example, from a parent to a child in piecemeal fashion (teaching one judgment after another), but through a holistic integration of the child into a preexisting *system*, and this system is a more primordial enabling condition for the intelligibility of social practices and cultural "know-how" than propositional knowledge represented in syntactical language. He writes: "The child learns to believe a host of things. I.e. it learns to act according to these beliefs. Bit by bit there forms a system of what is believed, and in that system some things stand unshakably fast and some are more or less liable to shift. What stands fast does so, not because it is intrinsically obvious or convincing; it is rather held fast by what lies around it."

272. Refer, for example, to Silvia Federici (2019): "The idea of social reproduction originated in the context of bourgeois economics to indicate the processes by which a social system reproduces itself" (p. 55) For a problematic account of colonial sexist racism and violence as a testing ground for the violence enacted on european women through witch-hunts, refer to Federici, 2004.

273. Refer to, for example, Herder's 1772 *Essay on the Origin of Language*, and the work of Johan Georg Hamann. The historical breadth of colonial ethnographic applications of these theories is staggering.

274. Ba, 2007.

275. "In this main portion of Africa, history is in fact out of the question. Life there consists of a succession of contingent happenings and surprises. No aim or state exists whose development could be followed; and there is no subjectivity, but merely a series of subjects who destroy one another" (Hegel, 1975, p. 176). For an extended treatment of Hegel's racism, refer to Tibebu, 2011. For an analysis of Hegel's exceptional treatment of Egypt, refer to https://www.pdcnet.org/hsaproceedings/content/hsaproceedings_2007_0018_0201_0216.

276. Eberhardt et al., 2006.

277. Houkamau & Sibley, 2015.

278. Smith, 1776, pp. 488–489.

279. Modern systems theory and complex adaptive systems theory (CST) grew out of the general systems research (GSR) movement of the late 1950s and early 1960s, when cybernetics and emerging computational paradigms of information processing transformed previous mechanical paradigms of interactive networks. The physical

concepts of "space, time, attraction, inertia, force, power" were "borrowed back," so to speak, from the physical sciences to produce a "relational mechanics" compatible with the functionalism exhibited in complex computational and biological systems, highlighting "continuous, boundary-maintaining" and adaptive abilities to "create, elaborate, or change structure as a prerequisite to remain viable, as ongoing systems" (Buckley, 1967, p. 5). (Refer also to the life science framing of CST in Capra's *The Systems View of Life*, 2014.) GSR popularized and refined vocabularies (like "feedback loops," "boundaries," and homeostatic regulation") developed in earlier organismic biological models in europe in the late nineteenth and early twentieth centuries. However, few systems theorists today emphasize the problematic history and designed compatibility of early GSR models developed in Viennese intellectual circles with Nazi ideology (e.g., the work of Karl Ludwig von Bertalanffy), preferring instead to narrate the influence of the european organismic biologists in ecological thinking and the later influence of string theory and other grand unifying theories of the 1980s. Attempts to develop CST into a social systems theory (especially those regarding the development of models of how to change a social structure) have mostly covered over these issues in their naturalized analyses of sociocultural systems. Talcott Parson's (1961) attempt to explain social change is an early case study for this.
280. Nimatuj, 2021, p. 106.
281. Omi & Winant, 1994, p. 71.
282. On racism: "We define racism as a fundamental characteristic of social projects which create or reproduce structures of domination based on essentialist categories of race" (1994, p. 162). On race: "We should think of race as an element of a social structure rather than as an irregularity within it; we should see race as a dimension of human representation rather than an illusion" (p. 55) and "race is strategic; race does ideological and political work" (2015, p. 111).
283. Such formations operate at different scales and across an expansive range of domains. At the interpersonal level, when individuals engage in the political process (in a Du Boisian sense) of making and remaking "race," so that one is not defined by one's oppressors, the process of racial formation is taking place. At the institutional level, when policies conspire to uphold hierarchies or violent structures of domination by singling out individual groups for surveillance, as in immigration and asylum policies or social work practices (as de facto policies), racial formation is also taking place. The diversity of examples and contexts captured by racial formations can be traced directly to naturalized framing of culturally relative "economic and political forces" that "determine the content and importance of racial categories" in each context (Omi & Winant, 1994).
284. Omi & Winant, 1994, p. 55.
285. *Racial formations* is an unstable process that still mimics the swing-counterswings dynamics of classic political theory from Hegel onward, only Omi and Winant transfer this process to the "micro" level identity formation and negotiation.
286. In the third edition of *Racial Formations*, Omi and Winant (2014) double down on this position by saying, as noted, that race is a "master category" that no other social conflict (class, sexism, colonialism) can be understood without (p. viii), especially

if we want to understand embodied experience (e.g., the phenomenological experience and bodily facticity of race as it is lived). This has drawn criticism as a "master interpretive move," as it further operationalizes a concept that is itself a product of settler epistemic dominance in order to account for a metaphysical dilemma also created by settler epistemologies (the dilemma that something can both exist and not exist at the same time, like the genetic fallacy of the existence of race alongside the social reality of race's continuing influence). Rather than undermine the dualism, race as a master concept becomes the analytic anchor for self-reflective action and negotiations of race, a problem Audrey Lorde and the radical Black feminist traditions (refer especially to Spillers, 2003; Dotson, 2015) and Indigenous feminism (refer especially to; Paredes, 2010; Silva, 2004; Simpson, 2004; Simpson, 2014) have swiftly rejected in favor of conjuring and affirmative politics (which does not minimize race). Previous to the third edition, the transcendental treatment of race led to claims like this: "We think that race is so profoundly a lived-in and lived-out part of both social structure and identity that it exceeds and transcends racism, thereby allowing for resistance to racism" (Omi & Winant, 2013, p. 264). Consider also Omi and Winant's (1994) responded to the question, "Some may argue that if the concept of race is so nebulous, so indeterminate, so flexible, and so susceptible to strategic manipulation by a range of political projects, why don't we simply dispense with it?" with the answer "It is rather difficult to jettison widely held beliefs, beliefs which moreover are central to everyone's identity and understanding of the social world." For contrasting view, Wolfe (2016) argues "race, being historically contingent, can be overcome" (p. 271).

287. I.e., the latter can be explained through intergroup political conflict or other intersecting categories of analysis that illuminate the contextual process of race-making.

288. Omi & Winant, 2014, p. 3; 2015, viii). "The effort must be made to understand race as an unstable and 'decentered' complex of social meanings constantly being transformed by political struggle" (Omi & Winant, 1994, p. 55).

289. Omi & Winant, 2015, p. x. Unsurprisingly, settler colonial history (alongside Indigenous perspectives) does not fare well in Omi and Winant's particular process-based metaphysics of continuous open-ended racial formation. This is because the explanatory priority is given to the "master concept" of race as an analytic paradigm, from which the "contextual" interpellation of the phenomenon of racism follows (just as in Farmer's work).

290. Mejia, 2022. This is an anti-Indigenous reference (based on anti-Blackness) to the large Zapotec community in LA that migrated from the Mexican state of Oaxaca. She also made racist remarks regarding the Black son of a councilmember. For decades, many scholars and activists like Shannon Speed have noted that Latin American states are settler colonial states that are sordidly racist, anti-Black, sexist, and profoundly anti-Indigenous, so this should not come as a surprise.

291. This includes providing cover for the US settler demographic project that introduced whiteness-reinforcing terms like "Hispanic" as census categories when other

NOTES 353

surveillance terms did not catch on. Refer to Rodríguez (2009) for a discussion on the statistical effort to make "Hispanics" a race.
292. Walker, 1983.
293. Thus, anti-Palestinian racism cannot be disconnected from the mycelial network of white dynastic social reproduction that maldistributed harm to Afro-Brazilian populations and to Pueblos Originarios throughout Abya Yala and First Nations peoples across Turtle Island.
294. Swain, 2007, p. 655.
295. For the white supremacist Nile valley historians in the back, the takeaway of "written" evidence (refer to Mignolo, 1995; Ong, 1982/2003) of "hue"-based differentiation associated with negative perceptions of "Egyptians and Ethiopians" in antiquity is not that color prejudice is a cultural, biological, or genetic truth. It is a social construction that is part of the same dynastic process of cultural reproduction that today provides cover and impunity for professional publications that demarcate Egypt as "outside" of Africa or part of the "white" west today.
296. Robinson, 1983, p. 2.
297. "Herodotus, the first of Europe's historians, traced Egyptian colonial settlements as far as the northern Black Sea region. Herodotus described a Black people, the Colchians ('they are black skinned and have woolly hair') living in what at present is Soviet Georgia" (p. 83).
298. He writes: "Yet despite their less than cordial relations with Africans, the Romans, like their Greek predecessors, did not evolve prejudices of color and race: [quoting Snowden] 'Social intercourse did not give rise among the Greeks and Romans to the color prejudice of certain later western societies. The Greeks and Romans developed no doctrines of white superiority unsupported by facts or theoretical justifications for a color bar. The presence of large numbers of Negroes in a white society, according to some modern views, gives rise to anti-Negro feeling. Ethiopians were far from rare sights in the Greco-Roman, particularly the Roman, world. Yet the intense color prejudice of the modern world was lacking. Although it is impossible to estimate the Negro element in the classical world in terms of precise statistics, it is obvious that the Black population in Greece and Italy was larger than has been generally realized'" (p. 85). For a historical context of Snowden's writings, refer to Parmenter, 2021. On modern color prejudice, refer to Du Bois 1899/2007; 1903/2007.
299. Racism never arrives fully formed—that much Omi and Winant got right—but it traveled a certain path—a modally possible path—to get where it got. One of the reasons I don't take the obvious Marxist route of value production and transmission to illustrate dynastic inequality is that the commodity form is historically associated with an act of magic: "The commodity-form, and the value-relation of the products of labour within which it appears, have absolutely no connection with the physical nature of the commodity and the material relations arising out of this. It is nothing but the definite social relation between men themselves which assumes here, for them, the *phantasmagorical* form of a relation between things."

300. Goldstein, 2022, pp. 65–77.
301. It cannot be unilaterally applied across all cultures to specify the particularities of "race-making" projects, but to the specific contexts where european colonialism reached to exert a historical influence (in all its processive and ongoing particularities).
302. The emphasis is on control. The study of complexity in natural systems illustrates how controlled succession is also distributive. Succession should therefore not be reduced to unbroken linear inheritance, as dynastic processes are dynamic, interactive, and irreducible to sequentially ordered units of historical progression. To survive transformations, succession adapts to value-transference mechanisms that reproduce the relations relevant to white dynastic formations. Today, we find examples of the link between controlled succession and value transference for white settler polities in lots of places, but the art market is one of the easiest to demonstrate this relationship because of the clear connection between gatekept "provenance" (e.g., logics of "pure lineage") and market value. The controlled succession of the global asset market, valued at nearly half a trillion dollars in 2022 (with an annual growth rate of over 60 percent), is unsurprisingly tied to the tunnels of impunity women and gender-nonconforming artists have to traverse when sexual violence and femicide are licensed by the art world (as the murder of artist Ana Mendieta illustrates).
303. Refer to Chapter 2 for an extended discussion of this through Athenian women's access to property and testimonial oaths. Also consider the case of Alessandro de Medici.
304. Settler white polities routinely attempt to discreet anticolonial liberation movements by invoking binary logic to argue that what we want as oppressed peoples is the same access to *violence* that white settler polities historically have (rather than equity, reparative action, and dignified peace). This note serves as a clear rebuking of any attempts to characterize this book as promoting "divisive politics" that fuel violence, especially when the actions necessary to address violence are within the power of the polities making such claims.
305. Jaleel, 2021, p. 178. Jaleel offers a poignant example of the dynastic dynamics of retrenchment in a comparative discussion of Title IX: in 2017, a federal judge dismissed a Title IX lawsuit brought by a former Haskell Indian Nations university student (who reported they were raped by two football players on November 15, 2014, in a university dorm) on grounds that the government and the university were immune under the doctrine of sovereign immunity (*Doe v. Haskell Indian Nations Univ.*, 266 F. Supp. 3d 1277, D. Kan. 2017). Jaleel is concerned with recurring patterns in the differential outcomes and uses of antidiscrimination legislation like Title IX, such as those that expose "trans/queer vulnerability to accusations of sexual assault in educational content" while closing off pathways for accountability when those harmed are from marginalized populations. For example, Jennifer Eller, an English teacher in Maryland, was subject to intense harassment, misgendering, threats, insults and physical assaults, but her repeated complaints and requests for support

were met with reclassifications of sexual harassment as nonactionable "disrespect" (*Eller v. Prince George's County Public Schools*, 580 F. Supp. 3d 154. D. Md. 2022).
306. Davis, 1998. The lesson for political organizing is cautionary—that "it's a mistake to assume that all we have to do is to guarantee the prosecution of the cop who killed Michael Brown" or to populate police departments with people of color (Davis, 2016, p. 15).
307. Davis, 2016, p. 16. Davis writes: "Racism is so dangerous because it is deeply embedded in the apparatus . . . it doesn't matter that a Black woman heads the national police [as one does in Markina, South Africa]. The technology, the regimes, the targets are the same. I fear that if we don't take seriously the ways in which racism is embedded in institutions, if we assume that there must be an identifiable racist . . . then we won't ever succeed in eradicating racism" (pp. 17–18).
308. Davis, 2016, p. 89.
309. Ruíz, 2019.
310. Lipsitz, 2006, p. vii.

Chapter 2

1. Komisaruk, 2008.
2. Krauze, 2016.
3. Agren, 2017; Rasgado, 2017; Sistema de Información Legislativa, 2017. Adapted from the judicial *writ of Amparo* (availabe at http://juristadelfuturo.org/wp-content/uploads/2017/03/AMPARO-159-2017-Diego-Gabriel-Cruz-Alonso.pdf) and social media reports. Refer also to Versión Estenográfica de la Agenda Política Comentarios Relativos a las Recientes Resoluciones Judiciales en Veracruz, 2017. http://sil.gobernacion.gob.mx/Archivos/Documentos/2017/04/asun_3516717_20170405_1491427079.pdf.
4. Because I draw on multiple disciplines, some terms can have multiple meanings (for instance, "wealth," "profit," and "family," have specific referents in sociology that do not track across Indigenous philosophy). In such cases, it is useful to keep in mind how terms function in relation to the three core arguments in this chapter: (1) epistemological notions of belief, credibility, and trustworthiness (as they emerge in the epistemology of testimony) function within a wider settler credibility economy that differs from mainstream philosophical accounts of how credibility functions in society (which yields whitewashed accounts of sexual violence); (2) gender-based violence is a primary tool of settler colonial processes of dispossession and, as such, plays a critical role in the settler economy; (3) A cost must be tallied and a bill presented for the existence of an invariant settler colonial structure of evidentiary address that precedes the legal structure of evidentiary proceedings in gender-based violence cases in settler colonial societies, as it structurally bars meaningful access to democratic institutions in ways that perpetuate, rather than alleviate, population-wide inequities. All three points rest on *structured profit views of violence*, where violence and profit are understood narrowly. First, violence is

understood as a multimodal cultural process rather than a specific event or series of events where the bourgeois nation-state's administrative dispersal of state power categorizes actions as either legal interventions or the extralegal use of force subject to a criminal code (be it in English common law, Napoleonic code and civil law, Portuguese civil law, the Law of Castile, etc., or in certain maritime zones, international law). Profit, though it will be expanded on in the next chapter, is understood dynamically as a socially licensed incentive structure to reproduce gain, particularly gain attained through artificially induced asymmetries between spent labor and generated earnings (including structured acquisition and accumulation of social capital goods like credibility, and protectives against exposure risks, like debt and its collection structures). Structured profit views of violence, as they are used here, go beyond quantitative and qualitative analyses of economically profitable exploitative harms like sex and labor trafficking; they reject the very structural innocence behind empirically reductive behavioral models of violence that are often used to explain cases and incidences of violent phenomena in settler colonial societies while drawing blanks on the structural causes. Structured profit views of violence correct this imbalance between our lives, realities, and social scientific research on racialized gender-based violence by aligning our experiences with diagnostic frameworks that can capture these experiences. It is not a fight over methods or frameworks—it is a fight for our lives. And that is a fight that not everyone doing research on violence has to fight.

5. Stolberg & Fandos, 2018.
6. Andersson et al., 2019; Salter, 2019; Stewart, 2019; Nackenoff, 2019; Winderman, 2019; Tuerkheimer, 2017.
7. Seo et al., 2019; refer also to Sohrs, 2016.
8. Welsh, 2017, p. 51.
9. Spohn & Horney, 1991, p. 137.
10. Coady, 1992; McMyler, 2011; Gelfert, 2014; Shieber, 2015.
11. Fricker, 2007.
12. Pohlhaus, 2017, paraphrasing Dotson, 2012.
13. Craig, 1990; Reynolds, 2017.
14. Prescod-Weinstein, 2020.
15. Democratic theorists propose a different origin of testimony. In democratic theory, testimony refers to the series of procedural mechanisms that codeveloped alongside the rise of legal systems in newly formed nation-states and constitutional democracies for the purposes of codifying normative social and political practices of vicinage. The purpose of such codification was to instill confidence in young independent legal and administrative systems by enshrining the presumed trust individuals have of local social networks (vicinage) into criminal and civil law, ranging from the rights of the accused to confront one's accuser to the right to "a trial by a jury of the vicinage," which is enshrined in the Sixth Amendment to the US Constitution. Such theories are most frequently traced back to Aristotle's description of a democratic citizen as one who is eligible to serve as a juror (*dikastes*). In reality, such renditions of testimony are designed to offer race-, gender-, and

power-neutral accounts of the epistemological relation between social knowledge and politico-administrative systems that favor white dynastic formations. As this chapter illustrates, such theories naturalize the history of testimony and erase the historical settler colonial uses of testimony as an apparatus that had to be formalized and developed and the specific lexical structure of which had to be "taught" to Indigenous peoples under conditions of supplication and torture (refer, for example, to Felipe Guamán Poma de Ayala's account of Indigenous testimonies to colonists, including his own supplication to Spain's King Phillip II to restore Indigenous governance structures in *El Primer Neva Crónica y Buen Gobierno* [1615]). The strategically political goal of extracting reliable information from Indigenous people was, for instance, to identify the whereabouts of gold and precious metals, and to ascertain european linguistic cognates for Indigenous political structures that could be used against Indigenous polities (consider, for example, the structures of european catholic power illustrated in the *Rhetorical Christiana* and the grammarian tradition of Native informancy exemplified in Diego de Landa's *Relación de las cosas de Yucatán* [1566]).

16. Under the Federal Rules of Evidence, for instance, a fact witness is not permitted to express an opinion while testifying that goes beyond limitations stipulated in Rule 701 (Opinion Testimony by Lay Witness), which states: "If the witness is not testifying as an expert, the witness' testimony in the form of opinions or inferences is limited to those opinions or inferences which are (a) rationally based on the perception of the witness, and (b) helpful to a clear understanding of the witness' testimony or the determination of a fact in issue and (c) not based on scientific, technical, or the specialized knowledge within the scope of Rule 702" (Testimony by Expert Witnesses).

17. For an extended example of naturalization as a method of critique in philosophy, refer to Chapter 3, "Naturalized Merits," in Charles Mills's *The Racial Contract* (1997/2014).

18. Benton, 2012.

19. Its older Indo-European root, *tris*, or "three," is a nod to this oral transition, referring to the third person present in an agreement between two men who could serve as a disinterested witness in a trial. This notion of *disinterested witnessing* and its links to evidentiary corroboration and correspondence has been attributed to the psychodynamics associated with the rise of alphabetic (from the Gr. letters *alpha* and *beta*) knowledge and writing in Asia Minor. Refer, for example, to Diringer (1962) and Ong (2003). This tradition focuses on the epistemic and neurocognitive consequences of the rise and internalization (the widespread cultural use) of alphabetic literacy since 720 BC (the date the greek alphabet is attributed to) on knowledge production, transmission, and preservation. For an account of the epistemic and hermeneutic mismatch between western alphabetic scripts and Indigenous writing systems, refer to Boone and Mignolo, 1994. For the violent features and political dimensions of this mismatch in colonial warfare and settlement, refer to Mignolo, 1995.

20. Fletcher, 2003, p. 29.

21. Dodds, 1991.
22. One of the only records of such oaths to survive paints a telling picture: "I live a holy life and am pure and unstained by all else that is not pure and by intercourse with a man" (Sommerstein & Torrance, 2014, p. 158).
23. The wealth-making parameters of the greco-roman world developed extensively after the fourth Macedonian and Achaean War, not only in expanding agrarian commercial infrastructures (especially in North Africa) but also in the rise of market institutions, including labor, capital, and credit markets. Historians of roman economy reject capital-neutral readings of ancient history by noting that "unlike the medieval period, the early Roman empire appears to have had well-functioning labor and capital markets" (Temin, 2006, p. 140). Historians also note the relation between these markets and the codevelopment of racial taxonomies (such as the one-drop rule) for the purposes of maintaining the roman slave supply through slave breeding (Bradley, 1987).
24. Think of the "rules" and vast network of socially blueprinted contextual cues (including land-based cues) necessary to distinguish a game of American basketball from the Aboriginal game of *buroinjin*.
25. Contextual history does not mean "cross-cultural" or "culturally relative," as in the western bioarcheological narrative of comparative accounts of "dynastic" social systems. Consider the use of western (Portuguese and British) colonial categories of caste in colonial India. Once overlaid over existing social categories, it became possible to recognize "caste" in India but to disappear it in England (Guha, 2013, as cited in Fárek et al., p. 9). Cultures with a "dynastic" appearance are often foils for the alleged absence of those patterns of domination in the societies that exerted violent influence over them. India's case is important because the narratives of inborn Brahminical dominance, and the theory of Aryan invasion (around 1500 BCE) and colonization of Indigenous peoples of South Asia (based on the european christian need to taxonomize populations through lineage to the sons of Noah), can be traced to sixteenth-century european scholars who tried to reconcile the linguistic similarities between Indian and european languages (e.g., to explain these similarities but establish orientalist-inspired differences to justify occupation). (Refer also to Keppens & Roover, 2020.) This does not negate the realities of caste-based sexual violence against Dalit women in India. It casts concern on western understandings of "caste" that allow that violence to be disconnected from colonialism and its producing mechanisms. Mainstream anthropology frequently naturalizes dynastic systems as lineal inheritance structures (or variations thereof, such as patrilineal priesthood), but which delink the patterned and the consequential. These maneuvers can graft a whitewashed hermeneutic lens (that produces internally consistent social scientific knowledge-claims) onto cultures that have different land-based epistemologies and metaphysical interrelations as social systems. For example, some nonwestern social structures are designed to reproduce dynastic formations that differ substantially from the successive lineages of hereditary systems conducive to the controlled transmission of transactional value, and are not designed to self-repair in comparable ways to western systems. Inca and Nahua systems governed by reciprocal ontologies like

camaquen or the metaphysically ambiguous concept of *teotl*, which are governed by principles of parity, are also governed by system goals of *cyclical destruction or enduring instability* that maintain a sustainable relationship with the land's caring capacity, and where beings and lands are not separate and can therefore not establish ownership relations analogous to occidental conceptions of material value.

26. I am referring to dynastic social systems rooted in controlled succession that adapt for the purposes of wielding power over the production, reproduction, and transmission of value, understood narrowly as defined in this chapter.
27. Or an adjacent system (since subsystems can themselves be analyzed as systems). System interaction and the *relation* between structures or elements in a structure are what is important here.
28. This general view of the (a) automated and (b) restructuring nature of oppression has been echoed by many theorists of color. Fanon, for example, conceptualized the relation between racism and culture as primarily structural, automated, and self-regenerating. He believed the intergenerational regeneration of racial inequality required "positive" (i.e., active agential enforcement) and "negative" (i.e., structural) forces to be able to outlast historical attempts to dismantle it. Trained as a medical doctor, Fanon's view was influenced by basic structural notions in developmental biology (such as cell regeneration and repair, angiogenesis) and by psychological adaptations of these notions (refer to Ruíz, 2019). Theorists like Fanon, Angela Davis (2016), and Neda Maghbouleh (2017) describe the regenerative and adaptive nature of oppression in more useful structural terms than classical philosophers such as Foucault. For instance, Foucault (1978) famously described sexuality as a "dense transfer point for relations of power" (p. 103), but his conception of power misses the mark on (1) the relation between power and colonial transference chains and (2) the payoff of the structural regeneration of enduring white supremacy through continuously created (and socially maintained) transfer points like racial systems, much less the hyperdense transfer points of intersectional oppressions.
29. A frequent question that arises when describing self-repairing white dynastic formations (and here I'm paraphrasing the question as it is generally put to me) is why white dynastic social structures "get" to regenerate when the social structures of Indigenous peoples and people of color don't "get to." They certainly do regenerate! And they have continued to do so despite the genocidal design of western imperialism. It's a question of the role of violence and its maintenance as a promoter agent of, to put it in agonistic settler imagery, metastatic colonization, where the adaptive features of an otherwise healthy system and its defenses are overpowered in the course of its self-defense. So we're describing different cultural systems, and different relations being regenerated at the systems level, which is a relational difference that makes a sociostructural difference. I maintain that western culture's particular history (e.g., its peculiar metaphysical commitments and epistemic orthodoxies that began emerging in Asia Minor from the eight century BCE onward, in the transition from oral to logographic and disembodied systems of knowledge, to the rise of the atomistic tradition and the logical relations built around it, to the well-known Platonic turn and subsequent christianization of Platonism alongside Alexandrian

imperial expansion) pose particular problems to nonhierarchical and sustainable relations with the earth and the inseparable diversity of life forms (i.e., the responsibility *to* sustaining care must be brought into the system from the outside; it is not easily generated as a systems property). So it is no surprise that a sociostructural process built on dynastic propensities toward patrilineal value transference and metaphysical reductivism that turns living land into inanimate property and accumulated wealth as a matter of irreflective logical course should produce the kind of oppressive social patterns that generations of Indigenous peoples and people of color claim are systemic, deep rooted, and built to harm some people so that other people may benefit. As Edward Said and many anticolonial thinkers have asserted, the question is not *that* other cultures exist and survive (we assuredly do), but of the persevering, staunch, persistent cultural domination and structural oppression that forces nondominant social structures to respond (often by establishing internally harmful interrelations) in order to survive the onslaught. So it's a two-pronged issue of asymmetric access to power (e.g., to cultural means of production, like lands and spaces tied to language) and cultural differences in the structural drivers of self-organized criticality of social systems (e.g., the specific aim of stabilizing processes toward the system goal).

30. *Takao Ozawa v. Unites States*, 260 U.S. 178 (1922); *United States v. Bhagat Singh Thind*, refer also to *Dow v. United States*, 226 F. 145 (4th Cir., 1915). U.S. Rev. Stat. § 2169 limited the Naturalization Act of June 29, 1906, through the provision that naturalization eligibility pertained only to "free white persons, and to aliens of African nativity and to persons of African descent." In the aftermath of abolition, the white settler state was actively searching for an adaptive domain of nonwhite labor to fill worker gaps created in the Industrial Revolution for dangerous jobs and disposable labor (e.g., in the building of the transcontinental railroad). And, while the Chinese exclusion act was not repealed until 1943, the unregulated legal domain of forced and coerced Chinese labor in mining and extractive camps is a case in point.
31. Qtd. in Chin, 2020, p. 1276.
32. Smith, 2002. For important discussions of Indigenous women's citizenship under Canada's Indian act, which made status conditional on the husband's status, refer to Cannon, 2019.
33. National Archives, 2021.
34. Smith, 1998, p. 152.
35. Smith, 2002.
36. Jaynes, 1982. The state's investment in racial arithmetic, particularly surrounding women's bodies, traced back to racial capitalism's investment in rape culture since slavery. Such investments can be linked historically to demographic practices requiring the geolocation of single freed Black women for white men's exploitation in Louisiana. "In New Orleans in the eighteenth century, quadroon balls, at which white men selected women who were one-quarter Negro to be their concubines, were extremely popular. The 1788 New Orleans city directory lists 1,500 free women of color who lived alone in little houses near the ramparts" (Jaynes, 1982, 16). The existence of quadroon balls has been questioned by white historians for lack of surviving written documentation, and by Black scholars who aptly point out the white settler male

fantasies (of swooning, beautiful women of color freely coveting and vying for the best financial arrangements from older, rich, white benefactors in exchange for sex) behind the widespread tales of quadroon balls (Clark, 2013). What isn't questioned is the explosion of human trafficking (what historians like to misdescribe as "sexual tourism") of free women of color in Louisiana initiated by the notoriety of these balls, whether they took place as described or not, as well as the common-law system of *plaçage* put in place by white planter society. The planter society that flourished in Louisiana had amassed the wealth to devise a formal system of informal workarounds to antimiscegenation laws and other regulations prohibiting mixed-race relations. It allowed white men to sexually exploit women of color (*une placée*—a placed woman), under the illusion of contractual arrangement that ended when the man found a white wife. *Plaçage* functioned as a distributive mechanism to align overarching system goals in settler colonial societies with that of subsystems, like legal codes limiting white men's unfettered access to women of color's bodies.

37. Maghbouleh, 2017, p. 5.
38. Maghbouleh, 2017.
39. MacFarlane, 1997; refer also to Hefny 2019. The reverse pattern of racial classification has also occurred, where light-skinned African nationals (in many cases, white settlers in Africa) have been reclassified as "Black." In the early twentieth century, a spate of cases on Syrian (today Lebanese) racial classification illuminated the colonial conflation between race and religion (where christianity can establish relational proximity to whiteness) through the disparate treatment of Syrian Muslims and Syrian christians (refer to *In re Najour*, 174 Fed.735 (1909), Ex parte *Shahid*, 205 Fed. 813 (1913), *In re Ellis*, 179 Fed. 1002 (1910)). In *Ellis* the government argued that while Ellis was "white," he was not from europe, and thus he was not an eligible "free white person."
40. Act of March 26, 1790.
41. Bureau of Indian Affairs, 1975.
42. Hearing before the subcommittee on immigration policy and enforcement, April 2011. https://www.govinfo.gov/content/pkg/CHRG-112hhrg65744/html/CHRG-112hhrg65744.htm.
43. Khimm & Silva, 2020.
44. *Rachel Moore v. Howard University*, et al., 2005. Retrieved from https://www.documentcloud.org/documents/2103329-the-rachel-moore-dolezal-vs-howard-university. Among her allegations, "Moore alleged that the decision of Dean Benjamin of Howard to remove some of her artworks from a February 2001 student exhibition was motivated by a discriminatory purpose to favor African-American students over Moore." Moore specifically alleged her work environment was "hostile" and that she was, as a white woman, subject to "intimidation, ridicule and insult" that had caused psychological distress. It is important to note her major claims were dismissed on statutory grounds.
45. Schapps, 1998.
46. Trümper, 2009.
47. Fanon, 1956, pp. 32–33.

48. The structuring sets of relations and valences that organize social hierarchies as, for example, reciprocal, nonreciprocal, complementary, or (the more familiar) exclusionary forms of hierarchy do so in light of broader system-level relationships to, for example, land (how land is conceptualized), language, how history and the social past are understood, relevant cosmologies, metaphysics, and salient relationships to the nonhuman world. Consider that western nonreciprocal dualisms yield exclusionary social hierarchies of out-groups and in-groups, whereas many nonwestern dualisms serve system goals of balance and reciprocity, so that what appear to western observers as exclusionary dualisms may in fact establish reciprocal and ethical responsibilities to land, air, waterways, and the animal world.

49. This point is important because it shows that the distributive design of social structures in white dynastic formations is not only a negative phenomenon (i.e., resulting in marginalized and exploited populations), but also a productive one that continuously reproduces reified value for white settler populations and their descendants. By reified value I mean the functional usefulness and worth produced through continuous transference chains that can turn nonfungible commodities into fungible ones and vice versa—into things that are "of worth" in a settler colonial economic system, and that can be traded and created by virtue of the epistemic structure of value in white dynastic formations. Why do mediocre white intellectuals make the grossly inflated salaries they do in the academy compared to Indigenous scholars and scholars of color? Why do the grand prizes in social and cultural fields recognize the theorists most aligned with settler colonial myths and agendas? Why do white european immigrants who speak English with an accent routinely represent Latinxs as people of color in award shows? Why are the people of color most often promoted into the highest echelons of public institutions despotically settler in their thinking? Structural respecification and its relation to settler colonial value transference is one way to think about this. Mythmaking, for instance, becomes real and valuable through its transmission and position in a structure, not though its content. This idea of respecification of value is inherently tied to the idea of social reproduction introduced in Chapter 1. Consider the case of Clarence Thomas. A basic gloss of Justice Thomas's conservative opinions and public comments on race has made him a darling of the Far Right for nearly three decades. While his conservatism is typically analyzed as a "colonized mind" situation (take, for example, Malcolm X's [1963] distinction between the enslaved person "who lived in the master's house" and was in the minority, versus the enslaved person "out in the field" who held no psychological allegiance to the enslaver), I take a view that is not psychologically reductive and does not locate the reproduction of white supremacy in mental models of racism. The transference of settler colonial white supremacy happens in a system context. Crucial to Justice Thomas's ascension to power, for instance, is that he was to replace Justice Thurgood Marshall on the US Supreme Court. Also crucial was the interpretive infrastructure created to receive Thomas's defense strategy to Dr. Hill's powerful testimony of having been sexually harassed by him. The core value being respecified can undergo many transference mechanisms, but impunity to sexual violence against racialized women is one of the oldest parameters for inducing respecification in white

dynastic formations. Moreover, while I think the structural transference mechanisms of social reproduction described here are an ancient epistemic technology of power developed in the wake of massive Athenian losses in the Peloponnesian War (structured to overcome the physical destruction of a polity by concentrating resources of cultural provenance in immaterial ideas, as illustrated in Plato's *Republic*, and developed as structural epistemic warfare through Alexander the Great's strategies of conquest), the origins are less important than the accumulative power and function this technology has today (transferences do not happen independent of accumulation; on the contrary, they support it, as Chapter 3 illustrates). I think it's important to bring this white dynastic technology of social reproduction into focus because the dominant alternative is a settler colonial narrative (typically used when analyzing the paradox of Latinxs as a disunified voting bloc) of oppressed peoples actively choosing their own oppression through the endorsement of conservative Republican platforms that actively target marginalized populations (i.e., lost is the role of settler white supremacy and the reproduction of Hispanic whiteness in nineteenth-century theories of *mestizaje* and in the US census creation of specific articulations of *Latinidad*). It's also important to bring this mechanism into focus because it dispels the demographic myth that structural violence and oppression will end when we reach a "minority white" point in the 2045 census (shrinking the "non-Hispanic White-alone population" from 199 million in 2020 to 179 million in 2060) (https://www.census.gov/newsroom/press-releases/2018/cb18-41-population-projections.html). It will not end; it will only be respecified, and potentially stronger than before. The German ideology of *Herrenvolk* (rule by an ethnic majority or "master race") propagated by the Nazi Party is part of a longer chain of transformations of the idea of pure lineage that remain consistent with the global distribution of wealth despite their transformations. A polity need not appear "Aryan" to maintain the infrastructure necessary for white dynastic formations to reproduce patterns of wealth distribution and maldistribution of burdens rooted in white supremacy, and to maintain the conditions under which racial regimes based on phenotypic whiteness can always emerge.

50. Nguyen, 2006.
51. Nguyen, 2006, p. 73.
52. Ngugen, 2006, p. 77.
53. As argued in Chapter 1, protoracism was, however, prominent in imperial rome. The writings of the greek geographer Strabo are particularly insightful in describing roman attitudes toward enslaved peoples and foreigners during the key transition from the roman republic to the roman empire that are characteristic of racial prejudice. For instance, in *Racial Prejudice in Imperial Rome*, Sherwin-White (1967) uses Strabo's distinctions between the peoples of Gaul, Germania, Britain, Greeks, and Iberians to indicate physical and anthropometric distinctions being made about "physical attributes such as size, pigment and type of hair" along with language and customs (p. 6).
54. Burks et al., 1837.
55. Smandych, 2006, p. 99.
56. Porter, 2019.

57. Isaac, 2006.
58. Isaac, 2006, p. 33. This is a stronger claim than "the ideology of modern racism is far more theoretically developed than ancient or medieval prejudices and is linked—whatever one's view, idealist or materialist, of causal priority—to a system of European domination" (Mills 1999, p. 63) because it roots european domination in longer nonaccidental conceptual formations and patterns of action that had to be kept up and supported through centuries of social practices.
59. Porter, 2019, p. 33.
60. Criticisms of slavery did exist in the greco-roman world, but as moral and intellectual exercises that mirrored the rise of the importance of rational reflection and contemplative introspection in public life and statecraft. Since most enslaved people were freeborn, becoming a slave was seen as having an element of "chance" (mediated by divine wills) and thus cause for introspection on the anxieties elicited by this potential. The roman stoic Seneca, arguably one of the most famous critics of slavery, argues against the perceived social class inequalities between slaves and nonslaves on this point: some people are enslaved quite late in their lives, so anxieties are well warranted and best addressed by dissolving *moral distinctions* between masters and slaves, not in abolishing the institution of slavery (*Epistulae Morales ad Lucilium*, 47, 10–12). This move will become foundational in the shift to democratic rule, where racist institutions can structurally coexist with antiracist thought and values.
61. Watson, 1983. The law on this was clear: "Whenever it is a question of ownership of slaves, if the truth cannot be uncovered by other proofs, the legal authorities approve the view that the slaves themselves can be interrogated, with torture" (C.9.41.12, Diocletion and Maximian, 291 CE).
62. Watson (1983) uses this fact to criticize modern scholars of roman law, even those who condemn roman slavery, for making it seem "more decent than it was" (p. 53). Refer also to the modern anglo-american legal system's treatment of torture in the Law of Evidence and evidentiary jurisprudence on when such torture is deemed permissible under admissibility standards (i.e., when racialized nonwhite defendants are involved) (Roberts, 2008). Calls are still being made for expanding the "exclusionary rule" that forbids judicial proceedings from admitting evidence obtained through torture—enshrined in Article 15 of the 1984 UN Convention against Torture and Other Cruel, Inhuman or Degrading Treatment or Punishment (UNCAT).
63. Ezgi Sertler (2019) has described this epistemological move, when codified in western democratic institutions such as international human rights law, as a "recognition bluff" that protects people (such as asylum seekers) in name only and which simultaneously provides the structural support for organized harms to target vulnerable populations via these same institutions. Refer also to Sara Ahmed's (2012) related notion of nonperformativity.
64. Benton, 2012, p. 168.
65. Seed, 1996, p. 68. John Locke's (1689) principle of first appropriation, by which English settlers can appropriate uncultivated land by "mixing their labor" or their

"slave's labor" with it, serves as an example. Refer also to Locke's *The Fundamental Constitutions of Carolina* (1669) for Locke's support of slavery ("Every freeman of Carolina shall have absolute power and authority over his negro slaves").
66. Refer to the *Dum Diversas*.
67. For an excellent example of how settler colonialism structurally positions white settler populations as epistemic arbiters and those with adjudicating power over communicative exchanges, refer to Dian Million's (2013) discussion in *Therapeutic Nations* of international human rights instruments and frameworks.
68. Shapiro, 2002.
69. This runs contrary to the view that legal orders developed "naturally" and without structural intent in their design.
70. This would become a critical administrative tool in the rise of the Holy Roman Empire, with its fusion of roman and christian values and the growth of a vast administrative bureaucratic monarchy that would eventually transform roman slavery into christian serfdom, and physical bondage into physical and spiritual supervision over land-bound serfs born into servitude.
71. Refer also to Sertler (2018) on "institutional comfort."
72. Hence the critical importance in understanding how interlocking oppression work as part of larger system-oriented social structures.
73. Goodell, 1853, p. 309. Michel Foucault (1926–1984) held a similar view about the normalizing role of state apparatuses in individual subject formation. It is through the (discontinuous and dispersed) exercise of disciplinary biopower that individuals are both constituted as "selves" in an epistemic field and, at the same time, as discrete biographical unities to be surveilled, monitored, statistically tracked, classified, written about, and documented by the new knowledge systems of modernity (such as the carceral state and social scientific disciplines like demography). What's important to know about Foucault, for the purposes of this project, is that, like many hermeneutic thinkers of his time, Foucault argued that there is simply no standpoint—objective or otherwise—outside of social power relations that could help in organizing resistance against organized oppression. Tracking coordinated violences through history via the self-repairing functions of dynastic cultural formations to illuminate an organizing set of principles based on white economic supremacy, Foucault might argue, is important critical historiography, but it cannot structurally legitimate a political standpoint like antiracism. For him, political positions are important things we take up as social beings, but they cannot be used to justify cultural or epistemological positions on independent grounds of any kind. This is often overlooked because Foucault wrote so much about institutional violence and the historical formations of knowledge that help coordinate specific forms of administrative harm that target populations, and which produce and maintain marginalized subjects. He wrote at length about the staggering scale of, and the vastly different modalities of, sociopolitical pressures (like state-sponsored violence and statistical surveillance) constantly exerted against social actors in public and private spheres—how knowledge is weaponized and institutions automated to reproduce specific outcomes based on power asymmetries in society. Power can

be spectacularly and panoptically oppressive when taking the form of juridical or administrative biopower—it can swarm like a mass of insects and work its influence at the most micrological and unexpected scales. But without power, there are also no human communities in which beings become subjects. In this respect, he follows Heidegger and other conservative and epistemically imperialist european hermeneuticists, in rejecting the idea of the possibility of an embodied critical social knowledge or of a minimal standpoint detached from colonial reason that could ever fully expose the governing structures of domination, or that continuously impact our lives to coordinate social and political liberation. In this respect, critics such as Gayatri Spivak and Edward Said have consistently critiqued Foucault for the blank spot in his thinking about how *colonial power* functions in relation to knowledge. Also, he stole a lot from the Black Panthers, so I say read them instead.
74. The use of torture to ascertain veracity was later introduced into roman legal rape proceedings (for those who had legal standing to bring forth charges). Art historians recount the Rome trial of the seventeenth-century painter Artemisa Gentileschi's rapist, "during which the then 17-year-old was forced to testify with ropes tied around her fingers that were progressively tightened in a test of her honesty" (Associated Press, 2022b).
75. Ruíz, 2020.
76. I draw on established and current research in inquisitorial europe and the Iberian colonies (Bethencourt, 2009; Silverblatt, 2004; Alberro, 1981; Herrera Sotillo, 1982; Lopez Don, 2008; O'Gorman, 1949; Perry & Cruz, 2018; Crew, 2019; Hill, 2019) as well as on the two large volumes of primary documents published by the Archivo General de la Nación (*Proceso inquisitorial del cacique de Tezcoco*, 1910) and Guamán Poma de Ayala's *Cronica de Buen Gobierno* (1615–1616) to frame my analysis.
77. The most notable of these aspects is the judicial use of torture, an aspect famously used throughout the various inquisitions that began sweeping the european continent in the thirteenth century and continued in the catholic Iberian colonies (especially in Mexico and Peru). Inquisitorial practice not only revived the use of torture in judicial procedure after it waned following the fall of the roman empire, but also tied testimonial practice to important new administrative procedures that would prove critical in the consolidation of newly unified continental states and their colonial holdings. It became especially important in the development of evidentiary aspects of pretrial criminal procedure, including interrogative procedures allowing deceit and pressure techniques for examining witnesses (Murphy, 2013; refer also to Murphy, 2012). On the truth-torture legal relation, as taken up in inquisitorial practice: the relation between truth and torture is functionally mediated by the enslaved, subjugated body in roman law, as earlier described. The medieval revival of torture in criminal proceedings, though well established (Peters, 1985; Ullmann, 1944; Lowell, 1897), is often narrated through the omission of the role socially stratified bodies play in torture. Lowell, for example, affirms "the use of torture was borrowed from the roman law, on the principle that heresy was *crimen laesae majistatis divinae*," and that the new inquisitorial procedure, which was "thoroughly in harmony with the spirit of Roman jurisprudence," was gradually adopted by the continental states

as a means to increase jurisdictional authority over large heterogeneous territories, "until at last prosecutions for crime were carried out almost exclusively by the judicial officers of *the government*" (p. 223, emphasis added). Torture, then, was a legal technology to produce political gain in the form of absorbed territories. Criticism of the view of inquisitorial practice as a political tool targeting minorities points to the persecution of high-ranking community members and elites across religious identifications in favor of the standard religious conversion function interpretation. A large body of scholarship points to the wide range of social positions subject to inquisitorial activity in medieval europe, including high-ranking officials and notable families, and thus minimizes the development of inquisitorial apparatuses for use on Indigenous populations during the colonial period. In fact, the scholarship on testimony, inquisitorial practice, and Indigenous populations is fairly recent (Silverblatt, 2004). This is significant because it downplays the power flows of communication and their structural relation to political goods in the colonies. For example, Derek Hill (2019) notes that "to make the truth pour forth through torments and bodily pain (*ad eruendam veritatem per tormenta et corporis dolorem*)" depends on the view interrogators had of who was speaking, especially in light of changing social contexts in the fourteenth century (p. 105). The context Hill refers to is the growing distinction between crimes of action and crimes of *belief* as part of jurisdictional claims and sacral authority. I reverse the power flow of this symbiotic relationship and dispense with the hermeneutical innocence narrative of contexts that shape beliefs, with reliably apolitical conclusions about an agent's knowledge. The political need to work out epistemological technologies of coercion and control (in response to dynamically changing contexts) led to the development of the specific uses of the first western administrative manuals that systematized practices like ruses, evasion, suggestive threats, and coercion.

78. The idea that western empires share structural features with the polities they colonized is called *Romanization*. This is a misleading approach to the structural study of dynastic racial systems and their origins. The Romanization paradigm refers to a scholarly debate that began in the twentieth century about the ethnogenesis of colonialism that has intellectual precursors in late eighteenth- and early nineteenth-century teleological narratives of european civilization in general (Ghisleni 2018). It takes up race-neutral questions like whether autochthonous cultures "adopted" roman culture and lifeways through cross-cultural contact, or whether Rome's civilizing mission imposed a culture of change in the process of imperial expansion (refer, for example, to Ghisleni 2018; Blagg 2002; and Dietler 2005). In recent years scholars have questioned or outright rejected the Romanization (or "Hellenization") paradigm as an inherently western epistemological narrative that provides the conceptual backdrop for comparative analyses of cultures in disciplines like archaeology (Luley 2020) and anthropology (Simpson 2020). In anthropology and ethnic studies especially, the Romanization paradigm has been largely rejected in favor of Indigenous-focused genealogies and archaeologies of cultural survivance, collective continuity, and cultural resurgence. However, a tension remains in fields like archaeology, which regard this trend as posing a conceptual divide between, for example,

structural analyses of roman imperialism as a process, and individual sociologies that focus on the resilience, agency, and self-determination of Indigenous and colonized peoples in response to european colonization: "There is a danger that if we limit our application of postcolonial theory to attempts to describe provincial cultures as composites of fragmentary, fluid, and hybrid identities, seemingly involving a fair degree of choice and flexibility, we will fail to analyze the power relationships that create and sustain inequality. Partly this requires us to recognize the continuing role of violence in imperial society, but also it necessitates a deeper engagement with theories of agency, personhood and the significance of material transformation to everyday life, and a concomitant interest in the structural characteristics of Roman imperialism as a process" (Gardner, qtd. in Luley 2020, 5). I think this is a false conceptual divide; it is possible to analyze the role of violence in colonial processes and the structural characteristics of roman imperialism and neoimperialism from within situated, land-based contexts that also stress collective identities. Critical geographies that focus on the historical processes of colonization and the various impacts on lands, dwellings, forests, airways, waterways, and food systems also call attention to how those processes began or are an extension of greco-roman cartographies and conceptual imaginaries of space and lifeways. Most importantly, they stress what is violent about this cartographical imperialism. It is also the case that, by contrast to the Romanization approach and its subsequent debate in archaeology, anticolonial approaches have long stressed the temporal and geographic continuity of western epistemological, hermeneutic, and political projects (as well as the cultural and exploitative social arrangements that accompanied these projects) that began in the greco-roman world. Refer, for example, to Said (1978), Césaire (1950), and Atalay (2006).
79. This is also where purity of blood statutes (*limpieza de sangre*) specific to Iberian colonization arose (Martínez 2008).
80. Bethencourt, 2009, p. 35. A common misconception about the Inquisition is that it was an anomalous period of religious violence concerning the struggle for ecclesiastical power and the suppression of heresy in the medieval period. While it is important to distinguish between, for example, the Spanish Inquisition and the 250-year-old roman inquisition that was active in France, Germany, and Italy, it is also important to stress continuities and how the shared use of new civil jurisdictional powers led to an extensively diffused administrative infrastructure that became critical for european state-building projects (Lopes Don, 2010, p. 22). Francisco Bethencourt (2009), using a Foucauldian analysis of the micropractices and technologies of administration developed by the Inquisition as a global enterprise, takes this line of argument. He approaches the Inquisition as a global phenomenon with shared features and technologies, focusing on "how the Inquisition was used as the first centralized institution, essential for the process of state-building in Italy, Spain, and Portugal" (p. 1). For my purposes, he makes an important link between (a) the statist political implications of inquisitorial practice, (b) the new administrative practices it required, and (c) how those practices enabled the strategic depopulation of Jewish and Arab strongholds in the south, thus making way

for Spanish state-building. These links can be understood as functional blueprints for strategic depopulation—and the extractive use of testimony in the pooling of Native information—that would become critical in european powers' genocidal projects in the colonies. Irene Silverblatt (2004) extends the statist analysis to colonial Mexico and Peru, showing how, amid the different manifestations and territorial realities, a blueprint for the colonial project existed through inquisitorial practice on Indigenous lands. Going around and systemically asking questions of specific populations under a punitive administrative structure is not a normatively neutral activity, as Castaño's (2014) work discussed in this chapter shows. It cannot be reduced to an ahistorical social practice distinct from settler epistemological systems and settler colonial projects. In Peru, the testimonial apparatus that arose in support of the colonial tributary labor system (used to force Amerindian people to work in the silver and copper mines, often on land that was stolen from them) was a direct challenge to the existing epistemological conventions and to the testimonial infrastructure that relied on quipus, for example, to narrate the past. European "information gathering" thus relied on the double move of extraction and suppression aimed at the destruction of a culture's material existence.

81. Sixtus IV, 1478.
82. Bethencourt, 2009, p. 35.
83. Refer to Shapiro, 1991.
84. Instead of Vatican oversight, "The monarchs set up a system of permanent tribunals, or Holy Offices, in the major cities, and these offices in turn sent out local tribunals to smaller communities as needed" (Lopes Don, 2010, p. 23). As Lopes Don argues, the move toward administrative centralization that culminated in state-building and an avaricious colonial system was rhetorically carried out through the project of expanding the christian imperium, but it was rooted in pragmatic economic interests. In the mid-fourteenth century the central Iberian kingdom of Castile fell under economic duress and increasing political pressures following the bubonic plague and civil wars.
85. While inquisitorial practice was steeped in violence, it was not reducible to a unilateral communication flow of ecclesiastic power between accuser and accused. The importance of inquisitorial practice for the development of testimony (and testator credibility in an evidentiary context) as a weapon of war cannot be dismissed as a sidebar example of a collectively shared structural identity prejudice that results in the marginalization of speakers by historical default, and which purports to be differentiated from the kind of naturalized picture of objective testimony discussed earlier. Only the most rudimentary ahistoricism and willful spellbinding of Iberian testimonial practice (for instance, through political science theories of vicinage) can delink inquisitorial practice from the rise of large-scale administrative machineries that produced state-building and established formal domains of nonliability for the state.
86. Testimony under duress is generally regarded as an especially poor source of microhistorical approaches that focus on the life experiences of the testator. One notable exception to this is Kagan and Dyer's *Inquisitorial Inquiries* (2004), which

recounts the lives of six european accusers of the Inquisition, including an important chapter on gender.
87. Hartman, 2008, p. 2; refer also to Carby, 2019. One of the goals of political epistemology, as Kristie Dotson (2012) envisions it, is to move beyond the analytics of oppression that continuously recenter oppressors' worldview and concerns (refer also to Lorde, 2000). This perspective is critical for grounding analyses of extractivism, depopulation, Native informancy, and jurisdictional power in early modern inquisitorial modalities. Such grounding provides a closer look at the inquisitorial formulas of testimony, and the material culture that surrounds it, as a blueprint for modern-day interrogative practices that perpetuate injustice without recentering the analytics of power that govern the historical decentering of our lives and voices. In the context of structurally manipulated reality and the persistence of structural epistemic gaslighting (Berenstain, 2020; Pohlhaus, 2020), taking names and sliding an abacus bead left for each offense found in (and in spite of) the colonial archive is a simple pretrial practice of justice.
88. Lopez Don, 2006; Williams & Pierce, 2004; refer also to Greenleaf, 1994 on the subordination of Indigenous leaders to european trials.
89. Lopes Don, 2010, p. 176.
90. Johnson 2016, pp. 31–36.
91. The Oztoticpac lands map, 1540, Retrieved from the Library of Congress, https://www.loc.gov/item/88690436/
92. Lopez Don, 2010. While the are no extant copies of the verdict, only of the ruler's fate, it is reasonable to conclude that a public burning was not the outcome of a winning case.
93. Such as communal attestation (making important statements in the presence of communal council. Testimony could not have functioned in the colonial era as contemporary social epistemologists understand the practice of (naturalized) testimony, for one thing, because of the centrality of Indigenous metonymies in linguistic understanding of the world. Metonymic relations involve adjoining parts to wholes to stress complexity and cyclical interconnections rather than linear causal necessity. It shows up in the speech forms of expressing one thing by way of speaking of another in detail without it being reduced to metaphor or metaphorical understanding. It is an inherently embodied process of speaking that cannot be divorced (like a written document) in distinctions between the speaker of testimony and the content of testimony (what one attests to). This is why song was a preferred speech modality of ritual utterance in Indigenous legal traditions: "It is not a questions of songs being like flowers but simply of songs *being* flowers" (Tomlinson 2007, p. 75). The evidence is right there, copresented in the testifiers' testament, not in an independently corroborated mind-independent reality. In Nahuatl, no word stands alone. "Even the most basic kernels of [Nahuatl's] complex grammar," which western linguists "present for pedagogical convenience as their stems or roots," do not have "the semantic generality and neutrality we expect in Indo-European roots. Instead of infinitives, the simplest form of a Nahuatl predicative word already assumes a substantive . . . instead of absolute nouns, the simplest form of a substantive includes a

predicate" (p. 29). In addition to the epistemic traditions violently suppressed by inquisitorial practice, inquisitorial jurisprudence also created written (Latinized) records of Native testimonial resistance using western epistemic conventions. The benefit for the system was that the testimonies could be co-opted for jurisdictional gain. Consider an English translation of the Spanish version of the testimony attributed to Ahuachpitzactzin, whom the first bishop of Mexico burned at the stake: "Who are those who tear us apart and disturb us, and live above us, and are upon us, and subjugate us? Here I am, and there is the Lord of Mexico, Yoanizi, and there is my nephew Tetzcapili, Lord of Tacuba, and there is Tlacahuepantli, Lord of Tula. We are all equal and act similarly. No one can equal us because this is our land and our property, and our jewel and our possession. This is our domain; it belongs to us. Who are these who come here to give us orders and subjugate us and who, they be not relatives nor share our blood, equate themselves to us" (trans. *Proceso inquisitorial del cacique de Tezcoco*). While some rhetorical elements of spoken Nahuatl are evident in the passage, it is doubtful that the metaphysical relations and substance ontologies behind western conceptions of property and inanimate objects—especially the concept of nature as sellable land—had been internalized to the degree trial records sought to show. It is also unlikely Nahua leaders collapsed regional differences between kin groups to create a homogenous population that provided for a "common enemy," and delivered such statements in a rhetorical structure common to the medieval duel and courtly oaths of challenge.

94. The link between settler claims to Indigenous lands and expanding jurisdictional authority over testimony can also be grasped in the New Zealand Land Claims Act of 1840. The law made special provisions for allowing Māori testimony "to enable investigation of who had acquired land from Māori before the signing of the Treaty of Waitangi" (Bowyer, 2022, p. 14) despite existing legal restrictions on all Indigenous testimony and on women's testimony (in New Zealand, women could not give testimony or appear as witnesses for much of the nineteenth century).
95. Murphy, 2012.
96. Alexander, 2010; Gilmore, 2007; Davis, 2003. While a host of papal bulls on jurisdiction over Native peoples were decreed, the Spanish Inquisition presented catholic monarchs with a unique opportunity because the pope had no direct control or jurisdiction over the Spanish Inquisition. This was not true of earlier inquisitions in europe.
97. Detailed manuals, notaries, schedules of inquisitorial visits, records of eyewitness statements, public courts and churches built through slave and forced tributary labor were all part of this material culture.
98. Hill, 2019, p. 116.
99. Mills, 1999, p. 100. Police violence is arguably a continuation of this tradition.
100. Efforts to pass such laws were repeatedly blocked until 2022, when the Emmett Till Antilynching Act finally passed, despite Republican votes against it (https://clerk.house.gov/Votes/202247). Scroll under right column for recorded "nay" votes.
101. Associated Press, 2022a.

102. One that upholds the functional reach of settler colonial democracy and precludes the structural relations necessary for consensual public governance.
103. National Defense Intelligence College.
104. Refer to *People v. Turner* for an illustration. It is well known that modern rape culture assigns gradients of blame and untrustworthiness to those who fail to meet the profile of the "perfect victim" in an idealized rape scenario—a strange man in a dark alley who overpowers a well-dressed white woman lost walking home, or some variant thereof. But victim service organizations, especially since their professionalization in the late 1980s, 1990s, and early 2000s, are also powerful organizations (typically run by white professional women administrators with university degrees) that reproduce a pathway-to-healing assembly line of services in which the victim emerges as a grateful, newly reconstituted subject of Republican motherhood, women whose stories and lives can be profiled in glossy annual reports to funders.
105. This is important because mainstream philosophers often differentiate special cases of "legal testimony" from the more idealized scenario of fact-fining from "the reports of others." The most common notions of testimony today—whether as a reductive communicative act bound to a proximate evidentiary context, or as a nonreductive general expression of thought that can be distinguished from noninformational expressions—share in the basic generalization of testimony as the "the reports of others" (Lackey & Sosa, 2006).
106. Ríos Castaño, 2014, p. 151. Ríos Castaño follows Klor de Alva's (1988) analysis of Fray Sahagún's work.
107. Those ethnographies would have already been known (or accessible through other records) in the Iberian context. This includes "sociological and biographical data regarding age, occupation, residence, and family genealogy, including relatives' occupations, residence, and marital status" as preludes to the questions pertaining to the accusation (Ríos Castaño, 2014, p. 161).
108. Gilmore, 2007, p. 28. Consider, as well, the difference between the scope and modalities of diffusion of inquisitorial practice in Tenochtitlán. Between 1536 and 1540, nearly 8 percent of the population were tried in the valley of central Mexico alone—"by any measure, this percentage was much higher than any Iberian city would have known in the first 50 years of the Inquisition" (Lopez Don, 2012, p. 8). Trials targeted Native leadership to symbolize supreme colonial authority, justify land dispossession, and economize prosecutorial resources. There was no need to interrogate the entire Indigenous populations in a formal trial. A vast system of interrogation that incorporated fact-finding and subordinated questioning had already been implemented in the administration of the sacraments.
109. Recent developments in inquisitorial scholarship focus on comparative approaches that illuminate structurally invariant and adaptive features behind the institution's resilience across the many different regional tribunals where the Inquisition took place. Focusing on identifying the operating structures and procedures (organizational form of rites, strategies of action, systems of representation, technologies of communication, sequences of ordered and repetitive acts), Francisco Bethencourt's (2009) research is led by the structural question: "How was it possible for an

institution created in the thirteenth century to survive, in different forms, until the eighteenth century, and even into the nineteenth century? How were the tribunals of faith able to entrench themselves in the most diverse environments, from southern Europe to the overseas territories of the Iberian empires?" (p. 28).
110. Biber, 2010.
111. Sarmiento Pérez, 2011; refer also to Romada Curto, 2020. While Sarmiento Pérez (2011) notes that "the kingdoms of the Iberian Peninsula used the Canary Archipelago as a testing ground for their later conquests and colonization in the Americas," he acknowledges the deep roots of this practice in Iberian relations in North and West Africa (p. 172).
112. Fayer, 2003.
113. He writes: "On my arrival at that sea [of Cuba], I had taken some Indians by force from the first island that I came to, in order that they might learn our language, and communicate to us what they knew respecting the country; which succeeded excellently, and was a great advantage to us, for in a short time, either by gestures and signs, or by word, we were enabled to understand each other." The slave-interpreter system came at great cost to Native lives. Most interpreters died soon after captivity. The Guanache of Tenerife faced genocide as a direct result of Iberian efforts to use the population for the slave-interpreter system.
114. Refer to Romada Curto, 2000.
115. Jager, 2015. "[European] memoirs consistently presented instrumental Native women as willing and gracious Indian princesses. From the white male perspective, the Indian princess was drawn to 'civilized' non-Indian culture; her help and generosity were characterized to reflect white male superiority to and to justify European colonization" (Jager, 2015, p. 4).
116. Alarcón, 1983, p. 182.
117. Collins, 1986; 1990.
118. Cohen, 2021.
119. Aviv, 2002.
120. Refer to *State v. Arica Waters* for the legal grounds of her acquittal.
121. Chamallas, 1998; 2004.
122. Lackey & Sosa, 2006.
123. Felipe Guamán Poma de Ayala's (Quechua) *Cronica de Buen Gobierno* (1615–16) illustrates the power asymmetries involved in the imposition of colonial structures of Native informancy, including the imposition of western linguistic conventions and the ontological assumptions that uphold them. Illustrations show the testimonial apparatus being imposed on Quechua and Aymara speakers by colonial officials. The process begins with familiarizing the Indigenous people with the inquisitorial prompt, "So tell me," which generates "tellings generally" (Fricker, 1995, p. 396). Colonial officials then assess the answers given to the prompt for epistemologically "relevant" content. It demonstrates the violent political structures of suppliance under which, following Rigoberta Menchú (1983), "That's the way it has to be," not because it is true, but because one is speaking to white settlers. Refer also

to Kristie Dotson's (2012) notion of strategic withholding by a testator and Ofelia Schutte's (1998) framing of power asymmetries in communication.

124. Spivak, 1985; 1988; 1999. Discussions of Native informancy in relation to epistemic discussions of testimonial evidence came to prominence in the twentieth century through South Asian historiographers' discussions of power and subordinated agency in colonial source materials (especially in the 1980s and 1990s). Since nonreductive accounts for testimony allow for information to be culled from the historical writings of extant peoples, the question of power, agency, and representation of Native informants in the colonial archives arose, leading Gayatri Spivak to coin the term "epistemic violence" (Spivak 1985; 1988; 1999). For Spivak, epistemic violence results from a dominant group's efforts to structurally foreclose (i.e., cut off in advance) the salience and intelligibility of oppressed groups' epistemological resources, leading to their silencing and marginalization as speakers in (western) textual history, and as knowers and interpreters of their own life stories. Epistemic violence is a "remotely orchestrated, far-flung, and heterogeneous project to constitute the colonial subject as Other" (Spivak, 1988, p. 280) that is not produced by interpersonal failures of understanding, but vice versa. Epistemic violence, as Spivak conceives it, is a cultural project used to create organized failures of understanding that produce structural benefits (predominantly in historiography) for some populations but not others. It produces the appearance of consistency, continuity, and the fulfillment of anticipated meaning within the regulated domain of western epistemic conventions (1999). Philosopher Kristie Dotson (2011) also gives an account of epistemic violence "as the failure, owing to pernicious ignorance, of hearers to meet the vulnerabilities of speakers in linguistic exchanges" that also homes in on the structural features of credibility deflation noted by Spivak. It likewise points our attention in the direction of power in communication exchanges, as Chandra Mohanty's and Ofelia Schutte's work long sought to illustrate.

125. Dotson, 2011.

126. A communicative context was created with specific formularies of inquiry (supported by administrative technologies) that guided what testimonial practice could and could not be. The failure to recognize the material substrate of inquisitorial practice can result in narrowly moralized analyses of colonial violence (and the use of the many weapons in the colonial arsenal), especially when framed as the ethical failure of one culture to recognize the equal worth of another (Mignolo 1995; 2000; 2011). Epistemic violence is not a hermeneutic lapse or a failure of ethical imagination. There is no "failure" in the deployment of alphabetic technologies in the colonies to suppress and supplant Indigenous forms of literacy (Boone & Mignolo, 2002). The cultural inheritance of a technique of violence was adapted and deployed as it had been in the past, adapting to new contexts and purposes. Speech forms like *huehuetlatolli*, reduced in translation to "the speech of elders," did not stand a chance in the political epistemological economy of colonialism. That system had no use for the paratactic conventions and nonexclusionary reciprocal binaries behind copresenting, speech forms that were spoken in the presence of others and as intermediaries with deceased elders.

NOTES 375

127. Yúdice, 1981.
128. Yúdice, 1991, p. 44; refer also to Beverly 2001; 2013; Gugelberger 1991; 1996; and Ahmed 2003.
129. In 2018, in what are conservative estimates, nearly one in five Black women in the military experienced sexual harassment (Breslin et al., 2022). Mil. R. Evid. 412 (b) (1) gives the following three exceptions: "(A) evidence of specific instances of sexual behavior by the alleged victim offered to prove that a person other than the accused was the source of semen, injury, or other physical evidence; (B) evidence of specific instances of sexual behavior by the alleged victim with respect to the person accused of the sexual misconduct offered by the accused to prove consent . . . ; and (C) evidence the exclusion of which would violate the constitutional rights of the accused."
130. Baldwin, 1998/1966, p. 738.
131. A settler colonial structure of address describes the epistemic and material conditions that license contexts of communicative exchange (e.g., what gets official uptake about what was said between asymmetrically positioned speakers within settler institutions) as valid and fair within a broader *network* of mutually reinforcing settler operatives, institutions, and their interrelations. Ofelia Schutte's (1993; 1998) work on the structurally produced power dynamics between dominant and nondominantly situated speakers offers some examples based on linguistic difference. For Schutte, the social power that institutions enact to operationalize a discourse in society as normative is not arbitrary; it follows the historical trajectory of colonial rule and the corresponding erasure of marginalized women's voices. Settler colonial structures of evidentiary address thus refers to the existence of structures of address in evidentiary legal processes and court proceedings that advance settler colonial futures yet pose as neutral and objective judicial reasoning through norm-enforcement practices. Such structures bar meaningful access to democratic institutions in ways that perpetuate rather than alleviate population-wide inequities. The institutions affected then mainline structural violence to marginalized populations as an actively reproduced social process that admits to no identifiable aggressors. The structure of evidentiary address simultaneously enacts harms and maintains control of the conceptualization of harms to evade identification and legal standing for their possible redress with particularly harsh consequences for women of color survivors of sexual violence.
132. Simon-Kerr, 2017, p. 158.
133. Simon-Kerr, 2017, p. 225.
134. The man impersonating a police officer acted through rape proxies (when a third party coerces rape, as when fundamentalist sect leader Warren Jeffs arranged the marriages of women and girls and adult men against their wishes using religion to coerce consent). Judge Edenfield disregarded criminal elements of coercion and applied implicit rationale of whether pleasure was derived from the assault to reconstruct intent to rape, labeling the impersonating offender a mere "prankster." *Fogal v. Coastal Restaurant Management, Inc.*, 452 F. Supp. 2d 1286 (S.D. Ga. 2004).

376 NOTES

135. "The existence of forcible compulsion in a rape case does not depend on the quantum of force that is applied but rather on whether the act is consummated against the victim's will." *Hillman v. State*, 569 S.W.3d 372 (Arkansas 2019).
136. "Courts should not be used to propagate a culture of victimology/entitlement that degrades the very sense of individual responsibility and hard work on which this great nation was founded. The best lessons learned are usually the most expensive. At tremendous expense, plaintiff hopefully will have learned to think for herself." *Fogal v. Coastal Restaurant Management, Inc.*, n. 15.
137. Simon-Kerr, 2017, p. 167.
138. Simon-Kerr, 2017, p. 154.
139. For Simon-Kerr, such standing is determined by dominant cultural communities' historical constructions of social identity and the accompanying assumptions about race, class, and gender that routinely situate white propertied men at the highest status registers of society. In linking the evolving evidentiary requirements in legal testimony to extralegal functions that are well outside courts' alleged truth-seeking purposes of these requirements, I think Simon-Kerr illuminates the functional features of the US settler colonial legal system, one where evidentiary rules purported exist to promote "truth-finding processes of trials." So I am framing their critique more broadly to attend to the dynastic dynamism of settler colonial violence, but in a way I think Simon-Kerr would support given their contentions about social stratification and the legal system.
140. The no-impeachment rule is an inheritance of colonial English law. Refer to *Vaise v. Delaval*, 1 T. R. 11, 99 Eng. Rep. 944 (K.B. 1785).
141. Had the case not reached the Supreme Court, Colorado Rule of Evidence 606(b) would have allowed the racist statements not to affect the verdict (the court of appeals upheld the ruling, citing *Tanner v. United States*, 483 U.S. 107 (1987); *Warger v. Shauers*, 574 U.S. (2014) as precent). Moreover, the Colorado Supreme Court held that Rule 606(b) did not violate the Sixth Amendment because jurors are able to be questioned during racial bias during voir dire (a known hot spot for systemic racism abated by procedural means).
142. The Court offered moving antiracist language in the majority opinion; the new rule holds that "where a juror makes a clear statement that indicates he or she relied on racial stereotypes or animus to convict a criminal defendant, the Sixth Amendment requires that the no-impeachment rule give way in order to permit the trial court to consider the evidence of the juror's statement and any resulting denial of the jury trial guarantee."
143. In the girl's case, although both separately identified the defendant as the perpetrator and testified to the sexual assault, the jury failed to convict the defendant on that charge, and in the defendant's case, because the Court offered no real remedy to the fact that a juror persisted in considering the defendant's alibi witness not credible as an "illegal" despite trial testimony that the witness was a legal resident. (As defense attorneys know all too well from the jury selection process of voir dire, jurors can always produce race-neutral rationale or simply withhold answers when probed about racist animus or beliefs.)

144. 596 N.W.2d 607 (Mich. 1999).
145. "An attack on a witness' credibility, like the one at issue, that is not an attack on the witness' character for truthfulness does not trigger MRE 608(a)(2). In the absence of an attack on complainant's character for truthfulness, the prosecution was not entitled, under MRE 608(a), to support her character for truthfulness."
146. Today, conflict-of-interest principles persist in evidence law as bias-based impeachment grounds (refer to Federal Rules of Evidence, Rule 610).
147. 25 F. Cas. 901, 902 (C.C.D. Md. 1840) No. 14,990.
148. In addition to existing testimonial restrictions on Black and Native peoples (free or enslaved on both accounts). Simon-Kerr, 2017, p. 165.
149. While legal historians often explain this shift through racially evasive terms that construct such changes as part of larger, naturally developmental, legal trends "towards conceiving of juries as the preferred arbiters of credibility," Simon-Kerr (2017) highlights the legal scholarship that clearly identifies federal efforts to force southern states "to remove overt bans on testimony form black witnesses" during Reconstruction as critical to understanding the legal response to this shift away from competency doctrines (p. 166).
150. Simon-Kerr, 2017, p. 167.
151. Siegel, 1996; 1997.
152. Siegel, 1996, p. 1111.
153. Simon-Kerr, 2017, p. 157.
154. Simon-Kerr (2017) writes, "In short, our impeachment system is racially-skewed because it places heightened constraints on testimony by black defendants and witnesses . . . the parallels to outright race-based competency rules of the nineteenth century are striking and troublesome" (p. 190, paraphrasing Bennet Capers's argument that "many of the witnesses to the use of police brutality, including the victim, will themselves be marked as . . . less credible witnesses").
155. Simon-Kerr, 2017, p. 174. The tightly guarded association between veracity, oath-keeping, male honor, and whiteness did not begin in the nineteenth century, but it can be particularly identified in legal developments of the time period. Refer, for example, to Jeremy Bentham's legal treatise on male honor and its inextricable link to veracity.
156. Simon-Kerr, 2017, p. 201.
157. Simon-Kerr, 2017, p. 193. One important consequence of this legal tradition that insists "convictions which rest on dishonest conduct relate to credibility whereas those of violence or assaultive crimes do not" is particularly damaging for the structural protectives offered to those who use *coercion and grooming* to carry out assaultive crimes.
158. Simon-Kerr, 2017, p. 197.
159. Simon-Kerr, 2017, 205.
160. Simon-Kerr, 2017, p. 201.
161. Simon-Kerr, 2017, quoting McKinney, 2016, N.Y. Crim. Proc. Law 60.4.
162. Refer, for example, to Spivak, 1988; Rifkin, 2014; Dotson, 2012; Ruíz, 2011; LaRocque, 2016.

378   NOTES

163. This is a move that is connected to the operationalization of white innocence in settler institutions and the rendering of white women's histories as categorically oppressed. As Jones-Rogers (2013) illustrates, many white women in the American South were proud slave owners after all, not duressed subjects recalcitrant in their role as slave owners.
164. Studying invariance structurally is important because it frames issues of violence, femicide, and political harnessing of women's reproductive rights on Turtle Island within political landscapes and social arrangements of power that have driven stratification and licensed gendered logics of abuse since colonialism began. It can tell us something useful about the political machinery and shifting geopolitical arrangements that coordinate over time to maintain functional power over racialized women's lives. As Chapter 1 illustrates, when divested from latent views of structure as apolitical (as in the view of structural violence as "having no identifiable aggressor") the notion of structural invariance can tell us something important about the role micro- and meso-level processes of violence play in maintaining these power arrangements, how they might restructure when challenged, and who stands to gain from them across various local and transnational contexts. As a systems-oriented method, it can connect seemingly unrelated patterns of violence to deep insights about gender and relational social systems that Indigenous peoples have long held. Finally, it can illuminate cases that show why there is good reason to think the oppressions we face today are more likely than not to continue to impact our lives and communities despite our best organizational efforts and (in some very limited cases that obscure genocides) historic (but probabilistically only temporary) gains in major quality-of-life sectors.
165. I introduce the concept of settler credibility economies to explain key features of the wider settler colonial economy within which testimonial credibility (and settler credit markets in general) operates. I'll use this framework to talk about sexual violence as part of this economy and the role testimonial evidence plays in maintaining that economy across generations.

Chapter 3

1. "Reagan had restricted land deeds," 1984.
2. Yglesias, 2007.
3. Reagan opposed making Martin Luther King Day a federal holiday because he thought that Dr. King was unworthy of the honor and that his contributions to American democracy "were based on an image (by 'them'—black people) not *reality*" (Clines, 1983). Although Reagan eventually relented and signed the bill making the day a federal holiday into law in 1983, it would take another seventeen years before all fifty states recognized it.
4. "Reagan's exit," 1966.
5. "Reagan's exit," 1966; refer also to Holden, 2013, p. 75.
6. Holden, 2013, p. 176.

NOTES 379

7. Refer to Chapter 1 for the distinction between *structural functionalist* views of system equilibrium (e.g., the view that "structural change occurs when disturbances in or around a system are sufficient to overcome the forces of equilibrium" [Parsons, 1961, p. 219]) and the view of *functional equilibrium* in white dynastic formations, which reinforces homeostasis in response to pressures for structural change to maintain oppressive (not "normalized") social relations. When I refer to "system equilibrium" I am referring to the latter.
8. Fields and Fields, 2012. In *Racecraft: The Soul of Inequality in American Life* (2012) Barbara Fields and Karen Fields offer a clue to the alchemy of racemaking in the United States that allowed Reagan, like other committed antiracists who perpetuate structural racism, to hold paraconsistent positions and actions on race so easily. Racecraft, they write, sets up a "powerful ideological undertow" that acts as a type of conjured magic to provide the conceptual resources necessary to justify very practical ends in a historical system of white supremacy: "The policies of the 1980s radically redistributed income upward.... It had a simple melody about the need to enrich the 'investing' classes (said to 'create jobs'), and an encoded percussion: 'culture wars'; 'welfare mothers'; 'race-and-IQ'; 'Black-on-Black crime'; 'criminal gene'; and on and on. Halfway through the decade, as the band played on, a huge economic revolution from above had got well under way" (p. 12). The phenomenon of racecraft is not otherworldly, even though it creates the "magical" effect of "race" that is unsupported by biological fact. Given Fields and Fields's examples, I interpret racecraft less as "ideology" than as a system process closely tied to accumulated profit and gain for some populations, so that, "sooner or later, tacitly or openly, any move to tackle inequality brings racecraft into play" (p. 283).
9. Fields & Fields, 2012.
10. E.g., it is not the universally applicable cultural inheritance of "tradition" passed on through common histories and languages that shapes the available social resources for interpretation. *Which* pathway activity chains are activated, and which are not, is based on intergenerational econo-epistemological projects that allow settler epistemic infrastructural activity to operate seamlessly in social institutions, which are themselves designed to preserve some traditions but not others. But if interpretive wealth is a stock, the obvious question is this: How does it start? To turn the tables on primitive accumulation, I suggest an equally plausible origin story for the epistemic capital that drives interpretive wealth. My story, however, is not predicated on colonial racism: we can imagine that epistemic accumulation of interpretive wealth is established through the structural epistemic violence required for white dynastic formations to emerge. And we can imagine how the western conceptual tradition that begins with Plato (and rests on the internalization of alphabetic literacy, which detaches human experience from meanings generated by physical environments) gets this going. Hence epistemic capital and the intergenerational hoarding of interpretive wealth begins to grow and accumulate at a pace that reproduces ongoing inequality, generation after generation.
11. The postcolonial feminist theorist Gayatri Spivak explained this idea in her famous essay "Can the Subaltern Speak?" (1988a). The word *subaltern* comes from an Italian Marxist (Antonio Gramsci), who used it as code for the working class (in Marx, the

"proletariat") in order to smuggle writings out of prison. "Subaltern" is a mashup of the words "alterity" (difference or otherness) and "sub-" (under, as in a submarine) that designates a kind of "difference that's below difference," as in people who, even if they spoke up, would not be "heard" (I now substitute "heard" with "understood" to flag the epistemic exclusion of Hard-of-hearing and Deaf communities) because of the way their difference is constructed by the dominant culture in power (and the power resources the dominant culture controls to keep such constructions of difference going over time) as unintelligible (particularly to dominantly situated agents and within dominant institutions). It's a social epistemological concern regarding the interrelation between "the semiosis of the social text" and individual "consciousness" (Spivak 1988a, p. 287). The idea is that when a marginalized knower (for Spivak, a racialized and caste-situated woman under British imperialism) expresses intent, the dominant social order is able to "foreclose" certain interpretive pathways necessary for marginalized knowers to be understood as they intended to be understood (refer also to Bierria, 2014; Dotson, 2012; Schutte, 1998). It's not that *no one* can understand marginalized "speakers" in culture; it's that, for Spivak (as for Edward Said), colonial warfare includes a project of planetary engineering that extends to human knowledge, not just to the land and labor resources colonialism violently seized and transformed to produce capital gain and profit for colonists. And such epistemic engineering means that there exist tools and methods for silencing marginalized knowers that may not be readily apparent (by design) but are nonetheless highly functional features of societies impacted by colonialism. So, for Spivak, there are agent-level (individual) and structural (social) considerations that are cofunctional in creating epistemic exclusion and cultural patterns of discrimination that nonaccidentally lead to death and dispossession for some populations and not others. And the analytic that shapes these considerations, for Spivak, is colonialism and its enduring power, even after India's 1947 formal independence from the British Empire. The "epistemic violence of imperialism gives us an imperfect allegory of the general violence that is the possibility of an episteme" (p. 286) as in the kind of "hermeneutic violence" described in Chapter 4.
12. Stern, 2019.
13. Stern, 2019.
14. On violence and colonial rule, for example, refer to Fashina, 1989 and Atiles-Osoria, 2012.
15. The equifinality built into the design of settler colonial social systems means that functionally, it does not matter whether one is believed or not because, even if one is believed, at a different scale (such as the level of populations) the end result of structured inequity persists. So interpretive power isn't power for power's sake, just as social systems are not systems because relations and connections exist between its individual elements, but because there is a *shared system goal or purpose that organizes those relations into a cohesive whole: profit*. Innocence cloaks only work by virtue of the concrete structural economic relations to social, institutional, and administrative apparatuses in settler colonial societies. To give one example of the importance of the economic valence in understanding the structural relations in settler colonial

NOTES 381

societies, the most likely types of social interventions to succeed in advanced industrial settler colonial societies are those for which a market is created, such as in the green building movement and LEED certification sustainability assessment process.

16. Allen, 2012; Ignatiev, 1995; Roediger, 2005. Contemporary uses of direct-to-consumer ancestry tests offer a parallel phenomenon of self-Indigenizing and colorwashing whiteness, which, regardless of motivation, function to move white settler populations closer to the final solution of settler colonialism, where Indigenous peoples are replaced by white settlers' descendants as the "original peoples" of stolen lands (refer to TallBear, 2013). In settler epistemic systems, this logic is perfectly compatible with the white supremacist political narrative of the "great replacement," which heralds a mendacious warning that nonwhite immigrants are intentionally being brought to replace white voters and has inspired acts of terrorism and mass shootings out of fear "the white race" is in threat of extinction. The movement's modern origins in anti-Arab French xenophobia (especially via the works of Jean Raspail and Renaud Camus) is important for grasping the global character and concerted intellectual project of settler colonial white supremacy.

17. This is as opposed to the more common, naturalized view of social knowledge as culturally relative variations of universal cognitive processes, according to which communal beliefs, or "folklore," purportedly derive from more general biological processes and universal properties of minds.

18. As Du Bois (1920) noted, "The discovery of personal whiteness among the world's peoples is a very modern thing—a nineteenth and twentieth century matter . . . whiteness is the ownership of the earth forever and ever" (1920/1996, pp. 184–185). For Du Bois, whiteness paid dividends even to the poorest of whites through a "public and psychological wage"—an idea echoed in Derrick Bell's (1988) relational economic theory of whiteness, where slavery "provided mainly propertyless whites with the property in their whiteness" (Bell, 1988, p. 733).

19. Consider the political discussions in the United States surrounding the division of the "Latino vote." There are many reconstituting pathways that allow nonwhites to access the privileges of white dynastic polities by establishing their proximity to setter colonial whiteness, so that it stops being a mystery why minorities like Justice Clarence Thomas rule (in jurisprudence terms) as they do, or why some minorities vote a straight white supremacist ticket on Election Day. It is a long-existing feature of white dynastic formations to dispense with a fixed form to retain a function. And this has been so since the greek city-state of Athens fell to Sparta, yet the conceptual substratum of Athenian culture endured in intellectual and political form. (Hence the critical adaptive role of epistemic capitalism in outlasting the social movements of the twenty-first century and the demographic shift toward so-called minority-majority states).

20. Refer to Ferreira Da Silva 2022. Generally speaking, this view of epistemology is different from the traditional empirical view of knowledge as the mind-dependent internal cognitive states of individuals that correspond to an external mind-independent reality in the world, so that our thoughts and ideas "represent" our experience of an empirical world that is thought to be separate and distinct from humans.

The idea that "epistemologies have power" (Berenstain & Ruíz 2021) is also different from the european "hermeneutic" view of knowledge, where the implicit understanding of our world—the one we grow into by virtue of simply coming into the fold of a given culture by being born into it—is neither good nor bad, but a historically relative template for cultural meaning relative to a time and place. There is certainly a core "generative" feature of social knowledge in philosophical hermeneutics that has a long tradition in western philosophy dating back to the eighteenth century, and later, of associating knowledge with power (most notably through Foucault and Nietzsche). While the functional view of knowledge associated with "value" has been obvious in western philosophy since Marx and Nietzsche, they way Nietzsche and others apply this insight (i.e., to human individuation in a social world that produces the experience of salience or meaning in our knowledge practices and shared languages) differs from identifying the strategic design of conquest and harm built into settler colonial and imperial formations of social structure that originated in Asia Minor in the aftermath of cataclysmic war in the Peloponnesus. Thus, while functional accounts of knowledge can be found in western thought, these are different ways of doing "genealogy" with very different liberatory aims.

21. As I've maintained throughout this book, what constitutes "white" is not reducible to phenotypic appearance. White settler populations, for example, can reorganize as epistemic polities throughout social transformations. Refer to Chapter 1 for further discussion of white dynastic formations.

22. "The inequality r > g implies that wealth accumulated in the past grows more rapidly than output and wages . . . Once constituted, capital reproduces itself faster than output increases. The past devours the future." Piketty, 2017, p. 572.

23. This feature nearly cost me my life many times over, as it routinely does for so many other survivors of violence. The experience of harm that accrues to collective resistance to these systems, generation after generation, is by design (Chapter 5). There's a reason why freedom is a constant struggle, and that reason, I maintain, can be understood through an anticolonial systems lens that links economics and epistemology within a shared network of dynamic relations shaped by history, just as it can be understood through the land-based epistemologies and Indigenous story work that lays out the historical patterns and gridlines of colonial violence and gender-based harm in Indian country, or through the Black radical and intersectional feminist tradition. This is just one way of approaching a problem we are all too familiar with.

24. Mills, 1997/2014, p. 19.

25. Gordon, 1980; 1982; Kotz et al., 1994; Lippit, 2010.

26. Brown 2021; Coulthard, 2014; Davis, 1983; Harris, 2019; Kelley, 2017; Marcos, 1997; Melamed, 2011, 2015; Mills, 1997/2014; Nichols, 2020; Robinson, 1983.

27. I also retain its rejection of individual agency as the primary driver, for example, the idea that SSA "is external to the decisions of individual capitalists, but it is internal to the macrodynamic of capitalist economies" (Gordon, 1982, p. 16). Moreover, I have developed my arguments on epistemic social structures of accumulation through the helpful lenses of anticolonial and extractive colonialism literatures. I use these literatures to move beyond SSA theory by connecting the dots between

profit, knowledge, colonial occupation, and epistemology, and to reject naturalized approaches to explanations of structurally stratifying economic forces in advanced industrial capitalist societies. Anticolonial practitioners begin with the assumption that such inequities are real and visceral, and that the collective work of theoretical action lies at the crossroads of critical analyses of power and the fight for justice as a livable future beyond pained survival for our communities. This is the heuristic function the framework epistemic capitalism offers beyond critique, but it is not prescriptive. It is one way of coming at the coordinated and sustained project of imperial and neocolonial violence that supports the automation of impunity in our lives.

28. Hardoon, 2017; Oxfam International, 2020; 2022.
29. Flynn et al., 2017, p. 2.
30. Steil et al., 2018; Baradaran, 2017; Taylor, 2019.
31. Betancur & Herring, 2012; Chakravartty & Ferreira da Silva, 2013; Rothstein, 2017.
32. Alexander, 2012; Haley, 2016; Hinton, 2016.
33. Pager, 2007.
34. Aalbers, 2012; Howell et al., 2021. Most stratification studies that centered race focused on men of color, creating data pathways for policy initiatives aimed at expanding opportunities for men and boys of color. For example, refer to https://obamawhitehouse.archives.gov/the-press-office/2014/02/27/presidential-memorandum-creating-and-expanding-ladders-opportunity-boys-.
35. Harris, 2021, p. 16.
36. Bhattacharyya, 2018; Day, 2016; Koshy et al., 2022; Leroy & Jenkins, 2021; Melamed, 2011; Zambrana, 2021.
37. Ben-Moshe, 2020; Bierria et al., 2022; Davis et al., 2022; Murch, 2022.
38. Gómez-Barris, 2017.
39. The resounding emphasis in these works is on the colonial project's aim to keep control of stolen Indigenous lands and to continue to reinvent racial regimes to uphold the asymmetrical structure of wealth accumulation for white settler populations and their descendants.
40. Escobar, 2017; Miñoso 2017; Quijano, 2000.
41. Mignolo, 2005. Since this manuscript was submitted, advances in the field have contextualized the widespread citation of the "cognitive empire" (Santos, 2018) with precursors and conceptual analogues in decolonial theory to reflect the wave of recent allegations of sexual misconduct and labor exploitation against Santos. Refer, for example, to https://www.buala.org/en/mukanda/without-taking-responsibility-for-concrete-acts-of-abuse-committed-there-is-no-self-criticis.
42. Furtado, 1948; 1958; Marini 1973; Prebisch, 1950; 1963; Street, 1967.
43. Wallerstein, 1999.
44. Refer to Bielshowski, 2009 for a review of the Latin American school of structuralism in economics.
45. *Arizona v. Youngblood*, 488 U.S. 51, 58 (1988).
46. Larry Youngblood was later exonerated through DNA evidence. The case established that *police have no duty to actually test items gathered as evidence*, and that the burden of proof falls on the defendant to establish that any failure on the part of the police to

test evidence, even potentially exculpatory evidence, was done out of malicious intent ("bad faith"). Youngblood, who is Black, died in 2007 without ever having received compensation (National Registry of Exonerations, 2022). The National Registry of Exonerations reports that "a black prisoner serving time for sexual assault is three-and-a-half times more likely to be innocent than a white sexual assault convict" (2017, pp. 12–13).
47. *Vega v. Tekoh*, 597 U.S. __ (2022).
48. Refer to *J.C. Penney Cas. Ins. Co. v. M.K.* (1991), in which the Supreme Court held that Insurance Code Section 533 bars recovery from insurance policies for child sexual assault.
49. *DeGraffenreid v. General Motors Assembly Div., Etc.*, 413 F. Supp. 142 (E.D. Mo. 1976); refer also to Ruíz, 2017.
50. Frey, 1991, p. 433. In the 1980s a wave of psychological studies emerged that differentiated between "emotional" and "sexual" motivations for child rape, informing the psychological assessment of intent (Frey, 1991).
51. *Old Republic Ins. Co. v. Comprehensive Health Care Associates, Inc.*, 2 F3d 105, 1993.
52. Refer, for example, to the class action suit brought for false arrest and wrongful imprisonment against Hertz rental car company (Sullivan, 2022) and the add-on coverage protections available for clergy. In the last decade, negligence principles have been used to trigger an insurer's duty to defend under the legal doctrine of negligent supervision, negligent hiring, and negligent retention (Swisher & Mason, 2010, pp. 358–589).
53. Zuckerman, 2021.
54. *LAUSD v. Superior Court*, B307389, May 21, 2021.
55. Chamallas, 2018, p. 7.
56. The anti-domestic violence movement also functions within the interpretive economy of white dynastic formations. For an excellent discussion refer to Bierria, 2007/2017.
57. For a discussion on the gendered dimensions of tort law, refer to Koening & Rustard, 1995. They argue that punitive damages verdicts awarded to men (e.g., for work-related accidents and vehicular accident injuries) exhibit different patterns than those awarded to women (e.g., damages from household consumer products and medical malpractice). They link policy reform efforts at the federal level (e.g., FDA's defense to punitive damages) to differential impacts of such laws on the basis of gender. Refer also to Finley, 2004 on the liability insurance market and noneconomic loss damages legal shifts.
58. Ruíz et al., unpublished manuscript (in review).
59. At first it can seem odd that an epistemic culture founded on the tripartite logical principles of identity, noncontradiction, and either/or binaries could support a discursive culture so distant from its own logical commitments, one where functional reality stands in an "opposite day" relation to many of the dominant discursive norms about who we are politically (a democracy), what is happening to whom, and why. But when considered in terms of the epistemic relations brought about in coordination

with inhabiting lands and the need to build systems for their expropriative and long-term occupation, it is not so difficult.
60. Structural invariance profits white settler populations and their descendants, even under the clout of western feminism. Epistemic capitalism is therefore also an anticolonial corrective to philosophical accounts of hermeneutical unfairness and injustice that efface the historically demonstrable patterns of structured malice and historical design of white dynastic wealth accumulation in settler epistemic systems; a design that functionalizes impunity when such harms do occur.
61. On philosophical agenda setting, refer to discussion of Dotson's work in Chapter 4.
62. Robinson, 1983.
63. On September 22, 2020, "in order to promote economy and efficiency in Federal contracting, to promote unity in the Federal workforce, and to combat offensive and anti-American race and sex stereotyping and scapegoating," Trump signed Executive Order 13950, "Combating Race and Sex Stereotyping," which forbade the kind of diversity training taking over corporate America from taking place in federal agencies. Constructed as a federal contracting and economic oversight decree, Executive Order 13950 became the basis of the "divisive and prohibited concepts" (DCP) House bills that swept through the 2021 legislative session in nearly every state (forty-one by the end of January 2021 alone). DCP legislation aimed to ban everything from "critical race theory" and the teaching of Black history, to the word "gay" in schools. What's structurally important about Executive Order 13950, at least from a systems perspective, is not its dog-whistling racist content, or the force of law with which it buttressed naturalized white supremacist rhetoric, or that it was in many ways unnecessary to achieve its stated aims—certainly, many corporate pledges of financial support were empty and self-serving, and EO 13950 came at the tail end of the Trump administration's four-year ban-a-thon of similar terms (including "diversity," "vulnerable," and "evidence-based") at the Centers for Disease Control and Environmental Protection Agency. On January 20, 2021, citing the "unbearable human costs of systemic racism," President Biden's Executive Order 13985, "Advancing Racial Equity and Support for Underserved Communities through the Federal Government," overtured EO 13950. And it did so with an antiracist rhetorical force meant to match and counter the white racial logic underwriting EO 13950. For many, Biden's executive order was a moral win for antiracism. It certainly felt good to read its clear rebuking of policies that upheld systemic racism. On a practical level, it was an immediate stopgap to a particular system flow that put groups of real people in harm's way and needed formal rebuking. But as 2021 rolled on, it became obvious that rather than putting an end to federal efforts targeting diversity training initiatives, EO 13985 simply triggered the relocation of antidiversity efforts to another point in the system: state legislatures and local governments. Moreover, DCP legislation efforts were not a proportional redistribution and proportional backlash against racial justice and diversity efforts; they were a deluge. Instead of stopping antidemocratic racist policies, the opposite occurred—*escalation* and *retrenchment*.
64. Philadelphia district attorney Larry Krasner and San Francisco district attorney Chesa Boudin, well-known advocates of restorative justice, progressive bail reform,

and community-based accountability anticrime policies, were famously subject to recall campaigns. To some extent, this is because progressive prosecutorial representation *is* a system threat (though minimally compared to abolitionist alternatives that cut off the adaptive pathways for system specification), the same way Section 5 of the Voting Rights Act posed a significant threat, so the self-correcting properties of settler epistemic systems went into effect. Attempts to rescue white innocence and self-improvement imperatives isolate transactional exchanges and redescribe system as outcomes or derivates of the interpersonal scale of social epistemological activity and the influence of structural injustices, like the "context ex machina" discussed in Chapter 1.

65. Bierria, 2014, p. 131. Dotson (2012) also locates epistemic oppression in a wider structural matrix and through an order-of-change model that links the structural and the individual domains of epistemology.

66. Bierria, 2014, p. 131. Because I read Bierria's agent-level account of epistemic violence as compatible with a network-systems description (e.g., of the interlocking operations of power necessary to maintain hermeneutic dominion over institutional infrastructures in settler colonial societies), epistemic capitalism can be taken to extend Bierria's insights about the hermeneutics of individual agency to a network model / logical ecosystems of economic relations in which value is traded, set, sold, adjusted, accumulated, and circulated in relation to settler epistemologies to produce interpretive "wealth" for some communities but not others, with real life consequences made visceral in legal and medical systems.

67. The "epistemic friction" advocated by Medina (2017) will thus be easily respecified as a frictionless system flow.

68. Scatton, 2022.

69. https://www.intelligent.com/34-of-white-college-students-lied-about-their-race-to-improve-chances-of-admission-financial-aid-benefits/?adfa. Lying about race in this context can even be construed as "entrepreneurial activity" under epistemic capitalism.

70. In 2022, Cop27 climate justice pledges included the creation of a "loss and damage fund" to compensate smaller nations (with less of a carbon emission footprint) that are disproportionately impacted by global warming. This climate justice "win" was accompanied by no substantive action on decarbonization, a fact that reporters quickly recognized as "greenwashing" (Dickie & Jessop, 2022). In the months following the announcement of the reparations fund, the fund had yet to receive a single pledge: "The fund, created to help poor nations grapple with unstoppable climate dangers, like rising seas, was seen as a major victory at the global climate talks in Egypt late last year. The absence of any financial commitments since then is raising concerns in developing countries that the fund could fail to deliver the historic help that was promised by world leaders" (Schonhardt, 2023).

71. Ruíz, 2019.

72. Goldstein, 2022, p. 73.

73. The Research Institute for Structural Change, https:structuralinstitute.org.

74. Doolittle et al., 2017.

75. According to the FBI's Uniform Crime Reports (2009–2014). https://github.com/BuzzFeedNews/2016-09-ucr-analysis/blob/master/notebooks/2016-09-ucr-analysis.ipynb. Scroll down to "Agencies with a High Percentage of 'Unfounded' Rape Reports" for breakdown of cities with highest percentages. Database compiled in Alex Campbell and Katie Baker's "Unfounded: This Police Department Tosses Aside Rape Reports When a Victim Doesn't Resist 'To the Best of Her Ability.'"
76. The Oxnard and Baltimore County data predate the #MeToo movement going viral on social media (dates are after the initial use of "Me Too" on social media by Tarana Burke in 2006 but before the movement received a viral-setting boost from Alyssa Milano in 2017).
77. Simon-Kerr, 2021, p. 112. In a Supreme Court case considering credibility determinations in asylum seekers' testimony, the court entertained arguments that distinguished between the capacity to be believed and the power to persuade, ultimately skeptical of the requirement to consider whether testimony is both "credible" and "persuasive" (8 U.S.C. § 1158(b)(1)(B)(ii). Refer to *Garland v. Ming Dai* (2021) and Simon-Kerr 2021, p. 113).
78. Gordon et al., 1982.
79. Collins, 2000.
80. Coulthard, 2014.
81. Kotz, 1994, p. 87.
82. Kotz, 1994, p. 60.
83. Johnstone, 1976, as cited in Nattrass, 1994, p. 253.
84. Kotz, et al., 1994, p. 58.
85. Kotz et al., 1994, p. 3.
86. Lippit, 2010, p. 4.
87. Kotz et al., 1994, p. 87.
88. Kotz et al., 1994, pp. 90–91.
89. Gordon et al., 1982, p. 23.
90. Albelda & Tilly, 1994.
91. Gordon, 1980; Gordon et al., 1982; Bowles et al., 1986; Weisskopf, 1981.
92. Mandel, 1980; Schumpeter, 1934; Kondratieff, 1935.
93. Coulthard, 2014; Nichols, 2020.
94. Gordon et al., 1982, p. 23.
95. Gordon et al., 1982, p. 20.
96. Kotz et al., 1994.
97. Gordon et al., 1982, p. 20.
98. Gordon et al., 1982, pp. 20–21.
99. Gordon et al., 1982, p. 21.
100. Gordon, 1982, p. 24.
101. Kotz, 1994, p. 53.
102. Gordon et al., 1982, p. 25.
103. Foucault, 1976.
104. Kotz et al., 1994, p. 61.
105. Kotz et al., 1994.

106. Albelda & Tilly, 1994, p. 218.
107. Albelda & Tilly, 1994, p. 218.
108. Albelda & Tilly, 1994, p. 223.
109. Christensen, 2017, p. 2. Christensen is paraphrasing features of the SSA view, on their account.
110. Marx, *Capital*, vol. 1.
111. Davis, 1983, p. 190.
112. Kotz et al., 1994, p. 67.
113. Kotz et al., 1994, p. 67.
114. Gómez-Barris, 2017, p. xvii.
115. Coulthard, 2014.
116. McDonough, 1994, p. 126.
117. Coulthard, 2014, p. 151.
118. Coulthard, 2014, p. 14.
119. Robinson, 1956, p. 334.
120. Robinson, 1956, p. 335.
121. Hermeneutic intersectionality is a form of philosophical analysis that focuses on how intersectional harms prevent meaningful access to social structures like law, education, and medicine—resulting in "access" in name only. It is connected to the notion of hermeneutic violence as "pre-structural violence" that is associated with "cultural gaslighting" (Ruíz, 2020). As Berenstain (2020) explains: "Ruíz . . . further conceives of gaslighting as something that occurs not only at structural scales but at a pre-structural one as well. In 'Theorizing Multiple Oppressions through Colonial History,' Ruíz (2012) shows how European colonization disrupted pre-colonial ways of knowing in what is now identified as Latin America and tracks how colonial lineages create public policies, institutions, and political structures that reify and solidify settler epistemologies as the only legitimate form of knowledge. Colonialism's foreclosure of Amerindian linguistic communities' ability to collectively engage in interpretive processes of culture—and be heard and understood as coherent—is thus not only essential to understanding the multiplicity of social oppressions and their intersections in contemporary Latin American contexts; it is also a form of pre-structural gaslighting. Colonial violence is built into the very foundation of the contemporary hermeneutic frameworks that structure human experience in settler societies. One outcome of this is that the concept of violence in settler epistemologies nonaccidentally excludes violence done to land, waterways, artifacts, and other loci of relations of meaning, particularly within Indigenous epistemologies—what Ruíz (2019) calls hermeneutic violence. Notably, the gaslighting Ruíz describes is not just a result of the structural automation of colonial epistemologies and institutions. As a central feature of the genocides that made and continue to make settler institutions possible, this gaslighting was a precondition on the existence of self-propagating systems of colonial epistemology. Thus, the gaslighting at the heart of colonial genocides—and the corresponding epistemicides—is pre-structural, rather than merely structural" (p. 734).

NOTES   389

122. https://viz.theinequalitylab.com/Animations/2-wealth-structure.html.
123. Speed, 2021, p. 18.
124. Million, 2009.
125. Maracle, 2015, p. 53.
126. Kendi, 2021. Refer to Chapter 1.
127. Siegel, 1997. Refer to Chapter 1.
128. Hannah-Jones, 2021, p. xvii–xx.
129. Lindsay, 2006.
130. Cillo et al., 2022; Jameson, 1986; Love 2005. It is an orientation I developed from Zapatista thinking on resistance to oppression and from Zapatista political economy, notably through the critique of the "capitalist hydra."
131. In the context of self-repairing white dynastic formations, wealth can also operate to uphold the structural inequalities associated with a lack of wealth. Consider Arline Geronimus's (2023) work on weathering, in which she demonstrates how higher incomes improve health among white people in Detroit but impair health of Mexicans in Detroit: "As our own findings on Stress Impact scores and telomere length suggest, Mexican immigrants and their children become weathered not only despite their extra years of education and higher incomes, but possibly because of them. The stress of trying to 'better' themselves socioeconomically takes a toll, as does the time spent in the kind of environments that their education and income allow (or require) them to enter" (pp. 158–160). I find this to be especially true of women of color and Indigenous women in the anglo-american academy, and perhaps nowhere more so than in the discipline of philosophy.
132. Collins, 2022.
133. Coulthard, 2014.
134. 2017, p. 572.
135. This allows, for example, epistemic wealth to amass over very long periods of time as powerful settler epistemological systems. Recall that in SSA theory, "Long-swing contractions cannot be self-correcting and [a] recovery cannot begin until individual actors are able to mobilize coherent and collective forces which . . . effect the necessary structural adjustments in the social structure of accumulation" (Gordon et al., 1994, p. 24), and the "core" theory refines the recovery process by giving greater explanatory power to a "core" set of institutions that keep the stability of the "external environment" going from one period to other.
136. In economies supported by settler epistemic systems, epistemic capital accumulated in the past reproduces itself faster than outputs of the (formal and informal) knowledge economy. Consider the growth rate of the dominant interpretive resources in multicultural democracies. In $r > g$, g can be conceptualized (for illustrative purposes) as an epistemic GDP that experiences an increased annual rate (e.g., think of how civil rights discourses became more popular or accepted each year, but that can conceivably shrink as well). Even with consecutive increases, interpretive resources underwriting multicultural democratic norms cannot keep *pace* with the inequalities structured by the concentrated accumulation of inherited epistemic

wealth set in motion by white dynastic formations. The accumulation, production, and circulation of epistemic resources is thus a key element in the resilience and adaptive transformational capacity of settler colonial capitalist economies. While epistemic capital reproduces itself faster than output increases, it does not mean that nondominant interpretive communities are resource poor or fated to toil under the exploitative conditions of epistemic capital. As aforementioned, it only means that the dominant interpretive ecology in which meaning operates in settler colonial societies is purposefully set up to make it very hard for formal institutional structures to bend toward justice for people of color and Indigenous peoples, and that many people die or suffer horribly because of this "very hard" feature of structural violence.

137. Rama, 1984.
138. Bhandar, 2018, p. 102.
139. I agree with Crenshaw that "in the context of white supremacy, engaging in rights discourse should be seen as an act of self-defense" (1988, p. 117). Of course, one of the goals of colonialism is to create subclasses of permanent defendants, to make self-defense a pervasive and profit-reaping condition in our lives across generations. In the long run, colonialism's goal also yields genocidal results. But if I'm right about the mycelial structural design of white dynastic formations, one thing to expect is a colonial social world that can predict white dynastic formations as a possible system output in response to repression, and can adjust by all-too-readily offering up armories of inaction, pessimism, and assimilation as a form of self-defense. What white dynastic formations can't do is out-design their own design; hence the work of refusal. It may also be possible to outpace the desing of colonial adaptive measures, as the current research on outpacing metastatic colonization illustrates. And, there is an incredible amount of political and emancipatory work that can be done from a space of scorn. Chapter 5 illustrates this through the "dignified rage" of Zapatista rebellion and world-building, with critical attention to how racialized women's lives fare in this space. Beyond Zapatista autonomous zones, thinking of incrementalism (a political strategy of achieving social change through incremental, battle-by-battle, progressive policy wins that safeguard civil rights in public domains like health, housing, voting, and education) as coordinated refusal is also important for creating structural bridges to efforts that can affect the elemental design of social systems in a network context. In isolation, those efforts are just random elements. But without them, oppressed peoples will die in the hands of willfully maltrained professionals, racist attorneys and their law professors, insurance denials of gender-affirming care, and beyond. The recent overturning of *Roe v. Wade* is a case in point.

Chapter 4

1. Refer, for example, to Cawthra et al., 1987; Kutcher, 1982.
2. It gained particular traction among antiviolence resource organizations as an educational outreach tool for intimate partner abuse cycles and, in more clinical settings, as a way to talk about somatic markers, neural pathways, and independent psychiatric

variables that could help explain impairments in social decision-making among individuals facing psychological trauma and/or emotional abuse (Humeny, 2014). Refer also to Ahern, 2018.
3. Kline 2006, quoted in Davis & Ernst 2017, 2.
4. Acuña Delgado 2006; Cameron et al. 2019; Jones et al. 2013; Ngāti Awa et al. 2013; Tuck & Yang 2012.
5. The probabilistic idea of "life chances" (*Lebenschancen*) comes from German sociologist Max Weber (1864– 1920), yet has a longer conceptual history in German philosophy, melding together theories of human agency from the existentialist and *Lebensphilosophie* tradition (especially Nietzsche) with socially determinist trends in the critique of political economy (as in Marx's *Produktionsverhältnisse*). Weber's original notion of the social power behind the distribution of life chances in a market economy (the opportunities each person has to access a better material life) highlighted "the probability that one actor within a social relationship will be in a position to carry out *his own will despite resistance*, regardless of the basis on which this probability rests" (Weber 1947, 53, emphasis added). The question of how the socially fated (by design) probabilistically defy the storm and stress of circumstance is not an appropriate starting point for thinking about responses to colonial violence and its aftermath. The descriptive tools of life chances were never meant to track the strategic maldistribution of life chances of Indigenous people and people of color, and need to be rethought as a framework, particularly in public health research.
6. Tuck & Yang, 2012; Mawhinney, 1998.
7. Sarkis, 2017.
8. Refer, for example, to Dotson, 2011; 2012; 2013; 2014a; 2014b; 2017.
9. The argument is not against the existence of the concept of systemic psychological abuse and its possible political uses. In fact, useful interpersonal accounts of gaslighting have long existed in women-of-color feminisms with little or no uptake in mainstream feminist discourses. Predictably, when the conditions of heuristic need arose in the domestic violence awareness campaigns of the early 1980s, which centered heavily on rescuing the future life chances of US white women, the term culled was not from our intellectual works and histories, but from the obscure works of a white male British playwright and its preservation in US settler cinema.
10. This includes experiences of embodiment that are wrongly medicalized as illness, particularly as mental pathology in psychiatry. More recently, medical gaslighting has been used to refer to a type of "identity-related abuse" observed by healthcare providers between patients and their healthcare proxies, or the parents of transgender children and adolescent patients (refer to Riggs & Bartholomaeus, 2018).
11. Harris & Woodlock, 2019, pp. 530–532; Johnson et al., 2017; Roberts & Andrews, 2013; Stark, 2007.
12. Refer, for example, to Bailey et al., 2017; Browne, 2017; Goodman et al., 2017; Hoffman et al., 2016; Washington, 2006. This pattern continues in philosophy. For years, progressive movements for racial justice have taken up structural analyses of gaslighting to little attention in mainstream analyses of gaslighting as a form of "epistemic injustice" (Fricker, 2007), with the exception of Pohlhaus, 2017.
13. Epstein & Goodman, 2019.

14. Design does not simply refer to the identification of patterns of distribution, *but the intent of distribution effects*, as in a grand design or master plan. A shift in thinking is needed from individual health "stressors" and bias to active structural "antagonists" in this regard.
15. Not only are these women disproportionately subjected to heightened mortality risk factors, they are often targets of state-sponsored epistemic warfare that promotes cultures of silence and violent retribution (Fregoso & Bejarano, 2009). For instance, the increasingly common phenomenon in Latin America of charging women who experience miscarriages with aggravated homicide has only recently attracted legal attention.
16. Russell, 2018. Russell also details the helpful notion of *structural competency*: "Physicians must learn what is called structural competency: the ability to discern how a host of issues defined clinically as symptoms, attitudes, or diseases ... also represent the downstream implications of upstream decisions about such matters as health care and food delivery systems, zoning laws, urban and rural infrastructure, medicalization, or even about the very definitions of illness and health" (Metzl, 2012, p. 216, cited in Russell, 2016, p. 52).
17. Dieke et al., 2017.
18. Nietzsche, 1873, p. 257.
19. Dieke et al., 2017, p. 605.
20. Particularly when no such comparative data are produced for white women and ARTs.
21. Stewart et al., 2013, p. 807.
22. Myles, 2013, pp. 2–10.
23. Centers for Disease Control and Prevention, 2015 Sexually Transmitted Diseases Surveillance: STDs in Racial and Ethnic Minorities 2015 Available at https://www.cdc.gov/std/stats/archive/STD-Surveillance-2015-print.pdf.
24. In her dissertation, "Unbearable Fruit: Black Women's Experiences with Uterine Fibroids," sociologist Ranell Myles finds that "their experiences negatively impact their quality of life by creating added stress, influencing their work lives, and in some cases affecting their ability to conceive and have safe pregnancies" (Myles, 2013, p. 145). Although "psychological distress" has been clinically shown to be a risk factor for death from cerebrovascular disease (Hamer et al., 2012), medical responses to psychological distress are often pathologized for women racialized as nonwhite but remedied with infrastructurally supported, provision-of-care models for women racialized as white.
25. Washington, 2006, p. 65.
26. Hoffman et al., 2016.
27. Bailey et al., 2017. Research on race itself was severely limited well into the late twentieth century, as race was routinely seen by high-ranking scientific journals as an ideological construct unsuited for inclusion in rigorous scientific study design and empirical research. This was, of course, methodologically compatible with generations of sexist racist research produced in American medicine and particularly in psychiatry. Today, health-disparities research lags significantly behind other public interest fields in intersectional analyses, with psychologically driven racial bias dominating the literature.

28. Such as a patient's alleged failures to report clinically significant symptoms or communicate effectively.
29. It is incumbent on researchers to anticipate this and design research with the social forces behind settler colonial market economies in mind, revolutionizing methodologies if need be.
30. Morgan Brinlee is citing a 2014 study by University of Cincinnati professor John Paul Wright that allowed the Trump administration to argue for policies based on the racist assumption that "Black children are just more disruptive in the classroom."
31. Cf. cases involving the expert testimony of Walter Quijano, state forensic psychiatrist for the state of Texas (Millhiser, 2016; *Buck v. Davis*).
32. Washington, 2006.
33. This in no way minimizes the range of socially legible public outbursts, tears, and emotive somersaults put on social display by white people mentally distressed by accusations of racism. In fact, the higher the pay grade, the more epistemic resources are often made available to license this behavior. The original claim of differential allostatic load remains the same.
34. Indigenous women fare similarly: they have produced robust scholarship on this phenomenon, yet remain peripheralized in western medical measures. Indigenous peoples have developed sophisticated knowledge-practices that incorporate wariness of white people with clipboards asking questions since the fifteenth century. The underserving of Indigenous populations is thus not due to "small data sets" but structured inattentions to the historical conditions for producing medical knowledges about Indigenous populations (Deer, 2015; Patrick, 2016). Scientific mystification of violence against Native and Indigenous women changes, of course, with border imaginaries that contain populations neatly in settler epistemic terms (island imaginaries), as the rising health literature on Australian Aboriginal women shows.
35. Refer to Flanders-Stepans, 2000; Howell et al., 2013.
36. Bailey & Trudy 2018, p. 762.
37. For example, refer to Braveman, 2001; Prussing, 2018.
38. Davis & Ernst, 2017.
39. Davis & Ernst, 2017, p. 3.
40. Davis & Ernst, 2017, p. 3.
41. Davis & Ernst, 2017, p. 5.
42. *Korematsu v. United States*, 323 U.S. 214 (1944).
43. *Braden v. Commonwealth*, 291 S.W.2d 843 (1956).
44. Davis & Ernst, 2017, p. 8.
45. Today, historical marker #2254 stands at the original site of the Wades' home. The State of Kentucky has rebranded the Wades as "open housing *pioneers*" who "benefited from the friendship and assistance of Carl and Anne Braden" (https://explorekyhistory.ky.gov/items/show/298). This is an example of gaslighting produced by settler geoscaping.
46. *Korematsu*, 224, qtd. in Rose & Ernst, 2017, p. 4.
47. *Stare decisis* refers to the procedural principle that decides which legal arguments have standing based on case precedent.
48. Rose & Ernst, 2017, p. 3, emphasis added.

49. Rose & Ernst, 2017, p. 4.
50. Rose & Ernst, 2017, p. 8.
51. Dotson, 2012.
52. Heston Tobias and Ameil Joseph make a related point, arguing gaslighting is a "historical form" of abuse that predates its coinage in settler aesthetics. It has been a technique of *communal incapacitation* through targeting noncompliance in Black communities, such that "gaslighting is part of a systemic, historical process of racism that has been used by the police and government organizations to both illegally target people of color and *deny complicity* in racial profiling" (2018, p. 22, emphasis added).
53. Gott, 2007; Speed, 2017.
54. Deloria, 1998.
55. Tuck & Yang, 2012, p. 7.
56. Tuck & Yang, 2012, p. 9.
57. Tuck & Yang, 2012, p. 9. As Tuck and Yang note, these can be redeployed by people of color and forced migrants, such as—following their logic—displaced victims of human trafficking, war, and global capitalism, hypothetically including (for illustrative purposes) Sonoran women asylum seekers who may have "stories of colonization" rather than "stories of creation" as part of their identity in settler Mexico (as the Mexican state coordinated the reclassification of Indigenous peoples as *campesinxs* under strategic settler configurations of labor and land politics). For a helpful distinction between claims to innocence and claims to pure innocence, which are untenable in late-stage settler colonial capitalist societies given the historical functioning of the settler-slave-Native triad, refer to Dotson, 2018a. I follow Dotson on this point.
58. Tuck & Yang, 2012, p. 10.
59. This is not only because one has it, but because of inhabiting social structures that nonaccidentally recognize *these* forms of capital but not others as social protectives or wealth. Understanding the structural relations behind motivations for settler moves to innocence is critical for recognizing the violent precarities that are structured to shape the aspirational experiences of people of color and racialized immigrants resettling on stolen lands, and whose own lands have often been stolen and/or removed from possibility of return.
60. The idea of "mobilization without emancipation" comes from late twentieth-century-century feminist interpretations of Latin American revolutionary theory, particularly of the Nicaraguan and Cuban revolutions (refer to AMNLAE, 1984; Ariza, 1999; Garzón et al., 2014; Molyneux, 1985; Randall, 1983; Viterna, 2005). Indeed, a great deal of feminist anticolonial approaches to structural oppressions (including lengthy treatments of ideological forces and epistemic oppressions responsible for thwarting women's liberation) arose out of these literatures, to little uptake in the global north. Along with feminist Zapatismo, it is these literatures that form my basic conceptions of social transformations, the predictive nature of counterrevolutionary forces, permutations of cultural power, and processes of functionalization. Stability across transformations is one of the lasting legacies of Latin American revolutions (Gleijeses, 1992; Winn, 1989); feminist interpretations of these histories, however, have been critical in dismantling deterministic accounts of cultural structural dependency on

the global north and envisioning paths for strategic responses to counterinsurgency (Kampwirth, 2004; Viterna, 2013).
61. Historically, one or two have always gone free—in fact some *must always go free* and in a statistically significant way for settler science to recognize, record, and study the paradox when it ebbs, thereby constructing the illusory puzzle of freedom to keep us busy as political theorists.
62. Simpson, 2007; 2014.
63. Spivak, 1988.
64. For example, citing Virginia Woolf's *A Room of One's Own* rather than Gertrude Mossell's "A Lofty Study" helps relieve pressure to enter the actual work and voices of women of color into the citational economy of the academy. A hundred women of color and Indigenous women can say it, but when a structurally privileged white woman says it, it becomes a potential cottage industry by design, irrespective of who the writer is. In fact, I fully expect terms like *cultural gaslighting* and *hermeneutic violence* to be unproblematically attributed to or associated with a white academic in the near future, or to be foreclosed by homologous terms that depoliticize or produce opposite effects (cf. the notion of academic mainstreaming of intersectionality in Ruíz, 2017).
65. Berenstain, 2016.
66. Dotson, 2019.
67. Mawhinney, 1998.
68. Fellows & Razack, 1998.
69. Tuck & Yang, 2012, p. 9.
70. Tuck & Yang, 2012, p. 9.
71. Berenstain, 2016. It enables journal referees to ask to have the term "settler colonial culture" explained to them, often with the presumption that no such thing exists. It is just another version of knowledge production based on Native informancy. It takes this form: "Prove to us we're bad, because we're inherently good," and where proof of harm, not *indication of harm*, is the baseline for motivating corrective action. Today, a slew of cutting-edge and important work is being done across the natural and social sciences to prove people of color are disproportionately harmed by policy, practice, and bias, but with the legitimating framework of unproven harm as the baseline of study design. Study design does not yet foreground the inverse, proof that harm *isn't* being done to our communities and lives. This would constitute corrective action and better align with the realities of the subjects that methodological positivism claims to be tracking. The gains may be short term, but they are necessary.
72. I think this power is wielded quite widely on a structural scale that has direct *economic* benefits and indirect benefits as social capital that are often economized for social mobility. It constitutes the nonaccidental accumulation of interpretive *wealth and capital* as a form of indirect intergenerational wealth transmissions between specific populations and their descendants. It is a form of wealth that performs as safety nets of social capital, yet (predictively) remain unaccounted for in studies of class wealth.
73. Dotson, 2019.
74. Dotson, 2012b.

75. Dotson, 2012b, p. 15.
76. Allen et al., 2008.
77. Whyte, 2018.
78. Dotson, 2018b.
79. Dotson, 2019.
80. Sertler, 2018, p. 5.
81. Sertler, 2018, p. 9.
82. McKinnon 2017, p. 168.
83. Ruíz, 2013.
84. Greene, 2019, p. 629.
85. Consolidatory domination and cultural recursion help us recognize how interpretive familiarity under colonialism is achieved, not by growing into a specific sociohistorical context held together by social acts and practices, but by the simultaneous erasure and repression of an alternative reference point that preconditions the emergence of *western interpretive frameworks*, acts, and practices. This productive repression is performed by hermeneutic violence. It is not a reflective political maneuver; it is the expressive outcome of western conceptual orthodoxies (such as substance ontology, hierarchical binaries, exclusionary logics) that are particularly adept at producing a worldview that structures social processes through agonism and domination, where what perseveres unchanged through struggle and change has its existence recognized as *real*. That's not a universal feature of human existence; it is the metaphysical provenance of western culture since the Greek atomists, and essential to the development of greco-roman slave law.
86. Ruíz, 2013; 2019.
87. Dotson, 2018b.
88. As one professor (one of Gadamer's students) in graduate school once told me, "Real Indigenous cultures are dead. All there is left are pastiches. Rain dances in high school gymnasiums." It didn't work. I recognized how the whitewashing of hermeneutic resources (including historiography) for the purposes of wielding monocultural authority over the instruments of knowledge production is one of the oldest tools of dispossession in the academy. Retaining monocultural control of institutional and infrastructural mechanisms such as law, history, and education that trade on whitewashed hermeneutical resources is critical to the formation of interpretive power, which discloses only those domains of intelligibility that recognize colonial cultural formations as the prereflective baseline for meaning, language, and social communication. The goal was not to get me to *believe* or adjudicate the claim of Indigenous terminal death, but to foreclose the possibility of epistemic disobedience based, for instance, on lived knowledge of Indigenous cultures, memories that outlive my life span, or simply the politics of refusal (refer to Dotson, 2018a; Simpson, 2007).
89. Million, 2013.
90. There's a deeper value inversion at play here, since monocultural epistemologies actually have the serious hermeneutical disadvantage when compared to the vast majority of the world's oppressed peoples that can track multiple cultural levels of salience. But this limitation is unsupported by the social infrastructures of settler culture.

91. Refer to Dotson, 2018b.
92. Rama, 1996.
93. Mayflowering is common in the discourses of ally culture, whether humanitarians, political liberals, white feminists, or structurally privileged peoples from colonized contexts who unproblematically resettle to Indigenous lives and lands, holding onto intergenerational wealth *or aspirations to restored settler status* through the social capital of assimilative recognition. (This is especially true of white and white-facing mestizx diasporic Latin Americans who expected to inherit privileged socioeconomic statuses in their countries of origin, and whose deflated social and economic standing as "Latinx" in the United States was interiorized to enable mayflowering, but also deep anti-Black racism, anti-Indigenous, sexist racism and complicity with US white settlers and their institutions.) What is imperial in the interpretive asymmetry enacted through mayflowering is more than an organized failure to recognize that their embodied can-do-ness takes place on stolen lands; it helps to organize the automation of structural violence. Mayflowerers are often some of the most virtued and principled humanists in the academy. Mayflowering is thus one reason to reject ethical views in social epistemology that tackle social injustices through the monocultural lenses of settler-imperial culture.
94. Pohlhaus, 2017.
95. Social epistemology under white feminisms has become the new clipboard-carrying ethnographer making the rounds on Native lands, the imperial social anthropologist who records as a matter of data, taking notes, assuming answers *are theirs* to interpret as truth, lies, or false belief and report back as objective knowledge. With universalism as a methodology, conquest is always near. That is why some prefer to fictionalize our lives to talk about them indirectly, so that you don't have to talk about actual hermeneutical injustices to, say, the actual women who have given *testimonio* of injustices, sexual violence, and femicide, for centuries. The literature on the epistemology of testimony is long and varied in Latin America, but to the global north, it might as well never have been written.
96. Dotson and Sertler, 2021.
97. Ruíz, 2017.
98. This does not mean colonialism is immaterial, or reducible to epistemic processes. I am thinking here of the interpretive wealth accumulation process discussed in the last chapter, which is rooted in historical processes that cannot be conceived without reference to existing material spaces and embodied social practices of dispossession.
99. Precarity is always a double-edged sword that requires structural countermoves to address. Since reproducing conditions of psychic exhaustion is part of the design of settler social structures, the trap set up is to respond by giving up on all empirical work and applied research, particularly on research that gives socially legitimate legal measure and cultural weight to communal impacts of trafficking, battery, femicide, rape, and associated gender-based violences. The fact remains that we need lawyers who won't advocate against our interests through cultural incompetence and doctors who won't get us killed while doing nothing legally recognized as

negligent, doctors who have "structural competence" (Russell, 2016). *We need structural competence across the board: policies that address regulatory lacunae and public servants who call racist policies and practices to task, even under a settler governance structure that on the long view skews advantage toward white settler populations and their descendants.* Strategically, we can marshal moves that force policies and laws to do what Section 5 of the Voting Rights Act of 1965 did, which was to shift the burden on states to first prove that proposed changes to voting procedures were *not* racist before being enacted. It had a nontrivial positive impact on the lives of many people of color in the United States, which is why it was foreseeable that it would be dismantled. But we can also stay ahead of predictive epistemic precarity by shifting the debate altogether and directing our citational economies to Indigenous social science research that doesn't rely on the interpretive assumptions of settler credibility economies, yet can move tactically within them to address community needs brought by structured harm (Walter & Andersen, 2016). When considering adverse racial climates in academia (Williams, 2019), flip the script. Make them keep up for a change.
100. And with metaphysically impoverished settler languages woefully unequipped for little more than prespecifying subject-object distinctions primed for regulating commercial transitions in settler market economies. There are other ways of being, living, and relating that the grammatical arrangements of settler languages do not enliven.
101. Rabasa, 2011.

Chapter 5

1. In most legends the three Moirai or "fates" are depicted with thread; Clotho spun it, Lachesis measured the length, and Atropos cut it, signifying their control over a person's length of life and moment of death. Later depictions emphasize the active interplay between human individuation and predetermination (hence the dice metaphor I use). The roman Parcae, for instance, refined the role of individuation in fate by emphasizing the limit of their powers to natal life, widening the field of interactions and choices mortals could take up as self-defining acts.
2. Despite their destinies foretold (by the oracle in *Oedipus Rex* and by the Fates, whom Sisyphus scorns by cheating death twice), both men are defined by their reactions to "bad fortune." This is the basis for Albert Camus's (1942/2018) famous existential interpretation of Homer's description of Sisyphus as the most cunning of mortals, one who found a way to defy the greek pantheon of gods despite the insurmountable odds against triumph: "Aye, and I saw Sisyphus in violent torment, seeking to raise a monstrous stone with both his hands. Verily he would brace himself with hands and feet, and thrust the stone toward the crest of a hill, but as often as he was about to heave it over the top, the weight would turn it back, and then down again to the plain would come rolling the ruthless stone. But he would strain again and thrust it

back [593–600] (1953). It is this last line that Camus relies on to define metaphysical rebellion as existential "scorn" that outwitted the God's eternal punishment.
3. This became particularly important for psychoanalysis, which refined the association between wounding and subjectivity in the notions of original trauma and constitutive loss (Beardsworth, 2009, p. 45). The notion of individuation is not exclusive to western culture, yet in the west it developed through particular epistemological and metaphysical commitments to (a) exclusionary logic (refer, for example, to Aristotle's laws of thought) and (b) nonreciprocal dualisms, and it is these commitments that pillared the rise of the particular model of modern individualism that underlies settler colonial cultures. While the principle of individuation (*principium individuationis*) took on slight variations in ecclesiastic, existential, and post-Renaissance notions of selfhood, they did not uproot the core of these commitments. One important consequence of the metaphysical and epistemological orthodoxies rooted in this view was the conceptual predevelopment of hierarchical binaries that allowed for clear and neat differentiations between alleged "races" as opposing in form and/or kind to one another. This is an example of the conceptual schemata that organizes social concepts pre-structurally.
4. Tragedy and trauma thus entered the *affective* realm of pain, where Euripides's *Trojan Women* dwelt, rather than a political realm that worked to directly dismantle organized violence against women. While affects can be powerfully political (refer to Lorde 1981; Chemaly 2018; Cooper 2018; Cherry 2021), the western intellectual tradition that encompasses Attic tragedy sought to contain organized resistance to state violence by internalizing conflicts, linking human agency to this internalization, and redirecting affects to this experience. Simultaneously, institutions were set up to formalize affects as public goods reserved for certain people and to function as sites for regulating the affective behavior of others. Delicts in roman law, for instance, carefully outlined how "outrage" as an injury (*Iniuria*) from a perceived insult were grievable harms for slave owners, but not slaves. This pattern continues today and can be found across a range of settler social institutions, from systemically racist pushout policies in education that target the behavior of girls of color for punishment, to the disparate dispensation of damages awarded for emotional injury in libel, defamation, and discrimination suits (cf. *Johnson v. Strive E. Harlem Emp't Grp*, *MacMillan v. Millennium Broadway Hotel*, *Cosmos Forms, Ltd. v. State Div. of Human Rights*, and *Laboy v. Office Equip. & Supply Corp* for cases where courts lower original damages awards and discuss the "N-word" as "garden variety" mental harms—a legal notion that in these cases is tied to the presumptive limited evidentiary value of Black plaintiffs' testimony about their own affective lives).
5. It should be noted that the conceptual shift argued for in this chapter is one that advocates and depends on a coalitional approach to solidarity among Indigenous feminisms and women-of-color feminisms, rather than one that collapses them or simplifies their political, geographic, and historical complexity. For more on interhemispheric structural feminisms, feminist anticolonial visions of coalition, and contingent collaborations, refer to Dotson, 2017; Speed, 2017, 2019; and Tuck et al., 2014.

6. Refer to discussion of "accumulation" in Chapter 3.
7. I do not use Butler's (2016) account of "grievability" (e.g., when and which lives can be grieved) because I find Million's (2014) framework much more useful and attentive to settler colonial sociostructural dynamics, as Million does not generalize the social consciousness (e.g., "the public") as western.
8. The Institutes of Justinian law, from where we get the term "institution" (from Latin *institutuere*—to set up, establish custom), formalized customs specific to conditions of war—the taking of live prisoners to extract profit in return for sparing their lives (from where the term "slave" derives, from the tribes [Slavs] mentioned) into an internal regulative social practice (Metzger, 1998). Institutions, on this view, were never value-free social phenomena or blank-slate structures universal across all cultures, but social formations set up to functionalize specific mechanisms of regulative power, like racial and gendered violence, for particular ends. Refer also to the discussion of testimony and slavery in Chapter 2.
9. Refer to Chapter 1 for self-organized criticality, a systems theory term.
10. Largely because of way they are interrelated to one another in a sociostructural fabric. In my view, such views are not mere aggregates, like sand particles put in a random pile, but interconnected in very particular ways that reinforce the self-regulation of critical systems states in settler social structures. They allow for the overall system state to retain functional regulation of supercritical conditions (where more epistemic resources are being produced than are lost), even if subcritical conditions (where designed events fail to release the sufficient number of epistemic resources necessary to sustain a chain of ongoing reactions) exist (typically brought on by system resistance, as illustrated in mass protests).
11. A settler epistemological system thus produces long-tailed distributions (like the skewed distribution of wealth) that can pass for the "bell curve" shape of normal distribution patterns, as noted in Chapter 1. This sleight of hand is easy enough to produce once we factor in the power laws and functional relationships between the elements of the settler epistemological conceptual grid and the institutions that rely on these concepts to exist. The epistemological whole is greater than the part. This is because settler concepts work as a system to produce the long-term dynamics of possession (based on dispossession) at the root of western social reproduction since antiquity, even though as individual elements conceptual dynamics can produce seemingly different outputs (like the appearance of democratic justice and one-off instances of fairness). There is thus consistency in the observed inconsistency. Moreover—and this bears repeating throughout this book—illustrating the functional contradiction between the master's tools (Lorde 1979/2018) and the purportedly egalitarian realities they are said to build does not always entail a political rejection of the "rights" toolkit (Crenshaw 1988). In many instances, settler epistemologies have created a genealogical distance between Indigenous legal traditions and settler reformulations of Indigenous democratic norms to make it appear as if Indigenous peoples are without egalitarian legal customs, in need of legal "civilizing" and humanist intervention that justifies occupation. (I owe this point

to the late Kwasi Wiredu, whose generous conversations with me often suggested a more radical politics than his philosophical writings suggested).
12. Coulthard, 2014.
13. Fregoso & Bejarano, 2009.
14. This notion of a prestructural groundwork for justifying continuing intervention is well documented by Indigenous scholars. Settler nations and international governance bodies rely on humanist logics of individuation to portray noneuropean peoples as trapped in a mythical past and as inherently predisposed to barbaric cultural norms that only european moral authority can guard against (through the continuing possibility of state intervention and occupation, and international human rights courts) (Fanon, 1952; Million 2017; Speed, 2008). The 2001 Mexican Law on Indigenous Rights and Culture, for instance, stipulates that Indigenous peoples can "obtain the recognition of their internal normative systems, to the extent that these are not contrary to constitutional guarantees and human rights" (Speed 2008, p. 224). Settler states, of course, know very little about consistency and fidelity to human rights.
15. This is a nonableist restatement of Spivak's conception of subalternity, where the speech claims of people marginalized by european colonialism are rendered "inaudible" by virtue of institutional (i.e., enforceable and materializable) control over the dominant hermeneutic resources (to be more specific, the social reproduction of "official" interpretive resources) in settler colonial societies (or "postcolonial" cultures—which, for Spivak, signifies a continuation of colonial occupation beyond national independence movements). Anglo-european cultural control over licensed epistemic maneuvers in culture constitutes "violence" and epistemic oppression for Spivak because dominant anglo-european governance structures try to pass off the ideological repertoire of colonial violence as a timeless truth and universal reality. Spivak thinks the broad range of conceptual schemata settler epistemologies work to produce is not accidental because it yields specific goods. This is one way inequality is sustained in democratic societies that depend on settler colonial social structures for the production of wealth: the reliance on prestructural conceptual schemata that uphold the unequal distribution of social goods through the power conferred to public institutions. Legal criteria for the right to sue for an injury (*locus standi*), the rights and immunities in castle doctrines, stand-your-ground laws, and other developments of common law illustrate this.
16. The logic of wounding tied to white settler populations, by contrast, uses the logic of individuation positively to create functional pathways for accessing infrastructural support from settler institutions like the legal system.
17. Consider, for example, Rousseau's (1781) contention that "the savage is a hunter, the barbarian a herdsman, civil man a tiller of the soil. So that regardless of whether one inquires into the origin of the arts or studies the earliest morals [or ways of life, *moeurs*] everything is seen to be related in its principle to the means by which men provide for their subsistence, and as for those among these means that unite men, they are a function of the climate and the nature of the soil. Hence the diversity

of languages and their opposite characteristics must also be explained by the same causes" (Rousseau 1781/2018, p. 282).
18. It performs a powerful value inversion, from the patent settler fantasy that it is, to a prize-worthy humanist narrative by rhetorically constructing structural violence and european hegemony as an impersonal force.
19. Taylor 1982, as cited in Maffie, 2009, p. 53.
20. Another example is Trump's Executive Order 13950 (2020) (the forerunner to divisive and prohibited concepts legislation discussed in Chapter 1), which prohibits "blame-focused" diversity training in federal work and contracting in order to eliminate antiracist educational initiatives in the United States, especially those that discuss whites' enslavement of nonwhite peoples: "Research also suggests that blame-focused diversity training reinforces biases and decrease opportunities for minorities." Refer also to Chapter 1.
21. Including in the cottage industry of bioarchaeological textbooks and popular histories that portray cultural entropy and decay as evolutionary features of societies that failed to adapt to change, rather than the result of ongoing *cultural genocide* (A term the Geneva Convention originally refused to include in its definition of genocide).
22. Speed, 2019, p. 1.
23. Deer, 2015, p. 51.
24. Such an approach is not necessary to reject structurally produced gendered violence in settler colonial societies. In keeping with Zapatismo, I remain strongly committed to the view that we cannot have conceptual protagonists in a settler colonial epistemic economy as a mainstay of strategies of self-defense against structural oppression; diversity is critical to responding to the homeostatic systems features and capacities of white dynastic formations. This is why I framed the notion of hermeneutic violence in Chapter 4 as I did. This does not mean that we do not need to cultivate cultural and intellectual traditions rooted in a feminist politics of citation (Ahmed, 2017). Quite the opposite. Such practices are necessary and that necessity holds in type and scale.
25. Wolfe, 1999; 2006.
26. Wolfe, 2006, p. 388.
27. Wolfe, 2006, p. 390.
28. The white supremacist (and debunked) rhetoric of "replacement theory" is a deceptively simple and transparent value inversion of the settler colonial project itself; it describes what white settlers have aimed to do for half a millennium, but assigns the value "bad" to it when ascribing it to people of color.
29. Refer to introduction, note 2. For extended analysis of the critique, refer, for example, to Barker, 2017; Kēhaulani Kauanui, 2016; Speed, 2017.
30. Wolfe, 1999, p. 2.
31. As the literature on environmental racism shows, while global warming and anthropogenic environmental change is rapidly raising the risks to a large number of the world's peoples, those who can afford to mitigate risk factors will continue to be associated with white dynastic polities and to the skewed access to socioeconomic resources of such polities.

32. Gilmore, 2007.
33. The concept of "the logic of containment" is useful here because it shows how colonial violence traversed various settler conceptual and biocultural strategies (such as the creation of controlling racial taxonomies) to achieve unified goals of providing enduring wealth for white lineages of settlement. It upends the settler conceptual schemata of racialization that controlled Black labor through (among other things) the one-drop rule, exploited Brown labor through reverse one-drop rules of Spanish blood, and dispossessed Native peoples of their lands through genocidal violence, spatial containment, and blood quantum rules. Containment and elimination are thus not mutually exclusive, even in the logic of containment's negative uses of force as noncontainment and impunity for violence. This is illustrated in the staggering rates of sexual violence and forced disappearance Native women face, but also in the structured impunity of non-Native perpetrators who rape Native women on Native lands (as is illustrated by the fact that the majority of rapes against Native women are perpetrated by non-Native men).
34. Méndez y Néstor Jiménez, 2020.
35. In 1987, a report funded by the Department of Justice suggested that the cost of convict lease and labor in private prison systems could not compete with cheap Mexican labor in and out of prisons (National Institute of Justice, 1987).
36. Mei-Singh, 2021, p. 76. I distinguish between carceral geographies, which are settler colonial administrative vehicles, and survivor-centered principles of restitution that incorporate the potential for punitive measures as part of restoring safety to survivors and communities. Industrial caging is a particularly western and modern approach to violence mitigation. Deer, for instance endorses "responses to rape that include elements of both retribution and restoration" (2015, p. 135) in the context of histories of US jurisdictional intrusions in tribal law and "male-dominated peacemaking models" (p. 135). Deer aptly notes that the inefficacy of some rehabilitation-based programs are due to the strategic underfunding and redirection of funds toward narrow state-licensed victim services (p. 147).
37. Young 2000; 2002.
38. Deer, 2015.
39. Kēhaulani Kauanui, 2016.
40. Marcos, 2014, n.p.
41. Ejército Zapatista de Liberación Nacional, 2015.
42. It should be clear by now that these logics are not self-caused; they arise as emergent phenomena from the social reproduction processes that have underpinned settler colonial dynastic formations since antiquity. As Chapter 4 highlights, a systems framing does not absolve individuals or cultures from responsibility over social processes. I only reject the agent-based modeling of structural oppression that is continuously used to place perpetrators at all levels (individual, institutional, cultural) in the tunnels of impunity that make accountability to the people targeted by such processes out of reach.
43. Valles 2018, p. 116.
44. Deer, 2015; Ritchie, 2017; Speed, 2021.

45. This is an example of the "leveling down" of settler epistemic concern. Refer to Valles, 2018, pp. 171–172.
46. Krystal, 1978; Stolorow, 2007.
47. In the humanities, two models have prevailed following the assumptive trends in Cartesian and post-Cartesian traditions: psychoanalysis and narrative theory, the latter of which approaches trauma from the notion of relationality, and both of which include corresponding feminist approaches. Some of these texts, such as Susan Brison's landmark work, *Aftermath*, have been curative in the healing processes of individuals recovering from experiences of violence, especially rape. They have helped some survivors make sense of experiences that were meant to undo us as individuals, to inflict a terror that has both has a bodily object and that proceeds in time without one—a dizzying and dislocating feeling. This account can also be found in Gloria Anzaldúa's work and her idea of "intimate terrorism" in psychic life (1987). The concern is thus not with what these texts do or don't do, it is with a wider structured inattention to how trauma has been used strategically as an institutional technology to consolidate colonial dispossession, whether in feminist theory or elsewhere.
48. Carson, 2006, p. 7.
49. This was a shaky time politically, with renewed calls for oligarchical rule in the aftermath of the Peloponnesian War and the need to contain the helot uprisings since the second Messenian War.
50. Diamond, 1997, p. 9, emphasis added.
51. Carson, 2006, p. 7.
52. For example, in a recent episode of *Black Mirror*, a twenty-two-year-old Black man is violently kidnapped at gunpoint by a white middle-aged man who killed his own fiancé and the driver of another vehicle while texting and driving, admittedly, out of sheer boredom. Unable to accept the outcome of his actions, he brutalizes and psychologically tortures his victim in order to attract the attention of the social media company he blames for addicting him to his phone. The script culminates in a late-staged apology to his victim. What is staged is not the apology, but the response: a hokey, *Oh, that's ok!* This is emblematic of the staging and restaging of (non)resistance to organized trauma. It has a function. And the mechanism is not just settler cinema (a modern version of tragic plays) and aesthetics, but education as well. Trauma has always been designed to create a pathos of distance from pain for some populations, so that others acquiesce and mirror what Amphitryon says to Lykos in Euripides's play *Herakles*: "Our death is your decree, we acquiesce. It must be as you say." But we do not acquiesce. This is why it is not accidental that *Birth of a Nation* maintains a near perfect (98 percent) critic score, for as long as there is resistance to the consolidation of the settler colonial project, resistance will be met with wide and ever-expansive nets of interconnected force.
53. Attanasio et al., 2019. One important point of these appeals to tragedy is to avoid broadening the reach of *Iniuria*. The 1989 Exxon-Valdez oil spill and other man-made disasters, for example, are similarly portrayed as environmental "tragedies" to prevent Indigenous peoples harmed by structurally foreseeable consequences of

human actions from seeking relief in response to injury, especially through settler legal mechanisms.
54. Combatimos La Tiranía, 2020 (my translation).
55. Fregoso, 2003, p. 14.
56. There's undoubtedly a varied human physiological reaction to pain from psychic or physical injury that is modulated by a complex range of biocultural factors. But the *special* connection of pain to the notion of tragedy—for example, the particular way it is operationalized, actualized, and in which it functions in an organized social system—is what I'm drawing attention to.
57. It must be kept alive (e.g., actively endorsed and continuously put to use to reinforce its narrow function over time), even if it originates in the historical design of settler colonial social structures. This is not analogous to the interactionist theories of social structuration discussed in Chapter 1. The dynamics involved in keeping alive specific interrelations made possible by a critically anchored cultural design (such as white dynastic formations) are more analogous to processes of optimization in complex systems and dual-phase evolution that arise in response to modifications in network interconnections. Social iterations of system design are critically important for interlocking oppressions because more iterations are often needed to create convergence; the fact that certain domains interlock with one another (and at disparate rates) is not a natural happenstance in human history.
58. IPN, 2022.
59. Deer, 2015, p. 44.
60. Stolorow, 2007, pp. 15–16.
61. This differs, for example, from calls to politicize deaths from gun violence, particularly on social media outlets. (The #IfIDieInaMassShooting campaign sought to mobilize efforts against the gun lobby and lax regulations of rapid-fire weaponry through the slogan "If I die in a mass shooting, politicize my death.")
62. Moreover, the elitist idea that most people don't really know about the worldly precarities they face is built on the settler colonial assumption that the world is generally *a safe place* that is worthy of trust until an unexpected, tragic event disrupts that tacit expectation of temporal flow through the fragmenting effects of trauma. This assumption of safeness is not rooted in universal normative grounds, such as in the idea that all children deserve to feel safe and physically secure in the world around them, but in the premise that the spatial and temporal coordinates around one *already belong to one's cultural tradition, giving one prereflective access to its interpretive resources*. This is the other side of the hermeneutic violence coin: that settler populations accumulate interpretive wealth for epistemic *profit* (Chapter 3).
63. Million, 2013, p. 90.
64. Patricia Hill Collins (2017) points out this aspect of Simone de Beauvoir's work when Beauvoir portrays Black Americans (and US Black women in particular) as pathologically traumatized by slavery, almost irredeemably broken as possible subjects of freedom.
65. Million, 2013, p. 102, emphasis added.
66. Million, 2013, p. 178.

406 NOTES

67. Wolfe, 1999, p. 167.
68. Million, 2013, p. 29.
69. The $6 billion "Maya Train" transportation megaproject in Mexico, which seeks to connect tourist ports to archaeological sites on predominantly Indigenous lands under the guise of connecting Indigenous infrastructure to public services, is another example.
70. McKittrick, 2006.
71. A recent study of PTSD in orphaned and homeless Haitian children who "experienced multiple traumas such as neglect, maltreatment, psychological, physical and sexual abuse" failed to obtain scores reaching clinical rates for PTSD for any more than 15 percent of the children studied (Cénat et al., 2018). The conclusion: Haitian "street children" are incredibly resilient, wherein "a large majority presented a level of resilience between moderate to very high." While Haitian children are undoubtedly resilient, the discourse of resilience is often applied to structurally traumatized populations to produce what Tuck and Yang (2012) call a "settler move to innocence" in an attempt to evade complicity in creating and maintaining colonial violences that force people to become resilient or die. As Williams and Mohammed (2013) have shown, resilience comes with a high cost; it has measurable health effects that contribute to population-level health inequities that not all populations face (refer also to Bassett et al., 2012).
72. Sertler, in press.
73. Maracle, 2015.
74. Berenstain, 2016.
75. Césaire, 1955/2000, p. 36.
76. Grand & Salberg, 2016.
77. In 2015, geneticist Rachel Yehuda led a team of researchers from Mount Sinai in a series of studies that showed descendants of Holocaust survivors have altered stress hormones that impact their ability to "bounce back" from stress or illness, particularly PTSD (Rodriguez 2015). Native geneticist LeManuel "Lee" Bitsoi (Navajo) aptly notes that epigeneticists' recent findings of historical traumas are hardly news to Native Americans, as "Native healers, medicine people and elders have always known this and it is common knowledge in Native oral traditions" (qtd. in Pember, 2016).
78. Sossenheimer, 2018.
79. Sossenheimer, 2018, pp. 537–538, emphasis added.
80. Brave Heart & DeBruyn, 1998; Fellner, 2018; Linklater, 2014; Methot, 2019; Million, 2013.
81. Ruíz & Sertler, 2019.
82. LaRocque, 1990, as paraphrased in Million, 2013, p. 93.
83. Rosa-Linda Fregoso (2003; Fregoso & Brejarano, 2010), for example, has powerfully laid out the case for asymmetry and siege in the torture and killing of Brown and Indigenous women. Her work has been critical to feminist efforts to stem the tide of femicide and forced disappearances of Mexican women and to linking gender-based

violence with structural violence. Victoria Sanford's forensic anthropological work documenting mass graves has also been important in this regard.
84. Valdivia & Okowí, 2021.
85. Secretaría de Relaciones Exteriores, 2007.
86. Speed, 2021, pp. 30–32. Refer also to Bird, 1997.
87. In "Trauma-Informed Social Policy: A Conceptual Framework for Policy Analysis and Advocacy" (2016) Elizabeth Bowen and Nadine Murshid apply the principles of trauma-informed care ("conceptualized as an organizational change process centered on principles intended to promote healing and reduce the risk of retraumatization for vulnerable individuals") to social policy (p, 223). Bowen and Murshid's proposal can prove helpful in developing examples of incidence approaches to trauma if structures are understood as nonaccidental relations between elements in settler societies rather than objectively neutral sets of social relations.
88. Speed, 2019, p. 286.
89. And this, again, functions in relation to the system goal of wealth concentration and accumulation for white dynastic polities, whose membership also dynamically interacts with the system to reproduce whiteness over long-term cultural and demographic transformations.
90. Blazina & Cox, 2022.
91. Young, 2000, p. 238.
92. Young, 2000, p. 237.
93. Young's "principles of postcolonial governance" call for a "global regulatory regime" surrounding "peace and security; environment; trade and finance; investment and capital utilization." Young is able to present this model of soft sovereignty by implying that what Indigenous peoples really care about is cultural expression and recognition—a position increasingly popular in social science research that reduces work in Indigenous political theory and the "Land Back" movement to exemplars of "cultural representation." It's an old hat trick that many Indigenous scholars have criticized (Coulthard, 2014). Moreover, while the argument against self-determination as a closed border system wielded by powerful and wealthy nations has critical and nuanced versions in international gender-based asylum and LGBTQ + rights policy work, Young does not sufficiently seize the opportunity to connect the idea that "states do not have the right to be indifferent to circumstances of those outside their borders" to these struggles in a colonial context. This is because Young understands the "post" in postcolonialism as temporal, political, and geographic term that signifies "after," not "continuing under different contexts" (as Said and most "postcolonial" thinkers use the term).
94. Young, 2000 p. 254, emphasis added.
95. Young, 2000, p. 249.
96. White feminist philosophers aren't the only ones to create neocolonial back routes, of course. As I've argued elsewhere (Ruíz 2019), Fanon's work can easily be a lifeline for colonialism. This is why I lean toward the systems framework. It is

compatible with intersectional framework I describe as doing the necessary work of counterformations (Ruíz 2017). The anticolonial systems framework draws on what I think are the systems features of intersectionality (so I'm emphasizing them), but they were already there. What I do think the anticolonial systems framework can be opposed to is the co-optation of intersectional narratives in academe that portray it as a toolkit for white people to think about the various dimensions of their identities.

97. This is just a restatement of what the system I'm describing is, and how it plausibly does what it does as a system. The importance of self-organization bears repeating. In nonlinear system dynamics, self-organization is simply a novel outcome that occurs without any agent in the system directing change toward the new pattern being observed (Banzaf, 2009).

98. Santos, 2018, p. 109. Refer to Chapter 3, note 41.

99. Young (2005) develops her earlier theory of a "decentered federalism" into a "horizontal federalism" (p. 144) of "mutual respect" in relation to Palestine/Israel relations. This (2005) work is typically cited as evidence Young backed away from her earlier stance against self-determination and now explicitly acknowledges the importance of land and control of land and resources in self-determination struggles. Moreover, in conceiving of self-determination as "nondomination" rather than as "self-determination," it is arguable that Young perhaps went even further than some Indigenous claims to self-determination (p. 140). I do not dispute that Young refined her theory of federalism to be less racist. The problem with Young's framework is that, throughout all its permutations, it is built to close off the possibility of ever removing white occupying settlements from the Indigenous lands they occupy (and maintain control of by force—an important distinction for diasporic communities living on Indigenous territories and Indigenous migrant communities displaced by settler capitalist violence). Instead, the global interconnectedness thesis and the melting pot psychology of being "together-in-difference" informs the analysis of "nondomination." Young reduces the "non-interference model of self-determination" into the "state" model (p. 144). "On this interpretation, for a group to be self-determining means that it controls a sphere over which others have no authority. The non-interference model makes a strong distinction between inside and outside . . . a non-interference model assumes that these autonomous units can be and are properly separate, and need have no interaction other than what they voluntary enter. . . . In fact, the world's peoples are often geographically mixed, or dwell in close proximity to one another, with physical and social environments that jointly affect them" (p. 155). For Young, such model "implicitly allows for domination within, to the extent that it forbids outsiders from interfering if they observe such internal domination" (p. 145). This is exactly how the Mexican government justifies paramilitary and military intervention in autonomous Indigenous regions. While Young agrees that self-determination "means autonomy," she qualifies that such autonomy must lie "within the limits of respect for, and cooperation with, other agents with whom one interacts and with whom one stands in relation"—a relation Young naturalizes into "self-determining units [that] dwell together," as if the settler colonial penetration is complete and irreversible. Young also seeks to apply

her normative criteria "anywhere that groups are interspersed with one another but claiming rights to sovereignty over a territory" (p. 141).
100. Deer, 2015.
101. Deer, 2015, p. 24.
102. Deer, 2015, p. xiv.
103. Deer, 2015, p. 34.
104. Deer, 2015, p. 100.
105. Deer, 2015, p. 106.
106. Ruíz et al., 2023.
107. Young, 2005, p. 146.
108. Moreover, Young purports to represent the true "aspirations" of Indigenous people by claiming that "almost no indigenous people take as their political goal secession from the state which now claims jurisdiction over them to establish their own state" and Young thinks of Indigenous peoples as "distinct" who dwell side by side other "distinct" peoples, leveling settler white polities to Indigenous status, "almost nowhere do indigenous people form a territorially concentrated large group" (p. 142). In the case of Chiapas and Oaxaca, this is patently wrong.
109. Felipe Guamán Poma de Ayala (1615) devoted over a thousand pages of pleas and plights to the Spanish Crown, asking for relief, just as the 2019 US congressional Subcommittee on the Constitution, Civil Rights, and Civil Liberties led by the late John Lewis assembled thousands of pages demonstrating the persistence of white supremacy in voting access regulations.
110. Chemaly, 2018, p. 134.
111. Ruíz et al., 2020. In 2018, it also proposed changing the definition of "gender" to a "biological, immutable condition determined by genitalia at birth" to specifically target the trans community. https://blogs.scientificamerican.com/voices/the-trump-administrations-proposed-redefinition-of-gender-is-scientifically-absurd/. Refer also to the proposed changes to EPA and CDC language.
112. This recalls a problem with Young's critique of the "liability model" of responsibility (Chapter 1), as the settler colonial reading of this critique questions the extent to which there ever was any real liability under this model. (And, as Chapter 2 illustrates, just because we can produce unbroken chains of physical evidence told and corroborated in western logic does not mean, of course, that a settler court will accept it.) Recall also the failure of John Lewis's evidence, referred to in note 109. (Note that the chain of evidence must be presented in causal chains that are consistent with western notions of causal knowledge. For further discussion of the history of western and neo-Aristotelian conception of causal knowledge versus, for example, Aztec thought, refer to Maffie 2014.)
113. Nimatuj, 2021.
114. Nimatuj, 2021, p. 111. The same relationship between sexual assault and enduring colonial matrixes of exploitation holds true for many Indigenous women who testified in the various "memory and reconciliation" tribunals in the late twentieth and early twenty-first centuries.
115. Refer to Gleijeses, 1992.

116. Broder, 1999. What allows the past to repeat itself is not the failure to learn from it. The notion of modal contextualism introduced in Chapter 1 undermines the ability to use history as a functional mechanism of structural innocence (one that admits to only vague and unenforceable claims of moral responsibility). It only does this to a partial and limited extent. As a systems thinker, I recognize how little concepts (that stay as concepts) can do to structure meaningful interventions in settler colonial societies, so the point is not to jot down or define modal contextualism for citational trafficking. No one cares. What I do care about is tracking the operational flow of the adaptive dynamics in white dynastic formations in real time. I think history, thought of in the systems way I explained earlier, can help do this (as can the various Indigenous conceptions of grounded normativity that illuminate the connections between seemingly disconnected aspects of colonial violence). But once you catch where the current is going and what's generating it, countercurrents and materials unsuitable for current transfer are far better weaponry than the abstract thought of knowing the "structure" of what's behind the oppressive phenomena we experience.
117. Another example: current global climate accords and negotiations over climate change reparations for poor and small nations, which bear little responsibility for global warming, illustrate the convergence of semantic (e.g., defining carbon footprints, greenhouse gasses, and emission rates) and causal liability distancing techniques by rich nations. Refer to Chapter 3 on COP27 climate agreements.
118. Coordinated restraint takes various official (policies) and unofficial (practices, or de facto policies) forms that do at least two things: one, they help flip the scripts necessary to justify present and continuing state violence and the need for future bureaucratic interventions, and two, they justify blanket policies of nonintervention for political gain.
119. The temporal splitting of structural causation and observable harms is central to the logic of wounding. It allows the downstream effects of these techniques to manifest in full view while settler states maintain plausible deniability of causal responsibility. A good example is spatial displacement of Indigenous peoples and perilous forced migration of people of color, particularly from South and Central America northward into Mexico, the United States, and Canada.
120. Things that seem only distantly connected are intimately linked through structural causation in settler colonial societies. So when narratives emerge that claim to tackle "structural violence," the majority of the world's inhabitants are impatiently tapping their fingers on a metaphoric court table waiting for obvious statements to be made about who is responsible at the structural level.
121. Koukkannen, 2019.
122. Cabnal, 2010; Colectivo Miradas Críticas, 2017; Marchese, 2019; Paredes, 2008.
123. Crenshaw, 1988, p. 1382.
124. Gramsci, 1948, p. 182. Derek Bell's (1980) interest convergence theory, where "the interest of blacks in achieving racial inequality will be accommodated only when it converges with the interest of whites" (p. 523), bears a family resemblance to Gramsci's framework.
125. Butler, 2016; Marcuse, 1969; Spade, 2011.

126. Ruíz, 2019.
127. Why would theoretical insights into system function be outside the recursive/self-healing capacities of systems? Moreover, I think the more important objection is that having citizenship is not a guarantee of safety and further establishes other pathways to claim jurisdiction over lives and personal decisions. Importantly, state power often penalizes, criminalizes, or otherwise makes it difficult to *not consent* to what the state "offers" as legal protections through marriage or naturalization, such as due process, access to public assistance and Medicaid/Medicare, healthcare decision-making, property rights, etc. So there are very good reasons to want to refuse the so-called options given over by the state.
128. Guevara, 1961.
129. Reif, 1986, p. 147.
130. Randall, 1981; Viterna, 2013.
131. Promoting the reclamation of cultural resources without also insisting on material chains of value transference simply provide recognizable settler pathways for the use of pluriethnic and multicultural recognition tactics to emerge as "solutions."
132. Speed, 2008.
133. Kēhaulani Kauanui, 2016.
134. The origins in leftist organization is longer. For detailed history, consult Muñoz Ramírez, 2008; Hayden, 2002.
135. Metz, 1978, p. 1261.
136. *Hearings before the subcommittee on inter-American economic relationships*, 1977.
137. Peterson, 1983, p. 1.
138. Babb, 2018, p. x.
139. Flores, 2005, p. 699.
140. Kelly, 1993–94, p. 544.
141. Oil was the only point Mexico contested in the negotiations, seeking to maintain national control over oil infrastructures (which benefited white settler and ladino political elites).
142. Behr, 2007.
143. Qtd. in Speed, 2008, p. 137.
144. Speed, 2008, p. 120.
145. Women's Revolutionary Law, qtd in. Speed, Hernández Castillo, Stephen 1990, pp. 3–4.
146. Sieder, 2015, p. 1133.
147. Marichuy, 2017, qtd. in Mora, 2017, p. 175.
148. Refer, for example, to Herrera & Martinez-Alvarez, 2022.
149. Hernández Castillo, 2010, p. 24.
150. Mora, 2017, p. 235.
151. Mora, 2017, p. 50.
152. Quoted in Mora, 2017, p. 87.
153. Collins, 1990.
154. Speed, 2008, p. 174.

155. This is another reason why the capacities-and-capabilities approach is so popular in humanitarian discourses.
156. But you can also get culturally gaslit when calling this out.
157. Cancik, 2002, p. 19.
158. "If we were to conduct an initial survey of how Roman masculinity is interpreted in modern historical analyses, we would perceive the predominance of two distinct types of masculine identities: one which highlights the noblemen, aristocrats, and righteous as the ones who commanded and held power, and the other which defined their clients, men hailing from the common or dependent class, those who served the first group and could be marginalized . . . two fundamental concepts for the formation of the roman ethos, dignitas and infamia, have been interpreted mainly as the first one refers to members of the elite, while the second almost always is associated with the lower classes. . . . Dignitas is almost always used to designate one with prestige, dignity, honor, and virtue, while infamia was its opposite, the mark of the dishonored, of ill repute, the discredited, the criminal" (Feitosa & Garrafoni 2010, pp. 60–61).
159. Cancik, 2002, pp. 20–21.
160. Escobar, 2020, p. 139.
161. Klein, 2009, p. x.

Bibliography

Aalbers, M. B. (Ed.). (2012). *Subprime cities: The political economy of mortgage markets.* Wiley-Blackwell.

Abrams, S. (2020). Statement of Stacey Y. Abrams, founder & chair, Fair Fight Action on continuing challenges to the Voting Rights Act since *Shelby County v. Holder* before the House Judiciary's Subcommittee on the Constitution, Civil Rights, and Civil Liberties, June 25, 2019, by Stacey Abrams. In H. C. Richardson, K. M. Kruse, C. Anderson, H. A. Thompson, & S. Abrams (Eds.), *Voter suppression in U.S. elections* (pp. 139–148). University of Georgia Press.

Acuña Delgado, A. (2006). *La construcción cultural del cuerpo en la sociedad rarámuri de la Sierra Tarahumara.* Abya-Yala.

Adler, J. (2012). Cognitive bias: Interracial homicide in New Orleans, 1921–1945. *Journal of Interdisciplinary History, 43*(1), 43–61. https://doi.org/10.1162/JINH_a_00338.

Adorno, R. (1992). The discursive encounter of Spain and America: The authority of eyewitness testimony in the writing of history. *William and Mary Quarterly, 49*(2), 210–228. https://doi.org/10.2307/2947270.

Aglietta, M. (1976). *A theory of capitalist regulation.* Verso Books.

Agren. D. (2017). Mexican man cleared in sexual assault of schoolgirl because he didn't "enjoy" it. *The Guardian.* March 28, 2017, https://www.theguardian.com/world/2017/mar/28/mexican-man-cleared-sexual-assault-schoolgirl-because-he-didnt-enjoy-it.

Ahern, K. (2018). Institutional betrayal and gaslighting: Why whistle-blowers are so traumatized. *Journal of Perinatal & Neonatal Nursing, 32*(1), 59–65.

Ahlskog, J. (2016). R. G. Collingwood and the concept of testimony: A story about autonomy and reliance. *Clio, 45*(2), 181–204.

Ahmed, S. (2003). The politics of fear in the making of worlds. *International Journal of Qualitative Studies in Education, 16*(3), 377–398.

Ahmed, S. (2004). Declarations of whiteness: The non-performativity of anti-racism. *Meridians, 7*(1), 104–126.

Ahmed, S. (2012). *On being included: Racism and diversity in institutional life.* Duke University Press.

Ahmed, S. (2017). *Living a Feminist life.* Duke University Press.

Ahmed, S. (2021). *Complaint!* Duke University Press.

Alabama State Board of Education. (2021). Resolution declaring the preservation of intellectual freedom and non-discrimination in Alabama public schools. Alabama State Archives. https://www.alabamaachieves.org/wp-content/uploads/2021/08/ALSBOE-Resolution-Declaring-the-Preservation-of-Intellectual-Freedom-and-Non-Discrimination-in-AL-Public-Schools.pdf.

Alarcón, N. (1983). Chicana's feminist literature: A re-vision through Malintzin/or Malintzin. Putting flesh back on the object. In C. Moraga & G. Anzaldúa (Eds.), *This bridge called my back: Writings by radical women of color* (2nd ed., pp. 182–190). Kitchen Table Women of Color Press.

Albelda, R., & Tilly, C. (1994). Towards a broader vision: Race, gender, and labor market segmentation in the social structure of accumulation framework. In D. M. Kotz, T. McDonough, & M. Reich (Eds.), *Social structures of accumulation: The political economy of growth and crisis* (pp. 212–230). Cambridge University Press.

Alberro, S. (1981). *La actividad del Santo Oficio de la Inquisición en Nueva España, 1571–1700.* INAH.

Alexander, M. (2012). *The new Jim Crow: Mass incarceration in the age of colorblindness* (rev. ed.). New Press.

Alexander, M. (2020). *The new Jim Crow: Mass incarceration in the age of colorblindness* (10th Anniversary ed.). New Press.

Alexander, M. J., & Mohanty, C. T. (1997). *Feminist genealogies, colonial legacies, democratic futures.* Routledge.

Allen, A., Mann, A., Marcano, D.-D., Moody-Adams, M., & Scott, J. (2008). Situated voices: Black women in/on the profession of philosophy. *Hypatia, 23*(2), 160–189.

Allen, T. W. (2012). *The invention of the white race* (Vol. 1). Verso Books.

Allport, G. W. (1954). *The nature of prejudice.* Addison-Wesley.

Alqaisiya, W. (2018). Decolonial queering: The politics of being queer in Palestine. *Journal of Palestine Studies, 47*(3), 29–44. https://doi/org/10.1525/jps.2018.47.3.29.

American Academy of Arts and Sciences. (2022). Is justice open to all? https://www.amacad.org/publication/measuring-civil-justice-all/section/3.

American Cancer Society. (2022). Cancer facts & figures for African American / Black people. American Cancer Society, Inc. https://www.cancer.org/research/cancer-facts-statistics/cancer-facts-figures-for-african-americans.html.

AMNLAE. (1984). *Por eso las mujeres respaldamos al F.S.L.N.!* Asociación de mujers Nicaragüenses Luisa Amanda Espinosa.

Andersson, U., Edgren, M., Karlsson, L., & Nilsson, G. (Eds.). (2019). *Rape narratives in motion.* Palgrave Macmillan.

Andreas, H., & Zenker, F. (2014). Basic concepts of structuralism. *Erkenntnis, 79*(Supp. 8), 1367–1372. https://doi.org/10.1007/s10670-013-9572-y.

Anzaldúa, G. (1987). *Borderlands / La Frontera: The New Mestiza.* Aunt Lute Books.

Archivo General de la Nación. (1910). *Proceso inquisitorial del cacique de Tetzcoco.* E. Gómez de la Puerte.

Aristotle. (2013). *Politics*, trans. Carnes Lord. University of Chicago Press.

Ariza, M., & De Oliveira, O. (1999). Inequidades de género y clase: Algunas consideraciones analíticas. *Nueva Sociedad, 164*(1), 70–81.

Arjava, A. (1996). *Women and law in late antiquity.* Oxford University Press.

Arwen, C., Silvano, M., & Ruiz i Altaba. (2022). On the origin of metastases: Induction of pro-metastatic states after impending cell death via ER stress, reprogramming, and a cytokine storm. *Cell Reports, 38*(10), 110490. https://doi/org/10.1016/j.celrep.2022.110490.

Ask, K., Rebelius, A., & Granhag, P. (2008). The "elasticity" of criminal evidence: A moderator of investigator bias. *Applied Cognitive Psychology, 22*(9), 1245–1259.

Associated Press. (2022a, August 9). A grand jury declined to indict a women whose accusations set off Emmett Till killing. *NPR.* https://www.npr.org/2022/08/09/1116562931/grand-jury-emmett-till-woman-carolyn-bryant-donham.

Associated Press. (2022b, November 13). Artemisa Gentileschi's censored nude painting to be digitally unveiled. *The Guardian.* https://www.theguardian.com/world/2022/nov/13/artemisia-gentileschi-nude-painting-allegory-of-inclination-restoration-italy.

Atiles-Osoria, J. M. (2012). The criminalisation of anti-colonial struggle in Puerto Rico. In S. Poynting & D. Whyte (Eds.), *Counter-terrorism and state political violence: The "war on terror" as terror* (pp. 156–177). Routledge.

Attanasio, C., Bleiberg, J., & Weber, P. J. (2019, August 9). Police: El Paso shooting suspect said he targeted Mexicans. *Associated Press*. https://apnews.com/article/shootings-el-paso-texas-mass-shooting-us-news-ap-top-news-immigration-456c0154218a4d378e2fb36cd40b709d.

Aviv, R. (2022, September 5). The victim who became the accused. *New Yorker*. New York Vol. XCVIII, September 12, 2022 https://www.newyorker.com/magazine/2022/09/12/the-victim-who-became-the-accused.

Ayto, J. (1994). *Dictionary of word origins*. Columbia Marketing.

Ba, D. (2007, September 5). Africans still seething over Sarkozy speech. *Reuters*. https://www.reuters.com/article/uk-africa-sarkozy/africans-still-seething-over-sarkozy-speech-idUKL0513034620070905.

Babb, S. (2018). *Managing Mexico: Economists from nationalism to neoliberalism*. Princeton University Press.

Bach, K. (2005). Context ex machina. In Zoltan Gendler Szabo (Ed.), *Semantics versus pragmatics* (pp. 15–44). Oxford University Press.

Bailey, A. (2007). Strategic ignorance. In S. Sullivan & N. Tuana (Eds.), *Race and epistemologies of ignorance* (pp. 77–94). State University of New York Press.

Bailey, M. & Trudy. (2018). On misogynoir: Citation, erasure, and plagiarism. *Feminist Media Studies*, 18(4), 762–768.

Bailey, Z., Krieger, N., Agénor, M., Graves, J., Linos, N., & Bassett, M. (2017). Structural racism and health inequities in the USA: Evidence and interventions. *The Lancet*, 389(10077), 1453–1463.

Bak, P., Tang, C., & Wiesenfeld, K. (1987). Self-organized criticality: An explanation of the 1/f noise. *Physical review letters*, 59(4), 381.

Baker, R. B., Fargo, J. D., Shambley-Ebron, D., & Sommers, M. S. (2010). A source of healthcare disparity: Race, skin color, and injuries after rape among adolescents and young adults. *Journal of Forensic Nursing*, 6(3), 144–150. https://doi.org/10.1111/j.1939-3938.2010.01070.

Baldwin, B. (2015). Backsliding: The United States Supreme Court, Shelby County v. Holder and the dismantling of Voting Rights Act of 1965. *Berkeley Journal of African-American Law and Policy*, 16(2), 251–262.

Banaji, M. R., Greenwald, A. G., Zanna, M. P., & Olson, J. M. (1994). Implicit stereotyping and prejudice. In Mark Zanna & James Olson (Eds.), *The psychology of prejudice: The Ontario symposium, volume 7* (pp. 55–76). L. Erlbaum Associates.

Banzhaf, W. (2009). Self-organizing systems. In R. Meyers (Ed.), *Encyclopedia of complexity and systems science* (pp. 8040–8050). Springer.

Baradaran, M. (2017). *The color of money: Black banks and the racial wealth gap*. Harvard University Press.

Barker, J. (2017). *Critically sovereign: Indigenous gender, sexuality, and feminist studies*. Duke University Press.

Bartky, S. L. (2015). *Femininity and domination: Studies in the phenomenology of oppression*. Taylor & Francis.

Bartscher, A. K., Schularick, M., Kuhn, M., & Wachtel, P. (2022). Monetary policy and racial inequality. *Brookings Papers on Economic Activity*, 2022(1), 1–63.

Bassett, D., Tsosie, U., & Nannauck, S. (2012). "Our culture is medicine": Perspectives of Native healers on post-trauma recovery among American Indian and Alaska Native patients. *Permanente Journal, 16*(1), 19–27. https://doi.org/10.7812/tpp/11-123.

Bazelon, E. (2014, November 25). Do online death threats count as free speech? *New York Times Magazine.* https://www.nytimes.com/2014/11/30/magazine/do-online-death-threats-count-as-free-speech.html.

Beardsworth, S. (2009). Overcoming the confusion of loss and trauma: The need of thinking historically. In K. B. Golden & B. G. Bergo (Eds.), *The trauma controversy: Philosophical and interdisciplinary dialogues* (pp. 45–70). State University of New York Press.

Beattie, G. (2013). *Our racist heart? An exploration of unconscious prejudice in everyday life.* Routledge.

Beattie, G., Cohen, D., & McGuire, L. (2013). An exploration of possible unconscious ethnic biases in higher education: The role of implicit attitudes on selection for university posts. *Semiotica, 2013*(197), 171–201.

Beckfield, J. (2018). *Political sociology and the people's health.* Oxford University Press.

Beilharz, P., & Cox, L. (2007). Settler capitalism revisited. *Thesis Eleven, 88,* 112–123.

Bell, D. (1980). Brown v. Board of Education and the interest-convergence dilemma. *Harvard Law Review, 93,* 518, 767–779.

Bell, D. (1988). White superiority in America: Its legal legacy, its economic costs. *Villanova Law Review, 33,* 767.

Bell, D. (1990). After we're gone: Prudent speculations on America in a post-racial epoch. *St. Louis University Law Journal, 34*(393), 393–397.

Bell, D. (1992). *Faces at the bottom of the well: The permanence of racism.* Basic Books.

Bell, D. (1993). The racism is permanent thesis: Courageous revelation or unconscious denial of racial genocide. *Capital University Law Review, 22*(571), 1–14.

Bellantuono, A. J., Bridge, D., & Martínez, D. E. (2015). Hydra as a tractable, long-lived model system for senescence. *Invertebrate Reproduction & Development, 9*(sup1), 39–44. https://doi.org/10.1080/07924259.2014.938196.

Ben-Moshe, L. (2020). *Decarcerating disability: Deinstitutionalization and prison abolition.* University of Minnesota Press.

Bensinger. K. (2022, October 28). Federal judge allows activists to stake out ballot boxes in Arizona. *New York Times.*

Benton, L. (2012). *Law and colonial cultures.* Columbia University Press.

Berenstain, N. (2016). Epistemic exploitation. *Ergo: An Open Access Journal of Philosophy, 3*(22) 569–590. http://dx.doi.org/10.3998/ergo.12405314.0003.022.

Berenstain, N. (2018). Stem cell clinics, medical gaslighting, and epistemic marginalization, *Symposium: Epistemology and injustice in stem cell clinics,* Pacific APA, San Diego, CA.

Berenstain. N. (2019). Intersectionality, modality, and structural oppression [paper presentation]. Bled Epistemology Conference: Social Epistemology and the Politics of Knowing, Bled, Slovenia.

Berenstain, N. (2020). White feminist gaslighting. *Hypatia, 35*(4), 733–758.

Berenstain, N., & Ruíz, E. (2021). Moving beyond epistemic oppression. *Contemporary Political Theory, 21*(2), 283–290. https://doi.org/10.1057/s41296-021-00483-z.

Berger, R. J., Searles, P., & Neuman, W. L. (1988). The dimensions of rape reform legislation. *Law and Society Review, 22*(2), 329–357.

Bernasconi, R. (2007). The return to Africa: Hegel and the question of the racial identity of the Egyptians. In Philip Grier (Ed.), *Identity and Difference* (pp. 201–216). State University of New York Press.

Betancur, J. J., & Herring, C. (Eds.). (2012). *Reinventing race, reinventing racism*. Brill.

Bethencourt, F. (2009). *The Inquisition: A global history, 1478–1834*. Cambridge University Press.

Beverley, J. (2001). What happens when the subaltern speaks. In Arturo Arias (Ed.), *The Rigoberta Menchú controversy* (pp. 219–236). University of Minnesota Press.

Beverly, J. (2013). Testimonio, subalternidad y autoridad narrativa. In Norman Denzin & Yvonne Lincol (Ed.), *Manual de investigación cualitativa* (pp. 343–360). Gedisa.

Beyer, J. (2022). Native American communities continue to face barriers to opportunity that stifle economic mobility. *Indigenous Policy Journal, 33*(1), 1–12.

Bhattacharyya, G. (2018). *Rethinking racial capitalism: Questions of reproduction and survival*. Rowman & Littlefield International.

Biber, K. (2010). Fact-finding, proof and Indigenous knowledge: Teaching evidence in Australia. *Alternative Law Journal, 35*(4), 208–212. https://doi.org/10.1177/1037969X1003500404.

Bielshowski, R. (2009, April). Sixty years of ECLAC: Structuralism and neo-structuralism, *CEPAL Review*, 171–192.

Bierria, A. (2014). Missing in action: Violence, power, and discerning agency. *Hypatia, 29*(1), 129–145. https://doi.org/10.1111/hypa.12074.

Bierria, A. (2007/2017). Pursuing a radical anti-violence agenda inside/outside a nonprofit structure. In Incite! Women of Color against Violence (Ed.), *The revolution will not be funded: Beyond the non-profit industrial complex* (pp. 151–163). Duke University Press.

Bierria, A., Caruthers J., & Lober, B. (Eds.). (2022). *Abolition feminisms* (Vol. 2). Haymarket Books.

Blazina, C., & Cox, K. (2022, November 28). Black and white Americans are far apart in their views of reparations for slavery. Pew Research Center. https://www.pewresearch.org/fact-tank/2022/11/28/black-and-white-americans-are-far-apart-in-their-views-of-reparations-for-slavery.

Bobo, L. D. (2001). Racial attitudes and relations at the close of the twentieth century. In N. Smelser, W. Wilson, & F. Mitchell (Eds.), *America becoming: Racial trends and their consequences* (pp. 262–299). National Academy Press.

Bohlander, M. (2001). International criminal tribunals and their power to punish contempt and false testimony. *Criminal Law Forum, 12*(1), 91–118.

Bøndergaard, J. (2017). *Forensic memory: Literature after testimony*. Springer.

Bonilla-Silva, E. (2015). The structure of racism in color-blind, "post-racial" America. *American Behavioral Scientist, 59*(11), 1358–1376.

Boone, E., & Mignolo, W. (1994/2002). *Writing without words*. Duke University Press.

Borrell, L. N., Elhawary, J. R., Fuentes-Afflick, E., Witonsky, J., Bhakta, N., Wu, A. H. B., Bibbins-Domingo, K., et al. (2021). Race and genetic ancestry in medicine—a time for reckoning with racism. *New England Journal of Medicine, 384*(5), 474–480.

Burchard, E. G., Ziv, E., Coyle, N., Gomez, S. L., Tang, H., Karter, A. J., Mountain, J. L., Pérez-Stable, E. J., Sheppard, D., & Risch, N. (2003). The importance of race and ethnic background in biomedical research and clinical practice. *New England Journal of Medicine, 234*(12), 1170–1175.

Bouchereau, P., & Coquio, C. (2017). *La grande coupure: Essai de philosophie testimoniale*. Classiques Garnier.
Bourdieu, P. (1990). *The logic of practice* (R. Nice, Trans.). Cambridge University Press.
Bowen, E. A., & Murshid, N. S. (2016). Trauma-informed social policy: A conceptual framework for policy analysis and advocacy. *American Journal of Public Health*, 106(2), 223–229. https://doi.org/10.2105/AJPH.2015.302970.
Bowles, S., Gordon, D. M., & Weisskopf, T. E. (1986). Power and profits: The social structure of accumulation and the profitability of the postwar US economy. *Review of radical political economics*, 18(1–2), 132–167.
Bowyer, E. (2022). Taking the stand: Women as witnesses in New Zealand's colonial courts, circa 1840–1900. *Law & History: Journal of the Australian and New Zealand Law and History Society*, 9(1), 1–28.
Bradley, K. (1987). On the Roman slave supply and slavebreeding. *Slavery & Abolition*, 8(1), 42–64.
Brave Heart, M. Y., & DeBruyn, L. M. (1998). The American Indian holocaust: Healing historical unresolved grief. *American Indian and Alaska Native Mental Health Research*, 8(2), 60–82. https://pubmed.ncbi.nlm.nih.gov/9842066/.
Braveman, P. (2001). Epidemiology and (neo-)colonialism. *Journal of Epidemiology and Community Health*, 55(3), 160–161.
Breslin, R. A., Daniel, S., and Hylton, K. (2022). Black women in the military: Prevalence, characteristics, and correlates of sexual harassment. *Public Administration Review*, 82, 410–419. https://doi.org/10.1111/puar.13464.
Brison, S. (2002). *Aftermath: Violence and the remaking of a self*. Princeton University Press.
Broder, J. M. (1999, March 11). Clinton offers his apologies to Guatemala. *New York Times*. https://www.nytimes.com/1999/03/11/world/clinton-offers-his-apologies-to-guatemala.html.
Brooker, C. (Writer), & Hawes, J. (Director). (2019, June 5). Smithereens (Season 5, Episode 2) [TV series episode]. In A. Jones & C. Brooker (Executive Producers), *Black Mirror*. Zeppotron; Channel 4 Television Corporation; Babieka; Gran Babieka; Netflix.
Brown, D. A. (2021). *The whiteness of wealth: How the tax system impoverishes Black Americans—and how we can fix it*. Crown Press.
Browne, A. J. (2017). Moving beyond description: Closing the health equity gap by redressing racism impacting Indigenous populations. *Social Science and Medicine*, 184(1), 23–26. https://doi.org/10.1016/j.socscimed.2017.04.045.
Buckley, W. (1967). *Sociology and modern systems theory*. Prentice-Hall.
Buckley, W. (1968). *Society—a complex adaptive system: Essays in social theory*. Routledge.
Bureau of Indian Affairs, US Department of the Interior. (1957, June 27). Memorandum. U.S. Department of the Interior. https://www.bia.gov/node/9302/printable/pdf.
Bureau of National Affairs. (2014). Confrontation: Rape-shield law doesn't block testimony about couple's history of "make-up sex." *Criminal Law Reporter*, 95(22), 642.
Burgess-Jackson, K. (1999). *A most detestable crime: New philosophical essays on rape*. Oxford University Press.
Burks, M. P., Robinson, C., Matthews, J. M., Leigh, B. W., Grattan, P. R., & Hansbrough, G. W. (1837). *Reports of cases in the Supreme Court of Appeals of Virginia*. D. Bottom, Superintendent of Public Print.
Butler, J. (2016). *Frames of war: When is life grievable?* Verso Books.
Byrd, J. A. (2011). *The transit of empire: Indigenous critiques of colonialism*. University of Minnesota Press.

Cabnal, L. (2010). *Feminismos diversos: El feminismo comunitario.* ACSUR-Las Segovias. https://porunavidavivible.files.wordpress.com/2012/09/feminismos-comunitario-lorena-cabnal.pdf.

Calveiro, P. (2009). El testigo narrador. *Puentes,* no. 24, 50–56.

Cameron, L., Courchene, D., Ijaz, S., & Mauro, I. (2019). The turtle lodge: Sustainable self-determination in practice. *AlterNative: An International Journal of Indigenous Peoples, 15*(1), 13–21.

Camus, A. (1942/2018). *The Myth of Sisyphus.* Knopf Doubleday Publishing Group.

Canaza-Choque, F. A. (2021). Nuestro legado: El Buen Vivir, la infaltable alternativa para desestructurar el modelo hegemónico de colonización de la naturaleza. *Revista revoluciones, 3*(6), 78–91.

Cancik, H. (2002). "Dignity of Man" and *"Persona"* in Stoic anthropology: Some remarks on Cicero, *De Officiis* I, 105–107. In D. Kretzmer & E. Klein (Eds.), *The concept of human dignity in human rights discourse* (pp. 19–39). Brill. https://doi.org/10.1163/9789004478190_003.

Cannon, M. J. (2019). *Men, masculinity, and the Indian Act.* UBC Press.

Capra, F. (1997). *The web of life: A new scientific understanding of living systems.* Anchor Books.

Carby, H. (2019). *Imperial intimacies.* Verso Books.

Carmon, I. (2014). Can women stand their ground? Depends on the target. *MSNBC.* https://www.msnbc.com/msnbc/can-women-stand-their-ground-msna288011.

Carson, A. (2006). Tragedy: A curious art form. In Euripides, *Grief lessons: Four plays by Euripides* (A. Carson, Trans., pp. 7–9). NYRB Classics.

Castanien, D. G. (1954). The Mexican inquisition censors a private library, 1655. *Hispanic American Historical Review, 34,* 374–392.

Caws, P. (1988). *Structuralism: The art of the intelligible.* Humanities Press International.

Cawthra, R., O'Brien, G., & Hassanyeh, F. (1987). "Imposed psychosis": A case variant of the gaslight phenomenon. *British Journal of Psychiatry, 150*(4), 553–556.

Cénat, J. M., Derivois, D., Hébert, M., Amédée, L. M., & Karray, A. (2018, May). Multiple traumas and resilience among street children in Haiti: Psychopathology of survival. *Child Abuse Neglect, 79,* 85–97. https://doi.org/10.1016/j.chiabu.2018.01.024.

Césaire, A. (1955/2001). *Discourse on colonialism.* Monthly Review Press.

Chakravartty, P., & Ferreira da Silva, D. (Eds.). (2013). *Race, empire, and the crisis of the subprime.* Johns Hopkins University Press.

Chamallas, M. (1998). The architecture of bias: Deep structures in tort law. *University of Pennsylvania Law Review, 146*(2), 463–531.

Chamallas, M. (2004). Civil rights in ordinary tort cases: Race, gender, and the calculation of economic loss. *Loyola of Los Angeles Las Rev*iew, *38,* 1435, article 11.

Chamallas, M. (2018). Will tort law have its #MeToo moment? *Journal of Tort Law, 11*(1), 39–70.

Chang, M. (2010). *Lifting as we climb: Women of color, wealth, and America's future. Insight Center for Community Economic Development.*

Chemaly, S. (2018). *Rage becomes her: The power of women's anger.* Atria Books.

Cherry, M. (2021). *The case for rage: Why anger is essential to anti-racist struggle.* Oxford University Press.

Cheung, T.-Y., & Zeng, W. (1998). Invariant-preserving transformations for the verification of place/transition systems. *IEEE Transactions on Systems, Man, and Cybernetics - Part A: Systems and Humans, 28*(1), 114–121.

Chin, G. J. (2020). A nation of white immigrants: State and federal racial preferences for white noncitizens. *Boston University Law Review, 100,* 1271–1313.

Christensen, K. (2020). The social structures of accumulation and the labor movement: A brief history and a modest proposal. *Review of Radical Political Economics, 52*(3), 487–505.

Cilliers, J., & Green, E. (2018). The land–labour hypothesis in a settler economy: Wealth, labour and household composition on the South African frontier. *International Review of Social History, 63*(2), 239–271.

Cillo, R., Docoa, L. F., Duque García, C. A., Cámara Izquierdo, S., Fineschi, R., Manigat, M. P., & Mariña Flores, A. (2022). *The general law of capitalist accumulation in Latin America and beyond: Actuality and pertinence.* Lexington Books.

Clark, E. (2013). *The strange history of the American quadroon: Free women of color in the revolutionary Atlantic world.* University of North Carolina Press.

Cline, F. (1983, October 22). Reagan's doubts on Dr. King disclosed. *New York Times.*

Coady, C. (1992). *Testimony: A philosophical study.* Clarendon Press; Oxford University Press.

Cohen, L. (2021, November 24). Former Baltimore County police officer convicted of raping 22-year old women sentenced to home detention. *CBS News.* https://www.cbsnews.com/news/anthony-westerman-rape-baltimore-county-police-officer-home-prison-suspended-sentence/.

Colar, A. (2011, May 30). Psychology Today, the misconception of racism, and the Kanazawa problem: End the racism misconception by removing Kanazawa from Psychology Today. https://www.psychologytoday.com/intl/blog/new-chapter/201105/psychology-today-the-misconception-racism-and-the-kanazawa-problem.

Colectivo Miradas Críticas del Territorio desde el Feminismo. (2017). Mapeando el cuerpo-territorio: Guía metodológica para mujeres que defienden sus territorios. Quito. https://miradascriticasdelterritoriodesdeelfeminismo.files.wordpress.com/2017/11/mapeando-el-cuerpo-territorio.pdf.

Collins, P. H. (1986). Learning from the outsider within: The sociological significance of Black feminist thought. *Social Problems, 33*(6), 14–s32. https://doi.org/10.2307/800672.

Collins, P. H. (1990). *Black feminist thought.* Routledge.

Collins, P. H. (2000). *Black feminist thought* (2nd ed.). Routledge.

Collins, P. H. (2006). *From Black power to hip hop: Racism, nationalism, and feminism.* Temple University Press.

Collins, P. H. (2017). Simone de Beauvoir, women's oppression and existential freedom. In L. Hengehold & N. Bauer (Eds.), *A companion to Simone de Beauvoir* (pp. 325–338). Wiley Blackwell.

Combahee River Collective. (1986/1995). A Black feminist statement. In B. Guy-Sheftall (Ed.), *Words of fire: An anthology of African-American feminist thought,* (pp. 232–240). New Press.

Combatimos La Tiranía. (2020, February 18). *Fuerte discurso de una madre que perdió a su hija.* [Video]. YouTube. https://www.youtube.com/watch?v=F70mqW1nEUg.

Connell, M. (2015). Expert testimony in sexual assault cases: Alcohol intoxication and memory. *International Journal of Law and Psychiatry, 42–43,* 98–105.

Cook-Lynn, E. (1997). Who stole Native American studies? *Wicazo Sa Review, 12*(1), 9–28.

Cooper, A. J. (1892). *A voice from the South.* Aldine Printing House.

Cooper, B. (2018). *Eloquent rage: A Black feminist discovers her superpower*. St. Martin's Press.
Coráñez Bolton, S. (2023). *Crip colony: Mestizaje, US imperialism, and the queer politics of disability in the Philippines*. Duke University Press.
Coulthard, G. S. (2014). *Red skin, white masks: Rejecting the colonial politics of recognition*. University of Minnesota Press.
Coutel, C., & Institut d'étude des faits religieux. (2017). *Témoigner, entre acte et parole: Une herméneutique du témoignage est-elle possible?* Parole et silence.
Cox, A. M. (2013, June 25). The supreme court guts the Voter [*sic*] Rights Act . . . since racism is over. *The Guardian*. https://www.theguardian.com/commentisfree/2013/jun/25/supreme-court-voter-rights-act-racism-over.
Craig. E. (1990). *Knowledge and the state of nature*. Oxford University Press.
Crane, P. T. (2006). "True threats" and the issue of intent. *Virginia Law Review, 92*(6), 1225–1277.
Crenshaw, K. W. (1988). Race, reform, and retrenchment: Transformation and legitimation in antidiscrimination law. *Harvard Law Review, 101*(7), 1331–1387. https://scholarship.law.columbia.edu/faculty_scholarship/2866.
Crenshaw, K. W. (1995). Race, reform, and retrenchment: Transformation and legitimation in antidiscrimination law. In C. West, K. Crenshaw, N. Gotanda, G. Peller, & K. Thomas (Eds.), *Critical race theory: The key writings that formed the movement* (pp. 103–126). New Press.
Crenshaw, K. W. [@sandylocks] (2021, February 22). "We cannot begin to address the obscene injustices in this country without grappling with whiteness—not as a simplistic racial categorization, but as a deeply structured relationship to power and group entitlement."
Crewe, R. D. (2019). *The Mexican mission: Indigenous reconstruction and mendicant enterprise in New Spain, 1521–1600*. Cambridge University Press.
Curiel, O., & Espinosa, Y. (2004). Forjando identidades y movimientos como lesbianas feministas y afro-caribeñas. In Juanita Ramos (Ed.), *Compañeras: Latina Lesbians, Lesbianas Latinoamericanas* (pp. 289–295).
Cusicanqui, S. R. (2019). *Ch'ixinakax utxiwa: On decolonising practices and discourses*. Wiley.
Danticat, E. (2000). *The farming of bones*. Abacus Press.
Davis, A. Y. (1983). *Women, race, and class*. Vintage.
Davis, A. Y. (1998). BBC Interview. https://www.youtube.com/watch?v=x3q_qV5mHg0
Davis, A. Y. (2016). *Freedom is a constant struggle: Ferguson, Palestine, and the foundations of a movement*. Haymarket Books.
Davis, A., & Ernst, R. (2017). Racial gaslighting. *Politics, Groups, and Identities, 7*(4), 1–14.
De Maio, F., & Ansell, D. (2018). "As natural as the air around us": On the origin and development of the concept of structural violence in health research. *International Journal of Health Services, 48*(4), 749–759.
Deer, S. (2015). *The beginning and end of rape: Confronting sexual violence in Native America*. University of Minnesota Press.
Deer, S., & Kronk Warner, E. A. (2019). Raping Indian country. *Columbia Journal of Gender & Law, 38*(1), 31–95.
Deines, P., Lachnit, T., & Bosch, T. C. (2017). Competing forces maintain the hydra metaorganism. *Immunological Reviews, 279*(1), 123–136.

Deleuze, G., & Guattari, F. (1987). *A thousand plateaus: capitalism and schizophrenia* (B. Massumi, Trans.). University of Minnesota Press.

Delgado Bernal, D., Burciaga, R., & Flores Carmona, J. (2016). *Chicana/Latina testimonios as pedagogical, methodological, and activist approaches to social justice.* Routledge.

Deloria, V., & Lytle, C. (1998). *The nations within: The past and future of American Indian sovereignty.* University of Texas Press.

Denoon, D. (1983). *Settler capitalism: The dynamics of dependent development in the southern hemisphere.* Oxford University Press.

Denoon, D. (1995). Settler capitalism unsettled. *New Zealand Journal of History, 29*(2), 129–141.

Dent, G., Davis, A. Y., Richie, B. E., & Meiners, E. R. (2022). *Abolition. Feminism. Now.* Haymarket Books.

Derenoncourt, E., Kim, C. H., Kuhn, M., & Schularick, M. (2022). *Wealth of two nations: The US racial wealth gap, 1860–2020.* (National Bureau for Economic Research Working Paper No. w30101). https://doi.org/10.3386/w30101.

Descola, P. (2016). Transformation transformed. *HAU: Journal of Ethnographic Theory, 6*(3), 33–44. https://www.journals.uchicago.edu/doi/pdfplus/10.14318/hau6.3.005.

Diamond, J. (1997). *Guns, germs, and steel.* Norton.

Diamond, S. (2006). *Anger, madness and the daimonic: The psychological genesis of violence, evil, and creativity.* State University of New York Press.

Dickie, G., & Jessop, S. (2022, November 8). COP27—Corporate climate pledges rife with greenwashing—U.N. Expert group. *Reuters.* https://www.reuters.com/business/cop/un-experts-cop27-corporate-climate-pledges-rife-with-greenwashing-2022-11-08/.

Dieke, A., Zhang, Y., Kissin, Y., Barfield, W., & Boulet, S. (2017). Disparities in assisted reproductive technology utilization by race and ethnicity, United States, 2014: A commentary. *Journal of Women's Health, 26*(6), 605–608.

Diringer, D. (1962). *Writing.* Praeger.

Doane, A. W., & Bonilla-Silva, E. (2013). *White out: The continuing significance of racism.* Taylor & Francis.

Dodds, J. (1991). The impact of the Roman law of succession and marriage on women's property and independence. *Melbourne University Law Review, 18,* 899–917.

Doolittle, R., Pereira, M., Blenkinsop, L., & Agius, J. (2017, February 3). Unfounded: Will the police believe you? *Globe and Mail.* https://www.theglobeandmail.com/news/investigations/compare-unfounded-sex-assault-rates-across-canada/article33855643/.

Dorch, E., & Fontaine, G. (1978). Rate of judges' gaze at different types of witnesses. *Perceptual and Motor Skills, 46*(3), 1103–1106.

Dotson, K. (2011). Tracking epistemic violence, tracking practices of silencing. *Hypatia, 26*(2), 236–257.

Dotson, K. (2012a). A cautionary tale: On limiting epistemic oppression. *Frontiers: A Journal of Women Studies, 33*(1), 24–47.

Dotson, K. (2012b). How is this paper philosophy? *Comparative Philosophy, 3*(1), 3–29.

Dotson, K. (2014a). Conceptualizing epistemic oppression. *Social Epistemology, 28*(2), 115–138.

Dotson, K. (2014b). Making sense: The multistability of oppression and the importance of intersectionality. In N. Goswami, M. O'Donovan, & L. Yount (Eds.), *Why race and gender still matter: An intersectional approach* (pp. 43–57). Pickering and Chatto.

Dotson, K. (2015). Inheriting Patricia Hill Collins's black feminist epistemology. *Ethnic and Racial Studies, 38*(13), 2322–2328.

Dotson, K. (2017a). On the way to decolonization in a settler colony: Re-introducing Black feminist identity politics. *AlterNative*, *14*(3), 190–199.
Dotson, K. (2017b). Theorizing Jane Crow, theorizing unknowability. *Social Epistemology*, *31*(5), 417–430.
Dotson, K. (2018a). Accumulating epistemic power: A problem with epistemology. *Philosophical Topics*, *46*(1), 129–154.
Dotson, K. (2018b). On the way to decolonization in a settler colony: Re-introducing Black feminist identity politics. *AlterNative: An International Journal of Indigenous Peoples*, *14*(3), 190–199.
Dotson, K. (2019). Tales from an apostate. *Philosophical Issues*, *29*(1), 1–15.
Dotson, K., and Sertler, E. (Forthcoming). When freeing your mind isn't enough: Framework approaches to social transformation and its discontents. In J. Lackey (Ed.), *Applied epistemology*. Oxford University Press.
Douglass, F. (1845/2021). *Narrative of the life of Frederick Douglass*. Wiley.
Dovidio, J. F., Kawakami, K., Johnson, C., Johnson, B., & Howard, A. (1997). On the nature of prejudice: Automatic and controlled processes. *Journal of Experimental Social Psychology*, *33*(5), 510–540.
Downs, J. (2020). Introduction. In H. C. Richardson, K. M. Kruse, C. Anderson, H. A. Thompson, & S. Abrams (Eds.), *Voter suppression in U.S. elections* (pp. 1–14). University of Georgia Press.
Du Bois, W. E. B. (1899/2007). *The Philadelphia Negro: A social study*. Oxford University Press.
Du Bois, W. E. B. (1903/2007). *The Souls of Black Folk*. Oxford University Press.
Du Bois, W. E. B. (1920/1996). The souls of whitefolk. In H. Huggins (Ed.), *W.E.B. Du Bois: Writings* (pp. 933–938). Library of America.
Dunbar-Ortiz, R. (2014). *An Indigenous peoples' history of the United States*. Beacon Press.
Durkheim, E. (1964/1894). *The rules of sociological method*. Free Press.
Dussel, E. (1977/2003). *Philosophy of liberation*. Wipf and Stock.
Eberhardt, J. L., Davies, P. G., Purdie-Vaughns, V. J., & Johnson, S. L. (2006). Looking deathworthy: Perceived stereotypicality of Black defendants predicts capital-sentencing outcomes. *Psychological Science*, *17*(5), 383–386.
Ejército Zapatista de Liberacion Nacional. (2015). *El pensamiento crítico frente a la hidra capitalista* (Vol. 1). Medios Libres, Alternativos, Autónomos o como se llamen.
Elder-Vass, D. 2011. *The causal power of social structures: Emergence, structure, agency*. Cambridge University Press.
Elias-Bursać, E. (2015). *Translating evidence and interpreting testimony at a war crimes tribunal: Working in a tug-of-war*. Palgrave Macmillan.
Ellison, L. (2005). Closing the credibility gap: The prosecutorial use of expert witness testimony in sexual assault cases. *International Journal of Evidence & Proof*, *9*(4), 239–268.
Epstein, D., & Goodman, L. (2019). Discounting women: Doubting domestic violence survivor's credibility and dismissing their experiences. *University of Pennsylvania Law Review*, *167*(2), 399–461.
Erevelles, N. (2011). *Disability and difference in global contexts: Enabling a transformative body politic*. Palgrave.
Erevelles, N. (2020). The color of violence: Reflecting on gender, race, and disability in wartime. In Carole McCann, Seung-kyung Kim, & Emek Ergun (Eds.), *Feminist theory reader* (pp. 434–441). Routledge.

Escobar, A. (2008). *Territories of difference: Place, movements, life, redes.* Duke University Press.
Escobar, A. (2017). *Other worlds are (already) possible: Social movements. Transformative shifts and turning points.* Routledge.
Escobar, A. (2020). *Pluriversal politics.* Duke University Press.
Eubanks, V. (2018). *Automating inequality: How high-tech tools profile, police, and punish the poor.* St. Martin's Press.
Fanon, F. (1956). Racism and culture. In Haakon Chevalier (trans.), *Toward the African revolution* (pp. 29–44). Grove Atlantic.
Fanon, F. (1964/2022). *Toward the African revolution.* Grove Atlantic.
Fanon, F. (1961/2007). *The wretched of the earth.* Grove Atlantic.
Farmer, P. (1996). On suffering and structural violence: A view from below. *Daedalus, 125*(1), 261–283.
Farmer, P. (1999a). *Infections and inequalities: The modern plagues.* University of California Press.
Farmer, P. (1999b). Invisible women: Class, gender, and HIV. In *Infections and inequalities: The modern plagues* (pp. 59–93). University of California Press.
Farmer, P. (2004). An anthropology of structural violence. *Current Anthropology, 45*(3), 305–325.
Farmer, P. (2010). *Partner to the poor: A Paul Farmer reader* (Haun Saussy, Ed.). University of California Press.
Farmer, P., Nizeye, B., Stulac, S., & Keshavjee, S. (2006). Structural violence and clinical medicine. *PloS Medicine 3*(10), e449. https://doi.org/10.1371/journal.pmed.0030449.
Fashina, O. (1989). Frantz Fanon and the ethical justification of anti-colonial violence. *Social Theory and Practice, 15*(2), 179–212.
Fayer, J. M. (2003). African interpreters in the Atlantic slave trade. *Anthropological Linguistics, 45*(3), 281–295.
Fazio, R. H., & Olson, M. A. (2003). Implicit measures in social cognition research: Their meaning and use. *Annual Review of Psychology, 54,* 297–327. https://doi.org/10.1146/annurev.psych.54.101601.145225.
Feagin, J. (2006). *Systemic racism: A theory of oppression.* Routledge.
Federici, S. (2004). The Caliban and the witch. Autonomedia.
Federici, S. (2019). Social reproduction theory: History, issues, and present challenges. *Radical Philosophy, 20*(4), 55–57.
Field, H. S. (1978). Attitudes toward rape: A comparative analysis of police, rapists, crisis counselors, and citizens. *Journal of Personality and Social Psychology, 36*(2), 156–179.
Fellner, K. D. (2018). Therapy as ceremony: Decolonizing and indigenizing our practice. In N. Arthur (Ed.), *Counselling in cultural contexts* (pp. 181–201). Springer. https://doi.org/10.1007/978-3-030-00090-5_8.
Fenner, T., Levene, M., & Loizou, G. (2010). Predicting the long tail of book sales: Unearthing the power-law exponent. *Physica A: Statistical Mechanics and Its Applications, 389*(12), 2416–2421.
Ferreira da Silva, D. (2022). *Unpayable debt.* MIT Press.
Fields, K. E., & Fields, B. J. (2012). *Racecraft: The soul of inequality in American life.* Verso Books.
Fields, S. (2022). White caller crime. In Shawn Fields (Ed.), *Neighborhood Watch: Policing white spaces in America* (pp. 31–60). Cambridge University Press. https://doi.org/10.1017/9781108878661.003.

Finley, L. M. (2004). The hidden victims of tort reform: Women, children, and the elderly. *Emory Law Journal*, 53(3), 1263–1314.

FitzGerald, C., & Hurst, S. (2017). Implicit bias in healthcare professionals: A systematic review. *BMC Medical Ethics* 18(1), 1–18. https://doi.org/10.1186/s12910-017-0179-8.

Flanders-Stepans, M. B. (2000). Alarming racial differences in maternal mortality. *Journal of Perinatal Education*, 9(2), 50–61.

Fletcher, J. (2003). Women and oaths in Euripides. *Theater Journal*, 55(1), 29–44.

Flores, I. B. (2005). Reconstituting constitutions—institutions and culture: The Mexican constitution and NAFTA. HUMAN rights vis-à-vis commerce. *Florida Journal of International Law*, 17, 693–718. https://scholarship.law.georgetown.edu/cgi/viewcontent.cgi?article=2128&context=facpub.

Flynn, A., Holmberg, S. R., Warren, D. T., & Wong, F. J. (2017). *The hidden rules of race: Barriers to an inclusive economy*. Cambridge University Press.

Fontaine, G., & Severance, L. (1990). Intercultural problems in the interpretation of evidence: A Yakuza trial. *International Journal of Intercultural Relations*, 14(2), 163–176.

Forscher, P. S., Lai, C. K., Axt, J., Ebersole, C. R., Herman, M., Devine, P. G., & Nosek, B. A. (2016, August 15). A meta-analysis of procedures to change implicit measures. *Journal of Personality and Social Psychology*, 117(3), 522–559. https://doi.org/10.1037/pspa0000160.

Fortmann, P. (2015). Did early German Romanticism impact systems theory? *Journal of Literary Theory*, 9(2), 271–292. https://doi.org/10.1515/jlt-2015-0014.

Foucault, M. (1976/2020). *The History of Sexuality: Vol. 1. The will to knowledge*. Penguin Books.

Foucault, M. (1978). *The history of sexuality: Vol. 1. An introduction* (R. Hurley, Trans.). Vintage.

Fraher, R. M. (1984). Criminal law of the high Middle Ages: "Rei publicae interest, ne crimina remaneant impunita." *University of Illinois Law Review*, 3, 577–596.

Frazee, G. (2019, October 16). Deadly police shootings keep happening: Data could be a missing piece. *PBS News Hour*. https://www.pbs.org/newshour/nation/deadly-police-shootings-keep-happening-data-could-be-a-missing-piece.

Fregoso, R. L. (2003). *MeXicana encounters: The making of social identities on the borderlands*. University of California Press.

Fregoso, R. L., & Bejarano, C. (Eds.). (2010). *Terrorizing women: Feminicide in the Américas*. Duke University Press.

Freire, P. (2018/1968). *Pedagogy of the oppressed* (Myra Bergman Ramos, Trans.). Bloomsbury Academic.

Frey, D. K. (1991). Allstate Ins. Co. v. Troelstrup: Application of the intentional acts exclusion under homeowner's insurance policies to acts of child molestation. *Denver University Law Review*, 68, 429–439.

Fricker, M. (2007). *Epistemic injustice*. Oxford University Press.

Fricker, M. (2013). How is hermeneutical injustice related to "White ignorance"? Reply to José Medina's "Hermeneutical injustice and polyphonic contextualism: Social silences and shared hermeneutical responsibilities." *Social Epistemology Review and Reply Collective*, 2(8), 49–53.

Furtado, C. (1948/2001). *Economia colonial no Brasil nos seculos XVI e XVII: Elementos de historia economica aplicados a analise de problemas economicos e sociais*. Hucitec.

Furtado, C. (1958). The external disequilibrium in the underdeveloped economies. *Indian Journal of Economics*, 38, 403–410.

Gabrielson, R., Sagara, E., & Jones, R. G. (2014, October 10). Deadly force, in black and white. *Propublica.* https://www.propublica.org/article/deadly-force-in-black-and-white.
Galarte, F. J. (2021). *Brown trans figurations: Rethinking race, gender, and sexuality in Chicanx/Latinx studies.* University of Texas Press.
Galeano [S.] (2015, May 10). The crack in the wall: First note on the Zapatista method. *Enlace Zapatista.* https://enlacezapatista.ezln.org.mx/2015/05/10/the-crack-in-the-wall-first-note-on-zapatista-method/.
Galtung, J. (1969). Violence, peace, and peace research. *Journal of Peace Research, 6*(3), 167–191.
Galtung, J. (1990). Cultural violence. *Journal of Peace Research, 27*(3), 291–305.
Galtung, J., & Fischer, D. (2013). *Johan Galtung: A pioneer of peace research.* Springer.
Gandolfo, D. I. (2010). Liberation philosophy. In S. Nuccetelli Ofelia Schutte, & Otávio Bueno (Eds.), *Companion to Latin American philosophy* vol. 40, (pp. 185–198).
Garzón Martínez, M. T., Cejas, M., Viera, M., Hernández Herse, L. F., & Villegas Mercado, L. D. (2014). Ninguna guerra en mi n ombre: Feminismo y estudios culturales en latinoamérica. *Nómadas, 40,* 159–173.
Gelfert, A. (2014). *A critical introduction to testimony.* Bloomsbury Publishing.
Geronimus, A. T. (1992). The weathering hypothesis and the health of African-American women and infants: Evidence and speculations. *Ethnicity & Disease, 2*(3), 207–221.
Geronimus, A. T. (2023). *Weathering: The extraordinary stress of ordinary life in an unjust society.* AK Press.
Giddens, A. (1979). *Central problems in social theory: Action, structure, and contradiction in social analysis.* University of California Press.
Gilboa, M. (2022). The color of pain: Racial bias in pain and suffering damages. *Georgia Law Review, 56*(2), 651–700. https://digitalcommons.law.uga.edu/glr/vol56/iss2/4.
Gilliam, W. S., Maupin, A. N., Reyes, C. R., Accavitti, M., & Shic, F. (2016). Do early educators' implicit biases regarding sex and race relate to behavior expectations and recommendations of preschool expulsions and suspensions? Yale University Child Study Center. https://arkansasearlychildhood.org/wp-content/uploads/2020/08/Preschool-Implicit-Bias-Policy-Brief-AAIMH.pdf.
Gilmore, R. W. (2007). *Golden gulag: Prisons, surplus, crisis, and opposition in globalizing California.* University of California Press.
Gilmore, R. W. (2022). *Abolition geography: Essays towards liberation.* Verso Books.
Givoni, M. (2016). *The care of the witness: A contemporary history of testimony in crises.* Cambridge University Press.
Glas, K. E., & Faloye, A. (2021). Unconscious (implicit) bias. *Journal of Cardiothoracic and Vascular Anesthesia, 35*(4), 991–992.
Glissant, É. (1997). *Poetics of relation.* University of Michigan Press.
Godstil, R., Tropp, L., Goff, P. A., and Powell, J. (2014). The science of equality, volume 1: Addressing implicit bias, racial anxiety, and stereotype threat in education and healthcare. The Haas Institution and the Perception Institute. http://perception.org/wp-content/uploads/2014/11/Science-of-Equality-111214_web.pdf.
Goeman, M. (2013). *Mark my words: Native women mapping our nations.* University of Minnesota Press.
Golding, J. M., Wasarhaley, N. E., Lynch, K. R., Lippert, A., & Magyarics, C. L. (2015). Improving the credibility of child sexual assault victims in court: The impact of a sexual assault nurse examiner. *Behavioral Sciences & the Law, 33*(4), 493–507.

Goldstein, A. (2022). "In the constant flux of its incessant renewal": The social reproduction of racial capitalism and settler colonial entitlement. In S. Koshy, Lisa Marie Cacho, Jodi A. Byrd, & Brian Jordan Jefferson. (Eds.), *Colonial racial capitalism* (pp. 60–87). Duke University Press.

Gómez-Barris, M. (2017). *The extractive zone: Social ecologies and decolonial perspectives.* Duke University Press.

González de Requena Farré, J. A. (2015). La injusticia epistémica y la justicia del testimonio. *Discusiones Filosóficas, 16*(26), 49–67. https://doi/org/10.17151/difil.2015.16.26.4.

Goodell, W. (1853). *The American slave code in theory and practice: Its distinctive features shown by its statutes, judicial decisions, and illustrative facts.* American and Foreign Anti-Slavery Society.

Goodman, A., Fleming, K., Markwick, N., Morrison, T., Lagimodiere, L., & Kerr, T. (2017). They treated me like crap and I know it was because I was Native: The healthcare experiences of Aboriginal peoples living in Vancouver's inner city. *Social Science and Medicine, 178,* 87–94.

Gordon, D. M. (1978). Up and down the long rollercoaster. In Bruce Steinberg and Union for Radical Political Economics (Ed.), *US capitalism in crisis* (pp. 22–34). New York Union for Radical Political Economics.

Gordon, D. M. (1980). Stages of accumulation and long economic cycles. In T. Hopkins & I. Wallerstein (Eds.), *Processes of the world-system* (pp. 9–45). Sage Publications.

Gordon, D. M., Edwards, R., & Reich, M. (1982). *Segmented work, divided workers: The historical transformation of labor in the United States.* Cambridge University Press.

Gott, R. (2007). Latin America as a white settler society. *Bulletin of Latin American Research 26*(2), 269–289.

Graham, M. (2017). Settler colonialism from the Neo-Assyrians to the Romans. In E. Cavanagh & L. Veracini (Eds.), *The Routledge handbook of the history of settler colonialism* (pp. 11–24). Routledge.

Grand, S., & Salberg, J. (Eds.) (2016). *Trans-generational trauma and the other: Dialogues across history and difference.* Routledge.

Grande, S. (2003). Whitestream feminism and the colonialist project: A review of contemporary feminist pedagogy and praxis. *Educational Theory, 53*(3), 329–346.

Grande, S. (2015). *Red pedagogy: Native American social and political thought.* Rowman & Littlefield.

Greene, J. (2019). Is Korematsu good law? *Yale Law Journal Forum, 128*(1), 629–640.

Greenleaf, R. E. (1994). Persistence of Native values: The Inquisition and the Indians of colonial Mexico. *The Americas, 50*(3), 351–376. https://doi.org/10.2307/1007165.

Greenwald, A. G., & Banaji, M. R. (1995). Implicit social cognition: Attitudes, self-esteem, and stereotypes. *Psychological Review, 102*(1), 4–27.

Greenwald, A. G., McGhee, D. E., & Schwartz, J. L. K. (1998). Measuring individual differences in implicit cognition: The Implicit Association Test. *Journal of Personality and Social Psychology, 74*(6), 1464–1480. https://doi.org/10.1037/0022-3514.74.6.1464.

Gross, S., Possley, M., & Stephens, K. (2017). Race and wrongful convictions in the United States. National Registry of Exonerations. https://www.law.umich.edu/special/exoneration/Documents/Race_and_Wrongful_Convictions.pdf.

Grzanka, P. R., & Cole, E. R. (2021). An argument for bad psychology: Disciplinary disruption, public engagement, and social transformation. *American Psychologist, 76*(8), 1334–1345. https://doi.org/10.1037/amp0000853.

Guaman Poma de Ayala, F. (1615–16). *Cronica de buen gobierno.* Biblioteca Ayacucho.

Guevara, E. (1961). *Guerrilla warfare*. Monthly Review Press.
Gugelberger, G. M. (1996). *The real thing: Testimonial discourse and Latin America*. Duke University Press.
Gugelberger, G. M., & Kearny, M. (1991). Voices for the voiceless: Testimonial literature in Latin America. *Latin American Perspectives*, 18(3), 3–14.
Guinier, L. (2004). Acquaintance rape and degrees of consent: "No" means "no," but what does "yes" mean? *Harvard Law Review*, 117, 2341–2342.
Gutiérrez, G. (1988). *A theology of liberation: History, politics, and salvation*. Orbis Books.
Haberkorn, J. (2012, November 6). Abortion, rape shaped key races. *Politico*. https://www.politico.com/story/2012/11/abortion-rape-shaped-key-races-083449.
Hale, M. (1677). *The primitive origination of mankind: Considered and examined according to the light of nature*. William Godbid.
Haley, S. (2016). *No mercy here: Gender, punishment, and the making of Jim Crow modernity*. University of North Carolina Press.
Hamer, M., Kivimaki, M., Stamatakis, E., & Batty, G. D. (2012). Psychological distress as a risk factor for death from cerebrovascular disease. *Canadian Medical Association Journal*, 184(13), 1461–1466.
Hamilton, D., & Darity, W. J. (2009, September 16). Race, wealth, and intergenerational poverty: There will never be a post-racial America if the wealth gap persists. *American Prospect*. https://prospect.org/special-report/race-wealth-intergenerational-poverty/.
Harbage, C., & Bloch, H. (2019, December 31). The 2010: a decade of protests around the world. *National Public Radio*. https://www.npr.org/sections/pictureshow/2019/12/31/790256816/the-2010s-a-decade-of-protests-around-the-world.
Hardoon, D. (2017, January 16). An economy for the 99 percent. Oxfam International. https://www.oxfam.org/en/research/economy-99.
Harrington, R. (2016, October 26). Courts routinely award women and minorities less money than white men in lost wage cases. *Yahoo News*. https://finance.yahoo.com/news/courts-routinely-award-women-minorities-190947076.html.
Harris, A. P. (2018). Anti-colonial pedagogies: "[X] justice" movements in the United States. *Canadian Journal of Women and the Law*, 30(3), 567–594.
Harris, A. P. (2021). Foreword: Racial capitalism and law. In Destin Jenkins (Ed.), *Histories of racial capitalism*, (pp. vii–xx). Columbia University Press.
Harris, B., and Woodlock, D. (2019). Digital coercive control: Insights from two landmark domestic violence studies. *British Journal of Criminology*, 59(3), 530–550.
Harris, C. (1993). Whiteness as property. *Harvard Law Review*, 106, 1707–1753.
Harris, C. (2019). Of Blackness and Indigeneity: Comments on Jodi A. Byrd's "Weather with you: Settler colonialism, antiblackness, and the grounded relationalities of resistance." *Critical Ethnic Studies*, 5(1–2), 215–228.
Hartman, S. (2008). Venus in two acts. *Small Axe*, no. 26, 12(2), 1–14.
Haruna, T., and Gunji, Y. P. (2019). Ordinal preferential attachment: A self-organizing principle generating dense scale-free networks. *Scientific Reports* 9(4130), 4130–4138. https://doi.org/10.1038/s41598-019-40716-1.
Haslanger, S. (2022). How to change a social structure. Paper delivered at Institute for Laws, Politics and Philosophy, University College London https://www.ucl.ac.uk/laws/site.s/laws/files/haslanger_how_to_change_a_social_structure_ucl.pdf.
Haslanger, S. (2023). Systemic and structural injustice: Is there a difference? *Philosophy*, 98(1), 1–27. https://doi.org/10.1017/S0031819122000353.

Hatch, A. R. (2022). The data will not save us: Afropessimism and racial antimatter in the COVID-19 pandemic. *Big Data & Society, 9*(1). https://doi.org/10.1177/2053951721 1067948.

Hecht, J. (2020). The whiteness of statehood: A review of Arizona and New Mexico 1848–1912. *Journal of the Southwest, 62*(4), 709–730.

Hegel, G. W. F. (1975). *Lectures on the philosophy of world history*. Cambridge University Press.

Herder, J. G. (1772). *Essay on the Origin of Language*. Cambridge University Press.

Herrera, J. S., & Martinez-Alvarez, C. B. (2022). Diversifying violence: Mining, export-agriculture, and criminal governance in Mexico. *World Development, 151*. https://doi.org/10.1016/j.worlddev.2021.105769.

Herrera Sotillo, M. A. (1982). *Ortodoxia y control social en México en el siglo XVII: El Tribunal del Santo Oficio* [Doctoral dissertation, Universidad Complutense de Madrid].

Herron, R. (2018, October 31). I used to be a 911 dispatcher. I had to respond to racist calls every day, *Vox*. https://www.vox.com/first-person/2018/5/30/17406092/racial-profiling-911-bbq-becky-living-while-black-babysitting-while-black.

Hey, M. (2019). *I am not a white man but the US government is forcing me to be one*. Africa World Press.

Hill, D. (2019). *Inquisition in the fourteenth century: The manuals of Bernard Gui and Nicholas Eymerich*. York Medieval Press.

Hinton, E. (2016). *From the war on poverty to the war on crime: The making of mass incarceration in America*. Harvard University Press.

Hoffman, K., Trawalter, S., Axt, J., & Oliver, N. (2016). Racial bias in pain assessment. *Proceedings of the National Academy of Sciences, 113*(16), 4296–4301.

Holden, K. (2013). *The making of the great communicator*. Rowman & Littlefield.

Honjo, K. (2004). Social epidemiology: Definition, history, and research examples. *Environmental Health and Preventive Medicine, 9*(5), 193–199. https://doi.org/10.1007/BF02898100.

hooks, b. (2000). *Feminist theory: From margin to center*. Pluto Press.

Hooper, K., & Kearins, K. (2004). Financing New Zealand 1860–1880: Maori land and the wealth tax effect. *Accounting History, 9*(2), 87–105.

Houkamau, C. A., & Sibley, C. G. (2015). Looking Māori predicts decreased rates of home ownership: Institutional racism in housing based on perceived appearance. *PloS One, 10*(3), e0118540.

Howell, E., Zeitlin, J., Herbert, P., Balbierz, A., & Egorova, N. (2013). Paradoxical trends and racial differences in obstetric quality and neonatal and maternal mortality. *Obstetrics and Gynecology, 121*(6), 1201–1208.

Howell, S., Kuchler, T., Snitkof, D., Stroebel, J., & Wong, J. (2021, October). *Racial disparities in access to small business credit: Evidence from the paycheck protection program* (CEPR Discussion Paper No. DP16623). https://ssrn.com/abstract=3960204.

Humeny, C. (2014). The aftermath of a romantic relationship with a psychopath: The effect of personality sub-factors. *Canadian Journal of Experimental Psychology / Revue Canadienne de Psychologie, 68*(4), 301.

Hurley, J. (2022). "I can't believe I'm still protesting this shit" sign, Women's March on Washington, 2017-01-21. Georgia State University Library Exhibits.

Ignatiev, N. (1995). *How the Irish became white*. Routledge.

India, F. (2021, March 4). Unconscious bias training doesn't work, but it's making billions. *Evie Magazine*. https://www.eviemagazine.com/post/unconscious-bias-training-doesnt-work-but-its-making-billions.

IPN (Instituto Politécnico Nacional). (2022, January 24). Pide IPN disculpa pública por caso de María de Jesús Jaimes Zamudio. National Polytechnic Institute (IPN). https://www.ipn.mx/imageninstitucional/comunicados/ver-comunicado.html?y=2022&n=10.

Isaac, B. (2006). Proto-racism in Graeco-Roman antiquity. *World Archaeology*, 38(1), 32–47.

Isaac, B. (2015). Witness to demographic catastrophe: Indigenous testimony in the Relaciones Geográficas of 1577–86 for Central Mexico. *Ethnohistory*, 62(2), 309–331.

Jackson, F. (1999). The impact of "dyconscious racism." *Multicultural perspectives*, 1(4), 15–18.

Jager, R. K. (2015). *Malinche, Pocahontas, and Sacagawea: Indian women as cultural intermediaries and national symbols*. University of Oklahoma Press.

Jaleel, R. (2021). *The work of rape*. Duke University Press.

Jameson, K. P. (1986). Latin American structuralism: A methodological perspective. *World Development*, 14(2), 223–232.

Jaynes, G. (1982, September 30). Suit on race recalls lines drawn under slavery. *New York Times*, B16.

Jeong, H., Néda, Z., & Barabási, A. L. (2003). Measuring preferential attachment in evolving networks. *EDP Sciences*, 567, 567–572. https://doi.org/10.1209/epl/i2003-00166-9.

Johnson, A. (2016). Rewriting Native imperial history in New Spain: The Texcocan dynasty. University of Michigan Dissertation. https://digitalrepository.unm.edu/cgi/viewcontent.cgi?article=1023&context=span_etds.

Johnson, C. (1982). Grass roots organizing: Women in anticolonial activity in southwestern Nigeria. *African Studies Review*, 25(2–3), 137–147.

Johnson, H., Eriksson, L., Mazerolle, P., & Wortley, R. (2017). Intimate femicide: The role of coercive control. *Feminist Criminology*, 14(1), 3–23.

Jones, B., Ingham, T., Cram, F., Dean, S., & Davies, C. (2013). An Indigenous approach to explore health-related experiences among Māori parents: The Pukapuka Hauora asthma study. *BMC Public Health*, 13, article 228, 228–239. https://doi.org/10.1186/1471-2458-13-228.

Jones-Rogers, S. E. (2020). *They were her property: White women as slave owners in the American South*. Yale University Press.

Jordan, J. (2012). Poem about my rights. In Jan Heller Levi & Sara Miles (Eds.), *Directed by desire: The collected poems of June Jordan* (pp. 309–312). Copper Canyon Press.

Kagan, R., & Dyer, A. (2004). *Inquisitorial inquiries*. Johns Hopkins University Press.

Karagiannis, G. S., Condeelis, J. S., & Oktay, M. H. (2018). Chemotherapy-induced metastasis: mechanisms and translational opportunities. *Clinical & Experimental Metastasis*, 35(4), 269–284. https://doi.org/10.1007/s10585-017-9870-x.

Karton, J. (2008). Lost in translation: International criminal tribunals and the legal implications of interpreted testimony. *Vanderbilt Journal of Transnational Law*, 41(1), 1.

Kauanui, J. K. (2008). *Hawaiian blood: Colonialism and the politics of sovereignty and indigeneity*. Duke University Press.

Kauanui, J. K. (2016, Spring). "A structure, not an event": Settler colonialism and enduring indigeneity. *Lateral*, 5(1), 1–7. https://doi.org/10.25158/L5.1.7.

Kawakami, K., Dovidio, J. F., & van Kamp, S. (2007). The impact of counterstereotypic training and related correction processes on the application of stereotypes. *Group Processes & Intergroup Relations*, *10*(2), 139–156. https://doi.org/10.1177/1368430207074725.

Kelley, R. D. G. (2017). The rest of us: Rethinking settler and Native. *American Quarterly*, *69*(2), 267–276. https://doi/org/10.1353/aq.2017.0020.

Kelly, J. J., Jr. (1993–94). Article 27 and Mexican land reform: The legacy of Zapata's dream. *Columbia Human Rights Law Review*, *25*, 541–570. https://scholarship.law.nd.edu/law_faculty_scholarship/668.

Kendi, I. X. [@DrIbram]. (2021, October 21). *Racism now, racism tomorrow, racism forever. #hastag* [Retweet of Kay Ivey @kayiveyforgov We have permanently BANNED Critical Race Theory in Alabama. We're focused on teaching our children how to read and write, not HATE.] [Tweet]. Twitter. https://twitter.com/dribram/status/1451263061382373382?lang=en.

Kenyon, T. (2016). Oral history and the epistemology of testimony. *Social Epistemology*, *30*(1), 45–66.

Khalidi, R. (2020). *The hundred years' war on Palestine: A history of settler colonialism and resistance, 1917–2017*. Macmillan.

Khimm, S., & Silva, D. (2020, July 29). Lured to America—then trapped. *NBC News*. https://www.nbcnews.com/specials/h2a-visa-program-for-farmworkers-surging-under-trump-and-labor-violations/.

King, K., & Meernik, J. (2019). The burden of bearing witness: The impact of testifying at war crimes tribunals. *Journal of Conflict Resolution*, *63*(2), 348–372.

King, T. L. (2016). New world grammars: The "unthought" Black discourses of conquest. *Theory & Event*, *19*(4), 77–93. https://www.muse.jhu.edu/article/633275.

King, T. L. (2019). *The black shoals: Offshore formations of Black and Native studies*. Duke University Press.

Kish, Z., & Leroy, J. (2015). Bonded life: Technologies of racial finance from slave insurance to philanthrocapital. *Cultural Studies*, *29*(5–6), 630–651. https://doi.org/10.1080/09502386.2015.1017137.

Klarfeld, J. (2011). A striking disconnect: Marital rape law's failure to keep up with domestic violence law. In David Kotz, Terrence McDonough, & Michael Reich (Eds.), *American Criminal Law Re*view, *48*, 1819–1841.

Klor de Alva, J. J. (1988). Sahagún and the birth of modern ethnography: Representing, confessing, and inscribing the Native other. In J. J. Klor de Alva, H. B. Nicholson, & E. Q. Keber (Eds.), *The work of Bernardino de Sahagún* (pp. 31–51). University of Texas Press.

Koenig, T., & Rustad, M. (1995). His and her tort reform: Gender injustice in disguise. *Washington Law Review*, *70*, 1.

Kohn, K. P., Underwood, S. M., & Cooper, M. M. (2018, June). Connecting structure-property and structure-function relationships across the disciplines of chemistry and biology: Exploring student perceptions. *CBE Life Sciences Education*, *17*(2), article 33. https://doi.org/10.1187/cbe.18-01-0004. PMID: 29786475; PMCID: PMC5998324.

Komisaruk, C. (2008). Rape narratives, rape silences: Sexual violence and judicial testimony in colonial Guatemala. *Biography*, *31*(3), 369–396, 552.

Kondratieff, N. D. (1935/2014). *The long waves in economic life*. Martino Publishing.

Koshy, S., Cacho, L. M., Byrd, J. A., & Jefferson, B. J. (Eds.). (2022). *Colonial racial capitalism*. Duke University Press.

Kotz, D. M. (1994). Interpreting the SSA theory. In David Kotz, Terrence McDonough, & Michael Reich (Eds.), *Social structures of accumulation: The political economy of growth and crisis* (pp. 50–71). Cambridge University Press.

Kotz, D. M., McDonough, T., & Reich, M. (1994). *Social structures of accumulation: The political economy of growth and crisis*. Cambridge University Press.

Krauze, L. (2016, April 14). Los porkys: The sexual-assault case that's shaking Mexico. *New Yorker*. https://www.newyorker.com/news/news-desk/los-porkys-the-sexual-assa ult-Ithats-shaking-mexico.

Kricken, T. R. (2019). Rape is not a contract: Recognizing the fundamental difficulties in applying economic theories of jurisprudence to criminal sexual assault. *Wyoming Law Review, 19*, 477–515.

Krystal, H. (1978). Trauma and affects. *The Psychoanalytic Study of the Child, 33*(1), 81–116.

Kümper, H. (2014). 3 learned men and skillful matrons: Medical expertise and the forensics of rape in the Middle Ages. In W. Turner & S. Butler (Eds.), *Medicine and the law in the Middle Ages* (pp. 88–108). Brill.

Kuokkanen, R. (2006). Indigenous peoples on two continents: Self-determination processes in Saami and First Nation societies, *European Review of Native American Studies, 20*(2), 1–5.

Kutcher, S. P. (1982). The gaslight syndrome. *Canadian Journal of Psychiatry, 27*(3), 224–227.

Lackey, J., & Sosa, E. (2006). *The epistemology of testimony*. Clarendon Press; Oxford University Press.

LaDuke, W. (2016). *Recovering the sacred: The power of naming and claiming*. Haymarket Books.

Lai, C., Marini, M., Lehr, S., Cerruti, C., Shin, J. E., Joy-Gaba, J., Ho, A., Teachman, B., Wojcik, S., Koleva, S., Frazier, R., Heiphetz, L., Chen, E., Turner, R., Haidt, J., Kesebir, S., Hawkins, C. B., Schaefer, H., Rubichi, S., . . . Nosek, B. (2016). Reducing implicit racial preferences: I. A comparative investigation of 17 interventions. *Journal of Experimental Psychology 143*(4), 1765–1785. https://dx.doi.org/10.2139/ssrn.2155175.

LaRocque, E. (2016). Preface or here are our voices—who will hear? In H. McFarlane & A. Ruffo (Eds.), *Introduction to Indigenous literary criticism in Canada* (pp. 47–60). Broadview Press, 2016.

Lee, B. X. (2016). Causes and cures VII: Structural violence. *Aggression and Violent Behavior, 28*, 109–114.

Lee, T., Anderson, J., Langsam, A., & Hatter, S. (2022). Disparate law enforcement practices against women of color and gender variant women: The more things change, the more they stay the same. *Journal of Law and Criminal Justice, 10*(1), 1–13.

Leroy, J., & Jenkins, D. (Eds). (2021). *Histories of racial capitalism*. Columbia University Press.

Lévi-Strauss, C. (1958/2008). *Structural anthropology*. Basic Books.

Li, Q., Yang, H., & Zhong, T. P. (2015). Regeneration across metazoan phylogeny: Lessons from model organisms. *Journal of Genetics and Genomics, 42*(2), 57–70.

Lindsay, M. J. (2006). How antidiscrimination law learned to live with racial inequality. *University of Cincinnati Law Review, 75*(1), 87–144.

Linklater, R. (2014). *Decolonizing trauma work: Indigenous stories and strategies. The hundred year's war on Palestine. A history of settler colonialism and resistance.* Fernwood Publishing.

Lippit, V. D. (2010). Social structure of accumulation theory. In T. McDonough, M. Reich, & D. M. Kotz (Eds.), *Contemporary capitalism and its crises: Social structure of accumulation theory for the 21st century* (pp. 45–71). Cambridge University Press.

Lipsitz, G. (2006). *The possessive investment in whiteness: How white people profit from identity politics.* Temple University Press.

Lithwick, D. (2015, June 1). Are you threatening me? The Supreme Court wants to know what this vile Facebook poster was thinking. *Slate.* https://slate.com/news-and-politics/2015/06/anthony-elonis-supreme-court-case-facebook-threats-must-surpass-a-reasonable-listener-standard.html.

Liu, M., Robles, B. J., Brewer, R. M., Adamson, R., & Leondar-Wright, B. (2006). *The color of wealth: The story behind the U.S. racial wealth divide.* New Press.

Lloyd, C., & Metzer, J. (2013). *Settler economies in world history.* Brill.

Lopez, B. (2021, October 15). The law that prompted a school administrator to call for an "opposing" perspective on the Holocaust is causing confusion across Texas. *Texas Tribune.* https://www.texastribune.org/2021/10/15/Texas-critical-race-theory-law-confuses-educators/.

Lopez Don, P. (2006). Franciscans, Indian sorcerers, and the Inquisition in New Spain, 1536–1543. *Journal of World History, 17*(1), 27–49.

Lopez Don, P. (2008). The 1539 inquisition and trial of Don Carlos of Texcoco in early Mexico. *Hispanic American Historical Review, 88*(4), 573–606.

Lopez Don, P. (2010). *Bonfires of culture: Franciscans, Indigenous leaders, and the Inquisition in early Mexico, 1524–1540.* University of Oklahoma Press.

Lorde, A. (1981). The uses of anger: Women responding to racism. *Women's Studies Quarterly, 25*(1–2), 278–285.

Lorde, A. (1984/2020). *Sister outsider: Essays and speeches.* Penguin.

Lorde, A. (2020). *The selected works of Audre Lorde.* Norton.

Love, J. L. (2005). The rise and decline of economic structuralism in Latin America: New dimensions. *Latin American Research Review, 40*(3), 100–125.

Loveday, T., Forster, E. S. (1985). Physiognomonics. In J. Barnes (Ed.), *Complete works of Aristotle* (Vol. 1, pp. 1237–1250). Princeton University Press.

Lowe, L. (2015). *The intimacies of four continents.* Duke University Press.

Lowell, A. L. (1897, November 25). The judicial use of torture, part I. *Harvard Law Review, 11*(4), 220–233.

Lugones, M. (2007). Heterosexualism and the colonial/modern gender system. *Hypatia, 22*(1), 186–219.

MacFarlane, J. (1997, July 16). Black or white? Egyptian immigrant fight for black classification. *CNN.* http://www.cnn.com/US/9707/16/racial.suit/.

MacLean, N. (2021, September 1). *How Milton Friedman exploited white supremacy to privatize education* (Institute for New Economic Thinking Working Paper Series No. 161). https://ssrn.com/abstract=3932454.

Maffie, J. (2009). "In the end, we have the Gatling gun, and they have not": Future prospects of Indigenous knowledges. *Futures, 41,* 53–65.

Maffie, J. (2014). *Aztec philosophy: Understanding a world in motion.* University Press of Colorado.

Maghbouleh, N. (2017). *The limits of whiteness: Iranian Americans and the everyday politics of race.* Stanford University Press.

Maitra, I. (2018). New words for old wrongs. *Episteme, 15*(3), 345–362.

Mamdani, M. (2020). *Neither settler nor native: The making and unmaking of permanent minorities*. Harvard University Press.

Mandel, E. (1980/1995). *Long waves of capitalist development: A Marxist interpretation*. Verso Books.

Manjapra, K. (2018). Plantation dispossessions: The global travel of agricultural racial capitalism. In S. Beckert & C. Desan (Eds.), *American capitalism: New histories* (pp. 361–388). Columbia University Press. https://doi.org/10.7312/beck18524-016.

Manley-Casimir, K. (2012). Creating space for Indigenous storytelling in courts. *Canadian Journal of Law and Society / Revue canadienne droit et societe*, 27(2), 231–248.

Maracle, L. (2015). *Memory serves: Oratories*. NeWest Press.

Marchese G. (2019). Del cuerpo en el territorio al cuerpo-territorio: Elementos para una genealogía feminista latinoamericana de la crítica a la violencia. *Entre diversidades*, 2(13), 9–41.

Marcos, S. I. (1997). The fourth world war has begun. In T. Hayden (Ed.), *The Zapatista reader* (pp. 270–85). Bold Type Books.

Marcos, S. I. (2014, July 22). The Zapatista Women's Revolutionary Law as it is lived today, (L. Quiquivix, Trans.). *Open Democracy*. https://www.opendemocracy.net/en/zapatista-womens-revolutionary-law-as-it-is-lived-today.

Marcos, S. I. (2018). *The Zapatistas' dignified rage: Final public speeches of Subcommander Marcos* (N. Henck, Ed.; H. Gales, Trans.). AK Press.

Mariátegui, J. C. (2014/1928). *Seven interpretive essays on Peruvian reality*. University of Texas Press.

Marini, R. M. (1973). *La dialectica de la dependencia*. Ediciones Era.

Martínez, M. E. (2008). *Genealogical fictions: Limpieza de sangre, religion, and gender in colonial Mexico*. Stanford University Press.

Marx, K. (1953/1993). *Grundrisse: Foundations of the critique of political economy*. Penguin.

Marx, K. (2004/1867). *Capital* (Vol. 1). Penguin.

Marx, K. (2011). *Capital: A critique of political economy*. Dover Publications.

Massagué, J., & Obenauf, A. C. (2016). Metastatic colonization by circulating tumour cells. *Nature*, 529(7586), 298–306. https://doi.org/10.1038/nature17038.

McDonald, E. (2009). And still we must talk about "real rape." [Review of the book *Sexual assault and the justice gap: A question of attitude* by J. Temkin & B. Krahe]. *Pace Law Review*, 29(2), 349–376.

McDonough, T. (1994). Social structures of accumulation, contingent history, and stages of capitalism. In D. M. Kotz, T. McDonough, & M. Reich (Eds.), *Social structures of accumulation: The political economy of growth and crisis* (pp. 72–84). Cambridge University Press.

McGrath, C. (2021). Highlight: Epigenetics help hydra get ahead, *Genome Biology and Evolution*, 13(12), 1–3.

McKinnon, R. (2017). Allies behaving badly: Gaslighting as epistemic injustice. In G. Pohlhaus Jr., I. J. Kidd, & J. Medina (Eds.), *The Routledge Handbook on Epistemic Injustice* (pp. 167–175). Routledge.

McKittrick, K. (2006). *Demonic grounds: Black women and the cartographies of struggle*. University of Minnesota Press.

McKittrick, K. (2013). Plantation futures. *Small Axe*, no. 42, 17(3), 1–15. https://doi.org/10.1215/07990537-2378892.

McKittrick, K. (2021). *Dear science and other stories*. Duke University Press.

McLeod-Henning, D. (2022, January 4). Improving bruise detection with alternate light. US Department of Justice. https://nij.ojp.gov/topics/articles/improving-bruise-detection-alternate-light.
McMyler, B. (2011). *Testimony, trust, and authority*. Oxford University Press.
Medina, J. (2012). Hermeneutical injustice and polyphonic contextualism: Social silences and shared hermeneutical responsibilities. *Social Epistemology, 26*(2), 201–220.
Medina, J. (2013). *The epistemology of resistance: Gender and racial oppression, epistemic injustice, and the social imagination*. Oxford University Press.
Mei-Singh, L. (2021). Accompaniment through carceral geographies: Abolitionist research partnerships with Indigenous communities. *Antipode, 53*(1), 74–94. https://doi.org/10.1111/anti.12589.
Mejia, B. (2022, October 15). Following city council members' racist remarks, hundreds of Oaxacans march for justice in L.A. *Los Angeles Times*. https://www.latimes.com/california/story/2022-10-15/los-angeles-city-council-members-racist-remarks-oaxacans-march.
Melamed, J. (2011). *Represent and destroy: Rationalizing violence in the new racial capitalism*. University of Minnesota Press.
Melamed, J. (2015). Racial capitalism. *Critical Ethnic Studies, 1*(1), 76–85.
Méndez y Néstor Jiménez, E. (2020, February 11). Gertz: Aumentaron los feminicidios 137% en cinco años. *La Jornada*. https://www.jornada.com.mx/ultimas/politica/2020/02/11/gertz-aumentaron-los-feminicidios-137-en-cinco-anos-4329.html.
Mendoza, B. (2022). The question of the coloniality of democracy. In Y. Espinosa-Miñoso, M. Lugones, & Nelson Maldonado-Torres (Eds.), *Decolonial feminism in Abya Yala: Caribbean, Meso, and South American contributions and challenges* (pp. 63–82). Rowman & Littlefield.
Methot, S. (2019). *Legacy: Trauma, story and Indigenous healing*. ECW Press.
Metz, W. D. (1978, December 22). Mexico: The premier oil discovery in the Western Hemisphere. *Science, 202*(4374), 1261–1265. https://doi.org/10.1126/science.202.4374.1261.
Metzger, E. (1998). *A companion to Justinian's Institutes*. Cornell University Press.
Middleton, J. D., Stover, D. G., & Hai, T. (2018). Chemotherapy-exacerbated breast cancer metastasis: A paradox explainable by dysregulated adaptive-response. *International Journal of Molecular Science, 19*(11), 3333. https://doi.org/10.3390/ijms19113333.
Mignolo, W. (1995). *The darker side of the Renaissance: Literacy, territoriality, and colonization*. University of Michigan Press.
Mignolo, W. (2000). *Local histories / global designs: Coloniality, subaltern knowledges, and border thinking*. Princeton University Press.
Mignolo, W. D. (2005). Cambiando las éticas y las políticas del conocimiento: lógica de la colonialidad y postcolonialidad imperial. *Tabula rasa, 3*, 47–72. https://doi.org/10.1080/09502380601162647.
Mignolo, W. (2011). *The darker side of western modernity: Global futures, decolonial options*. Duke University Press.
Mill, J. S. (1863). *Utilitarianism*. Parker and Bourn.
Miller, K. D., Sauer, A. G, Ortiz, A. P., Fedewa, S. A., Pinheiro, P. S., Tortolero-Luna, G., Martinez-Tyson, D., Jemal, A., & Siegel, R. L. (2018). Cancer statistics for Hispanics/Latinos. *CA: A Cancer Journal for Clinicians*. 68: 425–445. https://doi.org/10.3322/caac.21494.

Miller, M. (2011). Land and racial wealth inequality. *American Economic Review, 101*(3), 371–376. https://doi/org/10.1257/aer.101.3.371.
Million, D. (2009). Felt theory: An Indigenous feminist approach to affect and history. *Wicazo Sa Review, 24*(2), 53–76. https://doi/org/10.1353/wic.0.0043.
Million, D. (2013). *Therapeutic nations: Healing in an age of Indigenous rights*. University of Arizona Press.
Mills, C. (1997/2014). *The racial contract*. Cornell University Press.
Mills, C. (2005). "Ideal theory" as ideology. *Hypatia, 20*(3), 165–184.
Mills, C. (2015). Global white ignorance. In Matthias Gross, Linsey McGoey (Ed.), *Routledge international handbook of ignorance studies* (pp. 217–227). Routledge.
Mills, C. (2017). *Black rights / white wrongs: The critique of racial liberalism*. Oxford.
Min-ha, T. T. (1989). *Woman, Native, other: Writing postcoloniality and feminism*. Indiana University Press.
Miñoso, Y. E. (2017). Hacia la construcción de la historia de un (des) encuentro: La razón feminista y la agencia antiracista y decolonial en Abya Yala. *Revista Praxis, 76*, 1–14.
Moeke-Pickering, T. (2019). Indigenous worldviews and pedagogies in Indigenous-based programs: Social work and counselling. In S. Hameed, S. El-Kafafi, & R. Waretini-Karena (Eds.), *Handbook of research on Indigenous knowledge and biculturalism in a global context* (pp. 1–10). IGI Global. https://doi.org/10.4018/978-1-5225-6061-6.ch001.
Molyneux, M. (1985). Mobilization without emancipation? Women's interests, the state, and revolution in Nicaragua. *Feminist Studies, 11*(2), 227–254.
Monteith, M. J. (1993). Self-regulation of prejudiced responses: Implications for progress in prejudice-reduction efforts. *Journal of Personality and Social Psychology, 65*(3), 469–485. https://doi/org/10.1037/0022-3514.65.3.469.
Moore, K. (2022). *Legal spectatorship: Slavery and the visual culture of domestic violence*. Duke University Press.
Mora, M. (2017). *Kuxlejal politics: Indigenous autonomy, race, and decolonizing research in Zapatista communities*. University of Texas Press.
Moraga, C. (1995). From a long line of vendidas: Chicanas and feminism. In Teresa Lauretis (Ed.), *Feminist studies/critical studies* (pp. 173–190). Palgrave Macmillan.
Moraga, C., & Anzaldúa, G. (1981/2015). *This bridge called my back: Writings by radical women of color*. State University of New York Press.
Moran, R. (2018). *The exchange of words: Speech, testimony, and intersubjectivity*. Oxford University Press.
Moreton-Robinson, A. (2007). *Writing off Indigenous sovereignty: The discourse of security and patriarchal white sovereignty*. Routledge.
Moreton-Robinson, A. (2015). *The white possessive: Property, power, and Indigenous sovereignty*. University of Minnesota Press.
Morris, M. (2018). *Pushout: The criminalization of Black girls in schools*. New Press.
Morrison, T. (1998, January 2). Voir comme on ne v oit jamais: Dialogue entre Pierre Bourdieu et Toni Morrison. *Vacarme 6*, 58–60. https://doi.org/10.3917/vaca.006.0058.
Moulier-Boutang, Y. (2011). *Cognitive capitalism*. Wiley.
Muñoz Ramírez, G. (2008). *The fire and the word: A history of the Zapatista movement* (L Carlsen, Trans.). University of Michigan Press.
Murch, D. (2022). *Assata taught me: State violence, racial capitalism, and the movement for Black lives*. Haymarket Books.

Murphy, C. (2012, January 23). The Inquisition: A model for modern interrogators [Interview]. *NPR: Fresh Air.* https://www.npr.org/2012/01/23/145512271/the-inquisition-a-model-for-modern-interrogators.
Murphy, C. (2013). *God's jury: The Inquisition and the making of the modern world.* Mariner Books.
Myles, Ranell L. (2013). *Unbearable fruit: Black women's experiences with uterine fibroids* (doctoral dissertation, Georgia State University).
Nackenoff, C. (2019). Sexual harassment trajectories: Limits of (current) law and of the administrative state. *Journal of Women, Politics & Policy, 40*(1), 21–41.
Narayan, U. (1997). *Contesting cultures: Identities, traditions and third world feminisms.* Routledge.
Narayan, U. (1998). Essence of culture and a sense of history: A feminist critique of cultural essentialism. *Hypatia, 13*(2), 86–106.
National Archives. (2021). Chinese Exclusion Act case files. National Archives and Records Administration. https://chineseexclusionfiles.com/2021/03/28/rose-chin-born-in-seattle-lost-her-u-s-citizenship-when-she-married-a-chinese-native-in-1927/.
National Cancer Institute, National Institute of Health. (2017). Study uncovers previously unrecognized effects of chemotherapy. https://www.cancer.gov/news-events/cancer-currents-blog/2017/chemotherapy-effect-metastasis.
National Defense Intelligence College. (2006). Educing information interrogation; science and art, foundations for the future. http://www.lasorsa.com/wp-content/uploads/2015/02/Interrogation-Science-and-Art.pdf.
National Institute of Justice. (1987). *Private sector prison industries: A summary of findings.* U.S. Department of Justice. https://www.ojp.gov/library/publications/private-sector-prison-industries-summary-findings.
National Registry of Exonerations. (2022). Larry Youngblood. University of Michigan. https://www.law.umich.edu/special/exoneration/Pages/casedetail.aspx?caseid=3774#:~:text=In%202000%2C%20upon%20request%20from,against%20Larry%20Youngblood%20that%20year.
Nattrass, N. (1994). Apartheid and capitalism: Social structure of accumulation or contradiction? In D. M. Kotz, T. McDonough, & M. Reich (Eds.), *Social structures of accumulation: The political economy of growth and crisis* (pp 253–273). Cambridge University Press.
Ngāti Awa, T. A. (K. Raerino), Macmillan, A., & Kahungunu, N. (Rhys Jones). (2013). Indigenous Māori perspectives on urban transport patterns linked to health and wellbeing. *Health and Place, 23*(1), 54–62.
Nguyen, N. L. (2006). Roman rape: An overview of Roman rape laws from the republican period to Justinian's reign. *Michigan Journal of Gender and Law, 13*(1), 75–112.
Nichols, R. (2020). *Theft is property! Dispossession and critical theory.* Duke University Press.
Nielson, E., and Dennis, A. (2019). *Rap on trial: Lyrics, and guilt in America.* New Press.
Nietzsche, F. (2009). *Writings from the early notebooks.* Cambridge University Press.
Nimatuj, V. (2021). The case of Sepur Zarco and the challenge to the Colonial State. In L. Stephen & S. Speed (Eds.), *Indigenous women and violence: Feminist activist research in heightened states of injustice* (pp. 100–124). University of Arizona Press.
O'Gorman, E. (1949). *Primer libro de votos de la Inquisición de México, 1573–1600.* Archivo General de la Nación.

Obie, B. (2017, January 23). Woman in viral photo from Women's March to white female allies: "Listen to a Black woman." *The Root*. https://www.theroot.com/woman-in-viral-photo-from-women-s-march-to-white-female-1791524613.

Ojeda Martínez, R. I. (2021). Rape, body, and cognition: A case in Sierra Tarahumara. *Frontera norte*, *33*, 1–21. doi.org/10.33679/rfn.v1i1.2153.

Omi, M., & Winant, H. (1994). *Racial formation in the United States: From the 1960s to the 1990s*. Routledge.

Omi, M., & Winant, H. (2014). *Racial formation in the United States* (3rd ed.). Taylor & Francis.

Ong, W. J. (1982/2003). *Orality and literacy*. Routledge.

Ott, J. (2022). Why Is wealth white? *Southern Cultures*, *28*(4), 30–55.

Oxfam International. (2017, January 16). Just 8 men own same wealth as half the world. Oxfam publishing. oxfam.org/en/press-releases/just-8-men-own-same-wealth-half-world.

Oxfam International. (2022, January 17). Ten richest men double their fortunes in pandemic while incomes of 99 percent of humanity fall. Oxfam publishing. https://www.oxfam.org/en/press-releases/ten-richest-men-double-their-fortunes-pandemic-while-incomes-99-percent-humanity.

Páez, A. (Ed.). (2015). *Hechos, evidencia y estándares de prueba: Ensayos de epistemología jurídica*. Universidad de Los Andes, Facultad.

Pager, D. (2007). *Marked: Race, crime, and finding work in an era of mass incarceration*. University of Chicago Press.

Paredes, J. (2008). *Hilando fino: Desde el feminismo comunitario*. CEDEC.

Paredes, J. (2010). Hilando fino desde el feminismo indígena comunitario. In Y. Espinosa Miñoso (Comp.), *Aproximaciones críticas a las prácticas teórico-políticas del feminismo latinoamericano* (pp. 117–120).

Parmenter, C. (2021). "A happy coincidence": Race, the Cold War, and Frank M. Snowden, Jr's *Blacks in Antiquity*. *Classical Receptions Journal*, *13*(4), 485–506. https://doi.org/10.1093/crj/clab001.

Parsons. T. (1951/1991). *The social system*. Routledge.

Parsons, T. (1961). Some considerations on the theory of social change. *Rural Sociology*, *26*(3), 219–239.

Parsons, T. (1976). Social structure and the symbolic media of interchange. In Peter Blau (Ed.) *Approaches to the study of social structure* (pp. 94–120). Open Books.

Patrick, K. (2016). Not just justice: Inquiry into missing and murdered Aboriginal women needs public health input from the s tart. *Canadian Medical Association Journal*, *188*(5), 78–79.

Patterson, E., Roch, F., Plouffe-Malette, K., & Marquis, L. (2016). Reconciling Indigenous peoples with the judicial process: An examination of the recent genocide and sexual slavery trials in Guatemala and their integration of Mayan culture and customs. *Revue québécoise de droit international*, *29*(2), 225–252.

Pember, M. A. (2016). Intergenerational trauma: Understanding Natives' inherited pain. *Indian Country, Today Media Network*. U.S. Department of Commerce. https://amber-ic.org/wp-content/uploads/2017/01/ICMN-All-About-Generations-Trauma.pdf.

Peng, W. & Wallace, D. (1993). *Software error analysis*. National Institute of Standards and Technology.

Perry, M. E., & Cruz, A. J. (Eds.). (2018). *Cultural encounters: The impact of the Inquisition in Spain and the New World*. University of California Press.

Peters, E. (1985/2018). *Torture: An expert's confrontation with an everyday evil*. University of Pennsylvania Press.
Peterson, J. A. (1983). *Petroleum geology and resources of southeastern Mexico, northern Guatemala, and Belize*. Geological Survey Circular 760. US Department of the Interior. https://pubs.usgs.gov/circ/1983/0760/report.pdf.
Phelps, E. A., Cannistraci, C. J., & Cunningham, W. A. (2003). Intact performance on an indirect measure of race bias following amygdala damage. *Neuropsychologia, 41*(2), 203–208.
Phelps, E. A., O'Connor, K. J., Cunningham, W. A., Funayama, E. S., Gatenby, J. C., Gore, J. C., & Banaji, M. R. (2000). Performance on indirect measures of race evaluation predicts amygdala activation. *Journal of Cognitive Neuroscience, 12*(5), 729–738.
Piaget, J. (2015). *Structuralism*. Taylor & Francis.
Pico della Mirandola, G. (2012). *Oration on the Dignity of Man* (F. Borghesi, M. Papio, & M. Riva, Eds.). Cambridge University Press.
Piketty, T. (2017). *Capital in the twenty-first century*. Harvard University Press.
Pohlhaus, G. (2012). Relational knowing and epistemic injustice: Toward a theory of willful hermeneutical ignorance. *Hypatia, 27*(4), 715–735.
Pohlhaus, G. (2014). Discerning the primary epistemic harm in cases of testimonial injustice. *Social Epistemology, 28*(2), 99–114.
Pohlhaus, G. (2020). Gaslighting and echoing, or why collective epistemic resistance is not a "witch hunt." *Hypatia, 35*(4), 674–686. https://doi.org/10.1017/hyp.2020.29.
Pohlhaus, G. (2017a, September 23). Gaslighting, echoing, and gathering; or why collective epistemic resistance is not a "witch hunt." Gaslighting and Epistemic Injustice Conference, Claremont McKenna College.
Pohlhaus, G. (2017b). Introduction. In J. Kidd, J. Medina, and G. Pohlhaus Jr. (Eds.), *The Routledge handbook of epistemic injustice* (pp. 19–28). Routledge.
Poole, S. (1987). *Pedro Moya de Contreras: Catholic reform and royal power in New Spain, 1571–1591*. University of California Press.
Porpora, D. V. (1987). *The concept of social structure*. Greenwood Press.
Porter, J. (2019). Slavery and Athens' economic efflorescence. *Mare Nostrum, 10*(2), 25–50.
Powles, S. (2003). To testify or not to testify privilege from testimony at the ad hoc tribunals: The Randal decision. *Leiden Journal of International Law, 16*(3), 511–524.
Prebisch, R. (1950/1949). *The economic development of Latin America and its principal problems*. United Nations.
Prebisch, R. (1963). *Hacia una dinámica del desarrollo latinoamericano*. Fondo de Cultura Económica.
Prescod-Weinstein, C. (2020). Making Black women scientists under white empiricism: The racialization of epistemology in physics. *Signs: Journal of Women in Culture and Society, 45*(2), 421–447.
Pritchard, D. (2004). The epistemology of testimony. *Philosophical Issues, 14*, 326–348.
Prussing, E. (2018). Critical epidemiology in action: Research for and by Indigenous peoples. *SSM Population Health 6*, 98–106.
Psillos, S. (2006). The structure, the whole structure, and nothing but the structure? *Philosophy of Science, 73*(5), 560–570. https://doi.org/10.1086/518326.
Puar, J. K. (2007). *Terrorist assemblages: Homonationalism in queer times*. Duke University Press.
Puar, J. K. (2017). *The right to maim: Debility, capacity, disability*. Duke University Press.

Queirós, F. (2022). The (re)invocation of race in forensic genetics through forensic DNA phenotyping technology. In Sheila Khan, Nazir Ahmed Can, & Helena Machado (Eds.), *Racism and racial surveillance*. Taylor & Francis.

Quijano, A. (2000). Coloniality of power and Eurocentrism in Latin America. *International Sociology, 15*(2), 215–232.

Rabasa, J. (2011). *Tell me the story of how I conquered you: Elsewheres and ethnosuicide in the colonial Mesoamerican world*. University of Texas Press.

Rama, A. (1996). *The lettered city*. Duke University Press.

Randall, M. (1981). *Sandino's daughters: Testimonies of Nicaraguan women in struggle*. Rutgers University Press.

Randall, M. (1983). *Y también digo mujer: Testimonio de la mujer nicaragüense hoy*. Ediciones Populares Feministas.

Rasgado, G. (2017, March 27). Juez concede amparo a Porky: "No fue lascivo al tocar a joven." *Presencia*. https://www.presencia.mx/nota.aspx?id=120240&s=4

Rawls, J. (1971/1999). *A theory of justice*. Harvard University Press.

Reagan had restricted land deeds in 1940's. (1984, October 5). *New York Times*, D19.

Reagan's exit stirs Negro G.O.P. parley. (1966, March 7). *New York Times*, 16.

Reich, M. (1994). How social structures of accumulation decline and are built. In D. M. Kotz, T. McDonough, & M. Reich (Eds.), *Social structures of accumulation: The political economy of growth and crisis* (pp. 29–49). Cambridge University Press.

Reif, L. L. (1986). Women in Latin American guerrilla movements: A comparative perspective. *Comparative Politics, 18*(2), 147–169. https://doi.org/10.2307/421841.

Reilly, N., Bailey, D., & Global Tribunal on Violations of Women's Human Rights. (1994). Testimonies of the global tribunal on violations of women's human rights at the United Nations world conference on human rights: Vienna, June 1993. Center for Women's Global Leadership, Douglass College.

Reynolds, S. (2017). *Knowledge as acceptable testimony*. Cambridge University Press.

Richard, N. (2004). *The insubordination of signs: Political change, cultural transformation, and poetics of the crisis*. Duke University Press.

Richie, B. E. (2000). A Black feminist reflection on the antiviolence movement. *Signs: Journal of Women in Culture and Society, 25*(4), 1133–1137.

Rickford, J. R., & King, S. (2016). Language and linguistics on trial: Hearing Rachel Jeantel (and other vernacular speakers) in the courtroom and beyond. *Language, 92*(4), 948–988.

Riddle, E. (2019, March 8). The gaslighting of Jody Wilson-Raybould: Indigenous women have seen this before. *Global and Mail*. https://www.theglobeandmail.com/opinion/article-the-gaslighting-of-jody-wilson-raybould-indigenous-women-have-seen/.

Rifkin, M. (2014). *Settler common sense: Queerness and everyday colonialism in the American renaissance*. University of Minnesota Press.

Riggs, D., & Bartholomaeus, C. (2018). Gaslighting in the context of clinical interactions with parents of transgender children. *Sexual and Relationship Therapy, 33*(4), 382–394.

Ríos Castaño, V. (2014). Inquisitorial techniques as Sahagún's method of data collection. In *Translation as conquest: Sahagún and universal history of the things of New Spain* (pp. 151–198). Vervuert Verlagsgesellschaft. https://doi.org/10.31819/9783954871902-006.

Ritchie, A. (2017). *Invisible no more: Police violence against Black women and women of color*. Beacon Press.

Rives, J. M., & Yousefi, M. (1997). *Economic dimensions of gender inequality: A global perspective*. Praeger.

Roberts, D. (2002). *Shattered bonds: The color of child welfare*. Basic Books.
Roberts, D. (2008). Torture and the biopolitics of race. *Faculty Scholarship at Penn Law*, 575, 229–247. https://scholarship.law.upenn.edu/cgi/viewcontent.cgi?article=1574&context=faculty_scholarship.
Roberts, D. (2017). *Killing the Black body*. Vintage Books.
Roberts, T., & Andrews, D. C. (2013). A critical analysis of the gaslighting against African American teachers: Considerations for recruitment and retention. In D. C. Andrews & Frank Tuitt (Eds.), *Contesting the myth of the post racial era: The continued significance of race in U.S. education* (pp. 69–94). Peter Lang.
Robinson, C. J. (1983/2000). *Black Marxism: The making of the Black radical tradition*. University of North Carolina Press.
Robinson, J. (1956/2013). *The accumulation of capital*. Palgrave Macmillan.
Robinson, S. (2013). *Citizen strangers: Palestinians and the birth of Israel's liberal settler state*. Stanford University Press.
Rodríguez, C. (2009). Counting Latinos in the US census. In José Cobas, Jorge Duany, & Joe Feagin (Eds.), *How the United States racializes Latinos: White hegemony and its consequences* (pp. 37–43). Routledge.
Rodriguez, T. (2015, March 1). Descendants of Holocaust survivors have altered stress hormones. *Scientific American Mind*, 26(2), 10. https://doi.org/10.1038/scientificamericanmind0315-10a.
Roediger, D. (2005). *Working toward whiteness: How American immigrants became white*. Basic Books.
Rojas, M. (2010). *Women of color and feminism*. Seal Press.
Rolnick, A. (2018). Defending white space. *Cardozo Law Review*, 40(2), 1639–1717.
Romada Curto, D. (2020). *Imperial culture and colonial projects: The Portuguese-speaking world from the fifteenth to the eighteenth centuries*. Berghahn Books.
Rorty, R. (2010). Justice as a larger loyalty. In Christopher Voparil & Richard Bernstein (Eds.), *The Rorty reader* (pp. 433–434). Wiley.
Rothstein, R. (2017). *The color of law: A forgotten history of how our government segregated America*. Norton.
Rousseau, J.-J. (1762/1997). *The social contract and other later political writings* (V. Gourevitch, Ed.). Cambridge University Press.
Rousseau, J.-J. (2018). *Rousseau: The Discourses and other early political writings* (V. Gourevitch, Ed., 2nd ed.). Cambridge University Press. https://doi.org/10.1017/9781316584804.
Rubenstein, R. E. (2017). *Resolving structural conflicts: How violent systems can be transformed*. Routledge.
Ruffer, Galya. (2013). Testimony of sexual violence in the Democratic Republic of Congo and the injustice of rape: Moral outrage, epistemic injustice, and the failures of bearing witness. *Oregon Review of International Law*, 15(2), 225–270.
Ruíz, E. (2012). Theorizing multiple oppressions through colonial history: Cultural alterity and Latin American feminisms. *APA Newsletter on Hispanic/Latino Issues in Philosophy*, 11(2), 5–9.
Ruíz, E. (2016). Review of Beata Stawarska: *Saussure's philosophy of language as phenomenology: Undoing the doctrine of the course in general linguistics*. *Human Studies*, 39, 481–486.
Ruíz, E. (2017). Framing intersectionality. In L. Alcoff, P. Taylor, & L. Anderson, *The Routledge companion to the philosophy of race* (pp. 335–348). Routledge.

Ruíz, E. (2019). Between hermeneutic violence and alphabets of survival. In A. Pitts, J. Medina, & M. Ortega (Eds.), *Theories of the flesh: Latinx and Latin American feminisms, transformation, and resistance* (pp. 204–219). Oxford University Press.

Ruíz, E. (2020). Cultural gaslighting. *Hypatia, 35*(4), 687–713. https://doi.org/10.1017/hyp.2020.33.

Ruíz, E. (2021). Postcolonial and decolonial theories. In Ásta & K. Q. Hall (Eds.), *The Oxford handbook of feminist philosophy* (pp. 541–551). Oxford University Press.

Ruíz, E., Berenstain, N., & Paredes-Ruvalcaba, N. (2023). Reproductive violence and settler statecraft. In S. Khan & E. Schwebach (Eds.), *Globalization, displacement, and psychiatry: Global histories of trauma* (pp. 150–173). Routledge.

Ruíz, E., & Sertler, E. (2019, October 11). Asylum, credible fear tests, and colonial violence. *Biopolitical Philosophy*. https://biopoliticalphilosophy.com/2019/10/11/asylum-credible-fear-tests-and-colonial-violence-guest-post.

Ruíz y Flores, E. (2018). The hermeneutics of Mexican-American political philosophy. *Inter-American Journal of Philosophy, 9*(2), 45–57.

Ruíz y Flores, E. (2021). Women of color structural feminisms. In S. A. Tate & E. G. Rodríguez (Eds.), *The Palgrave handbook of critical race and gender* (pp. 167–188). Palgrave Macmillan.

Russell, C. (2016). Questions of race in bioethics: Deceit, disregard, disparity, and the work of decentering. *Philosophy Compass, 11*(1), 43–55.

Russell, C. (2018). *The assisted reproduction of race*. Indiana University Press.

Said, E. W. (1979). *Orientalism*. Knopf Doubleday Publishing Group.

Salter, M. (2019). Brett Kavanaugh's nomination and the moral context of trauma science. *Journal of Trauma & Dissociation, 20*(2), 135–139.

Sandoval, C. (2013). *Methodology of the oppressed*. University of Minnesota Press.

Santos, B. de S. (2007). *Another knowledge is possible: Beyond northern epistemologies*. Verso Books.

Santos, B. de S. (2018). *The end of the cognitive empire: The coming of age of epistemologies of the south*. Duke University Press.

Sañudo, J. E. P., Llanos, R. A., Orozco, C. A. M., & Sabatier, C. (1999). Estrés postraumático y resistencia psicológica en jóvenes desplazados. *Investigación & desarrollo, 10*, 16–29.

Sarkis, S. (2017, January 22). 11 warning signs of gaslighting, *Psychology Today*. https://www.psychologytoday.com/us/blog/here-there-and-everywhere/201701/11-warning-signs-gaslighting.

Sarmiento Pérez, M. (2011). The role of interpreters in the conquest and acculturation of the Canary archipelago. *Interpreting, 13*(2), 159–160.

Saul, S., Mazzei, P. & Gabriel, T. (2023, January 31). DeSantis takes on the education establishment, and builds his brand: A proposal by Gov. Ron DeSantis of Florida to overhaul higher education would mandate courses in Western civilization, eliminate diversity programs and reduce protections of tenure. *New York Times*. https://www.nytimes.com/2023/01/31/us/governor-desantis-higher-education-chris-rufo.html.

Saussure, F. D. (2011). *Course in general linguistics* (Haun Saussy & Pierry Meisel, Eds.). Columbia University Press.

Sawyer, K. (2005). *Social emergence as complex systems*. Cambridge University Press.

Scatton, R. (2022, November 17). 34% of white college students lied about their race to improve chances of admission, financial aid benefits. *Intelligent*. https://www.intellig

ent.com/34-of-white-college-students-lied-about-their-race-to-improve-chances-of-admission-financial-aid-benefits.

Schaps, D. M. (1998). What was free about a free Athenian woman? *Transactions of the American Philological Association, 128*, 161–188.

Schonhardt, S. (2023, January 11). A climate fund was born. It still doesn't have any money. *Climatewire*. https://www.eenews.net/articles/a-climate-fund-was-born-it-still-doesnt-have-any-money/.

Schuenemann, V. J., Peltzer, A., Welte, B., van Pelt, W. P., Molak, M., Chuan-Chao Wang, Anja Furtwängler, Christian Urban, Reiter, E., Nieselt, K., Tebmann, B., Francken, M., Harvati, K., Haak, W., Schiffels, S., & Krause, J. (2017). Ancient Egyptian mummy genomes suggest an increase of sub-Saharan African ancestry in post-Roman periods. *Nature Communications 8*, 15694 (May). https://doi.org/10.1038/ncomms15694.

Schumpeter, J. A. (1934). *The theory of economic development: An inquiry into profits, capital, credit, interest, and the business cycle.* Harvard University Press.

Schutte, O. (1993). *Cultural identity and social liberation in Latin American thought.* State University of New York Press.

Schutte, O. (1998). Cultural alterity: Cross-cultural communication and feminist theory in north-south contexts. *Hypatia, 13*(2), 53–72.

Searle. J. (1998). *Mind, language, and society: Philosophy in the real world.* Basic books.

Secretaría de Relaciones Exteriores. (2007). General Law on Women's Access to a Life Free of Violence. Estados Unidos Mexicanos. http://www.summit-americas.org/brief/docs/Law_on_access_to_a_life_free_violence.pdf.

Sedehi, K. T. (2019). Witnessing the unspoken truth: On residential school survivors' testimonies in Canada. *Theory and Practice in Language Studies, 9*(7), 755–761.

Seed, P. (1996). *Ceremonies of possession in Europe's conquest of the New World, 1492–1640.* Cambridge University Press.

Sellaro, R., Derks, B., Nitsche, M. A., Hommel, B., van den Wildenberg, W. P., van Dam, K., & Colzato, L. S. (2015). Reducing prejudice through brain stimulation. *Brain Stimulation, 8*(5), 891–897.

Selmi, M. (2018). The paradox of implicit bias and a plea for a new narrative. *Arizona State Law Journal, 50*, 193.

Seneca. (1971). *Ad Lucilium Epistulae Morales* (R. M. Gummere, Trans.). University of Michigan Press.

Seo, D., Rabinowitz, A., Douglas, R., & Sinha, R. (2019). Limbic response to stress linking life trauma and hypothalamus-pituitary-adrenal axis function. *Psychoneuroendocrinology, 99*, 38–46.

Sertler, E. (2018). The institution of gender-based asylum and epistemic injustice: A structural limit. *Feminist Philosophy Quarterly, 4*(3), 1–25.

Sertler, E. (2022). Epistemic dependence and oppression: A telling relationship. *Episteme, 19*(3), 394–408.

Sertler, E. (2023). Calling recognition bluffs: Structural epistemic injustice and administrative violence. In P. Giladi & N. McMillan (Eds.), *Epistemic injustice and the philosophy of recognition* (pp. 171–198). Routledge.

Sesardic, N. (2010). Race: A social destruction of a biological concept. *Biology & Philosophy. 25*, 143–162. https://link.springer.com/article/10.1007/s10539-009-9193-7.

Shapiro, B. J. (1991). *Beyond reasonable doubt and probable cause: Historical perspectives on the Anglo-American law of evidence.* University of California Press.

Shapiro, B. J. (2002). Testimony in seventeenth-century English natural philosophy: Legal origins and early development. *Studies in History and Philosophy of Science, Part A, 33*(2), 243–263.

Sheridan, C. (2003). "Another white race": Mexican Americans and the paradox of whiteness in jury selection. *Law and History Review, 21*(1), 109–144. www.jstor.org/stable/3595070.

Sherwin-White, A. N. (1967). *Racial prejudice in imperial Rome*. Cambridge University Press.

Shieber, J. (2015). *Testimony: A philosophical introduction*. Routledge.

Shonkoff, J. P., Boyce, W. T., & McEwen, B. S. (2009). Neuroscience, molecular biology, and the childhood roots of health disparities: Building a new framework for health promotion and disease prevention. *JAMA, 301*(21), 2252–2259. https://doi.org/10.1001/jama.2009.754.

Shors, T., & Millon, E. (2016). Sexual trauma and the female brain. *Frontiers in Neuroendocrinology, 41*, 87–98.

Sieder, R. (2015). Legal pluralism and Indigenous women's rights in Mexico: The ambiguities of recognition. *New York University Journal of International Law and Politics, 48*, 1125–1150. https://nyujilp.org/wp-content/uploads/2010/06/NYU_JILP_48_4_Sieder.pdf.

Siegel, R. (1996). "The rule of love": Wife beating as prerogative and privacy. *Yale Law Journal 106*, 2117–2207.

Siegel, R. (1997). Why equal protection no longer protects: The evolving forms of status-enforcing state action. *Stanford Law Review, 49*, 1111–1148. https://www.law.yale.edu/sites/default/files/documents/pdf/Faculty/Siegel_WhyEqualProtectionNoLongerProtects.pdf.

Silva, N. K. (2004). *Aloha betrayed: Native Hawaiian resistance to American colonialism*. Duke University Press.

Silverblatt, I. (2004). *Modern inquisitions: Peru and the colonial origins of the civilized world*. Duke University Press.

Simon-Kerr, J. (2017). Credibility by proxy. George *Washington Law Review, 85*, 155–225.

Simon-Kerr, J. (2021). Credibility in an age of algorithms. *Rutgers University Law Review, 74*, 111–159.

Simpson, A. (2007). On ethnographic refusal: Indigeneity, "voice" and colonial citizenship. *Junctures: The Journal for Thematic Dialogue, 9*, 67–80.

Simpson, A. (2014). *Mohawk interruptus: Political life across the borders of settler states*. Duke University Press.

Simpson, L. B. (2013). *Islands of decolonial love*. Arbeiter Publishing.

Simpson, L. B. (2014). Land as pedagogy: Nishnaabeg intelligence and rebellious transformation. *Decolonization: Indigeneity, Education & Society, 3*(3), 1–25.

Simpson, L. B. (2017). *As we have always done: Indigenous freedom through radical resistance*. University of Minnesota Press.

Sirota, D. (2021, January 1). Trump's impunity reflects the impunity of the entire class of American elites. *Jacobin*. https://jacobin.com/2021/01/kelly-loeffler-donald-trump-georgia-runoff-elections-senate-republicans-impunity.

Sixtus IV. (1478). *Exigit sincerae devotionis affectus* [Papal bull]. Rome, the Vatican.

Skocpol, T. (1979/2015). *States and social revolutions: A comparative analysis of France, Russia, and China*. Cambridge University Press.

Smandych, R. (2006). Contemplating the testimony of "others": James Stephen, the Colonial Office, and the fate of Australian Aboriginal Evidence Acts, circa 1839–1849. *Legal History, 10*(1–2), 97–143.

Smith, A. (1811). *An inquiry into the nature and causes of the wealth of nations*. S. Doig and A. Stirling, Lackington, Allen and Company, Cradock and Joy, and T. Hamilton, London, and Wilson and Son, York.

Smith, A. (2005). *Conquest: Sexual violence and American Indian genocide*. Duke University Press.

Smith, L. T. (2013/1999). *Decolonizing methodologies: Research and Indigenous peoples*. Zed Books.

Smith, M. L. (1998). Women and naturalization, ca. 1802–1940. *Prologue: The Journal of the National Archives, 30*(2). https://www.archives.gov/publications/prologue/1998/summer/women-and-naturalization-1.html

Smith, M. L. (2002). Race, nationality, and reality: INS administration of racial provisions in U.S. immigration and nationality law since 1898. *Prologue: The Journal of the National Archives, 34*(2). https://www.archives.gov/publications/prologue/2002/summer/immigration-law-1

Snitkof, D., Wong, J., Stroebel, J., Howell, S. T., & Kuchler, T. (2021). *Racial disparities in access to small business credit: Evidence from the paycheck protection program* (National Bureau of Economic Research Working Paper No. 29364).

Snorton, C. R. (2017). *Black on both sides: A racial history of trans identity*. University of Minnesota Press.

Sossenheimer, P. H., Andersen, M. J., Jr., Clermont, M. H., Hoppenot, C. V., Palma, A. A., & Rogers, S. O., Jr. (2018). Structural violence and trauma outcomes: An ethical framework for practical solutions. *Journal of the American College of Surgeons, 227*(5), 537–542.

Speed, S. (2017). Structures of settler capitalism in Abya Yala. *American Quarterly, 69*(4), 783–790. https://doi/org/10.1353/aq.2017.0064.

Speed, S. (2019). *Incarcerated stories: Indigenous women migrants and violence in the settler-capitalist state*. University of North Carolina Press.

Speed, S. (2021). Grief and Indigenous feminists' rage: The embodied field of knowledge production. In Shannon Speed & Stephen Lynn (Eds.), *Indigenous women and violence: Feminist activist research in heightened states of injustice* (pp. 26–42). University of Arizona Press.

Speed, S., & Lynn, S. (2021). *Indigenous women and violence: Feminist activist research in heightened states of injustice*. University of Arizona Press.

Spillers, H. J. (2003). *Black, white, and in color: Essays on American literature and culture*. University of Chicago Press.

Spinoza, B. D. (2018). *Ethics: Proved in geometrical order*. Cambridge University Press.

Spivak, G. C. (1985). The Rani of Sirmur: An essay in reading the archives. *History and Theory, 24*(3), 247–272.

Spivak, G. C. (1988a). Can the subaltern speak? In C. Nelson & L. Grossberg (Eds.), *Marxism and the interpretation of culture* (pp. 271–313). University of Illinois Press.

Spivak, G. C. (1988b). Subaltern studies: Deconstructing historiography. In R. Guha & G. C. Spivak (Eds.), *Selected subaltern studies* (pp. 3–34). Oxford University Press.

Spivak, G. C. (1999). A critique of postcolonial reason: Toward a history of the vanishing present. Harvard University Press.

Spohn, C., & Horney, J. (1991). "The law's the law, but fair is fair": Rape shield laws and officials' assessments of sexual history evidence. *Criminology, 29*(1), 137–161.

Stark, E. (2007). *Coercive control: The entrapment of women in personal life.* Oxford University Press.

Starr, S. B. (2022, May 6). *Race-norming and statistical discrimination: Beyond the NFL* (University of Chicago, Public Law Working Paper No. 805). https://ssrn.com/abstract=4101693 or http://dx.doi.org/10.2139/ssrn.4101693.

Steil, J. P., Albright, L., Rugh, J. S., & Massey, D. S. (2018). The social structure of mortgage discrimination. *Housing Studies, 33*(5), 759–776. https://doi.org/10.1080/02673037.2017.1390076.

Stern, M. J. (2019, April 12). Federal judge: Donald Trump is leading an "assault on our judiciary." *Slate.* https://slate.com/news-and-politics/2019/04/judge-carlton-reeves-donald-trump-assault-judiciary-scotus.html.

Stewart, E., Nicholson, W., Bradley, L., & Borah, B. (2013). The burden of uterine fibroids for African-American women: Results of a national survey. *Journal of Women's Health 22*(10), 807–816.

Stewart, H. (2019). "Why didn't she say something sooner?": Doubt, denial, silencing, and the epistemic harms of the #MeToo movement. *South Central Review, 36*(2), 68–94.

Stolberg, S. G., & Fandos, N. (2018, September 17). Brett Kavanaugh and Christine Blasey Ford duel with tears and fury. *New York Times.* https://www.nytimes.com/2018/09/27/us/politics/brett-kavanaugh-confirmation-hearings.html.

Stolorow, R. (2007). *Trauma and human existence.* Routledge.

Street, J. H. (1967/2017). The Latin American "structuralists" and the institutionalists: Convergence in development theory. In S. Warren (Ed.), *The economy as a system of power* (pp. 34–52). Routledge.

Subcommittee on the Constitution, Civil Rights, and Civil Liberties. (2019, June 25). *Continuing challenges to the Voting Rights Act since "Shelby County v. Holder."* U.S. Government Publishing Office. https://www.govinfo.gov/content/pkg/CHRG-116hhrg39717/html/CHRG-116hhrg39717.htm.

Sullivan, B. (2022, December 6). Hertz will pay $169 million to customers it falsely accused of stealing its cars. *National Public Radio.* https://www.npr.org/2022/12/06/1140998674/hertz-false-accusation-stealing-cars-settlement.

Sullivan, S., & Tuana, N. (Eds.). (2007). *Race and epistemologies of ignorance.* State University of New York Press.

Swain, S. (Ed.). (2007). *Seeing the face, seeing the soul: Polemon's Physiognomy from classical antiquity to medieval Islam.* Oxford University Press.

Sweatt, J., Nestler, E., Meaney, M., & Akbarian, S. (2012). An overview of the molecular basis of epigenetics. In J. David Sweatt, Michael J. Meaney, Eric J. Nestler, & Schahram Akbarian, *Epigenetic regulation in the nervous system: Basic mechanisms and clinical impact* (pp. 3–35). Elsevier Science.

Swisher, P. N., & Mason, R. C. (2010). Liability insurance coverage for clergy sexual abuse claims. *Connecticut Insurance Law Journal, 17,* 355–413.

Sye, D. (2022, March 8). Beyond book banning: Efforts to criminally charge librarians. Office for Intellectual Freedom of the American Library Association. Blog post. https://www.oif.ala.org/beyond-book-banning-efforts-to-criminally-charge-librarians/.

TallBear, K. (2013). *Native American DNA: Tribal belonging and the false promise of genetic science.* University of Minnesota Press.

TallBear, K. (2015). Theorizing queer inhumanisms: An Indigenous reflection on working beyond the human/nonhuman. *GLQ: A Journal of Lesbian and Gay Studies, 21*(2–3), 230–235.

Taylor, K. (2019). *Race for profit: How banks and the real estate industry undermined Black homeownership.* University of North Carolina Press.

Terbeck, S., Kahane, G., McTavish, S., Savulescu, J., Cowen, P. J., & Hewstone, M. (2012). Propranolol reduces implicit negative racial bias. *Psychopharmacology, 222*(3), 419–424.

The rape corroboration requirement: Repeal not reform. (1972). *Yale Law Journal, 81*(7), 1365–1391. https://doi.org/10.2307/795246.

Thiong'o, N. (1986). *Decolonising the mind: The politics of language in African literature.* East African Educational Publishers.

Thomas, C. (2011). Why don't we talk about "violence" in international relations? *Review of International Studies, 37*(4), 1815–1836.

Thomas, J., & Brunsma, D. (2014). Oh, you're racist? I've got a cure for that! *Ethnic and Racial Studies, 37*(9), 1467–1485, https://doi/org/10.1080/01419870.2013.783223.

Tibebu, T. (2011). *Hegel and the third world: The making of eurocentrism in world history.* Syracuse University Press.

Tobias, H., & Joseph, A. 2018. Sustaining systemic racism through psychological gaslighting: Denials of racial profiling and justifications of carding by police utilizing local news media. *Race and Justice, 10*(4), 424–455. https://doi.org/10.1177/2153368718760969.

Tomlinson, G. (2007). *The singing of the New World: Indigenous voice in the era of European contact.* Cambridge University Press.

Tremain, S. (2017). *Foucault and feminist philosophy of disability.* University of Michigan Press.

Trudel-Fitzgerald, C., & Ouellet-Morin I. (2022). The cost of resilience: How allostatic load may jeopardize health through repeated demands for (successful) adaptation. *Psychoneuroendocrinology, 144*, 105874. https://doi.org/10.1016/j.psyneuen.2022.105874.

Truitt, F. & Andrews, D. C. (2013). *Contesting the myth of a post racial era: The continued significance of race in U.S. education.* Peter Lang.

Trümper, M. (2009). *Graeco-Roman slave markets: Fact or fiction?* Oxbow Books.

Tuck, E. & Yang, K. W. (2012). Decolonization is not a metaphor. *Decolonization: Indigeneity, Education & Society, 1*(1), 1–40.

Tuck, E., McKenzie, M., & McCoy, K. (2014). Land education: Indigenous, post-colonial, and decolonizing perspectives on place and environmental education research. *Environmental Education Research, 20*(1), 1–23.

Tuerkheimer, D. (2017). Incredible women: Sexual violence as the credibility discount. *University of Pennsylvania Law Review, 166*(1), 1–58.

US Department of Health and Human Services. (n.d.). Cancer and American Indians / Alaska Natives. https://minorityhealth.hhs.gov/omh/browse.aspx?lvl=4&lvlid=31. Accessed August 29, 2023.

Uggen, C., Larson, R., Shannon, S., & Stewart, R. (2022, October 25). Locked out 2022: Estimates of people denied voting rights. The Sentencing Project. https://www.sentencingproject.org/publications/locked-out-2022-estimates-of-people-denied-voting-rights/.

Ullmann, W. (1944). Reflections on medieval torture, *Juridical Review, 56*, 123–137.

Valdivia, F. del R., & Okowí, J. (2021). Drug trafficking in the Tarahumara region, northern Mexico: An analysis of racism and dispossession. *World Development, 142*(3), 1–10. https://doi.org/10.1016/j.worlddev.2021.105426.

Valles, S. (2018). *Philosophy of population health: Philosophy for a new public health era.* Routledge.

Vimalassery, M. (2013). The wealth of the Natives: Toward a critique of settler colonial political economy. *Settler Colonial Studies, 3*(3–4), 295–310.

Viterna, J. (2005). Insurgent collective action and civil war in El Salvador. *The American Journal of Sociology 111*(1), 304–306.

Viterna, J. (2013). *Women in war: The micro-processes of mobilization in El Salvador.* Oxford University Press.

Vizenor, G. R. (1999). *Manifest manners: Narratives on post-Indian survivance.* University of Nebraska Press.

Wade, N. (2014). *A troublesome inheritance: Genes, race, and human history.* Penguin Press.

Walker, A. (1983). *In search of our mother's gardens.* Harcourt Brace Jovanovich.

Wallerstein, I. M. (2004). *World-systems analysis: An introduction.* Duke University Press.

Wang, C. (2018). The police are innocent as long as they honestly believe: the human rights problems with English self-defense law. *Columbia Human Rights Law Review, 49*(3), 373–414.

Ward, T. (2009). Usurping the role of the jury? Expert evidence and witness credibility in English criminal trials. *International Journal of Evidence & Proof, 13*(2), 83–101.

Washington, H. (2006). *Medical apartheid: The dark history of medical experimentation on Black Americans from colonial times to the present.* Doubleday.

Watson, A. (1983). Roman slave law and Romanist ideology. *Phoenix, 37*(1), 53–65.

Weisskopf, T. E., Bowles, S., Gordon, D. M., Baily, M. N., & Rees, A. (1983). Hearts and minds: A social model of US productivity growth. *Brookings Papers on Economic Activity, 1983*(2), 381–450.

Welsh, R. (2017). Tearing the face in grief and rape: Cheek rending in medieval Iberia, c. 1000–1300. In E. Connelly & S. Künzel (Eds.), *New approaches to disease, disability, and medicine in medieval Europe* (pp. 43–61). Archaeopress.

White, M. C., Espey, D. K., Swan, J., Wiggins, C. L., Eheman, C., & Kaur, J. S. (2014). Disparities in cancer mortality and incidence among American Indians and Alaska Natives in the United States. *American Journal of Public Health, 104*(suppl. 3), S377–S387. https://doi.org/10.2105/AJPH.2013.301673.

White, T. K. (2007). Initial conditions at emancipation: The long-run effect on black-white wealth and earnings inequality. *Journal of Economic Dynamics and Control, 31,* 3370–3395.

Whyte, K. (2018a). Critical investigations of resilience. *Daedalus: Journal of the American Academy of Arts and Sciences, 147*(2), 136–147.

Whyte, K. (2018b). Indigenous science (fiction) for the anthropocene: Ancestral dystopias and fantasies of climate change crises. *Environment and Planning E: Nature and Space 1*(1), 224–242.

Wildcat, D. R. (2001). The question of self-determination. In V. Deloria & D. Wildcat (Eds.), *Power and place: Indian education in America* (pp. 135–150). Fulcrum Publishing.

Wilder, R. (2008). Liberation theology, Christian base communities, and solidarity movements: A historical reflection. In R. Harris and J. Neff (Eds.), *Capital, power, and inequality in Latin America and the Caribbean* (pp. 225–251). Rowman & Littlefield.

Williams, B., & Pierce, J. (2014). Evidence of Acolhua science in pictorial land records. In J. Lee & G. Brokaw (Eds.), *Texcoco: Prehispanic and colonial perspectives* (pp. 147–164). University Press of Colorado.

Williams, D. R., & Mohammed, S. A. (2013). Racism and health I: Pathways and scientific evidence. *American Behavioral Scientist, 57*(8), 1152–1173. https://doi.org/10.1177/0002764213487340.

Williams, M. (2019). Adverse racial climates in academia: Conceptualization, interventions, and call to action. *New Ideas in Psychology 55*(1), 58–67.

Williams, R. B. (2022). Federal wealth policy and the perpetuation of white supremacy. *The Review of Black Political Economy, 49*(2), 130–151.

Winderman, E. (2019). Anger's volumes: Rhetorics of amplification and aggregation in #MeToo. *Women's Studies in Communication, 42*(3), 327–346.

Wittgenstein, L. (1969). *On Certainty*. Denis Paul and G.E.M Anscombe (trans.). Harper & Row.

Wolfe, P. (1999). *Settler colonialism and the transformation of anthropology: The politics and poetics of an ethnographic event*. Cassell.

Wolfe, P. (2006). Settler colonialism and the elimination of the Native. *Journal of Genocide Research*, 8(4), 387–409.

Wolfe, P. (2016). *Traces of history: Elementary structures of race*. Verso Books.

Woods, L. (1983). Book review: Rape in marriage. *Law & Inequality, 1*(1), 187–189. https://scholarship.law.umn.edu/lawineq/vol1/iss1/9.

Wright, R. (2019, December 30). The story of 2019: Protests in every corner of the globe. *New Yorker*. https://www.newyorker.com/news/our-columnists/the-story-of-2019-protests-in-every-corner-of-the-globe.

X. M. (1963, January 23). Malcolm X speaks at Michigan State University. MSU Archives and Historical Collections. Audio file. https://onthebanks.msu.edu/Object/162-565-2359/malcolm-x-speaks-at-michigan-state-university-1963.

Yeter, D., Banks, E. C., & Aschner, M. (2020). Disparity in risk factor severity for early childhood blood lead among predominantly African-American Black children: The 1999 to 2010 US NHANES. *International Journal of Environmental Research and Public Health, 17*(5), 1552. https://doi.org/10.3390/ijerph17051552.

Yglesias, M. (2007, November 9). Reagan's race record. *The Atlantic*. https://www.theatlantic.com/politics/archive/2007/11/reagans-race-record/46875.

Young, I. M. (1991/2022). *Justice and the politics of difference*. Princeton University Press.

Young, I. M. (2000). Hybrid democracy: Iroquois federalism and the postcolonial project. In Duncan Iveson, Paul Patton, and Will Sanders (Eds.), *Political theory and the rights of Indigenous peoples* (pp. 237–258). Cambridge University Press

Young, I. M. (2003). Political responsibility and structural injustice. The Lindley lecture delivered at the University of Kansas, Department of Philosophy. Available online https://kuscholarworks.ku.edu/bitstream/handle/1808/12416/politicalresponsibilityandstructuralinjustice-2003.pdf?sequence=1.

Young, I. M. (2005). Self-determination as non-domination: Ideals applied to Palestine/Israel. *Ethnicities, 5*(2), 139–159.

Young, I. M. (2006, Winter). Katrina: Too much blame, not enough responsibility. *Dissent, 53*(1), 41–46. doi:10.1353/dss.2006.0052. https://www.dissentmagazine.org/article/katrina-too-much-blame-not-enough-responsibility.

Young, I. M. (2011). *Responsibility for justice*. Oxford University Press.

Yúdice, G. (1991). Testimonio and postmodernism. *Latin American Perspectives*, *18*(3), 15–31.

Yúdice, G. (1992). Testimonio y concientización. *Revista de crítica literaria latinoamericana*, *18*(36), 211–232.

Zambrana, R. (2021). *Colonial debts: The case of Puerto Rico*. Duke University Press.

Zaragocin, S. (2019). Gendered geographies of elimination: Decolonial feminist geographies in Latin American settler contexts. *Antipode*, *51*(1), 373–392.

Zea, L. (1988). *Discurso desde la marginación y la barbarie*. Anthropos, Editorial del Hombre.

Zitawi, J., & Abdel Wahab, M. (2014). Translating and interpreting to win: The foreign language witness testimony dilemma in international arbitration. *The Translator*, *20*(3), 356–376.

Zuckerman, J. (2021, November 1). How a 2005 Ohio "tort reform" law has cost child rape victims: State Supreme Court agrees to hear second challenge to law. *Ohio Capital Journal*. https://ohiocapitaljournal.com/2021/11/01/how-a-2005-ohio-tort-reform-law-has-cost-child-rape-victims-millions/.

Index

For the benefit of digital users, indexed terms that span two pages (e.g., 52–53) may, on occasion, appear on only one of those pages.

#MeToo, 9, 274–75
1619 Project, 206

Aboriginal Witness Act, 129
abortion, 207–8
Abrams, Stacey, 37
abstraction in epistemic systems, 216, 263–64
Abu Ghraib, 140–41
Act for the Government and Protection of Indians, 147
Act Prohibiting the Importation of Slaves, 207–8
adaptive systems, 43, 45, 48–49, 52–53, 89, 90, 92–93, 98, 104, 105
  adaptive capacities, 40, 79, 110–11
  adaptive technologies, 32, 121–22, 128–29, 167, 195–96, 207, 266, 279
administrative dissimulation, 133
administrative violence, 211–12, 261–62, 278
Africa, 102, 108, 109, 124–25, 182–83
Aglietta, Michel, 184
Ahmed, Sara, 27
Alexander, Marissa, 53–54
Alexander, Michelle, 6–7
Allstate Ins. Co. v. Troelstrup, 171–72
Andean, 19–20, 22
Ansell, David, 84–85
anticolonial liberation movements, 15, 92, 104, 105
anticolonial literatures, 8
anticolonial systems theory, 43–44, 86–87, 95–106, 110, 139–40, 217, 249–50, 269–71
Aristotle, 108

Arizona v. Youngblood, 171
assisted reproductive technologies, 222–23
asylum, 71–72, 236–38, 263–64, 276
Australian Aboriginal Evidence Acts, 129, 142–43

Babb, Sara, 283–84
Baldwin, James, 120, 147
Barnes v. Felix, 52
Bartky, Sandra, 64–65
Beitz, Charles, 267–68
Bell, Derrick, 33, 35–36
Benton, Lauren, 131–32
Berenstain, Nora, 90, 92–95, 223–24, 233, 272
Bierria, Alisa, 177
Black women's reproductive health, 221–25, 226–27
blame, 48, 67–71, 77, 78, 79, 80, 83
blameless, tragedy as inherently, 246–47
Brazil, 143–45
Brown v. Board of Education, 35–36
Butler, Anthea, 6

Canada, 180–81, 198–99, 247, 260–61
Capra, Fritjof, 60–61
Carson, Anne, 255–56
casta system, 127–28, 132
Castilian law codes, 117–18, 132
Castillo, Rosalva Aída Hernández, 288
causal profiles, 92–93
Césaire, Aimé, 262
Chemaly, Soraya, 274
Chiapas, 282–95
Chilean youth protests, 104
Chin, Rose, 123–24
Ch'ol, 18, 283

citizenship, 108, 123, 262–63, 280
Civil Rights Act, 270–71
Clark, Rep. Katherine, 225
Collins, Patricia Hill, 32, 98, 143–45
Commonwealth of Kentucky v. Braden, 228–29
controlling images, 143–45
Coulthard, Glenn, 96, 160, 198–200, 201, 202, 209, 212–13
credibility, 146, 148, 164–65
　credibility and colonial law, 151–52
　credibility proxies, 148
　credibility redlining zones, 179–81
　credibility, settler economies of 57–58, 100, 133–34, 158, 159, 179–80
　credibility, testimonial, 115–16, 117–19, 155–59
Crenshaw, Kimberlé, 6, 33, 35–36, 110–11, 280
critical epidemiology, 226–27
critical race theory, 207–8
cuerpo-territorio, 278
culpability, 37, 278
cultural liability, 15
cultural transmission, 99
culture of justification, 234–36

Davis, Angela, 6–7, 111–12, 194–95
Davis, Angelique, 227–30
decolonization 231–32
Deer, Sara, 249–50, 252, 258, 271–75, 286–87
Diamond, Stephen, 256, 265–66
dignity, Enlightenment construction of, 290–92
dignity, Zapatista discourse on, 292
disinformation, 211–12
dispossession, 230–31, 232–33, 237–38, 252, 265–66, 273–74, 275
distribution of harm, 57–58
distributive design, 43–44, 57–59, 84, 101, 110–11, 115–16, 123, 127–29, 179, 214
divisive and prohibited concepts, 34, 38–39, 45
Dobbs v. Jackson, 5
Dotson, Kristie, 145, 221, 232–33, 234, 235–36, 242

dynastic chains of transmission, 7–8, 16–17, 29, 100–1, 110–11, 118–19, 162, 164, 247, 278, 280–82
dynastic design of settler colonial social systems, 6, 40, 110–11, 122, 153, 204, 217, 272, 280, 293
dynastic historical formations 12–14, 17–18, 63–64, 87, 95, 109–10, 253–54, 269–70
dynastic, white formations, 43, 45, 87–88, 96–97, 103–4, 106–12, 127, 155, 183–84, 196–97, 203, 207, 252–53, 267–68, 287

Elonis v. United States 53
epigenetic violence, 238
epistemic apartheid, 244
epistemic burden 9–10
epistemic capitalism, 16, 162–63, 164–67, 175, 178–79, 192, 206, 213–14, 215
epistemic complicity, 241–42
epistemic consolidation, 233, 235
epistemic currency and exchange networks, 211–18
epistemic exploitation 50–51, 232–38, 261–62
epistemic ignorance, 50–51, 92
epistemic impunity, 242–45
epistemic injustice, 221, 237–38
epistemic oppression, 221
epistemic reparations, 242
epistemic right to know, imperial, 141–42
Epistemic Social Structures of Accumulation (ESSAs), 202–18
epistemic spectacle, 239–40
epistemic territorial expansion, 241–42
epistemic violence, 215, 262–63
epistemic wealth, 16, 209, 289–90
equifinality, 27–28
Ernst, Rose, 227–30
Escobar, Arturo, 293

Fanon, Frantz, 6–7, 21–22, 92–93, 105, 112–13, 127–28
Farmer, Paul, 43–44, 79–87, 99–100
Fellows, Mary Louise, 233
femicide, 221, 243–45, 247, 248, 249–50, 252, 254–55, 257–58, 261–62, 279–80

Fields, Barbara, 162
Fields, Karen, 162
Fletcher, Judith, 120–21
forced disappearances, 249–50
formularies of inquiry, 138–39

Galtung, John, 82–84, 85, 91, 262–63
gaslighting, 219–21, 228–29, 237
  gaslighting, as abuse mechanism, 241–42
  gaslighting, cultural, 17–18, 166, 218, 233–34, 238, 241–42, 244
  gaslighting, legal, 221
  gaslighting, medical, 221–27
  gaslighting, racial, 227–31
gender-based violence, 41, 57–58, 74, 81–82, 246–47, 249–50, 254–55, 258, 265–66, 271–75
gendered terror, 248
Giddens, Anthony, 63, 72–73
Gilmore, Ruth Wilson 12
global south feminisms, 19–20
Goeman, Mishuana, 19–20
Goldstein, Alyosha, 109–10
Goodell, William, 133
Gorrostieta Salazar, María Santos, 264
Graham v. Connor, 52
Gramsci, 278–80
Green, Jamal, 237–38
grievable harms, 247–48, 258
Guantánamo, 140–41
Guatemala, 115, 277, 283–84
Guevara, Che, 92–93, 170–71, 278

Hampton, Fred, 46–47
Harris, Angela P., 169–70
Hartman, Saidiya, 135–36
Haslanger, Sally, 97–98
Hefny, Mostafa, 124–25, 126
hermeneutical resources, 240–41
hermeneutic intersectionality, 202–3
hermeneutic violence, 202–3, 232–33, 237–38, 239–41, 262–63, 288
Hill, Anita, 117, 147
Holocaust, 262
humanitarianism, 68, 82–83, 84, 260–61, 277
human rights, 260–61, 267, 278, 285, 289–91

Illinois v. Wardlow, 52
implicit-bias framework, 43, 45–57
impunity, 10–12, 15–17, 18, 26–27, 40–41, 48–49, 170–71, 174, 175, 177, 218, 248, 261–62, 264
Indian Evidence Act, 147
Indigenous autonomy, 9, 43, 267, 273, 286–87
Indigenous feminisims, 8, 18, 19–20, 21, 90–91, 111, 192, 252–53
Indigenous interpretive economies, 214–15, 234–35
Indigenous self-determination, 76, 91, 266–67, 271, 278
Indigenous sovereignty, 268–69, 276
individuation, 250–51
iniuria, 247
inquisitorial practice, 135, 141–42
institutional comfort, 236
insurrectionist knowledges, 235
interpretive counterplay, 266–67
interpretive ecologies, 197, 209, 278
interpretive wealth, 162–63, 202–3, 247
Ixil triangle, 204–5

Jakobson, Roman, 61
Jaleel, Rana, 111
Jim Crow, 33, 34–35, 36, 37, 38, 138, 188
Jordan, June, 87–88
jurisdictional power, 136–43
jurisdictional white supremacy, 123, 124–25

Kauanui, J. Kēhaulani, 252–53, 259–60, 282, 285
Kendi, Ibram X., 32, 38, 43–44
King, Martin Luther, 38–39
Korematsu v. United States, 228–31, 237–38
Kotz, David, 184, 195–97

LaRocque, Emma, 263–64
Latin America, 82–83, 218, 276, 280–81
Latin American economic structuralists, 170–71, 208
L.A.U.S.D. v. Superior Court, 172–73
Law of Burgos, 133
legal whiteness, 123–15
Lekil Kuxlejal, 252–53

Lévi-Strauss, Claude, 61
Lewis, John, 37
logic of containment, 251–52 , 261
logic of distancing, 268, 277
logic of elimination 250–52, 260–62
logical empiricism, 8
logics of wounding, 246–53, 262–63, 265, 277–78
loopholes, 119–29

Maghbouleh, Neda, 124
de Maio, Fernando, 84–85
Malintzin, 143–45
Mame, 18, 283
Mann, Annika, 234–35
Maracle, Lee, 204–5
Marcos, Sylvia, 252–53
Marichuy, 287
Martin, Trayvon, 46–47
Martínez, María de Jesús Patricio, 287–88. *See also* Marichuy
Marx, 101–2, 160, 184, 185–86, 194, 198, 200, 213, 269–70
Matoaka, 143–45
Mayan, 105
McKittrick, Katherine 19–20
mens rea, 53, 92, 230
metaphysical apostacy, 232–33, 234
metaphysics of science, 90, 92, 94
metastatic colonization, 1, 4–5
methodological racism, 242–43
"Mexicanization," 288
Mexico, 71–72, 201, 251, 264–65, 267–68, 282–95
Mill, John Stuart, 66, 283
Million, Dian, 14, 246, 260–62
Mills, Charles, 138–40, 165
misogynoir, 127–28, 147, 226–27
Mixtec, 19–20
modality, 92–93, 94, 197
modal profile, 92–93
Mon, Pong, 123
Mora, Mariana , 288
Moreton, Robinson, 276
Myanmar, 74
mycelial network, 145, 146, 202–3

Nahua, 19–20
Native informancy, 118–19, 130–31, 143–45, 147, 224–25, 237, 256, 263–64

Nguyen, Nghiem, 128–29
nondomination, 272
North American Free Trade Agreement, 282–95

Ocampo, Gisela Mota, 264
Oklahoma v. Castro-Huerta, 272
Oliphant v. Suquamish, 272
Omi and Winant, 106–7
Osage, 164
Otomí, 18

Pager, Devah, 55–56
paraprimary violence, 210
Paredes-Ruvalcaba, Nerli, 272
Parson, Talcott, 97–98
pathologizing narratives, 228
pathologizing noncompliance, 228–29
Pena-Rodriguez v. Colorado, 150
People v. Lukitty, 150
People v. Segovia, 154
Peoples, Angela, 5–6
Phills, Susie Guillory, 124 , –25
Piaget, Jean, 66
Pohlhaus, Gaile, 92, 242
poststructuralism, 62
preservation through transformation, 2, 3, 123, 205
prestructural violence, 238–42
prison-industrial complex, 138, 251
Proposition 14, 160–61
proto-racism, 109, 129–30, 214

R. v. Murrell, 129
race-neutral accounts of economic systems, 178, 200
race-neutral language, 32–33, 38–39
racial capitalism, 16, 44, 90, 94, 197, 198, 203, 206–7, 215
racial hinges, 123–27, 143–45
racial spectacles, 228
racial wealth gap, 3, 12–13, 202–3, 214
rage, 255–56, 257–58, 265–66
rage, dignified, 282–95
rape culture, 89, 116, 117–18, 202–3
rape shield laws, 111, 147, 153–55
rape, spousal exemptions, 3–4, 5
Rawls, John, 34–35, 68, 69–70, 71–72
Razack, Sherene, 233
reasonable perception, 53

recursive patterns, 207
regenerative settler colonial social structures, 38, 39–41, 42, 56–57, 89, 110, 249, 258
resilience in systems, 56–57, 62–63
res nullius, 132
respecification, 128, 244–45, 292
retrenchment, 35–36, 37, 38–44
Riddle, Emily, 219
Ríos Castaño, Victoria, 141–42
Roberts, Dorothy, 13–14, 35
Robinson, Cedric, 97, 109, 112–13
Robinson, Joan, 200–1
Roe v. Wade, 5, 35
roman law, 52–53, 131, 133, 134, 137, 146, 247, 248–49, 269–70
Rorty, Richard 67
Russell, Camisha, 222–23

Sacagawea, 143–45
San Andés Accords on Indigenous Rights and Culture, 286–87
de los Santos, María Micaela, 115
de Saussure, Ferdinand, 61
self-defense law, 52–57
self-organized criticality, 248
self-reparative settler colonial social reproduction, 252, 280, 281–82
　　self-reparative socio-legal process, 6, 105, 155
Selmi, Michael, 49
Sertler, Ezgi, 236–37, 261–62
settler colonial social systems, 2, 12, 16, 41–42, 82
settler colonial structure of address, 274
settler epistemic economies, 16–17, 58–59, 177, 205, 252, 253–54, 288
settler extractive accumulation processes, 197–201, 277
settler gold, 134, 232–33
settler innocence narratives, 220, 265–66
settler moves to innocence, 230–38
settler statecraft, 273, 276
sexual violence, 12–14, 15–16, 18
Shelby County v. Holder, 36–37, 38–39
Siege, Reva, 2, 152–53
Simon-Kerr, Julia, 148–49, 152
Simpson, Audra, 113–14
Simpson, Leanne Betasamosake, 6–7, 204–5

Sing, Ling, 129
social emergence, 95–99
social epidemiology, 57, 93–94, 219–20, 226–27, 244
Social Structure of Accumulation, 16, 167–68, 176, 181–201, 213
Speed, Shannon, 249–50, 265–66, 270–71, 285–86, 289–90
Spivak, Gayatri, 16, 145, 232–33
stand your ground laws, 53–54
stare decisis, 229–30
'structural' and 'systemic,' different uses of, 44, 62–65
structural epistemic warfare, 120, 175
structural gaslighting, 75
structural guerrilla warfare, 280–82
structural injustice, 44, 67–79, 252–53
structural innocence, 158, 242, 243–44
structural invariance, 43–44, 67, 115–16, 131–32, 139–40, 171, 195 , –210
structural iterative power, 230
structural justice, 122, 252
structural racism, 44–87, 120
structural resource transfers, 178
structural trauma, 252, 253–82
structural violence, 78, 79–95
structuralism, 59, 60–62, 65
structured inattention, 226–27
Subcomandante Galeano, 22, 204
surveillance, 54, 251
systemic racism, 13–15, 41
systems theories, 7–8, 12, 19–21, 40–41, 60–61, 103–4, 105, 216

Taylor, Breonna, 46–47
terra nullius, 132
Terry v. Ohio, 52
testigation, 147–48
testimonio, 146
testimony, 129, 136–37, 140–41, 156–59, 237–38
　　testimony and slavery 129–34
　　testimony as a technology of social power, 119–29, 133–56, 157–58
　　testimony, dismissal of, 129
　　testimony, legal, 128–29, 130–31, 133–34
　　testimony, naturalization of, 133–34
Texcocan trial records 136–37, 138
threat perception, 51–52

Till, Emmett, 139–40
Title IX, 35
tort calculation, 173–74
torture, 131, 133–34, 138–39, 140–41, 247, 251
trauma, 246–47
    trauma deserts, 262–63
    trauma, functionalized 262–63
    trauma models of care 254–55
    trauma-pain-tragedy triad, 255–58
    trauma's "redemptive" value, 258–60
Tribal Law and Order Act, 272
Tseltal, 18 , –283
Tsotsil, 18, 283
Tuck, Eve, 231–32, 233

United States v. Dow, 151
United States v. Estrada, 153–54

Vallejo Orea, Maricela, 246, 264, 295
Valles, Sean, 254
Vega v. Tekoh, 171
Veracruz, 246
Violence Against Women Act, 272
violence, construction of, 276–78
Voting Rights Act, 36, 160–61

Washington, Harriet, 224–25
Welsh, Rachel, 117–18

white feminism, 157
white innocence, 49, 65, 74–79, 102, 107–8
whitewashed theory of social justice, 75
Whyte, Kyle, 259–60
Williams, David, 10–11
witnessing, 120, 131, 132, 141–42
witnessing, credible, 132, 147
Wolfe, Patrick, 250, 260–61, 280–81
women of color feminisms, 8, 14, 15 , 21, 44, 59, 92
women of color-survivors, 4–5, 54–55, 89
Women's Revolutionary Law, 285–87
Wynter, Sylvia 19–20

Yang, Wayne, 231–32, 233
Young, Iris Marion, 15, 43–44, 67–87, 103, 252, 266–71, 272, 273
Yucatan, 201

Zamudio, María de Jesús Jaime, 230, 258
Zamudio, Yesenia, 256–58
Zapata, Emiliano, 284
Zapatismo, 252–53, 270–71, 282–95
Zapatistas, 105, 217, 252–53, 266, 267–68, 282–95
Zapotec, 18, 22
Zoque, 283

Printed in the USA/Agawam, MA
May 3, 2024

865425.007